INTRODUCTION TO

JAVA™

PROGRAMMING

FUNDAMENTALS FIRST

Sixth Edition

Y. Daniel Liang

Armstrong Atlantic State University

PEARSON

Prentice
Hall

Upper Saddle River, NJ 07458

Library of Congress Cataloging-in-Publication Data

Liang, Y. Daniel.
   Introduction to Java programming: fundamentals first/Y. Daniel Liang.--6 th ed.
     p.   cm.
   Includes index.
    ISBN 0-13-223738-5
   QA76.73.J38L523 2004
   005.2¢762—dc22

                                      2003065629

Vice President and Editorial Director, ECS: *Marcia J. Horton*
Executive Editor: *Tracy Dunkelberger*
Associate Editor: *Carole Snyder*
Editorial Assistant: *Christianna Lee*
Executive Managing Editor: *Vince O'Brien*
Managing Editor: *Camille Trentacoste*
Production Editor: *Craig Little*
Director of Creative Services: *Paul Belfanti*
Creative Director: *Juan Lopez*
Art Director and Cover Manager: *Maureen Eide*
Cover and Interior Designer: *Dina Curro*
Managing Editor, AV Management and Production: *Patricia Burns*
Art Editor: *Xiaohong Zhu*
Director, Image Resource Center: *Melinda Reo*
Manager, Rights and Permissions: *Zina Arabia*
Manager, Visual Research: *Beth Brenzel*
Manager, Cover Visual Research and Permissions: *Karen Sanatar*
Manufacturing Manager, ESM: *Alexis Heydt-Long*
Manufacturing Buyer: *Lisa McDowell*
Executive Marketing Manager: *Robin O'Brien*
Marketing Assistant: *Mack Patterson*
Photo Credits:
  Cover: The Pyramid of the Niches, El Tajin, Mexico. Photographer: Adalberto Rios Szalay/Sexto Sol. Courtesy Getty Images.
  Part Opener: The Goddess Chalchihuitlicue, found in the Valley of Mexico, 1300-1500 AD (stone), Aztec / Musée de l'Homme, Paris, France / Bridgeman Art Library.
  Chapter Opener: Mayan God Shel, Mexico. Photographer: Philip Coblentz. Courtesy Brand X Pictures.

© 2007, 2004, 2002, 2001 Pearson Education, Inc.
Pearson Prentice Hall
Pearson Education, Inc.
Upper Saddle River, NJ 07458

Printed in the United States of America

10 9 8 7 6 5 4 3 2 1

ISBN: 0-13-223738-5

Pearson Education Ltd., *London*
Pearson Education Australia Pty. Ltd., *Sydney*
Pearson Education Singapore, Pte. Ltd.
Pearson Education North Asia Ltd., *Hong Kong*
Pearson Education Canada, Inc., *Toronto*
Pearson Educación de Mexico, S.A. de C.V.
Pearson Education—Japan, *Tokyo*
Pearson Education Malaysia, Pte. Ltd.
Pearson Education, Inc., *Upper Saddle River, New Jersey*

To Samantha, Michael, and Michelle

PREFACE

Welcome to *Introduction to Java Programming, Sixth Edition*. This edition is a substantial improvement on the previous edition in respect to clarity, content, presentation, code listings, and exercises, thanks to comments and suggestions by instructors and students. Overall, it is a great leap forward. We invite you to take a close look and be the judge.

Versions

The book is available in two versions:

- The fundamentals first version (Chapters 1–19).
- The comprehensive version (Chapters 1–36).

The following diagram summarizes the contents:

Introduction to Java Programming, Sixth Edition

Part 1 Fundamentals of Programming
    Chapter 1 Introduction to Computers, Programs, and Java
    Chapter 2 Primitive Data Types and Operations
    Chapter 3 Selection Statements
    Chapter 4 Loops
    Chapter 5 Methods
    Chapter 6 Arrays

Part 2 Object-Oriented Programming
    Chapter 7 Objects and Classes
    Chapter 8 Strings and Text I/O
    Chapter 9 Inheritance and Polymorphism
    Chapter 10 Abstract Classes and Interfaces
    Chapter 11 Object-Oriented Design

Part 3 GUI Programming
    Chapter 12 Getting Started with GUI Programming
    Chapter 13 Graphics
    Chapter 14 Event-Driven Programming
    Chapter 15 Creating User Interfaces
    Chapter 16 Applets and Multimedia

Part 4 Exception Handling, I/O, and Recursion
    Chapter 17 Exceptions and Assertions
    Chapter 18 Binary I/O
    Chapter 19 Recursion

Part 5 Data Structures
    Chapter 20 Lists, Stacks, Queues, Trees, and Heaps
    Chapter 21 Generics
    Chapter 22 Java Collections Framework
    Chapter 23 Algorithm Efficiency and Sorting

Part 6 Concurrency, Networking, and Internationalization
    Chapter 24 Multithreading
    Chapter 25 Networking
    Chapter 26 Internationalization

Part 7 Advanced GUI Programming
    Chapter 27 JavaBeans and Bean Events
    Chapter 28 Containers, Layout Managers, and Borders
    Chapter 29 Menus, Toolbars, Dialogs, and Internal Frames
    Chapter 30 MVC and Swing Models
    Chapter 31 JTable and JTree

Part 8 Web Programming
    Chapter 32 Java Database Programming
    Chapter 33 Advanced Java Database Programming
    Chapter 34 Servlets
    Chapter 35 JavaServer Pages
    Chapter 36 Remote Method Invocations

Fundamentals First introduces the fundamentals of programming, problem-solving, object-oriented programming, and GUI programming. This version is suitable for an introductory course on problem-solving and object-oriented programming.

    The *Comprehensive Version* contains all the chapters in the fundamentals first version. Additionally, it covers data structures, networking, internationalization, advanced GUI programming, and Web programming.

fundamentals first

comprehensive version

Teaching Strategies

imperative and OOP

Both imperative and OOP are important programming paradigms with distinct advantages for certain applications. Some programs should be developed using the imperative approach and others are better developed using the object-oriented approach. Today's students need to know both paradigms and use them effectively. This book introduces both imperative and OOP paradigms. Students will learn when and how to apply these two paradigms effectively.

fundamentals first

There are several strategies in teaching Java. This book adopts the *fundamentals-first* strategy, proceeding at a steady pace through all the necessary and important basic concepts, then moving to object-oriented programming, and then to the use of the object-oriented approach to build interesting GUI applications and applets with exception handling, and advanced features.

fundamental programming techniques

My own experience, confirmed by the experience of many colleagues, demonstrates that learning basic logic and *fundamental programming techniques* like loops and step-wise refinement is essential for new programmers to succeed. Students who cannot write code in procedural programming are not able to learn object-oriented programming. A good introduction on primitive data types, control statements, methods, and arrays prepares students to learn object-oriented programming.

The fundamentals-first approach reinforces object-oriented programming by first presenting the procedural solutions and demonstrating how they can be improved using the object-oriented approach. Students can learn when and how to apply OOP effectively.

using OOP effectively

At every SIGCSE (Computer Science Education) conference prior to 2005, the object-early approach was trumpeted and the voice for the fundamentals-first approach was muted. This changed when some former proponents of object-early began to air their frustrations and declared that object-early was a failure. This book is fundamentals-first and *object-right*. OOP is introduced right after fundamental programming techniques are covered. Many instructors of this book, from research universities to community colleges, have embraced the approach and have succeeded.

object-early failed?
object-right

problem solving

Programming isn't just syntax, classes, or objects. It is really *problem solving*. Loops, methods, and arrays are fundamental techniques for problem solving. From fundamental programming techniques to object-oriented programming, there are many layers of abstraction. Classes are simply a layer of abstraction. Applying the concept of abstraction in the design and implementation of software projects is the key to developing software. The overriding objective of the book, therefore, is to teach students to use many layers of abstraction in solving problems and to see problems in small and in large. The examples and exercises throughout the book center on problem solving and foster the concept of developing reusable methods and classes and using them to create practical projects.

Learning Strategies

A programming course is quite different from other courses. In a programming course, you learn from examples, from *practice*, and from mistakes. You need to devote a lot of time to writing programs, testing them, and fixing errors.

practice

For first-time programmers, learning Java is like learning any high-level programming language. The fundamental point in learning programming is to develop the critical skills of formulating *programmatic solutions* for real problems and translating them into programs using selection statements, loops, and methods.

programmatic solution

Once you acquire the basic skills of writing programs using loops, methods, and arrays, you can begin to learn *object-oriented programming*. You will learn how to develop object-oriented software using class encapsulation and class inheritance.

object-oriented programming

Once you understand the concept of object-oriented programming, learning Java becomes a matter of learning the *Java API*. The Java API establishes a framework for programmers to develop applications using Java. You have to use the classes and interfaces in the API and follow their conventions and rules to create applications. The best way to learn the Java API is to imitate examples and do exercises. The following diagram highlights the API covered in the book.

Java API

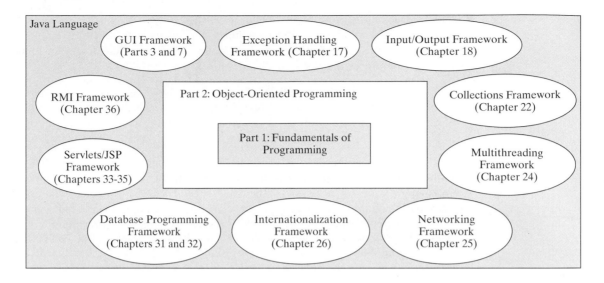

What's New in This Edition?

This edition substantially enhances *Introduction to Java Programming, Fifth Edition*. The major changes are as follows:

- All the Java code in the book now uses syntax coloring for keywords, literals, and comments. This makes the code more readable and understandable.   *syntax coloring*

- The Java 5 features are fully integrated in this edition. (Note: the fifth edition treats Java 5 features in separate optional sections.)   *full Java 5 update*

- The book is completely revised in every detail to enhance clarity, content, presentation, and exercises. All code samples and listings have been shortened and revised to be more compelling and to keep students even more engaged.   *complete revision*

- Optional GUI sections are provided at the end of Chapters 7–10 in Part 2, "Object-Oriented Programming," while a complete introduction of GUI programming is presented in Part 3, "GUI Programming," GUI components are excellent examples to demonstrate OOP. The optional GUI sections can be used as additional examples for OOP.   *GUI options in Part 2*

- Students can now write short, interesting, graphical game programs starting from Chapter 2.   *early interesting programs*

- Chapter 2, "Primitive Data Types and Operations," introduces the use of `JOptionPane` and `Scanner` to receive input. Students can use either `JOpationPane` or `Scanner` for obtaining input.   **`JOptionPane`** or **`Scanner`**

- The discussion of recursion is expanded to form Chapter 19, "Recursion," a brand-new chapter. It can be covered after Chapter 5, "Methods."   *new recursion chapter*

- High-level text I/O using the `Scanner` and `PrintWriter` classes is introduced in Chapter 8 along with strings. Binary I/O is covered in Chapter 18 "Binary I/O."   *early text I/O*

- `ArrayList` is introduced early in Chapter 9, "Inheritance and Polymorphism."   *early* **`ArrayList`**

- New exercises are provided in Part 2, "Object-Oriented Programming," for achieving three objectives: (1) design and draw UML for classes; (2) implement classes from the UML; (3) use classes to develop applications.   *UML exercises*

- Extensive supplements (e.g., installing and configuring JDK, IDE tutorials, design patterns, rapid GUI development, database design, SQL) are provided for instructors to customize a course.   *extensive supplements*

Part 1 enhancement

■ Part 1, "Fundamentals of Programming," is expanded into six chapters to focus on problem-solving and basic programming techniques with many new illustrations and practical examples, such as math tutor. New organization reinforces the teaching of fundamental problem-solving techniques.

Part 2 enhancement

■ Part 2, "Object-Oriented Programming," is expanded into five chapters to give a comprehensive introduction on OOP and how to use it to design programs. New organization enhances the presentation of object-oriented programming and enables GUI programming to be covered earlier.

Part 3 enhancement

■ Part 3, "GUI Programming," is expanded into five chapters to introduce GUI programming, graphics painting, event-driven programming, creating user interfaces, and applets.

Part 4 enhancements

■ Part 4, "Exception Handling, I/O, and Recursion," contains a brand new chapter on recursion. New short and simple examples are used to introduce the concept of exception handling. Since the text I/O has moved to Chapter 8, "Strings and Text I/O," the I/O chapter covers only the binary I/O.

Pedagogical Features

teaching by example
learning by doing

The philosophy of the Liang Java Series is *teaching by example and learning by doing*. Basic features are explained by example so that you can learn by doing. The book uses the following elements to get the most from the material:

■ **Objectives** list what students should have learned from the chapter. This will help them to determine whether they have met the objectives after completing the chapter.

■ **Introduction** opens the discussion with a brief overview of what to expect from the chapter.

■ **Code Listings** are used to teach programming concepts. Syntax coloring makes the code easier to follow.

■ **Chapter Summary** reviews the important subjects that students should understand and remember. It helps them to reinforce the key concepts they have learned in the chapter.

■ **Optional Sections** cover nonessential but valuable features. Instructors may choose to include or skip an optional section, or cover it later. The section headers of optional sections are marked by ✾.

■ **Review Questions** are grouped by sections to help students track their progress and evaluate their learning.

■ **Margin Notes** are featured throughout the book to emphasize key terms and important concepts.

■ **Programming Exercises** are grouped by sections to provide students with opportunities to apply on their own the new skills they have learned. The level of difficulty is rated as easy (no asterisk), moderate (*), hard (**), or challenging (***). The trick of learning programming is practice, practice, and practice. To that end, the book provides a great many exercises.

■ **Interactive Self-Test** lets students test their knowledge interactively online. The Self-Test is accessible from the Companion Website. It provides more than one thousand multiple-choice questions organized by sections in each chapter. The Instructor Resource Website contains the quiz generator with additional multiple-choice questions.

■ **Notes**, **Tips**, and **Cautions** are inserted throughout the text to offer valuable advice and insight on important aspects of program development.

Note
Provides additional information on the subject and reinforces important concepts.

 Tip
Teaches good programming style and practice.

 Caution
Helps students steer away from the pitfalls of programming errors.

Flexible Chapter Orderings

The book provides flexible chapter orderings to enable GUI, exception handling, generics, and the Java Collections Framework to be covered earlier. Three common alternative orderings are shown as follows:

	GUI Early
Chapter 9	Inheritance and Polymorphism
Chapter 12	GUI Basics
Chapter 13	Graphics
Chapter 10	Abstract Classes and Interfaces
Chapter 14	Event-Driven Programming
Chapter 15	Creating User Interfaces
Chapter 16	Applets and Multimedia

	Exception Early
Chapter 9	Inheritance and Polymorphism
Chapter 17	Exceptions and Assertions

	Data Structures Early
Chapter 9	Inheritance and Polymorphism
Chapter 10	Abstract Classes and Interfaces

Many of the chapters after Chapter 16 can be covered in any order. The following diagram shows the chapter dependencies.

Note

Some of the optional examples and exercises in later chapters may be dependent on earlier chapters. In such cases the examples and exercises can be omitted. For example, Chapter 17 has an example that uses GUI components from Chapter 15. If you have not covered Chapter 15, these examples and exercises can be skipped.

Java Development Tools

You can use a text editor, such as the Windows Notepad or WordPad, to create Java programs, and compile and run the programs from the command window. You can also use a Java development tool, such as TextPad, JBuilder, NetBeans, or Eclipse. These tools support an integrated development environment (IDE) for rapidly developing Java programs. Editing, compiling, building, executing, and debugging programs are integrated in one graphical user interface. Using these tools effectively will greatly increase your programming productivity. TextPad is a primitive IDE tool. JBuilder, NetBeans, and Eclipse are more sophisticated, but they are easy to use if you follow the tutorials. Tutorials on TextPad, JBuilder, NetBeans, and Eclipse will be found in the supplements on the Companion Website.

Companion Website

The Companion Website at www.prenhall.com/liang features a host of resources for students and instructors, including the following:

- Answers to review questions

- Solutions to programming exercises

- Source code for the code listings in the book

- Links to software and Web resources

- The **Online Quiz Generator** enables instructors to generate quizzes as well as assign students to take quizzes online with the results emailed to the instructor. This can be done in a closed lab or at home. Instructors may assign a set of 10, 15, or 20 questions and specify that the questions to be randomly generated. Go to www.prenhall.com/liang to access the Online Quiz.

Supplements

The text covers the essential subjects. The supplements extend the text to introduce additional topics that might be of interest to readers. The supplements that are available from the Companion Website are listed in this table.

Supplements for Introduction to Java Programming, 6E

Part I General Supplements
  A Glossary
  B Installing and Configuring JDK
  C Compiling and Running Java from the
     Command Window
  D Java Coding Style Guidelines
  E Creating Desktop Shortcuts for Java
     Applications on Windows

Part II IDE Supplements
  A TextPad Tutorial
  B JBuilder Tutorial
  C Learning Java Effectively with JBuilder
  D NetBeans Tutorial
  E Learning Java Effectively with NetBeans
  F Eclipse Tutorial
  G Learning Java Effectively with Eclipse

Supplements for Introduction to Java Programming, 6E (*Continued*)

Part III Data Structures Supplements
  A Hashing
  B B-Tree
  C Graph Algorithms

Part IV Database Supplements
  A SQL Statements for Creating and
     Initializing Tables Used in the Book
  B MySQL Tutorial
  C Oracle Tutorial
  D Microsoft Access Tutorial
  E Introduction to Database Systems
  F Relational Database Concept
  G Database Design
  H SQL Basics
  I Advanced SQL

Part V Java Supplements
  A More on Regular Expressions
  B Enumerated Types (Java 5)
  C Java 2D
  D Security
  E Java Media Framework
  F Java Sound
  G Java Mail
  H Design Patterns

Part VI Obsolete Java Features
  A StringTokenizer
  B Text I/O using Reader and Writer

Part VII Web Programming Supplements
  A HTML and XHTML Tutorial
  B CSS Tutorial
  C XML
  D Java and XML
  E Tomcat Tutorial

Part VIII Visual GUI Development Using
    NetBeans
  A Getting Started with NetBeans
  B Visual Design Using NetBeans
  C Rapid Component Development Using
    NetBeans
  D Customizing Property Editors in
    NetBeans

Part IX Visual GUI Development Using
    JBuilder
  A Getting Started with JBuilder
  B Basic UI Design Using JBuilder
  C Rapid Component Development Using
    JBuilder
  D Customizing Property Editors in JBuilder

Part X Visual GUI Development Using Eclipse
  A Getting Started with Eclipse
  B Basic UI Design Using Eclipse
  C Rapid Component Development Using
    Eclipse
  D Customizing Property Editors in Eclipse

Instructor Resource Center

The Instructor Resource Center, accessible from www.prenhall.com/liang, contains the following resources:

- Over 2000 Microsoft PowerPoint lecture slides. They bring the illustrations from the text to life in the classroom. Featuring full-color, syntax-highlighted source code and the ability to run programs live without leaving the slides and trace program execution using animation.

- Sample exams. In general, each exam has four parts:
  1. Multiple-choice questions or short-answer questions (most of these are different from the questions in the self-test on the Companion Website)
  2. Correct programming errors
  3. Trace programs
  4. Write programs

- Solutions to all the exercises (available to instructors only). Students will have access to the solutions of even-numbered exercises.

- UML Diagram Solutions to all the UML exercises (for instructors only). Students are provided solutions to even-numbered exercises.

- TestGen, a test bank of over 2000 programming questions.

- Online quiz. (Students can take the online quiz for each chapter and a quiz report will be sent to the instructor.)

- Ten sample exams, each with multiple choice or short-answer questions. They test how students correct programming errors, test programs, and write their own programs.

- Online Homework and Assessment. GOAL (Gradiance Online Accelerated Learning) is a sophisticated online homework tool that can be purchased and used alongside the textbook. Multiple choice problems based on the concept of a "root question" and challenging programming labs are designed to save instructors time grading programming assignments and to deliver meaningful feedback to students immediately. All code is tested against a real data set. Contact your local Pearson Prentice Hall sales representative to learn more about GOAL.

Some readers have requested the materials from the Instructor Resource Website. Please understand that these are for instructors only. Such requests will not be answered.

Acknowledgments

I would like to thank Ray Greenlaw and my colleagues at Armstrong Atlantic State University for enabling me to teach what I write and for supporting me in writing what I teach. Teaching is the source of inspiration for continuing to improve the book. I am grateful to the instructors and students who have offered comments, suggestions, bug reports, and praise.

This book was greatly enhanced thanks to outstanding reviews. The reviewers for the previous editions were:

Yang Ang	University of Wollongong (Australia)
David Champion	DeVry Institute
James Chegwidden	Tarrant County College
Harold Grossman	Clemson University
Ron Hofman	Red River College (Canada)
Hong Lin	DeVry Institute
Dan Lipsa	Armstrong Atlantic State University
Vladan Jovanovic	Georgia Southern University
Larry King	University of Texas at Dallas
Nana Kofi	Langara College (Canada)
Roger Kraft	Purdue University at Calumet
Debbie Masada	Sun Microsystems
Blayne Mayfield	Oklahoma State University
Michel Mitri	James Madison University
Kenrick Mock	University of Alaska Anchorage
Jun Ni	University of Iowa
Gavin Osborne	University of Sakatchewan
Kevin Parker	Idaho State University
Mary Ann Pumphrey	De Anza Junior College
Ronald F. Taylor	Wright State University
Carolyn Schauble	Colorado State University
David Scuse	University of Manitoba
Ashraf Shirani	San Jose State University
Daniel Spiegel	Kutztown University
Lixin Tao	Pace University
Russ Tront	Simon Fraser University
Deborah Trytten	University of Oklahoma
Kent Vidrine	George Washington University
Bahram Zartoshty	California State University at Northridge

The reviewers for this edition are:

Kevin Bierre	Rochester Institute of Technology
James Chegwidden	Tarrant County College
Charles Dierbach	Towson University
Deena Engel	New York University
Vladan Jovanovic	Georgia Southern University
Frank Malinowski	Aelera Corporation
John McGrath	J.P. McGrath Consulting
Shyamal Mitra	University of Texas at Austin
Benjamin Nystuen	University of Colorado at Colorado
Roger Priebe	University of Texas at Austin

It is a great pleasure, honor, and privilege to work with Prentice Hall. I would like to thank Marcia Horton, Tracy Dunkelberger, Robin O'Brien, Christianna Lee, Jennifer Cappello, Vince O'Brien, Camille Trentacoste, Craig Little, Xiaohong Zhu, and their colleagues for organizing, producing, and promoting this project, and Robert Milch for copy editing.

As always, I am indebted to my wife, Samantha, for her love, support, and encouragement.

Y. Daniel Liang
liang@armstrong.edu
www.cs.armstrong.edu/liang/intro6e

BRIEF CONTENTS

CONTENTS

INTRODUCTION TO

JAVA™

PROGRAMMING

FUNDAMENTALS FIRST

Sixth Edition

PART 1

FUNDAMENTALS OF PROGRAMMING

By now you have heard a lot about Java and are anxious to start writing Java programs. The first part of the book is a stepping stone that will prepare you to embark on the journey of learning Java. You will begin to know Java and will develop fundamental programming skills. Specifically, you will learn how to write simple Java programs with primitive data types, control statements, methods, and arrays.

Prerequisites for Part I

basic computer skills

This book does not require any prior programming experience, nor any mathematics, other than elementary high school algebra and *basic computer skills* such as using Windows, Internet Explorer, and Microsoft Word.

recursion

You may cover the concept and simple examples of recursive programming in §§19.1–19.3 in Chapter 19, *"Recursion,"* after Chapter 5, "Methods."

sorting algorithms

You may cover Chapter 23, "Algorithm Efficiency and Sorting," after Chapter 6, "Arrays." Two simple *sorting algorithms* are introduced in Chapter 6. Chapter 23 introduces several advanced sorting algorithms.

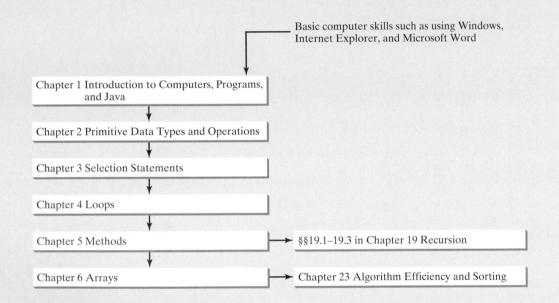

Basic computer skills such as using Windows,
Internet Explorer, and Microsoft Word

Chapter 1 Introduction to Computers, Programs, and Java

Chapter 2 Primitive Data Types and Operations

Chapter 3 Selection Statements

Chapter 4 Loops

Chapter 5 Methods → §§19.1–19.3 in Chapter 19 Recursion

Chapter 6 Arrays → Chapter 23 Algorithm Efficiency and Sorting

INTRODUCTION TO COMPUTERS, PROGRAMS, AND JAVA

Objectives

- To review computer basics, programs, and operating systems (§§1.2–1.4).

- (Optional) To represent numbers in binary, decimal, and hexadecimal (§1.5).

- To understand the relationship between Java and the World Wide Web (§1.6).

- To distinguish the terms API, IDE, and JDK (§1.7).

- To write a simple Java program (§1.8).

- To create, compile, and run Java programs (§1.9).

- To know the basic syntax of a Java program (§1.10).

- To display output in a dialog box (§1.11).

1.1 Introduction

You use word processors to write documents, Web browsers to explore the Internet, and email programs to send email over the Internet. Word processors, browsers, and email programs are all examples of software that runs on computers. Software is developed using programming languages. There are many programming languages. So why Java? The answer is that Java enables users to develop and deploy applications on the Internet for servers, desktop computers, and small hand-held devices. The future of computing is being profoundly influenced by the Internet, and Java promises to remain a big part of that future. Java is *the* Internet programming language.

You are about to begin an exciting journey, learning a powerful programming language. Before the journey, it is helpful to review computer basics, programs, and operating systems, and to become familiar with number systems. You may skip the review in §§1.2–1.4 if you are familiar with such terms as CPU, memory, disks, operating systems, and programming languages. You may also skip §1.5 and use it as reference when you have questions regarding binary and hexadecimal numbers.

1.2 What Is a Computer?

hardware
software

A computer is an electronic device that stores and processes data. A computer includes both *hardware* and *software*. In general, hardware is the physical aspect of the computer that can be seen, and software is the invisible instructions that control the hardware and make it perform specific tasks. Computer programming consists of writing instructions for computers to perform. You can learn a programming language without knowing computer hardware, but you will be better able to understand the effect of the instructions in the program if you do. This section gives a brief introduction to computer hardware components and their functionality.

A computer consists of the following major hardware components, as shown in Figure 1.1.

- Central Processing Unit (CPU)

- Memory (main memory)

- Storage Devices (disks, CDs, tapes)

- Input and Output Devices (monitors, keyboards, mice, printers)

- Communication Devices (modems and network interface cards (NICs))

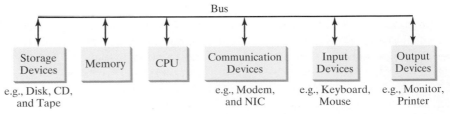

FIGURE 1.1   A computer consists of a CPU, memory, hard disk, floppy disk, monitor, printer, and communication devices.

The components are connected through a subsystem called a *bus* that transfers data or power between the components.

1.2.1 Central Processing Unit

CPU

The *central processing unit* (*CPU*) is the brain of a computer. It retrieves instructions from memory and executes them. The CPU usually has two components: a *control unit* and an *arithmetic/logic unit*. The control unit controls and coordinates the actions of the other components. The arithmetic and logic unit performs numeric operations (addition, subtraction, multiplication, division) and logical operations (comparisons).

    Today's CPU is built on a small silicon semiconductor chip with millions of transistors. The *speed* of the CPU is mainly determined by clock speed. Every computer has an internal clock. The faster the clock speed, the more instructions are executed in a given period of time. The clock emits electronic pulses at a constant rate, and these are used to control and synchronize the pace of operations. The unit of measurement is called a *hertz* (Hz), with 1 hertz equaling 1 pulse per second. The clock speed of computers is usually measured in *megahertz* (MHz) (1 MHz is 1 million Hz). The speed of the CPU has been improved continuously. If you buy a PC now, you can get an Intel Pentium 4 Processor at 3 *gigahertz* (GHz) (1 GHz is 1000 MHz). *[margin: speed, hertz, megahertz, gigahertz]*

1.2.2 Memory

Computers use zeros and ones because digital devices have two stable states, referred to as *zero* and *one* by convention. Data of various kinds, such as numbers, characters, and strings, are encoded as a series of *bits* (binary dig*its*: zeros and ones). *Memory* stores data and program instructions for the CPU to execute. A memory unit is an ordered sequence of *bytes*, each holding eight bits, as shown in Figure 1.2. *[margin: bit, byte]*

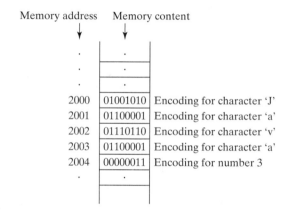

FIGURE 1.2 Memory stores data and program instructions.

    The programmer need not be concerned about the encoding and decoding of data, which is performed automatically by the system based on the encoding scheme. The encoding scheme varies. For example, character 'J' is represented by 01001010 in one byte in the popular ASCII encoding. A small number such as 3 can be stored in a single byte. If a computer needs to store a large number that cannot fit into a single byte, it uses several adjacent bytes. No two data items can share or split the same byte. A byte is the minimum storage unit.

    A program and its data must be brought to memory before they can be executed. A memory byte is never empty, but its initial content may be meaningless to your program. The current content of a memory byte is lost whenever new information is placed in it.

    Every byte has a unique address. The address is used to locate the byte for storing and retrieving data. Since the bytes can be accessed in any order, the memory is also referred to as *RAM* (random-access memory). Today's personal computers usually have at least 128 megabytes of RAM. A *megabyte* (abbreviated MB) is about 1 million bytes. For a precise definition of megabyte, please see http://en.wikipedia.org/wiki/Megabyte. Like the CPU, memory is built on silicon semiconductor chips containing thousands of transistors embedded on their surface. Compared to the CPU chips, memory chips are less complicated, slower, and less expensive. *[margin: RAM, megabyte, megabyte URL]*

1.2.3 Storage Devices

Memory is volatile, because information is lost when the power is turned off. Programs and data are permanently stored on storage devices and are moved to memory when the computer actually uses them. The reason for this is that memory is much faster than storage devices. There are four main types of storage devices:

- Disk drives (hard disks and floppy disks)

- CD drives (CD-R, CD-RW, and DVD)

- Tape drives

- USB flash drives

drive   *Drives* are devices for operating a medium, such as disks, CDs, and tapes.

Disks

hard disk
floppy disk

There are two kinds of disks: *hard disks* and *floppy disks*. Personal computers usually have a 3.5-inch floppy disk drive and a hard drive. A floppy disk has a fixed capacity of about 1.44 MB. Hard disk capacities vary. The capacity of the hard disks of the latest PCs is in the range of 30 gigabytes to 160 gigabytes. Hard disks provide much faster performance and larger capacity than floppy disks. Both disk drives are often encased inside the computer. A floppy disk is removable. A hard disk is mounted inside the case of the computer. Removable hard disks are also available. Floppy disks will eventually be replaced by CD-RW and flash drives.

CDs and DVDs

CD-R

CD-RW

CD stands for compact disc. There are two types of CD drives: CD-R and CD-RW. A *CD-R* is for read-only permanent storage, and the user cannot modify its contents once they are recorded. A *CD-RW* can be used like a floppy disk, and thus can be read and rewritten. A single CD can hold up to 700 MB. Most software is distributed through CD-ROMs. Most new PCs are equipped with a CD-RW drive that can work with both CD-R and CD-RW.

DVD stands for digital versatile disc. DVDs and CDs look alike. You can store data using a CD or DVD. A DVD can hold more information than a CD. A standard DVD storage is 4.7 GB in capacity.

Tapes

Tapes are mainly used for backup of data and programs. Unlike disks and CDs, tapes store information sequentially. The computer must retrieve information in the order it was stored. Tapes are very slow. It would take one to two hours to back up a 1-gigabyte hard disk.

USB Flash Drives

USB flash drives are popular new devices for storing and transporting data. They are small—about the size of a package of gum. They act like a portable hard disk that can be plugged into the USB port of your computer. USB flash drives are currently available with up to 2 GB storage capacity.

1.2.4 Input and Output Devices

Input and output devices let the user communicate with the computer. The common input devices are *keyboards* and *mice*. The common output devices are *monitors* and *printers*.

The Keyboard

A computer *keyboard* resembles a typewriter keyboard except that it has extra keys for certain special functions.

Function keys are located at the top of the keyboard with prefix F. Their use depends on the software.

A *modifier key* is special key (e.g., Shift, Alt, Ctrl) that modifies the normal action of another key when the two are pressed in combination.

The *numeric keypad,* located on the right-hand corner of the keyboard, is a separate set of number keys for quick input of numbers.

Arrow keys, located between the main keypad and the numeric keypad, are used to move the cursor up, down, left, and right.

The *insert, delete, page up,* and *page down keys*, located above the arrow keys, are used in word processing for performing insert, delete, page up, and page down.

The Mouse

A *mouse* is a pointing device. It is used to move an electronic pointer called a cursor around the screen or to click on an object on the screen to trigger it to respond.

The Monitor

The *monitor* displays information (text and graphics). The resolution and dot pitch determine the quality of the display.

The *resolution* specifies the number of pixels per square inch. Pixels (short for "picture elements") are tiny dots that form an image on the screen. A common resolution for a 17-inch screen, for example, is 1024 pixels wide and 768 pixels high. The resolution can be set manually. The higher the resolution, the sharper and clearer the image is. *(screen resolution)*

The *dot pitch* is the amount of space between pixels. Typically, it has a range from 0.21 to 0.81 millimeters. The smaller the dot pitch, the better the display. *(dot pitch)*

1.2.5 Communication Devices

Computers can be networked through communication devices. Commonly used communication devices are the dialup *modem, DSL,* cable modem, and network interface card. A dialup modem uses a phone line and can transfer data at a speed up to 56,000 bps (bits per second). A DSL (digital subscriber line) also uses a phone line and can transfer data at a speed 20 times faster than a dialup modem. A cable modem uses the TV cable line maintained by the cable company. A cable modem is as fast as DSL. A network interface card (*NIC*) is a device that connects a computer to a local area network (*LAN*). The LAN is commonly used in business, universities, and government organizations. A typical NIC called *10BaseT* can transfer data at 10 *mbps* (million bits per second). *(modem, DSL, NIC, LAN, mbps)*

1.3 Programs

Computer *programs*, known as *software*, are instructions to the computer. You tell a computer what to do through programs. Without programs, a computer is an empty machine. Computers do not understand human languages, so you need to use computer languages to communicate with them. *(software)*

The language a computer speaks is the computer's native language or machine language. The *machine language* is a set of primitive instructions built into every computer. Machine languages are different for different type of computers. The instructions are in the form of binary code, so you have to enter binary codes for various instructions. Programming using *(machine language)* a native machine language is a tedious process. Moreover, the programs are highly difficult to read and modify. For example, to add two numbers, you might have to write an instruction in binary like this:

    1101101010011010

assembly language

Assembly language is a low-level programming language in which a mnemonic is used to represent each of the machine-language instructions. For example, to add two numbers, you might write an instruction in assembly code like this:

    ADDF3 R1, R2, R3

assembler

Assembly languages were developed to make programming easy. Since the computer cannot understand assembly language, however, a program called *assembler* is used to convert assembly language programs into machine code, as shown in Figure 1.3.

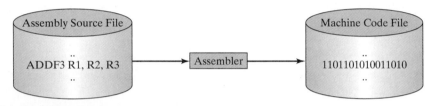

FIGURE 1.3   Assembler translates assembly language instructions to machine code.

Since assembly language is machine-dependent, an assembly program can only be executed on a particular machine. Assembly programs are written in terms of machine instructions with easy-to-remember mnemonic names. The high-level languages were developed in order to overcome the platform-specific problem and make programming easier.

high-level language

The *high-level languages* are English-like and easy to learn and program. Here, for example, is a high-level language statement that computes the area of a circle with radius 5:

    area = 5 * 5 * 3.1415;

There are over one hundred high-level languages. The popular languages used today are:

- COBOL (COmmon Business Oriented Language)
- FORTRAN (FORmula TRANslation)
- BASIC (Beginner All-purpose Symbolic Instructional Code)
- Pascal (named for Blaise Pascal)
- Ada (named for Ada Lovelace)
- C (whose developer designed B first)
- Visual Basic (Basic-like visual language developed by Microsoft)
- Delphi (Pascal-like visual language developed by Borland)
- C++ (an object-oriented language, based on C)
- C# (a Java-like language developed by Microsoft)
- Java

Each of these languages was designed for a specific purpose. COBOL was designed for business applications and now is used primarily for business data processing. FORTRAN was designed for mathematical computations and is used mainly for numeric computations. BASIC, as its name suggests, was designed to be learned and used easily. Ada was developed for the Department of Defense and is mainly used in defense projects. C combines the power of an assembly language with the ease of use and portability of a high-level language. Visual Basic and Delphi are used in developing graphical user interfaces and in rapid application development. C++ is popular for system software projects like writing compilers and operating systems. The Microsoft Windows operating system was coded using C++.

A program written in a high-level language is called a *source program*. Since a computer cannot understand a source program, a program called a *compiler* is used to translate the source program into a machine-language program. The machine-language program is often then linked with other supporting library code to form an executable file. The executable file can be executed on the machine, as shown in Figure 1.4. On Windows, executable files have extension .exe.

source program
compiler

FIGURE 1.4 A source program is compiled into a machine-language file, which is then linked with the system library to form an executable file.

You can port (i.e., move) a source program to any machine with appropriate compilers. The source program must be recompiled, however, because the machine-language program can only run on a specific machine. Nowadays computers are networked to work together. Java was designed to run on any platform. With Java, you write the program once and compile the source program into a special type of machine-language code known as *bytecode*. The bytecode can then run on any computer with a Java Virtual Machine (*JVM*), as shown in Figure 1.5. The Java Virtual Machine is software that interprets Java bytecode.

bytecode
JVM

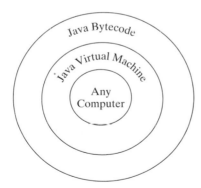

FIGURE 1.5 Java bytecode can be executed on any computer with a Java Virtual Machine.

Note

Java bytecode is interpreted. The difference between compiling and interpreting is as follows. Compiling translates the high-level code into a target language code as a single unit. Interpreting translates the individual steps in a high-level program one at a time rather than the whole program as a single unit. Each step is executed immediately after it is translated.

compiling vs. interpreting

1.4 Operating Systems

OS

The *operating system* (*OS*) is the most important program that runs on a computer to manage and control its activities. You are probably using Windows (98, NT, 2000, XP, or ME), Mac OS, or Linux. Windows is currently the most popular PC operating system. Application programs, such as a Web browser or a word processor, cannot run without an operating system. The interrelationship of hardware, operating system, application software, and the user is shown in Figure 1.6.

FIGURE 1.6   The operating system is the software that controls and manages the system.

The major tasks of the operating systems are:

■ Controlling and monitoring system activities

■ Allocating and assigning system resources

■ Scheduling operations

1.4.1   Controlling and Monitoring System Activities

Operating systems are responsible for security, ensuring that unauthorized users do not access the system. Operating systems perform basic tasks, such as recognizing input from the keyboard, sending output to the monitor, keeping track of files and directories on the disk, and controlling peripheral devices, such as disk drives and printers. Operating systems also make sure that different programs and users running at the same time do not interfere with one other.

1.4.2   Allocating and Assigning System Resources

The OS is responsible for determining what computer resources a program needs (e.g., CPU, memory, disks, input and output devices) and for allocating and assigning them to run the program.

1.4.3   Scheduling Operations

The OS is responsible for scheduling programs to use the system resources efficiently. Many of today's operating systems support such techniques as *multiprogramming*, *multithreading*, or *multiprocessing* to increase system performance.

multiprogramming

Multiprogramming allows multiple programs to run simultaneously by sharing the CPU. The CPU is much faster than the other components. As a result, it is idle most of the time; for example, while waiting for data to be transferred from the disk or from other sources. A multiprogramming OS takes advantage of this by allowing multiple programs to use the CPU when it would otherwise be idle. For example, you may use a word processor to edit a file while the Web browser is downloading a file at the same time.

Multithreading allows concurrency within a program, so that its subunits can run at the same time. For example, a word-processing program allows users to simultaneously edit text and save it to a file. In this example, editing and saving are two tasks within the same application. These two tasks may run on separate threads concurrently.

multithreading

Multiprocessing, or parallel processing, uses two or more processors together to perform a task. It is like a surgical operation where several doctors work together on one patient.

multiprocessing

1.5 (Optional) Number Systems

 Note
You can skip this section and use it as reference when you have questions regarding binary and hexadecimal numbers.

Computers use *binary numbers* internally because storage devices like memory and disk are made to store 0s and 1s. A number or a character inside a computer is stored as a sequence of 0s and 1s. Each 0 or 1 is called a *bit*. The binary number system has two digits, 0 and 1.

binary number

Since we use *decimal numbers* in our daily life, binary numbers are not intuitive. When you write a number like 20 in a program, it is assumed to be a decimal number. Internally, computer software is used to convert decimal numbers into binary numbers, and vice versa.

decimal number

You write programs using decimal number systems. However, if you write programs to deal with a system like an operating system, you need to use binary numbers to reach down to the "machine-level." Binary numbers tend to be very long and cumbersome. *Hexadecimal numbers* are often used to abbreviate binary numbers, with each hexadecimal digit representing exactly four binary digits. The hexadecimal number system has sixteen digits: 0, 1, 2, 3, 4, 5, 6, 7, 8, 9, A, B, C, D, E, and F. The letters A, B, C, D, E, and F correspond to the decimal numbers 10, 11, 12, 13, 14, and 15.

hexadecimal number

The digits in the decimal number system are 0, 1, 2, 3, 4, 5, 6, 7, 8, and 9. A decimal number is represented using a sequence of one or more of these digits. The value that each digit in the sequence represents depends on its position. A position in a sequence has a value that is an integral power of 10. For example, the digits 7, 4, 2, and 3 in decimal number 7423 represent 7000, 400, 20, and 3, respectively, as shown below:

$$\boxed{7 \mid 4 \mid 2 \mid 3} = 7 \times 10^3 + 4 \times 10^2 + 2 \times 10^1 + 3 \times 10^0$$
$$10^3 \ 10^2 \ 10^1 \ 10^0 \ = 7000 + 400 + 20 + 3 = 7423$$

The decimal number system has ten digits, and the position values are integral powers of 10. We say that 10 is the *base* or *radix* of the decimal number system. Similarly, the base of the binary number system is 2 since the binary number system has two digits, and the base of the hex number system is 16 since the hex number system has sixteen digits.

base

radix

1.5.1 Conversions Between Binary Numbers and Decimal Numbers

Given a binary number $b_n b_{n-1} b_{n-2} \cdots b_2 b_1 b_0$, the equivalent decimal value is

$$b_n \times 2^n + b_{n-1} \times 2^{n-1} + b_{n-2} \times 2^{n-2} + \cdots + b_2 \times 2^2 + b_1 \times 2^1 + b_0 \times 2^0$$

The following are examples of converting binary numbers to decimals:

binary to decimal

Binary	Conversion Formula	Decimal
10	$1 \times 2^1 + 0 \times 2^0$	2
1000	$1 \times 2^3 + 0 \times 2^2 + 0 \times 2^1 + 0 \times 2^0$	8
10101011	$1 \times 2^7 + 0 \times 2^6 + 1 \times 2^5 + 0 \times 2^4 + 1 \times 2^3 + 0 \times 2^2 +$	
	$1 \times 2^1 + 1 \times 2^0$	171

decimal to binary

To convert a decimal number d to a binary number is to find the bits $b_n, b_{n-1}, b_{n-2}, \ldots, b_2, b_1$, and b_0 such that

$$d = b_n \times 2^n + b_{n-1} \times 2^{n-1} + b_{n-2} \times 2^{n-2} + \cdots + b_2 \times 2^2 + b_1 \times 2^1 + b_0 \times 2^0$$

These bits can be found by successively dividing d by 2 until the quotient is 0. The remainders are $b_0, b_1, b_2, \ldots, b_{n-2}, b_{n-1}$, and b_n.

For example, the decimal number 123 is 1111011 in binary. The conversion is done as follows:

 Tip

The Windows Calculator, as shown in Figure 1.7, is a useful tool for performing number conversions. To run it, choose *Programs*, *Accessories*, and *Calculator* from the Start button.

FIGURE 1.7 You can perform number conversions using the Windows Calculator.

1.5.2 Conversions Between Hexadecimal Numbers and Decimal Numbers

Given a hexadecimal number $h_n h_{n-1} h_{n-2} \cdots h_2 h_1 h_0$, the equivalent decimal value is

$$h_n \times 16^n + h_{n-1} \times 16^{n-1} + h_{n-2} \times 16^{n-2} + \cdots + h_2 \times 16^2 + h_1 \times 16^1 + h_0 \times 16^0$$

hex to decimal

The following are examples of converting hexadecimal numbers to decimals:

Hexadecimal	Conversion Formula	Decimal
7F	$7 \times 16^1 + 15 \times 16^0$	127
FFFF	$15 \times 16^3 + 15 \times 16^2 + 15 \times 16^1 + 15 \times 16^0$	65535
431	$4 \times 16^2 + 3 \times 16^1 + 1 \times 16^0$	1073

To convert a decimal number d to a hexadecimal number is to find the hexadecimal digits $h_n, h_{n-1}, h_{n-2}, \ldots, h_2, h_1$, and h_0 such that

$$d = h_n \times 16^n + h_{n-1} \times 16^{n-1} + h_{n-2} \times 16^{n-2} + \cdots + h_2 \times 16^2$$
$$+ h_1 \times 16^1 + h_0 \times 16^0$$

decimal to hex

These numbers can be found by successively dividing d by 16 until the quotient is 0. The remainders are $h_0, h_1, h_2, \ldots, h_{n-2}, h_{n-1}$, and h_n.

For example, the decimal number 123 is 7B in hexadecimal. The conversion is done as follows:

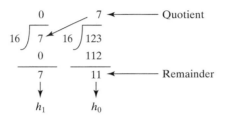

1.5.3 Conversions Between Binary Numbers and Hexadecimal Numbers

To convert a hexadecimal number to a binary number, simply convert each digit in the hexadecimal number into a four-digit binary number using Table 1.1.

hex to binary

TABLE 1.1 Converting Hexadecimal to Binary

Hexadecimal	Binary	Decimal
0	0	0
1	1	1
2	10	2
3	11	3
4	100	4
5	101	5
6	110	6
7	111	7
8	1000	8
9	1001	9
A	1010	10
B	1011	11
C	1100	12
D	1101	13
E	1110	14
F	1111	15

For example, the hexadecimal number 7B is 1111011, where 7 is 111 in binary, and B is 1011 in binary.

binary to hex

To convert a binary number to a hexadecimal, convert every four binary digits from right to left in the binary number into a hexadecimal number.

For example, the binary number 1110001101 is 38D, since 1101 is D, 1000 is 8, and 11 is 3, as shown below.

Note

Octal numbers are also useful. The octal number system has eight digits, 0 to 7. A decimal number 8 is represented as 10 in the octal system.

1.6 Java, the World Wide Web, and Beyond

This book introduces Java programming. Java was developed by a team led by James Gosling at Sun Microsystems. Originally called *Oak*, it was designed in 1991 for use in embedded consumer electronic appliances. In 1995, renamed *Java*, it was redesigned for developing Internet applications. For the history of Java, see java.sun.com/features/1998/05/birthday.html.

Java history URL

Java has become enormously popular. Java's rapid rise and wide acceptance can be traced to its design characteristics, particularly its promise that you can write a program once and run it anywhere. As stated in the Java language white paper by Sun, Java is *simple*, *object-oriented*, *distributed*, *interpreted*, *robust*, *secure*, *architecture-neutral*, *portable*, *high-performance*, *multi-threaded*, and *dynamic*. For the anatomy of Java characteristics, see www.cs.armstrong.edu/liang/intro6e/JavaCharacteristics.pdf.

Java characteristics URL
Java's versatility

Java is a full-featured, general-purpose programming language that is capable of developing robust mission-critical applications. Today, it is used not only for Web programming, but also for developing standalone applications across platforms on servers, desktops, and mobile devices. It was used to develop the code to communicate with and control the robotic rover that rolled on Mars. Many companies that once considered Java to be more hype than substance are now using it to create distributed applications accessed by customers and partners across the Internet. For every new project being developed today, companies are asking how they can use Java to make their work easier.

The World Wide Web is an electronic information repository that can be accessed on the Internet from anywhere in the world. You can use the Web to book a hotel room, buy an airline ticket, register for a college course, download the *New York Times*, chat with friends, or listen to live radio. There are countless activities you can do on the Internet. Many people spend a good part of their computer time surfing the Web for fun and profit.

The Internet is the infrastructure of the Web. The Internet has been around for more than thirty years, but has only recently become popular. The colorful World Wide Web and sophisticated Web browsers are the major reason for its popularity.

The primary authoring language for the Web is the Hypertext Markup Language (HTML). HTML is a markup language: a simple language for laying out documents, linking documents on the Internet, and bringing images, sound, and video alive on the Web. However, it cannot interact with the user except through simple forms. Web pages in HTML are essentially static and flat.

applet

Java initially became attractive because Java programs can be run from a Web browser. Java programs that run from a Web browser are called *applets*. Applets use a modern graphical user interface with buttons, text fields, text areas, radio buttons, and so on, to interact with users on the Web and process their requests. Applets make the Web responsive, interactive, and fun to use. Figure 1.8 shows an applet running from a Web browser.

Enter this URL from a
Web browser

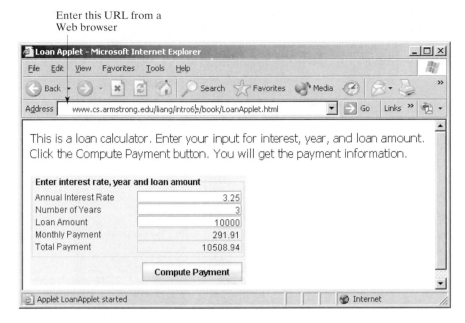

FIGURE 1.8 A Java applet for computing loan payments is embedded in an HTML page.
The user can use the applet to compute the loan payments.

 Tip

For a demonstration of Java applets, visit java.sun.com/applets. This site provides a rich Java resource
as well as links to other cool applet demo sites. java.sun.com is the official Sun Java website.

Java can also be used to develop applications on the server side. These applications, called *Java
servlets* or *JavaServer Pages (JSP)*, can be run from a Web server to generate dynamic Web
pages. The Self-Test website for this book, as shown in Figure 1.9, was developed using Java
servlets. The Web pages for the questions and answers are dynamically generated by the servlets.

servlet
JSP

Enter this URL from a
Web browser

FIGURE 1.9 Java was used to develop the self-test in the Companion Website for this book.

Java is a versatile programming language. You can use it to develop applications on your desktop and on the server. You can also use it to develop applications for small hand-held devices, such as personal digital assistants and cell phones. Figure 1.10 shows a Java program that displays the calendar on a BlackBerry® and on a cell phone.

FIGURE 1.10 Java can be used to develop applications for hand-held and wireless devices, such as a BlackBerry (left) and a cell phone (right).

1.7 The Java Language Specification, API, JDK, and IDE

Computer languages have strict rules of usage. If you do not follow the rules when writing a program, the computer will be unable to understand it. Sun Microsystems, the originator of Java, intends to retain control of this important new computer language—and for a very good reason: to prevent it from losing its unified standards. The Java language specification and Java API define the Java standard.

The Java language specification is a technical definition of the language that includes the syntax and semantics of the Java programming language. The complete Java language specification can be found at java.sun.com/docs/books/jls.

API

The *application program interface* (*API*) contains predefined classes and interfaces for developing Java programs. The Java language specification is stable, but the API is still expanding. At the Sun Java website (java.sun.com), you can view and download the latest version of the Java API.

Java was introduced in 1995. Sun announced the Java 2 platform in December 1998. Java 2 is the overarching brand that applies to current Java technology. There are three editions of the Java API: *Java 2 Standard Edition (J2SE)*, *Java 2 Enterprise Edition (J2EE)*, and *Java 2 Micro Edition (J2ME)*. Java is a full-fledged and powerful language that can be used in many ways. J2SE can be used to develop client-side standalone applications or applets. J2EE can be used to develop server-side applications, such as Java servlets and JavaServer Pages. J2ME can be used to develop applications for mobile devices, such as cell phones. This book uses J2SE to introduce Java programming.

There are many versions of J2SE. The latest version is J2SE 5.0, which will be used in this book. Sun releases each version of J2SE with a *Java Development Toolkit* (JDK). For J2SE 5.0, the Java Development Toolkit is called JDK 5.0. JDK 5.0 was formerly known as JDK 1.5.

Since most Java programmers are familiar with the name JDK 1.5, this book uses the names
JDK 5.0 and JDK 1.5 interchangeably.

JDK 1.5 = JDK 5.0

JDK consists of a set of separate programs for developing and testing Java programs, each
of which is invoked from a command line. Besides JDK, there are more than a dozen Java
development tools on the market today. Three major development tools are:

- JBuilder by Borland (www.borland.com)
- NetBeans Open Source by Sun (www.netbeans.org)
- Eclipse Open Source by IBM (www.eclipse.org)

Other useful tools are:

- Code Warrior by Metrowerks (www.metrowerks.com)
- TextPad Editor (www.textpad.com)
- JCreator LE (www.jcreator.com)
- JEdit (www.jedit.org)
- JGrasp (www.jgrasp.org)
- BlueJ (www.bluej.org)
- DrJava (http://drjava.sourceforge.net)

A Java development tool is software that provides an *integrated development environment* (*IDE*) for
rapidly developing Java programs. Editing, compiling, building, debugging, and online help are
integrated in one graphical user interface. Just enter source code in one window or open an existing
file in a window, then click a button, menu item, or function key to compile and run the program.

Java IDE

1.8 A Simple Java Program

A Java program can be written in many ways. This book introduces Java *applications*, applets,
and servlets. Applications are standalone programs that can be executed from any computer
with a JVM. *Applets* are special kinds of Java programs that run from a Web browser. Servlets
are special kinds of Java programs that run from a Web server to generate dynamic Web contents. Applets will be introduced in Chapter 16, and servlets will be introduced in Chapter 34.

application

applet

Let us begin with a simple Java program that displays the message "Welcome to Java!" on
the console. The program is shown in Listing 1.1.

LISTING 1.1 `Welcome.java`

```
Comments ──▶  // This application program prints Welcome to Java!

Class          public class Welcome {   Class Name
heading ──▶    public static void main(String[] args) {
Main method
  signature
                 System.out.println("Welcome to Java!");   String
               }
             }
```

Every Java program must have at least one class. A class is a construct that defines data and
methods. Each class has a name. By convention, *class names* start with an uppercase letter.
In this example, the class name is `Welcome`.

class name

In order to run a class, the class must contain a method named `main`. The JVM executes
the program by invoking the `main` method.

`main` method

A method is a construct that contains statements. The `main` method in this program contains the `System.out.println` statement. This statement prints a message "Welcome to
Java!" to the console.

console output

Note

You are probably wondering about such points as why the `main` method is declared this way and why `System.out.println(...)` is used to display a message to the console. Your questions cannot be fully answered yet. For the time being, you will just have to accept that this is how things are done. You will find the answers in the coming chapters.

Note

syntax rules

Like any other programming language, Java has its own syntax, and you need to write code that obeys the *syntax rules*. The Java compiler will report syntax errors if your program violates the syntax rules.

1.9 Creating, Compiling, and Executing a Java Program

You have to create your program and compile it before it can be executed. This process is repetitive, as shown in Figure 1.11. If your program has compilation errors, you have to fix them by modifying the program, then recompile it. If your program has runtime errors or does not produce the correct result, you have to modify the program, recompile it, and execute it again.

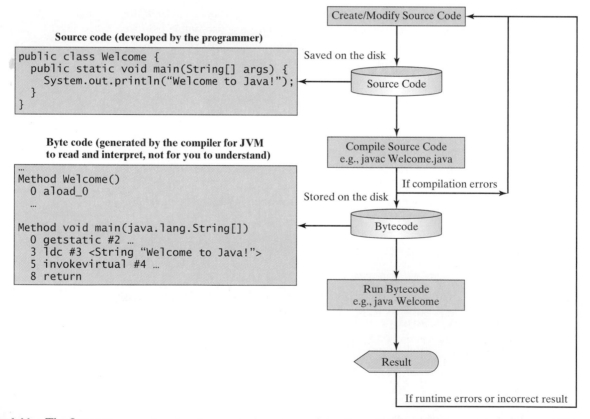

FIGURE 1.11 The Java programming-development process consists of creating/modifying source code, compiling, and executing programs.

editor

You can use any text *editor* to create and edit a Java source code file, or you can use an IDE like Eclipse, JBuilder or NetBeans. Figure 1.12 shows how to use NotePad to create and edit the source code file.

FIGURE 1.12   You can create the Java source file using Windows NotePad.

This file must end with the extension .java and must have the exact same name as the public class name. For example, the file for the source code in Listing 1.1 should be named Welcome.java, since the public class name is `Welcome`.

A Java compiler translates a *Java source file* into a Java bytecode file. The following command *compiles* Welcome.java:

.java source file

compile

```
javac Welcome.java
```

Note
You must first install and configure JDK before compiling and running programs. See *Supplement I.B,* "Installing and Configuring JDK 5.0," on how to install JDK and how to set up the environment to compile and run Java programs. If you have trouble compiling and running programs, please see *Supplement I.C,* "Compiling and Running Java from the Command Window." This supplement also explains how to use basic DOS commands and how to use Windows NotePad and WordPad to create and edit files. All the supplements are accessible from the Companion Website.

Supplement I.B

Supplement I.C

Caution
Java source programs are *case-sensitive*. It would be wrong, for example, to replace `main` in the program with `Main`. Program filenames are case-sensitive on UNIX but generally not on Windows; JDK treats filenames as case-sensitive on any platform. If you try to compile the program using `javac welcome.java`, you will get a file-not-found error.

case-sensitive

If there are no syntax errors, the *compiler* generates a bytecode file with a .class extension. So the preceding command generates a file named **Welcome.class**. The bytecode is similar to machine instructions but is architecture-neutral and can run on any platform that has a JVM. This is one of Java's primary advantages: *Java bytecode can run on a variety of hardware platforms and operating systems.*

.class bytecode file

To execute a Java program is to *run* the program's bytecode. You can execute the bytecode on any platform with a JVM. The following command runs the bytecode:

run

```
java Welcome
```

Figure 1.13 shows the **javac** command for compiling Welcome.java. The compiler generated the Welcome.class file. This file is executed using the **java** command.

FIGURE 1.13   The output of Listing 1.1 displays the message Welcome to Java!

Caution

Do not use the extension .class in the command line when executing the program. The JVM assumes that the first argument in the command is the filename and then fetches **filename.class** to execute. It would attempt to fetch **filename.class.class** if you used **java filename.class** in the command line.

NoClassDefFoundError

NoSuchMethodError

Tip

If you execute a class file that does not exist, a `NoClassDefFoundError` exception will occur. If you execute a class file that does not have a `main` method or you mistype the `main` method (e.g., by typing `Main` instead of `main`), a `NoSuchMethodError` will occur.

Note

class loader

bytecode verifier

When executing a Java program, the JVM first loads the bytecode of the class to memory using a program called the *class loader*. If your program uses other classes, the class loader dynamically loads them just before they are needed. After a class is loaded, the JVM uses a program called *bytecode verifier* to check the validity of the bytecode and ensure that the bytecode does not violate Java's security restrictions. Java enforces strict security to make sure that Java programs arriving from the network do not harm your computer.

1.10 Anatomy of a Java Program

The application program in Listing 1.1 has the following components:

- Comments
- Reserved words
- Modifiers
- Statements
- Blocks
- Classes
- Methods
- The `main` method

To build a program, you need to understand these basic elements. They are explained in the sections that follow.

1.10.1 Comments

The first line in Welcome.java in Listing 1.1 is a *comment* that documents what the program is and how the program is constructed. Comments help programmers to communicate and understand the program. Comments are not programming statements and thus are ignored by the compiler. In Java, comments are preceded by two slashes (//) on a line, called a *line comment*, or enclosed between /* and */ on one or several lines, called a *paragraph comment*. When the compiler sees //, it ignores all text after // on the same line. When it sees /*, it scans for the next */ and ignores any text between /* and */.

line comment
paragraph comment

Here are examples of the two types of comments:

```
// This application program prints Welcome to Java!
/* This application program prints Welcome to Java! */
/* This application program
   prints Welcome to Java! */
```

Note

In addition to the two comment styles, `//` and `/*`, Java supports comments of a special type, referred to as *javadoc comments*. javadoc comments begin with `/**` and end with `*/`. They are used for documenting classes, data, and methods. They can be extracted into an HTML file using JDK's **javadoc** command. For more information, see java.sun.com/j2se/javadoc.

javadoc comment

1.10.2   Reserved Words

Reserved words, or *keywords*, are words that have a specific meaning to the compiler and cannot be used for other purposes in the program. For example, when the compiler sees the word **class**, it understands that the word after **class** is the name for the class. Other reserved words in Listing 1.1 are **public**, **static**, and **void**. Their use will be introduced later in the book.

reserved word

Tip

Because Java is *case-sensitive*, **public** is a reserved word, but **Public** is not. Nonetheless, for clarity and readability, it would be best to avoid using reserved words in other forms. (See Appendix A, "Java Keywords.")

case-sensitive

1.10.3   Modifiers

Java uses certain reserved words called *modifiers* that specify the properties of the data, methods, and classes and how they can be used. Examples of modifiers are **public** and **static**. Other modifiers are **private**, **final**, **abstract**, and **protected**. A **public** datum, method, or class can be accessed by other classes. A **private** datum or method cannot be accessed by other classes.

modifier

1.10.4   Statements

A *statement* represents an action or a sequence of actions. The statement `System.out.println("Welcome to Java!");` in the program in Listing 1.1 is a statement to display the greeting "Welcome to Java!" Every statement in Java ends with a *semicolon (;)*.

statement

semicolon

1.10.5   Blocks

The braces in the program form a *block* that groups the components of the program. In Java, each block begins with an opening brace ({) and ends with a closing brace (}). Every class has a *class block* that groups the data and methods of the class. Every method has a *method block* that groups the statements in the method. Blocks can be *nested*, meaning that one block can be placed within another, as shown in the following code.

block

```
public class Test {              ◄
    public static void main(String[] args) {  ◄          Class block
        System.out.println("Welcome to Java!");  Method block
    }  ◄
}  ◄
```

1.10.6   Classes

The *class* is the essential Java construct. To program in Java, you must understand classes and be able to write and use them. The mystery of classes will be unveiled throughout the book. For now, though, it is enough to know that a program is defined by using one or more classes.

class

1.10.7 Methods

method

What is `System.out.println`? `System.out` is known as the *standard output object*. `println` is a *method* in the object, which consists of a collection of statements that perform a sequence of operations to display a message to the standard output device. If you run the program from the command window, the output from the `System.out.println` is displayed in the command window. The method can be used even without fully understanding the details of how it works. It is used by invoking a statement with a string argument. The string argument is enclosed in parentheses. In this case, the argument is `"Welcome to Java!"` You can call the same `println` method with a different argument to print a different message.

1.10.8 The `main` Method

main method

Every Java application must have a user-declared `main` method that defines where the program execution begins. The JVM executes the application by invoking the `main` method. The `main` method looks like this:

```
public static void main(String[] args) {
  // Statements;
}
```

1.11 Displaying Text in a Message Dialog Box

JOptionPane

showMessageDialog

The program in Listing 1.1 displays the text on the console, as shown in Figure 1.13. You can rewrite the program to display the text in a message dialog box. To do so, you need to use the `showMessageDialog` method in the `JOptionPane` class. `JOptionPane` is one of the many predefined classes in the Java system that you can reuse rather than "reinventing the wheel." You can use the `showMessageDialog` method to display any text in a message dialog box, as shown in Figure 1.14. The new program is given in Listing 1.2.

FIGURE 1.14 "Welcome to Java!" is displayed in a message box.

LISTING 1.2 WelcomeInMessageDialogBox.java

paragraph comment

import

main method

display message

```
 1  /** This application program displays Welcome to Java!
 2   *  in a message dialog box.
 3   */
 4  import javax.swing.JOptionPane;
 5
 6  public class WelcomeInMessageDialogBox {
 7    public static void main(String[] args) {
 8      // Display Welcome to Java! in a message dialog box
 9      JOptionPane.showMessageDialog(null, "Welcome to Java!",
10        "Display Message", JOptionPane.INFORMATION_MESSAGE);
11    }
12  }
```

The line numbers are not part of the program, but are displayed for reference purposes.

This program uses a Java class **JOptionPane** (line 9). Java's predefined classes are grouped into packages. **JOptionPane** is in the **javax.swing** package. **JOptionPane** is imported to the program using the **import** statement in line 4 so that the compiler can locate the class. Recall that you have used the **System** class in the statement *System.out. println("Welcome to Java");* in Listing 1.1. The **System** class is not imported because it is in the **java.lang** package. All the classes in the **java.lang** package are implicitly imported in every Java program.

Note

If you replace **JOptionPane** on line 9 with **javax.swing.JOptionPane**, you don't need to import it in line 4. **javax.swing.JOptionPane** is the full name for the **JOptionPane** class.

The **showMessageDialog** method is a *static* method. Such a method should be invoked by using the class name followed by a dot operator (.) and the method name with arguments. Static methods will be introduced in Chapter 5, "Methods." The **showMessageDialog** method can be invoked with four arguments, as in lines 9–10.

The first argument can always be **null**. **null** is a Java keyword that will be fully introduced in Part II, "Object-Oriented Programming." The second argument can be a string for text to be displayed. The third argument is the title of the message box. The fourth argument can be **JOptionPane.INFORMATION_MESSAGE**, which causes the icon ( ) to be displayed in the message box.

Note

There are several ways to use the **showMessageDialog** method. For the time being, all you need to know are two ways to invoke it. One is to use a statement, as shown in the example:

```
JOptionPane.showMessageDialog(null, x,
  y, JOptionPane.INFORMATION_MESSAGE);
```

where x is a string for the text to be displayed, and y is a string for the title of the message box. The other is to use a statement like this one:

```
JOptionPane.showMessageDialog(null, x);
```

where x is a string for the text to be displayed.

KEY TERMS

Supplement I.A

 Note

The above terms are defined in this chapter. *Supplement I.A,* "Glossary," lists all the key terms and descriptions in the book, organized by chapters.

CHAPTER SUMMARY

■   A computer is an electronic device that stores and processes data. A computer includes both *hardware* and *software*. In general, hardware is the physical aspect of the computer that can be seen, and software is the invisible instructions that control the hardware and make it perform tasks.

■   Computer *programs*, known as *software*, are instructions to the computer. You tell a computer what to do through programs. Computer programming consists of writing instructions for computers to perform.

■   The *machine language* is a set of primitive instructions built into every computer. *Assembly language* is a low-level programming language in which a mnemonic is used to represent each of the machine-language instructions.

■   *High-level languages* are English-like and easy to learn and program. There are over one hundred high-level languages. A program written in a high-level language is called a s*ource program*. Since a computer cannot understand a source program, a program called a *compiler* is used to translate the source program into a machine language program, which is then linked with other supporting library code to form an executable file.

■   The *operating system* (OS) is a program that manages and controls a computer's activities. Application programs, such as Web browsers and word processors, cannot run without an operating system.

■   Java was developed by a team led by James Gosling at Sun Microsystems. It is an Internet programming language. Since its inception in 1995, it has quickly become a premier language for building software.

■   Java is platform-independent, meaning that you can write a program once and run it anywhere.

- Java programs can be embedded in HTML pages and downloaded by Web browsers to bring live animation and interaction to Web clients.

- Java source files end with the .java extension. Every class is compiled into a separate file bytecode that has the same name as the class and ends with the .class extension.

- To compile a Java source code file, use the **javac** command. To run a Java class, use the **java** command.

- Every Java program is a set of class definitions. The keyword `class` introduces a class definition. The contents of the class are included in a block. A block begins with an opening brace ({) and ends with a closing brace (}). Methods are contained in a class.

- A Java application must have a `main` method. The `main` method is the entry point where the application program starts when it is executed.

REVIEW QUESTIONS

 Note
Answers to review questions are on the Companion Website.

Sections 1.2–1.4

1.1   Define hardware and software.

1.2   Define machine language, assembly language, and high-level programming language.

1.3   What is an operating system?

Section 1.5

1.4   Convert the following decimal numbers into hexadecimal and binary numbers.

    100; 4340; 2000

1.5   Convert the following binary numbers into hexadecimal numbers and decimal numbers.

    1000011001; 100000000; 100111

1.6   Convert the following hexdecimal numbers into binary and decimal numbers.

    FEFA9; 93; 2000

Sections 1.6–1.8

1.7   Describe the history of Java. Can Java run on any machine? What is needed to run Java on a computer?

1.8   What are the input and output of a Java compiler?

1.9   List some Java development tools. Are tools like Eclipse, NetBeans, and JBuilder different languages from Java, or are they dialects or extensions of Java?

1.10   What is the relationship between Java and HTML?

Sections 1.9–1.11

1.11 Explain the Java keywords. List some Java keywords you learned in this chapter.

1.12 Is Java case-sensitive? What is the case for Java keywords?

1.13 What is the Java source filename extension, and what is the Java bytecode filename extension?

1.14 What is a comment? What is the syntax for a comment in Java? Is the comment ignored by the compiler?

1.15 What is the statement to display a string on the console? What is the statement to display the message "Hello world" in a message dialog box?

1.16 Identify and fix the errors in the following code:

```
1 public class Welcome {
2   public void Main(String[] args) {
3     System.out.println('Welcome to Java!);
4   }
5 }
```

1.17 What is the command to compile a Java program? What is the command to run a Java application?

1.18 If the exception NoClassFoundError is raised when you run a program, what is the cause of the error?

1.19 If the exception "NoSuchMethodError: main" is raised when you run a program, what is the cause of the error?

PROGRAMMING EXERCISES

1.1 (*Creating, compiling, and running a Java program*) Create a source file containing a Java program. Perform the following steps to compile the program and run it (see §1.9, "Creating, Compiling, and Executing a Java Program"):

1. Create a file named **Welcome.java** for Listing 1.1. You can use any editor that will save your file in text format.
2. Compile the source file.
3. Run the bytecode.
4. Replace "Welcome to Java" with "My first program" in the program; save, compile, and run the program. You will see the message "My first program" displayed.
5. Replace main with Main, and recompile the source code. The compiler returns an error message because the Java program is case-sensitive.
6. Change it back, and compile the program again.
7. Instead of the command javac Welcome.java, use javac welcome.java. What happens?
8. Instead of the command java Welcome, use java Welcome.class. What happens?

CHAPTER 2

PRIMITIVE DATA TYPES AND OPERATIONS

Objectives

- To write Java programs to perform simple calculations (§2.2).

- To use identifiers to name variables, constants, methods, and classes (§2.3).

- To use variables to store data (§§2.4–2.5).

- To program with assignment statements and assignment expressions (§2.5).

- To use constants to store permanent data (§2.6).

- To declare Java primitive data types: `byte`, `short`, `int`, `long`, `float`, `double`, and `char` (§§2.7–2.9).

- To use Java operators to write numeric expressions (§§2.7–2.8).

- To represent characters using the `char` type (§2.9).

- To represent a string using the `String` type (§2.10).

- To obtain input using the `JOptionPane` input dialog boxes (§2.11).

- To obtain input from the console using the `Scanner` class (§2.13).

- To become familiar with Java documentation, programming style, and naming conventions (§2.14).

- To distinguish syntax errors, runtime errors, and logic errors (§2.15).

- To debug logic errors (§2.16).

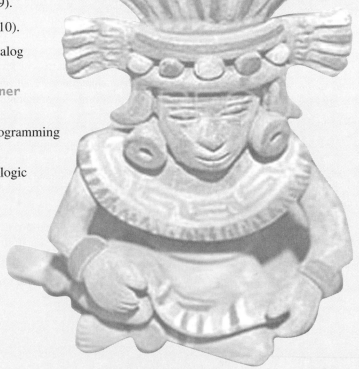

2.1 Introduction

In the preceding chapter, you learned how to create, compile, and run a Java program. In this chapter, you will be introduced to Java primitive data types and related subjects, such as variables, constants, data types, operators, and expressions. You will learn how to write programs using primitive data types, input and output, and simple calculations.

2.2 Writing Simple Programs

To begin, let's look at a simple program that computes the area of a circle. The program reads in the radius of a circle and displays its area. The program will use variables to store the radius and the area, and will use an expression to compute the area.

algorithm

Writing this program involves designing simple program and data structures, as well as translating algorithms into programming code. An *algorithm* describes how a problem is solved in terms of the actions to be executed, and it specifies the order in which the actions should be executed. Algorithms can help the programmer plan a program before writing it in a programming language. The algorithm for this program can be described as follows:

1. Read in the radius.

2. Compute the area using the following formula:

$$area = radius \times radius \times \pi$$

3. Display the area.

Many of the problems you will meet when taking an introductory course in programming using this text can be described with simple, straightforward algorithms. As your education progresses, and you take courses on data structures or on algorithm design and analysis, you will encounter complex problems that require sophisticated solutions. You will need to design accurate, efficient algorithms with appropriate data structures in order to solve such problems.

primitive data types

Data structures involve data representation and manipulation. Java provides data types for representing integers, floating-point numbers (i.e., numbers with a decimal point), characters, and Boolean types. These types are known as *primitive data types*. Java also supports array and string types as objects. Some advanced data structures, such as stacks, sets, and lists, have built-in implementation in Java.

To novice programmers, coding is a daunting task. When you *code*, you translate an algorithm into a programming language understood by the computer. You already know that every Java program begins with a class declaration in which the keyword `class` is followed by the class name. Assume that you have chosen `ComputeArea` as the class name. The outline of the program would look like this:

```java
public class ComputeArea {
  // Data and methods to be given later
}
```

As you know, every application must have a `main` method where program execution begins. So the program is expanded as follows:

```java
public class ComputeArea {
  public static void main(String[] args) {
    // Step 1: Read in radius

    // Step 2: Compute area

    // Step 3: Display the area
  }
}
```

The program needs to read the radius entered by the user from the keyboard. This raises two important issues:

- Reading the radius.

- Storing the radius in the program.

Let's address the second issue first. In order to store the radius, the program needs to declare a symbol called a *variable* that will represent the radius. Variables are used to store data and computational results in the program.

variable

Rather than using x and y, choose *descriptive names*: in this case, `radius` for radius, and `area` for area. Specify their data types to let the compiler know what `radius` and `area` are, indicating whether they are integer, float, or something else. Declare `radius` and `area` as double-precision floating-point numbers. The program can be expanded as follows:

descriptive names

```java
public class ComputeArea {
  public static void main(String[] args) {
    double radius;
    double area;

    // Step 1: Read in radius

    // Step 2: Compute area

    // Step 3: Display the area
  }
}
```

The program declares `radius` and `area` as variables. The reserved word `double` indicates that `radius` and `area` are double-precision floating-point values stored in the computer.

The first step is to read in `radius`. Reading a number is not a simple matter. For the time being, let us assign a fixed number to `radius` in the program. In §2.11, "Getting Input from Input Dialogs," and §2.13, "Getting Input from the Console," you will learn how to obtain a numeric value from an input dialog and from the console.

The second step is to compute `area` by assigning the expression `radius * radius * 3.14159` to `area`.

In the final step, print `area` on the console by using the `System.out.println` method.

The complete program is shown in Listing 2.1. A sample run of the program is shown in Figure 2.1.

LISTING 2.1 ComputeArea.java

```java
1 public class ComputeArea {
2   /** Main method */
3   public static void main(String[] args) {
4     double radius; // Declare radius          radius [no value]
5     double area; // Declare area              area [no value]
6
7     // Assign a radius
8     radius = 20; // New value is radius        radius [20]
9
10    // Compute area
11    area = radius * radius * 3.14159;          area [1256.636]
12
```

```
13      // Display results
14      System.out.println("The area for the circle of radius " +
15        radius + " is " + area);
16    }
17  }
```

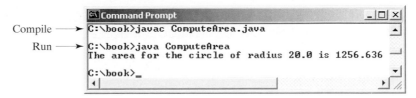

Compile ⟶
Run ⟶

FIGURE 2.1 The program displays the area of a circle.

declaring variable

assign value

Variables such as `radius` and `area` correspond to memory locations. Every variable has a name, a type, a size, and a value. Line 4 declares that `radius` can store a `double` value. The value is not defined until you assign a value. Line 8 assigns 20 into `radius`. Similarly, line 5 declares variable `area`, and line 11 assigns a value into `area`.

concatenating strings

concatenating strings with numbers

The plus sign (+) has two meanings: one for addition and the other for *concatenating strings*. The plus sign (+) in lines 14–15 is called a *string concatenation operator*. The string concatenation operator connects two strings if two operands are strings. If one of the operands is a non-string (e.g., a number), the non-string value is converted into a string and concatenated with the other string. So the plus signs (+) in lines 14–15 concatenate strings into a longer string, which is then displayed in the output. More on strings and string concatenation will be discussed in §2.10, "The `String` Type."

Caution

A string constant cannot cross lines in the source code. Thus the following statement would result in a compilation error:

```
System.out.println("Introduction to Java Programming,
  by Y. Daniel Liang");
```

breaking a long string

To fix the error, break the string into substrings, and use the concatenation operator (+) to combine them:

```
System.out.println("Introduction to Java Programming, " +
  "by Y. Daniel Liang");
```

Tip

incremental development and testing

This example consists of three steps. It is a good approach to develop and test these steps incrementally by adding one step at a time. You should apply this approach to all the programs, although the problem-solving steps are not explicitly stated in many programs in this book.

2.3 Identifiers

identifier

Just as every entity in the real world has a name, so you need to choose names for the things you will refer to in your programs. Programming languages use special symbols called *identifiers* to name such programming entities as variables, constants, methods, classes, and packages. Here are the rules for naming identifiers:

- An identifier is a sequence of characters that consists of letters, digits, underscores (_), and dollar signs ($).

- An identifier must start with a letter, an underscore (_), or a dollar sign ($). It cannot start with a digit.

- An identifier cannot be a reserved word. (See Appendix A, "Java Keywords," for a list of reserved words.)

- An identifier cannot be `true`, `false`, or `null`.

- An identifier can be of any length.

For example, `$2`, `ComputeArea`, `area`, `radius`, and `showMessageDialog` are legal identifiers, whereas `2A` and `d+4` are illegal identifiers because they do not follow the rules. The Java compiler detects illegal identifiers and reports syntax errors.

 Note

Since Java is *case-sensitive*, `X` and `x` are different identifiers.

case-sensitive

 Tip

Identifiers are used for naming variables, constants, methods, classes, and packages. Descriptive identifiers make programs easy to read. Besides choosing *descriptive names* for identifiers, there are naming conventions for different kinds of identifiers. Naming conventions are summarized in §2.14, "Programming Style and Documentation."

descriptive names

 Tip

Do not name identifiers with *the $ character*. By convention, the $ character should be used only in mechanically generated source code.

the $ character

2.4 Variables

Variables are used to store data in a program. In the program in Listing 2.1, `radius` and `area` are variables of double-precision, floating-point type. You can assign any numerical value to `radius` and `area`, and the values of `radius` and `area` can be reassigned. For example, you can write the code shown below to compute the area for different radii:

```
// Compute the first area
radius = 1.0;
area = radius * radius * 3.14159;
System.out.println("The area is " + area + " for radius " + radius);

// Compute the second area
radius = 2.0;
area = radius * radius * 3.14159;
System.out.println("The area is " + area + " for radius " + radius);
```

2.4.1 Declaring Variables

Variables are for representing data of a certain type. To use a variable, you declare it by telling the compiler the name of the variable as well as what type of data it represents. This is called a *variable declaration*. Declaring a variable tells the compiler to allocate appropriate memory space for the variable based on its data type. The syntax for declaring a variable is:

```
datatype variableName;
```

Here are some examples of variable declarations:

declaring variable

```
int x;               // Declare x to be an integer variable;
double radius;       // Declare radius to be a double variable;
double interestRate; // Declare interestRate to be a double variable;
char a;              // Declare a to be a character variable;
```

The examples use the data types `int`, `double`, and `char`. Later you will be introduced to additional data types, such as `byte`, `short`, `long`, `float`, and `boolean`.

If variables are of the same type, they can be declared together, as follows:

```
datatype variable1, variable2, ..., variablen;
```

The variables are separated by commas. For example,

```
int i, j, k; // Declare i, j, and k as int variables
```

naming variables

 Note

By convention, variable names are in lowercase. If a name consists of several words, concatenate all of them and capitalize the first letter of each word except the first. Examples of variables are `radius` and `interestRate`.

2.5 Assignment Statements and Assignment Expressions

assignment statement
assignment operator

After a variable is declared, you can assign a value to it by using an *assignment statement*. In Java, the equal sign (=) is used as the *assignment operator*. The syntax for assignment statements is as follows:

```
variable = expression;
```

expression

An *expression* represents a computation involving values, variables, and operators that together evaluates to a value. For example, consider the following code:

```
int x = 1;                  // Assign 1 to variable x;
double radius = 1.0;        // Assign 1.0 to variable radius;
x = 5 * (3 / 2) + 3 * 2;    // Assign the value of the expression to x;
x = y + 1;                  // Assign the addition of y and 1 to x;
area = radius * radius * 3.14159; // Compute area
```

A variable can also be used in an expression. For example,

```
x = x + 1;
```

In this assignment statement, the result of x + 1 is assigned to x. If x is 1 before the statement is executed, then it becomes 2 after the statement is executed.

To assign a value to a variable, the variable name must be on the left of the assignment operator. Thus, 1 = x would be wrong.

assignment expression

In Java, an assignment statement can also be treated as an expression that evaluates to the value being assigned to the variable on the left-hand side of the assignment operator. For this reason, an assignment statement is also known as an *assignment expression*. For example, the following statement is correct:

```
System.out.println(x = 1);
```

which is equivalent to

```
x = 1;
System.out.println(x);
```

The following statement is also correct:

```
i = j = k = 1;
```

which is equivalent to

```
k = 1;
j = k;
i = j;
```

Note

In an assignment statement, the data type of the variable on the left must be compatible with the data type of the value on the right. For example, `int x = 1.0` would be illegal because the data type of `x` is `int`. You cannot assign a `double` value (`1.0`) to an `int` variable without using type casting. Type casting is introduced in §2.8, "Numeric Type Conversions."

2.5.1 Declaring and Initializing Variables in One Step

Variables often have initial values. You can declare a variable and initialize it in one step. Consider, for instance, the following code:

```
int x = 1;
```

This is equivalent to the next two statements:

```
int x;
x = 1;
```

You can also use a shorthand form to declare and initialize variables of the same type together. For example,

```
int i = 1, j = 2;
```

Tip

A variable must be declared before it can be assigned a value. A variable declared in a method must be assigned a value before it can be used. Whenever possible, declare a variable and assign its initial value in one step. This will make the program easy to read and avoid programming errors.

2.6 Constants

The value of a variable may change during the execution of the program, but a *constant* represents permanent data that never changes. In our `ComputeArea` program, π is a constant. If you use it frequently, you don't want to keep typing `3.14159`; instead, you can define a constant for π. Here is the syntax for declaring a constant:

constant

```
final datatype CONSTANTNAME = VALUE;
```

A constant must be declared and initialized in the same statement. The word `final` is a Java keyword which means that the constant cannot be changed. For example, in the `ComputeArea` program, you could define π as a constant and rewrite the program as follows:

```
// ComputeArea.java: Compute the area of a circle
public class ComputeArea {
  /** Main method */
  public static void main(String[] args) {
    final double PI = 3.14159; // Declare a constant

    // Assign a radius
    double radius = 20;
```

```
    // Compute area
    double area = radius * radius * PI;

    // Display results
    System.out.println("The area for the circle of radius " +
      radius + " is " + area);
  }
}
```

Caution

naming constants

By convention, constants are named in uppercase: `PI`, not `pi` or `Pi`.

Note

benefits of constants

There are three benefits of using constants: (1) you don't have to repeatedly type the same value; (2) the value can be changed in a single location if necessary; (3) a descriptive name for a constant makes the program easy to read.

2.7 Numeric Data Types and Operations

Every data type has a range of values. The compiler allocates memory space to store each variable or constant according to its data type. Java provides eight primitive data types for numeric values, characters, and Boolean values. In this section, numeric data types are introduced.

Table 2.1 lists the six numeric data types, their ranges, and their storage sizes.

TABLE 2.1 Numeric Data Types

Name	Range	Storage Size
byte	-2^7 (-128) to $2^7 - 1$ (127)	8-bit signed
short	-2^{15} (-32768) to $2^{15} - 1$ (32767)	16-bit signed
int	-2^{31} (-2147483648) to $2^{31} - 1$ (2147483647)	32-bit signed
long	-2^{63} to $2^{63} - 1$	64-bit signed
	(i.e., -9223372036854775808 to 9223372036854775807)	
float	Negative range: $-3.4028235E+38$ to $-1.4E-45$	32-bit IEEE 754
	Positive range: $1.4E-45$ to $3.4028235E+38$	
double	Negative range: $-1.7976931348623157E+308$ to $-4.9E-324$	64-bit IEEE 754
	Positive range: $4.9E-324$ to $1.7976931348623157E+308$	

Note

IEEE 754 is a standard approved by the Institute of Electrical and Electronics Engineers for representing floating-point numbers on computers. The standard has been widely adopted. Java has adopted the 32-bit **IEEE 754** for the `float` type and the 64-bit **IEEE 754** for the `double` type. The **IEEE 754** standard also defines special values and operations in Appendix F, "Special Floating-Point Values."

integer

Java uses four types for integers: `byte`, `short`, `int`, and `long`. Choose the type that is most appropriate for your variable. For example, if you know an integer stored in a variable is within a range of byte, declare the variable as a `byte`.

floating-point

Java uses two types for *floating-point* numbers: `float` and `double`. The `double` type is twice as big as `float`. So, the `double` is known as *double precision*, while `float` is known as *single precision*. Normally, you should use the `double` type because it is more accurate than the `float` type.

2.7.1   Numeric Operators

The operators for numeric data types include the standard arithmetic operators: addition (+),   *operators + , − , *, /, %*
subtraction (−), multiplication (*), division (/), and remainder (%), as shown in Table 2.2.

TABLE 2.2   Numeric Operators

Name	Meaning	Example	Result
+	Addition	34 + 1	35
−	Subtraction	34.0 − 0.1	33.9
*	Multiplication	300 * 30	9000
/	Division	1.0 / 2.0	0.5
%	Remainder	20 % 3	2

The result of *integer division* is an integer. The fractional part is truncated. For example,   *integer division*
5 / 2 yields 2, not 2.5, and −5 / 2 yields −2, not −2.5.

The % operator yields the remainder after division. The left-hand operand is the dividend, and the right-hand operand is the divisor. Therefore, 7 % 3 yields 1, 12 % 4 yields 0, 26 % 8 yields 2, and 20 % 13 yields 7.

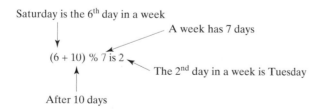

The % operator is often used for positive integers but also can be used with negative integers and floating-point values. The remainder is negative only if the dividend is negative. For example, −7 % 3 yields −1, −12 % 4 yields 0, −26 % −8 yields −2, and 20 % −13 yields 7.

Remainder is very useful in programming. For example, an even number % 2 is always 0, and an odd number % 2 is always 1. So you can use this property to determine whether a number is even or odd. Suppose today is Saturday, you and your friend are going to meet in 10 days. What day is in 10 days? You can find that day is Tuesday using the following expression:

```
Saturday is the 6th day in a week
            │
            ▼                    A week has 7 days
       (6 + 10) % 7 is 2
            ▲              The 2nd day in a week is Tuesday
            │
       After 10 days
```

Listing 2.2 gives a program that obtains minutes and remaining seconds from an amount of time in seconds. For example, 500 seconds contains 8 minutes and 20 seconds.

LISTING 2.2   `DisplayTime.java`

```java
1 import javax.swing.JOptionPane;
2
3 public class DisplayTime {
4   public static void main(String[] args) {
5     int seconds = 500;
```

```
 6      int minutes = seconds / 60;
 7      int remainingSeconds = seconds % 60;
 8      JOptionPane.showMessageDialog(null,
 9        seconds + " seconds is " + minutes +
10        " minutes and " + remainingSeconds
11        + " seconds");
12  }
13 }
```

Line 6 obtains the minutes using **seconds / 60**. Line 7 (**seconds % 60**) obtains the remaining seconds after taking away the minutes.

unary operator
binary operator

The + and − operators can be both unary and binary. A *unary* operator only one operand; a *binary* operator has two operands. For example, the − operator in −5 can be considered a unary operator to negate number 5, whereas the − operator in 4 − 5 is a binary operator for subtracting 5 from 4.

 Note

approximation

Calculations involving floating-point numbers are approximated because these numbers are not stored with complete accuracy. For example,

```
System.out.println(1.0 - 0.1 - 0.1 - 0.1 - 0.1 - 0.1);
```

displays 0.5000000000000001, not 0.5, and

```
System.out.println(1.0 - 0.9);
```

displays 0.09999999999999998, not 0.1. Integers are stored precisely. Therefore, calculations with integers yield a precise integer result.

2.7.2　Numeric Literals

literal

A *literal* is a constant value that appears directly in a program. For example, 34, 1000000, and 5.0 are literals in the following statements:

```
int i = 34;
long k = 1000000;
double d = 5.0;
```

Integer Literals

An integer literal can be assigned to an integer variable as long as it can fit into the variable. A compilation error would occur if the literal were too large for the variable to hold. The statement **byte b = 128**, for example, would cause a compilation error, because 128 cannot be stored in a variable of the **byte** type. (Note that the range for a byte value is from −128 to 127.)

An integer literal is assumed to be of the **int** type, whose value is between -2^{31} (−2147483648) and $2^{31}-1$ (2147483647). The statement **System.out.println (2147483648)**, for example, would cause a compilation error, because 2147483648 is too long as an **int** value.

To denote an integer literal of the **long** type, append the letter **L** or **l** to it (e.g., **2147483648L**). **L** is preferred because **l** (lowercase L) can easily be confused with 1 (the digit one). Since **2147483648** exceeds the range for the **int** type, it must be denoted as **2147483648L**.

long literal

Note

By default, an integer literal is a decimal number. To denote an octal integer literal, use a leading *0* (zero), and to denote a hexadecimal integer literal, use a leading *0x* or *0X* (zero x). For example, the following code displays the decimal value **65535** for hexadecimal number **FFFF**.

octal and hex literals

```
System.out.println(0xFFFF);
```

Hexadecimal numbers, binary numbers, and octal numbers were introduced in §1.5, "Number Systems."

Floating-Point Literals

Floating-point literals are written with a decimal point. By default, a floating-point literal is treated as a **double** type value. For example, **5.0** is considered a **double** value, not a **float** value. You can make a number a **float** by appending the letter **f** or **F**, and you can make a number a **double** by appending the letter **d** or **D**. For example, you can use **100.2f** or **100.2F** for a **float** number, and **100.2d** or **100.2D** for a **double** number.

suffix **f** or **F**
suffix **d** or **D**

Note

The **double** type values are more accurate than the **float** type values. For example,

double vs. **float**

```
System.out.println("1.0 / 3.0 is " + 1.0 / 3.0);
```

displays **1.0 / 3.0 is 0.3333333333333333**.

```
System.out.println("1.0F / 3.0F is " + 1.0F / 3.0F);
```

displays **1.0F / 3.0F is 0.33333334**.

Scientific Notations

Floating-point literals can also be specified in scientific notation; for example, **1.23456e+2**, the same as **1.23456e2**, is equivalent to **1.23456 x 10^2 = 123.456** and **1.23456e−2** is equivalent to **1.23456 x 10^{-2} = 0.0123456**. E (or **e**) represents an exponent and can be either in lowercase or uppercase.

Note

The **float** and **double** types are used to represent numbers with a decimal point. Why are they called *floating-point numbers*? These numbers are stored into scientific notation. When a number such as **50.534** is converted into scientific notation such as **5.053e1**, its decimal point is moved (i.e., floated) to a new position.

why called floating-point?

2.7.3 Arithmetic Expressions

Writing numeric expressions in Java involves a straightforward translation of an arithmetic expression using Java operators. For example, the arithmetic expression

$$\frac{3 + 4x}{5} - \frac{10(y - 5)(a + b + c)}{x} + 9\left(\frac{4}{x} + \frac{9 + x}{y}\right)$$

can be translated into a Java expression as:

```
(3 + 4 * x) / 5 - 10 * (y - 5) * (a + b + c) / x +
9 * (4 / x + (9 + x) / y)
```

The numeric operators in a Java expression are applied the same way as in an arithmetic expression. Operators contained within pairs of parentheses are evaluated first. Parentheses can be nested, in which case the expression in the inner parentheses is evaluated first. Multiplication, division, and remainder operators are applied next. If an expression contains several multiplication, division, and remainder operators, they are applied from left to right. Addition and subtraction operators are applied last. If an expression contains several addition and subtraction operators, they are applied from left to right.

Listing 2.3 gives a program that converts a Fahrenheit degree to Celsius using the formula $celsius = \left(\frac{5}{9}\right)(fahrenheit - 32)$.

LISTING 2.3 FahrenheitToCelsius.java

```
1 public class FahrenheitToCelsius {
2   public static void main(String[] args) {
3     double fahrenheit = 100; // Say 100;
4     double celsius = (5.0 / 9) * (fahrenheit - 32);
5     System.out.println("Fahrenheit " + fahrenheit + " is " +
6       celsius + " in Celsius");
7   }
8 }
```

integer vs. decimal division

Be careful when applying division. Division of two integers yields an integer in Java. $\frac{5}{9}$ is translated to **5.0 / 9** instead of **5 / 9** in line 4, because **5 / 9** yields **0** in Java.

2.7.4 Shorthand Operators

Very often the current value of a variable is used, modified, and then reassigned back to the same variable. For example, the following statement adds the current value of i with 8 and assigns the result back to i.

```
i = i + 8;
```

shorthand operator

Java allows you to combine assignment and addition operators using a *shorthand operator*. For example, the preceding statement can be written as:

```
i += 8;
```

shorthand operator

The += is called the *addition assignment operator*. Other *shorthand operators* are shown in Table 2.3.

TABLE 2.3 Shorthand Operators

Operator	Name	Example	Equivalent
+=	Addition assignment	i += 8	i = i + 8
-=	Subtraction assignment	f -= 8.0	f = f - 8.0
*=	Multiplication assignment	i *= 8	i = i * 8
/=	Division assignment	i /= 8	i = i / 8
%=	Remainder assignment	i %= 8	i = i % 8

++ and --

There are two more shorthand operators for incrementing and decrementing a variable by 1. This is handy because that is often how much the value needs to be changed. These two operators are ++ and --. They can be used in prefix or suffix notation, as shown in Table 2.4.

TABLE 2.4   Increment and Decrement Operators

Operator	Name	Description
++var	preincrement	The expression (++var) increments var by 1 and evaluates to the *new* value in var *after* the increment.
var++	postincrement	The expression (var++) evaluates to the *original* value in var and increments var by 1.
--var	predecrement	The expression (--var) decrements var by 1 and evaluates to the *new* value in var *after* the decrement.
var--	postdecrement	The expression (var--) evaluates to the *original* value in var and decrements var by 1.

If the operator is *before* (prefixed to) the variable, the variable is incremented or decremented by 1, then the *new* value of the variable is returned. If the operator is *after* (suffixed to) the variable, the original *old* value of the variable is returned, then the variable is incremented or decremented by 1. Therefore, the prefixes ++x and --x are referred to, respectively, as the *preincrement operator* and the *predecrement operator*; and the suffixes x++ and x-- are referred to, respectively, as the *postincrement operator* and the *postdecrement operator*. The prefix form of ++ (or --) and the suffix form of ++ (or --) are the same if they are used in isolation, but they cause different effects when used in an expression. The following code illustrates this:

preincrement, predecrement
postincrement, postdecrement

```
int i = 10;
int newNum = 10 * i++;
```
Same effect as →
```
int newNum = 10 * i;
i = i + 1;
```

In this case, i is incremented by 1, then the *old* value of i is returned and used in the multiplication. So newNum becomes 100. If i++ is replaced by ++i as follows,

```
int i = 10;
int newNum = 10 * (++i);
```
Same effect as →
```
i = i + 1;
int newNum = 10 * i;
```

i is incremented by 1, and the new value of i is returned and used in the multiplication. Thus newNum becomes 110.

Here is another example:

```
double x = 1.0;
double y = 5.0;
double z = x-- + (++y);
```

After all three lines are executed, y becomes 6.0, z becomes 7.0, and x becomes 0.0.

The increment operator ++ and the decrement operator -- can be applied to all integer and floating-point types. These operators are often used in loop statements . A *loop statement* is a structure that controls how many times an operation or a sequence of operations is performed in succession. This structure, and the subject of loop statements, is introduced in Chapter 4, "Loops."

Tip

Using increment and decrement operators makes expressions short, but it also makes them complex and difficult to read. Avoid using these operators in expressions that modify multiple variables or the same variable multiple times, such as this one: int k = ++i + i.

Note

Like the assignment operator (=), the operators (+=, -=, *=, /=, %=, ++, and --) can be used to form an assignment statement as well as an expression. For example, in the following code, x = 2 is a statement in the first line and is an expression in the second line.

```
x = 2; // statement
System.out.println(x = 2); // expression
```

expression statement

If a statement is used as an expression, it is called an *expression statement*.

Caution

There are no spaces in the shorthand operators. For example, + = should be +=.

2.8 Numeric Type Conversions

Sometimes it is necessary to mix numeric values of different types in a computation. Consider the following statements:

```
byte i = 100;
long k = i * 3 + 4;
double d = i * 3.1 + k / 2;
```

Are these statements correct? Java allows binary operations on values of different types. When performing a binary operation involving two operands of different types, Java automatically converts the operand based on the following rules:

converting operands

1. If one of the operands is **double**, the other is converted into **double**.

2. Otherwise, if one of the operands is **float**, the other is converted into **float**.

3. Otherwise, if one of the operands is **long**, the other is converted into **long**.

4. Otherwise, both operands are converted into **int**.

For example, the result of **1 / 2** is **0**, because both operands **int** values. The result of **1.0 / 2** is **0.5**, because **1.0** is **double** and **2** is converted to **2.0**.

The range of numeric types increases in this order:

range increases →

`byte, short, int, long, float, double`

You can always assign a value to a numeric variable whose type supports a larger range of values; thus, for instance, you can assign a **long** value to a **float** variable. You cannot, however, assign a value to a variable of a type with smaller range unless you use *type casting*. Casting is an operation that converts a value of one data type into a value of another data type. Casting a variable of a type with a small range to a variable of a type with a larger range is known as *widening a type*. Casting a variable of a type with a large range to a variable of a type with a smaller range is known as *narrowing a type*. Widening a type can be performed automatically without explicit casting. Narrowing a type must be performed explicitly.

type casting

widening a type
narrowing a type

The syntax for casting gives the target type in parentheses, followed by the variable's name or the value to be cast. For example:

```
float f = (float)10.1;
int i = (int)f;
```

In the first line, the `double` value `10.1` is cast into `float`. In the second line, `i` has a value of `10`; the fractional part in `f` is truncated.

Caution

Casting is necessary if you are assigning a value to a variable of a smaller type range, such as assigning a `double` value to an `int` variable. A compilation error will occur if casting is not used in situations of this kind. Be careful when using casting. Lost information might lead to inaccurate results.

possible loss of precision

Note

Casting does not change the variable being cast. For example, `d` is not changed after casting in the following code:

```
double d = 4.5;
int i = (int)d;   // d is not changed
```

Note

To assign a variable of the `int` type to a variable of the `short` or `byte` type, explicit casting must be used. For example, the following statements have a syntax error:

```
int i = 1;
byte b = i; // Error because explicit casting is required
```

However, so long as the integer literal is within the permissible range of the target variable, explicit casting is not needed to assign an integer literal to a variable of the `short` or `byte` type. Please refer to §2.7.2, "Numeric Literals."

Listing 2.4 gives a program that displays the sales tax with two digits after the decimal point.

LISTING 2.4 SalesTax.java

```
1 public class SalesTax {
2   public static void main(String[] args) {
3     double purchaseAmount = 197.55;
4     double tax = purchaseAmount * 0.06;
5     System.out.println((int)(tax * 100) / 100.0);
6   }
7 }
```

Variable `purchaseAmount` is `197.55` (line 3). The sales tax is 6% of the purchase, so the `tax` is evaluated as `11.853` (line 4). The statement in line 5 displays the tax `11.85` with two digits after the decimal point. Note that `(int)(tax * 100)` is 1185, so `(int)(tax * 100) / 100.0` is `11.85`.

formatting numbers

2.9 Character Data Type and Operations

The character data type, `char`, is used to represent a single character. A character literal is enclosed in single quotation marks. Consider the following code:

char type

```
char letter = 'A';
char numChar = '4';
```

The first statement assigns character `A` to the `char` variable `letter`. The second statement assigns the digit character `4` to the `char` variable `numChar`.

Caution

A string literal must be enclosed in quotation marks. A character literal is a single character enclosed in single quotation marks. So `"A"` is a string, and `'A'` is a character.

char literal

2.9.1 Unicode and ASCII Code

character encoding

Computers use binary numbers internally. A character is stored as a sequence of 0s and 1s in a computer. The process of converting a character to its binary representation is called *encoding*. There are different ways to encode a character. How characters are encoded is defined by an *encoding scheme*.

Unicode

original Unicode

Java supports *Unicode*, an encoding scheme established by the Unicode Consortium to support the interchange, processing, and display of written texts in the world's diverse languages. Unicode was originally designed as a 16-bit character encoding. The primitive data type **char** was intended to take advantage of this design by providing a simple data type that could hold any character. However, it turned out that the 65,536 characters possible in a 16-bit encoding are not sufficient to represent all the characters in the world. The Unicode standard therefore has been extended to allow up to 1,112,064 characters. Those characters that go beyond the original 16-bit limit are called *supplementary characters*. JDK 1.5 supports supplementary characters. Processing and representing supplementary characters are beyond the scope of this book. For simplicity, this book considers only the original 16-bit Unicode characters. These characters can be stored in a **char** type variable.

supplementary Unicode

A 16-bit Unicode takes two bytes, preceded by **\u**, expressed in four hexadecimal digits that run from **'\u0000'** to **'\uFFFF'**. For example, the word "welcome" is translated into Chinese using two characters, 欢迎. The Unicodes of these two characters are **"\u6B22\u8FCE"**. Listing 2.5 gives a program that displays two Chinese characters and three Greek letters.

LISTING 2.5 DisplayUnicode.java

```java
import javax.swing.JOptionPane;

public class DisplayUnicode {
  public static void main(String[] args) {
    JOptionPane.showMessageDialog(null,
      "\u6B22\u8FCE \u03b1 \u03b2 \u03b3",
      "\u6B22\u8FCE Welcome",
      JOptionPane.INFORMATION_MESSAGE);
  }
}
```

If no Chinese font is installed on your system, you will not be able to see the Chinese characters. The Unicodes for the Greek letters α β γ are **\u03b1 \u03b2 \u03b3**.

ASCII

Most computers use *ASCII* (*American Standard Code for Information Interchange*), a 7-bit encoding scheme for representing all uppercase and lowercase letters, digits, punctuation marks, and control characters. Unicode includes ASCII code, with **'\u0000'** to **'\u007F'** corresponding to the 128 ASCII characters. (See Appendix B, "The ASCII Character Set," for a list of ASCII characters and their decimal and hexadecimal codes.) You can use ASCII characters like **'X'**, **'1'**, and **'$'** in a Java program as well as Unicodes. Thus, for example, the following statements are equivalent:

```java
char letter = 'A';
char letter = '\u0041'; // Character A's Unicode is 0041
```

Both statements assign character **A** to **char** variable **letter**.

Note

char increment and decrement

The increment and decrement operators can also be used on **char** variables to get the next or preceding Unicode character. For example, the following statements display character **b**.

```java
char ch = 'a';
System.out.println(++ch);
```

2.9.2   Escape Sequences for Special Characters

Java allows you to use escape sequences to represent special characters, as shown in Table 2.5. An escape sequence begins with the backslash character (\) followed by a character that has a special meaning to the compiler.

TABLE 2.5   Java Escape Sequences

Character Escape Sequence	Name	Unicode Code
\b	Backspace	\u0008
\t	Tab	\u0009
\n	Linefeed	\u000A
\f	Formfeed	\u000C
\r	Carriage Return	\u000D
\\	Backslash	\u005C
\'	Single Quote	\u0027
\"	Double Quote	\u0022

Suppose you want to print the quoted message shown below:

```
He said "Java is fun"
```

The statement to print it should be

```
System.out.println("He said \"Java is fun\"");
```

2.9.3   Casting Between `char` and Numeric Types

A `char` can be cast into any numeric type, and vice versa. When an integer is cast into a `char`, only its lower sixteen bits of data are used; the other part is ignored.
For example, see the following code:

```
char c = (char)0XAB0041; // the lower 16 bits hex code 0041 is
                         // assigned to c
System.out.println(c);   // c is character A
```

When a floating-point value is cast into a `char`, the integral part of the floating-point value is cast into a `char`.

```
char c = (char)65.25;    // decimal 65 is assigned to t
System.out.println(c);   // c is character A
```

When a `char` is cast into a numeric type, the character's Unicode is cast into the specified numeric type.

```
int i = (int)'A';        // the Unicode of character A is assigned to i
System.out.println(i);   // i is 65
```

Implicit casting can be used if the result of a casting fits into the target variable. Otherwise, explicit casting must be used. For example, since the Unicode of `'a'` is **97**, which is within the range of a byte, these implicit castings are fine:

```
byte b = 'a';
int i = 'a';
```

But the following casting is incorrect, because the Unicode \uFFF4 cannot fit into a byte:

```
byte b = '\uFFF4';
```

To force assignment, use explicit casting, as follows:

```
byte b = (byte)'\uFFF4';
```

Any positive integer between **0** and **FFFF** in hexadecimal can be cast into a character implicitly. Any number not in this range must be cast into a **char** explicitly.

Note

numeric operators
on characters

All numeric operators can be applied to **char** operands. A **char** operand is automatically cast into a number if the other operand is a number or a character. If the other operand is a string, the character is concatenated with the string. For example, the following statements

```
int i = '2' + '3'; // (int)'2' is 50 and (int)'3' is 51
System.out.println("i is " + i);

int j = 2 + 'a'; // (int)'a' is 97
System.out.println("j is " + j);
System.out.println(j + " is the Unicode for character " + (char)j);

System.out.println("Chapter " + '2');
```

display

```
i is 101
j is 99
99 is the Unicode for character c
Chapter 2
```

Note

The Unicodes for lowercase letters are consecutive integers starting from the Unicode for **'a'**, then for **'b'**, **'c'**, ..., and **'z'**. The same is true for the uppercase letters. Furthermore, the Unicode for **'a'** is greater than the Unicode for **'A'**. So **'a'** – **'A'** is the same as **'b'** – **'B'**. For a lowercase letter *ch*, its corresponding uppercase letter is **(char)('A' + (ch - 'a'))**.

2.10 The **String** Type

The **char** type only represents one character. To represent a string of characters, use the data type called **String**. For example, the following code declares the message to be a string that has an initial value of "Welcome to Java".

```
String message = "Welcome to Java";
```

String is actually a predefined class in the Java library just like the **System** class and **JOptionPane** class. The **String** type is not a primitive type. It is known as a *reference type*. Any Java class can be used as a reference type for a variable. Reference data types will be thoroughly discussed in Chapter 7, "Classes and Objects." For the time being, you only need to know how to declare a **String** variable, how to assign a string to the variable, and how to concatenate strings.

As first shown in Listing 2.1, two strings can be concatenated. The plus sign (+) is the concatenation operator if one of the operands is a string. If one of the operands is a non-string (e.g., a number), the non-string value is converted into a string and concatenated with the other string. Here are some examples:

concatenating strings
and numbers

```
// Three strings are concatenated
String message = "Welcome " + "to " + "Java";

// String Chapter is concatenated with number 2
String s = "Chapter" + 2; // s becomes Chapter2
```

```
// String Supplement is concatenated with character B
String s1 = "Supplement" + 'B'; // s becomes SupplementB
```

If neither of the operands is a string, the plus sign (+) is the addition operator that adds two numbers.

The shorthand += operator can also be used for string concatenation. For example, the following code appends the string "and Java is fun" with the string "Welcome to Java" in message.

```
message += " and Java is fun";
```

So the new message is "Welcome to Java and Java is fun".

Suppose that i = 1 and j = 2, what is the output of the following statement?

```
System.out.println("i + j is " + i + j);
```

The output is "i + j is 12" because "i + j is " is concatenated with the value of i first. To force i + j to be executed first, enclose i + j in the parentheses, as follows:

```
System.out.println("i + j is " + (i + j));
```

2.11 Getting Input from Input Dialogs

In Listing 2.1, the radius is fixed in the source code. To use a different radius, you have to modify the source code and recompile it. Obviously, this is not convenient. You can use the showInputDialog method in the JOptionPane class to get input at runtime. When this method is executed, a dialog is displayed to enable you to enter an input value, as shown in Figure 2.2.

JOptionPane class

FIGURE 2.2   The input dialog box enables the user to enter a string.

After entering a string, click OK to accept the input and dismiss the dialog box. The input is returned from the method as a string. You can invoke the method with four arguments, as follows:

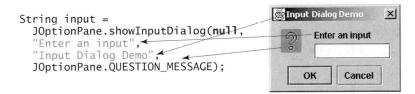

```
String input =
    JOptionPane.showInputDialog(null,
    "Enter an input",
    "Input Dialog Demo",
    JOptionPane.QUESTION_MESSAGE);
```

The first argument can always be null. The second argument is a string that prompts the user. The third argument is the title of the input box. The fourth argument can be JOptionPane.QUESTION_MESSAGE, which causes the icon ( ) to be displayed in the input box.

Note

There are several ways to use the showInputDialog method. For the time being, you only need to know two ways to invoke it.

showInputDialog method

One is to use a statement as shown in the example:

```
String string = JOptionPane.showInputDialog(null, x,
   y, JOptionPane.QUESTION_MESSAGE));
```

where x is a string for the prompting message, and y is a string for the title of the input dialog box.

The other is to use a statement like this one:

```
JOptionPane.showInputDialog(x);
```

where x is a string for the prompting message.

2.11.1 Converting Strings to Numbers

The input returned from the input dialog box is a string. If you enter a numeric value such as **123**, it returns **"123"**. You have to convert a string into a number to obtain the input as a number.

Integer.parseInt method

To convert a string into an **int** value, use the **parseInt** method in the **Integer** class, as follows:

```
int intValue = Integer.parseInt(intString);
```

where **intString** is a numeric string such as **"123"**.

Double.parseDouble method

To convert a string into a **double** value, use the **parseDouble** method in the **Double** class, as follows:

```
double doubleValue = Double.parseDouble(doubleString);
```

where **doubleString** is a numeric string such as **"123.45"**.

The **Integer** and **Double** classes are both included in the **java.lang** package, and thus are automatically imported.

2.12 Case Studies

In the preceding sections, you learned about variables, constants, primitive data types, operators, and expressions. You are now ready to use them to write interesting programs. This section presents three examples: computing loan payments, breaking a sum of money down into smaller units, and displaying the current time.

2.12.1 Example: Computing Loan Payments

This example shows you how to write a program that computes loan payments. The loan can be a car loan, a student loan, or a home mortgage loan. The program lets the user enter the interest rate, number of years, and loan amount, and then computes the monthly payment and the total payment. It concludes by displaying the monthly and total payments.

The formula to compute the monthly payment is as follows:

$$\frac{\text{loanAmount} \times \text{monthlyInterestRate}}{1 - \dfrac{1}{(1 + \text{monthlyInterestRate})^{\text{numberOfYears} \times 12}}}$$

You don't have to know how this formula is derived. Nonetheless, given the monthly interest rate, number of years, and loan amount, you can use it to compute the monthly payment. Here are the steps in developing the program:

1. Prompt the user to enter the annual interest rate, number of years, and loan amount.

2. Obtain the monthly interest rate from the annual interest rate.

3. Compute the monthly payment using the preceding formula.

4. Compute the total payment, which is the monthly payment multiplied by 12 and multi-plied by the number of years.

5. Display the monthly payment and total payment in a message dialog.

In the formula, you have to compute $(1 + monthlyInterestRate)^{number\ Of\ Years \times 12}$. The `pow(a, b)` method in the `Math` class can be used to compute a^b. The `Math` class, which comes with the Java API, is available to all Java programs. Other useful methods in the `Math` class will be introduced in Chapter 5, "Methods."

`pow(a, b)` method

Listing 2.6 gives the complete program. Figure 2.3 shows a sample run of the program.

FIGURE 2.3   The program accepts the annual interest rate, number of years, and loan amount, then displays the monthly payment and total payment.

LISTING 2.6 ComputeLoan.java

```
1 import javax.swing.JOptionPane;
2
3 public class ComputeLoan {
4   /** Main method */
5   public static void main(String[] args) {
6     // Enter yearly interest rate
7     String annualInterestRateString = JOptionPane.showInputDialog(
8       "Enter yearly interest rate, for example 8.25:");
9
10    // Convert string to double
11    double annualInterestRate =
12      Double.parseDouble(annualInterestRateString);
13
14    // Obtain monthly interest rate
15    double monthlyInterestRate = annualInterestRate / 1200;
16
17    // Enter number of years
18    String numberOfYearsString = JOptionPane.showInputDialog(
19      "Enter number of years as an integer, \nfor example 5:");
20
21    // Convert string to int
22    int numberOfYears = Integer.parseInt(numberOfYearsString);
23
24    // Enter loan amount
25    String loanString = JOptionPane.showInputDialog(
26      "Enter loan amount, for example 120000.95:");
27
```

enter interest rate

convert string
to double

```
28        // Convert string to double
29        double loanAmount = Double.parseDouble(loanString);
30
31        // Calculate payment
32        double monthlyPayment = loanAmount * monthlyInterestRate / (1
33          - 1 / Math.pow(1 + monthlyInterestRate, numberOfYears * 12));
34        double totalPayment = monthlyPayment * numberOfYears * 12;
35
36        // Format to keep two digits after the decimal point
37        monthlyPayment = (int)(monthlyPayment * 100) / 100.0;
38        totalPayment = (int)(totalPayment * 100) / 100.0;
39
40        // Display results
41        String output = "The monthly payment is " + monthlyPayment +
42          "\nThe total payment is " + totalPayment;
43        JOptionPane.showMessageDialog(null, output);
44    }
45 }
```

monthlyPayment (line 32)
totalPayment (line 34)
preparing output (lines 37–38)

The `showInputDialog` method in lines 7–8 displays an input dialog. Enter the interest rate as a double value and click OK to accept the input. The value is returned as a string that is assigned to the `String` variable `annualInterestRateString`. The `Double.parseDouble (annualInterestRateString)` (line 12) is used to convert the string into a `double` value. If you entered an input other than a numeric value, a runtime error would occur. In Chapter 17, "Exceptions and Assertions," you will learn how to handle the exception so that the program can continue to run.

Each new variable in a method must be declared once and only once. Choose the most appropriate data type for the variable. For example, `numberOfYears` is best declared as an `int` (line 22), although it could be declared as a `long`, `float`, or `double`. Note that `byte` might be the most appropriate for `numberOfYears`. For simplicity, however, the examples in this book will use `int` for integer and `double` for floating-point values.

The formula for computing the monthly payment is translated into Java code in lines 32–33.

formatting numbers

The statements in lines 37–38 are for formatting the number to keep two digits after the decimal point. For example, if `monthlyPayment` is `2076.0252175`, `(int)(monthlyPayment * 100)` is `207602`. Therefore, `(int)(monthlyPayment * 100) / 100.0` yields `2076.02`.

The strings are concatenated into `output` in lines 11–25. The linefeed escape character `'\n'` is in the string to display the text after `'\n'` in the next line.

Note

If you click *Cancel* in the input dialog box, no string is returned. A runtime error would occur.

2.12.2 Example: Counting Monetary Units

This section presents a program that classifies a given amount of money into smaller monetary units. The program lets the user enter an amount as a `double` value representing a total in dollars and cents, and outputs a report listing the monetary equivalent in dollars, quarters, dimes, nickels, and pennies, as shown in Figure 2.4.

Your program should report the maximum number of dollars, then the maximum number of quarters, and so on, in this order.

Here are the steps in developing the program:

1. Prompt the user to enter the amount as a decimal number such as `11.56`.

2. Convert the amount (e.g., `11.56`) into cents (`1156`).

FIGURE 2.4   The program receives an amount in decimals and breaks it into dollars, quarters, dimes, nickels, and pennies.

3. Divide the cents by **100** to find the number of dollars. Obtain the remaining cents using the cents remainder **100**.

4. Divide the remaining cents by **25** to find the number of quarters. Obtain the remaining cents using the remaining cents remainder **25**.

5. Divide the remaining cents by **10** to find the number of dimes. Obtain the remaining cents using the remaining cents remainder **10**.

6. Divide the remaining cents by **5** to find the number of nickels. Obtain the remaining cents using the remaining cents remainder **5**.

7. The remaining cents are the pennies.

8. Display the result.

The complete program is given in Listing 2.7.

LISTING 2.7   ComputeChange.java

```java
1  import javax.swing.JOptionPane;
2
3  public class ComputeChange {
4    /** Main method */
5    public static void main(String[] args) {
6      // Receive the amount
7      String amountString = JOptionPane.showInputDialog(
8        "Enter an amount in double, for example 11.56");
9
10     // Convert string to double
11     double amount = Double.parseDouble(amountString);
12
13     int remainingAmount = (int)(amount * 100);
14
15     // Find the number of one dollars
16     int numberOfOneDollars = remainingAmount / 100;            dollars
17     remainingAmount = remainingAmount % 100;
18
19     // Find the number of quarters in the remaining amount
20     int numberOfQuarters = remainingAmount / 25;               quarters
21     remainingAmount = remainingAmount % 25;
22
23     // Find the number of dimes in the remaining amount
24     int numberOfDimes = remainingAmount / 10;                  dimes
25     remainingAmount = remainingAmount % 10;
26
```

nickels

pennies

```
27      // Find the number of nickels in the remaining amount
28      int numberOfNickels = remainingAmount / 5;
29      remainingAmount = remainingAmount % 5;
30
31      // Find the number of pennies in the remaining amount
32      int numberOfPennies = remainingAmount;
33
34      // Display results
35      String output = "Your amount " + amount + " consists of \n" +
36        numberOfOneDollars + " dollars\n" +
37        numberOfQuarters + " quarters\n" +
38        numberOfDimes + " dimes\n" +
39        numberOfNickels + " nickels\n" +
40        numberOfPennies + " pennies";
41      JOptionPane.showMessageDialog(null, output);
42    }
43  }
```

The variable `amount` stores the amount entered from the input dialog box (lines 7–11). This variable is not changed because the amount has to be used at the end of the program to display the results. The program introduces the variable `remainingAmount` (line 13) to store the changing `remainingAmount`.

The variable `amount` is a `double` decimal representing dollars and cents. It is converted to an `int` variable `remainingAmount`, which represents all the cents. For instance, if `amount` is `11.56`, then the initial `remainingAmount` is `1156`. The division operator yields the integer part of the division. So `1156 / 100` is `11`. The remainder operator obtains the remainder of the division. So `1156 % 100` is `56`.

The program extracts the maximum number of singles from the total amount and obtains the remaining amount in the variable `remainingAmount` (lines 16–17). It then extracts the maximum number of quarters from `remainingAmount` and obtains a new `remainingAmount` (lines 20–21). Continuing the same process, the program finds the maximum number of dimes, nickels, and pennies in the remaining amount.

loss of precision

One serious problem with this example is the possible *loss of precision* when casting a `double` amount to an `int remainingAmount`. This could lead to an inaccurate result. If you try to enter the amount `10.03`, `10.03 * 100` becomes `1002.9999999999999`. You will find that the program displays `10` dollars and `2` pennies. To fix the problem, enter the amount as an integer value representing cents (see Exercise 2.10).

As shown in Figure 2.4, `0` dimes, `1` nickels, and `1` pennies are displayed in the result. It would be better not to display `0` dimes, and to display `1` nickel and `1` penny using the singular forms of the words. You will learn how to use selection statements to modify this program in the next chapter (see Exercise 3.7).

2.12.3   Example: Displaying the Current Time

This section presents a program that displays the current time in GMT (Greenwich Mean Time) in the format hour:minute:second, such as `13:19:8`, as shown in Figure 2.5.

FIGURE 2.5   The program displays the current GMT.

currentTimeMillis

The `currentTimeMillis` method in the `System` class returns the current time in milliseconds elapsed since the time `00:00:00` on January 1, 1970 GMT, as shown in Figure 2.6.

FIGURE 2.6 The `System.currentTimeMillis()` returns the number of milliseconds since the Unix epoch.

This time is known as the *Unix epoch* because 1970 was the year when the Unix operating system was formally introduced.

Unix epoch

You can use this method to obtain the current time, and then compute the current second, minute, and hour as follows.

1. Obtain the total milliseconds since midnight, Jan 1, 1970 in `totalMilliseconds` by invoking `System.currentTimeMillis()` (e.g., 1103203148368 milliseconds).

2. Obtain the total seconds `totalSeconds` by dividing `totalMilliseconds` by 1000 (e.g., 1103203148368 milliseconds / 1000 = 1103203148 seconds).

3. Compute the current second from `totalSeconds % 60` (e.g., 1103203148 seconds % 60 = 8, which is the current second).

4. Obtain the total minutes `totalMinutes` by dividing `totalSeconds` by 60 (e.g., 1103203148 seconds / 60 = 18386719 minutes).

5. Compute the current minute from `totalMinutes % 60` (e.g., 18386719 minutes % 60 = 19, which is the current minute).

6. Obtain the total hours `totalHours` by dividing `totalMinutes` by 60 (e.g., 18386719 minutes / 60 = 306445 hours).

7. Compute the current hour from `totalHours % 24` (e.g., 306445 hours % 24 = 19, which is the current hour).

The program follows, and the output is shown in Figure 2.5.

LISTING 2.8   ShowCurrentTime.java

```
1  import javax.swing.JOptionPane;
2
3  public class ShowCurrentTime {
4    public static void main(String[] args) {
5      // Obtain the total milliseconds since the midnight, Jan 1, 1970
6      long totalMilliseconds = System.currentTimeMillis();
7
8      // Obtain the total seconds since the midnight, Jan 1, 1970
9      long totalSeconds = totalMilliseconds / 1000;                  totalSeconds
10
11     // Compute the current second in the minute in the hour
12     int currentSecond = (int)(totalSeconds % 60);                  currentSecond
13
14     // Obtain the total minutes
15     long totalMinutes = totalSeconds / 60;                         totalMinutes
16
17     // Compute the current minute in the hour
18     int currentMinute = (int)(totalMinutes % 60);                  currentMinute
19
20     // Obtain the total hours
21     long totalHours = totalMinutes / 60;                           totalHours
22
```

currentHour

preparing output

```
23     // Compute the current hour
24     int currentHour = (int)(totalHours % 24);
25
26     // Display results
27     String output = "Current time is " + currentHour + ":"
28       + currentMinute + ":" + currentSecond + " GMT";
29
30     JOptionPane.showMessageDialog(null, output);
31   }
32 }
```

When `System.currentTimeMillis()` (line 6) is invoked, it returns the difference, measured in milliseconds, between the current GMT and midnight, January 1, 1970 GMT. This method returns the milliseconds as a `long` value.

2.13 Getting Input from the Console

You can obtain input from an input dialog box using the `JOptionPane.showInputDialog` method. Alternatively, you may obtain input from the console.

Java uses `System.out` to refer to the standard output device, and `System.in` to the standard input device. By default the output device is the console, and the input device is the keyboard. To perform console output, you simply use the `println` method to display a primitive value or a string to the console. Console input is not directly supported in Java, but you can use the `Scanner` class to create an object to read input from `System.in`, as follows:

```
Scanner scanner = new Scanner(System.in);
```

`Scanner` is a new class in JDK 1.5. The syntax *new Scanner(System.in)* creates an object of the `Scanner` type. The syntax *Scanner scanner* declares that `scanner` is a variable whose type is `Scanner`. The whole line *Scanner scanner = new Scanner(System.in)* creates a `Scanner` object and assigns its reference to the variable `scanner`. An object may contain methods. Invoking a method on an object is to ask the object to perform a task. A `Scanner` object contains the following methods for reading an input:

- `next()`: reading a string. A string is delimited by spaces.

- `nextByte()`: reading an integer of the `byte` type.

- `nextShort()`: reading an integer of the `short` type.

- `nextInt()`: reading an integer of the `int` type.

- `nextLong()`: reading an integer of the `long` type.

- `nextFloat()`: reading a number of the `float` type.

- `nextDouble()`: reading a number of the `double` type.

For example, the following statements prompt the user to enter a double value from the console.

```
System.out.print("Enter a double value: ");
Scanner scanner = new Scanner(System.in);
double d = scanner.nextDouble();
```

 Note

More details on classes and objects will be introduced in Chapter 7, "Classes and Objects." For the time being, you will just have to accept that this is how to obtain input from the console.

Note
The `print` method is identical to the `println` method except that `println` moves the cursor to the next line after displaying the string, but `print` does not advance the cursor to the next line when completed.

print vs. println

Listing 2.9 gives an example that reads various types of data from the console using the `Scanner` class. A sample run of this program is shown in Figure 2.7.

FIGURE 2.7   You can enter input from a command window.

LISTING 2.9   TestScanner.java

```
1 import java.util.Scanner; // Scanner is in java.util
2
3 public class TestScanner {
4   public static void main(String args[]) {
5     // Create a Scanner
6     Scanner scanner = new Scanner(System.in);
7
8     // Prompt the user to enter an integer
9     System.out.print("Enter an integer: ");
10    int intValue = scanner.nextInt();
11    System.out.println("You entered the integer " + intValue);
12
13    // Prompt the user to enter a double value
14    System.out.print("Enter a double value: ");
15    double doubleValue = scanner.nextDouble();
16    System.out.println("You entered the double value "
17      + doubleValue);
18
19    // Prompt the user to enter a string
20    System.out.print("Enter a string without space: ");
21    String string = scanner.next();
22    System.out.println("You entered the string " + string);
23  }
24 }
```

Tip
One benefit of using the console input is that you can store the input values in a text file and pass the file from the command line using the following command:

```
java TestScanner < input.txt
```

where input.txt is a text file that contains the data, as shown in Figure 2.8(a). The output of **java TestScanner < input.txt** is shown in Figure 2.8(b).

You can also save the output into a file using the following command:

```
java TestScanner < input.txt > out.txt
```

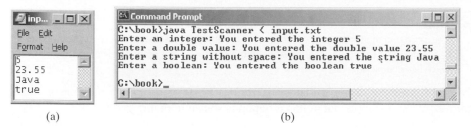

(a)   (b)

FIGURE 2.8 (a) You can create a text file using NotePad. (b) The data in the text file is passed to the program.

whitespace

Caution

By default, a **Scanner** object reads a string separated by *whitespaces* (i.e., `' '`, `'\t'`, `'\f'`, `'\r'`, and `'\n'`). To read a string with embedded spaces, see §8.8.2, "Reading Data Using **Scanner**."

JOptionPane or **Scanner**?

Pedagogical NOTE

You can use **JOptionPane** or **Scanner** for obtaining input, whichever is convenient. The examples in the book use **JOptionPane** for getting input for consistency. You can easily revise the examples using **Scanner** for getting input.

Listing 2.6 uses input dialog boxes to obtain input. Alternatively, you can read input from the console in Listing 2.10. A sample run of the new program is shown in Figure 2.9.

FIGURE 2.9 The program receives input from the console.

LISTING 2.10 ComputeLoanAlternative.java

```
1  import java.util.Scanner;
2
3  public class ComputeLoanAlternative {
4    /** Main method */
5    public static void main(String[] args) {
6      // Create a scanner for input
7      Scanner input = new Scanner(System.in);
8
9      // Enter yearly interest rate
10     System.out.print("Enter yearly interest rate, for example 8.25: ");
11     double annualInterestRate = input.nextDouble();
12
13     // Obtain monthly interest rate
14     double monthlyInterestRate = annualInterestRate / 1200;
15
16     // Enter number of years
17     System.out.print(
18       "Enter number of years as an integer, \nfor example 5: ");
19     int numberOfYears = input.nextInt();
20
21     // Enter loan amount
22     System.out.print("Enter loan amount, for example 120000.95: ");
```

create a scanner (line 7)

annualInterestRate (line 11)

monthlyInterestRate (line 14)

numberOfYears (line 19)

```
23      double loanAmount = input.nextDouble();                    loanAmount
24
25      // Calculate payment
26      double monthlyPayment = loanAmount * monthlyInterestRate / (1    monthlyPayment
27        - 1 / Math.pow(1 + monthlyInterestRate, numberOfYears * 12));
28      double totalPayment = monthlyPayment * numberOfYears * 12;   totalPayment
29
30      // Format to keep two digits after the decimal point
31      monthlyPayment = (int)(monthlyPayment * 100) / 100.0;       formatting output
32      totalPayment = (int)(totalPayment * 100) / 100.0;
33
34      // Display results
35      System.out.println("The monthly payment is " + monthlyPayment);
36      System.out.println("The total payment is " + totalPayment);
37    }
38 }
```

2.14 Programming Style and Documentation

Programming style deals with what programs look like. A program can compile and run properly even if written on only one line, but writing it all on one line would be bad programming style because it would be hard to read. *Documentation* is the body of explanatory remarks and comments pertaining to a program. Programming style and documentation are as important as coding. Good programming style and appropriate documentation reduce the chance of errors and make programs easy to read. So far you have learned some good programming styles. This section summarizes them and gives several guidelines. More detailed guidelines on programming style and documentation can be found in Supplement I.D, "Java Coding Style Guidelines," on the Companion Website.

programming style

2.14.1 Appropriate Comments and Comment Styles

Include a summary at the beginning of the program to explain what the program does, its key features, its supporting data structures, and any unique techniques it uses. In a long program, you should also include comments that introduce each major step and explain anything that is difficult to read. It is important to make comments concise so that they do not crowd the program or make it difficult to read.

Use *javadoc comments* (/** ... */) for commenting on an entire class or an entire method. These comments must precede the class or the method header, and can be extracted in a javadoc HTML file. For commenting on steps inside a method, use line comments (//).

javadoc comments

2.14.2 Naming Conventions

Make sure that you choose descriptive names with straightforward meanings for the variables, constants, classes, and methods in your program. Names are case-sensitive. Listed below are the conventions for naming variables, methods, and classes.

- Use lowercase for variables and methods. If a name consists of several words, concatenate them into one, making the first word lowercase and capitalizing the first letter of each subsequent word; for example, the variables `radius` and `area` and the method `showInputDialog`.

naming variables and methods

- Capitalize the first letter of each word in a class name; for example, the class names `ComputeArea`, `Math`, and `JOptionPane`.

naming classes

- Capitalize every letter in a constant, and use underscores between words; for example, the constants `PI` and `MAX_VALUE`.

naming constants

naming conventions

Tip
It is important to become familiar with the *naming conventions*. Understanding them will help you to understand Java programs. If you stick with the naming conventions, other programmers will be more willing to accept your program.

naming classes

Caution
Do not choose class names that are already used in the Java library. For example, since the `Math` class is defined in Java, you should not name your class `Math`.

using full descriptive names

Tip
Avoid using abbreviation for identifiers. Using complete words is more descriptive. For example, `numberOfStudents` is better than `numStuds`, `numOfStuds`, or `numOfStudents`.

2.14.3 Proper Indentation and Spacing

indent code

A consistent indentation style makes programs clear and easy to read. *Indentation* is used to illustrate the structural relationships between a program's components or statements. Java can read the program even if all of the statements are in a straight line, but it is easier to read and maintain code that is aligned properly. Indent each subcomponent or statement *two* spaces more than the structure within which it is nested.

A single space should be added on both sides of a binary operator, as shown in the following statement:

A single space line should be used to separate segments of the code to make the program easier to read.

2.14.4 Block Styles

A block is a group of statements surrounded by braces. There are two popular styles, *next-line* style and *end-of-line* style, as shown in Figure 2.10. The next-line style aligns braces vertically and makes programs easy to read, whereas the end-of-line style saves space and may help avoid some subtle programming errors. Both are acceptable block styles. The choice

FIGURE 2.10 The opening brace is placed at the beginning of a new line for next-line style and at the end of the line for end-of-line style.

depends on personal or organizational preference. You should use a style consistently. Mixing styles is not recommended. This book uses the *end-of-line* style to be consistent with the Java API source code.

2.15 Programming Errors

Programming errors are unavoidable, even for experienced programmers. Errors can be categorized into three types: syntax errors, runtime errors, and logic errors.

2.15.1 Syntax Errors

Errors that occur during compilation are called *syntax errors* or *compilation errors*. Syntax errors result from errors in code construction, such as mistyping a keyword, omitting some necessary punctuation, or using an opening brace without a corresponding closing brace. These errors are usually easy to detect, because the compiler tells you where they are and what caused them. For example, compiling the following program results in a syntax error, as shown in Figure 2.11.

syntax errors

```
// ShowSyntaxErrors.java: The program contains syntax errors
public class ShowSyntaxErrors {
  public static void main(String[] args) {
    i = 30;
    System.out.println(i + 4);
  }
}
```

syntax error

FIGURE 2.11 The compiler reports syntax errors.

Two errors are detected. Both are the result of not declaring variable i. Since a single error will often display many lines of compilation errors, it is a good practice to start debugging from the top line and work downward. Fixing errors that occur earlier in the program may also fix additional errors that occur later.

2.15.2 Runtime Errors

Runtime errors are errors that cause a program to terminate abnormally. Runtime errors occur while an application is running if the environment detects an operation that is impossible to carry out. Input errors are typical runtime errors.

runtime errors

An *input error* occurs when the user enters an unexpected input value that the program cannot handle. For instance, if the program expects to read in a number, but instead the user enters a string, this causes data-type errors to occur in the program. To prevent input errors, the program should prompt the user to enter the correct type of values. It may display a message like "`Please enter an integer`" before reading an integer from the keyboard.

Another common source of runtime errors is division by zero. This happens when the divisor is zero for integer divisions. For instance, the following program would cause a runtime error, as shown in Figure 2.12.

runtime error

```
// ShowRuntimeErrors.java: Program contains runtime errors
public class ShowRuntimeErrors {
  public static void main(String[] args) {
    int i = 1 / 0 ;
  }
}
```

```
Command Prompt                                              _ □ ×
C:\book>java ShowRuntimeErrors
Exception in thread "main" java.lang.ArithmeticException: / by zero
        at ShowRuntimeErrors.main(ShowRuntimeErrors.java:4)

C:\book>
```

FIGURE 2.12   The runtime error causes the program to terminate abnormally.

2.15.3   Logic Errors

Logic errors occur when a program does not perform the way it was intended to. Errors of this kind occur for many different reasons. For example, suppose you wrote the following program to add **number1** to **number2**.

```
// ShowLogicErrors.java: The program contains a logic error
public class ShowLogicErrors {
  public static void main(String[] args) {
    // Add number1 to number2
    int number1 = 3;
    int number2 = 3;
    number2 += number1 + number2;
    System.out.println("number2 is " + number2);
  }
}
```

The program does not have syntax errors or runtime errors, but it does not print the correct result for **number2**. See if you can find the error.

2.16   Debugging

In general, syntax errors are easy to find and easy to correct, because the compiler gives indications as to where the errors came from and why they are there. Runtime errors are not difficult to find either, since the Java interpreter displays them on the console when the program aborts. Finding logic errors, on the other hand, can be very challenging.

bugs
debugging
hand-traces

Logic errors are called *bugs*. The process of finding and correcting errors is called *debugging*. A common approach to debugging is to use a combination of methods to narrow down to the part of the program where the bug is located. You can *hand-trace* the program (i.e., catch errors by reading the program), or you can insert print statements in order to show the values of the variables or the execution flow of the program. This approach might work for a short, simple program. But for a large, complex program, the most effective approach for debugging is to use a debugger utility.

JDK includes a command-line debugger (jdb), which is invoked with a class name. jdb is itself a Java program, running its own copy of Java interpreter. All the Java IDE tools, such as JBuilder, NetBeans, and Eclipse, include integrated debuggers. The debugger utilities let you follow the execution of a program. They vary from one system to another, but they all support most of the following helpful features:

■ **Executing a single statement at a time:** The debugger allows you to execute one statement at a time so that you can see the effect of each statement.

■ **Tracing into or stepping over a method:** If a method is being executed, you can ask the debugger to enter the method and execute one statement at a time in the method, or you can ask it to step over the entire method. You should step over the entire method if you know that the method works. For example, always step over system-supplied methods, such as `System.out.println`.

- **Setting breakpoints:** You can also set a breakpoint at a specific statement. Your program pauses when it reaches a breakpoint and displays the line with the breakpoint. You can set as many breakpoints as you want. Breakpoints are particularly useful when you know where your programming error starts. You can set a breakpoint at that line and have the program execute until it reaches the breakpoint.

- **Displaying variables:** The debugger lets you select several variables and display their values. As you trace through a program, the content of a variable is continuously updated.

- **Displaying call stacks:** The debugger lets you trace all of the method calls and lists all pending methods. This feature is helpful when you need to see a large picture of the program-execution flow.

- **Modifying variables:** Some debuggers enable you to modify the value of a variable when debugging. This is convenient when you want to test a program with different samples but do not want to leave the debugger.

Tip
If you use an IDE such as JBuilder, NetBeans, or Eclipse, please refer to *Learning Java Effectively with JBuilder/NetBeans/Eclipse* in the supplement on the Companion Website. The supplement shows you how to use a debugger to trace programs and how debugging can help in learning Java effectively.

debugging in IDE

KEY TERMS

algorithm   28
assignment operator (=)   32
assignment statement   32
backslash (\)   43
`byte` type   34
casting   40
`char` type   41
constant   33
data type   28
debugger   58
debugging   58
declaration   31
decrement operator (--)   39
`double` type   34
encoding   42
`final`   33
`float` type   34
floating-point number   28
expression   32
expression statement   40

identifier   30
increment operator (++)   39
incremental development and testing   30
indentation   56
`int` type   34
literal   36
logic error   58
`long` type   34
narrowing (of types)   40
operator   32
primitive data type   28
runtime error   57
`short` type   34
syntax error   57
supplementary Unicode   42
Unicode   42
Unix epoch   51
variable   29
widening (of types)   54
whitespace   54

CHAPTER SUMMARY

- Java provides four integer types (`byte`, `short`, `int`, `long`) that represent integers of four different sizes, and two floating-point types (`float`, `double`) that represent floating-point numbers of two different precisions. Character type (`char`) represents a single character. These are called primitive data types. Java's primitive types are portable across all computer platforms. They have exactly the same values on all platforms. When they are declared, the variables of these types are created and assigned memory space.

■ Java provides operators that perform numeric operations: + (addition), − (subtraction), * (multiplication), / (division), and % (remainder). Integer division (/) yields an integer result. The remainder operator (%) yields the remainder of the division.

■ The increment operator (++) and the decrement operator (−−) increment or decrement a variable by 1. If the operator is prefixed to the variable, the variable is first incremented or decremented by 1, then used in the expression. If the operator is a suffix to the variable, the variable is incremented or decremented by 1, but then the original old value is used in the expression.

■ All the numeric operators can be applied to characters. When an operand is a character, the character's Unicode value is used in the operation.

■ You can use casting to convert a value of one type into another type. Casting a variable of a type with a small range to a variable of a type with a larger range is known as *widening a type*. Casting a variable of a type with a large range to a variable of a type with a smaller range is known as *narrowing a type*. Widening a type can be performed automatically without explicit casting. Narrowing a type must be performed explicitly.

■ Programming errors can be categorized into three types: syntax errors, runtime errors, and logic errors. Errors that occur during compilation are called *syntax errors* or *compilation errors*. *Runtime errors* are errors that cause a program to terminate abnormally. *Logic errors* occur when a program does not perform the way it was intended to.

REVIEW QUESTIONS

Sections 2.2–2.6

2.1 Which of the following identifiers are valid?

`applet`, `Applet`, `a++`, `−−a`, `4#R`, `$4`, `#44`, `apps`

2.2 Which of the following are Java keywords?

`class`, `public`, `int`, `x`, `y`, `radius`

2.3 Translate the following pseudocode into Java code:
- Step 1: Declare a `double` variable named `miles` with initial value `100`;
- Step 2: Declare a `double` constant named `MILE_TO_KILOMETER` with value `1.609`;
- Step 3: Declare a `double` variable named `kilometer`, multiply miles and `MILE_TO_KILOMETER` and assign the result to `kilometer`;
- Step 4: Display `kilometer` to the console.

What is `kilometer` after Step 4?

2.4 What are the benefits of using constants? Declare an `int` constant `SIZE` with value `20`.

Section 2.7 Numeric Data Types and Operations

2.5 Assume that `int a = 1` and `double d = 1.0`, and that each expression is independent. What are the results of the following expressions?

```
a = 46 / 9;
a = 46 % 9 + 4 * 4 - 2;
a = 45 + 43 % 5 * (23 * 3 % 2);
```

```
a %= 3 / a + 3;
d = 4 + d * d + 4;
d += 1.5 * 3 + (++a);
d -= 1.5 * 3 + a++;
```

2.6   Show the result of the following remainders.

```
56 % 6
78 % -4
-34 % 5
-34 % -5
5 % 1
1 % 5
```

2.7   Find the largest and smallest `byte`, `short`, `int`, `long`, `float`, and `double`. Which of these data types requires the least amount of memory?

2.8   What is the result of `25 / 4`? How would you rewrite the expression if you wished the result to be a floating-point number?

2.9   Are the following statements correct? If so, show the output.

```
System.out.println("the output for 25 / 4 is " + 25 / 4);
System.out.println("the output for 25 / 4.0 is " + 25 / 4.0);
```

2.10   How would you write the following arithmetic expression in Java?

$$\frac{4}{3(r + 34)} - 9(a + bc) + \frac{3 + d(2 + a)}{a + bd}$$

2.11   Which of these statements are true?

(a)   Any expression can be used as a statement.
(b)   The expression `x++` can be used as a statement.
(c)   The statement `x = x + 5` is also an expression.
(d)   The statement `x = y = x = 0` is illegal.

2.12   Which of the following are correct literals for floating-point numbers?

`12.3, 12.3e+2, 23.4e-2, -334.4, 20, 39F, 40D`

2.13   Identify and fix the errors in the following code:

```
 1 public class Test {
 2   public void main(string[] args) {
 3     int i;
 4     int k = 100.0;
 5     int j = i + 1;
 6
 7     System.out.println("j is " + j + " and
 8       k is " + k);
 9   }
10 }
```

Section 2.8 Numeric Type Conversions

2.14   Can different types of numeric values be used together in a computation?

2.15   What does an explicit conversion from a `double` to an `int` do with the fractional part of the *double* value? Does casting change the variable being cast?

2.16   Show the following output:

```
float f = 12.5F;
int i = (int)f;
System.out.println("f is " + f);
System.out.println("i is " + i);
```

Section 2.9 Character Data Type and Operations

2.17 Use print statements to find out the ASCII code for `'1'`, `'A'`, `'B'`, `'a'`, `'b'`. Use print statements to find out the character for the decimal code 40, 59, 79, 85, 90. Use print statements to find out the character for the hexadecimal code 40, 5A, 71, 72, 7A.

2.18 Which of the following are correct literals for characters?

$$'1', '\backslash u345dE', '\backslash u3fFa', '\backslash b', \backslash t$$

2.19 How do you display characters \ and "?

2.20 Evaluate the following:

```
int i = '1';
int j = '1' + '2';
int k = 'a';
char c = 90;
```

2.21 Can the following conversions involving casting be allowed? If so, find the converted result.

```
char c = 'A';
i = (int)c;

float f = 1000.34f;
int i = (int)f;

double d = 1000.34;
int i = (int)d;

int i = 97;
char c = (char)i;
```

Section 2.10 The `String` Type

2.22 Show the output of the following statements:

```
System.out.println("1" + 1);
System.out.println('1' + 1);
System.out.println("1" + 1 + 1);
System.out.println("1" + (1 + 1));
System.out.println('1' + 1 + 1);
```

2.23 Evaluate the following expressions:

```
1 + "Welcome " + 1 + 1
1 + "Welcome " + (1 + 1)
1 + "Welcome " + ('\u0001'  + 1)
1 + "Welcome " + 'a'  + 1
```

Sections 2.11–2.12

2.24 How do you convert a decimal string into a `double` value? How do you convert an integer string into an `int` value?

2.25 How do you obtain the current minute using the `System.currentTimeMillis()` method?

Sections 2.14–2.15

2.26 How do you denote a comment line and a comment paragraph?

2.27 What are the naming conventions for class names, method names, constants, and variables? Which of the following items can be a constant, a method, a variable, or a class according to the Java naming conventions?

```
MAX_VALUE, Test, read, readInt
```

2.28 Reformat the following program according to the programming style and documentation guidelines. Use the next-line brace style.

```java
public class Test
{
  // Main method
  public static void main(String[] args) {
  /** Print a line */
  System.out.println("2 % 3 = "+2%3);
  }
}
```

2.29 Describe syntax errors, runtime errors, and logic errors.

PROGRAMMING EXERCISES

Note

Solutions to even-numbered exercises are on the Companion website. Solutions to all exercises are on the Instructor Resource website. The *level of difficulty* is rated as easy (no star), moderate (*), hard (**), or challenging (***).

level of difficulty

Pedagogical Note

Students may first write a program with a *fixed input* value and later modify it using an input dialog box or using the console input.

fixed input

Debugging Tip

The compiler usually gives a reason for a syntax error. If you don't know how to correct it, compare your program closely with similar examples in the text character by character.

learn from examples

Sections 2.2–2.8

2.1 (*Converting Fahrenheit to Celsius*) Write a program that reads a Fahrenheit degree in double from an input dialog box, then converts it to Celsius and displays the result in a message dialog box. The formula for the conversion is as follows:

$$\text{celsius} = (5/9) * (\text{fahrenheit} - 32)$$

Hint

In Java, `5 / 9` is 0, so you need to write `5.0 / 9` in the program to obtain the correct result.

2.2 (*Computing the volume of a cylinder*) Write a program that reads in the radius and length of a cylinder and computes its volume using the following formulas:

$$\text{area} = \text{radius} * \text{radius} * \pi$$
$$\text{volume} = \text{area} * \text{length}$$

2.3 (*Converting feet into meters*) Write a program that reads a number in feet, converts it to meters, and displays the result. One foot is `0.305` meters.

2.4 (*Converting pounds into kilograms*) Write a program that converts pounds into kilograms. The program prompts the user to enter a number in pounds, converts it to kilograms, and displays the result. One pound is `0.454` kilograms.

2.5* (*Calculating tips*) Write a program that reads the subtotal and the gratuity rate, and computes the gratuity and total. For example, if the user enters `10` for subtotal and `15%` for gratuity rate, the program displays `$1.5` as gratuity and `$11.5` as total.

2.6** (*Summing the digits in an integer*) Write a program that reads an integer between 0 and 1000 and adds all the digits in the integer. For example, if an integer is 932, the sum of all its digits is 14.

Hint

Use the % operator to extract digits, and use the / operator to remove the extracted digit. For instance, 932 % 10 = 2 and 932 / 10 = 93

Section 2.9 Character Data Type and Operations

2.7* (*Converting an uppercase letter to lowercase*) Write a program that converts an uppercase letter to a lowercase letter. The character is typed in the source code as a literal value. In Chapter 8, "Strings and Text I/O," you will learn how to enter a character from an input dialog box.

Hint

In the ASCII table (see Appendix B), uppercase letters appear before lowercase letters. The offset between any uppercase letter and its corresponding lowercase letter is the same. So you can find a lowercase letter from its corresponding uppercase letter, as follows:

```
int offset = (int)'a' - (int)'A';
char lowercase = (char)((int)uppercase + offset);
```

2.8* (*Finding the character of an ASCII code*) Write a program that receives an ASCII code (an integer between 0 and 127) and displays its character. For example, if the user enters 97, the program displays character a.

Sections 2.10–2.12

2.9* (*Calculating the future investment value*) Write a program that reads in investment amount, annual interest rate, and number of years, and displays the future investment value using the following formula:

```
futureInvestmentValue =
    investmentAmount x (1 + monthlyInterestRate)
```
^{numberOfYears*12}

For example, if you entered amount 1000, annual interest rate 3.25%, and number of years 1, the future investment value is 1032.98.

Hint

Use the Math.pow(a, b) method to compute a raised to the power of b.

2.10* (*Monetary units*) Rewrite Listing 2.7, ComputeChange.java, to fix the possible loss of accuracy when converting a double value to an int value. Enter the input as an integer whose last two digits represent the cents. For example, the input 1156 represents 11 dollars and 56 cents.

Section 2.13 Getting Input from the Console

2.11* (*Using the console input*) Rewrite Listing 2.7, ComputeChange.java, using the console input and output.

2.12* (*Payroll*) Write a program that reads the following information and prints a payroll statement:

■ Employee's name (e.g., Smith)
■ Number of hours worked in a week (e.g., 10)
■ Hourly pay rate (e.g., 6.75)

- Federal tax withholding rate (e.g., 20%)
- State tax withholding rate (e.g., 9%)

Write this program in two versions: (a) Use dialog boxes to obtain input and display output; (b) Use console input and output. A sample run of the console input and output is shown in Figure 2.13.

Obtain input ⟶

Display output ⟶

FIGURE 2.13 The program prints a payroll statement.

2.13* (*Calculating interest*) If you know the balance and the annual percentage interest rate, you can compute the interest on the next monthly payment using the following formula:

$$interest = balance \times (annualInterestRate / 1200)$$

Write a program that reads the balance and the annual percentage interest rate and displays the interest for the next month in two versions: (a) Use dialog boxes to obtain input and display output; (b) Use console input and output. A sample run of the console input and output is shown in Figure 2.14.

FIGURE 2.14 The program prints interest.

CHAPTER 3

SELECTION STATEMENTS

Objectives

- To declare `boolean` type and write Boolean expressions (§3.2).

- To distinguish between conditional and unconditional `&&` and `||` operators (§3.2.1).

- To use Boolean expressions to control selection statements (§§3.3–3.5).

- To implement selection control using `if` and nested `if` statements (§3.3).

- To implement selection control using `switch` statements (§3.4).

- To write expressions using the conditional operator (§3.5).

- To display formatted output using the `System.out.printf` method and to format strings using the `String.format` method (§3.6).

- To know the rules governing operand evaluation order, operator precedence, and operator associativity (§§3.7–3.8).

3.1 Introduction

why selection?
pseudocode

In Chapter 2, "Primitive Data Types and Operations," if you assigned a negative value for `radius` in Listing 2.1, ComputeArea.java, the program would print an invalid result. If the radius is negative, you don't want the program to compute the area. Like all high-level programming languages, Java provides selection statements that let you choose actions with two or more alternative courses. You can use selection statements in the following *pseudocode* (i.e., natural language mixed with programming code) to rewrite Listing 2.1:

```
if the radius is negative
    the program displays a message indicating a wrong input;
else
    the program computes the area and displays the result;
```

Selection statements use conditions. Conditions are Boolean expressions. This chapter first introduces Boolean types, values, operators, and expressions.

3.2 `boolean` Data Type and Operations

comparison operators

Often in a program you need to compare two values, such as whether i is greater than j. Java provides six *comparison operators* (also known as *relational operators*), shown in Table 3.1, which can be used to compare two values. The result of the comparison is a Boolean value: `true` or `false`. For example, the following statement displays `true`:

```
System.out.println(1 < 2);
```

TABLE 3.1 Comparison Operators

Operator	Name	Example	Answer
<	less than	1 < 2	true
<=	less than or equal to	1 <= 2	true
>	greater than	1 > 2	false
>=	greater than or equal to	1 >= 2	false
==	equal to	1 == 2	false
!=	not equal to	1 != 2	true

compare characters

Note

You can also *compare characters*. Comparing characters is the same as comparing the Unicodes of the characters. For example, 'a' is larger than 'A' because the Unicode of 'a' is larger than the Unicode of 'A.'

Caution

== *vs.* =

The equality comparison operator is two equal signs (==), not a single equal sign (=). The latter symbol is for assignment.

Boolean variable

A variable that holds a Boolean value is known as a *Boolean variable*. The `boolean` data type is used to declare Boolean variables. The domain of the `boolean` type consists of two literal values: `true` and `false`. For example, the following statement assigns `true` to the variable `lightsOn`:

```
boolean lightsOn = true;
```

Boolean operators, also known as *logical operators*, operate on Boolean values to create a new Boolean value. Table 3.2 contains a list of Boolean operators. Table 3.3 defines the not (!) operator. The not (!) operator negates **true** to **false** and **false** to **true**. Table 3.4 defines the and (&&) operator. The and (&&) of two Boolean operands is **true** if and only if both operands are **true**. Table 3.5 defines the or (||) operator. The **or** (||) of two Boolean operands is **true** if at least one of the operands is **true**. Table 3.6 defines the exclusive or (^) operator. The exclusive or (^) of two Boolean operands is **true** if and only if the two operands have different Boolean values.

Boolean operators

TABLE 3.2 Boolean Operators

Operator	Name	Description
!	not	logical negation
&&	and	logical conjunction
||	or	logical disjunction
^	exclusive or	logical exclusion

TABLE 3.3 Truth Table for Operator !

p	!p	Example
true	false	!(1 > 2) is **true**, because (1 > 2) is **false**.
false	true	!(1 > 0) is **false**, because (1 > 0) is **true**.

TABLE 3.4 Truth Table for Operator &&

p1	p2	p1 && p2	Example
false	false	false	(2 > 3) && (5 > 5) is **false**, because
false	true	false	either (2 > 3) or (5 > 5) is **false**.
true	false	false	(3 > 2) && (5 > 5) is **false**, because (5 > 5) is **false**.
true	true	true	(3 > 2) && (5 >= 5) is **true**, because (3 > 2) and (5 >= 5) are both **true**.

TABLE 3.5 Truth Table for Operator ||

p1	p2	p1 || p2	Example
false	false	false	(2 > 3) || (5 > 5) is **false**, because (2 > 3)
false	true	true	and (5 > 5) are both **false**.
true	false	true	(3 > 2) || (5 > 5) is **true**, because (3 > 2)
true	true	true	is **true**.

TABLE 3.6 Truth Table for Operator ^

p1	p2	p1 ^ p2	Example
false	false	false	(2 > 3)^(5 > 5) is **true**, because (2 > 3)
false	true	true	is **false** and (5 > 1) is **true**.
true	false	true	(3 > 2)^(5 > 1) is **false**, because both
true	true	false	(3 > 2) and (5 > 1) are **true**.

Listing 3.1 gives a program that checks whether a number is divisible by 2 and 3, whether a number is divisible by 2 or 3, and whether a number is divisible by 2 or 3 but not both:

LISTING 3.1 TestBoolean.java

```java
 1 import javax.swin ptionPane;
 2
 3 public class TestBoolean {
 4   public static void main(String[] args) {
 5     int number = 18;
 6
 7     JOptionPane.showMessageDialog(null,
 8       "Is " + number +
 9       "\n divisible by 2 and 3? " +
10       (number % 2 == 0 && number % 3 == 0)
11       + "\ndivisible by 2 or 3? " +
12       (number % 2 == 0 || number % 3 == 0) +
13       "\ndivisible by 2 or 3, but not both? "
14       + (number % 2 == 0 ∧ number % 3 == 0));
15   }
16 }
```

A long string is formed by concatenating the substrings in lines 8–14. The three \n characters display the string in four lines. (number % 2 == 0 && number % 3 == 0) (line 10) checks whether the number is divisible by 2 and 3. (number % 2 == 0 || number % 3 == 0) (line 12) checks whether the number is divisible by 2 or 3. (number % 2 == 0 ∧ number % 3 == 0) (line 14) checks whether the number is divisible by 2 or 3, but not both.

3.2.1 Unconditional vs. Conditional Boolean Operators

If one of the operands of an && operator is false, the expression is false; if one of the operands of an || operand is true, the expression is true. Java uses these properties to improve the performance of these operators.

When evaluating p1 && p2, Java first evaluates p1 and then evaluates p2 if p1 is true; if p1 is false, it does not evaluate p2. When evaluating p1 || p2, Java first evaluates p1 and then evaluates p2 if p1 is false; if p1 is true, it does not evaluate p2. Therefore, && is referred to as the *conditional* or *short-circuit AND* operator, and || is referred to as the *conditional* or *short-circuit OR* operator.

conditional operator
short-circuit operator

Java also provides the & and | operators. The & operator works exactly the same as the && operator, and the | operator works exactly the same as the || operator with one exception: the & and | operators always evaluate both operands. Therefore, & is referred to as the *unconditional AND* operator, and | is referred to as the *unconditional OR* operator. In some rare situations when needed, you can use the & and | operators to guarantee that the right-hand operand is evaluated regardless of whether the left-hand operand is true or false. For example, the expression (width < 2) & (height-- < 2) guarantees that (height-- < 2) is evaluated. Thus the variable height will be decremented regardless of whether width is less than 2 or not.

unconditional operator

Tip

Avoid using the **&** and **|** operators. The benefits of the **&** and **|** operators are marginal. Using them will make the program difficult to read and could cause errors. For example, the expression **(x != 0) & (100 / x)** results in a runtime error if x is 0. However, **(x != 0) && (100 / x)** is fine. If **x** is **0**, **(x != 0)** is false. Since **&&** is a short-circuit operator, Java does not evaluate **(100 / x)** and returns the result as false for the entire expression **(x != 0) && (100 / x).**

 Note

The **&** and **|** operators can also apply to *bitwise operations*. See Appendix G, "Bit Manipulations," for details.

bitwise operations

 Note

As shown in the preceding chapter, a **char** value can be cast into an **int** value, and vice versa. A Boolean value, however, cannot be cast into a value of other types, nor can a value of other types be cast into a Boolean value.

 Note

true and **false** are literals, just like a number such as **10**, so they are not keywords, but you cannot use them as identifiers, just as you cannot use **10** as an identifier.

Boolean literals

3.2.2 Example: Determining Leap Year

This section presents a program that lets the user enter a year in a dialog box and checks whether it is a leap year.

A year is a *leap year* if it is divisible by **4** but not by **100** or if it is divisible by **400**. So you can use the following Boolean expression to check whether a year is a leap year:

leap year

```
(year % 4 == 0 && year % 100 != 0) || (year % 400 == 0)
```

Listing 3.2 gives the program. Two sample runs of the program are shown in Figure 3.1.

FIGURE 3.1   The program determines whether a year is a leap year.

LISTING 3.2 LeapYear.java

```
1 import javax.swing.JOptionPane;
2
3 public class LeapYear {
4   public static void main(String args[]) {
5     // Prompt the user to enter a year
```

show input dialog

```
 6    String yearString = JOptionPane.showInputDialog("Enter a year");
 7
 8    // Convert the string into an int value
 9    int year = Integer.parseInt(yearString);
10
11    // Check if the year is a leap year
12    boolean isLeapYear =
13      (year % 4 == 0 && year % 100 != 0) || (year % 400 == 0);
14
15    // Display the result in a message dialog box
16    JOptionPane.showMessageDialog(null,
17      year + " is a leap year? " + isLeapYear);
18  }
19 }
```

convert to **int** — lines 8–9

leap year? — lines 11–13

show message dialog — lines 15–17

3.2.3 Example: A Simple Math Learning Tool

This example creates a program to let a first grader practice addition. The program randomly generates two single-digit integers **number1** and **number2** and displays a question such as **"What is 7 + 9?"** to the student, as shown in Figure 3.2(a). After the student types the answer in the input dialog box, the program displays a message dialog box to indicate whether the answer is true or false, as shown in Figure 3.2(b).

(a) (b) (c) (d)

FIGURE 3.2 The program generates an addition question and grades the student's answer.

There are many good ways to generate random numbers. For now, generate the first integer using **System.currentTimeMillis() % 10** and the second using **System.current-TimeMillis() * 7 % 10**. Listing 3.3 gives the program. Lines 5–6 generate two numbers, **number1** and **number2**. Line 11 displays a dialog box and obtains an answer from the user. The answer is graded in line 15 using a Boolean expression **number1 + number2 == answer**.

LISTING 3.3 AdditionTutor.java

```
 1 import javax.swing.*;
 2
 3 public class AdditionTutor {
 4   public static void main(String[] args) {
 5     int number1 = (int)(System.currentTimeMillis() % 10);
 6     int number2 = (int)(System.currentTimeMillis() * 7 % 10);
 7
 8     String answerString = JOptionPane.showInputDialog
 9       ("What is " + number1 + " + " + number2 + "?");
10
11     int answer = Integer.parseInt(answerString);
12
13     JOptionPane.showMessageDialog(null,
14       number1 + " + " + number2 + " = " + answer + " is " +
15       (number1 + number2 == answer));
16   }
17 }
```

generate **number1** — line 5

generate **number2** — line 6

show question — lines 8–9

display result — lines 13–15

3.3 **if** Statements

The example in Listing 3.3 displays a message such as "6 + 2 = 7 is false." If you wish the message to be "6 + 2 = 7 is incorrect," you have to use a selection statement.

This section introduces selection statements. Java has several types of selection statements: simple **if** statements, **if ... else** statements, nested **if** statements, **switch** statements, and conditional expressions.

3.3.1 Simple **if** Statements

A simple **if** statement executes an action if and only if the condition is **true**. The syntax for a simple **if** statement is shown below:

```
if (booleanExpression) {
   statement(s);
}
```
if statement

The execution flow chart is shown in Figure 3.3(a).

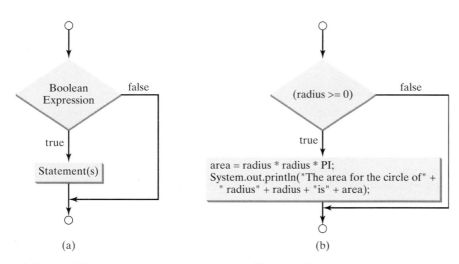

(a)   (b)

FIGURE 3.3   An **if** statement executes statements if the **booleanExpression** evaluates to **true**.

If the **booleanExpression** evaluates to **true**, the statements in the block are executed. As an example, see the following code:

```
if (radius >= 0) {
   area = radius * radius * PI;
   System.out.println("The area for the circle of radius " +
      radius + " is " + area);
}
```

The flow chart of the preceding statement is shown in Figure 3.3(b). If the value of **radius** is greater than or equal to 0, then the **area** is computed and the result is displayed; otherwise, the two statements in the block will not be executed.

 Note

The **booleanExpression** is enclosed in parentheses for all forms of the **if** statement. Thus, for example, the outer parentheses in the following **if** statements are required.

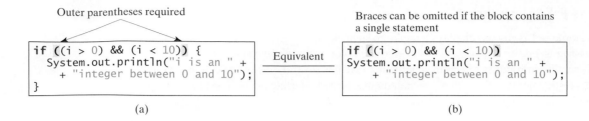

Outer parentheses required

Braces can be omitted if the block contains a single statement

```
if ((i > 0) && (i < 10)) {
  System.out.println("i is an " +
    + "integer between 0 and 10");
}
```

Equivalent

```
if ((i > 0) && (i < 10))
  System.out.println("i is an " +
    + "integer between 0 and 10");
```

(a)   (b)

The braces can be omitted if they enclose a single statement.

Caution

Forgetting the braces when they are needed for grouping multiple statements is a common programming error. If you modify the code by adding new statements in an `if` statement without braces, you will have to insert the braces if they are not already in place.

The following statement determines whether a number is even or odd:

```
// Prompt the user to enter an integer
String intString = JOptionPane.showInputDialog(
  "Enter an integer:");

// Convert string into int
int number = Integer.parseInt(intString);

if (number % 2 == 0)
  System.out.println(number + " is even.");

if (number % 2 != 0)
  System.out.println(number + " is odd.");
```

Caution

Adding a semicolon at the end of an `if` clause, as shown in (a) in the following code, is a common mistake.

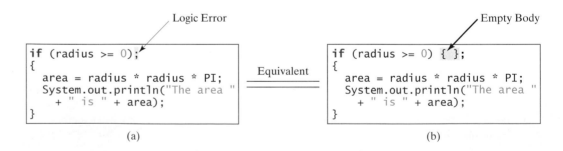

Logic Error

Empty Body

```
if (radius >= 0);
{
  area = radius * radius * PI;
  System.out.println("The area "
    + " is " + area);
}
```

Equivalent

```
if (radius >= 0) { };
{
  area = radius * radius * PI;
  System.out.println("The area "
    + " is " + area);
}
```

(a)   (b)

This mistake is hard to find because it is neither a compilation error nor a runtime error, it is a logic error. The code in (a) is equivalent to (b) with an empty body.

This error often occurs when you use the next-line block style. Using the end-of-line block style will prevent this error.

3.3.2 `if ... else` Statements

A simple `if` statement takes an action if the specified condition is **true**. If the condition is **false**, nothing is done. But what if you want to take alternative actions when the condition is **false**? You can use an `if ... else` statement. The actions that an `if ... else` statement specifies differ based on whether the condition is **true** or **false**.

Here is the syntax for this type of statement:

```
if (booleanExpression) {
  statement(s)-for-the-true-case;
}
else {
  statement(s)-for-the-false-case;
}
```

The flow chart of the statement is shown in Figure 3.4.

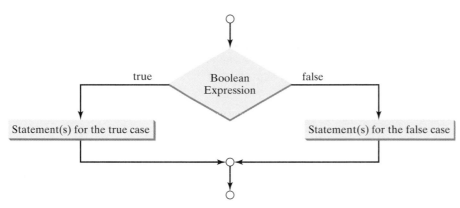

FIGURE 3.4   An `if ... else` statement executes statements for the `true` case if the `boolean` expression evaluates to `true`; otherwise, statements for the `false` case are executed.

If the `booleanExpression` evaluates to `true`, the `statement(s)` for the true case is executed; otherwise, the `statement(s)` for the false case is executed. For example, consider the following code:

```
if (radius >= 0) {
  area = radius * radius * PI;
  System.out.println("The area for the circle of radius " +
    radius + " is " + area);
}
else {
  System.out.println("Negative input");
}
```

if-else statement

If `radius >= 0` is `true`, `area` is computed and displayed; if it is `false`, the message `"Negative input"` is printed.

As usual, the braces can be omitted if there is only one statement within them. The braces enclosing the `System.out.println("Negative input")` statement can therefore be omitted in the preceding example.

Using the `if ... else` statement, you can rewrite the code for determining whether a number is even or odd in the preceding section, as follows:

```
if (number % 2 == 0)
  System.out.println(number + " is even.");
else
  System.out.println(number + " is odd.");
```

This is more efficient because whether `number % 2` is `0` is tested only once.

3.3.3 Nested `if` Statements

The statement in an `if` or `if ... else` statement can be any legal Java statement, including another `if` or `if ... else` statement. The inner `if` statement is said to be *nested* inside the outer `if` statement. The inner `if` statement can contain another `if` statement; in fact, there is no limit to the depth of the nesting. For example, the following is a nested `if` statement:

nested **if** statement

```java
if (i > k) {
  if (j > k)
    System.out.println("i and j are greater than k");
}
else
  System.out.println("i is less than or equal to k");
```

The `if (j > k)` statement is nested inside the `if (i > k)` statement.

The nested `if` statement can be used to implement multiple alternatives. The statement given in Figure 3.5(a), for instance, assigns a letter grade to the variable **grade** according to the score, with multiple alternatives.

```java
if (score >= 90.0)
  grade = 'A';
else
  if (score >= 80.0)
    grade = 'B';
  else
    if (score >= 70.0)
      grade = 'C';
    else
      if (score >= 60.0)
        grade = 'D';
      else
        grade = 'F';
```

Equivalent

This is better

```java
if (score >= 90.0)
  grade = 'A';
else if (score >= 80.0)
  grade = 'B';
else if (score >= 70.0)
  grade = 'C';
else if (score >= 60.0)
  grade = 'D';
else
  grade = 'F';
```

(a)   (b)

FIGURE 3.5 A preferred format for multiple alternative `if` statements is shown in (b).

The execution of this `if` statement proceeds as follows. The first condition (`score >= 90.0`) is tested. If it is `true`, the grade becomes `'A'`. If it is `false`, the second condition (`score >= 80.0`) is tested. If the second condition is `true`, the grade becomes `'B'`. If that condition is `false`, the third condition and the rest of the conditions (if necessary) continue to be tested until a condition is met or all of the conditions prove to be `false`. If all of the conditions are `false`, the grade becomes `'F'`. Note that a condition is tested only when all of the conditions that come before it are `false`.

The `if` statement in Figure 3.5(a) is equivalent to the `if` statement in Figure 3.5(b). In fact, Figure 3.5(b) is the preferred writing style for multiple alternative `if` statements. This style avoids deep indentation and makes the program easy to read.

matching **else** with **if**

 Note

The `else` clause matches the most recent unmatched `if` clause in the same block. For example, the following statement in (a) is equivalent to the statement in (b).

The compiler ignores indentation. Nothing is printed from the statements in (a) and (b). To force the `else` clause to match the first `if` clause, you must add a pair of braces:

```java
int i = 1; int j = 2; int k = 3;
if (i > j) {
```

```
int i = 1;
int j = 2;
int k = 3;

if (i > j)
  if (i > k)
    System.out.println("A");
else
    System.out.println("B");
```

Equivalent

This is better
with correct →
indentation

```
int i = 1;
int j = 2;
int k = 3;

if (i > j)
  if (i > k)
    System.out.println("A");
  else
    System.out.println("B");
```

(a)   (b)

```
  if (i > k)
    System.out.println("A");
}
else
  System.out.println("B");
```

This statement prints **B**.

Tip

Often new programmers write the code that assigns a test condition to a **boolean** variable like   assign boolean variable
the code in (a):

```
if (number % 2 == 0)
  even = true;
else
  even = false;
```

Equivalent
───────────
This is better

```
boolean even
  = number % 2 == 0;
```

(a)   (b)

The code can be simplified by assigning the test value directly to the variable, as shown in (b).

Caution

To test whether a **boolean** variable is **true** or **false** in a test condition, it is redundant to use   test boolean value
the equality comparison operator like the code in (a):

```
if (even == true)
  System.out.println(
    "It is even.");
```

Equivalent
═══════════
This is better

```
if (even)
  System.out.println(
    "It is even.");
```

(a)   (b)

Instead, it is better to use the **boolean** variable directly, as shown in (b). Another good reason
to use the **boolean** variable directly is to avoid errors that are difficult to detect. Using the =
operator instead of the == operator to compare equality of two items in a test condition is a common error. It could lead to the following erroneous statement:

```
if (even = true)
  System.out.println("It is even.");
```

This statement does not have syntax errors. It assigns **true** to **even** so that **even** is always
true.

debugging in IDE

Tip

If you use an IDE such as JBuilder, NetBeans, or Eclipse, please refer to *Learning Java Effectively with JBuilder/NetBeans/Eclipse* in the supplements. This supplement shows you how to use a debugger to trace a simple **if-else** statement.

3.3.4 Example: Computing Taxes

This section uses nested **if** statements to write a program to compute personal income tax. The United States federal personal income tax is calculated based on filing status and taxable income. There are four filing statuses: single filers, married filing jointly, married filing separately, and head of household. The tax rates for 2002 are shown in Table 3.7. If you are, say, single with a taxable income of $10,000, the first $6,000 is taxed at 10% and the other $4,000 is taxed at 15%. So your tax is $1,200.

TABLE 3.7 2002 U.S. Federal Personal Tax Rates

Tax rate	Single filers	Married filing jointly or qualifying widow/widower	Married filing separately	Head of household
10%	Up to $6,000	Up to $12,000	Up to $6,000	Up to $10,000
15%	$6,001–$27,950	$12,001–$46,700	$6,001–$23,350	$10,001–$37,450
27%	$27,951–$67,700	$46,701–$112,850	$23,351–$56,425	$37,451–$96,700
30%	$67,701–$141,250	$112,851–$171,950	$56,426–$85,975	$96,701–$156,600
35%	$141,251–$307,050	$171,951–$307,050	$85,976–$153,525	$156,601–$307,050
38.6%	$307,051 or more	$307,051 or more	$153,526 or more	$307,051 or more

Your program should prompt the user to enter the filing status and taxable income and computes the tax for the year 2002. Enter 0 for single filers, 1 for married filing jointly, 2 for married filing separately, and 3 for head of household. A sample run of the program is shown in Figure 3.6.

(a) (b) (c)

FIGURE 3.6 The program computes the tax using **if** statements.

Your program computes the tax for the taxable income based on the filing status. The filing status can be determined using **if** statements outlined as follows:

```
if (status == 0) {
  // Compute tax for single filers
}
else if (status == 1) {
  // Compute tax for married file jointly
}
else if (status == 2) {
  // Compute tax for married file separately
}
```

```
  else if (status == 3) {
    // Compute tax for head of household
  }
  else {
    // Display wrong status
  }
```

For each filing status, there are six tax rates. Each rate is applied to a certain amount of taxable income. For example, of a taxable income of $400,000 for single filers, $6,000 is taxed at 10%, (27950 – 6000) at 15%, (67700 – 27950) at 27%, (141250 – 67700) at 35%, and (400000 – 307050) at 38.6%.

Listing 3.4 gives the solution to compute taxes for single filers. The complete solution is left as an exercise.

LISTING 3.4 ComputeTaxWithSelectionStatement.java

```
 1 import javax.swing.JOptionPane;                                    import class
 2
 3 public class ComputeTaxWithSelectionStatement {
 4   public static void main(String[] args) {
 5     // Prompt the user to enter filing status
 6     String statusString = JOptionPane.showInputDialog(              input dialog
 7       "Enter the filing status:\n" +
 8       "(0-single filer, 1-married jointly,\n" +
 9       "2-married separately, 3-head of household)");
10     int status = Integer.parseInt(statusString);                    convert string
11                                                                       to int
12     // Prompt the user to enter taxable income
13     String incomeString = JOptionPane.showInputDialog(              input dialog
14       "Enter the taxable income:");
15     double income = Double.parseDouble(incomeString);               convert string
16                                                                       to double
17     // Compute tax
18     double tax = 0;                                                 compute tax
19
20     if (status == 0) { // Compute tax for single filers
21       if (income <= 6000)
22         tax = income * 0.10;
23       else if (income <= 27950)
24         tax = 6000 * 0.10 + (income - 6000) * 0.15;
25       else if (income <= 67700)
26         tax = 6000 * 0.10 + (27950 - 6000) * 0.15 +
27           (income - 27950) * 0.27;
28       else if (income <= 141250)
29         tax = 6000 * 0.10 + (27950 - 6000) * 0.15 +
30           (67700 - 27950) * 0.27 + (income - 67700) * 0.30;
31       else if (income <= 307050)
32         tax = 6000 * 0.10 + (27950 - 6000) * 0.15 +
33           (67700 - 27950) * 0.27 + (141250 - 67700) * 0.30 +
34           (income - 141250) * 0.35;
35       else
36         tax = 6000 * 0.10 + (27950 - 6000) * 0.15 +
37           (67700 - 27950) * 0.27 + (141250 - 67700) * 0.30 +
38           (307050 - 141250) * 0.35 + (income - 307050) * 0.386;
39     }
40     else if (status == 1) { // Compute tax for married file jointly
41       // Left as exercise
42     }
```

```
43    else if (status == 2) { // Compute tax for married separately
44       // Left as exercise
45    }
46    else if (status == 3) { // Compute tax for head of household
47       // Left as exercise
48    }
49    else {
50       System.out.println("Error: invalid status");
51       System.exit(0);
52    }
53
54    // Display the result
55    JOptionPane.showMessageDialog(null, "Tax is " +
56       (int)(tax * 100) / 100.0);
57  }
58 }
```

exit program (line 51)

message dialog (line 55)

The `import` statement (line 1) makes the class `javax.swing.JOptionPane` available for use in this example.

The program receives the filing status and taxable income. The multiple alternative `if` statements (lines 22, 42, 45, 48, 51) check the filing status and compute the tax based on the filing status.

exit method

Like the `showMessageDialog` method, `System.exit(0)` (line 53) is also a static method. This method is defined in the `System` class. Invoking this method terminates the program. The argument `0` indicates that the program is terminated normally.

Note

An initial value of `0` is assigned to `tax` (line 20). A syntax error would occur if it had no initial value because all of the other statements that assign values to `tax` are within the `if` statement. The compiler thinks that these statements may not be executed and therefore reports a syntax error.

3.3.5 Example: An Improved Math Learning Tool

This example creates a program for a first grader to practice subtraction. The program randomly generates two single-digit integers `number1` and `number2` with `number1 > number2` and displays a question such as "`What is 9–2?`" to the student, as shown in Figure 3.7(a). After the student types the answer in the input dialog box, the program displays a message dialog box to indicate whether the answer is correct, as shown in Figure 3.7(b).

(a)   (b)   (c)   (d)

Figure 3.7 The program generates a subtraction question and grades the student's answer.

random() method

To generate a random number, use the `random()` method in the `Math` class. Invoking this method returns a random double value `d` such that `0.0 ≤ d < 1.0` So `(int)(Math.random() * 10)` returns a random single-digit integer (i.e., a number between `0` and `9`).

The program may work as follows:

- Generate two single-digit integers into `number1` and `number2`.

- If `number1 < number2`, swap `number1` with `number2`.

- Prompt the student to answer `"what is number1 - number2?"`
- Check the student's answer and display whether the answer is correct.

The complete program is shown in Listing 3.5.

LISTING 3.5 SubtractionTutor.java

```
 1 import javax.swing.JOptionPane;                                      import class
 2
 3 public class SubtractionTutor {
 4   public static void main(String[] args) {
 5     // 1. Generate two random single-digit integers
 6     int number1 = (int)(Math.random() * 10);                          random numbers
 7     int number2 = (int)(Math.random() * 10);
 8
 9     // 2. If number1 < number2, swap number1 with number2
10     if (number1 < number2) {
11       int temp = number1;
12       number1 = number2;
13       number2 = temp;
14     }
15
16     // 3. Prompt the student to answer "what is number1 - number2?"
17     String answerString = JOptionPane.showInputDialog             input dialog
18       ("What is " + number1 + " - " + number2 + "?");
19     int answer = Integer.parseInt(answerString);
20
21     // 4. Grade the answer and display the result
22     String replyString;
23     if (number1 - number2 == answer)
24       replyString = "You are correct!";
25     else
26       replyString = "Your answer is wrong.\n" + number1 + " - "
27         + number2 + " should be " + (number1 - number2);
28     JOptionPane.showMessageDialog(null, replyString);             message dialog
29   }
30 }
```

To swap two variables `number1` and `number2`, a temporary variable `temp` (line 11) is used to first hold the value in `number1`. The value in `number2` is assigned to `number1` (line 12), and the value in `temp` is assigned to `number2`.

3.4 **switch** Statements

The `if` statement in Listing 3.4 makes selections based on a single `true` or `false` condition. There are four cases for computing taxes, which depend on the value of `status`. To fully account for all the cases, nested `if` statements were used. Overuse of nested `if` statements makes a program difficult to read. Java provides a `switch` statement to handle multiple conditions efficiently. You could write the following `switch` statement to replace the nested `if` statement in Listing 3.4:

```
switch (status) {
  case 0:  compute taxes for single filers;
           break;
  case 1:  compute taxes for married file jointly;
           break;
```

```
    case 2:  compute taxes for married file separately;
             break;
    case 3:  compute taxes for head of household;
             break;
    default: System.out.println("Errors: invalid status");
             System.exit(0);
}
```

The flow chart of the preceding `switch` statement is shown in Figure 3.8.

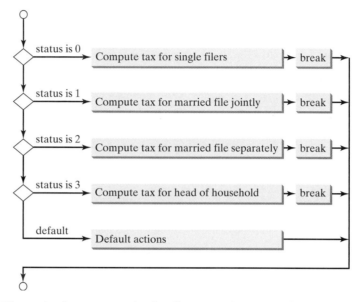

FIGURE 3.8 The `switch` statement checks all cases and executes the statements in the matched case.

This statement checks to see whether the status matches the value 0, 1, 2, or 3, in that order. If matched, the corresponding tax is computed; if not matched, a message is displayed. Here is the full syntax for the `switch` statement:

`switch` statement

```
switch (switch-expression) {
    case value1: statement(s)1;
                 break;
    case value2: statement(s)2;
                 break;
    ...
    case valueN: statement(s)N;
                 break;
    default:     statement(s)-for-default;
}
```

The `switch` statement observes the following rules:

- The **switch-expression** must yield a value of **char**, **byte**, **short**, or **int** type and must always be enclosed in parentheses.

- The **value1**, ..., and **valueN** must have the same data type as the value of the **switch-expression**. Note that **value1**, ..., and **valueN** are constant expressions, meaning that they cannot contain variables in the expression, such as 1 + x.

- When the value in a `case` statement matches the value of the `switch-expression`, the statements *starting from this case* are executed until either a `break` statement or the end of the switch statement is reached.

- The keyword `break` is optional. The `break` statement immediately ends the `switch` statement.

- The `default` case, which is optional, can be used to perform actions when none of the specified cases matches the `switch-expression`.

- The `case` statements are checked in sequential order, but the order of the cases (including the default case) does not matter. However, it is good programming style to follow the logical sequence of the cases and place the default case at the end.

Caution

Do not forget to use a `break` statement when one is needed. Once a case is matched, the statements starting from the matched case are executed until a `break` statement or the end of the `switch` statement is reached. This phenomenon is referred to as the *fall-through* behavior. For example, the following code prints character a three times if `ch` is `'a'`:

without **break**

fall-through behavior

```
switch (ch) {
  case 'a': System.out.println(ch);
  case 'b': System.out.println(ch);
  case 'c': System.out.println(ch);
}
```

ch is 'c' —true→ System.out.println(ch)
false
ch is 'b' —true→ System.out.println(ch)
false
ch is 'c' —true→ System.out.println(ch)
false

Tip

To avoid programming errors and improve code maintainability, it is a good idea to put a comment in a case clause if `break` is purposely omitted.

3.5 Conditional Expressions

You might want to assign a value to a variable that is restricted by certain conditions. For example, the following statement assigns 1 to y if x is greater than 0, and −1 to y if x is less than or equal to 0.

```
if (x > 0)
  y = 1
else
  y = -1;
```

Alternatively, as in this example, you can use a conditional expression to achieve the same result.

```
y = (x > 0) ? 1 : -1;
```

Conditional expressions are in a completely different style, with no explicit `if` in the statement. The syntax is shown below:

```
booleanExpression ? expression1 : expression2;
```

conditional expression

The result of this conditional expression is `expression1` if `booleanExpression` is `true`; otherwise the result is `expression2`.

Suppose you want to assign the larger number between variable `num1` and `num2` to `max`. You can simply write a statement using the conditional expression:

```
max = (num1 > num2) ? num1 : num2;
```

For another example, the following statement displays the message `"num is even"` if `num` is even, and otherwise displays `"num is odd."`

```
System.out.println((num % 2 == 0) ? "num is even" : "num is odd");
```

Note

The symbols `?` and `:` appear together in a conditional expression. They form a conditional operator. This operator is called a *ternary operator* because it uses three operands. It is the only ternary operator in Java.

3.6 Formatting Console Output and Strings

You already know how to display console output using the `println` method. JDK 1.5 introduced a new `printf` method that enables you to format output. The syntax to invoke this method is

printf

```
System.out.printf(format, item1, item2, ..., itemk)
```

specifier

where `format` is a string that may consist of substrings and format specifiers. A format specifier specifies how an item should be displayed. An item may be a numeric value, a character, a boolean value, or a string. Each specifier begins with a percent sign. Table 3.8 lists some frequently used specifiers.

TABLE 3.8 Frequently Used Specifiers

Specifier	Output	Example
%b	a boolean value	true or false
%c	a character	'a'
%d	a decimal integer	200
%f	a floating-point number	45.460000
%e	a number in standard scientific notation	4.556000e+01
%s	a string	"Java is cool"

Here is an example:

```
int count = 5;
double amount = 45.56;
System.out.printf("count is %d and amount is %f", count, amount);
```
items

display   count is 5 and amount is 45.560000

Items must match the specifiers in order, in number, and in exact type. For example, the specifier for `count` is `%d` and for `amount` is `%f`. By default, a floating-point value is displayed with six digits after the decimal point. You can specify the width and precision in a specifier, as shown in the examples in Table 3.9.

TABLE 3.9   Examples of Specifying Width and Precision

Example	Output
`%5c`	Output the character and add four spaces before the character item.
`%6b`	Output the boolean value and add one space before the false value and two spaces before the true value.
`%5d`	Output the integer item with width at least 5. If the number of digits in the item is <5, add spaces before the number. If the number of digits in the item is >5, the width is automatically increased.
`%10.2f`	Output the floating-point item with width at least 10 including a decimal point and two digits after the point. Thus there are 7 digits allocated before the decimal point. If the number of digits before the decimal in the item is <7, add spaces before the number. If the number of digits before the decimal in the item is >7, the width is automatically increased.
`%10.2e`	Output the floating-point item with width at least 10 including a decimal point, two digits after the point and the exponent part. If the displayed number in scientific notation has width less than 10, add spaces before the number.
`%12s`	Output the string with width at least 12 characters. If the string item has less than 12 characters, add spaces before the string. If the string item has more than 12 characters, the width is automatically increased.

You can put the minus sign (−) in the specifier to specify that the item is left-justified in the output within the specified field. For example, the following statement

left justify

```
System.out.printf("%8d%-8s\n", 1234, "Java");
System.out.printf("%-8d%-8s\n", 1234, "Java");
```

displays

```
    1234Java
1234    Java
```

Caution

The items must match the specifiers in exact type. The item for the specifier `%f` or `%e` must be a floating-point type value such as `40.0`, not `40`. Thus an `int` variable cannot match `%f` or `%e`.

Tip

The `%` sign denotes a specifier. To output a literal `%` in the format string, use `%%`.

You can print formatted output to the console using the `printf` method. Can you display formatted output in a message dialog box? To accomplish this, use the static `format` method in the `String` class to create a formatted string. The syntax to invoke this method is

formatting strings

```
String.format(format, item1, item2, ..., itemk)
```

This method is similar to the `printf` method except that the `format` method returns a formatted string, whereas the `printf` method displays a formatted string. For example,

```
String s = String.format("count is %d and amount is %f", 5, 45.56));
```

creates a formatted string `"count is 5 and amount is 45.560000"`.

The following statement displays a formatted string in a message dialog box:

```
JOptionPane.showMessageDialog(null,
    String.format("Sales tax is %1.2f",
    24.3454));
```

3.7 Operator Precedence and Associativity

Operator precedence and associativity determine the order in which operators are evaluated. Suppose that you have this expression:

$$3 + 4 * 4 > 5 * (4 + 3) - 1$$

precedence

What is its value? How does the compiler know the execution order of the operators? The expression in the parentheses is evaluated first. (Parentheses can be nested, in which case the expression in the inner parentheses is executed first.) When evaluating an expression without parentheses, the operators are applied according to the precedence rule and the associativity rule. The precedence rule defines precedence for operators, as shown in Table 3.10, which contains the operators you have learned so far. Operators are listed in decreasing order of precedence from top to bottom. Operators with the same precedence appear in the same group. (See Appendix C, "Operator Precedence Chart," for a complete list of Java operators and their precedence.)

TABLE 3.10 Operator Precedence Chart

Precedence	Operator
Highest Order	**var++** and **var−−** (Postfix)
	+, **−** (Unary plus and minus), **++var** and **−−var** (Prefix)
	(type) (Casting)
	! (Not)
	*, **/**, **%** (Multiplication, division, and remainder)
	+, **−** (Binary addition and subtraction)
	<, **<=**, **>**, **>=** (Comparison)
	==, **!=** (Equality)
	& (Unconditional AND)
	^ (Exclusive OR)
	| (Unconditional OR)
	&& (Conditional AND)
	|| (Conditional OR)
Lowest Order	**=**, **+=**, **−=**, ***=**, **/=**, **%=** (Assignment operator)

associativity

If operators with the same precedence are next to each other, their *associativity* determines the order of evaluation. All binary operators except assignment operators are *left-associative*. For example, since + and − are of the same precedence and are left-associative, the expression

$$a - b + c - d \qquad \underline{\text{equivalent}} \qquad ((a - b) + c) - d$$

Assignment operators are *right-associative*. Therefore, the expression

a = b += c = 5 _____ equivalent _____ a = (b += (c = 5))

Suppose **a**, **b**, and **c** are **1** before the assignment; after the whole expression is evaluated, **a** becomes **6**, **b** becomes **6**, and **c** becomes **5**. Note that left associativity for the assignment operator would not make sense.

Applying the operator precedence and associativity rule, the expression **3 + 4 * 4 > 5 * (4 + 3) - 1** is evaluated as follows:

```
3 + 4 * 4 > 5 * (4 + 3) - 1
                     ┕━━━━━━━━━━━━━━ (1) inside parentheses first
3 + 4 * 4 > 5 * 7 - 1
   ┕━━━━━━━━━━━━━━━━━━━━━━━━━━━ (2) multiplication
3 + 16 > 5 * 7 - 1
           ┕━━━━━━━━━━━━━━━━━━━ (3) multiplication
3 + 16 > 35 - 1
 ┕━━━━━━━━━━━━━━━━━━━━━━━━━━━━━ (4) addition
19 > 35 - 1
       ┕━━━━━━━━━━━━━━━━━━━━━━━ (5) subtraction
19 > 34
 ┕━━━━━━━━━━━━━━━━━━━━━━━━━━━━━ (6) greater than
false
```

Tip
You can use parentheses to force an evaluation order as well as to make a program easy to read. Use of redundant parentheses does not slow down the execution of the expression.

3.8 Operand Evaluation Order

The precedence and associativity rules specify the order of the operators but not the order in which the operands of a binary operator are evaluated. Operands are evaluated strictly *from left to right* in Java. *The left-hand operand of a binary operator is evaluated before any part of the right-hand operand is evaluated.* This rule takes precedence over any other rules that govern expressions. Consider this expression:

from left to right

a + b * (c + **10** * d) / e

a, **b**, **c**, **d**, and **e** are evaluated in this order. *If no operands have side effects that change the value of a variable, the order of operand evaluation is irrelevant.* Interesting cases arise when operands do have a side effect. For example, **x** becomes 1 in the following code because **a** is evaluated to 0 before **++a** is evaluated to **1**.

```
int a = 0;
int x = a + (++a);
```

But **x** becomes **2** in the following code because **++a** is evaluated to **1**, and then **a** is evaluated to **1**.

```
int a = 0;
int x = ++a + a;
```

The order for evaluating operands takes precedence over the operator precedence rule. In the former case, **(++a)** has higher precedence than addition (+), but since **a** is a left-hand operand of the addition (+), it is evaluated before any part of its right-hand operand (e.g., ++**a** in this case).

evaluation rule   In summary, the rule of evaluating an expression is:

- Rule 1: Evaluate whatever subexpressions you can possibly evaluate from left to right.

- Rule 2: The operators are applied according to their precedence, as shown in Table 3.10.

- Rule 3: The associativity rule applies for two operators next to each other with the same precedence.

Applying the rule, the expression 3 + 4 * 4 > 5 * (4 + 3) - 1 is evaluated as follows:

```
3 + 4 * 4 > 5 * (4 + 3) - 1
```
(1) 4 * 4 is the first subexpression that can be evaluated from the left.

```
3 + 16 > 5 * (4 + 3) - 1
```
(2) 3 + 16 is evaluated now.

```
19 > 5 * (4 + 3) - 1
```
(3) 4 + 3 is now the leftmost subexpression that should be evaluated.

```
19 > 5 * 7 - 1
```
(4) 5 * 7 is evaluated now.

```
19 > 35 - 1
```
(5) 35 - 1 is evaluated now.

```
19 > 34
```
(6) 19 > 34 is evaluated now.

false

The result happens to be the same as applying Rule 2 and Rule 3 without applying Rule 1. In fact, Rule 1 is not necessary if no operands have side effects that change the value of a variable in an expression.

KEY TERMS

boolean expression 68	operand evaluation order 87
boolean value 68	operator associativity 86
boolean type 68	operator precedence 86
break statement 81, 101	selection statement 73
conditional operator 84	short-circuit evaluation 70
fall-through behavior 83	

CHAPTER SUMMARY

- Java has eight primitive data types. The preceding chapter introduced **byte**, **short**, **int**, **long**, **float**, **double**, and **char**. This chapter introduced the **boolean** type that represents a **true** or **false** value.

- The Boolean operators &&, &, | |, |, !, and ^ operate with Boolean values and variables. The relational operators (<, <=, ==, !=, >, >=) work with numbers and characters, and yield a Boolean value.

- When evaluating **p1** && **p2**, Java first evaluates **p1** and then evaluates **p2** if **p1** is **true**; if **p1** is **false**, it does not evaluate **p2**. When evaluating **p1** | | **p2**, Java first evaluates **p1** and then evaluates **p2** if **p1** is **false**; if **p1** is **true**, it does not evaluate p2. Therefore, **&&** is referred to as the *conditional* or *short-circuit AND* operator, and | | is referred to as the *conditional* or *short-circuit OR* operator.

- Java also provides the **&** and | operators. The **&** operator works exactly the same as the **&&** operator, and the | operator works exactly the same as the | | operator with one exception: the **&** and | operators always evaluate both operands. Therefore, **&** is referred to as the *unconditional AND* operator, and | is referred to as the *unconditional OR* operator.

- Selection statements are used for building selection steps into programs. There are several types of selection statements: `if` statements, `if ... else` statements, nested `if` statements, `switch` statements, and conditional expressions.

- The various `if` statements all make control decisions based on a Boolean expression. Based on the `true` or `false` evaluation of the expression, these statements take one of two possible courses.

- The `switch` statement makes control decisions based on a switch expression of type `char`, `byte`, `short`, `int`, or `boolean`.

- The keyword `break` is optional in a `switch` statement, but it is normally used at the end of each case in order to terminate the remainder of the `switch` statement. If the `break` statement is not present, the next `case` statement will be executed.

- The operands of a binary operator are evaluated from left to right. No part of the right-hand operand is evaluated until all the operands before the binary operator are evaluated.

- The operators in arithmetic expressions are evaluated in the order determined by the rules of parentheses, operator precedence, and associativity.

- Parentheses can be used to force the order of evaluation to occur in any sequence. Operators with higher precedence are evaluated earlier. The associativity of the operators determines the order of evaluation for operators of the same precedence.

- All binary operators except assignment operators are left-associative, and assignment operators are right-associative.

REVIEW QUESTIONS

Section 3.2 `boolean` Data Type and Operations

3.1 List six comparison operators.

3.2 Assume that x is 1, show the result of the following Boolean expressions:

```
(true) && (3 > 4)
!(x > 0) && (x > 0)
(x > 0) || (x < 0)
(x != 0) || (x == 0)
(x >= 0) || (x < 0)
(x != 1) == !(x == 1)
```

3.3 Write a Boolean expression that evaluates to `true` if a number stored in variable `num` is between 1 and 100.

3.4 Write a Boolean expression that evaluates to `true` if a number stored in variable `num` is between 1 and 100 or the number is negative.

3.5 Assume that `x` and `y` are `int` type. Which of the following are correct Java expressions?

```
x > y > 0
x = y && y
x /= y
x or y
x and y
(x != 0) || (x = 0)
```

3.6 Can the following conversions involving casting be allowed? If so, find the converted result.

```
boolean b = true;
i = (int)b;
int i = 1;
boolean b = (boolean)i;
```

3.7 Suppose that `x` is 1. What is `x` after the evaluation of the following expression?

```
(x > 1) & (x++ > 1)
```

3.8 Suppose that `x` is 1. What is `x` after the evaluation of the following expression?

```
(x > 1) && (x++ > 1)
```

3.9 Show the output of the following program:

```java
public class Test {
  public static void main(String[] args) {
    char x = 'a';
    char y = 'c';

    System.out.println(++y);
    System.out.println(y++);
    System.out.println(x > y);
    System.out.println(x - y);
  }
}
```

Section 3.3 `if` Statements

3.10 Suppose `x = 3` and `y = 2`, show the output, if any, of the following code. What is the output if `x = 3` and `y = 4`? What is the output if `x = 2` and `y = 2`? Draw a flowchart of the following code:

```java
if (x > 2) {
  if (y > 2) {
    int z = x + y;
    System.out.println("z is " + z);
  }
}
else
  System.out.println("x is " + x);
```

3.11 Which of the following statements are equivalent? Which ones are correctly indented?

```
if (i > 0) if
(j > 0)
x = 0; else
if (k > 0) y = 0;
else z = 0;
```
(a)

```
if (i > 0) {
  if (j > 0)
    x = 0;
  else if (k > 0)
    y = 0;
}
else
  z = 0;
```
(b)

```
if (i > 0)
  if (j > 0)
    x = 0;
  else if (k > 0)
    y = 0;
  else
    z = 0;
```
(c)

```
if (i > 0)
  if (j > 0)
    x = 0;
  else if (k > 0)
    y = 0;
else
  z = 0;
```
(d)

3.12   Suppose x = 2 and y = 3, show the output, if any, of the following code. What is the output if x = 3 and y = 2? What is the output if x = 3 and y = 3? (Hint: please indent the statement correctly first.)

```
if (x > 2)
  if (y > 2) {
    int z = x + y;
    System.out.println("z is " + z);
  }
else
  System.out.println("x is " + x);
```

3.13   Are the following two statements equivalent?

```
if (income <= 10000)
  tax = income * 0.1;
else if (income <= 20000)
  tax = 1000 +
    (income - 10000) * 0.15;
```

```
if (income <= 10000)
  tax = income * 0.1;
else if (income > 10000 &&
         income <= 20000)
  tax = 1000 +
    (income - 10000) * 0.15;
```

3.14   Which of the following is a possible output from invoking `Math.random()`?

```
323.4, 0.5, 34, 1.0, 0.0, 0.234
```

3.15   How do you generate a random integer i such that $0 \le i < 20$?
       How do you generate a random integer i such that $10 \le i < 20$?
       How do you generate a random integer i such that $10 \le i \le 50$?

Section 3.4 `switch` Statements

3.16   What data types are required for a `switch` variable? If the keyword **break** is not used after a case is processed, what is the next statement to be executed? Can you convert a `switch` statement to an equivalent `if` statement, or vice versa? What are the advantages of using a `switch` statement?

3.17   What is y after the following `switch` statement is executed?

```
x = 3; y = 3;
switch (x + 3) {
  case 6:  y = 1;
  default: y += 1;
}
```

3.18 Use a `switch` statement to rewrite the following `if` statement and draw the flowchart for the `switch` statement:

```
if (a == 1)
  x += 5;
else if (a == 2)
  x += 10;
else if (a == 3)
  x += 16;
else if (a == 4)
  x += 34;
```

Section 3.5 Conditional Expressions

3.19 Rewrite the following `if` statement using the conditional operator:

```
if (count % 10 == 0)
  System.out.print(count + "\n");
else
  System.out.print(count + " ");
```

Section 3.6 Formatting Console Output and Strings

3.20 What are the specifiers for outputting a boolean value, a character, a decimal integer, a floating-point number, and a string?

3.21 What is wrong in the following statements?

(a) `System.out.printf("%5d %d", 1, 2, 3);`
(b) `System.out.printf("%5d %f", 1);`
(c) `System.out.printf("%5d %f", 1, 2);`

3.22 Show the output of the following statements.

(a) `System.out.printf("amount is %f %e\n", 32.32, 32.32);`
(b) `System.out.printf("amount is %5.4f %5.4e\n", 32.32, 32.32);`
(c) `System.out.printf("%6b\n", (1 > 2));`
(d) `System.out.printf("%6s\n", "Java");`
(e) `System.out.printf("%-6b%s\n", (1 > 2), "Java");`
(f) `System.out.printf("%6b%-s\n", (1 > 2), "Java");`

3.23 How do you create a formatted string?

Sections 3.7–3.8

3.24 List the precedence order of the Boolean operators. Evaluate the following expressions:

```
true | true && false
true || true && false
true | true & false
```

3.25 Show and explain the output of the following code:

(a)
```
int i = 0;
System.out.println(--i + i + i++);
System.out.println(i + ++i);
```

(b)
```
int i = 0;
i = i + (i = 1);
System.out.println(i);
```

```
(c)        int i = 0;
           i = (i = 1) + i;
           System.out.println(i);
```

3.26 Assume that `int a = 1` and `double d = 1.0`, and that each expression is independent. What are the results of the following expressions?

```
a = (a = 3) + a;
a = a + (a = 3);
a += a + (a = 3);
a = 5 + 5 * 2 % a--;
a = 4 + 1 + 4 * 5 % (++a + 1);
d += 1.5 * 3 + (++d);
d -= 1.5 * 3 + d++;
```

PROGRAMMING EXERCISES

Section 3.2 `boolean` Data Type and Operations

Pedagogical Note

For each exercise, students should carefully analyze the problem requirements and the design strategies for solving the problem before coding.

think before coding

Pedagogical Note

Instructors may ask students to *document analysis and design* for selected exercises. Students should use their own words to analyze the problem, including the input, output, and what needs to be computed and describe how to solve the problem using pseudocode. This has two benefits: (1) it mandates students to think before typing code; (2) it fosters writing skills.

document analysis and design

Debugging Tip

Before you ask for help, read and explain the program to yourself, and trace it using several representative inputs by hand or using an IDE debugger. You learn how to program by debugging your own mistakes.

learn from mistakes

Note

Do not use selection statements for Exercises 3.1–3.6.

3.1* (*Validating triangles*) Write a program that reads three edges for a triangle and determines whether the input is valid. The input is valid if the sum of any two edges is greater than the third edge. For example, if your input for three edges is 1, 2, 1, the output should be:

```
Can edges 1, 2, and 1 form a triangle? false
```

If your input for three edges is 2, 2, 1, the output should be:

```
Can edges 2, 2, and 1 form a triangle? true
```

3.2 (*Checking whether a number is even*) Write a program that reads an integer and checks whether it is even. For example, if your input is 25, the output should be:

```
Is 25 an even number? false
```

If your input is 2000, the output should be:

```
Is 2000 an even number? true
```

3.3* (*Using the* **&&,** **||** *and* ∧ *operators*) Write a program that prompts the user to enter an integer and determines whether it is divisible by **5** and **6**, whether it is divisible by **5** or **6**, and whether it is divisible by **5** or **6**, but not both. For example, if your input is **10**, the output should be

```
Is 10 divisible by 5 and 6? false
Is 10 divisible by 5 or 6? true
Is 10 divisible by 5 or 6, but not both? true
```

3.4** (*Learning addition*) Write a program that generates two integers under **100** and prompts the user to enter the addition of these two integers. The program then reports **true** if the answer is correct, **false** otherwise. The program is similar to Listing 3.3.

3.5** (*Addition for three numbers*) The program in Listing 3.3 generates two integers and prompts the user to enter the addition of these two integers. Revise the program to generate three single-digit integers and prompt the user to enter the addition of these three integers.

3.6* (*Using the console input*) Rewrite Listing 3.2, LeapYear.java, using the console input.

Section 3.3 Selection Statements

3.7 (*Monetary units*) Modify Listing 2.4 to display the non-zero denominations only, using singular words for single units like **1** dollar and **1** penny, and plural words for more than one unit like **2** dollars and **3** pennies. (Use **23.67** to test your program.)

3.8* (*Sorting three integers*) Write a program that sorts three integers. The integers are entered from the input dialogs and stored in variables **num1**, **num2**, and **num3**, respectively. The program sorts the numbers so that *num1* ≤ *num2* ≤ *num3*.

3.9 (*Computing the perimeter of a triangle*) Write a program that reads three edges for a triangle and computes the perimeter if the input is valid. Otherwise, display that the input is invalid. The input is valid if the sum of any two edges is greater than the third edge (also see Exercise 3.1).

3.10 (*Computing taxes*) Listing 3.4 gives the source code to compute taxes for single filers. Complete Listing 3.4 to give the complete source code.

3.11* (*Finding the number of days in a month*) Write a program that prompts the user to enter the month and year, and displays the number of days in the month. For example, if the user entered month 2 and year 2000, the program should display that February 2000 has 29 days. If the user entered month 3 and year 2005, the program should display that March 2005 has 31 days.

3.12 (*Checking a number*) Write a program that prompts the user to enter an integer and checks whether the number is divisible by both **5** and **6**, neither, or just one of them. Here are some sample outputs for inputs **10**, **30**, and **23**.

```
10 is divisible by 5 or 6, but not both
30 is divisible by both 5 and 6
23 is not divisible by either 5 or 6
```

3.13 (*An addition learning tool*) Listing 3.5, SubtractionTutor.java, randomly generates a subtraction question. Revise the program to randomly generate an addition question with two integers less than **100**.

CHAPTER 4

LOOPS

Objectives

- To use **while**, **do-while**, and **for** loop statements to control the repetition of statements (§§4.2–4.4).

- To understand the flow of control in loop statements (§§4.2–4.4).

- To use Boolean expressions to control loop statements (§§4.2–4.4).

- To know the similarities and differences between three types of loops (§4.5).

- To write nested loops (§4.6).

- To implement program control with **break** and **continue** (§4.9).

4.1 Introduction

Suppose that you need to print a string (e.g., `"Welcome to Java!"`) a hundred times. It would be tedious to have to write the following statement a hundred times:

```
System.out.println("Welcome to Java!");
```

why loop?

Java provides a powerful control structure called a *loop* that controls how many times an operation or a sequence of operations is performed in succession. Using a loop statement, you simply tell the computer to print a string a hundred times without having to code the print statement a hundred times.

Loops are structures that control repeated executions of a block of statements. The concept of looping is fundamental to programming. Java provides three types of loop statements: `while` loops, `do-while` loops, and `for` loops.

4.2 The `while` Loop

The syntax for the `while` loop is as follows:

while loop

```
while (loop-continuation-condition) {
  // Loop body
  Statement(s);
}
```

loop body
iteration

The `while` loop flow chart is shown in Figure 4.1(a). The part of the loop that contains the statements to be repeated is called the *loop body*. A one-time execution of a loop body is referred to as an *iteration of the loop*. Each loop contains a loop-continuation condition, a Boolean expression that controls the execution of the body. It is always evaluated before the loop body is executed. If its evaluation is true, the loop body is executed; if its evaluation is false, the entire loop terminates and the program control turns to the statement that follows the `while` loop. For example, the following `while` loop prints `"Welcome to Java!"` a hundred times.

```
int count = 0;
while (count < 100) {
  System.out.println("Welcome to Java!");
  count++;
}
```

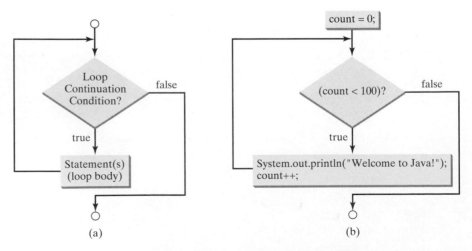

(a)   (b)

FIGURE 4.1 The `while` loop repeatedly executes the statements in the loop body when the `loop-continuation-condition` evaluates to `true`.

The flow chart of the preceding statement is shown in Figure 4.1(b). The variable `count` is initially `0`. The loop checks whether (`count < 100`) is true. If so, it executes the loop body to print the message `"Welcome to Java!"` and increments count by `1`. It repeatedly executes the loop body until (`count < 100`) becomes `false`. When (`count < 100`) is `false` (i.e., when `count` reaches `100`), the loop terminates and the next statement after the loop statement is executed.

Note
The `loop-continuation-condition` must always appear inside the parentheses. The braces enclosing the loop body can be omitted only if the loop body contains one or no statement.

Caution
Make sure that the `loop-continuation-condition` eventually becomes `false` so that the program will terminate. A common programming error involves infinite loops. That is, the program cannot terminate because of a mistake in the `loop-continuation-condition`. For instance, if you forgot to increase `count` (`count++`) in the code, the program would not stop. To terminate the program, press CTRL+C.

infinite loop

Tip
If you use an IDE such as JBuilder, NetBeans, or Eclipse, please refer to *Learning Java Effectively with JBuilder/NetBeans/Eclipse* in the supplements. This supplement shows you how to use a debugger to trace a simple loop statement.

debugging in IDE

4.2.1   Example: An Advanced Math Learning Tool

The Math subtraction learning tool program in Listing 3.5, SubtractionTutor.java, generates just one question for each run. You can use a loop to generate questions repeatedly. Listing 4.1 gives a program that generates ten questions and reports the number of correct answers after a student answers all ten questions. The program also displays the time spent on the test and lists all the questions, as shown in Figure 4.2.

FIGURE 4.2   (a) The program prompts the user to answer the first question. (b) The program grades the answer. (c) The program displays a summary of the answers.

LISTING 4.1   SubtractionTutorLoop.java

```java
1 import javax.swing.JOptionPane;
2
3 public class SubtractionTutorLoop {
4   public static void main(String[] args) {
```

```
              5      int correctCount = 0; // Count the number of correct answers
              6      int count = 0; // Count the number of questions
get start time   7      long startTime = System.currentTimeMillis();
              8      String output = "";
              9
loop            10     while (count < 10) {
              11       // 1. Generate two random single-digit integers
              12       int number1 = (int)(Math.random() * 10);
              13       int number2 = (int)(Math.random() * 10);
              14
              15       // 2. If number1 < number2, swap number1 with number2
              16       if (number1 < number2) {
              17         int temp = number1;
              18         number1 = number2;
              19         number2 = temp;
              20       }
              21
              22       // 3. Prompt the student to answer "what is number1 - number2?"
display a question 23     String answerString = JOptionPane.showInputDialog
              24         ("What is " + number1 + " - " + number2 + "?");
              25       int answer = Integer.parseInt(answerString);
              26
              27       // 4. Grade the answer and display the result
              28       String replyString;
grade an answer  29       if (number1 - number2 == answer) {
              30         replyString = "You are correct!";
increase correct 31         correctCount++;
  count         32       }
              33       else
              34         replyString = "Your answer is wrong.\n" + number1 + " - "
              35           + number2 + " should be " + (number1 - number2);
              36       JOptionPane.showMessageDialog(null, replyString);
              37
              38       // Increase the count
increase control 39       count++;
  variable       40
prepare output  41       output += "\n" + number1 + "-" + number2 + "=" + answerString +
              42         ((number1 - number2 == answer) ? " correct" : " wrong");
              43     }
              44
get end time    45     long endTime = System.currentTimeMillis();
test time       46     long testTime = endTime - startTime;
              47
display result  48     JOptionPane.showMessageDialog(null,
              49       "Correct count is " + correctCount + "\nTest time is " +
              50       testTime / 1000 + " seconds\n" + output);
              51   }
              52 }
```

The program uses the control variable count to control the execution of the loop. **count** is initially **0** (line 6) and is increased by **1** in each iteration (line 39). A subtraction question is displayed and processed in each iteration. The program obtains the time before the test starts in line 7 and the time after the test ends in line 45, and computes the test time in line 46. The test time is in milliseconds and is converted to seconds in line 50.

4.2.2 Controlling a Loop with a Confirmation Dialog

confirmation dialog

The preceding example executes the loop ten times. If you want the user to decide whether to take another question, you can use a confirmation dialog to control the loop. A confirmation dialog can be created using the following statement:

```
int option =
    JOptionPane.showConfirmDialog
        (null, "Continue");
```

When a button is clicked, the method returns an option value. The value is `JOptionPane.YES_OPTION` (0) for the Yes button, `JOptionPane.NO_OPTION` (1) for the No button, and `JOptionPane.CANCEL_OPTION` (2) for the Cancel button. For example, the following loop continues to execute until the user clicks the No or Cancel button.

```
int option = 0;
while (option == JOptionPane.YES_OPTION) {
    System.out.println("continue loop");
    option = JOptionPane.showConfirmDialog(null, "Continue?");
}
```

You can rewrite Listing 4.1 using a confirmation dialog to let the user decide whether to continue the next question.

4.2.3 Controlling a Loop with a Sentinel Value

Another common technique for controlling a loop is to designate a special value when reading and processing a set of values. This special input value, known as a *sentinel value*, signifies the end of the loop.

sentinel value

Listing 4.2 writes a program that reads and calculates the sum of an unspecified number of integers. The input 0 signifies the end of the input. Do you need to declare a new variable for each input value? No. Just use one variable named `data` (line 9) to store the input value and use a variable named `sum` (line 12) to store the total. Whenever a value is read, assign it to `data` and added to `sum` (line 14) if it is not zero.

LISTING 4.2 SentinelValue.java

```
 1 import javax.swing.JOptionPane;
 2
 3 public class SentinelValue {
 4   /** Main method */
 5   public static void main(String[] args) {
 6     // Read an initial data
 7     String dataString = JOptionPane.showInputDialog(        input dialog
 8       "Enter an int value:\n(the program exits if the input is 0)");
 9     int data = Integer.parseInt(dataString);               convert string
10                                                                 to int
11     // Keep reading data until the input is 0
12     int sum = 0;
13     while (data != 0) {                                     loop
14       sum += data;
15
16       // Read the next data
17       dataString = JOptionPane.showInputDialog(
18         "Enter an int value:\n(the program exits if the input is 0)");
19       data = Integer.parseInt(dataString);
20     }
21
22     JOptionPane.showMessageDialog(null, "The sum is " + sum);   message dialog
23   }
24 }
```

A sample run of the program is shown in Figure 4.3. If data is not 0, it is added to the sum (line 14) and the next items of input data are read (lines 12–19). If data is 0, the loop body is no longer executed and the while loop terminates. The input value 0 is the sentinel value for this loop. Note that if the first input read is 0, the loop body never executes, and the resulting sum is 0.

FIGURE 4.3 The program uses a while loop to add an unspecified number of integers.

 Caution

Don't use floating-point values for equality checking in a loop control. Since floating-point values are approximations for some values, using them could result in imprecise counter values and inaccurate results. This example uses int value for data. If a floating-point type value is used for data, (data != 0) may be true even though data is exactly 0.

Here is a good example provided by a reviewer of this book:

```
// data should be zero
double data = Math.pow(Math.sqrt(2), 2) - 2;

if (data == 0)
  System.out.println("data is zero");
else
  System.out.println("data is not zero");
```

numeric error

Like pow, sqrt is a method in the Math class for computing the square root of a number. The variable data in the above code should be zero, but it is not, because of rounding-off errors.

4.3 The do-while Loop

The do-while loop is a variation of the while loop. Its syntax is given below:

do-while loop

```
do {
  // Loop body;
  Statement(s);
} while (loop-continuation-condition);
```

Its execution flow chart is shown in Figure 4.4.

The loop body is executed first. Then the loop-continuation-condition is evaluated. If the evaluation is true, the loop body is executed again; if it is false, the do-while loop terminates. The major difference between a while loop and a do-while loop is the order in which the loop-continuation-condition is evaluated and the loop body executed.

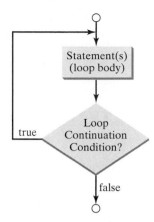

FIGURE 4.4 The `do-while` loop executes the loop body first, and then checks the `loop-continuation-condition` to determine whether to continue or terminate the loop.

The `while` loop and the `do-while` loop have equal expressive power. Sometimes one is a more convenient choice than the other. For example, you can rewrite the `while` loop in Listing 4.2 using a `do-while` loop, as shown in Listing 4.3.

LISTING 4.3 TestDo.java

```
1 import javax.swing.JOptionPane;
2
3 public class TestDoWhile {
4   /** Main method */
5   public static void main(String[] args) {
6     int data;
7     int sum = 0;
8
9     // Keep reading data until the input is 0
10     do {                                                          loop
11       // Read the next data
12       String dataString = JOptionPane.showInputDialog(null,
13         "Enter an int value:\n(the program exits if the input is 0)",
14         "TestDo", JOptionPane.QUESTION_MESSAGE);
15
16       data = Integer.parseInt(dataString);
17
18       sum += data;
19     } while (data != 0);
20
21     JOptionPane.showMessageDialog(null, "The sum is " + sum,
22       "TestDo", JOptionPane.INFORMATION_MESSAGE);
23   }
24 }
```

Tip
Use the `do-while` loop if you have statements inside the loop that must be executed at least once, as in the case of the `do-while` loop in the preceding `TestDoWhile` program. These statements must appear before the loop as well as inside the loop if you use a `while` loop.

4.4 The **for** Loop

Often you write a loop in the following common form:

```
i = initialValue; // Initialize loop control variable
while (i < endValue) {
  // Loop body
  ...
  i++; // Adjust loop control variable
}
```

A **for** loop can be used to simplify the preceding loop:

```
for (i = initialValue; i < endValue; i++) {
  // Loop body
  ...
}
```

In general, the syntax of a **for** loop is as shown below:

for loop

```
for (initial-action; loop-continuation-condition;
      action-after-each-iteration) {
  // Loop body;
  Statement(s);
}
```

The flow chart of the **for** loop is shown in Figure 4.5(a).

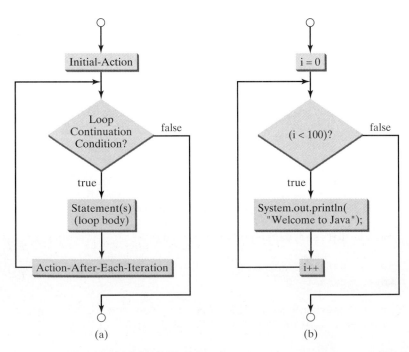

(a)　　　　(b)

FIGURE 4.5 A **for** loop performs an initial action once, then repeatedly executes the statements in the loop body, and performs an action after an iteration when the **loop-continuation-condition** evaluates to **true**.

The **for** loop statement starts with the keyword **for**, followed by a pair of parentheses enclosing **initial-action**, **loop-continuation-condition**, and **action-after-each-iteration**, and followed by the loop body enclosed inside braces. **initial-action**, `loop-continuation-condition`, and `action-after-each-iteration` are separated by semicolons.

    A **for** loop generally uses a variable to control how many times the loop body is executed and when the loop terminates. This variable is referred to as a *control variable*. The `initial-action` often initializes a control variable, the `action-after-each-iteration` usually increments or decrements the control variable, and the `loop-continuation-condition` tests whether the control variable has reached a termination value. For example, the following **for** loop prints `"Welcome to Java!"` a hundred times:

control variable

```
int i;
for (i = 0; i < 100; i++) {
  System.out.println("Welcome to Java!");
}
```

The flow chart of the statement is shown in Figure 4.5(b). The **for** loop initializes i to 0, then repeatedly executes the `println` statement and evaluates i++ while i is less than 100.

    The `initial-action`, i = 0, initializes the control variable, i. The `loop-continuation-condition`, i < 100 is a Boolean expression. The expression is evaluated at the beginning of each iteration. If this condition is **true**, execute the loop body. If it is **false**, the loop terminates and the program control turns to the line following the loop.

    The `action-after-each-iteration`, i++, is a statement that adjusts the control variable. This statement is executed after each iteration. It increments the control variable. Eventually, the value of the control variable should force the `loop-continuation-condition` to become false. Otherwise the loop is infinite.

```
for (int i = 0; i < 100; i++) {
  System.out.println("Welcome to Java!");
}
```

If there is only one statement in the loop body, as in this example, the braces can be omitted.

Tip

The control variable must always be declared inside the control structure of the loop or before the loop. If the loop control variable is used only in the loop, and not elsewhere, it is good programming practice to declare it in the `initial-action` of the **for** loop. If the variable is declared inside the loop control structure, it cannot be referenced outside the loop. For example, you cannot reference i outside the **for** loop in the preceding code, because it is declared inside the **for** loop.

Note

The `initial-action` in a **for** loop can be a list of zero or more comma-separated variable declaration statements or assignment expressions. For example,

```
for (int i = 0, j = 0; (i + j < 10); i++, j++) {
  // Do something
}
```

The `action-after-each-iteration` in a **for** loop can be a list of zero or more comma-separated statements. For example,

```
for (int i = 1; i < 100; System.out.println(i), i++);
```

This example is correct, but it is not a good example, because it makes the code difficult to read. Normally, you declare and initialize a control variable as initial action, and increment or decrement the control variable as an action after each iteration.

Note

If the `loop-continuation-condition` in a `for` loop is omitted, it is implicitly `true`. Thus the statement given below in (a), which is an infinite loop, is correct. Nevertheless, it is better to use the equivalent loop in (b) to avoid confusion:

```
for ( ; ; ) {
   // Do something
}
```
(a)

Equivalent

This is better

```
while (true) {
   // Do something
}
```
(b)

4.5 Which Loop to Use?

pre-test loop

post-test loop

The `while` loop and `for` loop are called *pre-test loops* because the continuation condition is checked before the loop body is executed. The `do-while` loop is called a *post-test loop* because the condition is checked after the loop body is executed. The three forms of loop statements, `while`, `do-while`, and `for`, are expressively equivalent; that is, you can write a loop in any of these three forms. For example, a `while` loop in (a) in the following figure can always be converted into the `for` loop in (b):

```
while (loop-continuation-condition) {
   // Loop body
}
```
(a)

Equivalent

```
for ( ; loop-continuation-condition; ) {
   // Loop body
}
```
(b)

A `for` loop in (a) in the next figure can generally be converted into the `while` loop in (b) except in certain special cases (see Review Question 4.12 for such a case):

```
for (initial-action;
     loop-continuation-condition;
     action-after-each-iteration) {
   // Loop body;
}
```
(a)

Equivalent

```
initial-action;
while (loop-continuation-condition) {
   // Loop body;
   action-after-each-iteration;
}
```
(b)

Use the loop statement that is most intuitive and comfortable for you. In general, a `for` loop may be used if the number of repetitions is known, as, for example, when you need to print a message a hundred times. A `while` loop may be used if the number of repetitions is not known, as in the case of reading the numbers until the input is 0. A `do-while` loop can be used to replace a `while` loop if the loop body has to be executed before the continuation condition is tested.

Caution

Adding a semicolon at the end of the `for` clause before the loop body is a common mistake, as shown below in (a). In (a), the semicolon signifies the end of the loop prematurely. The loop body is actually empty, as shown in (b). (a) and (b) are equivalent.

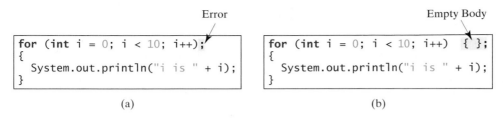

Error

Empty Body

```
for (int i = 0; i < 10; i++);
{
  System.out.println("i is " + i);
}
```
(a)

```
for (int i = 0; i < 10; i++)  { };
{
  System.out.println("i is " + i);
}
```
(b)

Similarly, the loop in (c) is also wrong. (c) is equivalent to (d).

Error

Empty Body

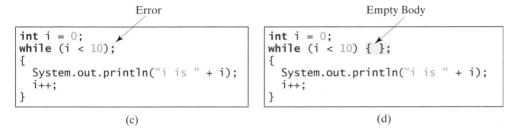

```
int i = 0;
while (i < 10);
{
  System.out.println("i is " + i);
  i++;
}
```
(c)

```
int i = 0;
while (i < 10) { };
{
  System.out.println("i is " + i);
  i++;
}
```
(d)

These errors often occur when you use the next-line block style.

In the case of the `do-while` loop, the semicolon is needed to end the loop.

```
int i = 0;
do {
  System.out.println("i is " + i);
  i++;
} while (i < 10);  ←——— Correct
```

4.6 Nested Loops

Nested loops consist of an outer loop and one or more inner loops. Each time the outer loop is repeated, the inner loops are reentered, and started anew.

Listing 4.4 presents a program that uses nested **for** loops to print a multiplication table, as shown in Figure 4.6.

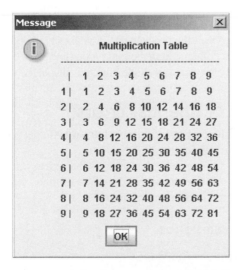

FIGURE 4.6 The program uses nested **for** loops to print a multiplication table.

LISTING 4.4 `MultiplicationTable.java`

table title

table body

nested loop

```java
1 import javax.swing.JOptionPane;
2
3 public class MultiplicationTable {
4   /** Main method */
5   public static void main(String[] args) {
6     // Display the table heading
7     String output = "                      Multiplication Table\n";
8     output += "-------------------------------------------------\n";
9
10    // Display the number title
11    output += "    | ";
12    for (int j = 1; j <= 9; j++)
13      output += "    " + j;
14
15    output += "\n";
16
17    // Print table body
18    for (int i = 1; i <= 9; i++) {
19      output += i + " | ";
20      for (int j = 1; j <= 9; j++) {
21        // Display the product and align properly
22        if (i * j < 10)
23          output += "    " + i * j;
24        else
25          output += "   " + i * j;
26      }
27      output += "\n";
28    }
29
30    // Display result
31    JOptionPane.showMessageDialog(null, output);
32  }
33 }
```

The program displays a title (line 7) on the first line and dashes (-) (line 8) on the second line. The first `for` loop (lines 12–13) displays the numbers **1** through **9** on the third line.

The next loop (lines 18–28) is a nested `for` loop with the control variable `i` in the outer loop and `j` in the inner loop. For each `i`, the product `i * j` is displayed on a line in the inner loop, with `j` being **1, 2, 3, ..., 9**. The `if` statement in the inner loop (lines 22–25) is used so that the product will be aligned properly. If the product is a single digit, it is displayed with an extra space before it.

4.7 Minimizing Numerical Errors

Numeric errors involving floating-point numbers are inevitable. This section discusses how to minimize such errors through an example.

Listing 4.5 presents an example that sums a series that starts with **0.01** and ends with **1.0**. The numbers in the series will increment by **0.01**, as follows: **0.01 + 0.02 + 0.03** and so on. The output of the program appears in Figure 4.7.

LISTING 4.5 `TestSum.java`

```java
1 import javax.swing.JOptionPane;
2
3 public class TestSum {
4   public static void main(String[] args) {
```

```
 5      // Initialize sum
 6      float sum = 0;
 7
 8      // Add 0.01, 0.02, ..., 0.99, 1 to sum
 9      for (float i = 0.01f; i <= 1.0f; i = i + 0.01f)          loop
10        sum += i;
11
12      // Display result
13      JOptionPane.showMessageDialog(null, "The sum is " + sum);
14    }
15 }
```

FIGURE 4.7   The program uses a `for` loop to sum a series from `0.01` to `1.0` in increments of `0.01`.

The `for` loop (lines 9–10) repeatedly adds the control variable `i` to the sum. This variable, which begins with `0.01`, is incremented by `0.01` after each iteration. The loop terminates when `i` exceeds `1.0`.

The `for` loop initial action can be any statement, but it is often used to initialize a control variable. From this example, you can see that a control variable can be a `float` type. In fact, it can be any data type.

The exact `sum` should be `50.50`, but the answer is `50.499985`. The result is not precise because computers use a fixed number of bits to represent floating-point numbers, and thus cannot represent some floating-point numbers exactly. If you change `float` in the program to `double` as follows, you should see a slight improvement in precision because a `double` variable takes sixty-four bits, whereas a `float` variable takes thirty-two bits.   double precision

```
// Initialize sum
double sum = 0;

// Add 0.01, 0.02, ..., 0.99, 1 to sum
for (double i = 0.01; i <= 1.0; i = i + 0.01)
  sum += i;
```

However, you will be stunned to see that the result is actually `49.50000000000003`. What went wrong? If you print out `i` for each iteration in the loop, you will see that the last `i` is slightly larger than `1` (not exactly `1`). This causes the last `i` not to be added into `sum`. The fundamental problem is that the floating-point numbers are represented by approximation. Errors commonly occur. There are two ways to fix the problem:

- Minimizing errors by processing large numbers first.   numeric error

- Using an integer count to ensure that all the numbers are processed.

- To minimize errors, add numbers from `1.0`, `0.99`, down to `0.1`, as follows:

```
// Add 1, 0.99, ..., 0.01 to sum
for (double i = 1.0; i >= 0.01; i = i - 0.01)
  sum += i;
```

To ensure that all the items are added to sum, use an integer variable to count the items. Here is the new loop:

```
double currentValue = 0.01;

for (int count = 0; count < 100; count++) {
  sum += currentValue;
  currentValue += 0.01;
}
```

After this loop, sum is 50.50000000000003.

4.8 Case Studies

Control statements are fundamental in programming. The ability to write control statements is essential in learning Java programming. *If you can write programs using loops, you know how to program!* For this reason, this section presents three additional examples of how to solve problems using loops.

4.8.1 Example: Finding the Greatest Common Divisor

This section presents a program that prompts the user to enter two positive integers and finds their greatest common divisor.

GCD

The greatest common divisor of two integers 4 and 2 is 2. The greatest common divisor of two integers 16 and 24 is 8. How do you find the greatest common divisor? Let the two input integers be n1 and n2. You know that number 1 is a common divisor, but it may not be the greatest common divisor. So you can check whether k (for k = 2, 3, 4 and so on) is a common divisor for n1 and n2, until k is greater than n1 or n2. Store the common divisor in a variable named gcd. Initially, gcd is 1. Whenever a new common divisor is found, it becomes the new gcd. When you have checked all the possible common divisors from 2 up to n1 or n2, the value in variable gcd is the greatest common divisor. The idea can be translated into the following loop:

```
int gcd = 1;
int k = 1;

while (k <= n1 && k <= n2) {
  if (n1 % k == 0 && n2 % k == 0)
    gcd = k;
  k++;
}

// After the loop, gcd is the greatest common divisor for n1 and n2
```

The complete program is given in Listing 4.6, and a sample run of the program is shown in Figure 4.8.

LISTING 4.6 GreatestCommonDivisor.java

```
 1 import javax.swing.JOptionPane;
 2
 3 public class GreatestCommonDivisor {
 4   /** Main method */
 5   public static void main(String[] args) {
 6     // Prompt the user to enter two integers
 7     String s1 = JOptionPane.showInputDialog("Enter first integer");
 8     int n1 = Integer.parseInt(s1);
 9
10     String s2 = JOptionPane.showInputDialog("Enter second integer");
11     int n2 = Integer.parseInt(s2);
12
13     int gcd = 1;
```

input

input

```
14      int k = 1;
15      while (k <= n1 && k <= n2) {
16        if (n1 % k == 0 && n2 % k == 0)
17          gcd = k;                                          gcd
18        k++;
19      }
20
21      String output = "The greatest common divisor for " + n1 + " and "
22        + n2 + " is " + gcd;
23      JOptionPane.showMessageDialog(null, output);           output
24    }
25 }
```

FIGURE 4.8 The program finds the greatest common divisor for two integers.

How did you write this program? Did you immediately begin to write the code? No. It is important to *think before you type*. Thinking enables you to generate a logical solution for the problem without concern about how to write the code. Once you have a logical solution, type the code to translate the solution into a Java program. The translation is not unique. For example, you could use a `for` loop to rewrite the code as follows:

think before you type

```
for (int k = 1; k <= n1 && k <= n2; k++) {
  if (n1 % k == 0 && n2 % k == 0)
    gcd = k;
}
```

A problem often has multiple solutions. The GCD problem can be solved in many ways. Exercise 4.15 suggests another solution. A more efficient solution is to use the classic Euclidean algorithm. See http://www.cut-the-knot.org/blue/Euclid.shtml for more information.

multiple solutions

You might think that a divisor for a number `n1` cannot be greater than `n1 / 2`. So you would attempt to improve the program using the following loop:

erroneous solutions

```
for (int k = 1; k <= n1 / 2 && k <= n2 / 2; k++) {
  if (n1 % k == 0 && n2 % k == 0)
    gcd = k;
}
```

This revision is wrong. Can you find the reason? See Review Question 4.9 for the answer.

4.8.2 Example: Finding the Sales Amount

You have just started a sales job in a department store. Your pay consists of a base salary and a commission. The base salary is $5,000. The scheme shown below is used to determine the commission rate.

Sales Amount	Commission Rate
$0.01–$5,000	8 percent
$5,000.01–$10,000	10 percent
$10,000.01 and above	12 percent

Your goal is to earn $30,000 a year. This section writes a program that finds the minimum amount of sales you have to generate in order to make $30,000.

Since your base salary is $5,000, you have to make $25,000 in commissions to earn $30,000 a year. What is the sales amount for a $25,000 commission? If you know the sales amount, the commission can be computed as follows:

```
if (salesAmount >= 10000.01)
  commission =
    5000 * 0.08 + 5000 * 0.1 + (salesAmount - 10000) * 0.12;
else if (salesAmount >= 5000.01)
  commission = 5000 * 0.08 + (salesAmount - 5000) * 0.10;
else
  commission = salesAmount * 0.08;
```

This suggests that you can try to find the salesAmount to match a given commission through incremental approximation. For a salesAmount of $0.01 (1 cent), find commission. If commission is less than $25,000, increment salesAmount by 0.01 and find commission again. If commission is still less than $25,000, repeat the process until it is greater than or equal to $25,000. This is a tedious job for humans, but it is exactly what a computer is good for. You can write a loop and let a computer execute it painlessly. The idea can be translated into the following loop:

```
Set COMMISSION_SOUGHT as a constant;
Set an initial salesAmount;

do {
  Increase salesAmount by 1 cent;
  Compute the commission from the current salesAmount;
} while (commission < COMMISSION_SOUGHT);
```

The complete program is given in Listing 4.7, and a sample run of the program is shown in Figure 4.9.

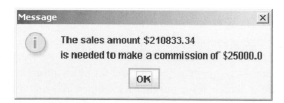

FIGURE 4.9   The program finds the sales amount for the given commission.

LISTING 4.7   FindSalesAmount.java

```
1  import javax.swing.JOptionPane;
2
3  public class FindSalesAmount {
4    /** Main method */
5    public static void main(String[] args) {
6      // The commission sought
7      final double COMMISSION_SOUGHT = 25000;
8      final double INITIAL_SALES_AMOUNT = 0.01;
```

constants

```
 9      double commission = 0;
10      double salesAmount = INITIAL_SALES_AMOUNT;
11
12      do {                                                                   loop
13        // Increase salesAmount by 1 cent
14        salesAmount += 0.01;
15
16        // Compute the commission from the current salesAmount;
17        if (salesAmount >= 10000.01)
18          commission =
19            5000 * 0.08 + 5000 * 0.1 + (salesAmount - 10000) * 0.12;
20        else if (salesAmount >= 5000.01)
21          commission = 5000 * 0.08 + (salesAmount - 5000) * 0.10;
22        else
23          commission = salesAmount * 0.08;
24      } while (commission < COMMISSION_SOUGHT);
25
26      // Display the sales amount
27      String output =                                                        prepare output
28        "The sales amount $" + (int)(salesAmount * 100) / 100.0 +
29        "\nis needed to make a commission of $" + COMMISSION_SOUGHT;
30      JOptionPane.showMessageDialog(null, output);                           output
31    }
32 }
```

The **do-while** loop (lines 12–24) is used to repeatedly compute **commission** for an incremental **salesAmount**. The loop terminates when **commission** is greater than or equal to a constant COMMISSION_SOUGHT.

In Exercise 4.17, you will rewrite this program to let the user enter COMMISSION_SOUGHT dynamically from an input dialog.

You can improve the performance of this program by estimating a higher INITIAL_SALES_AMOUNT (e.g., **25000**).

What is wrong if **saleAmount** is incremented after the commission is computed, as follows?

```
do {
  // Compute the commission from the current salesAmount;
  if (salesAmount >= 10000.01)
    commission =
      5000 * 0.08 + 5000 * 0.1 + (salesAmount - 10000) * 0.12;
  else if (salesAmount >= 5000.01)
    commission = 5000 * 0.08 + (salesAmount - 5000) * 0.10;
  else
    commission = salesAmount * 0.08;

  // Increase salesAmount by 1 cent
  salesAmount += 0.01;
} while (commission < COMMISSION_SOUGHT);
```

The change is erroneous because **saleAmount** is 1 cent more than is needed for the commission when the loop ends. This is a common error in loops, known as the *off-by-one* error.

off-by-one error

Tip
This example uses *constants* COMMISSION_SOUGHT and INITIAL_SALES_AMOUNT. Using   constants
constants makes programs easy to read and maintain.

4.8.3   Example: Displaying a Pyramid of Numbers

This section presents a program that prompts the user to enter an integer from **1** to **15** and displays a pyramid. If the input integer is **12**, for example, the output is shown in Figure 4.10.

FIGURE 4.10 The program uses nested loops to print numbers in a triangular pattern.

Your program receives the input for an integer (numberOfLines) that represents the total number of lines. It displays all the lines one by one. Each line has three parts. The first part comprises the spaces before the numbers; the second part, the leading numbers, such as 3 2 1 in line 3; and the last part, the ending numbers, such as 2 3 in line 3.

Each number occupies three spaces. Display an empty space before a double-digit number, and display two empty spaces before a single-digit number.

You can use an outer loop to control the lines. At the nth row, there are (numberOfLines – n) * 3 leading spaces, the leading numbers are n, n-1, ..., 1, and the ending numbers are 2, ..., n. You can use three separate inner loops to print each part.

Here is the algorithm for the problem:

```
Input numberOfLines;

for (int row = 1; row <= numberOfLines; row++) {
  Print (numberOfLines – row) * 3 leading spaces;
  Print leading numbers row, row – 1, ..., 1;
  Print ending numbers 2, 3, ..., row – 1, row;
  Start a new line;
}
```

The complete program is given in Listing 4.8.

LISTING 4.8   PrintPyramid.java

```
 1 import javax.swing.JOptionPane;
 2
 3 public class PrintPyramid {
 4   /** Main method */
 5   public static void main(String[] args) {
 6     // Prompt the user to enter the number of lines
 7     String input = JOptionPane.showInputDialog(
 8       "Enter the number of lines:");
 9     int numberOfLines = Integer.parseInt(input);
10
11     if (numberOfLines < 1 || numberOfLines > 15) {
12       System.out.println("You must enter a number from 1 to 15");
13       System.exit(0);
14     }
15
16     // Print lines
17     for (int row = 1; row <= numberOfLines; row++) {
18       // Print NUMBER OF LINES – row) leading spaces
19       for (int column = 1; column <= numberOfLines - row; column++)
20         System.out.print("   ");
21
```

print lines

print spaces

```
22          // Print leading numbers row, row - 1, ..., 1
23          for (int num = row; num >= 1; num-)
24            System.out.print((num >= 10) ? " " + num : "  " + num);
25
26          // Print ending numbers 2, 3, ..., row - 1, row
27          for (int num = 2; num <= row; num++)
28            System.out.print((num >= 10) ? " " + num : "  " + num);
29
30          // Start a new line
31          System.out.println();
32        }
33      }
34  }
```

print leading numbers

print ending numbers

a new line

The program uses the print method (lines 20, 24, and 28) to display a string to the console. The conditional expression `(num >= 10) ? " " + num : "  " + num` in lines 24 and 28 returns a string with a single empty space before the number if the number is greater than or equal to 10, and otherwise returns a string with two empty spaces before the number.

Printing patterns like this one and the ones in Exercises 4.18 and 4.19 is a good exercise for practicing loop control statements. The key is to understand the pattern and to describe it using loop control variables.

The last line in the outer loop (line 31), `System.out.println()`, does not have any argument in the method. This call moves the cursor to the next line.

4.9 Keywords **break** and `continue`

Two statements, break and `continue`, can be used in loop statements to provide the loop with additional control.

■ break immediately ends the innermost loop that contains it. It is generally used with an `if` statement.   break

■ `continue` only ends the current iteration. Program control goes to the end of the loop body. This keyword is generally used with an `if` statement.   continue

You have already used the keyword break in a `switch` statement. You can also use break and `continue` in a loop. Listings 4.9 and 4.10 present two programs to demonstrate the effect of the break and `continue` keywords in a loop.

The program in Listing 4.9 adds the integers from 1 to 20 in this order to sum until sum is greater than or equal to 100. Without the `if` statement (line 10), the program calculates the sum of the numbers from 1 to 20. But with the `if` statement, the loop terminates when the sum becomes greater than or equal to 100. The output of the program is shown in Figure 4.11(a).

(a)   (b)

FIGURE 4.11   (a) The break statement in the `TestBreak` program forces the `while` loop to exit when sum is greater than or equal to 100. (b) The break statement is not executed in the modified `TestBreak` program because sum `== 100` cannot be `true`.

If you changed the `if` statement as shown below, the output would resemble that in Figure 4.11(b).

```
if (sum == 100) break;
```

In this case, the `if` condition will never be true. Therefore, the `break` statement will never be executed.

LISTING 4.9 TestBreak.java

```
 1 public class TestBreak {
 2   /** Main method */
 3   public static void main(String[] args) {
 4     int sum = 0;
 5     int number = 0;
 6
 7     while (number < 20) {
 8       number++;
 9       sum += number;
10       if (sum >= 100) break;
11     }
12
13     System.out.println("The number is " + number);
14     System.out.println("The sum is " + sum);
15   }
16 }
```

break

The program in Listing 4.10 adds all the integers from 1 to 20 except 10 and 11 to `sum`. With the `if` statement in the program (line 9), the `continue` statement is executed when number becomes 10 or 11. The `continue` statement ends the current iteration so that the rest of the statement in the loop body is not executed; therefore, number is not added to `sum` when it is 10 or 11. The output of the program is shown in Figure 4.12(a).

(a)   (b)

FIGURE 4.12   (a) The `continue` statement in the `TestContinue` program forces the current iteration to end when `number` equals 10 or 11. (b) Since the modified `TestContinue` program has no `continue` statement, every number is added to `sum`.

Without the `if` statement in the program, the output would look like Figure 4.12(b). In this case, all of the numbers are added to `sum`, even when `number` is 10 or 11. Therefore, the result is 210, which is 21 more than it was with the `if` statement.

LISTING 4.10 TestContinue.java

```
1 public class TestContinue {
2   /** Main method */
3   public static void main(String[] args) {
4     int sum = 0;
5     int number = 0;
6
```

```
7      while (number < 20) {
8        number++;
9        if (number == 10 || number == 11) continue;
10       sum += number;
11     }
12
13     System.out.println("The sum is " + sum);
14   }
15 }
```

continue

Note

The `continue` statement is always inside a loop. In the `while` and `do-while` loops, the `loop-continuation-condition` is evaluated immediately after the `continue` statement. In the `for` loop, the `action-after-each-iteration` is performed, then the `loop-continuation-condition` is evaluated immediately after the `continue` statement.

Tip

You can always write a program without using **break** or **continue** in a loop. See Review Question 4.13. In general, it is appropriate to use **break** and **continue** if their use simplifies coding and makes programs easier to read.

4.9.1   (Optional) Statement Labels and Breaking with Labels

Every statement in Java can have an optional label as an identifier. Labels are often associated with loops. You can use a **break** statement with a label to break out of the labeled loop, and a **continue** statement with a label to break out of the current iteration of the labeled loop.

The **break** statement given below, for example, breaks out of the outer loop if ($i * j > 50$) and transfers control to the statement immediately following the outer loop.

```
outer:
  for (int i = 1; i < 10; i++) {
  inner:
    for (int j = 1; j < 10; j++) {
      if (i * j > 50)
        break outer;

      System.out.println(i * j);
    }
  }
```

If you replace **breakouter** with **break** in the preceding statement, the **break** statement would break out of the inner loop and continue to stay inside the outer loop.

The following continue statement breaks out of the inner loop if ($i * j > 50$) and starts a new iteration of the outer loop if $i < 10$ is **true** after i is incremented by 1.

```
outer:
  for (int i = 1; i < 10; i++) {
  inner:
    for (int j = 1; j < 10; j++) {
      if (i * j > 50)
        continue outer;

      System.out.println(i * j);
    }
  }
```

If you replace `continue outer` with `continue` in the preceding statement, the `continue` statement would break out of the current iteration of the inner loop and continue the next iteration of the inner loop if `j < 10` is true after `j` is incremented by `1`.

Note

goto

Some programming languages have a `goto` statement, but labeled `break` statements and labeled `continue` statements in Java are completely different from `goto` statements. The `goto label` statement would indiscriminately transfer the control to any labeled statement in the program and execute it. The `break label` statement breaks out of the labeled loop, and the `continue label` statement breaks out of the current iteration in the labeled loop.

 ### 4.9.2   (Optional) Example: Displaying Prime Numbers

This section presents a program that displays the first fifty prime numbers in five lines, each of which contains ten numbers, as shown in Figure 4.13. An integer greater than 1 is *prime* if its only positive divisor is 1 or itself. For example, 2, 3, 5, and 7 are prime numbers, but 4, 6, 8, and 9 are not.

FIGURE 4.13   The program displays the first fifty prime numbers.

The problem can be broken into the following tasks:

- Determine whether a given number is prime.
- For `number = 2, 3, 4, 5, 6, . . .`, test whether it is prime.
- Count the prime numbers.
- Print each prime number, and print ten numbers per line.

Obviously, you need to write a loop and repeatedly test whether a new `number` is prime. If the `number` is prime, increase the count by 1. The `count` is `0` initially. When it reaches `50`, the loop terminates.

Here is the algorithm for the problem:

```
Set the number of prime numbers to be printed as
  a constant NUMBER_OF_PRIMES;
Use count to track the number of prime numbers and
  set an initial count to 0;
Set an initial number to 2;

while (count < NUMBER_OF_PRIMES) {
  Test if number is prime;

  if number is prime {
    Print the prime number and increase the count;
  }

  Increment number by 1;
}
```

To test whether a number is prime, check whether it is divisible by 2, 3, 4, up to number/2. If a divisor is found, the number is not a prime. The algorithm can be described as follows:

```
Use a boolean variable isPrime to denote whether
  the number is prime; Set isPrime to true initially;
for (int divisor = 2; divisor <= number / 2; divisor++) {
  if (number % divisor == 0) {
    Set isPrime to false
    Exit the loop;
  }
}
```

The complete program is given in Listing 4.11.

LISTING 4.11   PrimeNumber.java

```java
1 public class PrimeNumber {
2   /** Main method */
3   public static void main(String[] args) {
4     final int NUMBER_OF_PRIMES = 50; // Number of primes to display
5     final int NUMBER_OF_PRIMES_PER_LINE = 10; // Display 10 per line
6     int count = 0; // Count the number of prime numbers
7     int number = 2; // A number to be tested for primeness
8
9     System.out.println("The first 50 prime numbers are \n");
10
11     // Repeatedly find prime numbers
12     while (count < NUMBER_OF_PRIMES) {               count prime numbers
13       // Assume the number is prime                   subproblem
14       boolean isPrime = true; // Is the current number prime?
15
16       // Test if number is prime
17       for (int divisor = 2; divisor <= number / 2; divisor++) {   check primeness
18         if (number % divisor == 0) { // the number is not prime
19           isPrime = false; // Set isPrime to false
20           break; // Exit the for loop                exit loop
21         }
22       }
23
24       // Print the prime number and increase the count
25       if (isPrime) {                                 print if prime
26         count++; // Increase the count
27
28         if (count % NUMBER_OF_PRIMES_PER_LINE == 0) {
29           // Print the number and advance to the new line
30           System.out.println(number);
31         }
32         else
33           System.out.print(number + " ");
34       }
35
36       // Check if the next number is prime
37       number++;
38     }
39   }
40 }
```

This is a complex example for novice programmers. The key to developing a programmatic solution to this problem, and to many other problems, is to break it into subproblems and develop solutions for each of them in turn. Do not attempt to develop a complete solution in the first trial. Instead, begin by writing the code to determine whether a given number is prime, then expand the program to test whether other numbers are prime in a loop.

To determine whether a number is prime, check whether it is divisible by a number between 2 and `number/2` inclusive. If so, it is not a prime number; otherwise, it is a prime number. For a prime number, display it. If the count is divisible by 10, advance to a new line. The program ends when the count reaches 50.

 Note

The program uses the `break` statement in line 23 to exit the `for` loop as soon as the number is found to be a nonprime. You can rewrite the loop (lines 17–22) without using the `break` statement, as follows:

```
for (int divisor = 2; divisor <= number / 2 && isPrime;
     divisor++) {
  // If true, the number is not prime
  if (number % divisor == 0) {
    // Set isPrime to false, if the number is not prime
    isPrime = false;
  }
}
```

However, using the `break` statement makes the program simpler and easier to read in this case.

KEY TERMS

`break` statement 89, 113	loop 96
`continue` statement 113	`loop-continuation-condition` 96
infinite loop 97	loop body 96
iteration 96	nested loop 105
labeled break statement 115	off-by-one error 111
labled continue statement 115	sentinel value 99

CHAPTER SUMMARY

- Program control specifies the order in which statements are executed in a program. There are three types of control statements: sequence, selection, and repetition. The preceding chapters introduced sequence and selection statements. This chapter introduced repetition statements.

- There are three types of repetition statements: the `while` loop, the `do-while` loop, and the `for` loop. In designing loops, you need to consider both the loop control structure and the loop body.

- The `while` loop checks the `loop-continuation-condition` first. If the condition is `true`, the loop body is executed; if it is `false`, the loop terminates. The `do-while` loop is similar to the `while` loop, except that the `do-while` loop executes the loop body first and then checks the `loop-continuation-condition` to decide whether to continue or to terminate.

- Since the `while` loop and the `do-while` loop contain the `loop-continuation-condition`, which is dependent on the loop body, the number of repetitions is determined by the loop body. The `while` loop and the `do-while` loop are often used when the number of repetitions is unspecified.

- The **for** loop is generally used to execute a loop body a predictable number of times; this number is not determined by the loop body. The loop control has three parts. The first part is an initial action that often initializes a control variable. The second part, the **loop-continuation-condition**, determines whether the loop body is to be executed. The third part is executed after each iteration and is often used to adjust the control variable. Usually, the loop control variables are initialized and changed in the control structure.

- Two keywords, **break** and **continue**, can be used in a loop. The keyword **break** immediately ends the innermost loop, which contains the break. The keyword **continue** only ends the current iteration.

REVIEW QUESTIONS

Sections 4.2–4.8

4.1 How many times is the following loop body repeated? What is the printout of the loop?

```
int i = 1;
while (i > 10)
  if ((i++) % 2 == 0)
    System.out.println(i);
```
(a)

```
int i = 1;
while (i < 10)
  if ((i++) % 2 == 0)
    System.out.println(i);
```
(b)

4.2 What are the differences between a **while** loop and a **do-while** loop?

4.3 Do the following two loops result in the same value in **sum**?

```
for (int i = 0; i < 10; ++i) {
  sum += i;
}
```
(a)

```
for (int i = 0; i < 10; i++ ) {
  sum += i;
}
```
(b)

4.4 What are the three parts of a **for** loop control? Write a **for** loop that prints the numbers from **1** to **100**.

4.5 What does the following statement do?

```
for ( ; ; ) {
  do something;
}
```

4.6 If a variable is declared in the **for** loop control, can it be used after the loop exits?

4.7 Can you convert a **for** loop to a **while** loop? List the advantages of using **for** loops.

4.8 Convert the following **for** loop statement to a **while** loop and to a **do-while** loop:

```
long sum = 0;
for (int i = 0; i <= 1000; i++)
  sum = sum + i;
```

4.9 Will the program work if **n1** and **n2** are replaced by **n1 / 2** and **n2 / 2** in line 15 in Listing 4.6?

Section 4.9 Keywords **break** and `continue`

4.10 What is the keyword break for? What is the keyword `continue` for? Will the following program terminate? If so, give the output.

```
int balance = 1000;
while (true) {
  if (balance < 9)
    break;
  balance = balance - 9;
}
System.out.println("Balance is "
  + balance);
int balance = 1000;
```
(a)

```
while (true) {
  if (balance < 9)
    continue;
  balance = balance - 9;
}
System.out.println("Balance is "
  + balance);
```
(b)

4.11 Can you always convert a `while` loop into a `for` loop? Convert the following `while` loop into a `for` loop.

```
int i = 1;
int sum = 0;
while (sum < 10000) {
  sum = sum + i;
  i++;
}
```

4.12 The `for` loop on the left is converted into the `while` loop on the right. What is wrong? Correct it.

```
for (int i = 0; i < 4; i++) {
  if (i % 3 == 0) continue;
  sum += i;
}
```
Converted → Wrong Conversion
```
int i = 0;
while (i < 4) {
  if (i % 3 == 0) continue;
  sum += i;
  i++;
}
```

4.13 Rewrite the programs `TestBreak` and `TestContinue` in Listings 4.9 and 4.10 without using `break` and `continue`.

4.14 After the `break outer` statement is executed in the following loop, which statement is executed?

```
outer:
  for (int i = 1; i < 10; i++) {
  inner:
    for (int j = 1; j < 10; j++) {
      if (i * j > 50)
        break outer;

      System.out.println(i * j);
    }
  }

next:
```

4.15 After the `continue outer` statement is executed in the following loop, which statement is executed?

```
outer:
  for (int i = 1; i < 10; i++) {
```

```
      inner:
        for (int j = 1; j < 10; j++) {
          if (i * j > 50)
            continue outer;
          System.out.println(i * j);
        }
      }

    next:
```

Comprehensive

4.16   Identify and fix the errors in the following code:

```
 1 public class Test {
 2   public void main(String[] args) {
 3     for (int i = 0; i < 10; i++);
 4       sum += i;
 5
 6     if (i < j);
 7       System.out.println(i)
 8     else
 9       System.out.println(j);
10
11     while (j < 10);
12     {
13       j++;
14     };
15
16     do {
17       j++;
18     } while (j < 10)
19   }
20 }
```

4.17   What is wrong with the following program?

```
1 public class ShowErrors {
2   public static void main(String[] args) {
3     int i;
4     int j = 5;
5
6     if (j > 3)
7       System.out.println(i + 4);
8   }
9 }
```
(a)

```
1 public class ShowErrors {
2   public static void main(String[] args) {
3     for (int i = 0; i < 10; i++);
4       System.out.println(i + 4);
5   }
6 }
```
(b)

4.18   Show the output of the following programs:

```
public class Test {
  /** Main method */
  public static void main(String[] args) {
    for (int i = 1; i < 5; i++) {
      int j = 0;
      while (j < i) {
        System.out.print(j + " ");
        j++;
      }
    }
  }
}
```
(a)

```
public class Test {
  /** Main method */
  public static void main(String[] args) {
    int i = 0;
    while (i < 5) {
      for (int j = i; j > 1; j--)
        System.out.print(j + " ");
      System.out.println("****");
      i++;
    }
  }
}
```
(b)

```
public class Test {
  public static void main(String[] args) {
    int i = 5;
    while (i >= 1) {
      int num = 1;
      for (int j = 1; j <= i; j++) {
        System.out.print(num + "xxx");
        num *= 2;
      }

      System.out.println();
      i--;
    }
  }
}
```
(c)

```
public class Test {
  public static void main(String[] args) {
    int i = 1;
    do {
      int num = 1;
      for (int j = 1; j <= i; j++) {
        System.out.print(num + "G");
        num += 2;
      }

      System.out.println();
      i++;
    } while (i <= 5);
  }
}
```
(d)

4.19 Reformat the following programs according to the programming style and documentation guidelines proposed in §2.14. Use the next-line brace style.

```
public class Test {
  public static void main(String[] args) {
    int i = 0;
    if (i>0)
    i++;
    else
    i--;

    char grade;

    if (i >= 90)
     grade = 'A';
    else
      if (i >= 80)
        grade = 'B';

  }
}
```
(a)

```
public class Test {
  public static void main(String[] args) {
    for (int i = 0; i<10; i++)
      if (i>0)
        i++;
      else
        i--;
    }
  }
```
(b)

PROGRAMMING EXERCISES

Pedagogical Note

A problem often can be solved in many different ways. Students are encouraged to explore various solutions.

explore solutions

Sections 4.2–4.7

4.1* (*Repeating additions*) Listing 4.1, SubtractionTutorLoop.java, generates ten random subtraction questions. Revise the program to generate ten random addition questions for two integers between 1 and 15. Display the number of correct answers and test time.

4.2* (*Counting positive and negative numbers and computing the average of numbers*) Write a program that reads an unspecified number of integers, determines how many positive and negative values have been read, and computes the total and average of the input values, not counting zeros. Your program ends with the input 0. Display the average as a floating-point number. (For example, if you entered 1, 2, and 0, the average should be 1.5.)

4.3   (*Conversion from kilograms to pounds*) Write a program that displays the following table (note that 1 kilogram is 2.2 pounds):

```
Kilograms      Pounds

1              2.2
3              6.6
...
197            433.4
199            437.8
```

4.4   (*Conversion from miles to kilometers*) Write a program that displays the following table (note that 1 mile is 1.609 kilometers):

```
Miles      Kilometers

1          1.609
2          3.218
...
9          14.481
10         16.09
```

4.5   (*Conversion from kilograms to pounds*) Write a program that displays the following two tables side-by-side (note that 1 kilogram is 2.2 pounds):

```
Kilograms      Pounds      Pounds      Kilograms

1              2.2         20          9.09
3              6.6         25          11.36
...
197            433.4       510         231.82
199            437.8       515         234.09
```

4.6   (*Conversion from miles to kilometers*) Write a program that displays the following two tables side-by-side (note that 1 mile is 1.609 kilometers):

```
Miles      Kilometers      Kilometers      Miles

1          1.609           20              12.430
2          3.218           25              15.538
...
9          14.481          60              37.290
10         16.09           65              40.398
```

4.7**   (*Computing future tuition*) Suppose that the tuition for a university is $10,000 this year and increases 5% every year. Write a program that uses a loop to compute the tuition in ten years. Write another program that computes the total cost of four years' worth of tuition starting ten years from now.

4.8   (*Finding the highest score*) Write a program that prompts the user to enter the number of students and each student's name and score, and finally displays the student with the highest score.

4.9*   (*Finding the two highest scores*) Write a program that prompts the user to enter the number of students and each student's name and score, and finally displays the student with the highest score and the student with the second-highest score.

4.10   (*Finding numbers divisible by 5 and 6*) Write a program that displays all the numbers from 100 to 1000, ten per line, that are divisible by 5 and 6.

4.11   (*Finding numbers divisible by 5 or 6, but not both*) Write a program that displays all the numbers from 100 to 200, ten per line, that are divisible by 5 or 6, but not both.

4.12   (*Finding the smallest n such that $n^2 > 12000$*) Use a `while` loop to find the smallest integer n such that n is greater than 12,000.

4.13 (*Finding the largest n such that $n^3 < 12000$*) Use a `while` loop to find the largest integer **n** such that **n** is less than **12,000**.

4.14* (*Displaying the ACSII character table*) Write a program that prints the characters in the ASCII character table from '!' to '~'. Print ten characters per line.

Section 4.8 Case Studies

4.15* (*Computing the greatest common divisor*) Another solution for Listing 4.6 to find the greatest common divisor of two integers **n1** and **n2** is as follows: First find **d** to be the minimum of **n1** and **n2**, then check whether **d, d-1, d-2, ..., 2,** or **1** is a divisor for both **n1** and **n2** in this order. The first such common divisor is the greatest common divisor for **n1** and **n2**.

4.16** (*Finding the factors of an integer*) Write a program that reads an integer and displays all its smallest factors. For example, if the input integer is **120**, the output should be as follows: **2, 2, 2, 3, 5**.

4.17* (*Finding the sales amount*) Rewrite Listing 4.7, FindSalesAmount.java, as follows:

- Use a `for` loop instead of a `do-while` loop.

- Let the user enter `COMMISSION_SOUGHT` instead of fixing it as a constant.

4.18* (*Printing four patterns using loops*) Use nested loops that print the following patterns in four separate programs:

```
Pattern I        Pattern II       Pattern III      Pattern IV
1                1 2 3 4 5 6                1       1 2 3 4 5 6
1 2              1 2 3 4 5               2 1         1 2 3 4 5
1 2 3            1 2 3 4              3 2 1            1 2 3 4
1 2 3 4          1 2 3             4 3 2 1              1 2 3
1 2 3 4 5        1 2            5 4 3 2 1                1 2
1 2 3 4 5 6      1           6 5 4 3 2 1                   1
```

4.19** (*Printing numbers in a pyramid pattern*) Write a nested `for` loop that prints the following output:

```
                              1
                        1     2     1
                  1     2     4     2     1
            1     2     4     8     4     2     1
      1     2     4     8    16     8     4     2     1
1     2     4     8    16    32    16     8     4     2     1
1     2     4     8    16    32    64    32    16     8     4     2     1
1     2     4     8    16    32    64   128    64    32    16     8     4     2     1
```

Hint

Here is the pseudocode solution:

```
for the row from 0 to 7 {
  Pad leading blanks in a row using a loop like this:
  for the column from 1 to 7-row
    System.out.print("   ");

  Print left half of the row for numbers 1, 2, 4, up to
    2^row using a look like this:
  for the column from 0 to row
    System.out.print("   " + (int)Math.pow(2, column));

  Print the right half of the row for numbers
    2^row-1, 2^row-2, ..., 1 using a loop like this:
```

```
    for (int column = row - 1; column >= 0; col--)
        System.out.print("     " + (int)Math.pow(2, column));

    Start a new line
    System.out.println();
}
```

You need to figure out how many spaces to print before the number. This is dependent on the number. If a number is a single digit, print four spaces. If a number has two digits, print three spaces. If a number has three digits, print two spaces.

The `Math.pow()` method was introduced in §2.12.1, "Example: Computing Loan Payments." Can you write this program without using it?

4.20* (*Printing prime numbers between 2 and 1000*) Modify Listing 4.11 to print all the prime numbers between 2 and 1000, inclusively. Display eight prime numbers per line.

Comprehensive

4.21** (*Comparing loans with various interest rates*) Write a program that lets the user enter the loan amount and loan period in number of years and displays the monthly and total payments for each interest rate starting from 5% to 8%, with an increment of 1/8. Suppose you enter the loan amount 10,000 for five years; display a table as follows:

```
Loan Amount: 10000
Number of Years: 5
Interest Rate      Monthly Payment      Total Payment

5%                 188.71               11322.74
5.125%             189.28               11357.13
5.25%              189.85               11391.59
...
7.85%              202.16               12129.97
8.0%               202.76               12165.83
```

4.22** (*Displaying the loan amortization schedule*) The monthly payment for a given loan pays the principal and the interest. The monthly interest is computed by multiplying the monthly interest rate and the balance (the remaining principal). The principal paid for the month is therefore the monthly payment minus the monthly interest. Write a program that lets the user enter the loan amount, number of years, and interest rate, and displays the amortization schedule for the loan. Suppose you enter the loan amount 10,000 for one year with an interest rate of 7%; display a table as follows:

```
Loan Amount: 10000
Number of Years: 1
Annual Interest Rate: 7%

Monthly Payment: 865.26
Total Payment: 10383.21

Payment#      Interest      Principal      Balance

1             58.33         806.93         9193.07
2             53.62         811.64         8381.43
...
11            10.0          855.26         860.27
12            5.01          860.25         0.01
```

Note

The balance after the last payment may not be zero. If so, the last payment should be the normal monthly payment plus the final balance.

Hint

Write a loop to print the table. Since monthly payment is the same for each month, it should be computed before the loop. The balance is initially the loan amount. For each iteration in the loop, compute the interest and principal, and update the balance. The loop may look like this:

```
for (i = 1; i <= numberOfYears * 12; i++) {
  interest = monthlyInterestRate * balance;
  principal = monthlyPayment - interest;
  balance = balance - principal;
  System.out.println(i + "\t\t" + interest
    + "\t\t" + principal + "\t\t" + balance);
}
```

4.23* (*Demonstrating cancellation errors*) A cancellation error occurs when you are manipulating a very large number with a very small number. The large number may cancel out the smaller number. For example, the result of **100000000.0 +** **0.000000001** is equal to **100000000.0**. To avoid cancellation errors and obtain more accurate results, carefully select the order of computation. For example, in computing the following series, you will obtain more accurate results by computing from right to left rather than from left to right:

$$1 + \frac{1}{2} + \frac{1}{3} + \cdots + \frac{1}{n}$$

Write a program that compares the results of the summation of the preceding series, computing from left to right and from right to left with **n = 50000**.

4.24* (*Summing a series*) Write a program to sum the following series:

$$\frac{1}{3} + \frac{3}{5} + \frac{5}{7} + \frac{7}{9} + \frac{9}{11} + \frac{11}{13} + \cdots + \frac{95}{97} + \frac{97}{99}$$

4.25** (*Computing* π) You can approximate π by using the following series:

$$\pi = 4\left(1 - \frac{1}{3} + \frac{1}{5} - \frac{1}{7} + \frac{1}{9} - \frac{1}{11} + \frac{1}{13} - \cdots - \frac{1}{2i-1} + \frac{1}{2i+1}\right)$$

Write a program that displays the π value for **i = 10000, 20000, . . .,** and **100000**.

4.26** (*Computing e*) You can approximate **e** by using the following series:

$$e = 1 + \frac{1}{1!} + \frac{1}{2!} + \frac{1}{3!} + \frac{1}{4!} + \cdots + \frac{1}{i!}$$

Write a program that displays the **e** value for **i = 10000, 20000, . . .,** and **100000**.

Hint

Since $i! = i \times (i-1) \times \cdots \times 2 \times 1$, $\frac{1}{i!}$ is $\frac{1}{i(i-1)!}$. Initialize **e** and **item** to be 1 and keep adding a new **item** to **e**. The new item is the previous item divided by **i** for $i = 2, 3, 4, \ldots$.

4.27** (*Displaying leap years*) Write a program that displays all the leap years, ten per line, in the twenty-first century (from **2001** to **2100**).

4.28** (*Displaying the first days of each month*) Write a program that prompts the user to enter the year and first day of the year, and displays the first day of each month in the year on the console. For example, if the user entered the year 2005, and 6 for Saturday, January 1, 2005, your program should display the following output:

```
January 1, 2005 is Saturday
...
December 1, 2005 is Thursday
```

4.29**(*Displaying calendars*) Write a program that prompts the user to enter the year and first day of the year, and displays the calendar table for the year on the console. For example, if the user entered the year 2005, and 6 for Saturday, January 1, 2005, your program should display the calendar for each month in the year, as follows:

January 2005

Sun	Mon	Tue	Wed	Thu	Fri	Sat
						1
2	3	4	5	6	7	8
9	10	11	12	13	14	15
16	17	18	19	20	21	22
23	24	25	26	27	28	29
30	31					

. . .

December 2005

Sun	Mon	Tue	Wed	Thu	Fri	Sat
				1	2	3
4	5	6	7	8	9	10
11	12	13	14	15	16	17
18	19	20	21	22	23	24
25	26	27	28	29	30	31

METHODS

Objectives

- To create methods, invoke methods, and pass arguments to a method (§§5.2–5.5).
- To use method overloading and understand ambiguous overloading (§5.6).
- To determine the scope of variables (§5.8).
- To know how to use the methods in the `Math` class (§5.9).
- To learn the concept of method abstraction (§5.11).
- To design and implement methods using stepwise refinement (§5.11).
- (Optional) To group classes into packages (§5.12).

5.1 Introduction

In the preceding chapters, you learned about such methods as `System.out.println`, `JOptionPane.showMessageDialog`, `JOptionPane.showInputDialog`, `Integer.parseInt`, `Double.parseDouble`, `System.exit`, `Math.pow`, and `Math.random()`. A method is a collection of statements that are grouped together to perform an operation. When you call the `System.out.println` method, for example, the system actually executes several statements in order to display a message on the console.

This chapter introduces methods. You will learn how to create your own methods with or without return values, invoke a method with or without parameters, overload methods using the same names, and apply method abstraction in the program design.

5.2 Creating a Method

In general, a method has the following syntax:

```
modifier returnValueType methodName(list of parameters) {
    // Method body;
}
```

Let's take a look at a method created to find which of two integers is bigger. This method, named `max`, has two `int` parameters, `num1` and `num2`, the larger of which is returned by the method. Figure 5.1 illustrates the components of this method.

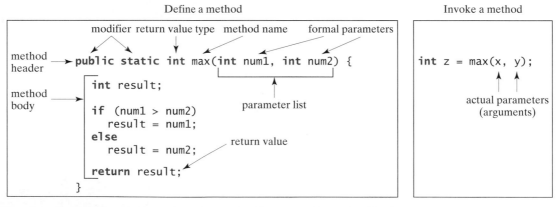

FIGURE 5.1   A method declaration consists of a method header and a method body.

The method header specifies the *modifiers*, *return value type*, *method name*, and *parameters* of the method. The modifier, which is optional, tells the compiler how to call the method. The static modifier is used for all the methods in this chapter. The reason for using it will be discussed in Chapter 7, "Objects and Classes."

A method may return a value. The `returnValueType` is the data type of the value the method returns. Some methods perform the desired operations without returning a value. In this case, the `returnValueType` is the keyword `void`. For example, the `returnValueType` in the `main` method is `void`, as well as in `System.exit`, `System.out.println`, and `JOptionPane.showMessageDialog`. The method that returns a value is called a *nonvoid method*, and the method that does not return a value is called a *void method*.

nonvoid method

void method

parameter

argument

parameter list

The variables defined in the method header are known as *formal parameters* or simply *parameters*. A parameter is like a placeholder. When a method is invoked, you pass a value to the parameter. This value is referred to as *actual parameter or argument*. The *parameter list* refers to the type, order, and number of the parameters of a method. The method name and the parameter list together constitute the *method signature*. Parameters are optional; that is, a method may contain no parameters.   method signature

The method body contains a collection of statements that define what the method does. The method body of the `max` method uses an `if` statement to determine which number is larger and return the value of that number. A return statement using the keyword `return` is *required* for a nonvoid method to return a result. The method terminates when a return statement is executed.

Note

In certain other languages, methods are referred to as *procedures* and *functions*. A method with a nonvoid return value type is called a *function*; a method with a `void` return value type is called a *procedure*.

Caution

You need to declare a separate data type for each parameter. For instance, `int num1, num2` should be replaced by `int num1, int num2`.

5.3 Calling a Method

In creating a method, you give a definition of what the method is to do. To use a method, you have to *call* or *invoke* it. There are two ways to call a method; the choice is based on whether the method returns a value or not.

If the method returns a value, a call to the method is usually treated as a value. For example,

```
int larger = max(3, 4);
```

calls `max(3, 4)` and assigns the result of the method to the variable `larger`. Another example of a call that is treated as a value is

```
System.out.println(max(3, 4));
```

which prints the return value of the method call `max(3, 4)`.

If the method returns `void`, a call to the method must be a statement. For example, the method `println` returns `void`. The following call is a statement:

```
System.out.println("Welcome to Java!");
```

Note

A method with a nonvoid return value type can also be invoked as a statement in Java. In this case, the caller simply ignores the return value. This is rare, but permissible if the caller is not interested in the return value.

When a program calls a method, program control is transferred to the called method. A called method returns control to the caller when its return statement is executed or when its method-ending closing brace is reached.

Listing 5.1 shows a complete program that is used to test the `max` method. The output of the program is shown in Figure 5.2.

FIGURE 5.2   The program invokes `max(i, j)` in order to get the maximum value between `i` and `j`.

LISTING 5.1 TestMax.java

```
 1  public class TestMax {
 2    /** Main method */
 3    public static void main(String[] args) {
 4      int i = 5;
 5      int j = 2;
 6      int k = max(i, j);
 7      System.out.println("The maximum between " + i +
 8        " and " + j + " is " + k);
 9    }
10
11    /** Return the max between two numbers */
12    public static int max(int num1, int num2) {
13      int result;
14
15      if (num1 > num2)
16        result = num1;
17      else
18        result = num2;
19
20      return result;
21    }
22  }
```

main method — line 3
invoke max — line 6
declare method — line 12

main method

This program contains the `main` method and the `max` method. The `main` method is just like any other method except that it is invoked by the JVM.

The `main` method's header is always the same, like the one in this example, with the modifiers `public` and `static`, return value type `void`, method name `main`, and a parameter of the `String[]` type. `String[]` indicates that the parameter is an array of `String`, a subject addressed in Chapter 6, "Arrays."

The statements in `main` may invoke other methods that are defined in the class that contains the `main` method or in other classes. In this example, the `main` method invokes `max(i, j)`, which is defined in the same class with the `main` method.

max method

When the `max` method is invoked (line 6), variable `i`'s value 5 is passed to `num1`, and variable `j`'s value 2 is passed to `num2` in the `max` method. The flow of control transfers to the `max` method. The `max` method is executed. When the `return` statement in the `max` method is executed, the `max` method returns the control to its caller (in this case the caller is the `main` method). This process is illustrated in Figure 5.3.

pass the value i

pass the value j

```
public static void main(String[] args) {
  int i = 5;
  int j = 2;
  int k = max(i, j);

  System.out.println(
    "The maximum between " + i +
    " and " + j + " is " + k);
}
```

```
public static int max(int num1, int num2) {
  int result;

  if (num1 > num2)
    result = num1;
  else
    result = num2;

  return result;
}
```

FIGURE 5.3 When the `max` method is invoked, the flow of control transfers to the `max` method. Once the `max` method is finished, it returns the control back to the caller.

Caution

A `return` statement is required for a nonvoid method. The method shown below in (a) is logically correct, but it has a compilation error because the Java compiler thinks it possible that this method does not return any value.

```
public static int sign(int n) {
  if (n > 0) return 1;
  else if (n == 0) return 0;
  else if (n < 0) return -1;
}
```
                                 Should be →
```
public static int sign(int n) {
  if (n > 0) return 1;
  else if (n == 0) return 0;
  else return -1;
}
```

(a)   (b)

To fix this problem, delete `if (n < 0)` in (a), so that the compiler will see a `return` statement to be reached regardless of how the `if` statement is evaluated.

Note

One of the benefits of methods is for reuse. The `max` method can be invoked from any class besides `TestMax`. If you create a new class, `Test`, you can invoke the `max` method using `ClassName.methodName` (i.e., `TestMax.max`).

reusing method

5.3.1   Call Stacks

Each time a method is invoked, the system stores parameters and variables in an area of memory, known as a *stack*, which stores elements in last-in first-out fashion. When a method calls another method, the caller's stack space is kept intact, and new space is created to handle the new method call. When a method finishes its work and returns to its caller, its associated space is released.

stack

Understanding call stacks helps you to comprehend how methods are invoked. The variables defined in the `main` method are `i`, `j`, and `k`. The variables defined in the `max` method are `num1`, `num2`, and `result`. The variables `num1` and `num2` are defined in the method signature and are parameters of the method. Their values are passed through method invocation. Figure 5.4 illustrates the variables in the stack.

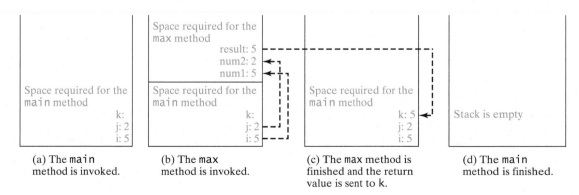

(a) The `main`   (b) The `max`   (c) The `max` method is   (d) The `main`
method is invoked.   method is invoked.   finished and the return   method is finished.
                                                              value is sent to `k`.

FIGURE 5.4   When the `max` method is invoked, the flow of control transfers to the `max` method. Once the `max` method is finished, it returns the control back to the caller.

Tip

If you use an IDE such as JBuilder, NetBeans, or Eclipse, please refer to *Learning Java Effectively with JBuilder/NetBeans/Eclipse* in the supplements. This supplement shows you how to use a debugger to trace method invocations.

debugging in IDE

5.4 **void** Method Example

The preceding section gives an example of a nonvoid method. This section shows how to declare and invoke a void method. Listing 5.2 gives a program that declares a method named `printGrade` and invokes it to print the grade for a given score.

LISTING 5.2   TestVoidMethod.java

```
 1  public class TestVoidMethod {
 2    public static void main(String[] args) {
 3      printGrade(78.5);
 4    }
 5
 6    public static void printGrade(double score) {
 7      if (score >= 90.0) {
 8        System.out.println('A');
 9      }
10      else if (score >= 80.0) {
11        System.out.println('B');
12      }
13      else if (score >= 70.0) {
14        System.out.println('C');
15      }
16      else if (score >= 60.0) {
17        System.out.println('D');
18      }
19      else {
20        System.out.println('F');
21      }
22    }
23  }
```

main method
invoke **printGrade**

printGrade method

invoke **void** method

The `printGrade` method is a **void** method. It does not return any value. A call to a **void** method must be a statement. So, it is invoked as a statement in line 3 in the `main` method. This statement is like any Java statement terminated with a semicolon.

return in **void** method

Note

A `return` statement is not needed for a **void** method, but it can be used for terminating the method and returning to the method's caller. The syntax is simply

return;

This is rare, but sometimes useful for circumventing the normal flow of control in a **void** function. For example, the following code has a `return` statement to terminate the function when the score is invalid.

```
public static void printGrade(double score) {
  if (score < 0 || score > 100)
    System.out.println("Invalid score");
    return;
  }

  if (score >= 90.0) {
    System.out.println('A');
  }
  else if (score >= 80.0) {
    System.out.println('B');
  }
  else if (score >= 70.0) {
```

```
      System.out.println('C');
    }
    else if (score >= 60.0) {
      System.out.println('D');
    }
    else {
      System.out.println('F');
    }
  }
```

5.5 Passing Parameters by Values

The power of a method is its ability to work with parameters. You can use `println` to print any string and `max` to find the maximum between any two `int` values. When calling a method, you need to provide arguments, which must be given in the same order as their respective parameters in the method specification. This is known as *parameter order association*. For example, the following method prints a message `n` times:

parameter order association

```
public static void nPrintln(String message, int n) {
  for (int i = 0; i < n; i++)
    System.out.println(message);
}
```

You can use `nPrintln("Hello", 3)` to print "Hello" three times. The `nPrintln("Hello", 3)` statement passes the actual string parameter, `"Hello"`, to the parameter, `message`; passes `3` to `n`; and prints `"Hello"` three times. However, the statement `nPrintln(3, "Hello")` would be wrong. The data type of `3` does not match the data type for the first parameter, `message`, nor does the second parameter, `"Hello"`, match the second parameter, `n`.

 Caution

The arguments must match the parameters in *order*, *number*, and *compatible type*, as defined in the method signature. Compatible type means that you can pass an argument to a parameter without explicit casting, such as passing an `int` value argument to a `double` value parameter.

parameter matching

When you invoke a method with a parameter, the value of the argument is passed to the parameter. This is referred to as *pass-by-value*. If the argument is a variable rather than a literal value, the value of the variable is passed to the parameter. The variable is not affected, regardless of the changes made to the parameter inside the method. We will examine an interesting scenario in the following example, in which the parameters are changed in the method but the arguments are not affected.

pass-by-value

Listing 5.3 is a program that demonstrates the effect of passing by value. The program creates a method for swapping two variables. The `swap` method is invoked by passing two arguments. Interestingly, the values of the arguments are not changed after the method is invoked. The output of the program is shown in Figure 5.5.

```
Command Prompt                                      _ □ ×
C:\book>java TestPassByValue
Before invoking the swap method, num1 is 1 and num2 is 2
        Inside the swap method
                Before swapping n1 is 1 n2 is 2
                After swapping n1 is 2 n2 is 1
After invoking the swap method, num1 is 1 and num2 is 2

C:\book>_
```

FIGURE 5.5   The contents of the arguments are not swapped after the `swap` method is invoked.

LISTING 5.3   TestPassByValue.java

```
 1  public class TestPassByValue {
 2    /** Main method */
 3    public static void main(String[] args) {
 4      // Declare and initialize variables
 5      int num1 = 1;
 6      int num2 = 2;
 7
 8      System.out.println("Before invoking the swap method, num1 is " +
 9        num1 + " and num2 is " + num2);
10
11      // Invoke the swap method to attempt to swap two variables
12      swap(num1, num2);
13
14      System.out.println("After invoking the swap method, num1 is " +
15        num1 + " and num2 is " + num2);
16    }
17
18    /** Swap two variables */
19    public static void swap(int n1, int n2) {
20      System.out.println("\tInside the swap method");
21      System.out.println("\t\tBefore swapping n1 is " + n1
22        + " n2 is " + n2);
23
24      // Swap n1 with n2
25      int temp = n1;
26      n1 = n2;
27      n2 = temp;
28
29      System.out.println("\t\tAfter swapping n1 is " + n1
30        + " n2 is " + n2);
31    }
32  }
```

false swap

Before the **swap** method is invoked (line 12), **num1** is 1 and **num2** is 2. After the **swap** method is invoked, **num1** is still 1 and **num2** is still 2. Their values are not swapped after the **swap** method is invoked. As shown in Figure 5.6, the values of the arguments **num1** and **num2** are passed to **n1** and **n2**, but **n1** and **n2** have their own memory locations independent of **num1** and **num2**. Therefore, changes in **n1** and **n2** do not affect the contents of **num1** and **num2**.

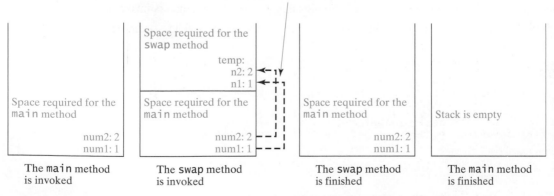

The values of num1 and num2 are passed to n1 and n2. Executing swap does not affect num1 and num2.

FIGURE 5.6   The values of the variables are passed to the parameters of the method.

Another twist is to change the parameter name `n1` in `swap` to `num1`. What effect does this have? No change occurs because it makes no difference whether the parameter and the argument have the same name. The parameter is a variable in the method with its own memory space. The variable is allocated when the method is invoked, and it disappears when the method is returned to its caller.

Note

For simplicity, Java programmers often say *passing an argument* x *to a parameter* y, which actually means *passing the value of* x *to* y.

5.6 Overloading Methods

The `max` method that was used earlier works only with the `int` data type. But what if you need to find which of two floating-point numbers has the maximum value? The solution is to create another method with the same name but different parameters, as shown in the following code:

```
public static double max(double num1, double num2) {
  if (num1 > num2)
    return num1;
  else
    return num2;
}
```

If you call `max` with `int` parameters, the `max` method that expects `int` parameters will be invoked; if you call `max` with `double` parameters, the `max` method that expects `double` parameters will be invoked. This is referred to as *method overloading*; that is, two methods have the same name but different parameter lists within one class. The Java compiler determines which method is used based on the method signature.

method overloading

Listing 5.4 is a program that creates three methods. The first finds the maximum integer, the second finds the maximum double, and the third finds the maximum among three double values. All three methods are named `max`. The output of the program is shown in Figure 5.7.

FIGURE 5.7 The program invokes three different `max` methods that all have the same name: `max(3, 4)`, `max(3.0, 5.4)`, and `max(3.0, 5.4, 10.14)`.

LISTING 5.4 TestMethodOverloading.java

```
1  public class TestMethodOverloading {
2    /** Main method */
3    public static void main(String[] args) {
4      // Invoke the max method with int parameters
5      System.out.println("The maximum between 3 and 4 is "
6        + max(3, 4));
7
```

```
 8        // Invoke the max method with the double parameters
 9        System.out.println("The maximum between 3.0 and 5.4 is "
10          + max(3.0, 5.4) );
11
12        // Invoke the max method with three double parameters
13        System.out.println("The maximum between 3.0, 5.4, and 10.14 is "
14          + max(3.0, 5.4, 10.14) );
15     }
16
17     /** Return the max between two int values */
18     public static int max(int num1, int num2) {
19       if (num1 > num2)
20         return num1;
21       else
22         return num2;
23     }
24
25     /** Find the max between two double values */
26     public static double max(double num1, double num2) {
27       if (num1 > num2)
28         return num1;
29       else
30         return num2;
31     }
32
33     /** Return the max among three double values */
34     public static double max(double num1, double num2, double num3) {
35       return max(max(num1, num2), num3);
36     }
37  }
```

When calling `max(3, 4)` (line 6), the `max` method for finding the maximum of two integers is invoked. When calling `max(3.0, 5.4)` (line 10), the `max` method for finding the maximum of two doubles is invoked. When calling `max(3.0, 5.4, 10.14)` (line 14), the `max` method for finding the maximum of three double values is invoked.

Can you invoke the `max` method with an `int` value and a `double` value, such as `max(2, 2.5)`? If so, which of the `max` methods is invoked? The answer to the first question is yes. The answer to the second is that the `max` method for finding the maximum of two `double` values is invoked. The argument value `2` is automatically converted into a `double` value and passed to this method.

You may be wondering why the method `max(double, double)` is not invoked for the call `max(3, 4)`. Both `max(double, double)` and `max(int, int)` are possible matches for `max(3, 4)`. The Java compiler finds the most specific method for a method invocation. Since the method `max(int, int)` is more specific than `max(double, double)`, `max(int, int)` is used to invoke `max(3, 4)`.

Tip

Overloading methods can make programs clearer and more readable. Methods that perform closely related tasks should be given the same name.

Note

Overloaded methods must have different parameter lists. You cannot overload methods based on different modifiers or return types.

Note

Sometimes there are two or more possible matches for an invocation of a method, but the compiler cannot determine the most specific match. This is referred to as *ambiguous invocation*. Ambiguous invocation causes a compilation error. Consider the following code:

ambiguous invocation

```java
public class AmbiguousOverloading {
  public static void main(String[] args) {
    System.out.println(max(1, 2));
  }

  public static double max(int num1, double num2) {
    if (num1 > num2)
      return num1;
    else
      return num2;
  }

  public static double max(double num1, int num2) {
    if (num1 > num2)
      return num1;
    else
      return num2;
  }
}
```

Both `max(int, double)` and `max(double, int)` are possible candidates to match `max(1, 2)`. Since neither of them is more specific than the other, the invocation is ambiguous, resulting in a compilation error.

5.7 Case Study: Computing Taxes with Methods

The program in Listing 3.4 uses `if` statements to check the filing status and computes the tax based on the filing status. This example uses methods to simplify Listing 3.4.

Each filing status has six brackets. The code for computing taxes is nearly the same regardless of filing status except that each filing status has different bracket ranges. For example, the brackets of the single-filer status are [0, 6000], (6000, 27950], (27950, 67700], (67700, 141250], (141250, 307050], (307050, ∞), and the six brackets of the married–file jointly status are [0, 12000], (12000, 46700], (46700, 112850], (112850, 171950], (171950, 307050], (307050, ∞). The first bracket of each filing status is taxed at 10%, the second at 15%, the third at 27%, the fourth at 30%, the fifth at 35%, and the sixth at 38.6%. So you can write a method with the brackets as arguments to compute the tax for the filing status. The header of the method is:

```
public static double computeTax(double income,  ◄─────────── 400000
    int r1, int r2, int r3, int r4, int r5)
```

[0, 6000], [6000, 27950], [27950, 67700], [67700, 141250], [141250, 307050], (307050, ∞)

For example, you can invoke `computeTax(400000, 6000, 27950, 67700, 141250, 307050)` to compute the tax for single filers with $400,000 of taxable income.

Listing 5.5 gives the solution to the problem. The output of the program is similar to Figure 3.3.

LISTING 5.5 ComputeTaxWithMethod.java

```
1  import javax.swing.JOptionPane;
2
3  public class ComputeTaxWithMethod {
4    public static void main(String[] args) {
5      // Prompt the user to enter filing status
6      String statusString = JOptionPane.showInputDialog(
7        "Enter the filing status:");
8      int status = Integer.parseInt(statusString);
9
10     // Prompt the user to enter taxable income
11     String incomeString = JOptionPane.showInputDialog(
12       "Enter the taxable income:");
13     double income = Double.parseDouble(incomeString);
14
15     // Display the result
16     JOptionPane.showMessageDialog(null, "Tax is " +
17       (int)(computeTax(status, income) * 100) / 100.0);
18   }
19
20   public static double computeTax(double income,
21     int r1, int r2, int r3, int r4, int r5) {
22     double tax = 0;
23
24     if (income <= r1)
25       tax = income * 0.10;
26     else if (income <= r2)
27       tax = r1 * 0.10 + (income - r1) * 0.15;
28     else if (income <= r3)
29       tax = r1 * 0.10 + (r2 - r1) * 0.15 + (income - r2) * 0.27;
30     else if (income <= r4)
31       tax = r1 * 0.10 + (r2 - r1) * 0.15 +
32         (r3 - r2) * 0.27 + (income - r3) * 0.30;
33     else if (income <= r5)
34       tax = r1 * 0.10 + (r2 - r1) * 0.15 + (r3 - r2) * 0.27 +
35         (r4 - r3) * 0.30 + (income - r4) * 0.35;
36     else
37       tax = r1 * 0.10 + (r2 - r1) * 0.15 + (r3 - r2) * 0.27 +
38         (r4 - r3) * 0.30 + (r5 - r4) * 0.35 + (income - r5) * 0.386;
39
40     return tax;
41   }
42
43   public static double computeTax(int status, double income) {
44     switch (status) {
45       case 0: return
46         computeTax(income, 6000, 27950, 67700, 141250, 307050);
47       case 1: return
48         computeTax(income, 12000, 46700, 112850, 171950, 307050);
49       case 2: return
50         computeTax(income, 6000, 23350, 56425, 85975, 153525);
51       case 3: return
52         computeTax(income, 10000, 37450, 96700, 156600, 307050);
53       default: return 0;
54     }
55   }
56 }
```

This program does the same thing as the one in Listing 3.4. Instead of writing the same code for computing taxes for different filing statuses, the new program uses a method for computing taxes. Using the method not only shortens the program, it also makes the program simpler, easy to read, and easy to maintain.

The program uses two overloaded `computeTax` methods (lines 20, 43). The first `computeTax` method in line 20 computes the tax for the specified brackets and taxable income. The second `computeTax` method in line 43 computes the tax for the specified status and taxable income.

5.8 The Scope of Variables

The *scope of a variable* is the part of the program where the variable can be referenced. A variable defined inside a method is referred to as a *local variable*.

The scope of a local variable starts from its declaration and continues to the end of the block that contains the variable. A local variable must be declared before it can be used.

A *parameter* is actually a local variable. The scope of a method parameter covers the entire method.

A variable declared in the initial action part of a `for` loop header has its scope in the entire loop. But a variable declared inside a `for` loop body has its scope limited in the loop body from its declaration to the end of the block that contains the variable, as shown in Figure 5.8.

scope
local variable

parameter

for loop control variable

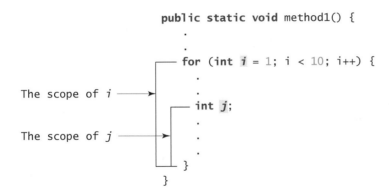

FIGURE 5.8   A variable declared in the initial action part of a `for` loop header has its scope in the entire loop.

You can declare a local variable with the same name multiple times in different non-nesting blocks in a method, but you cannot declare a local variable twice in nested blocks, as shown in Figure 5.9.

multiple declarations

 Caution

Do not declare a variable inside a block and then attempt to use it outside the block. Here is an example of a common mistake:

```
for (int i = 0; i < 10; i++) {
}

System.out.println(i);
```

The last statement would cause a syntax error because variable `i` is not defined outside of the `for` loop.

It is fine to declare *i* in two
non-nesting blocks

It is wrong to declare *i* in two
nesting blocks

```
public static void method1() {
  int x = 1;
  int y = 1;

  for (int i = 1; i < 10; i++) {
    x += i;
  }

  for (int i = 1; i < 10; i++) {
    y += i;
  }
}
```

```
public static void method2() {

  int i = 1;
  int sum = 0;

  for (int i = 1; i < 10; i++)
    sum += i;
  }

}
```

FIGURE 5.9   A variable can be declared multiple times in non-nested blocks, but can be declared only once in nested blocks.

5.9 The `Math` Class

The `Math` class contains the methods needed to perform basic mathematical functions. You have already used the `pow(a, b)` method to compute a^b in Listing 2.6, ComputeLoan.java, and the Math.random() in Listing 3.5, SubtractionTutor.java. This section introduces other useful methods in the `Math` class. They can be categorized as *trigonometric methods*, *exponent methods*, and *service methods*. Besides methods, the `Math` class provides two useful `double` constants, `PI` and `E` (the base of natural logarithms). You can use these constants as `Math.PI` and `Math.E` in any program.

5.9.1   Trigonometric Methods

The `Math` class contains the following trigonometric methods:

```
public static double sin(double radians)
public static double cos(double radians)
public static double tan(double radians)
public static double asin(double radians)
public static double acos(double radians)
public static double atan(double radians)
public static double toRadians(double degree)
public static double toDegrees(double radians)
```

Each method has a single `double` parameter, and its return type is `double`. The parameter represents an angle in radians. One degree is equal to $\pi/180$ in radians. For example, `Math.sin(Math.PI)` returns the trigonometric sine of π. Since JDK 1.2, the `Math` class has also provided the method `toRadians(double angdeg)` for converting an angle in degrees to radians, and the method `toDegrees(double angrad)` for converting an angle in radians to degrees.

For example,

```
Math.sin(0) returns 0.0
Math.sin(Math.toRadians(270)) returns -1.0
Math.sin(Math.PI / 6) returns 0.5
Math.sin(Math.PI / 2) returns 1.0
Math.cos(0) returns 1.0
Math.cos(Math.PI / 6) returns 0.866
Math.cos(Math.PI / 2) returns 0
```

5.9.2   Exponent Methods

There are five methods related to exponents in the **Math** class:

```
/** Return e raised to the power of x (ex) */
public static double exp(double x)

/** Return the natural logarithm of x (ln(x) = loge(x)) */
public static double log(double x)

/** Return the base 10 logarithm of x (log10(x)) */
public static double log10(double x)

/** Return a raised to the power of b (xb) */
public static double pow(double x, double b)

/** Return the square root of a (√x) */
public static double sqrt(double x)
```

Note that the parameter in the **sqrt** method must not be negative.
  For example,

```
Math.exp(1) returns 2.71828
Math.log(Math.E) returns 1.0
Math.log10(10) returns 1.0
Math.pow(2, 3) returns 8.0
Math.pow(3, 2) returns 9.0
Math.pow(3.5, 2.5) returns 22.91765
Math.sqrt(4) returns 2.0
Math.sqrt(10.5) returns 3.24
```

5.9.3   The Rounding Methods

The **Math** class contains five rounding methods:

```
/** x rounded up to its nearest integer. This integer is
  * returned as a double value. */
public static double ceil(double x)

/** x is rounded down to its nearest integer. This integer is
  * returned as a double value. */
public static double floor(double x)

/** x is rounded to its nearest integer. If x is equally close
  * to two integers, the even one is returned as a double. */
public static double rint(double x)

/** Return (int)Math.floor(x + 0.5). */
public static int round(float x)

/** Return (long)Math.floor(x + 0.5). */
public static long round(double x)
```

For example,

```
Math.ceil(2.1) returns 3.0
Math.ceil(2.0) returns 2.0
Math.ceil(-2.0) returns -2.0
Math.ceil(-2.1) returns -2.0
Math.floor(2.1) returns 2.0
Math.floor(2.0) returns 2.0
```

```
Math.floor(-2.0) returns -2.0
Math.floor(-2.1) returns -3.0
Math.rint(2.1) returns 2.0
Math.rint(2.0) returns 2.0
Math.rint(-2.0) returns -2.0
Math.rint(-2.1) returns -2.0
Math.rint(2.5) returns 2.0
Math.rint(-2.5) returns -2.0
Math.round(2.6f) returns 3  // Returns int
Math.round(2.0) returns 2   // Returns long
Math.round(-2.0f) returns -2
Math.round(-2.6) returns -3
```

5.9.4 The `min`, `max`, and `abs` Methods

The `min` and `max` methods are overloaded to return the minimum and maximum numbers between two numbers (`int`, `long`, `float`, or `double`). For example, `max(3.4, 5.0)` returns `5.0`, and `min(3, 2)` returns `2`.

The `abs` method is overloaded to return the absolute value of the number (`int`, `long`, `float`, and `double`). For example,

```
Math.max(2, 3) returns 3
Math.max(2.5, 3) returns 3.0
Math.min(2.5, 3.6) returns 2.5
Math.abs(-2) returns 2
Math.abs(-2.1) returns 2.1
```

5.9.5 The `random` Method

The `Math` class also has a powerful method, `random`, which generates a random `double` value greater than or equal to 0.0 and less than 1.0 (`0.0 <= Math.random() < 1.0`). This method is very useful. Listing 3.5, SubtractionTutor.java, uses this method to generate a single-digit integer. You can use it to write a simple expression to generate random numbers in any range. For example,

$$(\textbf{int})(\text{Math. random}() * 10) \longrightarrow$$ Returns a random integer between 0 and 9.

$$50 + (\textbf{int})(\text{Math. random}() * 50) \longrightarrow$$ Returns a random integer between 50 and 99.

In general,

$$a + \text{Math. random}() * b \longrightarrow$$ Returns a random number between a and a + b, excluding a + b.

Tip
You can view the complete documentation for the `Math` class online at http://java.sun.com/j2se/1.5.0/docs/api/index.html, as shown in Figure 5.10. You can also download `jdk-1_5_0-doc.zip` from the same website and install it on your PC so that you can browse the documents locally.

Note
Not all classes need a `main` method. The `Math` class and `JOptionPane` class do not have `main` methods. These classes contain methods for other classes to use.

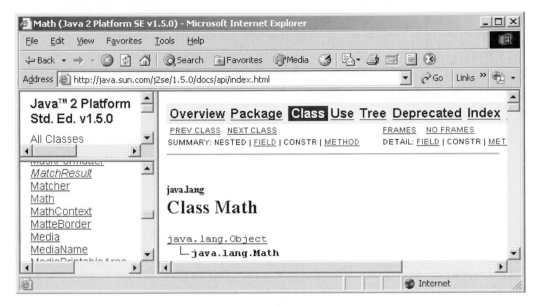

FIGURE 5.10 You can view the documentation for Java API online.

5.10 Case Study: Generating Random Characters

Computer programs process numerical data and characters. You have seen many examples that involve numerical data. It is also important to understand characters and how to process them. This section presents an example for generating random characters.

As introduced in §2.9, every character has a unique Unicode between 0 and FFFF in hexadecimal (65535 in decimal). To generate a random character is to generate a random integer between 0 and 65535 using the following expression (note that since 0.0 <= Math.random() < 1.0, you have to add 1 to 65535):

```
(int)(Math.random() * (65535 + 1))
```

Now let us consider how to generate a random lowercase letter. The Unicodes for lowercase letters are consecutive integers starting from the Unicode for 'a,' then for 'b', 'c', ..., and 'z.' The Unicode for 'a' is

```
(int)'a'
```

So a random integer between (int)'a' and (int)'z' is

```
(int)((int)'a' + Math.random() * ((int)'z' - (int)'a' + 1)
```

As discussed in §2.9.4, all numeric operators can be applied to the char operands. The char operand is cast into a number if the other operand is a number or a character. Thus the preceding expression can be simplified as follows:

```
'a' + Math.random() * ('z' - 'a' + 1)
```

and a random lowercase letter is

```
(char)('a' + Math.random() * ('z' - 'a' + 1))
```

To generalize the foregoing discussion, a random character between any two characters ch1 and ch2 with ch1 < ch2 can be generated as follows:

```
(char)(ch1 + Math.random() * (ch2 - ch1 + 1))
```

This is a simple but useful discovery. Let us create a class named **RandomCharacter** in Listing 5.6 with five methods to get a certain type of character randomly. You can use these methods in your future projects.

LISTING 5.6 RandomCharacter.java

```java
1  public class RandomCharacter {
2    /** Generate a random character between ch1 and ch2 */
3    public static char getRandomCharacter(char ch1, char ch2) {
4      return (char)(ch1 + Math.random() * (ch2 - ch1 + 1));
5    }
6
7    /** Generate a random lowercase letter */
8    public static char getRandomLowerCaseLetter() {
9      return getRandomCharacter('a', 'z');
10   }
11
12   /** Generate a random uppercase letter */
13   public static char getRandomUpperCaseLetter() {
14     return getRandomCharacter('A', 'Z');
15   }
16
17   /** Generate a random digit character */
18   public static char getRandomDigitCharacter() {
19     return getRandomCharacter('0', '9');
20   }
21
22   /** Generate a random character */
23   public static char getRandomCharacter() {
24     return getRandomCharacter('\u0000', '\uFFFF');
25   }
26 }
```

Listing 5.7 gives a test program that displays one hundred lowercase letters.

LISTING 5.7 TestRandomCharacter.java

```java
1  public class TestRandomCharacter {
2    /** Main method */
3    public static void main(String args[]) {
4      final int NUMBER_OF_CHARS = 175;
5      final int CHARS_PER_LINE = 25;
6
7      // Print random characters between '!' and '~', 25 chars per line
8      for (int i = 0; i < NUMBER_OF_CHARS; i++) {
9        char ch = RandomCharacter.getRandomLowerCaseLetter();
10       if ((i + 1) % CHARS_PER_LINE == 0)
11         System.out.println(ch);
12       else
13         System.out.print(ch);
14     }
15   }
16 }
```

constants

lowercase letter

5.11 Method Abstraction and Stepwise Refinement

method abstraction

The key to developing software is to apply the concept of abstraction. You will learn many levels of abstraction from this book. *Method abstraction* is achieved by separating the use of a method from its implementation. The client can use a method without knowing how it is implemented.

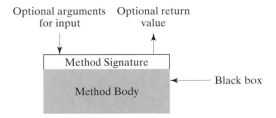

FIGURE 5.11 The method body can be thought of as a black box that contains the detailed implementation for the method.

The details of the implementation are encapsulated in the method and hidden from the client who invokes the method. This is known as *information hiding* or *encapsulation*. If you decide to change the implementation, the client program will not be affected, provided that you do not change the method signature. The implementation of the method is hidden from the client in a "black box," as shown in Figure 5.11.

information hiding

You have already used the `System.out.print` method to display a string, the `JOptionPane.showInputDialog` method to read a string from a dialog box, and the `max` method to find the maximum number. You know how to write the code to invoke these methods in your program, but as a user of these methods, you are not required to know how they are implemented.

The concept of method abstraction can be applied to the process of developing programs. When writing a large program, you can use the "divide and conquer" strategy, also known as *stepwise refinement*, to decompose it into subproblems. The subproblems can be further decomposed into smaller, more manageable problems.

divide and conquer
stepwise refinement

Suppose you write a program that displays the calendar for a given month of the year. The program prompts the user to enter the year and the month, and then displays the entire calendar for the month, as shown in Figure 5.12.

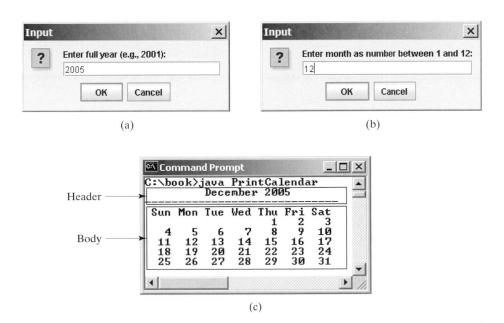

FIGURE 5.12 After prompting the user to enter the year and the month, the program displays the calendar for that month.

Let us use this example to demonstrate the divide-and-conquer approach.

5.11.1   Top-Down Design

How would you get started on such a program? Would you immediately start coding? Beginning programmers often start by trying to work out the solution to every detail. Although details are important in the final program, concern for detail in the early stages may block the problem-solving process. To make problem-solving flow as smoothly as possible, this example begins by using method abstraction to isolate details from design and only later implements the details.

For this example, the problem is first broken into two subproblems: get input from the user, and print the calendar for the month. At this stage, the creator of the program should be concerned with what the subproblems will achieve, not with how to get input and print the calendar for the month. You can draw a structure chart to help visualize the decomposition of the problem (see Figure 5.13(a)).

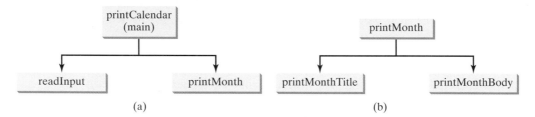

(a)   (b)

FIGURE 5.13   The structure chart shows that the `printCalendar` problem is divided into two subproblems, `readInput` and `printMonth`, and that `printMonth` is divided into two smaller subproblems, `printMonthTitle` and `printMonthBody`.

Use the `JOptionPane.showInputDialog` method to display input dialog boxes that prompt the user to enter the year and the month.

The problem of printing the calendar for a given month can be broken into two subproblems: print the month title, and print the month body, as shown in Figure 5.13(b). The month title consists of three lines: month and year, a dash line, and the names of the seven days of the week. You need to get the month name (e.g., January) from the numeric month (e.g., 1). This is accomplished in `getMonthName` (see Figure 5.14(a)).

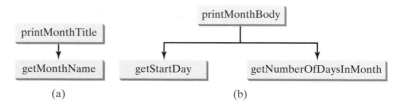

(a)   (b)

FIGURE 5.14   (a) To `printMonthTitle`, you need `getMonthName`. (b) The `printMonthBody` problem is refined into several smaller problems.

In order to print the month body, you need to know which day of the week is the first day of the month (`getStartDay`) and how many days the month has (`getNumberOfDaysInMonth`), as shown in Figure 5.14(b). For example, December 2005 has thirty-one days, and the first of the month is Thursday, as shown in Figure 5.12.

How would you get the start day for the first date in a month? There are several ways to find the start day. The simplest approach is to use the `Calendar` class in §9.3, "The `Calendar` and `GregorianCalendar` Classes." For now, an alternative approach is used. Assume that you know that the start day (`startDay1800 = 3`) for January 1, 1800 was Wednesday. You could compute the total number of days (`totalNumberOfDays`) between January 1, 1800 and the first date of the calendar month. The start day for the calendar month is (`totalNumberOfDays + startDay1800`) `% 7`, since every week has seven days. So the `getStartDay` problem can be further refined as `getTotalNumberOfDays`, as shown in Figure 5.15(a).

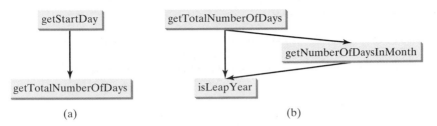

FIGURE 5.15   (a) To `getStartDay`, you need `getTotalNumberOfDays`. (b) The `getTotalNumberOfDays` problem is refined into two smaller problems.

To get the total number of days, you need to know whether the year is a leap year and the number of days in each month. So `getTotalNumberOfDays` is further refined into two subproblems: `isLeapYear` and `getNumberOfDaysInMonth`, as shown in Figure 5.15(b). The complete structure chart is shown in Figure 5.16.

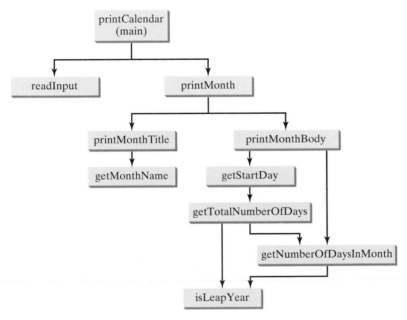

FIGURE 5.16   The structure chart shows the hierarchical relationship of the subproblems in the program.

5.11.2   Top-Down or Bottom-Up Implementation

Now we turn our attention to implementation. In general, a subproblem corresponds to a method in the implementation, although some are so simple that this is unnecessary. You would need to decide which modules to implement as methods and which to combine in other methods. Decisions of this kind should be based on whether the overall program will be easier to read as a result of your choice. In this example, the subproblem `readInput` can be simply implemented in the `main` method.

You can use either a "top-down" approach or a "bottom-up" approach. The "top-down" approach implements one method in the structure chart at a time from the top to the bottom. Stubs can be used for the methods waiting to be implemented. A *stub* is a simple but incomplete version of a method. The use of stubs enables you to test invoking the method from a caller. Implement the `main` method first, and then use a stub for the `printMonth` method. For example, let `printMonth` display the year and the month in the stub. Thus, your program may begin like this:

top-down approach

stub

```java
public class PrintCalendar {
  /** Main method */
  public static void main(String[] args) {
    // Prompt the user to enter year
    String yearString = JOptionPane.showInputDialog(
      "Enter full year (e.g., 2001):");

    // Convert string into integer
    int year = Integer.parseInt(yearString);

    // Prompt the user to enter month
    String monthString = JOptionPane.showInputDialog(
      "Enter month as number between 1 and 12:");

    // Convert string into integer
    int month = Integer.parseInt(monthString);

    // Print calendar for the month of the year
    printMonth(year, month);
  }

  /** A stub for printMonth may look like this */
  public static void printMonth(int year, int month) {
    System.out.print(month + " " + year);
  }

  /** A stub for printMonthTitle may look like this */
  public static void printMonthTitle(int year, int month) {
  }

  /** A stub for getMonthName may look like this */
  public static String getMonthName(int month) {
    return "January"; // a dummy value
  }

  /** A stub for getMonthNmae may look like this */
  public static int getStartDay(int year, int month) {
    return 1; // a dummy value
  }

  /** A stub for getNumberOfDaysInMonth may look like this */
  public static int getNumberOfDaysInMonth(int year, int month) {
    return 31; // a dummy value
  }

  /** A stub for getTotalNumberOfDays may look like this */
  public static int getTotalNumberOfDays(int year, int month) {
    return 10000; // a dummy value
  }

  /** A stub for getTotalNumberOfDays may look like this */
  public static boolean isLeapYear(int year) {
    return true; // a dummy value
  }
}
```

Compile and test the program, and fix any errors. You can now implement the `printMonth` method. For methods invoked from the `printMonth` method, you can again use stubs.

The bottom-up approach implements one method in the structure chart at a time from the bottom to the top. For each method implemented, write a test program to test it. The top-down and bottom-up approaches are both fine. Both approaches implement methods incrementally, help to isolate programming errors, and make debugging easy. Sometimes they can be used together.

5.11.3 Implementation Details

The `isLeapYear(int year)` method can be implemented using the following code:

```
return (year % 400 == 0 || (year % 4 == 0 && year % 100 != 0));
```

Use the following facts to implement `getTotalNumberOfDaysInMonth(int year, int month)`:

- January, March, May, July, August, October, and December have thirty-one days.

- April, June, September, and November have thirty days.

- February has twenty-eight days during a regular year and twenty-nine days during a leap year. A regular year, therefore, has 365 days, whereas a leap year has 366 days.

To implement `getTotalNumberOfDays(int year, int month)`, you need to compute the total number of days (`totalNumberOfDays`) between January 1, 1800 and the first day of the calendar month. You could find the total number of days between the year 1800 and the calendar year and then figure out the total number of days prior to the calendar month in the calendar year. The sum of these two totals is `totalNumberOfDays`.

To print a body, first pad some space before the start day and then print the lines for every week, as shown for December 2005 (see Figure 5.12).

The complete program is given in Listing 5.8.

Listing 5.8 PrintCalendar.java

```java
1  import javax.swing.JOptionPane;
2
3  public class PrintCalendar {
4    /** Main method */
5    public static void main(String[] args) {
6      // Prompt the user to enter year
7      String yearString = JOptionPane.showInputDialog(
8        "Enter full year (e.g., 2001):");
9
10     // Convert string into integer
11     int year = Integer.parseInt(yearString);
12
13     // Prompt the user to enter month
14     String monthString = JOptionPane.showInputDialog(
15       "Enter month in number between 1 and 12:");
16
17     // Convert string into integer
18     int month = Integer.parseInt(monthString);
19
20     // Print calendar for the month of the year
21     printMonth(year, month);
22   }
23
24   /** Print the calendar for a month in a year */
25   static void printMonth(int year, int month) {
26     // Print the headings of the calendar
27     printMonthTitle(year, month);
28
```

```
29        // Print the body of the calendar
30        printMonthBody(year, month);
31      }
32
33      /** Print the month title, e.g., May, 1999 */
34      static void printMonthTitle(int year, int month) {
35        System.out.println("           " + getMonthName(month)
36          + " " + year);
37        System.out.println("-----------------------------");
38        System.out.println(" Sun Mon Tue Wed Thu Fri Sat");
39      }
40
41      /** Get the English name for the month */
42      static String getMonthName(int month) {
43        String monthName = null;
44        switch (month) {
45          case 1: monthName = "January"; break;
46          case 2: monthName = "February"; break;
47          case 3: monthName = "March"; break;
48          case 4: monthName = "April"; break;
49          case 5: monthName = "May"; break;
50          case 6: monthName = "June"; break;
51          case 7: monthName = "July"; break;
52          case 8: monthName = "August"; break;
53          case 9: monthName = "September"; break;
54          case 10: monthName = "October"; break;
55          case 11: monthName = "November"; break;
56          case 12: monthName = "December";
57        }
58
59        return monthName;
60      }
61
62      /** Print month body */
63      static void printMonthBody(int year, int month) {
64        // Get start day of the week for the first date in the month
65        int startDay = getStartDay(year, month);
66
67        // Get number of days in the month
68        int numberOfDaysInMonth = getNumberOfDaysInMonth(year, month);
69
70        // Pad space before the first day of the month
71        int i = 0;
72        for (i = 0; i < startDay; i++)
73          System.out.print("    ");
74
75        for (i = 1; i <= numberOfDaysInMonth; i++) {
76          if (i < 10)
77            System.out.print("    " + i);
78          else
79            System.out.print("   " + i);
80
81          if ((i + startDay) % 7 == 0)
82            System.out.println();
83        }
84
85        System.out.println();
86      }
87
88      /** Get the start day of the first day in a month */
89      static int getStartDay(int year, int month) {
```

```
90          // Get total number of days since 1/1/1800
91          int startDay1800 = 3;
92          int totalNumberOfDays = getTotalNumberOfDays(year, month);
93
94          // Return the start day
95          return (totalNumberOfDays + startDay1800) % 7;
96        }
97
98      /** Get the total number of days since January 1, 1800 */
99      static int getTotalNumberOfDays(int year, int month) {
100         int total = 0;
101
102         // Get the total days from 1800 to year - 1
103         for (int i = 1800; i < year; i++)
104           if (isLeapYear(i))
105             total = total + 366;
106           else
107             total = total + 365;
108
109         // Add days from January to the month prior to the calendar month
110         for (int i = 1; i < month; i++)
111           total = total + getNumberOfDaysInMonth(year, i);
112
113         return total;
114       }
115
116     /** Get the number of days in a month */
117     static int getNumberOfDaysInMonth(int year, int month) {
118         if (month == 1 || month == 3 || month == 5 || month == 7 ||
119           month == 8 || month == 10 || month == 12)
120           return 31;
121
122         if (month == 4 || month == 6 || month == 9 || month == 11)
123           return 30;
124
125         if (month == 2) return isLeapYear(year) ? 29 : 28;
126
127         return 0; // If month is incorrect
128       }
129
130     /** Determine if it is a leap year */
131     static boolean isLeapYear(int year) {
132         return year % 400 == 0 || (year % 4 == 0 && year % 100 != 0);
133       }
134   }
```

The program does not validate user input. For instance, if the user enters either a month not in the range between 1 and 12 or a year before 1800, the program would display an erroneous calendar. To avoid this error, add an `if` statement to check the input before printing the calendar.

This program prints calendars for a month but could easily be modified to print calendars for a whole year. Although it can only print months after January 1800, it could be modified to trace the day of a month before 1800.

Note

Method abstraction modularizes programs in a neat, hierarchical manner. Programs written as collections of concise methods are easier to write, debug, maintain, and modify than would otherwise be the case. This writing style also promotes method reusability.

Tip

When implementing a large program, use the top-down or bottom-up approach. Do not write the entire program at once. This approach seems to take more time for coding (because you are repeatedly compiling and running the program), but it actually saves time and makes debugging easier.

 # 5.12 (Optional) Packages

Packages are used to group classes. So far, all the classes in this book are grouped into a default package. You can explicitly specify a package for each class. There are four reasons for using packages.

why package

■ **To locate classes.** Classes with similar functions can be placed in the same package to make them easy to locate.

■ **To avoid naming conflicts.** When you develop reusable classes to be shared by other programmers, naming conflicts often occur, i.e., two classes with the same name. To prevent this, put your classes into packages so that they can be referenced through package names.

■ **To distribute software conveniently.** Packages group related classes so that they can be easily distributed.

■ **To protect classes.** Packages provide protection so that the protected members of the classes are accessible to the classes in the same package, but not to the external classes.

5.12.1 Package-Naming Conventions

Packages are hierarchical, and you can have packages within packages. For example, `java.lang.Math` indicates that `Math` is a class in the package `lang` and that `lang` is a package in the package `java`. Levels of nesting can be used to ensure the uniqueness of package names.

Choosing a unique name is important because your package may be used on the Internet by other programs. Java designers recommend that you use your Internet domain name in reverse order as a package prefix. Since Internet domain names are unique, this prevents naming conflicts. Suppose you want to create a package named `mypackage` on a host machine with the Internet domain name `prenhall.com`. To follow the naming convention, you would name the entire package `com.prenhall.mypackage`. By convention, package names are all in lowercase.

5.12.2 Package Directories

Java expects one-to-one mapping of the package name and the file system directory structure. For the package named `com.prenhall.mypackage`, you must create a directory, as shown in Figure 5.17(a). In other words, a package is actually a directory that contains the bytecode of the classes.

(a)   (b)

FIGURE 5.17 The package `com.prenhall.mypackage` is mapped to a directory structure in the file system.

The `com` directory does not have to be the root directory. In order for Java to know where your package is in the file system, you must modify the environment variable `classpath` so that it points to the directory in which your package resides. Such a directory is known as the *classpath* for the class. Suppose the `com` directory is under `c:\book`, as shown in Figure 5.17(b). The following line adds `c:\book` into the `classpath`:

classpath

```
set classpath=.;c:\book;
```

The period (.) indicating the current directory is always in `classpath`. The directory `c:\book` is in `classpath` so that you can use the package `com.prenhall.mypackage` in the program.

current directory

You can add as many directories as necessary in `classpath`. The order in which the directories are specified is the order in which the classes are searched. If you have two classes of the same name in different directories, Java uses the first one it finds.

The `classpath` variable is set differently in Windows and Unix, as outlined below.

classpath

- Windows 98: Edit autoexec.bat using a text editor, such as Microsoft Notepad.

- Windows NT/2000/XP: Go to the start button and choose control panel, select the system icon, then modify `classpath` in the Environment Variables.

- UNIX: Use the `setenv` command to set `classpath`, such as

    ```
    setenv classpath .:/home/book
    ```

    If you insert this line into the .cshrc file, the `classpath` variable will be set automatically when you log on.

Note

On Windows 95 and Window 98, you must restart the system in order for the `classpath` variable to take effect. On Windows NT/2000/ME/XP, however, the settings are effective immediately. They affect any new command windows, but not the existing command windows.

5.12.3   Putting Classes into Packages

Every class in Java belongs to a package. The class is added to a package when it is compiled. All the classes that you have used so far in this book were placed in the current directory (a default package) when the Java source programs were compiled. To put a class in a specific package, you need to add the following line as the first noncomment and nonblank statement in the program:

```
package packagename;
```

Let us create a class named `Format` and place it in the package `com.prenhall.mypackage`. The `Format` class contains the `format(number, numberOfDecimalDigits)` method, which returns a new number with the specified number of digits after the decimal point. For example, `format(10.3422345, 2)` returns `10.34`, and format `(-0.343434, 3)` returns `-0.343`.

1. Create Format.java in Listing 5.9 and save it into `c:\book\com\prenhall\mypackage`.

LISTING 5.9   `Format.java`

```
1  package com.prenhall.mypackage;
2
3  public class Format {
4    public static double format(
5        double number, int numberOfDecimalDigits) {
```

specify a package

```
6        return Math.round(number * Math.pow(10, numberOfDecimalDigits)) /
7            Math.pow(10, numberOfDecimalDigits);
8    }
9 }
```

2. Compile Format.java and place it in `c:\book\com\prenhall\mypackage`.

A class must be defined as public in order to be accessed by other programs. If you want to put several classes into the package, you have to create separate source files for them, because each file can have only one public class.

Format.java can be placed under **anyDir\com\prenhall\mypackage**, Format.class in **anyOtherDir\com\prenhall\mypackage**, and **anyDir** and **anyOtherDir** may be the same or different. To make the class available, add **anyOtherDir** in the classpath, using the command:

`set classpath=%classpath%;anyOtherDir`

 Note

Class files can be archived into a single file for convenience. For instance, you may compress all the class files in the folder mypackage into a single zip file named mypackage.zip with subfolder information kept as shown in Figure 5.18. To make the classes in the zip file available for use, add the zip file to the classpath like this:

`classpath=%classpath%;c:\mypackage.zip`

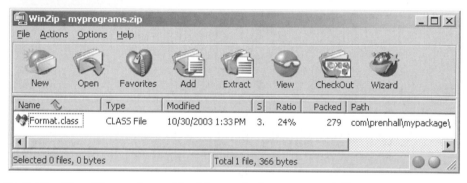

FIGURE 5.18   Class files can be archived into a single compressed file.

 Note

An IDE such as JBuilder uses the *source directory path* to specify where the source files are stored and uses the *class directory path* to specify where the compiled class files are stored.

A source file must be stored in a package directory under the source directory path. For example, if the source directory is `c:\mysource`, and the package statement in the source code is **package com.prenhall.mypackage**, then the source code file is automatically stored in `c:\mysource\com\prenhall\mypackage`.

A class file must be stored in a package directory under the class directory path. For example, if the class directory is `c:\myclass`, and the package statement in the source code is **package com.prenhall.mypackage**, then the class file is automatically stored in `c:\myclass\com\prenhall\mypackage`.

5.12.4   Using Classes from Packages

There are two ways to use classes from a package. One way is to use the fully qualified name of the class. For example, the fully qualified name for **JOptionPane** is **javax.swing.JOptionPane**. For **Format** in the preceding example, it is **com.prenhall.**

(margin notes:) IDE source path
IDE class path

`mypackage.Format`. This is convenient if the class is used only a few times in the program. The other way is to use the `import` statement. For example, to import all the classes in the `javax.swing` package, you can use

```
import javax.swing.*;
```

An import that uses an `*` is called *an import on demand* declaration. You can also import a specific class. For example, this statement imports `javax.swing.JOptionPane`:

```
import javax.swing.JOptionPane;
```

The information for the classes in an imported package is not read in at compile time or runtime unless the class is used in the program. The import statement simply tells the compiler where to locate the classes. There is no performance difference between an import on demand declaration and a specific class import declaration.

Let us write a program that uses the `Format` class in the `com.prenhall.mypackage.mypackage` package.

1. Create TestFormatClass.java in Listing 5.10 and save it into `c:\book`.

LISTING 5.10 `TestFormatClass.java`

```
1  import com.prenhall.mypackage.Format;
2
3  public class TestFormatClass {
4    /** Main method */
5    public static void main(String[] args) {
6      System.out.println(Format.format(10.3422345, 2));
7      System.out.println(Format.format(-0.343434, 3));
8    }
9  }
```
import class

2. Run TestFormatClass, as shown in Figure 5.19.

FIGURE 5.19 `TestFormatClass` uses `Format` defined in `com.prenhall.mypackage`.

TestFormatClass.java can be placed anywhere as long as `c:\book` is in the classpath so that the `Format` class can be found. Please note that `Format` is defined as public so that it can be used by classes in other packages.

The program uses an `import` statement to get the class `Format`. You cannot import entire packages, such as `com.prenhall.*.*`. Only one asterisk (*) can be used in an `import` statement.

Note

The `format` method can be invoked from any class. If you create a new class in the same package with `Format`, you can invoke the `format` method using `ClassName.methodName` (e.g., `Format.format`). If you create a new class in a different package, you can invoke the `format` method using `packagename.ClassName.methodName` (e.g., `com.prenhall.mypackage.Format.format`).

KEY TERMS

actual parameter   131
argument   131
ambiguous invocation   139
divide and conquer   147
formal parameter (i.e., parameter)   130
information hiding   147
method   130
method abstraction   146
method overloading   137
method signature   131

modifier   130
package   154
pass-by-value   135
parameter   130
return type   130
return value   130
scope of variable   141
stepwise refinement   146
stub   149

CHAPTER SUMMARY

■ Making programs modular and reusable is one of the central goals in software engineering. Java provides many powerful constructs that help to achieve this goal. Methods are one such construct.

■ The method header specifies the *modifiers*, *return value type*, *method name*, and *parameters* of the method. The modifier, which is optional, tells the compiler how to call the method. The static modifier is used for all the methods in this chapter.

■ A method may return a value. The `returnValueType` is the data type of the value the method returns. If the method does not return a value, the `returnValueType` is the keyword `void`.

■ The *parameter list* refers to the type, order, and number of the parameters of a method. The method name and the parameter list together constitute the *method signature*. Parameters are optional; that is, a method may contain no parameters.

■ A return statement can also be used in a `void` method for terminating the method and returning to the method's caller. This is useful occasionally for circumventing the normal flow of control in a method.

■ The arguments that are passed to a method should have the same number, type, and order as the parameters in the method definition.

■ When a program calls a method, program control is transferred to the called method. A called method returns control to the caller when its return statement is executed or when its method-ending closing brace is reached.

■ A method with a nonvoid return value type can also be invoked as a statement in Java. In this case, the caller simply ignores the return value. In the majority of cases, a call to a method with return value is treated as a value. In some cases, however, the caller is not interested in the return value.

■ Each time a method is invoked, the system stores parameters, local variables, and system registers in a space known as a *stack*. When a method calls another method, the caller's stack space is kept intact, and new space is created to handle the new method call. When a method finishes its work and returns to its caller, its associated space is released.

■ A method can be overloaded. This means that two methods can have the same name as long as their method parameter lists differ.

■ The scope of a local variable is limited locally to a method. The scope of a local variable starts from its declaration and continues to the end of the block that contains the variable. A local variable must be declared before it can be used, and it must be initialized before it is referenced.

■ *Method abstraction* is achieved by separating the use of a method from its implementation. The client can use a method without knowing how it is implemented. The details of the implementation are encapsulated in the method and hidden from the client who invokes the method. This is known as *information hiding* or *encapsulation.*

■ Method abstraction modularizes programs in a neat, hierarchical manner. Programs written as collections of concise methods are easier to write, debug, maintain, and modify than would otherwise be the case. This writing style also promotes method reusability.

■ When implementing a large program, use the top-down or bottom-up coding approach. Do not write the entire program at once. This approach seems to take more time for coding (because you are repeatedly compiling and running the program), but it actually saves time and makes debugging easier.

REVIEW QUESTIONS

Sections 5.2–5.3

5.1   What are the benefits of using a method? How do you declare a method? How do you invoke a method?

5.2   What is the `return` type of a `main` method?

5.3   Can you simplify the `max` method in Listing 5.1 using the conditional operator?

5.4   True of false? A call to a method with a `void` return type is always a statement itself, but a call to a method with a nonvoid return type is always a component of an expression.

5.5   What would be wrong with not writing a `return` statement in a nonvoid method? Can you have a `return` statement in a `void` method, such as the following?

```java
public static void main(String[] args) {
  int i;
  while (true) {
    // Prompt the user to enter an integer
    String intString = JOptionPane.showInputDialog(
      "Enter an integer:");

    // Convert a string into int
    int i = Integer.parseInt(intString);
```

```
      if (i == 0)
        return;
      System.out.println("i = " + i);
    }
  }
```

Does the `return` statement in the following method cause syntax errors?

```java
public static void xMethod(double x, double y) {
  System.out.println(x + y);
  return x + y;
}
```

5.6 Define the terms parameter, argument, method signature.

5.7 Write method headers for the following methods:

- Computing a sales commission, given the sales amount and the commission rate.
- Printing the calendar for a month, given the month and year.
- Computing a square root.
- Testing whether a number is even, and returning `true` if it is.
- Printing a message a specified number of times.
- Computing the monthly payment, given the loan amount, number of years, and annual interest rate.
- Finding the corresponding uppercase letter, given a lowercase letter.

5.8 Identify and correct the errors in the following program:

```java
1  public class Test {
2    public static method1(int n, m) {
3      n += m;
4      xMethod(3.4);
5    }
6
7    public static int xMethod(int n) {
8      if (n > 0) return 1;
9      else if (n == 0) return 0;
10     else if (n < 0) return -1;
11   }
12 }
```

5.9 Reformat the following program according to the programming style and documentation guidelines proposed in §2.14, "Programming Style and Documentation." Use the next-line brace style.

```java
public class Test {
  public static double xMethod(double i,double j)
  {
  while (i<j) {
    j--;
  }
  return j;
  }
}
```

Section 5.5 Passing Parameters

5.10 How is an argument passed to a method? Can the argument have the same name as its parameter?

5.11 What is pass-by-value? Show the result of the following programs:

```
public class Test {
  public static void main(String[] args) {
    int max = 0;
    max(1, 2, max);
    System.out.println(max);
  }

  public static void max(
      int value1, int value2, int max) {
    if (value1 > value2)
      max = value1;
    else
      max = value2;
  }
}
```

(a)

```
public class Test {
  public static void main(String[] args) {
    // Initialize times
    int times = 3;
    System.out.println("Before the call,"
      + " variable times is " + times);

    // Invoke nPrintln and display times
    nPrintln("Welcome to Java!", times);
    System.out.println("After the call,"
      + "variable times is " + times);
  }

  // Print the message n times
  public static void nPrintln(
      String message, int n) {
    while (n > 0) {
      System.out.println("n = " + n);
      System.out.println(message);
      n--;
    }
  }
}
```

(b)

```
public class Test {
  public static void main(String[] args) {
    int i = 1;
    while (i <= 6) {
      xMethod(i, 2);
      i++;
    }
  }

  public static void xMethod(
      int i, int num) {
    for (int j = 1; j <= i; j++) {
      System.out.print(num + " ");
      num *= 2;
    }

    System.out.println();
  }
}
```

(c)

```
public class Test {
  public static void main(String[] args) {
    int i = 0;
    while (i <= 4) {
      xMethod(i);
      i++;
    }

    System.out.println("i is " + i);
  }

  public static void xMethod(int i) {
    do {
      if (i % 3 != 0)
        System.out.print(i + " ");
      i--;
    }
    while (i >= 1);

    System.out.println();
  }
}
```

(d)

5.12 For (a) in the preceding question, show the contents of the stack just before the method `max` is invoked, just entering `max`, just before `max` is returned, and right after `max` is returned.

Section 5.6 Overloading Methods

5.13 What is method overloading? Is it possible to define two methods that have the same name but different parameter types? Is it possible to define two methods in a class that have identical method names and parameter lists but with different return value types or different modifiers?

5.14   What is wrong in the following program?

```java
public class Test {
  public static void method(int x) {
  }

  public static int method(int y) {
    return y;
  }
}
```

Section 5.8 The Scope of Local Variables

5.15   Identify and correct the errors in the following program:

```java
1 public class Test {
2   public static void main(String[] args) {
3     nPrintln("Welcome to Java!", 5);
4   }
5
6   public static void nPrintln(String message, int n) {
7     int n = 1;
8     for (int i = 0; i < n; i++)
9       System.out.println(message);
10  }
11 }
```

Section 5.9 The Math Class

5.16   True or false? The argument for trigonometric methods represents an angle in radians.

5.17   Write an expression that returns a random integer between 34 and 55. Write an expression that returns a random integer between 0 and 999. Write an expression that returns a random number between 5.5 and 55.5. Write an expression that returns a random lowercase letter.

5.18   Evaluate the following method calls:

```
A. Math.sqrt(4)
B. Math.sin(2 * Math.PI)
C. Math.cos(2 * Math.PI)
D. Math.pow(2, 2)
E. Math.log(Math.E)
F. Math.exp(1)
G. Math.max(2, Math.min(3, 4))
H. Math.rint(-2.5)
I. Math.ceil(-2.5)
J. Math.floor(-2.5)
K. Math.round(-2.5f)
L. Math.round(-2.5)
M. Math.rint(2.5)
N. Math.ceil(2.5)
O. Math.floor(2.5)
P. Math.round(2.5f)
Q. Math.round(2.5)
R. Math.round(Math.abs(-2.5))
```

Section 5.12 (Optional) Packages

5.19   What are the benefits of using packages?

5.20   If a class uses the package statement "package java.chapter5", where should the source code be stored, and where should the .class files be stored? How do you make the class available for use by other programs?

5.21   Why do you have to import JOptionPane but not the Math class?

PROGRAMMING EXERCISES

Sections 5.2–5.7

5.1 (*Converting an uppercase letter to lowercase*) Write a method that converts an uppercase letter to a lowercase letter. Use the following method header:

```
public static char upperCaseToLowerCase(char ch)
```

For example, `upperCaseToLowerCase('B')` returns `b`. See Exercise 2.7 on how to convert an uppercase letter to lowercase.

5.2* (*Summing the digits in an integer*) Write a method that computes the sum of the digits in an integer. Use the following method header:

```
public static int sumDigits(long n)
```

For example, `sumDigits(234)` returns 2 + 3 + 4 = 9.

Hint

Use the % operator to extract digits, and the / operator to remove the extracted digit. For instance, to extract 4 from 234, use 234 % 10 (= 4). To remove 4 from 234, use 234 / 10 (= 23) Use a loop to repeatedly extract and remove the digit until all the digits are extracted.

5.3* (*Displaying an integer reversed*) Write the following method to display an integer in reverse order:

```
public static void reverse(int number)
```

For example, `reverse(3456)` displays `6543`.

5.4** (*Returning an integer reversed*) Write the following method to return an integer reversed:

```
public static int reverse(int number)
```

For example, `reverse(3456)` returns `6543`.

5.5* (*Sorting three numbers*) Write the following method to display three numbers in increasing order:

```
public static void sort(double num1, double num2, double num3)
```

5.6* (*Displaying patterns*) Write a method to display a pattern as follows:

```
        1
      2 1
    3 2 1
...
n n-1 ... 3 2 1
```

The method header is

```
public static void displayPattern(int n)
```

5.7* (*Computing the future investment value*) Write a method that computes future investment value at a given interest rate for a specified number of years. The future investment is determined using the formula in Exercise 2.9.

Use the following method header:

```
public static double futureInvestmentValue(
    double investmentAmount, double monthlyInterestRate, int years)
```

For example, `futureInvestmentValue(10000, 0.05/12, 5)` returns `12833.59`.

Write a test program that prompts the user to enter the investment amount (e.g., `1000`) and the interest rate (e.g., `9%`), and print a table that displays future value for the years from `1` to `30`, as shown below:

```
The amount invested: 1000
Annual interest rate: 9%
Years          Future Value
  1              1093.8
  2              1196.41
...
 29             13467.25
 30             14730.57
```

5.8 (*Conversions between Celsius and Fahrenheit*) Write a class that contains the following two methods:

```
/** Converts from Celsius to Fahrenheit */
public static double celsiusToFahrenheit(double celsius)
```

```
/** Converts from Fahrenheit to Celsius */
public static double fahrenheitToCelsius(double fahrenheit)
```

The formula for the conversion is:

```
fahrenheit = (9.0 / 5) * celsius + 32
```

Write a test program that invokes these methods to display the following tables:

Celsius	Fahrenheit	Fahrenheit	Celsius
40.0	105.0	120.0	48.89
39.0	102.2	110.0	43.33
...			
32.0	89.6	40.0	5.44
31.0	87.8	30.0	−1.11

5.9 (*Conversions between feet and meters*) Write a class that contains the following two methods:

```
/** Converts from feet to meters */
public static double footToMeter(double foot)
```

```
/** Converts from meters to feet */
public static double meterToFoot(double meter)
```

The formula for the conversion is:

```
meter = 0.305 * foot
```

Write a test program that invokes these methods to display the following tables:

Feet	Meters	Meters	Feet
1.0	0.305	20.0	65.574
2.0	0.61	25.0	81.967
...			
9.0	2.745	60.0	195.721
10.0	3.05	65.0	213.115

5.10   (*Computing GCD*) Write a method that returns the greatest common divisor between two positive integers, using the following header:

```
public static int gcd(int m, int n)
```

Write a test program that computes **gcd(24, 16)** and **gcd(255, 25)**.

5.11   (*Computing commissions*) Write a method that computes the commission, using the scheme in §4.8.2 "Example: Finding the Sales Amount." The header of the method is:

```
public static double computeCommission(double salesAmount)
```

Write a test program that displays the following table:

SalesAmount	Commission
10000	900.0
15000	1500.0
...	
95000	11100.0
100000	11700.0

5.12   (*Displaying characters*) Write a method that prints characters using the following header:

```
public static void printChars(char ch1, char ch2,
  int numberPerLine)
```

This method prints the characters between **ch1** and **ch2** with the specified numbers per line. Write a test program that prints ten characters per line from '**1**' and '**Z**.'

5.13*   (*Summing series*) Write a method to compute the following series:

$$m(i) = \frac{1}{2} + \frac{2}{3} + \cdots + \frac{i}{i + 1}$$

Write a test program that displays the following table:

i	m(i)
2	0.5
3	1.1667
...	
19	15.4523
20	16.4023

5.14*   (*Computing series*) Write a method to compute the following series:

$$m(i) = 4\left(1 - \frac{1}{3} + \frac{1}{5} - \frac{1}{7} + \frac{1}{9} - \frac{1}{11} + \frac{1}{13} - \cdots - \frac{1}{2i - 1} + \frac{1}{2i + 1}\right)$$

5.15*   (*Printing a tax table*) Use the **computeTax** methods in Listing 5.5, ComputeTaxWithMethod.java, to write a program that prints a 2002 tax table for taxable income from $50,000 to $60,000 with intervals of $50 for all four statuses, as follows:

Taxable Income	Single	Married Joint	Married Separate	Head of a House
50000	9846	7296	10398	8506
50050	9859	7309	10411	8519
...				
59950	12532	9982	13190	11192
60000	12546	9996	13205	11206

5.16* (*Revising Listing 4.11, PrimeNumber.java*) Write a program that meets the following requirements:

- Declare a method to determine whether an integer is a prime number. Use the following method header:

```
public static boolean isPrime(int num)
```

An integer greater than 1 is a *prime number* if its only divisor is 1 or itself. For example, `isPrime(11)` returns `true`, and `isPrime(9)` returns `false`.
- Use the `isPrime` method to find the first thousand prime numbers and display every ten prime numbers in a row, as follows:

```
2    3    5    7    11   13   17   19   23   29
31   37   41   43   47   53   59   61   67   71
73   79   83   89   97   ...
...
```

Section 5.9 The Math Class

5.17* (*Displaying matrix of 0s and 1s*) Write a method that displays an n by n matrix using the following header:

```
public static void printMatrix(int n)
```

Each element is 0 or 1, which is generated randomly. Write a test program that prints a 3 by 3 matrix that may look like this:

```
0 1 0
0 0 0
1 1 1
```

5.18 (*Using the Math.sqrt method*) Write a program that prints the following table using the `sqrt` method in the `Math` class.

Number	SquareRoot
0	0.0000
2	1.4142
...	
18	5.2426
20	5.4721

5.19* (*The MyTriangle class*) Create a class named `MyTriangle` that contains the following two methods:

```
/** Returns true if the sum of any two sides is
 *  greater than the third side. */
public static boolean isValid(
   double side1, double side2, double side3)

/** Returns the area of the triangle. */
public static double area(
   double side1, double side2, double side3)
```

The formula for computing the area is

$$s = (side1 + side2 + side3)/2;$$

$$area = \sqrt{s(s - side1)(s - side2)(s - side3)}$$

Write a test program that reads three sides for a triangle and computes the area if the input is valid. Otherwise, it displays that the input is invalid.

5.20   (*Using trigonometric methods*) Print the following table to display the `sin` value and `cos` value of degrees from **0** to **360** with increments of **10** degrees. Round the value to keep four digits after the decimal point.

Degree	Sin	Cos
0	0.0	1.0
10	0.1736	0.9848
...		
350	−0.1736	0.9848
360	0.0	1.0

5.21**(*Computing mean and standard deviation*) In business applications, you are often asked to compute the mean and standard deviation of data. The mean is simply the average of the numbers. The standard deviation is a statistic that tells you how tightly all the various data are clustered around the mean in a set of data. For example, what is the average age of the students in a class? How close are the ages? If all the students are the same age, the deviation is **0**. Write a program that generates ten random numbers between **0** and **1000**, and computes the mean and standard deviations of these numbers using the following formula:

$$mean = \frac{\sum_{i=1}^{n} x_i}{n} = \frac{x_1 + x_2 + \cdots + x_n}{n} \qquad deviation = \sqrt{\frac{\sum_{i=1}^{n} x_i^2 - \frac{\left(\sum_{i=1}^{n} x_i\right)^2}{n}}{n-1}}$$

5.22**(*Approximating the square root*) Implement the `sqrt` method. The square root of a number, `num`, can be approximated by repeatedly performing a calculation using the following formula:

`nextGuess = (lastGuess + (num / lastGuess)) / 2`

When `nextGuess` and `lastGuess` are almost identical, `nextGuess` is the approximated square root.

The initial guess will be the starting value of `lastGuess`. If the difference between `nextGuess` and `lastGuess` is less than a very small number, such as 0.0001, you can claim that `nextGuess` is the approximated square root of `num`.

Sections 5.10–5.11

5.23* (*Generating random characters*) Use the methods in `RandomCharacter` in Listing 5.6 to print one hundred uppercase letters and then one hundred single digits, and print ten per line.

5.24**(*Displaying current date and time*) Listing 2.8, ShowCurrentTime.java, displays the current time. Improve this example to display the current date and time. The calendar example in §5.11, "Method Abstraction and Stepwise Refinement," should give you some ideas on how to find year, month, and day.

5.25**(*Converting milliseconds to hours, minutes, and seconds*) Write a method that converts milliseconds to hours, minutes, and seconds using the following header:

`public static String convertMillis(long millis)`

The method returns a string as `hours:minutes:seconds`. For example, `convertMillis(5500)` returns a string `0:0:5`, `convertMillis(100000)` returns a string `0:1:40`, and `convertMillis(555550000)` returns a string `154:19:10`.

CHAPTER 6

ARRAYS

Objectives

- To describe why arrays are necessary in programming (§6.1).
- To learn the steps involved in using arrays: declaring array reference variables and creating arrays (§§6.2.1–6.2.2).
- To initialize the values in an array (§6.2.3).
- To access array elements using indexed variables (§6.2.4).
- To simplify programming using the JDK 1.5 `foreach` loops (§6.2.5).
- To declare, create, and initialize an array using an array initializer (§6.2.6).
- To copy contents from one array to another (§6.3).
- To develop and invoke methods with array arguments and return values (§§6.4–6.5).
- (Optional) To declare a method with variable-length argument list (§6.6).
- To search elements using the linear (§6.7.1) or binary (§6.7.2) search algorithm.
- To sort an array using the selection sort (§6.8.1).
- (Optional) To sort an array using the insertion sort algorithms (§6.8.2).
- To use the methods in the `Arrays` class (§6.9).
- To declare and create two-dimensional arrays (§6.10).
- (Optional) To declare and create multidimensional arrays (§6.11).

6.1 Introduction

Often you will have to store a large number of values during the execution of a program. Suppose, for instance, that you want to read one hundred numbers, compute their average, and find out how many numbers are above the average. Your program first reads the numbers and computes their average, and then compares each number with the average to determine whether it is above the average. The numbers must all be stored in variables in order to accomplish this task. You have to declare one hundred variables and repeatedly write almost identical code one hundred times. From the standpoint of practicality, it is impossible to write a program this way. An efficient, organized approach is needed. Java and all other high-level languages provide a data structure, the *array*, which stores a fixed-size sequential collection of elements of the same type.

6.2 Array Basics

An array is used to store a collection of data, but it is often more useful to think of an array as a collection of variables of the same type. Instead of declaring individual variables, such as `number0`, `number1`, ..., and `number99`, you declare one array variable such as `numbers` and use `numbers[0]`, `numbers[1]`, ..., and `numbers[99]` to represent individual variables. This section introduces how to declare array variables, create arrays, and process arrays using indexed variables.

6.2.1 Declaring Array Variables

To use an array in a program, you must declare a variable to reference the array, and you must specify the type of array the variable can reference. Here is the syntax for declaring an array variable:

```
dataType[] arrayRefVar;
```

or

```
dataType arrayRefVar[]; // This style is allowed, but not preferred
```

The following code snippets are examples of this syntax:

```
double[] myList;
```

or

```
double myList[]; // This style is allowed, but not preferred
```

 Note

The style `dataType[] arrayRefVar` is preferred. The style `dataType arrayRefVar[]` comes from the C/C++ language and was adopted in Java to accommodate C/C++ programmers.

6.2.2 Creating Arrays

Unlike declarations for primitive data type variables, the declaration of an array variable does not allocate any space in memory for the array. Only a storage location for the reference to an array is created. If a variable does not reference to an array, the value of the variable is `null`. You cannot assign elements to an array unless it has already been created. After an array variable is declared, you can create an array by using the `new` operator with the following syntax:

```
arrayRefVar = new dataType[arraySize];
```

This statement does two things: (1) it creates an array using `new dataType[arraySize]`; (2) it assigns the reference of the newly created array to the variable `arrayRefVar`.

Declaring an array variable, creating an array, and assigning the reference of the array to the variable can be combined in one statement, as shown below:

```
dataType[] arrayRefVar = new dataType[arraySize];
```

or

```
dataType arrayRefVar[] = new dataType[arraySize];
```

Here is an example of such a statement:

```
double[] myList = new double[10];
```

This statement declares an array variable, `myList`, creates an array of ten elements of `double` type, and assigns its reference to `myList`. Figure 6.1 illustrates an array with sample element values.

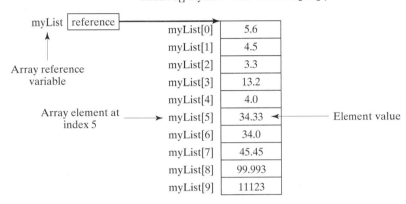

FIGURE 6.1   The array `myList` has ten elements of `double` type and `int` indices from 0 to 9.

 Note

An array variable that appears to hold an array actually contains a reference to that array. Strictly speaking, an array variable and an array are different, but most of the time the distinction between them can be ignored. Thus it is all right to say, for simplicity, that `myList` is an array, instead of stating, at greater length, that `myList` is a variable that contains a reference to an array of ten double elements. When the distinction makes a subtle difference, the longer phrase should be used.

array vs. array variable

6.2.3 Array Size and Default Values

When space for an array is allocated, the array size must be given, to specify the number of elements that can be stored in it. The size of an array cannot be changed after the array is created. Size can be obtained using `arrayRefVar.length`. For example, `myList.length` is 10.

array length

When an array is created, its elements are assigned the *default value* of `0` for the numeric primitive data types, `'\u0000'` for `char` types, and `false` for `boolean` types.

default values

6.2.4 Array Indexed Variables

The array elements are accessed through the index. Array indices are *0-based*; that is, they start from `0` to `arrayRefVar.length-1`. In the example in Figure 6.1, `myList` holds ten `double` values and the indices are from `0` to `9`.

array index
0-based

Each element in the array is represented using the following syntax, known as an *indexed variable*:

indexed variables

```
arrayRefVar[index];
```

For example, `myList[9]` represents the last element in the array `myList`.

Caution

Some languages use parentheses to reference an array element, as in `myList(9)`. But Java uses brackets, as in `myList[9]`.

After an array is created, an indexed variable can be used in the same way as a regular variable. For example, the following code adds the values in `myList[0]` and `myList[1]` to `myList[2]`:

```
myList[2] = myList[0] + myList[1];
```

The following loop assigns 0 to `myList[0]`, 1 to `myList[1]`, ..., and 9 to `myList[9]`:

```
for (int i = 0; i < myList.length; i++) {
  myList[i] = i;
}
```

6.2.5 Array Initializers

array initializer

Java has a shorthand notation, known as the *array initializer*, which combines declaring an array, creating an array, and initializing in one statement using the following syntax:

```
dataType[] arrayRefVar = {value0, value1, ..., valuek};
```

For example,

```
double[] myList = {1.9, 2.9, 3.4, 3.5};
```

This statement declares, creates, and initializes the array `myList` with four elements, which is equivalent to the statements shown below:

```
double[] myList = new double[4];
myList[0] = 1.9;
myList[1] = 2.9;
myList[2] = 3.4;
myList[3] = 3.5;
```

Caution

The **new** operator is not used in the array initializer syntax. Using an array initializer, you have to declare, create, and initialize the array all in one statement. Splitting it would cause a syntax error. Thus the next statement is wrong:

```
double[] myList;
myList = {1.9, 2.9, 3.4, 3.5};
```

6.2.6 Processing Arrays

When processing array elements, you will often use a **for** loop. Here are the reasons why:

- All of the elements in an array are of the same type. They are evenly processed in the same fashion by repeatedly using a loop.

- Since the size of the array is known, it is natural to use a **for** loop.

Here are some examples of processing arrays:

1. (*Initializing arrays with random values*) The following loop initializes the array `myList` with random values between `0.0` and `99.0`:

```
for (int i = 0; i < myList.length; i++) {
  myList[i] = Math.random() * 100;
}
```

2. (*Printing arrays*) To print an array, you have to print each element in the array using a loop like the one shown below.

```
for (int i = 0; i < myList.length; i++) {
  System.out.print(myList[i] + " ");
}
```

Tip

For an array of the `char[]` type, it can be printed using one print statement. For example, the following code displays `Dallas`:

print character array

```
char[] city = {'D', 'a', 'l', 'l', 'a', 's'};
System.out.println(city);
```

3. (*Summing all elements*) Use a variable named `total` to store the sum. Initially `total` is `0`. Add each element in the array to `total`, using a loop like this:

```
double total = 0;
for (int i = 0; i < myList.length; i++) {
  total += myList[i];
}
```

4. (*Finding the largest element*) Use a variable named `max` to store the largest element. Initially `max` is `myList[0]`. To find the largest element in the array `myList`, compare each element in `myList` with `max`, and update `max` if the element is greater than `max`.

```
double max = myList[0];
for (int i = 1; i < myList.length; i++) {
  if (myList[i] > max) max = myList[i];
}
```

5. (*Finding the smallest index of the largest element*) Often you need to locate the largest element in an array. If an array has more than one largest element, find the smallest index of such an element. Suppose the array `myList` is {1, 5, 3, 4, 5, 5}. The largest element is 5, and the smallest index for 5 is 1. Use a variable named `max` to store the largest element and a variable named `indexOfMax` to denote the index of the largest element. Initially `max` is `myList[0]`, and `indexOfMax` is `0`. Compare each element in `myList` with `max`, and update `max` and `indexOfMax` if the element is greater than `max`.

```
double max = myList[0];
int indexOfMax = 0;
for (int i = 1; i < myList.length; i++) {
  if (myList[i] > max) {
    max = myList[i];
    indexOfMax = i;
  }
}
```

What is the consequence if `(myList[i] > max)` is replaced by `(myList[i] >= max)`?

6.2.7 foreach Loops

JDK 1.5 introduced a new **for** loop, known as **foreach** *loop* or *enhanced* **for** *loop*, which enables you to traverse the complete array sequentially without using an index variable. For example, the following code displays all the elements in the array **myList**:

```
for (double element: myList) {
   System.out.println(element);
}
```

You can read the code as "for each element in **myList** do the following." Note that the variable, **element**, must be declared the same type as the elements in **myList**.

In general, the syntax for a **foreach** loop is

```
for (elementType element: arrayRefVar) {
   // Process the element
}
```

You still have to use an index variable if you wish to traverse the array in a different order or change the elements in the array.

6.2.8 Example: Testing Arrays

This section presents a program that reads six integers, finds the largest of them, and counts its occurrences. Suppose that you entered 3, 5, 2, 5, 5, 5, as shown in Figure 6.2; the program finds that the largest is 5 and that the occurrence count for 5 is 4.

FIGURE 6.2   The program finds the largest number and counts its occurrences.

An intuitive solution is to first read the numbers and store them in an array, then find the largest number in the array, and finally count the occurrences of the largest number in the array. The program is given in Listing 6.1.

LISTING 6.1 TestArray.java

```
1  import javax.swing.JOptionPane;
2
3  public class TestArray {
4    /** Main method */
5    public static void main(String[] args) {
6      final int TOTAL NUMBERS = 6;
7      int[] numbers = new int[TOTAL NUMBERS];
8
```

create array

```
9      // Read all numbers
10     for (int i = 0; i < numbers.length;  i++) {
11       String numString = JOptionPane.showInputDialog(
12         "Enter a number:");
13
14       // Convert string into integer
15       numbers[i] = Integer.parseInt(numString);
16     }
17
18     // Find the largest
19     int max = numbers[0];
20     for (int i = 1;  i < numbers.length ; i++) {
21       if (max < numbers[i] )
22         max = numbers[i];
23     }
24
25     // Find the occurrence of the largest number
26     int count = 0;
27     for (int i = 0;  i < numbers.length ; i++) {
28       if (numbers[i] == max ) count++;
29     }
30
31     // Prepare the result
32     String output = "The array is ";
33     for (int i = 0;  i < numbers.length ; i++) {
34       output += numbers[i] + " ";
35     }
36
37     output += "\nThe largest number is " + max;
38     output += "\nThe occurrence count of the largest number "
39       + "is " + count;
40
41     // Display the result
42     JOptionPane.showMessageDialog(null, output);
43   }
44 }
```

store numbers

update max

count occurrence

prepare output

output

The program declares and creates an array of six integers (line 7). It finds the largest number in the array (lines 19–23), counts its occurrences (lines 26–29), and displays the result (lines 32–42). To display the array, you need to display each element in the array using a loop.

Without using the **numbers** array, you would have to declare a variable for each number entered, because all the numbers are compared to the largest number to count its occurrences after it is found.

Caution

Accessing an array out of bounds is a common programming error that throws a runtime `ArrayIndexOutOfBoundsException`. To avoid it, make sure that you do not use an index beyond `arrayRefVar.length - 1`.

Programmers often mistakenly reference the first element in an array with index 1, so that the index of the tenth element becomes 10. This is called the *off-by-one error*.

`ArrayIndexOutOfBounds`
  Exception

off-by-one error

Tip

If you use an IDE such as JBuilder, NetBeans, or Eclipse, please refer to *Learning Java Effectively with JBuilder/NetBeans/Eclipse* in the supplements. It will show you how to use a debugger to inspect arrays.

debugging in IDE

6.2.9 Example: Assigning Grades

This example writes a program that reads student scores, gets the best score, and then assigns grades based on the following scheme:

$$\text{Grade is A if score is} >= \text{best} - 10;$$

$$\text{Grade is B if score is} >= \text{best} - 20;$$

$$\text{Grade is C if score is} >= \text{best} - 30;$$

$$\text{Grade is D if score is} >= \text{best} - 40;$$

$$\text{Grade is F otherwise.}$$

The program prompts the user to enter the total number of students, then prompts the user to enter all of the scores, and concludes by displaying the grades.

The program reads the scores, then finds the best score, and finally assigns grades to the students based on the preceding scheme. Listing 6.2 gives the solution to the problem. The output of a sample run of the program is shown in Figure 6.3.

LISTING 6.2 AssignGrade.java

```
1  import javax.swing.JOptionPane;
2
3  public class AssignGrade {
4    /** Main method */
5    public static void main(String[] args) {
6      // Get number of students
7      String numberOfStudentsString = JOptionPane.showInputDialog(
8        "Please enter number of students:");
9
10     // Convert string into integer
11     int numberOfStudents = Integer.parseInt(numberOfStudentsString);
12
13     int[] scores = new int[numberOfStudents]; // Array scores
14     int best = 0; // The best score
15     char grade; // The grade
16
17     // Read scores and find the best score
18     for (int i = 0; i < scores.length ; i++) {
19       String scoreString = JOptionPane.showInputDialog(
20         "Please enter a score:");
21
22       // Convert string into integer
23       scores[i] = Integer.parseInt(scoreString);
24       if (scores[i] > best)
25         best = scores[i];
26     }
27
28     // Declare and initialize output string
29     String output = "";
30
31     // Assign and display grades
32     for (int i = 0; i < scores.length ; i++) {
33       if (scores[i] >= best - 10)
34         grade = 'A';
35       else if (scores[i] >= best - 20)
36         grade = 'B';
```

number of students

create array

get a score

update best

assign grade

```
37        else if (scores[i] >= best - 30)
38          grade = 'C';
39        else if (scores[i] >= best - 40)
40          grade = 'D';
41        else
42          grade = 'F';
43
44        output += "Student " + i + " score is " +
45          scores[i] + " and grade is " + grade + "\n";
46      }
47
48      // Display the result
49      JOptionPane.showMessageDialog(null, output);
50    }
51  }
```

FIGURE 6.3   The program receives the number of students and their scores, and then assigns grades.

The program declares and creates scores as an array of int type in order to store the students' scores (line 13) after the user enters the number of students into numberOfStudents in lines 7–11. The size of the array is set at runtime; it cannot be changed once the array is created.

The array is not needed to find the best score, but it is needed to keep all of the scores so that grades can be assigned later on, and it is needed when scores are printed along with the students' grades.

6.3 Copying Arrays

Often, in a program, you need to duplicate an array or a part of an array. In such cases you could attempt to use the assignment statement (=), as follows:

```
list2 = list1;
```

This statement does not copy the contents of the array referenced by list1 to list2, but merely copies the reference value from list1 to list2. After this statement, list1 and list2 reference to the same array, as shown in Figure 6.4. The array previously referenced by list2 is no longer referenced; it becomes garbage, which will be automatically collected by the Java Virtual Machine.

In Java, you can use assignment statements to copy primitive data type variables, but not arrays. Assigning one array variable to another array variable actually copies one reference to another and makes both variables point to the same memory location.

copy reference

FIGURE 6.4   Before the assignment statement, `list1` and `list2` point to separate memory locations. After the assignment, the reference of the `list1` array is passed to `list2`.

There are three ways to copy arrays:

■ Use a loop to copy individual elements one by one.

■ Use the static `arraycopy` method in the `System` class.

■ Use the `clone` method to copy arrays; this will be introduced in Chapter 9, "Inheritance and Polymorphism."

You can write a loop to copy every element from the source array to the corresponding element in the target array. The following code, for instance, copies `sourceArray` to `targetArray` using a `for` loop:

```java
int[] sourceArray = {2, 3, 1, 5, 10};
int[] targetArray = new int[sourceArray.length];
for (int i = 0; i < sourceArray.length; i++) {
  targetArray[i] = sourceArray[i];
}
```

Another approach is to use the `arraycopy` method in the `java.lang.System` class to copy arrays instead of using a loop. The syntax for `arraycopy` is shown below:

```java
arraycopy(sourceArray, srcPos, targetArray, tarPos, length);
```

The parameters `srcPos` and `tarPos` indicate the starting positions in `sourceArray` and `targetArray`, respectively. The number of elements copied from `sourceArray` to `targetArray` is indicated by `length`. For example, you can rewrite the loop using the following statement:

```java
System.arraycopy(sourceArray, 0, targetArray, 0, sourceArray.length);
```

arraycopy method

The `arraycopy` *method* does not allocate memory space for the target array. The target array must have already been created with its memory space allocated. After the copying takes place, `targetArray` and `sourceArray` have the same content but independent memory locations.

 Note

The `arraycopy` method violates the Java naming convention. By convention, this method should be named **arrayCopy** (i.e., with an uppercase **C**).

6.4 Passing Arrays to Methods

Just as you can pass primitive type values to methods, you can also pass arrays to methods. For example, the following method displays the elements in an `int` array:

```
public static void printArray(int[] array) {
  for (int i = 0; i < array.length; i++) {
    System.out.print(array[i] + " ");
  }
}
```

You can invoke it by passing an array. For example, the following statement invokes the `printArray` method to display 3, 1, 2, 6, 4, and 2:

```
printArray(new int[]{3, 1, 2, 6, 4, 2});
```

 Note

The preceding statement creates an array using the following syntax:

```
new dataType[]{value0, value1, ..., valuek};
```

There is no explicit reference variable for the array. Such an array is called an *anonymous array*.

anonymous arrays

Java uses *pass-by-value* to pass arguments to a method. There are important differences between passing the values of variables of primitive data types and passing arrays.

pass-by-value

■ For an argument of a primitive type, the argument's value is passed.

■ For an argument of an array type, the value of the argument contains a reference to an array; this reference is passed to the method.

Take the following code, for example:

```
public class Test {
  public static void main(String[] args) {
    int x = 1; // x represents an int value
    int[] y = new int[10]; // y represents an array of int values

    m(x, y); // Invoke m with arguments x and y
    System.out.println("x is " + x);
    System.out.println("y[0] is " + y[0]);
  }

  public static void m(int number, int[] numbers) {
    number = 1001; // Assign a new value to number
    numbers[0] = 5555; // Assign a new value to numbers[0]
  }
}
```

You will see that after `m` is invoked, `x` remains 1, but `y[0]` is 5555. This is because `y` and `numbers` reference to the same array, although `y` and `numbers` are independent variables, as illustrated in Figure 6.5. When invoking `m(x, y)`, the values of `x` and `y` are passed to `number` and `numbers`. Since `y` contains the reference value to the array, `numbers` now contains the same reference value to the same array.

 Note

The JVM stores the array in an area of memory called the *heap*, which is used for dynamic memory allocation where blocks of memory are allocated and freed in an arbitrary order.

heap

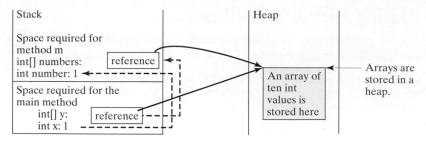

FIGURE 6.5 The primitive type value in x is passed to number, and the reference value in y is passed to numbers.

6.4.1   Example: Passing Array Arguments

Listing 6.3 gives another example that shows the difference between passing a primitive data type value and an array reference variable to a method.

The example contains two methods for swapping elements in an array. The first method, named swap, fails to swap two int arguments. The second method, named swapFirst-TwoInArray, successfully swaps the first two elements in the array argument. Figure 6.6 shows a sample run of the program.

LISTING 6.3   TestPassArray.java

false swap

swap array elements

```java
1  public class TestPassArray {
2    /** Main method */
3    public static void main(String[] args) {
4      int[] a = {1, 2};
5
6      // Swap elements using the swap method
7      System.out.println("Before invoking swap");
8      System.out.println("array is {" + a[0] + ", " + a[1] + "}");
9      swap(a[0], a[1]);
10     System.out.println("After invoking swap");
11     System.out.println("array is {" + a[0] + ", " + a[1] + "}");
12
13     // Swap elements using the swapFirstTwoInArray method
14     System.out.println("Before invoking swapFirstTwoInArray");
15     System.out.println("array is {" + a[0] + ", " + a[1] + "}");
16     swapFirstTwoInArray(a);
17     System.out.println("After invoking swapFirstTwoInArray");
18     System.out.println("array is {" + a[0] + ", " + a[1] + "}");
19   }
20
21   /** Swap two variables */
22   public static void swap(int n1, int n2) {
23     int temp = n1;
24     n1 = n2;
25     n2 = temp;
26   }
27
28   /** Swap the first two elements in the array */
29   public static void swapFirstTwoInArray(int[] array) {
30     int temp = array[0];
```

```
31      array[0] = array[1];
32      array[1] = temp;
33   }
34 }
```

```
Command Prompt                        _ □ X
C:\book>java TestPassArray
Before invoking swap
array is {1, 2}
After invoking swap
array is {1, 2}
Before invoking swapFirstTwoInArray
array is {1, 2}
After invoking swapFirstTwoInArray
array is {2, 1}

C:\book>_
```

FIGURE 6.6   The program attempts to swap two elements using the **swap** method and the **swapFirstTwoInArray** method.

As shown in Figure 6.6, the two elements are not swapped using the **swap** method. However, they are swapped using the **swapFirstTwoInArray** method. Since the parameters in the **swap** method are primitive type, the values of **a[0]** and **a[1]** are passed to **n1** and **n2** inside the method when invoking **swap(a[0], a[1])**. The memory locations for **n1** and **n2** are independent of the ones for **a[0]** and **a[1]**. The contents of the array are not affected by this call. This is pictured in Figure 6.7.

Invoke **swap(int n1, int n2)**. The primitive type values in **a[0]** and **a[1]** are passed to the **swap** method.

The arrays are stored in a heap.

Invoke **swapFirstTwoInArray(int[] array)**. The reference value in **a** is passed to the **swapFirstTwoInArray** method.

FIGURE 6.7   When passing an array to a method, the reference of the array is passed to the method.

The parameter in the **swapFirstTwoInArray** method is an array. As shown in Figure 6.7, the reference of the array is passed to the method. Thus the variables **a** (outside the method) and **array** (inside the method) both refer to the same array in the same memory location. Therefore, swapping **array[0]** with **array[1]** inside the method **swapFirstTwoInArray** is the same as swapping **a[0]** with **a[1]** outside of the method.

6.5 Returning an Array from a Method

You can pass arrays when invoking a method. A method may also return an array. For example, the method shown below returns an array that is the reversal of another array:

```
 1 public static int[] reverse(int[] list) {
 2   int[] result = new int[list.length];
 3
 4   for (int i = 0, j = result.length - 1;
 5        i < list.length; i++, j--) {
 6     result[j] = list[i];
 7   }
 8
 9   return result;
10 }
```

return array

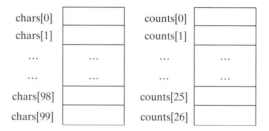

Line 2 creates a new array `result`. Lines 4–7 copies elements from array `list` to array `result`. Line 9 returns the array. For example, the following statement returns a new array `list2` with elements 6, 5, 4, 3, 2, 1:

```
int[] list1 = {1, 2, 3, 4, 5, 6};
int[] list2 = reverse(list1);
```

6.5.1 Example: Counting the Occurrences of Each Letter

Listing 6.4 presents a program to count the occurrences of each letter in an array of characters. The program does the following:

1. Generate one hundred lowercase letters randomly and assign them to an array of characters, as shown in Figure 6.8. You can obtain a random letter by using the **getRandom-LowerCaseLetter()** method in the **RandomCharacter** class in Listing 5.6.

chars[0]		counts[0]	
chars[1]		counts[1]	
...	...	...	...
...	...	...	...
chars[98]		counts[25]	
chars[99]		counts[26]	

FIGURE 6.8 The `chars` array stores 100 characters, and the `counts` array stores 26 counts, each of which counts the occurrences of a letter.

2. Count the occurrences of each letter in the array. To count the occurrences of each letter in the array, create an array, say `counts`, of twenty-six `int` values, each of which counts the occurrences of a letter, as shown in Figure 6.8. That is, `counts[0]` counts the number of a's, `counts[1]` counts the number of b's, and so on. Figure 6.9 shows a sample run of the program.

LISTING 6.4 CountLettersInArray.java

```
1 public class CountLettersInArray {
2   /** Main method */
3   public static void main(String args[]) {
4     // Declare and create an array
5     char[] chars = createArray();
6
7     // Display the array
8     System.out.println("The lowercase letters are:");
9     displayArray(chars);
```

create array

pass array

```
10
11      // Count the occurrences of each letter
12      int[] counts = countLetters(chars);                              return array
13
14      // Display counts
15      System.out.println();
16      System.out.println("The occurrences of each letter are:");
17       displayCounts(counts);                                          pass array
18    }
19
20    /** Create an array of characters */
21    public static char[] createArray() {
22      // Declare an array of characters and create it
23      char[] chars = new char[100];
24
25      // Create lowercase letters randomly and assign
26      // them to the array
27      for (int i = 0; i < chars.length; i++)
28        chars[i] = RandomCharacter.getRandomLowerCaseLetter();
29
30      // Return the array
31      return chars;
32    }
33
34    /** Display the array of characters */
35    public static void displayArray(char[] chars) {
36      // Display the characters in the array 20 on each line
37      for (int i = 0; i < chars.length; i++) {
38        if ((i + 1) % 20 == 0)
39          System.out.println(chars[i] + " ");
40        else
41          System.out.print(chars[i] + " ");
42      }
43    }
44
45    /** Count the occurrences of each letter */
46    public static int[] countLetters(char[] chars) {
47      // Declare and create an array of 26 int
48      int[] counts = new int[26];
49
50      // For each lowercase letter in the array, count it
51      for (int i = 0; i < chars.length; i++)
52        counts[chars[i] - 'a']++;                                       count
53
54      return counts;
55    }
56
57    /** Display counts */
58    public static void displayCounts(int[] counts) {
59      for (int i = 0; i < counts.length; i++) {
60        if ((i + 1) % 10 == 0)
61          System.out.println(counts[i] + " " + (char)(i + 'a'));
62        else
63          System.out.print(counts[i] + " " + (char)(i + 'a') + " ");
64      }
65    }
66 }
```

```
Command Prompt                                    _ □ ×
C:\book>java CountLettersInArray
The lowercase letters are:
a q e n s g a w g f o p e q q k w c d b
z e w p k x j g z j c z i t v b l r a q
m f b x z q p r s l u p u e g x v b l u
x x h t q y d z f x z y e n u o u d n k
a h o r s g b x l e u a c u l e j o l w

The occurrences of each letter are:
5 a 5 b 3 c 3 d 7 e 3 f 5 g 2 h 1 i 3 j
3 k 6 l 1 m 3 n 4 o 4 p 6 q 3 r 3 s 2 t
7 u 2 v 4 w 7 x 2 y 6 z
C:\book>_
```

Figure 6.9   The program generates one hundred lowercase letters randomly and counts the occurrences of each letter.

The `createArray` method (lines 21–32) generates an array of one hundred random lowercase letters. Line 5 invokes the method and assigns the array to `chars`. What would be wrong if you rewrote the code as follows?

```java
char[] chars = new char[100];
chars = createArray();
```

You would be creating two arrays. The first line would create an array by using `new char[100]`. The second line would create an array by invoking `createArray()` and assign the reference of the array to `chars`. The array created in the first line would be garbage because it is no longer referenced. Java automatically collects garbage behind the scenes. Your program would compile and run correctly, but it would create an array unnecessarily.

Invoking `getRandomLowerCaseLetter()` (line 28) returns a random lowercase letter. This method is defined in the `RandomCharacter` class in Listing 5.6.

The `countLetters` method (lines 46–55) returns an array of twenty-six `int` values, each of which stores the number of occurrences of a letter. The method processes each letter in the array and increases its count by one. A brute-force approach to count the occurrences of each letter might be as follows:

```java
for (int i = 0; i < chars.length; i++)
  if (counts[chars[i] == 'a')
    count[0]++;
  else if (counts[chars[i] == 'b')
    count[1]++;
  ...
```

But a better solution is given in lines 51–52.

```java
for (int i = 0; i < chars.length; i++)
  counts[chars[i] - 'a']++;
```

If the letter (`chars[i]`) is `'a'`, the corresponding count is `counts['a' - 'a']` (i.e., `counts[0]`). If the letter is `'b'`, the corresponding count is `counts['b' - 'a']` (i.e., `counts[1]`), since the Unicode of `'b'` is one more than that of `'a'`. If the letter is `'z'`, the corresponding count is `counts['z' - 'a']` (i.e., `counts[25]`), since the Unicode of `'z'` is `25` more than that of `'a'`.

Figure 6.10 shows the call stack and heap *during* and *after* executing `createArray`. See Review Question 6.14 to show the call stack and heap for other methods in the program.

(a) Executing
createArray in Line 5

(b) After exiting
createArray in Line 5

FIGURE 6.10   (a) An array of one hundred characters is created when executing `createArray`.
(b) This array is returned and assigned to the variable `chars` in the `main` method.

 ## 6.6 (Optional) Variable-Length Argument Lists

JDK 1.5 enables you to pass a variable number of arguments of the same type to a method.
The parameter in the method is declared as follows:

```
typeName... parameterName
```

In the method declaration, you specify the type followed by an ellipsis (. . .) Only one variable-length parameter may be specified in a method, and this parameter must be the last
parameter. Any regular parameters must precede it.

Java treats a variable-length parameter as an array. You can pass an array or a variable
number of arguments to a variable-length parameter. When invoking a method with a
variable number of arguments, Java creates an array and passes the arguments to it.
Listing 6.5 contains a method that prints the maximum value in a list of an unspecified
number of values.

LISTING 6.5 VarargsDemo.java

```
 1 public class VarargsDemo {
 2   public static void main(String args[]) {
 3     printMax(34, 3, 3, 2, 56.5);                          pass variable-
 4     printMax(new double[]{1, 2, 3});                        length arg list
 5   }                                                      pass an array arg
 6
 7   public static void printMax( double... numbers) {      a variable-
 8     if (numbers.length == 0) {                              length arg
 9       System.out.println("No argument passed");            parameter
10       return;
11     }
12
13     double result = numbers[0];
14
15     for (int i = 1; i < numbers.length; i++)
16       if (numbers[i] > result)
17         result = numbers[i];
18
19     System.out.println("The max value is " + result);
20   }
21 }
```

Line 3 invokes the `printMax` method with a variable-length argument list passed to the array
`numbers`. If no arguments are passed, the length of the array is `0` (line 7).

Line 4 invokes the `printMax` method with an array.

linear search
binary search

6.7 Searching Arrays

Searching is the process of looking for a specific element in an array; for example, discovering whether a certain score is included in a list of scores. Searching is a common task in computer programming. There are many algorithms and data structures devoted to searching. In this section, two commonly used approaches are discussed, *linear search* and *binary search*.

6.7.1 The Linear Search Approach

The linear search approach compares the key element **key** sequentially with each element in the array. The method continues to do so until the key matches an element in the array or the array is exhausted without a match being found. If a match is made, the linear search returns the index of the element in the array that matches the key. If no match is found, the search returns -1. The `linearSearch` method in Listing 6.6 gives the solution.

LISTING 6.6 LinearSearch.java

```
 1 public class LinearSearch {
 2   /** The method for finding a key in the list */
 3   public static int linearSearch(int[] list, int key) {
 4     for (int i = 0; i < list.length; i++) {
 5       if (key == list[i])
 6         return i;
 7     }
 8
 9     return -1;
10   }
11 }
```

```
                                          [0] [1] [2] ...
                                     list
                                     key  Compare key with list[i] for i = 0, 1, ...
```

Please trace the method using the following statements:

```
int[] list = {1, 4, 4, 2, 5, -3, 6, 2};
int i = linearSearch(list, 4);   // returns 1
int j = linearSearch(list, -4);  // returns -1
int k = linearSearch(list, -3);  // returns 5
```

The linear search method compares the key with each element in the array. The elements in the array can be in any order. On average, the algorithm will have to compare half of the elements in an array before finding the key if it exists. Since the execution time of a linear search increases linearly as the number of array elements increases, linear search is inefficient for a large array.

6.7.2 The Binary Search Approach

Binary search is the other common search approach for a list of values. For binary search to work, the elements in the array must already be ordered. Without loss of generality, assume that the array is in ascending order. The binary search first compares the key with the element in the middle of the array. Consider the following three cases:

- If the key is less than the middle element, you only need to continue to search for the key in the first half of the array.

- If the key is equal to the middle element, the search ends with a match.

- If the key is greater than the middle element, you only need to continue to search for the key in the second half of the array.

Clearly, the binary search method eliminates half of the array after each comparison. Suppose that the array has n elements. For convenience, let **n** be a power of **2**. After the first comparison, there are **n/2** elements left for further search; after the second comparison, there are **(n/2)/2** elements left for further search. After the kth comparison, there are $n/2^k$ elements left for further search. When $k = \log_2 n$, only one element is left in the array, and you only need one more comparison. Therefore, in the worst case, you need $\log_2 n + 1$ comparisons to find an element in the sorted array when using the binary search approach. For a list of **1024**

(2^{10}) elements, binary search requires only eleven comparisons in the worst case, whereas a linear search would take 1024 comparisons in the worst case.

The portion of the array being searched shrinks by half after each comparison. Let low and high denote, respectively, the first index and last index of the array that is currently being searched. Initially, low is 0 and high is list.length−1. Let mid denote the index of the middle element. So mid is (low + high)/2. Figure 6.11 shows how to find key 11 in the list {2, 4, 7, 10, 11, 45, 50, 59, 60, 66, 69, 70, 79} using binary search.

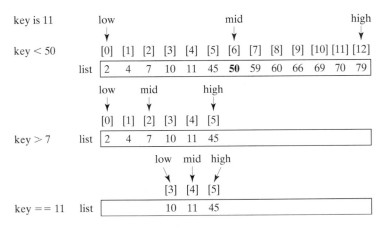

FIGURE 6.11   Binary search eliminates half of the list from further consideration after each comparison.

The binary search returns the index of the search key if it is contained in the list. Otherwise, it returns −(**insertion point + 1**). The insertion point is the point at which the key would be inserted into the list. For example, the insertion point for key 5 is 2, so the binary search returns −3; the insertion point for key 51 is 7, so the binary search returns −8.

You now know how the binary approach works. The next task is to implement it in Java, as shown in Listing 6.7.

LISTING 6.7   BinarySearch.java

```java
public class BinarySearch {
  /** Use binary search to find the key in the list */
  public static int binarySearch(int[] list, int key) {
    int low = 0;
    int high = list.length - 1;

    while (high >= low) {
      int mid = (low + high) / 2;
      if (key < list[mid])
        high = mid - 1;
      else if (key == list[mid])
        return mid;
      else
        low = mid + 1;
    }

    return -low - 1;
  }
}
```

You start by comparing the key with the middle element in the list whose low index is 0 and high index is list.length−1. If key < list[mid], set the high index to mid−1; if `key == list[mid]`, a match is found and return `mid`; if `key > list[mid]`, set the low index to `mid+1`. Continue the search until `low > high` or a match is found. If `low > high`, return `-1 - low`, where `low` is the insertion point.

What happens if `(high >= low)` in line 7 is replaced by `(high > low)`? The search would miss a possible matching element. Consider a list with just one element. The search would miss the element.

Does the method still work if there are duplicate elements in the list? Yes, as long as the elements are sorted in increasing order in the list. The method returns the index of one of the matching elements if the element is in the list.

Please trace the program using the following statements:

```
int[] list = {2, 4, 7, 10, 11, 45, 50, 59, 60, 66, 69, 70, 79};
int i = binarySearch(list, 2);   // returns 0
int j = binarySearch(list, 11);  // returns 4
int k = binarySearch(list, 12);  // returns -6
```

Note

Linear search is useful for finding an element in a small array or an unsorted array, but it is inefficient for large arrays. Binary search is more efficient, but requires that the array be pre-sorted.

6.8 Sorting Arrays

Sorting, like searching, is a common task in computer programming. It would be used, for instance, if you wanted to display the grades from Listing 6.2 in alphabetical order. Many different algorithms have been developed for sorting. This section introduces two simple, intuitive sorting algorithms: `selection sort` and `insertion sort`.

6.8.1 Selection Sort

Suppose that you want to sort a list in ascending order. Selection sort finds the largest number in the list and places it last. It then finds the largest number remaining and places it next to last, and so on until the list contains only a single number. Figure 6.12 shows how to sort a list {2, 9, 5, 4, 8, 1, 6} using selection sort.

You know how the selection sort approach works. The task now is to implement it in Java. Beginners find it difficult to develop a complete solution on the first attempt. Start by writing the code for the first iteration to find the largest element in the list and swap it with the last element, and then observe what would be different for the second iteration, the third, and so on. The insight this gives will enable you to write a loop that generalizes all the iterations.

The solution can be described as follows:

```
for (int i = list.length - 1; i >= 1; i--) {
  select the largest element in list[0..i];
  swap the largest with list[i], if necessary;
  // list[i] is in its correct position
  // The next iteration apply on list[0..i-1]
}
```

Listing 6.8 implements the solution.

LISTING **6.8** SelectionSort.java

```
1 public class SelectionSort {
2   /** The method for sorting the numbers */
3   public static void selectionSort(double[] list) {
4     for (int i = list.length - 1; i >= 1; i--) {
5       // Find the maximum in the list[0..i]
6       double currentMax = list[0];
7       int currentMaxIndex = 0;
```

```
 8
 9        for (int j = 1; j <= i; j++) {
10          if (currentMax < list[j]) {
11            currentMax = list[j];
12            currentMaxIndex = j;
13          }
14        }
15
16        // Swap list[i] with list[currentMaxIndex] if necessary;
17        if (currentMaxIndex != i) {
18          list[currentMaxIndex] = list[i];
19          list[i] = currentMax;
20        }
21      }
22    }
23 }
```

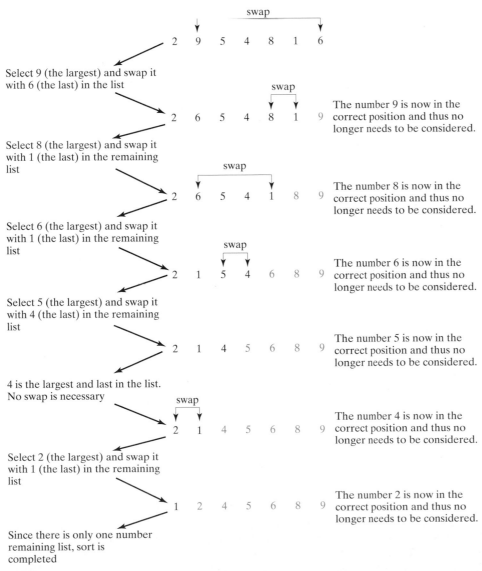

FIGURE 6.12   Selection sort repeatedly selects the largest number and swaps it with the last number in the list.

The `selectionSort(double[] list)` method sorts any array of double elements. The method is implemented with a nested **for** loop. The outer loop (with the loop control variable `i`) (line 4) is iterated in order to find the largest element in the list, which ranges from `list[0]` to `list[i]`, and exchange it with the current last element, `list[i]`.

The variable `i` is initially `list.length-1`. After each iteration of the outer loop, `list[i]` is in the right place. Eventually, all the elements are put in the right place; therefore, the whole list is sorted.

Please trace the method with the following statements:

```
selectionSort(new double[]{2, 1});
selectionSort(new double[]{2, 3, 1});
selectionSort(new double[]{1, 2, 1});
```

 ### 6.8.2   (Optional) Insertion Sort

Suppose that you want to sort a list in ascending order. The insertion-sort algorithm sorts a list of values by repeatedly inserting a new element into a sorted sublist until the whole list is sorted. Figure 6.13 shows how to sort a list {2, 9, 5, 4, 8, 1, 6} using insertion sort.

Step 1: Initially, the sorted sublist contains the first element in the list. Insert 9 to the sublist.   2 9 5 4 8 1 6

Step 2: The sorted sublist is {2, 9}. Insert 5 to the sublist.   2 9 5 4 8 1 6

Step 3: The sorted sublist is {2, 5, 9}. Insert 4 to the sublist.   2 5 9 4 8 1 6

Step 4: The sorted sublist is {2, 4, 5, 9}. Insert 8 to the sublist.   2 4 5 9 8 1 6

Step 5: The sorted sublist is {2, 4, 5, 8, 9}. Insert 1 to the sublist.   2 4 5 8 9 1 6

Step 6: The sorted sublist is {1, 2, 4, 5, 8, 9}. Insert 6 to the sublist.   1 2 4 5 8 9 6

Step 7: The entire list is now sorted   1 2 4 5 6 8 9

FIGURE 6.13   Insertion sort repeatedly inserts a new element into a sorted sublist.

The algorithm can be described as follows:

```
for (int i = 1; i < list.length; i++) {
  insert list[i] into a sorted sublist list[0..i-1] so that
  list[0..i] is sorted.
}
```

To insert `list[i]` into `list[0..i-1]`, save `list[i]` into a temporary variable, say `currentElement`. Move `list[i-1]` to `list[i]` if `list[i-1]` > `currentElement`, move `list[i-2]` to `list[i-1]` if `list[i-2]` > `currentElement`, and so on, until `list[i-k]` <= `currentElement`. Assign `currentElement` to `list[i-k+1]`. For example, to insert 4 into {2, 5, 9} in Step 3 in Figure 6.13, move `list[2]` (9) to `list[3]` since 9 > 4, move list[1] (5) to list[2] since 5 > 4. Finally, move currentElement (4) to list[1], as shown in Figure 6.14.

The algorithm can be expanded and implemented in Listing 6.9.

LISTING 6.9 `InsertionSort.java`

```
 1 public class InsertionSort {
 2   /** The method for sorting the numbers */
 3   public static void insertionSort(double[] list) {
 4     for (int i = 1; i < list.length; i++) {
 5       /** insert list[i] into a sorted sublist list[0..i-1] so that
 6            list[0..i] is sorted. */
 7       double currentElement = list[i];
 8       int k;
 9       for (k = i - 1; k >= 0 && list[k] > currentElement; k--) {
10         list[k + 1] = list[k];
11       }
12
13       // Insert the current element into list[k+1]
14       list[k + 1] = currentElement;
15     }
16   }
17 }
```

```
       [0] [1] [2] [3] [4] [5] [6]
list   | 2   5   9   4            |    Step 1: Save 4 to a temporary variable currentElement

       [0] [1] [2] [3] [4] [5] [6]
list   | 2   5       9            |    Step 2: Move list[2] to list[3]

       [0] [1] [2] [3] [4] [5] [6]
list   | 2       5   9            |    Step 3: Move list[1] to list[2]

       [0] [1] [2] [3] [4] [5] [6]
list   | 2   4   5   9            |    Step 4: Assign currentElement to list[1]
```

FIGURE 6.14   A new element is inserted into a sorted sublist.

The insertionSort(double[] list) method sorts any array of double elements. The method is implemented with a nested **for** loop. The outer loop (with the loop control variable i) (line 4) is iterated in order to obtain a sorted sublist, which ranges from list[0] to list[i]. The inner loop (with the loop control variable k) inserts list[i] into the sublist from list[0] to list[i-1].

Please trace the method with the following statements:

```
insertionSort(new double[]{2, 1});
insertionSort(new double[]{2, 3, 1});
insertionSort(new double[]{1, 2, 1});
```

6.9 The **Arrays** Class

The java.util.Arrays class contains various static methods for sorting and searching arrays, comparing arrays, and filling array elements. These methods are overloaded for all primitive types.

sort

You can use the `sort` method to sort a whole array or a partial array. For example, the following code sorts an array of numbers and an array of characters:

```
double[] numbers = {6.0, 4.4, 1.9, 2.9, 3.4, 3.5};
java.util.Arrays.sort(numbers);  // Sort the whole array

char[] chars = {'a', 'A', '4', 'F', 'D', 'P'};
java.util.Arrays.sort(chars, 1, 3);  // Sort part of the array
```

Invoking `sort(numbers)` sorts the whole array `numbers`. Invoking `sort(chars, 1, 3)` sorts a partial array from `chars[1]` to `chars[3-1]`.

binarySearch

You can use the `binarySearch` method to search for a key in an array. The array must be pre-sorted in increasing order. If the key is not in the array, the method returns −(*insertion point* + *1*). For example, the following code searches the keys in an array of integers and an array of characters:

```
int[] list = {2, 4, 7, 10, 11, 45, 50, 59, 60, 66, 69, 70, 79};
System.out.println("(1) Index is " +
  java.util.Arrays.binarySearch(list, 11));
System.out.println("(2) Index is " +
  java.util.Arrays.binarySearch(list, 12));

char[] chars = {'a', 'c', 'g', 'x', 'y', 'z'};
System.out.println("(3) Index is " +
  java.util.Arrays.binarySearch(chars, 'a'));
System.out.println("(4) Index is " +
  java.util.Arrays.binarySearch(chars, 't'));
```

The output of the preceding code is

(1) Index is 4

(2) Index is −6

(3) Index is 0

(4) Index is −4

equals example

You can use the `equals` method to check whether two arrays are equal. Two arrays are equal if they have the same contents. In the following code, `list1` and `list2` are equal, but `list2` and `list3` are not:

```
int[] list1 = {2, 4, 7, 10};
int[] list2 = {2, 4, 7, 10};
int[] list3 = {4, 2, 7, 10};
System.out.println(java.util.Arrays.equals(list1, list2) ); // true
System.out.println(java.util.Arrays.equals(list2, list3) ); // false
```

fill example

You can use the `fill` method to fill in the whole array or part of the array. For example, the following code fills `list1` with 5 and fills 8 into elements `list2[1]` and `list2[3-1]`:

```
int[] list1 = {2, 4, 7, 10};
int[] list2 = {2, 4, 7, 10};
java.util.Arrays.fill(list1, 5); // fill 5 to the whole array
java.util.Arrays.fill(list2, 1, 3, 8); // fill 8 to a partial array
```

6.10 Two-Dimensional Arrays

Thus far, you have used one-dimensional arrays to model linear collections of elements. You can use a two-dimensional array to represent a matrix or a table.

6.10.1 Declaring Variables of Two-Dimensional Arrays and Creating Two-Dimensional Arrays

Here is the syntax for declaring a two-dimensional array:

```
dataType[][] arrayRefVar;
```

or

```
dataType arrayRefVar[][]; // This style is allowed, but not preferred
```

As an example, here is how you would declare a two-dimensional array variable `matrix` of `int` values:

```
int[][] matrix;
```

or

```
int matrix[][]; // This style is allowed, but not preferred
```

You can create a two-dimensional array of 5 by 5 `int` values and assign it to `matrix` using this syntax:

```
matrix = new int[5][5];
```

Two subscripts are used in a two-dimensional array, one for the row, and the other for the column. As in a one-dimensional array, the index for each subscript is of the `int` type and starts from 0, as shown in Figure 6.15(a).

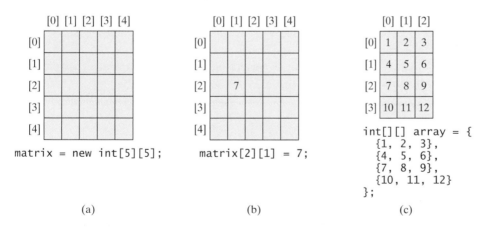

```
                                                    int[][] array = {
                                                      {1, 2, 3},
                                                      {4, 5, 6},
                                                      {7, 8, 9},
                                                      {10, 11, 12}
                                                    };
```

matrix = new int[5][5];   matrix[2][1] = 7;

(a)   (b)   (c)

FIGURE 6.15   The index of each subscript of a two-dimensional array is an `int` value starting from 0.

To assign the value 7 to a specific element at row 2 and column 1, as shown in Figure 6.15(b), you can use the following:

```
matrix[2][1] = 7;
```

 Caution

It is a common mistake to use `matrix[2, 1]` to access the element at row 2 and column 1. In Java, each subscript must be enclosed in a pair of square brackets.

You can also use an array initializer to declare, create, and initialize a two-dimensional array. For example, the following code in (a) creates an array with the specified initial values, as shown in Figure 6.15(c). This is equivalent to the code in (b).

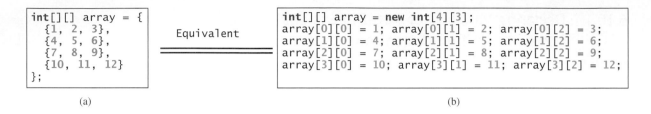

```
int[][] array = {
   {1, 2, 3},
   {4, 5, 6},
   {7, 8, 9},
   {10, 11, 12}
};
```

Equivalent

```
int[][] array = new int[4][3];
array[0][0] = 1; array[0][1] = 2; array[0][2] = 3;
array[1][0] = 4; array[1][1] = 5; array[1][2] = 6;
array[2][0] = 7; array[2][1] = 8; array[2][2] = 9;
array[3][0] = 10; array[3][1] = 11; array[3][2] = 12;
```

(a)   (b)

6.10.2. Obtaining the Lengths of Two-Dimensional Arrays

A two-dimensional array is actually an array in which each element is a one-dimensional array. The length of an array x is the number of elements in the array, which can be obtained using x.length. x[0], x[1], ..., and x[x.length-1] are arrays. Their lengths can be obtained using x[0].length, x[1].length, ..., and x[x.length-1].length.

For example, suppose x = new int[3][4], x[0], x[1], and x[2] are one-dimensional arrays and each contains four elements, as shown in Figure 6.16. x.length is 3, and x[0].length, x[1].length, and x[2].length are 4.

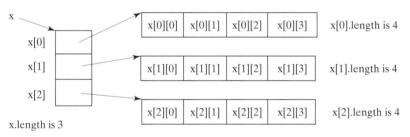

FIGURE 6.16   A two-dimensional array is a one-dimensional array in which each element is another one-dimensional array.

6.10.3   Ragged Arrays

Each row in a two-dimensional array is itself an array. Thus the rows can have different lengths. An array of this kind is known as a *ragged array*. Here is an example of creating a ragged array:

ragged array

```
int[][] triangleArray = {
   {1, 2, 3, 4, 5},
   {2, 3, 4, 5},
   {3, 4, 5},
   {4, 5},
   {5}
};
```

| 1 | 2 | 3 | 4 | 5 |

| 2 | 3 | 4 | 5 |

| 3 | 4 | 5 |

| 4 | 5 |

| 5 |

As can be seen, triangleArray[0].length is 5, triangleArray[1].length is 4, triangleArray[2].length is 3, triangleArray[3].length is 2, and triangle Array[4].length is 1.

If you don't know the values in a ragged array in advance, but you know the sizes, say the same as before, you can create a ragged array using the syntax that follows:

```
int[][] triangleArray = new int[5][];
triangleArray[0] = new int[5];
triangleArray[1] = new int[4];
triangleArray[2] = new int[3];
triangleArray[3] = new int[2];
triangleArray[4] = new int[1];
```

You can now assign values to the array. For example,

```
triangleArray[0][3] = 50;
triangleArray[4][0] = 45;
```

Note

The syntax `new int[5][]` for creating an array requires the first index to be specified. The syntax `new int[][]` would be wrong.

6.10.4. Processing Two-Dimensional Arrays

Suppose an array `matrix` is declared as follows:

```
int[][] matrix = new int[10][10];
```

Here are some examples of processing two-dimensional arrays:

1. (*Initializing arrays with random values*) The following loop initializes the array with random values between **0** and **99**:

```
for (int row = 0; row < matrix.length; row++) {
  for (int column = 0; column < matrix[row].length; column++) {
    matrix[row][column] = (int)(Math.random() * 100);
  }
}
```

2. (*Printing arrays*) To print a two-dimensional array, you have to print each element in the array using a loop like the following:

```
for (int row = 0; row < matrix.length; row++) {
  for (int column = 0; column < matrix[row].length; column++) {
    System.out.print(matrix[row][column] + " ");
  }

  System.out.println();
}
```

3. (*Summing all elements*) Use a variable named **total** to store the sum. Initially **total** is **0**. Add each element in the array to **total** using a loop like this:

```
int total = 0;
for (int row = 0; row < matrix.length; row++) {
  for (int column = 0; column < matrix[row].length; column++) {
    total += matrix[row][column];
  }
}
```

4. (*Summing elements by column*) For each column, use a variable named **total** to store its sum. Add each element in the column to **total** using a loop like this:

```
for (int column = 0; column < matrix[0].length; column++) {
  int total = 0;
  for (int row = 0; row < matrix.length; row++)
```

```
                     total += matrix[row][column];
          System.out.println("Sum for column " + column + " is " + total);
       }
```

5. (*Which row has the largest sum?*) Use variables `maxRow` and `indexOfMaxRow` to track the largest sum and index of the row. For each row, compute its sum, and update `maxRow` and `indexOfMaxRow` if the new sum is greater.

```
int maxRow = 0;
int indexOfMaxRow = 0;

// Get sum of the first row in maxRow
for (int column = 0; column < matrix[0].length; column++) {
  maxRow += matrix[0][column];
}

for (int row = 1; row < matrix.length; row++) {
  int totalOfThisRow = 0;
  for (int column = 0; column < matrix[row].length; column++) {
    totalOfThisRow += matrix[row][column];
    if (totalOfThisRow > maxRow) {
      maxRow = totalOfThisRow;
      indexOfMaxRow = row;
    }
  }
}

System.out.println("Row " + indexOfMaxRow
  + " has the maximum sum" + " of " + maxRow);
```

6.10.5 Example: Grading a Multiple-Choice Test

This example presents a program that grades multiple-choice tests. Suppose there are eight students and ten questions, and the answers are stored in a two-dimensional array. Each row records a student's answers to the questions. For example, the array shown below stores the test.

```
                        Students' Answers to the Questions:
                        0 1 2 3 4 5 6 7 8 9

            Student 0   A B A C C D E E A D
            Student 1   D B A B C A E E A D
            Student 2   E D D A C B E E A D
            Student 3   C B A E D C E E A D
            Student 4   A B D C C D E E A D
            Student 5   B B E C C D E E A D
            Student 6   B B A C C D E E A D
            Student 7   E B E C C D E E A D
```

The key is stored in a one-dimensional array:

```
                        Key to the Questions:
                        0 1 2 3 4 5 6 7 8 9
            Key        D B D C C D A E A D
```

Your program grades the test and displays the result, as shown in Figure 6.17.

The program compares each student's answers with the key, counts the number of correct answers, and displays it. Listing 6.10 gives the program.

LISTING 6.10   GradeExam.java

```java
1 public class GradeExam {
2   /** Main method */
3   public static void main(String args[]) {
4     // Students' answers to the questions
5     char[][] answers = {
6       {'A', 'B', 'A', 'C', 'C', 'D', 'E', 'E', 'A', 'D'},
7       {'D', 'B', 'A', 'B', 'C', 'A', 'E', 'E', 'A', 'D'},
8       {'E', 'D', 'D', 'A', 'C', 'B', 'E', 'E', 'A', 'D'},
9       {'C', 'B', 'A', 'E', 'D', 'C', 'E', 'E', 'A', 'D'},
10      {'A', 'B', 'D', 'C', 'C', 'D', 'E', 'E', 'A', 'D'},
11      {'B', 'B', 'E', 'C', 'C', 'D', 'E', 'E', 'A', 'D'},
12      {'B', 'B', 'A', 'C', 'C', 'D', 'E', 'E', 'A', 'D'},
13      {'E', 'B', 'E', 'C', 'C', 'D', 'E', 'E', 'A', 'D'}};
14
15    // Key to the questions
16    char[] keys = {'D', 'B', 'D', 'C', 'C', 'D', 'A', 'E', 'A', 'D'};
17
18    // Grade all answers
19    for (int i = 0; i < answers.length ; i++) {
20      // Grade one student
21      int correctCount = 0;
22      for (int j = 0; j < answers[i].length ; j++) {
23        if (answers[i][j] == keys[j] )
24          correctCount++;
25      }
26
27      System.out.println("Student " + i + "'s correct count is " +
28        correctCount);
29    }
30  }
31 }
```

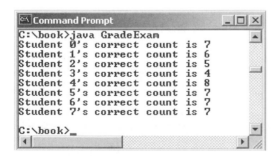

FIGURE 6.17   The program grades students' answers to the multiple-choice questions.

The statement in lines 5–13 declares, creates, and initializes a two-dimensional array of characters and assigns the reference to **answers** of the **char[][]** type.

The statement in line 16 declares, creates, and initializes an array of **char** values and assigns the reference to **keys** of the **char[][]** type.

Each row in the array **answers** stores a student's answer, which is graded by comparing it with the key in the array **keys**. The result is displayed immediately after a student's answer is graded.

6.10.6 (Optional) Example: Computing Taxes

Listing 5.5, ComputeTaxWithMethod.java, simplified Listing 3.4, ComputeTaxWithSelection-Statement.java. Listing 5.5 can be further improved using arrays. For each filing status, there are six tax rates. Each rate is applied to a certain amount of taxable income. For example, from the taxable income of $400,000 for a single filer, $6,000 is taxed at 10%, (27950 − 6000) at 15%, (67700 − 27950) at 27%, (141250 − 67700) at 30%, (307050 − 141250) at 35%, and (400000 − 307050) at 38.6%. The six rates are the same for all filing statuses, which can be represented in the following array:

```
double[] rates = {0.10, 0.15, 0.27, 0.30, 0.35, 0.386};
```

The brackets for each rate for all the filing statuses can be represented in a two-dimensional array as follows:

```
int[][] brackets = {
  {6000, 27950, 67700, 141250, 307050}, // Single filer
  {12000, 46700, 112850, 171950, 307050}, // Married jointly
  {6000, 23350, 56425, 85975, 153525}, // Married separately
  {10000, 37450, 96700, 156600, 307050} // Head of household
};
```

Suppose the taxable income is $400,000 for single filers, the tax can be computed as follows:

```
brackets[0][0] * rates[0] +
(brackets[0][1] - brackets[0][0]) * rates[1] +
(brackets[0][2] - brackets[0][1]) * rates[2] +
(brackets[0][3] - brackets[0][2]) * rates[3] +
(brackets[0][4] - brackets[0][3]) * rates[4] +
(400000 - brackets[0][4]) * rates[5]
```

Listing 6.11 gives the solution to the program.

LISTING 6.11 ComputeTax.java

```
1 import javax.swing.JOptionPane;
2
3 public class ComputeTax {
4   public static void main(String[] args) {
5     // Prompt the user to enter filing status
6     String statusString = JOptionPane.showInputDialog(
7       "Enter the filing status:\n" +
8       "(0-single filer, 1-married jointly,\n" +
9       "2-married separately, 3-head of household)");
10    int status = Integer.parseInt(statusString);
11
12    // Prompt the user to enter taxable income
13    String incomeString = JOptionPane.showInputDialog(
14      "Enter the taxable income:");
15    double income = Double.parseDouble(incomeString);
16
17    // Compute and display the result
18    JOptionPane.showMessageDialog(null, "Tax is " +
19      (int)(computeTax(status, income)  * 100) / 100.0);
20  }
21
22  public static double computeTax(int status, double income) {
23    double[] rates = {0.10, 0.15, 0.27, 0.30, 0.35, 0.386};
24
```

```
25      int[][] brackets = {
26        {6000, 27950, 67700, 141250, 307050}, // Single filer
27        {12000, 46700, 112850, 171950, 307050}, // Married jointly
28        {6000, 23350, 56425, 85975, 153525}, // Married separately
29        {10000, 37450, 96700, 156600, 307050} // Head of household
30      };
31
32      double tax = 0; // Tax to be computed
33
34      // Compute tax in the first bracket
35      if (income <= brackets[status][0])
36        return tax = income * rates[0]; //Done
37      else
38        tax = brackets[status][0] * rates[0];
39
40      // Compute tax in the 2nd, 3rd, 4th, and 5th brackets, if needed
41      for (int i = 1; i < brackets[0].length; i++) {
42        if (income > brackets[status][i])
43          tax += (brackets[status][i] - brackets[status][i - 1]) *
44            rates[i];
45        else {
46          tax += (income - brackets[status][i - 1]) * rates[i];
47          return tax; // Done
48        }
49      }
50
51      // Compute tax in the last (i.e., 6th) bracket
52      return  tax += (income - brackets[status][4]) * rates[5];
53    }
54  }
```

The `computeTax` method computes the tax for the taxable income of a given filing status. The tax for the first bracket (`0` to `brackets[status][0]`) is computed in lines 35–38. The taxes for the second, third, fourth, and fifth brackets are computed in the loop in lines 41–49. The tax for the last bracket is computed in line 52.

6.11 (Optional) Multidimensional Arrays

In the preceding section, you used a two-dimensional array to represent a matrix or a table. Occasionally, you will need to represent *n*-dimensional data structures. In Java, you can create *n*-dimensional arrays for any integer *n*.

The way to declare two-dimensional array variables and create two-dimensional arrays can be generalized to declare *n*-dimensional array variables and create *n*-dimensional arrays for *n* >= 3. For example, the following syntax declares a three-dimensional array variable `scores`, creates an array, and assigns its reference to `scores`:

```
double[][][] scores = new double[10][5][2];
```

A multidimensional array is actually an array in which each element is another array. A three-dimensional array consists of an array of two-dimensional arrays, each of which is an array of one-dimensional arrays. For example, suppose `x = new int[2][2][6]`, `x[0]`, and `x[1]` are two-dimensional arrays. `X[0][0]`, `x[0][1]`, `x[1][0]`, and `x[1][1]` are one-dimensional arrays and each contains five elements. `x.length` is `2`, `x[0].length` and `x[1].length` are `2`, and `X[0][0].length`, `x[0][1].length`, `x[1][0].length`, and `x[1][1].length` are `6`.

6.11.1 Example: Computing Student Scores

Listing 6.12 gives a program that calculates the total score for the students in a class. Suppose the scores are stored in a three-dimensional array named **scores**. The first index in **scores** refers to a student, the second refers to an exam, and the third refers to a part of the exam. Suppose there are seven students, five exams, and each exam has two parts: a multiple-choice part and a programming part. **scores[i][j][0]** represents the score on the multiple-choice part for the **i**'s student on the **j**'s exam. **scores[i][j][1]** represents the score on the programming part for the **i**'s student on the **j**'s exam. The program processes the **scores** array for all the students. For each student, it adds the two scores from all exams to **totalScore** and displays **totalScore**. Your program displays the total score for each student, as shown in Figure 6.18.

LISTING 6.12 TotalScore.java

```
 1 public class TotalScore {
 2   /** Main method */
 3   public static void main(String args[]) {
 4     double[][][] scores = {
 5       {{7.5, 20.5}, {9.0, 22.5}, {15, 33.5}, {13, 21.5}, {15, 2.5}},
 6       {{4.5, 21.5}, {9.0, 22.5}, {15, 34.5}, {12, 20.5}, {14, 9.5}},
 7       {{6.5, 30.5}, {9.4, 10.5}, {11, 33.5}, {11, 23.5}, {10, 2.5}},
 8       {{6.5, 23.5}, {9.4, 32.5}, {13, 34.5}, {11, 20.5}, {16, 7.5}},
 9       {{8.5, 26.5}, {9.4, 52.5}, {13, 36.5}, {13, 24.5}, {16, 2.5}},
10       {{9.5, 20.5}, {9.4, 42.5}, {13, 31.5}, {12, 20.5}, {16, 6.5}},
11       {{1.5, 29.5}, {6.4, 22.5}, {14, 30.5}, {10, 30.5}, {16, 6.0}}};
12
13     // Calculate and display total score for each student
14     for (int i = 0; i < scores.length; i++) {
15       double totalScore = 0;
16       for (int j = 0; j < scores[i].length; j++)
17         for (int k = 0; k < scores[i][j].length; k++)
18           totalScore += scores[i][j][k] ;
19
20       System.out.println("Student " + i + "'s score is " +
21         totalScore);
22     }
23   }
24 }
```

scores[0][3][0]

scores[0][3][1]

scores[6][4][1]

FIGURE 6.18 The program displays the total score for each student.

To understand this example, it is essential to know how data in the three-dimensional array are interpreted. **scores[0]** is a two-dimensional array that stores all the exam scores for the first student. **scores[0][0]** is {7.5, 20.5}, a one-dimensional array, which stores two scores for the two parts of the first student's first exam. **scores[0][0][0]** is 7.5, which is the score for the first part of the first student's first exam. `scores[5]` is a two-dimensional array that stores all the exam scores for the sixth student. `scores[5][4]` is {16, 6.5}, a one-dimensional array, which stores two scores for the two parts of the sixth student's fifth exam. `scores[5][4][1]` is 6.5, which is the score for the second part of the sixth student's fifth exam.

The statement in lines 4–11 declares, creates, and initializes a three-dimensional array of `double` values and assigns the reference to `scores` of the `double[][][]` type.

The scores for each student are added in lines 16–18, and the result is displayed in lines 20–21. The `for` loop in line 14 process the scores for all the students.

KEY TERMS

anonymous array 179	indexed variable 174
array 172	insertion sort 188
array initializer 172	linear search 188
binary search 185	multidimensional array 199
garbage collection 177	ragged array 194
index 171	selection sort 188

CHAPTER SUMMARY

- A variable is declared as an array type using the syntax `dataType[] arrayRefVar` or `dataType arrayRefVar[]`. The style `dataType[] arrayRefVar` is preferred, although `dataType arrayRefVar[]` is legal.

- Unlike declarations for primitive data type variables, the declaration of an array variable does not allocate any space in memory for the array. An array variable is not a primitive data type variable. An array variable contains a reference to an array.

- You cannot assign elements to an array unless it has already been created. You can create an array by using the `new` operator with the following syntax: `new dataType[arraySize]`.

- Each element in the array is represented using the syntax `arrayRefVar[index]`. An index must be an integer or an integer expression.

- After an array is created, its size becomes permanent and can be obtained using `arrayRefVar.length`. Since the index of an array always begins with 0, the last index is always `arrayRefVar.length - 1`. An out-of-bounds error will occur if you attempt to reference elements beyond the bounds of an array.

- Programmers often mistakenly reference the first element in an array with index 1, so that the index of the tenth element becomes 10. This is called the *index off-by-one error*.

- Java has a shorthand notation, known as the *array initializer*, which combines declaring an array, creating an array, and initializing in one statement using the syntax: `dataType[] arrayRefVar = {value0, value1, ..., valuek}`.

- When you pass an array argument to a method, you are actually passing the reference of the array; that is, the called method can modify the elements in the caller's original array.

- You can use arrays of arrays to form multidimensional arrays. For example, a two-dimensional array is declared as an array of arrays using the syntax `dataType[][] arrayRefVar` or `dataType arrayRefVar[][]`.

REVIEW QUESTIONS

Section 6.2 Array Basics

6.1 How do you declare and create an array?

6.2 How do you access elements of an array?

6.3 Is memory allocated when an array is declared? When is the memory allocated for an array? What is the printout of the following code?

```
int x = 30;
int[] numbers = new int[x];
x = 60;
System.out.println("x is " + x);
System.out.println("The size of numbers is " + numbers.length);
```

6.4 Indicate true or false for the following statements:

- Every element in an array has the same type.
- The array size is fixed after it is declared.
- The array size is fixed after it is created.
- The elements in an array must be of primitive data type.

6.5 Which of the following statements are valid array declarations?

```
int i = new int(30);
double d[] = new double[30];
char[] r = new char(1..30);
int i[] = (3, 4, 3, 2);
float f[] = {2.3, 4.5, 6.6};
char[] c = new char();
```

6.6 What is the array index type? What is the lowest index?

6.7 What is the representation of the third element in an array named a?

6.8 What happens when your program attempts to access an array element with an invalid index?

6.9 Identify and fix the errors in the following code:

```
1 public class Test {
2   public static void main(String[] args) {
3     double[100] r;
4
5     for (int i = 0; i < r.length(); i++);
6       r(i) = Math.random * 100;
7   }
8 }
```

Section 6.3 Copying Arrays

6.10 Use the arraycopy() method to copy the following array to a target array t:

```
int[] source = {3, 4, 5};
```

6.11 Once an array is created, its size cannot be changed. Does the following code resize the array?

```
int[] myList;
myList = new int[10];
// Some time later you want to assign a new array to myList
myList = new int[20];
```

Sections 6.4–6.5

6.12   When an array is passed to a method, a new array is created and passed to the method. Is this true?

6.13   Show the output of the following two programs:

```java
public class Test {
  public static void main(String[] args) {
    int number = 0;
    int[] numbers = new int[1];

    m(number, numbers);

    System.out.println("number is " + number
      + " and numbers[0] is " + numbers[0]);
  }

  public static void m(int x, int[] y) {
    x = 3;
    y[0] = 3;
  }
}
```

(a)

```java
public class Test {
  public static void main(String[] args) {
    int[] list = {1, 2, 3, 4, 5};
    reverse(list);
    for (int i = 0; i < list.length; i++)
      System.out.print(list[i] + " ");
  }

  public static void reverse(int[] list) {
    int[] newList = new int[list.length];

    for (int i = 0; i < list.length; i++)
      newList[i] = list[list.length - 1 - i];

    list = newList;
  }
}
```

(b)

6.14   Where are the arrays stored during execution? Show the contents of the stack and heap during and after executing createArray, displayArray, countLetters, displayCounts in Listing 6.4,

Section 6.6 Variable-Length Argument Lists

6.15   What is wrong in the following method declaration?

```java
public static void print(String... strings, double... numbers)
public static void print(double... numbers, String name)
public static double... print(double d1, double d2)
```

6.16   Can you invoke the printMax method in Listing 6.5 using the following statements?

```java
printMax(1, 2, 2, 1, 4);
printMax(new double[]{1, 2, 3});
printMax(new int[]{1, 2, 3});
```

Sections 6.7–6.8

6.17   Use Figure 6.11 as an example to show how to apply the binary search approach to a search for key 10 and key 12 in list {2, 4, 7, 10, 11, 45, 50, 59, 60, 66, 69, 70, 79}.

6.18   Use Figure 6.12 as an example to show how to apply the selection sort approach to sort {3.4, 5, 3, 3.5, 2.2, 1.9, 2}.

6.19   Use Figure 6.13 as an example to show how to apply the insertion sort approach to sort {3.4, 5, 3, 3.5, 2.2, 1.9, 2}.

6.20   How do you modify the selectionSort method in Listing 6.8 to sort numbers in decreasing order?

6.21   How do you modify the insertionSort method in Listing 6.9 to sort numbers in decreasing order?

Section 6.9 The **Arrays** Class

6.22 What types of array can be sorted using the `java.util.Arrays.sort` method? Does this `sort` method create a new array?

6.23 To apply `java.util.Arrays.binarySearch(array, key)`, should the array be sorted in increasing order, in decreasing order, or either?

6.24 Show the contents of the array after the execution of each line.

```
int[] list = {2, 4, 7, 10};
java.util.Arrays.fill(list, 7);
java.util.Arrays.fill(list, 1, 3, 8);
System.out.print(java.util.Arrays.equals(list, list));
```

Section 6.10 Two-Dimensional Arrays

6.25 Declare and create a 4 × 5 `int` matrix.

6.26 Can the rows in a two-dimensional array have different lengths?

6.27 What is the output of the following code?

```
int[][] array = new int[5][6];
int[] x = {1, 2};
array[0] = x;
System.out.println("array[0][1] is " + array[0][1]);
```

6.28 Which of the following statements are valid array declarations?

```
int[][] r = new int[2];
int[] x = new int[];
int[][] y = new int[3][];
```

PROGRAMMING EXERCISES

Section 6.2 Array Basics

6.1 (*Analyzing input*) Write a program that reads ten numbers, computes their average, and finds out how many numbers are above the average.

6.2 (*Alternative solution to Listing 6.1, TestArray.java*) The solution of Listing 6.1 counts the occurrences of the largest number by comparing *each number* with the largest. So you have to use an array to store all the numbers. Another way to solve the problem is to maintain two variables, `max` and `count`. `max` stores the current max number, and `count` stores its occurrences. Initially, assign the first number to `max` and `1` to `count`. Compare each subsequent number with `max`. If the number is greater than `max`, assign it to `max` and reset `count` to `1`. If the number is equal to `max`, increment `count` by `1`. Use this approach to rewrite Listing 6.1.

6.3 (*Reversing the numbers entered*) Write a program that reads ten integers and displays them in the reverse of the order in which they were read.

6.4 (*Analyzing scores*) Write a program that reads an unspecified number of scores and determines how many scores are above or equal to the average and how many scores are below the average. Enter a negative number to signify the end of the input. Assume that the maximum number of scores is `100`.

6.5** (*Printing distinct numbers*) Write a program that reads in ten numbers and displays distinct numbers (i.e., if a number appears multiple times, it is displayed only once). Hint: Read a number and store it to an array if it is new. If the number is already in the array, discard it. After the input, the array contains the distinct numbers.

6.6* (*Revising Listing 4.11, PrimeNumber.java*) Listing 4.11 determines whether a number n is prime by checking whether 2, 3, 4, 5, 6, ..., n/2 is a divisor. If a divisor is found, n is not prime. A more efficient approach to determine whether n is prime is to check whether any of the prime numbers less than or equal to $\sqrt{n}$ can divide n evenly. If not, n is prime. Rewrite Listing 4.11 to display the first fifty prime numbers using this approach. You need to use an array to store the prime numbers and later use them to check whether they are possible divisors for n.

6.7* (*Counting single digits*) Write a program that generates one hundred random integers between 0 and 9 and displays the count for each number. Hint: Use `(int)(Math.random() * 10)` to generate a random integer between 0 and 9. Use an array of ten integers, say `counts`, to store the counts for the number of 0's, 1's, ..., 9's.

Sections 6.4–6.5

6.8 (*Averaging an array*) Write two overloaded methods that return the average of an array with the following headers:

```
public static int average(int[] array);
public static double average(double[] array);
```

Use {1, 2, 3, 4, 5, 6} and {6.0, 4.4, 1.9, 2.9, 3.4, 3.5} to test the methods.

6.9 (*Finding the smallest element*) Write a method that finds the smallest element in an array of integers. Use {1, 2, 4, 5, 10, 100, 2, -22} to test the method.

6.10 (*Finding the index of the smallest element*) Write a method that returns the index of the smallest element in an array of integers. If there are more than one such elements, return the smallest index. Use {1, 2, 4, 5, 10, 100, 2, -22} to test the method.

6.11* (*Computing deviation*) Exercise 5.21 computes the standard deviation of numbers. This exercise uses a different but equivalent formula to compute the standard deviation of n numbers.

$$mean = \frac{\sum_{i=1}^{n} x_i}{n} = \frac{x_1 + x_2 + \cdots + x_n}{n} \qquad deviation = \sqrt{\frac{\sum_{i=1}^{n} (x_i - mean)^2}{n - 1}}$$

To compute deviation with this formula, you have to store the individual numbers using an array, so that they can be used after the mean is obtained. Use {1, 2, 3, 4, 5, 6, 7, 8, 9, 10} to test the method.

6.12* (*Reversing an array*) The `reverse` method in §6.5 reverses an array by copying it to a new array. Rewrite the method without creating new arrays.

6.13* (*Increasing array size*) Once an array is created, its size is fixed. Occasionally, you need to add more values to an array, but it is full. In such cases, you can create a new, larger array to replace the existing array. Write a method with the following header:

```
public static int[] doubleCapacity(int[] list)
```

The method returns a new array that doubles the size of the parameter `list`.

Section 6.6 Variable-Length Argument Lists

6.14 (*Computing average*) Write a method that returns the average of an unspecified number of numeric arguments.

Sections 6.7–6.9

6.15 (*Finding the sales amount*) Rewrite Listing 4.7, FindSalesAmount.java, using the binary search approach. Since the sales amount is between 1 and COMMISSION_SOUGHT/0.08, you can use a binary search to improve Listing 4.7.

6.16 (*Timing execution*) Write a program that randomly generates an array of 100000 integers and a key. Estimate the execution time of invoking the linearSearch method in Listing 6.6. Sort the array and estimate the execution time of invoking the binarySearch method in Listing 6.7. You can use the following code template to obtain the execution time:

```
long startTime = System.currentTimeMillis();
perform the task;
long endTime = System.currentTimeMillis();
long executionTime = endTime - startTime;
```

6.17* (*Revising selection sort*) In §6.8, you used selection sort to sort an array. The selection sort method repeatedly finds the largest number in the current array and swaps it with the last number in the array. Rewrite this example by finding the smallest number and swapping it with the first number in the array.

6.18* * (*Bubble sort*) Write a sort method that uses the bubble-sort algorithm. The bubble-sort algorithm makes several passes through the array. On each pass, successive neighboring pairs are compared. If a pair is in decreasing order, its values are swapped; otherwise, the values remain unchanged. The technique is called a *bubble sort* or *sinking sort* because the smaller values gradually "bubble" their way to the top and the larger values sink to the bottom.

The algorithm can be described as follows:

```
boolean changed = true;
do {
  changed = false;
  for (int j = 0; j < list.length - 1; j++)
    if (list[j] > list[j + 1]) {
      swap list[j] with list[j + 1];
      changed = true;
    }
} while (changed);
```

Clearly, the list is in increasing order when the loop terminates. It is easy to show that the **do** loop executes at most list.length –1 times.

Use {6.0, 4.4, 1.9, 2.9, 3.4, 2.9, 3.5} to test the method.

6.19* * (*Sorting students*) Write a program that prompts the user to enter the number of students, and student names and their scores, and prints the student names in decreasing order of their scores.

Section 6.10 Two-Dimensional Arrays

6.20* (*Summing all the numbers in a matrix*) Write a method that sums all the integers in a matrix of integers. Use {{1, 2, 4, 5}, {6, 7, 8, 9}, {10, 11, 12, 13}, {14, 15, 16, 17}} to test the method.

6.21* (*Summing the major diagonal in a matrix*) Write a method that sums all the integers in the major diagonal in a matrix of integers. Use {{1, 2, 4, 5}, {6, 7, 8, 9}, {10, 11, 12, 13}, {14, 15, 16, 17}} to test the method.

6.22* (*Sorting students on grades*) Rewrite Listing 6.10, GradeExam.java, to display the students in increasing order of the number of correct answers.

6.23* (*Computing the weekly hours for each employee*) Suppose the weekly hours for all employees are stored in a two-dimensional array. Each row records an employee's seven-day work hours with seven columns. For example, the following array stores the work hours for eight employees. Write a program that displays employees and their total hours in decreasing order of the total hours.

	Su	M	T	W	H	F	Sa
Employee 0	2	4	3	4	5	8	8
Employee 1	7	3	4	3	3	4	4
Employee 2	3	3	4	3	3	2	2
Employee 3	9	3	4	7	3	4	1
Employee 4	3	5	4	3	6	3	8
Employee 5	3	4	4	6	3	4	4
Employee 6	3	7	4	8	3	8	4
Employee 7	6	3	5	9	2	7	9

6.24 (*Adding two matrices*) Write a method to add two matrices. The header of the method is as follows:

```
public static int[][] addMatrix(int[][] a, int[][] b)
```

In order to be added, the two matrices must have the same dimensions and the same or compatible types of elements. As shown below, two matrices are added by adding the two elements of the arrays with the same index:

$$
\begin{pmatrix}
a_{11} & a_{12} & a_{13} & a_{14} & a_{15} \\
a_{21} & a_{22} & a_{23} & a_{24} & a_{25} \\
a_{31} & a_{32} & a_{33} & a_{34} & a_{35} \\
a_{41} & a_{42} & a_{43} & a_{44} & a_{45} \\
a_{51} & a_{52} & a_{53} & a_{54} & a_{55}
\end{pmatrix}
+
\begin{pmatrix}
b_{11} & b_{12} & b_{13} & b_{14} & b_{15} \\
b_{21} & b_{22} & b_{23} & b_{24} & b_{25} \\
b_{31} & b_{32} & b_{33} & b_{34} & b_{35} \\
b_{41} & b_{42} & b_{43} & b_{44} & b_{45} \\
b_{51} & b_{52} & b_{53} & b_{54} & b_{55}
\end{pmatrix}
$$

$$
=
\begin{pmatrix}
a_{11}+b_{11} & a_{12}+b_{12} & a_{13}+b_{13} & a_{14}+b_{14} & a_{15}+b_{15} \\
a_{21}+b_{21} & a_{22}+b_{22} & a_{23}+b_{23} & a_{24}+b_{24} & a_{25}+b_{25} \\
a_{31}+b_{31} & a_{32}+b_{32} & a_{33}+b_{33} & a_{34}+b_{34} & a_{35}+b_{35} \\
a_{41}+b_{41} & a_{42}+b_{42} & a_{43}+b_{43} & a_{44}+b_{44} & a_{45}+b_{45} \\
a_{51}+b_{51} & a_{52}+b_{52} & a_{53}+b_{53} & a_{54}+b_{54} & a_{55}+b_{55}
\end{pmatrix}
$$

6.25** (*Multiplying two matrices*) Write a method to multiply two matrices. The header of the method is as follows:

```
public static int[][] multiplyMatrix(int[][] a, int[][] b)
```

To multiply matrix **a** by matrix **b**, the number of columns in **a** must be the same as the number of rows in **b**, and the two matrices must have elements of the same or compatible types. Let **c** be the result of the multiplication, and **a**, **b**, and **c** are denoted as follows:

$$\begin{pmatrix} a_{11} & a_{12} & a_{13} & a_{14} & a_{15} \\ a_{21} & a_{22} & a_{23} & a_{24} & a_{25} \\ a_{31} & a_{32} & a_{33} & a_{34} & a_{35} \\ a_{41} & a_{42} & a_{43} & a_{44} & a_{45} \\ a_{51} & a_{52} & a_{53} & a_{54} & a_{55} \end{pmatrix} \times \begin{pmatrix} b_{11} & b_{12} & b_{13} & b_{14} & b_{15} \\ b_{21} & b_{22} & b_{23} & b_{24} & b_{25} \\ b_{31} & b_{32} & b_{33} & b_{34} & b_{34} \\ b_{41} & b_{42} & b_{43} & b_{44} & b_{44} \\ b_{51} & b_{52} & b_{53} & b_{54} & b_{54} \end{pmatrix} =$$

$$\begin{pmatrix} c_{11} & c_{12} & c_{13} & c_{14} & c_{15} \\ c_{21} & c_{22} & c_{23} & c_{24} & c_{25} \\ c_{31} & c_{32} & c_{33} & c_{34} & c_{35} \\ c_{41} & c_{42} & c_{43} & c_{44} & c_{45} \\ c_{51} & c_{52} & c_{53} & c_{54} & c_{55} \end{pmatrix}$$

where $c_{ij} = a_{i1} \times b_{1j} + a_{i2} \times b_{2j} + a_{i3} \times b_{3j} + a_{i4} \times b_{4j} + a_{i5} \times b_{5j}$.

6.26* (*TicTacToe board*) Write a program that randomly fills in 0s and 1s into a TicTacToe board, prints the board, and finds the rows, columns, or diagonals with all 0s or 1s. Use a two-dimensional array to represent a TicTacToe board. Here is a sample run of the program:

```
001
001
111
All 0's on row 0
All 1's on row 2
All 1's on column 2
```

6.27** (*Checker board*) Write a program that randomly fills in 0s and 1s into an 8×8 checker board, prints the board, and finds the rows, columns, or diagonals with all 0s or 1s. Use a two-dimensional array to represent a checker board. Here is a sample run of the program:

```
10101000
10100001
11100011
10100001
11100111
10000001
10100111
00100001
All 0's on subdiagonal
```

6.28***(*Playing a TicTacToe game*) In a game of TicTacToe, two players take turns marking an available cell in a 3×3 grid with their respective tokens (either X or O). When one player has placed three tokens in a horizontal, vertical, or diagonal row on the grid, the game is over and that player has won. A draw (no winner) occurs when all the cells on the grid have been filled with tokens and neither player has achieved a win. Create a program for playing TicTacToe, as follows:

1. The program prompts the first player to enter an X token, and then prompts the second player to enter an O token. Whenever a token is entered,

the program refreshes the board and determines the status of the game (win, draw, or unfinished).

2. To place a token, display two dialog boxes to prompt the user to enter the row and the column for the token.

6.29*** (*Least common multiple*) Write a program that prompts the user to enter two integers and finds their least common multiple (LCM). The LCM of two numbers is the smallest number that is a multiple of both. For example, the LCM for 8 and 12 is 24, for 15 and 25 it is 75, and for 120 and 150 it is 600. There are many ways to find the LCM. In this exercise, you will use the approach described as follows:

To find the LCM of two numbers, first create a prime factor table for each number. The first column of the table consists of all the prime factors, and the second column tracks the occurrence of the corresponding prime factor in the number. For example, the prime factors for 120 are 2, 2, 2, 3, 5, so the prime factor table for number 120 is shown as follows:

prime factors for 120	# of occurrence		
2	3	table[0][0] = 2	table[0][1] = 3
3	1	table[1][0] = 3	table[1][1] = 1
5	1	table[2][0] = 5	table[2][1] = 1

The prime factors for 150 are 2, 3, 5, 5, so the prime factor table for number 150 is shown as follows:

prime factors for 120	# of occurrence		
2	1	table[0][0] = 2	table[0][1] = 1
3	1	table[1][0] = 3	table[1][1] = 1
5	2	table[2][0] = 5	table[2][1] = 2

The LCM of the two numbers consists of the factors with the most frequent occurrence in the two numbers. So the LCM for 120 and 150 is $2 \times 2 \times 2 \times 3 \times 5 \times 5$, where 2 appears three times in 120, 3 one time in 120, and 5 two times in 150.

Hint

The prime factor table can be represented using a two-dimensional array. Write a method named `getPrimeFactors(int number)` that returns a two-dimensional array for the prime factor table.

PART 2

OBJECT-ORIENTED PROGRAMMING

In Part 1, "Fundamentals of Programming," you learned how to write simple Java applications using primitive data types, control statements, methods, and arrays, all of which are features commonly available in procedural programming languages. Java, however, is an object-oriented programming language that uses abstraction, encapsulation, inheritance, and polymorphism to provide great flexibility, modularity, and reusability for developing software. In this part of the book you will learn how to define, extend, and work with classes and their objects.

Prerequisites for Part 2

optional GUI sections

Optional GUI sections are provided at the end of Chapters 7–10 in Part 2, while a complete introduction to GUI programming is presented in Part 3. This serves two purposes: (1) GUI can be covered early to stimulate student interest in programming; (2) GUI components are excellent examples to demonstrate object-oriented programming. The optional GUI sections can be used as additional examples to teach OOP.

text I/O

The *text I/O* in Chapter 8, "Strings and Text I/O," can be covered whenever text I/O is needed.

exception

Exception handling and binary I/O can be covered after Chapter 9, "Inheritance and Polymorphism."

Part 3, "GUI Programming," may be intertwined with Part 2. You can cover GUI programming in Chapters 12 and 13, "GUI Basics" and "Graphics," after you have covered

abstract classes

abstract classes in Chapter 10, "Abstract Classes and Interfaces."

interfaces

Interfaces in Chapter 10, "Abstract Classes and Interfaces," can be covered just before introducing Chapter 14, "Event-Driven Programming."

Chapter 11

The sections in *Chapter 11*, "Object-Oriented Design," can be covered selectively. For example, if you want to use sequence diagrams to model dynamic behaviors, you can cover sequence diagrams at that time.

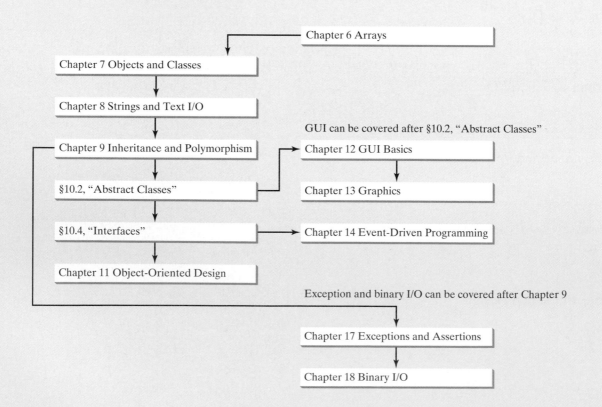

CHAPTER 7

OBJECTS AND CLASSES

Objectives

- To understand objects and classes, and use classes to model objects (§7.2).

- To use UML graphical notations to describe classes and objects (§7.2).

- To learn how to declare a class and how to create an object of a class (§7.3).

- To understand the role of constructors when creating objects (§7.3).

- To distinguish between object reference variables and primitive data type variables (§7.4).

- To use classes in the Java library (§7.5).

- To understand the difference between instance and static variables and methods (§7.6).

- To declare private data fields with appropriate `get` and `set` methods for data field encapsulation to make classes easy to maintain (§§7.7–7.8).

- To create immutable objects from immutable classes (§7.9).

- To develop methods with object arguments (§7.10).

- To determine the scope of variables in the context of a class (§7.11).

- To use the keyword `this` to refer to the calling object (§7.12).

- To store and process objects in arrays (§7.13).

- To apply class abstraction to develop software (§§7.14–7.17).

- (Optional GUI) To create windows using `JFrame` (§7.18).

7.1 Introduction

Programming in procedural languages like C, Pascal, BASIC, Ada, and COBOL involves choosing data structures, designing algorithms, and translating algorithms into code. An object-oriented language like Java combines the power of procedural languages with an added dimension that provides more flexibility, modularity, clarity, and reusability through abstraction, encapsulation, inheritance, and polymorphism.

In procedural programming, data and operations on the data are separate, and this methodology requires sending data to methods. Object-oriented programming places data and the operations that pertain to them within a single entity called an *object*; this approach solves many of the problems inherent in procedural programming. The object-oriented programming approach organizes programs in a way that mirrors the real world, in which all objects are associated with both attributes and activities. Using objects improves software reusability and makes programs easier to develop and easier to maintain. Programming in Java involves thinking in terms of objects; a Java program can be viewed as a collection of cooperating objects.

This chapter introduces declaring classes, creating objects, manipulating objects, and making objects work together.

7.2 Defining Classes for Objects

object-oriented programming

Object-oriented programming (OOP) involves programming using objects. An *object* represents an entity in the real world that can be distinctly identified. For example, a student, a desk, a circle, a button, and even a loan can all be viewed as objects. An object has a unique identity, state, and behaviors.

state

■ The *state* of an object is represented by *data fields* (also known as *properties*) with their current values.

behavior

■ The *behavior* of an object is defined by a set of methods. Invoking a method on an object means that you ask the object to perform a task.

A circle object, for example, has a data field, `radius`, which is the property that characterizes a circle. One behavior of a circle is that its area can be computed using the method `getArea()`.

Objects of the same type are defined using a common class. A class is a template or blueprint that defines what an object's data and methods will be. An object is an instance of a class.
instantiation
object
instance
You can create many instances of a class. Creating an instance is referred to as *instantiation*. The terms *object* and *instance* are often interchangeable. The relationship between classes and objects is analogous to the relationship between apple pie recipes and apple pies. You can make as many apple pies as you want from a single recipe. Figure 7.1 shows a class named `Circle` and its three objects.

class
data field
method
constructor

A Java *class* uses variables to define *data fields* and *methods* to define behaviors. Additionally, a class provides methods of a special type, known as *constructors*, which are invoked when

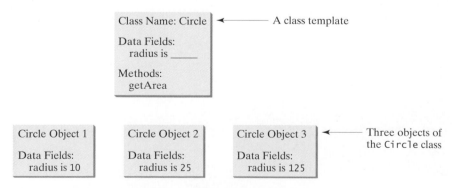

FIGURE 7.1 A class is a template for creating objects.

a new object is created. A constructor is a special kind of method. A constructor can perform any action, but constructors are designed to perform initializing actions, such as initializing the data fields of objects. Figure 7.2 shows an example of the class for `Circle` objects.

```
class Circle {
  /** The radius of this circle */
  double radius = 1.0;              ◄────── Data field

  /** Construct a circle object */
  Circle() {
  }
                                    ◄────── Constructors
  /** Construct a circle object */
  Circle(double newRadius) {
    radius = newRadius;
  }

  /** Return the area of this circle */
  double getArea() {                ◄────── Method
    return radius * radius * Math.PI;
  }
}
```

FIGURE 7.2   A class is a construct that defines objects of the same type.

The `Circle` class is different from all of the other classes you have seen thus far. It does not have a `main` method and therefore cannot be run; it is merely a definition used to declare and create `Circle` objects. For convenience, the class that contains the `main` method will be referred to as the *main class* in this book.

main class

The illustration of class templates and objects in Figure 7.1 can be standardized using UML (Unified Modeling Language) notations. This notation, as shown in Figure 7.3, is called a *UML class diagram*, or simply a *class diagram*. For more information on UML, see www.rational.com/uml/.

UML class diagram

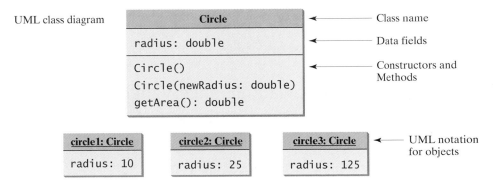

FIGURE 7.3   Classes and objects can be represented using UML notations.

In the class diagram, the data field is denoted as

    dataFieldName: dataFieldType

The constructor is denoted as

    ClassName(parameterName: parameterType)

The method is denoted as

```
methodName(parameterName: parameterType): returnType
```

7.3 Constructors

overloading constructors

The constructor has exactly the same name as the defining class. Like regular methods, constructors can be overloaded (i.e., multiple constructors with the same name but different signatures), making it easy to construct objects with different initial data values.

To construct an object from a class, invoke a constructor of the class using the **new** operator, as follows:

```
new ClassName(arguments);
```

For example, **new Circle()** creates an object of the **Circle** class using the first constructor defined in the **Circle** class, and **new Circle(5)** creates an object using the second constructor defined in the **Circle** class.

no-arg constructor

A class normally provides a constructor without arguments (e.g., **Circle()**). Such a constructor is called a *no-arg* or *no-argument constructor*.

default constructor

A class may be declared without constructors. In this case, a no-arg constructor with an empty body is implicitly declared in the class. This constructor, called *a default constructor*, is provided automatically *only if no constructors are explicitly declared in the class*.

Note

Constructors are a special kind of method, with three differences:

constructor's name

■ Constructors must have the same name as the class itself.

no return type

■ Constructors do not have a return type—not even **void**.

new operator

■ Constructors are invoked using the **new** operator when an object is created. Constructors play the role of initializing objects.

Caution

It is a common mistake to put the **void** keyword in front of a constructor. For example,

```
public void Circle() {
}
```

In this case, **Circle()** is a method, not a constructor.

7.4 Accessing Objects via Reference Variables

Newly created objects are allocated in the memory. How can they be accessed? The answer is given in this section.

7.4.1 Reference Variables and Reference Types

reference variable

Objects are accessed via object *reference variables*, which contain references to the objects. Such variables are declared using the following syntax:

```
ClassName objectRefVar;
```

reference type

A class defines a type, known as a *reference type*. Any variable of the class type can reference to an instance of the class. The following statement declares the variable **myCircle** to be of the **Circle** type:

```
Circle myCircle;
```

The variable `myCircle` can reference a `Circle` object. The next statement creates an object and assigns its reference to `myCircle`.

```
myCircle = new Circle();
```

Using the syntax shown below, you can write one statement that combines the declaration of an object reference variable, the creation of an object, and the assigning of an object reference to the variable.

```
ClassName objectRefVar = new ClassName();
```

Here is an example:

```
Circle myCircle = new Circle();
```

The variable `myCircle` holds a reference to a `Circle` object.

Note

An object reference variable that appears to hold an object actually contains a reference to that object. Strictly speaking, an object reference variable and an object are different, but most of the time the distinction between them can be ignored. So it is fine, for simplicity, to say that `myCircle` is a `Circle` object rather than a more long-winded phrase stating that `myCircle` is a variable that contains a reference to a `Circle` object. When the distinction makes a subtle difference, the long phrase should be used.

object vs. object reference variable

Note

Arrays are treated as objects in Java. Arrays are created using the `new` operator. An array variable is actually a variable that contains a reference to an array.

array object

7.4.2 Accessing an Object's Data and Methods

After an object is created, its data can be accessed and its methods invoked using the *dot operator* (`.`), also known as the *object member access operator*:

dot operator

- `objectRefVar.dataField` references a data field in the object.

- `objectRefVar.method(arguments)` invokes a method on the object.

For example, `myCircle.radius` references the radius in `myCircle`, and `myCircle.getArea()` invokes the `getArea` method on `myCircle`. Methods are invoked as operations on objects.

The data field `radius` is referred to as an *instance variable* because it is dependent on a specific instance. For the same reason, the method `getArea` is referred to as an *instance method*, because you can only invoke it on a specific instance. The object on which an instance method is invoked is referred to as a *calling object*.

instance variable

instance method

calling object

Note

Most of the time, you create an object and assign it to a variable. Later you can use the variable to reference the object. Occasionally, an object does not need to be referenced later. In this case, you can create an object without explicitly assigning it to a variable, as shown below:

```
new Circle();
```

or

```
System.out.println("Area is " + new Circle(5).getArea());
```

anonymous object

The former statement creates a `Circle` object. The latter statement creates a `Circle` object and invokes its `getArea` method to return its area. An object created in this way is known as an *anonymous object.*

7.4.3 Example: Declaring Classes and Creating Objects

Listing 7.1 is a program that declares a circle class. To avoid a naming conflict with several improved versions of the `Circle` class introduced later in this book, the `Circle` class in this example is named `Circle1`.

The program constructs a circle object with radius 5 and an object with radius 1 and displays the radius and area of each of the two circles. Change the radius of the second object to 100 and display its new radius and area, as shown in Figure 7.4.

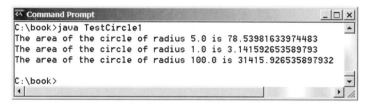

FIGURE 7.4 The program constructs two circles with radii of 5 and 1, and displays their radii and areas.

LISTING 7.1 TestCircle1.java

```java
 1 public class TestCircle1 {
 2   /** Main method */
 3   public static void main(String[] args) {
 4     // Create a circle with radius 5.0
 5     Circle1 myCircle = new Circle1(5.0);
 6     System.out.println("The area of the circle of radius "
 7       + myCircle.radius + " is " + myCircle.getArea());
 8
 9     // Create a circle with radius 1
10     Circle1 yourCircle = new Circle1();
11     System.out.println("The area of the circle of radius "
12       + yourCircle.radius + " is " + yourCircle.getArea());
13
14     // Modify circle radius
15     yourCircle.radius = 100;
16     System.out.println("The area of the circle of radius "
17       + yourCircle.radius + " is " + yourCircle.getArea());
18   }
19 }
20
21 // Define the circle class with two constructors
22 class Circle1 {
23   double radius;
24
25   /** Construct a circle with radius 1 */
26   Circle1() {
27     radius = 1.0;
28   }
29
30   /** Construct a circle with a specified radius */
31   Circle1(double newRadius) {
32     radius = newRadius;
33   }
```

no-arg constructor

second constructor

```
34
35   /** Return the area of this circle */
36   double getArea() {
37     return radius * radius * Math.PI;
38   }
39 }
```

The program contains two classes. The first class, `TestCircle1`, is the main class. Its sole purpose is to test the second class, `Circle1`. Every time you run the program, the JVM invokes the `main` method in the main class.

You can put the two classes into one file, but only one class in the file can be a public class. Furthermore, the public class must have the same name as the file name and the main method must be in a public class. Therefore, the file name is `TestCircle1.java` if the `TestCircle1` and `Circle1` classes are both in the same file.

The main class contains the `main` method (line 3) that creates two objects. The constructor `Circle1(5.0)` was used to create `myCircle` with a radius of `5.0` (line 5), and the constructor `Circle1()` was used to create `yourCircle` with a radius of `1.0` (line 10).

These two objects (referenced by `myCircle` and `yourCircle`) have different data but share the same methods. Therefore, you can compute their respective areas by using the `getArea()` method.

To write the `getArea` method in a procedural programming language like Pascal, you would pass radius as an argument to the method. But in object-oriented programming, `radius` and `getArea` are defined in the object. The `radius` is a data member in the object, which is accessible by the `getArea` method. In procedural programming languages, data and methods are separated, but in an object-oriented programming language, data and methods are grouped together.

The `getArea` method is an instance method that is always invoked by an instance in which the `radius` is specified.

There are many ways to write Java programs. For instance, you can combine the two classes in the example into one, as shown in Listing 7.2.

LISTING 7.2 Circle1.java

```
1 public class Circle1 {
2   /** Main method */
3   public static void main(String[] args) {                          main method
4     // Create a circle with radius 5.0
5     Circle1 myCircle = new Circle1(5.0);
6     System.out.println("The area of the circle of radius "
7       + myCircle.radius + " is " + myCircle.getArea());
8
9     // Create a circle with radius 1
10    Circle1 yourCircle = new Circle1();
11    System.out.println("The area of the circle of radius "
12      + yourCircle.radius + " is " + yourCircle.getArea());
13
14    // Modify circle radius
15    yourCircle.radius = 100;
16    System.out.println("The area of the circle of radius "
17      + yourCircle.radius + " is " + yourCircle.getArea());
18  }
19
20  double radius;
21
22  /** Construct a circle with radius 1 */
23  Circle1() {                                                        no-arg constructor
```

```
24        radius = 1.0;
25    }
26
27    /** Construct a circle with a specified radius */
```

second constructor

```
28    Circle1(double newRadius) {
29        radius = newRadius;
30    }
31
32    /** Return the area of this circle */
33    double getArea() {
34        return radius * radius * Math.PI;
35    }
36 }
```

Since the combined class has a `main` method, it can be executed by the Java interpreter. The `main` method creates `myCircle` as a `Circle1` object and then displays radius and finds area in `myCircle`. This demonstrates that you can test a class by simply adding a `main` method in the same class.

Caution

invoking methods

Recall that you use `Math.methodName(arguments)` (e.g., `Math.pow(3,2.5)`) to invoke a method in the `Math` class. Can you invoke `getArea()` using `Circle1.getArea()`? The answer is no. All the methods in the `Math` class are static methods, which are defined using the **static** keyword. However, `getArea()` is an instance method, and thus non-static. It must be invoked from an object using `objectRefVar.methodName(arguments)` (e.g., `myCircle.getArea()`). More explanations will follow in §7.6, "Static Variables, Constants, and Methods."

Tip

If you use an IDE such as JBuilder, NetBeans, or Eclipse, please refer to *Learning Java Effectively with JBuilder/NetBeans/Eclipse* in the supplements. This supplement shows you how to use a debugger to inspect objects.

debugging in IDE

7.4.4 Reference Data Fields and the `null` Value

reference data fields

The data fields can be of reference types. For example, the following `Student` class contains a data field `name` of the `String` type. `String` is a predefined Java class.

```
class Student {
    String name; // name has default value null
    int age; // age has default value 0
    boolean isScienceMajor; // isScienceMajor has default value false
    char gender; // c has default value '\u0000'
}
```

null value

If a data field of a reference type does not reference any object, the data field holds a special Java value, `null`. `null` is a literal just like `true` and `false`. While `true` and `false` are Boolean literals, `null` is a literal for a reference type.

default field values

The default value of a data field is `null` for a reference type, `0` for a numeric type, `false` for a `boolean` type, and `'\u0000'` for a `char` type. However, Java assigns no default value to a local variable inside a method. The following code displays the default values of data fields `name`, `age`, `isScienceMajor`, and `gender` for a `Student` object:

```
class Test {
    public static void main(String[] args) {
        Student student = new Student();
```

```
        System.out.println("name? " + student.name);
        System.out.println("age? " + student.age);
        System.out.println("isScienceMajor? " + student.isScienceMajor);
        System.out.println("gender? " + student.gender);
    }
}
```

The following code has a compilation error because local variables x and y are not initialized:

```
class Test {
    public static void main(String[] args) {
        int x; // x has no default value
        String y; // y has no default value
        System.out.println("x is " + x);
        System.out.println("y is " + y);
    }
}
```

Caution

NullPointerException is a common runtime error. It happens when you invoke a method on a reference variable with **null** value. Make sure you assign an object reference to the variable before invoking the method through the reference variable.

NullPointerException

7.4.5 Differences Between Variables of Primitive Types and Reference Types

Every variable represents a memory location that holds a value. When you declare a variable, you are telling the compiler what type of value the variable can hold. For a variable of a primitive type, the value is of the primitive type. For a variable of a reference type, the value is a reference to where an object is located. For example, as shown in Figure 7.5, the value of **int** variable i is **int** value 1, and the value of **Circle** object c holds a reference to where the contents of the **Circle** object are stored in the memory.

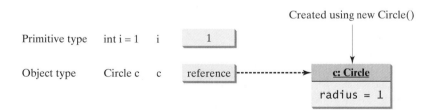

FIGURE 7.5 A variable of a primitive type holds a value of the primitive type, and a variable of a reference type holds a reference to where an object is stored in the memory.

When you assign one variable to another, the other variable is set to the same value. For a variable of a primitive type, the real value of one variable is assigned to the other variable. For a variable of a reference type, the reference of one variable is assigned to the other variable. As shown in Figure 7.6, the assignment statement i = j copies the contents of j into i for primitive variables. As shown in Figure 7.7, the assignment statement c1 = c2 copies the reference of c2 into c1 for reference variables. After the assignment, variables c1 and c2 refer to the same object.

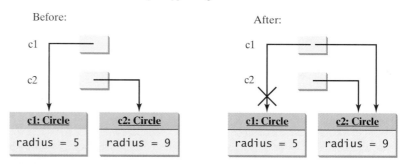

FIGURE 7.6 Primitive variable `j` is copied to variable `i`.

Object type assignment c1 = c2

FIGURE 7.7 Reference variable `c2` is copied to variable `c1`.

Note

As shown in Figure 7.7, after the assignment statement `c1 = c2`, `c1` points to the same object referenced by `c2`. The object previously referenced by `c1` is no longer useful and therefore is now known as *garbage*. Garbage occupies memory space. The JVM detects garbage and automatically reclaims the space it occupies. This process is called *garbage collection*.

garbage
garbage collection

Tip

If you know that an object is no longer needed, you can explicitly assign `null` to a reference variable for the object. The JVM will automatically collect the space if the object is not referenced by any reference variable.

7.5 Using Classes from the Java Library

Listing 7.1 declared the `Circle1` class and created objects from the class. You will frequently use the classes in the Java library to develop programs. This section gives some examples of the classes in the Java library.

7.5.1 The `Date` Class

In Listing 2.5, ShowCurrentTime.java, you learned how to obtain the current time using `System.currentTimeMillis()`. You used the division and remainder operators to extract the current second, minute, and hour. Java provides a system-independent encapsulation of date and time in the `java.util.Date` class, as shown in Figure 7.8.

`java.util.Date` class

You can use the no-arg constructor in the `Date` class to create an instance for the current date and time, its `getTime()` method to return the elapsed time since January 1, 1970, GMT, and its `toString` method to return the date and time as a string. For example, the following code

The + sign indicates public modifer

java.util.Date	
+Date()	Constructs a Date object for the current time.
+Date(elapseTime: long)	Constructs a Date object for a given time in milliseconds elapsed since January 1, 1970, GMT.
+toString(): String	Returns a string representing the date and time.
+getTime(): long	Returns the number of milliseconds since January 1, 1970, GMT.
+setTime(elapseTime: long): void	Sets a new elapse time in the object.

FIGURE 7.8   A Date object represents a specific date and time.

```
java.util.Date date = new java.util.Date();                            create object
System.out.println("The elapsed time since Jan 1, 1970 is " +
  date.getTime() + " milliseconds");                                   get elapsed time
System.out.println(date.toString());                                   invoke toString
```

displays the output like this:

```
The elapse time since Jan 1, 1970 is 1100547210284 milliseconds
Mon Nov 15 14:33:30 EST 2004
```

The Date class has another constructor, Date(long elapseTime), which can be used to construct a Date object for a given time in milliseconds elapsed since January 1, 1970, GMT.

7.5.2   The Random Class

You have used Math.random() to obtain a random double value between 0.0 and 1.0 (excluding 1.0). A more useful random number generator is provided in the java.util.Random class, as shown in Figure 7.9.

java.util.Random	
+Random()	Constructs a Random object with the current time as its seed.
+Random(seed: long)	Constructs a Random object with a specified seed.
+nextInt(): int	Returns a random int value.
+nextInt(n: int): int	Returns a random int value between 0 and n (exclusive).
+nextLong(): long	Returns a random long value.
+nextDouble(): double	Returns a random double value between 0.0 and 1.0 (exclusive).
+nextFloat(): float	Returns a random float value between 0.0F and 1.0F (exclusive).
+nextBoolean(): boolean	Returns a random boolean value.

FIGURE 7.9   A Random object can be used to generate random values.

You can create a Random object for generating random values using its no-arg constructor with the current elapse time as its seed. You can also create a Random object using new Random(seed) with a specified seed. If two Random objects have the same seed, they will generate identical sequences of numbers. For example, the following code creates two Random objects with the same seed, 3:

```
Random random1 = new Random(3);
System.out.print("From random1: ");
for (int i = 0; i < 10; i++)
  System.out.print(random1.nextInt(1000) + " ");
```

```
Random random2 = new Random(3);
System.out.print("\nFrom random2: ");
for (int i = 0; i < 10; i++)
    System.out.print(random2.nextInt(1000) + " ");
```

The code generates the same sequence of random `int` values:

```
From random1: 734 660 210 581 128 202 549 564 459 961
From random2: 734 660 210 581 128 202 549 564 459 961
```

7.6 Static Variables, Constants, and Methods

instance variable

The data field `radius` in the circle class in Listing 7.1 is known as an *instance variable*. An instance variable is tied to a specific instance of the class; it is not shared among objects of the same class. For example, suppose that you create the following objects:

```
Circle circle1 = new Circle();
Circle circle2 = new Circle(5);
```

The `radius` in `circle1` is independent of the `radius` in `circle2`, and is stored in a different memory location. Changes made to `circle1`'s `radius` do not affect `circle2`'s `radius`, and vice versa.

static variable

If you want all the instances of a class to share data, use *static variables*. Static variables store values for the variables in a common memory location. Because of this common location, all objects of the same class are affected if one object changes the value of a static variable. Java supports static methods as well as static variables. *Static methods* can be called without creating an instance of the class.

static method

Let us modify the `Circle` class by adding a static variable `numberOfObjects` to count the number of circle objects created. When the first object of this class is created, `numberOfObjects` is 1. When the second object is created, `numberOfObjects` becomes 2. The UML of the new circle class is shown in Figure 7.10. The `Circle` class defines the instance variable `radius` and the static variable `numberOfObjects`, the instance methods `getRadius`, `setRadius`, and `getArea`, and the static method `getNumberOfObjects`. (Note that static variables and functions are *underlined* in the UML class diagram.)

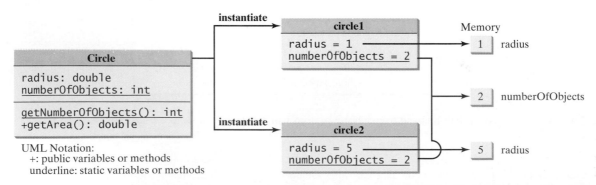

FIGURE 7.10 Instance variables belong to the instances and have memory storage independent of one another. Static variables are shared by all the instances of the same class.

To declare a static variable or a static method, put the modifier `static` in the variable or method declaration. The static variable `numberOfObjects` and the static method `getNumberOfObjects()` can be declared as follows:

```
static int numberOfObjects;                                    declare static
                                                                  variable
static int getNumberObjects() {                                declare static
  return numberOfObjects;                                         method
}
```

Constants in a class are shared by all objects of the class. Thus, constants should be declared
`final static`. For example, the constant `PI` in the `Math` class is defined as:

```
final static double PI = 3.14159265358979323846;
```

The new circle class, named `Circle2`, is declared in Listing 7.3.   declare constant

LISTING 7.3 `Circle2.java`

```
 1 public class Circle2 {
 2   /** The radius of the circle */
 3   double radius;
 4
 5   /** The number of the objects created */
 6   static int numberOfObjects = 0;                          static variable
 7
 8   /** Construct a circle with radius 1 */
 9   Circle2() {
10     radius = 1.0;
11     numberOfObjects++;                                     increase by 1
12   }
13
14   /** Construct a circle with a specified radius */
15   Circle2(double newRadius) {
16     radius = newRadius;
17     numberOfObjects++;                                     increase by 1
18   }
19
20   /** Return numberOfObjects */
21   static int getNumberOfObjects() {                        static method
22     return numberOfObjects;
23   }
24
25   /** Return the area of this circle */
26   double getArea() {
27     return radius * radius * Math.PI;
28   }
29 }
```

Method `getNumberOfObjects()` in `Circle2` is a static method. Other examples of static
methods are `showMessageDialog` and `showInputDialog` in the `JOptionPane` class, and
all the methods in the `Math` class. In fact, so are all the methods used in Part 1 of this book,
including the `main` method.

Instance methods (e.g., `getArea()`) and instance data (e.g., `radius`) belong to
instances and can only be used after the instances are created. They are accessed via a
reference variable. Static methods (e.g., `getNumberOfObjects()`) and static data
(e.g., `numberOfObjects`) can be accessed from a reference variable or from their class
name.

The program in Listing 7.4 demonstrates how to use instance and static variables and methods, and illustrates the effects of using them. Its output is shown in Figure 7.11.

LISTING 7.4 TestCircle2.java

```
 1 public class TestCircle2 {
 2   /** Main method */
 3   public static void main(String[] args) {
 4     // Create c1
 5     Circle2 c1 = new Circle2();
 6
 7     // Display c1 BEFORE c2 is created
 8     System.out.println("Before creating c2");
 9     System.out.println("c1 is : radius (" + c1.radius +
10       ") and number of Circle objects (" +
11       c1.numberOfObjects + ")");
12
13     // Create c2
14     Circle2 c2 = new Circle2(5);
15
16     // Change the radius in c1
17     c1.radius = 9;
18
19     // Display c1 and c2 AFTER c2 was created
20     System.out.println("\nAfter creating c2 and modifying " +
21       "c1's radius to 9");
22     System.out.println("c1 is : radius (" + c1.radius +
23       ") and number of Circle objects (" +
24       c1.numberOfObjects + ")");
25     System.out.println("c2 is : radius (" + c2.radius +
26       ") and number of Circle objects (" +
27       c2.numberOfObjects +")");
28   }
29 }
```

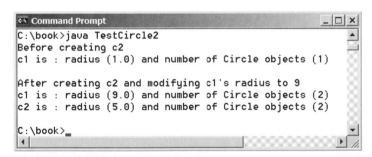

FIGURE 7.11 The program uses the instance variable `radius` as well as the static variable `numberOfObjects`. All of the objects share the same `numberOfObjects`.

The `main` method creates two circles, `c1` and `c2` (lines 5, 14). The instance variable `radius` in `c1` is modified to become 9 (line 17). This change does not affect the instance variable `radius` in `c2`, since these two instance variables are independent. The static variable `numberOfObjects` becomes 1 after `c1` is created (line 5), and it becomes 2 after `c2` is created (line 14).

Note that `PI` is a constant defined in `Math` and `Math.PI` access the constant. `c1.numberOfObjects` and `c2.numberOfObjects` could be replaced by `Circle2.numberOfObjects`. This improves readability. You can also replace `Circle2.numberOfObjects` by `Circle2.getNumberOfObjects()`.

Tip

Use `ClassName.methodName(arguments)` to invoke a static method and `ClassName.staticVariable`. This improves readability because the user can easily recognize the static method and data in the class.

use class name

Note

You can use a new JDK 1.5 feature to directly import static variables and methods from a class. The imported data and methods can be referenced or called without specifying a class. For example, you can use `PI` (instead of `Math.PI`), and `random()` (instead of `Math.random()`), if you have the following import statement in the class:

static import

```
import static java.lang.Math.*;
```

Caution

Static variables and methods can be used from instance or static methods in the class. However, instance variables and methods can only be used from instance methods, not from static methods, since static variables and methods belong to the class as a whole and not to particular objects. Thus the code given below would be wrong.

```java
public class Foo {
  int i = 5;
  static int k = 2;

  public static void main(String[] args) {
    int j = i;  // Wrong because i is an instance variable
    m1(); // Wrong because m1() is an instance method
  }

  public void m1() {
    // Correct since instance and static variables and methods
    // can be used in an instance method
    i = i + k + m2(i, k);
  }

  public static int m2(int i, int j) {
    return (int)(Math.pow(i, j));
  }
}
```

Tip

How do you decide whether a variable or method should be an instance one or a static one? A variable or method that is dependent on a specific instance of the class should be an instance variable or method. A variable or method that is not dependent on a specific instance of the class should be a static variable or method. For example, every circle has its own radius. Radius is dependent on a specific circle. Therefore, `radius` is an instance variable of the `Circle` class. Since the `getArea` method is dependent on a specific circle, it is an instance method. None of the methods in the `Math` class, such as `random`, `pow`, `sin`, and `cos`, is dependent on a specific instance. Therefore, these methods are static methods. The `main` method is static, and can be invoked directly from a class.

instance or static?

Caution

It is a *common design error* to declare an instance method that should have been declared static. For example, the following method `factorial(int n)` should be declared static, because it is independent of any specific instance.

common design error

```
public class Test {
  public int factorial(int n) {
    int result = 1;
    for (int i = 1; i <= n; i++)
      result *= i;

    return result;
  }
}
```

```
public class Test {
  public static int factorial(int n) {
    int result = 1;
    for (int i = 1; i <= n; i++)
      result *= i;

    return result;
  }
}
```

(a) Wrong design

(b) Correct design

7.7 Visibility Modifiers

Java provides several modifiers that control access to data fields, methods, and classes. This section introduces the **public**, **private**, and default modifiers.

public

■   **public** makes classes, methods, and data fields accessible from any class.

private

■   **private** makes methods and data fields accessible only from within its own class.

package-private

■   If **public** or **private** is not used, then by default the classes, methods, and data fields are accessible by any class in the same package. This is known as *package-private* or *package-access*.

Figure 7.12 illustrates how a public, default, and private data field or method in class C1 can be accessed from a class C2 in the same package, and from a class C3 in a different package.

```
package p1;

public class C1 {
  public int x;
  int y;
  private int z;

  public void m1() {
  }
  void m2() {
  }
  private void m3() {
  }
}
```

```
public class C2 {
  void aMethod() {
    C1 o = new C1();
    can access o.x;
    can access o.y;
    cannot access o.z;

    can invoke o.m1();
    can invoke o.m2();
    cannot invoke o.m3();
  }
}
```

```
package p2;

public class C3 {
  void aMethod() {
    C1 o = new C1();
    can access o.x;
    cannot access o.y;
    cannot access o.z;

    can invoke o.m1();
    cannot invoke o.m2();
    cannot invoke o.m3();
  }
}
```

FIGURE 7.12   The private modifier restricts access to its defining a class, the default modifier restricts access to a package, and the public modifier enables unrestricted access.

If a class is not declared public, it can only be accessed within the same package, as shown in Figure 7.13.

A visibility modifier specifies how data fields and methods in a class can be accessed from the outside of the class. There is no restriction on accessing data fields and methods from inside the class. As shown in Figure 7.14(b), an object foo of the Foo class cannot access its private members, because foo is in the Test class. As shown in Figure 7.14(a), an object foo of the Foo class can access its private members, because foo is declared inside its own class.

inside access

Note

private data field
private method

The **private** modifier applies solely to the members of a class (e.g., data fields or methods). The various Java modifiers are summarized in the table in Appendix D, "Java Modifiers."

```
package p1;

class C1 {        public class C2 {
  ...               can access C1
}                 }
```

```
package p2;

public class C3 {
  cannot access C1;
  can access C2;
}
```

FIGURE 7.13   A non-public class has package-access.

```
public class Foo {
  private boolean x;

  public static void main(String[] args) {
    Foo foo = new Foo();
    System.out.println(foo.x);
    System.out.println(foo.convert());
  }

  private int convert() {
    return x ? 1 : -1;
  }
}
```

```
public class Test {
  public static void main(String[] args) {
    Foo foo = new Foo();
    System.out.println(foo.x);
    System.out.println(foo.convert());
  }
}
```

(a) This is OK because object foo is used inside the Foo class   (b) This is wrong because x and convert are private in Foo.

FIGURE 7.14   An object can access its private members if it is declared in its own class.

Note
Visibility modifiers are used for the members of the class, not local variables inside the methods. Using a visibility modifier on local variables would cause a compilation error.

Note
In most cases, the constructor should be public. However, if you want to prohibit the user from creating an instance of a class, you can use a *private constructor*. For example, there is no reason to create an instance from the `Math` class because all of the data fields and methods are static. One solution is to define a dummy private constructor in the class. The `Math` class cannot be instantiated because it has a private constructor, as follows:

private constructor

```
private Math() {
}
```

The `Math` class that comes with the Java system was introduced in §5.8, "The `Math` Class."

7.8 Data Field Encapsulation

The data fields `radius` and `numberOfObjects` in the `Circle2` class in Listing 7.2 can be modified directly (e.g., `myCircle.radius = 5` or `Circle2.numberOfObjects = 10`). This is not a good practice for two reasons:

■ First, data may be tampered. For example, `numberOfObjects` is to count the number of objects created, but it may be set to an arbitrary value (e.g., `Circle2.numberOfObjects = 10`).

■ Second, it makes the class difficult to maintain and vulnerable to bugs. Suppose you want to modify the `Circle2` class to ensure that the radius is non-negative after other programs have already used the class. You have to change not only the `Circle2` class, but also the programs that use the `Circle2` class. Such programs

client

are often referred to as *clients*. This is because the clients may have modified the radius directly (e.g., `myCircle.radius = -5`).

data field encapsulation

To prevent direct modifications of properties, you should declare the field private, using the `private` modifier. This is known as *data field encapsulation*.

A private data field cannot be accessed by an object through a direct reference outside the class that defines the private field. But often a client needs to retrieve and modify a data field. To make a private data field accessible, provide a *get* method to return the value of the data field. To enable a private data field to be updated, provide a *set* method to set a new value.

 Note

accessor
mutator

Colloquially, a `get` method is referred to as a *getter* (or *accessor*), and a `set` method is referred to as a *setter* (or *mutator*).

A `get` method has the following signature:

    public returnType get*PropertyName*()

boolean accessor

If the `returnType` is `boolean`, the `get` method should be defined as follows by convention:

    public boolean is*PropertyName*()

A set method has the following signature:

    public void set*PropertyName*(*dataType propertyValue*)

Let us create a new circle class with a private data field radius and its associated accessor and mutator methods. The class diagram is shown in Figure 7.15. The new circle class, named `Circle3`, is declared in Listing 7.5.

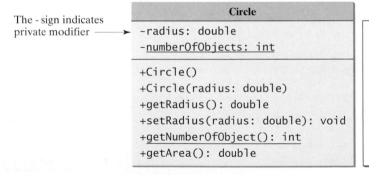

FIGURE 7.15 The `Circle` class encapsulates circle properties and provides get/set and other methods.

LISTING 7.5 `Circle3.java`

encapsulate radius

encapsulate
numberOfObjects

```java
1 public class Circle3 {
2   /** The radius of the circle */
3   private double radius = 1;
4
5   /** The number of the objects created */
6   private static int numberOfObjects = 0;
7
8   /** Construct a circle with radius 1 */
9   public Circle3() {
10    numberOfObjects++;
11  }
```

```
12
13   /** Construct a circle with a specified radius */
14   public Circle3(double newRadius) {
15     radius = newRadius;
16     numberOfObjects++;
17   }
18
19   /** Return radius */
20   public double getRadius() {
21     return radius;
22   }
23
24   /** Set a new radius */
25   public void setRadius(double newRadius) {
26     radius = (newRadius >= 0) ? newRadius : 0;
27   }
28
29   /** Return numberOfObjects */
30   public static int getNumberOfObjects() {
31     return numberOfObjects;
32   }
33
34   /** Return the area of this circle */
35   public double getArea() {
36     return radius * radius * Math.PI;
37   }
38 }
```

access method *(lines 20)*
mutator method *(lines 25)*
access method *(lines 30)*

The `getRadius()` method (lines 20–22) returns the radius, and the `setRadius(newRadius)` method (lines 25–27) sets a new radius into the object. If the new radius is negative, `0` is set to the radius in the object. Since these methods are the only ways to read and modify radius, you have total control over how the `radius` property is accessed. If you have to change the implementation of these methods, you need not change the client programs. This makes the class easy to maintain.

Here is a client program that uses the `Circle3` class to create a `Circle3` object and modifies the radius using the `setRadius` method.

```
1  // TestCircle3.java: Demonstrate private modifier
2  public class TestCircle3 {
3    /** Main method */
4    public static void main(String[] args) {
5      // Create a Circle with radius 5.0
6      Circle myCircle = new Circle(5.0);
7      System.out.println("The area of the circle of radius "
8        + myCircle.getRadius() + " is " + myCircle.getArea());
9
10     // Increase myCircle's radius by 10%
11     myCircle.setRadius(myCircle.getRadius() * 1.1);
12     System.out.println("The area of the circle of radius "
13       + myCircle.getRadius() + " is " + myCircle.getArea());
14   }
15 }
```

The data field `radius` is declared private. Private data can only be accessed within their defining class. You cannot use `myCircle.radius` in the client program. A compilation error would occur if you attempted to access private data from a client.

Since `numberOfObjects` is private, it cannot be modified. This prevents tampering. For example, the user cannot set `numberOfObjects` to 100. The only way to make it 100 is to create one hundred objects of the `Circle3` class.

Suppose you combined `TestCircle3` and `Circle3` into one class by moving the `main` method in `TestCircle3` into `Circle3`. Could you use `myCircle.radius` in the `main` method? See Review Question 7.15 for the answer.

Note

When you compile `TestCircle3.java`, the Java compiler automatically compiles `Circle3.java` if it has not been compiled since the last change.

Tip

To prevent data from being tampered with and to make the class easy to maintain, most of the data fields in this book will be private.

7.9 Immutable Objects and Classes

immutable object
immutable class

If the contents of an object cannot be changed once the object is created, the object is called an *immutable object* and its class is called an *immutable class*. If you delete the `set` method in the `Circle3` class in the preceding example, the class would be immutable because radius is private and cannot be changed without a `set` method.

A class with all private data fields and no mutators is not necessarily immutable. For example, the following class `Student` has all private data fields and no mutators, but it is mutable.

Student class

```java
public class Student {
  private int id;
  private BirthDate birthDate;

  public Student(int ssn, int year, int month, int day) {
    id = ssn;
    birthDate = new BirthDate(year, month, day);
  }

  public int getId() {
    return id;
  }

  public BirthDate getBirthDate() {
    return birthDate;
  }
}
```

BirthDate class

```java
public class BirthDate {
  private int year;
  private int month;
  private int day;

  public BirthDate(int newYear, int newMonth, int newDay) {
    year = newYear;
    month = newMonth;
    day = newDay;
  }

  public void setYear(int newYear) {
    year = newYear;
  }
}
```

As shown in the following code, the data field `birthDate` is returned using the `getBirthDate()` method. This is a reference to a `BirthDate` object. Through this reference, the year of the birth date is changed, which effectively changes the contents of the `Student` object.

```
public class Test {
  public static void main(String[] args) {
    Student student = new Student(111223333, 1970, 5, 3);
    BirthDate date = student.getBirthDate();
    date.setYear(2010); //Now the student birth year is changed!
  }
}
```

For a class to be immutable, it must mark all data fields private and provide no mutator methods and no accessor methods that would return a reference to a mutable data field object.

7.10 Passing Objects to Methods

So far, you have learned how to pass arguments of primitive types and array types to methods. You can also pass objects to methods. Like passing an array, passing an object is actually passing the reference of the object. The following code passes the `myCircle` object as an argument to the `printCircle` method:

```
public class TestPassObject {
  public static void main(String[] args) {
    Circle3 myCircle = new Circle3(5.0);
    printCircle(myCircle);
  }

  public static void printCircle(Circle3 c) {
    System.out.println("The area of the circle of radius "
      + c.getRadius() + " is " + c.getArea());
  }
}
```

Java uses exactly one mode of passing arguments: *pass-by-value*. In the preceding code, the value of `myCircle` is passed to the `printCircle` method. This value is a reference to a `Circle3` object.

pass-by-value

Let us demonstrate the difference between passing a primitive type value and passing a reference value with the program in Listing 7.6.

LISTING 7.6 TestPassObject.java

```
 1 public class TestPassObject {
 2   /** Main method */
 3   public static void main(String[] args) {
 4     // Create a Circle object with radius 1
 5     Circle3 myCircle = new Circle3(1);
 6
 7     // Print areas for radius 1, 2, 3, 4, and 5.
 8     int n = 5;
 9     printAreas(myCircle, n);
10
11     // See myCircle.radius and times
12     System.out.println("\n" + "Radius is " + myCircle.getRadius());
13     System.out.println("n is " + n);
14   }
15
```

```
16    /** Print a table of areas for radius */
17    public static void printAreas(Circle3 c, int times) {
18      System.out.println("Radius \t\tArea");
19      while (times >= 1) {
20        System.out.println(c.getRadius() + "\t\t" + c.getArea());
21        c.setRadius(c.getRadius() + 1);
22        times--;
23      }
24    }
25 }
```

The program passes a `Circle3` object `myCircle` and an integer value from `n` to invoke `printAreas(myCircle, n)` (line 19), which prints a table of areas for radii 1, 2, 3, 4, and 5, as shown in Figure 7.16.

FIGURE 7.16   The program passes a `Circle` object `myCircle` and an integer value `n` as arguments to the `printAreas` method, which displays a table of the areas for radii 1, 2, 3, 4, and 5.

Figure 7.17 shows the call stack for executing the methods in the program. Note that the objects are stored in a heap.

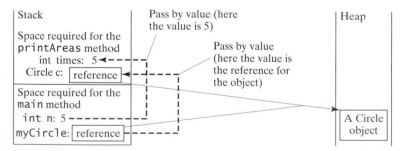

FIGURE 7.17   The value of `n` is passed to `times`, and the reference of `myCircle` is passed to `c` in the `printAreas` method.

When passing an argument of a primitive data type, the value of the argument is passed. In this case, the value of `n` (5) is passed to `times`. Inside the `printAreas` method, the content of `times` is changed; this does not affect the content of `n`. When passing an argument of a reference type, the reference of the object is passed. In this case, `c` contains a reference for the object that is also referenced via `myCircle`. Therefore, changing the properties of the object through `c` inside the `printAreas` method has the same effect as doing so outside the method through the variable `myCircle`.

7.11 The Scope of Variables

Chapter 5, "Methods," discussed local variables and their scope rules. Local variables are declared and used inside a method locally. This section discusses the scope rules of all the variables in the context of a class.

Instance and static variables in a class are referred to as the *class's variables* or *data fields*. A variable defined inside a method is referred to as a local variable. The scope of a class's variables is the entire class, regardless of where the variables are declared. A class's variables and methods can be declared in any order in the class, as shown in Figure 7.18(a). The exception is when a data field is initialized based on a reference to another data field. In such cases, the other data field must be declared first, as shown in Figure 7.18(b).

```
public class Circle {
  public double find getArea() {
    return radius * radius * Math.PI;
  }

  private double radius = 1;
}
```

(a) variable radius and method getArea() can be declared in any order

```
public class Foo {
  private int i;
  private int j = i + 1;
}
```

(b) i has to be declared before j because j's initial value is dependent on i.

FIGURE 7.18   Members of a class can be declared in any order, with one exception.

You can declare a class's variable only once, but you can declare the same variable name in a method many times in different non-nesting blocks.

If a local variable has the same name as a class's variable, the local variable takes precedence and the class's variable with the same name is hidden. For example, in the following program, x is defined as an instance variable and as a local variable in the method.

```
class Foo {
  int x = 0; // instance variable
  int y = 0;

  Foo() {
  }

  void p() {
    int x = 1; // local variable
    System.out.println("x = " + x);
    System.out.println("y = " + y);
  }
}
```

What is the printout for `f.p()`, where `f` is an instance of `Foo`? The printout for `f.p()` is `1` for x and `0` for y. Here is why:

- x is declared as a data field with the initial value of `0` in the class, but is also defined in the method `p()` with an initial value of `1`. The latter x is referenced in the `System.out.println` statement.

- y is declared outside the method `p()`, but is accessible inside it.

Tip
As demonstrated in the example, it is easy to make mistakes. To avoid confusion, do not declare the same variable name twice in a class, except for method parameters.

7.12 The **this** Keyword

hidden variable

Sometimes you need to reference a class's *hidden variable* in a method. For example, a property name is often used as the parameter name in a **set** method for the property. In this case, you need to reference the hidden property name in the method in order to set a new value to it. A hidden static variable can be accessed simply by using the `ClassName.StaticVariable` reference. A hidden instance variable can be accessed by using the keyword **this**, as shown in Figure 7.19(a).

```
class Foo {
  int i = 5;
  static double k = 0;

  void setI(int i) {
    this.i = i;
  }

  static void setK(double k) {
    Foo.k = k;
  }
}
```
```
Suppose that f1 and f2 are two objects of Foo.

Invoking f1.setI(10) is to execute
  ►f1.i = 10, where this is replaced by f1

Invoking f2.setI(45) is to execute
  ►f2.i = 45, where this is replaced by f2
```

(a)   (b)

FIGURE 7.19 The keyword **this** serves as the proxy for the object that invokes the method.

The line `this.i = i` means "assign the value of parameter `i` to the data field `i` of the calling object." The keyword **this** serves as a proxy for the object that invokes the instance method `setI`, as shown in Figure 7.19(b). The line `Foo.k = k` means that the value in parameter `k` is assigned to the static data field `k` of the class, which is shared by all the objects of the class.

call another constructor

The keyword **this** can also be used inside a constructor to invoke another constructor of the same class. For example, you can redefine the `Circle` class as follows:

```
public class Circle {
  private double radius;

  public Circle(double radius) {
    this.radius = radius;
  }

  public Circle() {
    this(1.0);
  }

  public double getArea() {
    return this.radius * this.radius * Math.PI;
  }
}
```

This must be explicitly used to reference the data field radius of the object being constructed

this is used to invoke another constructor

Every instance variable belongs to an instance represented by **this**, which is normally omitted

The line `this(1.0)` invokes the constructor with a **double** value argument in the class.

Tip

If a class has multiple constructors, it is better to implement them using `this(arg-list)` as much as possible. In general, a constructor with no or fewer arguments can invoke the constructor with more arguments using `this(arg-list)`. This often simplifies coding and makes the class easier to read and to maintain.

Note

Java requires that the `this(arg-list)` statement appear first in the constructor before any other statements.

7.13 Array of Objects

In Chapter 6, "Arrays," arrays of primitive type elements were created. You can also create arrays of objects. For example, the following statement declares and creates an array of ten `Circle` objects:

```
Circle[] circleArray = new Circle[10];
```

To initialize the `circleArray`, you can use a `for` loop like this one:

```
for (int i = 0; i < circleArray.length; i++) {
  circleArray[i] = new Circle();
}
```

An array of objects is actually an *array of reference variables*. So invoking `circleArray[1].getArea()` involves two levels of referencing, as shown in Figure 7.20. `circleArray` references the entire array. `circleArray[1]` references a `Circle` object.

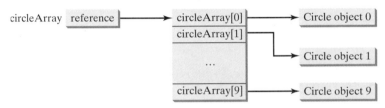

FIGURE 7.20 In an array of objects, an element of the array contains a reference to an object.

Note

When an array of objects is created using the **new** operator, each element is a reference variable with a default value of `null`.

Listing 7.7 gives an example that demonstrates how to use an array of objects. The program summarizes the areas of an array of circles. The program creates `circleArray`, an array composed of ten `Circle3` objects; it then initializes circle radii with random values, and displays the total area of the circles in the array. The output of a sample run of the program is shown in Figure 7.21.

LISTING 7.7 TotalArea.java

```
1 public class TotalArea {
2   /** Main method */
3   public static void main(String[] args) {
4     // Declare circleArray
5     Circle3[] circleArray;
6
7     // Create circleArray
8     circleArray = createCircleArray();
9
10    // Print circleArray and total areas of the circles
11    printCircleArray(circleArray);
12  }
13
```

```java
14    /** Create an array of Circle objects */
15    public static Circle3[] createCircleArray() {
16      Circle3[] circleArray = new Circle3[10];
17
18      for (int i = 0; i < circleArray.length; i++) {
19        circleArray[i] = new Circle3(Math.random() * 100);
20      }
21
22      // Return Circle array
23      return circleArray;
24    }
25
26    /** Print an array of circles and their total area */
27    public static void printCircleArray
28        (Circle3[] circleArray) {
29      System.out.println("Radius\t\t\t\t" + "Area");
30      for (int i = 0; i < circleArray.length; i++) {
31        System.out.print(circleArray[i].getRadius() + "\t\t" +
32          circleArray[i].getArea() + '\n');
33      }
34
35      System.out.println("--------------");
36
37      // Compute and display the result
38      System.out.println("The total areas of circles is \t" +
39        sum(circleArray));
40    }
41
42    /** Add circle areas */
43    public static double sum(Circle3[] circleArray) {
44      // Initialize sum
45      double sum = 0;
46
47      // Add areas to sum
48      for (int i = 0; i < circleArray.length; i++)
49        sum += circleArray[i].getArea();
50
51      return sum;
52    }
53 }
```

FIGURE 7.21   The program creates an array of `Circle3` objects, then displays their total area.

The program invokes `createCircleArray()` (line 8) to create an array of ten `Circle3` objects. Several `Circle` classes were introduced in this chapter. This example uses the `Circle3` class introduced in §7.8, "Data Field Encapsulation."

The circle radii are randomly generated using the `Math.random()` method (line 19). The `createCircleArray` method returns an array of `Circle3` objects (line 23). The array is passed to the `printCircleArray` method, which displays the radii of the total area of the circles.

The sum of the areas of the circle is computed using the `sum` method (line 39), which takes the array of `Circle3` objects as the argument and returns a `double` value for the total area.

7.14 Class Abstraction and Encapsulation

In Chapter 5, "Methods," you learned about method abstraction and used it in program development. Java provides many levels of abstraction. *Class abstraction* is the separation of class implementation from the use of a class. The creator of a class provides a description of the class and lets the user know how the class can be used. The collection of methods and fields that are accessible from outside the class, together with the description of how these members are expected to behave, serves as the *class's contract*. As shown in Figure 7.22, the user of the class does not need to know how the class is implemented. The details of implementation are encapsulated and hidden from the user. This is known as *class encapsulation*. For example, you can create a `Circle` object and find the area of the circle without knowing how the area is computed.

class abstraction

class encapsulation

FIGURE 7.22   Class abstraction separates class implementation from the use of the class.

Class abstraction and encapsulation are two sides of the same coin. There are many real-life examples that illustrate the concept of class abstraction. Consider building a computer system, for instance. Your personal computer is made up of many components, such as a CPU, CD-ROM, floppy disk, motherboard, fan, and so on. Each component can be viewed as an object that has properties and methods. To get the components to work together, all you need to know is how each component is used and how it interacts with the others. You don't need to know how it works internally. The internal implementation is encapsulated and hidden from you. You can build a computer without knowing how a component is implemented.

The computer-system analogy precisely mirrors the object-oriented approach. Each component can be viewed as an object of the class for the component. For example, you might have a class that models all kinds of fans for use in a computer, with properties like fan size and speed, and methods like start, stop, and so on. A specific fan is an instance of this class with specific property values.

Consider getting a loan, for another example. A specific loan can be viewed as an object of a `Loan` class. Interest rate, loan amount, and loan period are its data properties, and computing monthly payment and total payment are its methods. When you buy a car, a loan object is created by instantiating the class with your loan interest rate, loan amount, and loan period. You can then use the methods to find the monthly payment and total payment of your loan. As a user of the `Loan` class, you don't need to know how these methods are implemented.

7.15 Case Study: The **Loan** Class

Let us use the `Loan` class as an example to demonstrate the creation and use of classes. `Loan` has the data fields: `annualInterestRate`, `numberOfYears`, `loanAmount`, and `loanDate`, and the methods `getAnnualInterestRate`, `getNumberOfYears`, `getLoanAmount`, `getLoanDate`, `setAnnualInterestRate`, `setNumberOfYears`, `setLoanAmount`, `getMonthlyPayment`, and `getTotalPayment`, as shown in Figure 7.23.

Loan
-annualInterestRate: double
-numberOfYears: int
-loanAmount: double
-loanDate: Date
+Loan()
+Loan(annualInterestRate: double, numberOfYears: int, loanAmount: double)
+getAnnualInterestRate(): double
+getNumberOfYears(): int
+getLoanAmount(): double
+getLoanDate(): Date
+setAnnualInterestRate(annualInterestRate: double): void
+setNumberOfYears(numberOfYears: int): void
+setLoanAmount(loanAmount: double): void
+getMonthlyPayment(): double
+getTotalPayment(): double

The annual interest rate of the loan (default: 2.5).
The number of years for the loan (default: 1).
The loan amount (default: 1000).
The date this loan was created.

Constructs a default Loan object.
Constructs a loan with specified interest rate, years, and loan amount.

Returns the annual interest rate of this loan.
Returns the number of the years of this loan.
Returns the amount of this loan.
Returns the date of the creation of this loan.
Sets a new annual interest rate for this loan.

Sets a new number of years for this loan.

Sets a new amount for this loan.

Returns the monthly payment of this loan.
Returns the total payment of this loan.

FIGURE 7.23 The Loan class models the properties and behaviors of loans.

composition

 Note

An object can contain another object. The relationship between the two is called *composition*. In this example, a Loan object contains a Date object.

The UML diagram in Figure 7.23 serves as the contract for the Loan class. Throughout the book, you will play the role of both class user and class writer. The user can use the class without knowing how the class is implemented. Assume that the Loan class is available. Let us begin by writing a test program that uses the Loan class in Listing 7.8.

LISTING 7.8 TestLoanClass.java

```java
1  import javax.swing.JOptionPane;
2
3  public class TestLoanClass {
4    /** Main method */
5    public static void main(String[] args) {
6      // Enter yearly interest rate
7      String annualInterestRateString = JOptionPane.showInputDialog(
8        "Enter yearly interest rate, for example 8.25:");
9
10     // Convert string to double
11     double annualInterestRate =
12       Double.parseDouble(annualInterestRateString);
13
14     // Enter number of years
15     String numberOfYearsString = JOptionPane.showInputDialog(
16       "Enter number of years as an integer, \nfor example 5:");
17
18     // Convert string to int
19     int numberOfYears = Integer.parseInt(numberOfYearsString);
```

```
20
21      // Enter loan amount
22      String loanString = JOptionPane.showInputDialog(
23        "Enter loan amount, for example 120000.95:");
24
25      // Convert string to double
26      double loanAmount = Double.parseDouble(loanString);
27
28      // Create Loan object
29      Loan loan =
30        new Loan(annualInterestRate, numberOfYears, loanAmount);
31
32      // Format to keep two digits after the decimal point
33      double monthlyPayment =
34        (int)(loan.getMonthlyPayment() * 100) / 100.0;
35      double totalPayment =
36        (int)(loan.getTotalPayment() * 100) / 100.0;
37
38      // Display results
39      String output = "The loan was created on " +
40        loan.getLoanDate().toString() + "\nThe monthly payment is " +
41        monthlyPayment + "\nThe total payment is " + totalPayment;
42      JOptionPane.showMessageDialog(null, output);
43    }
44 }
```

The `main` method reads interest rate, payment period (in years), and loan amount; creates a `Loan` object; and then obtains the monthly payment (lines 33–34) and total payment (lines 35–36) using the instance methods in the `Loan` class. Figure 7.24 shows the output of a sample run of the program.

FIGURE 7.24   The program creates a `Loan` instance with the annual interest rate, number of years, and loan amount, and displays the loan date, monthly payment, and total payment by invoking the methods of the instance.

The `Loan` class can be implemented in Listing 7.9.

LISTING 7.9   Loan.java

```
1 public class Loan {
2    private double annualInterestRate;
3    private int numberOfYears;
4    private double loanAmount;
```

```
 5    private java.util.Date loanDate;
 6
 7    /** Default constructor */
 8    public Loan() {
 9      this(7.5, 30, 100000);
10    }
11
12    /** Construct a loan with specified annual interest rate,
13        number of years and loan amount
14     */
15    public Loan(double annualInterestRate, int numberOfYears,
16        double loanAmount) {
17      this.annualInterestRate = annualInterestRate;
18      this.numberOfYears = numberOfYears;
19      this.loanAmount = loanAmount;
20      loanDate = new java.util.Date();
21    }
22
23    /** Return annualInterestRate */
24    public double getAnnualInterestRate() {
25      return annualInterestRate;
26    }
27
28    /** Set a new annualInterestRate */
29    public void setAnnualInterestRate(double annualInterestRate) {
30      this.annualInterestRate = annualInterestRate;
31    }
32
33    /** Return numberOfYears */
34    public int getNumberOfYears() {
35      return numberOfYears;
36    }
37
38    /** Set a new numberOfYears */
39    public void setNumberOfYears(int numberOfYears) {
40      this.numberOfYears = numberOfYears;
41    }
42
43    /** Return loanAmount */
44    public double getLoanAmount() {
45      return loanAmount;
46    }
47
48    /** Set a newloanAmount */
49    public void setLoanAmount(double loanAmount) {
50      this.loanAmount = loanAmount;
51    }
52
53    /** Find monthly payment */
54    public double getMonthlyPayment() {
55      double monthlyInterestRate = annualInterestRate / 1200;
56      return loanAmount * monthlyInterestRate / (1 -
57        (Math.pow(1 / (1 + monthlyInterestRate), numberOfYears * 12)));
58    }
59
60    /** Find total payment */
61    public double getTotalPayment() {
62      return getMonthlyPayment() * numberOfYears * 12;
63    }
```

no-arg constructor

constructor

```
64
65    /** Return loan date */
66    public java.util.Date getLoanDate() {
67      return loanDate;
68    }
69 }
```

From a class developer's perspective, a class is designed for use by many different customers. In order to be useful in a wide range of applications, a class should provide a variety of ways for customization through constructors, properties, and methods.

The Loan class contains two constructors, four get methods, three set methods, and the methods for finding monthly payment and total payment. You can construct a Loan object by using the no-arg constructor or the one with three parameters: annual interest rate, number of years, and loan amount. When a loan object is created, its date is stored in the loanDate field. The getLoanDate method returns the date. The three get methods, getAnnualInterest, getNumberOfYears, and getLoanAmount, return annual interest rate, payment years, and loan amount, respectively. All the data properties and methods in this class are tied to a specific instance of the Loan class. Therefore, they are instance variables or methods.

Recall that the java.util.Date can be used to create an instance to represent current date and time in §7.5.1, "The Date Class." The Loan class contains the accessor method for loanDate, but no mutator method for it. Does this mean that the contents of loanDate cannot be changed? See Review Question 7.24.

Important Pedagogical Tip

The UML diagram for the Loan class is shown in Figure 7.23. Students should begin by writing a test program that uses the Loan class even though they don't know how the Loan class is implemented. This has three benefits:

- It demonstrates that developing a class and using a class are two separate tasks.
- It makes it possible to skip the complex implementation of certain classes without interrupting the sequence of the book.
- It is easier to learn how to implement a class if you are familiar with the class through using it.

For all the examples from now on, you may first create an object from the class and try to use its methods and then turn your attention to its implementation.

7.16 Case Study: The **Course** Class

This section uses the Course class to demonstrate the creation and use of classes. The UML diagram for the class is shown in Figure 7.25.

Course
-name: String
-students: String[]
-numberOfStudents: int
+Course(name: String)
+getName(): String
+addStudent(student: String): void
+getStudents(): String[]
+getNumberOfStudents(): int

The name of the course.
The students who take the course.
The number of students (default: 0).
Creates a course with the specified name.
Returns the course name.
Adds a new student to the course list.
Returns the students for the course.
Returns the number of students for the course.

FIGURE 7.25 The Course class models the courses.

A `Course` object can be created using the constructor `Course(String name)` by passing a course name. You can add students to the course using the `addStudent (String student)` method and return all the students for the course using the `getStudents()` method. Suppose the class is available, Listing 7.10 gives a test class that creates two courses and adds students to the courses.

LISTING 7.10 TestCourse.java

```
 1 public class TestCourse {
 2   public static void main(String[] args) {
 3     Course course1 = new Course("Data Structures");
 4     Course course2 = new Course("Database Systems");
 5
 6     course1.addStudent("Peter Jones");
 7     course1.addStudent("Brian Smith");
 8     course1.addStudent("Anne Kennedy");
 9
10     course2.addStudent("Peter Jones");
11     course2.addStudent("Steve Smith");
12
13     System.out.println("Number of students in course1: "
14       + course1.getNumberOfStudents());
15     String[] students = course1.getStudents();
16     for (int i = 0; i < course1.getNumberOfStudents(); i++)
17       System.out.print(students[i] + ", ");
18
19     System.out.println();
20     System.out.print("Number of students in course2: "
21       + course2.getNumberOfStudents());
22   }
23 }
```

create a course

add a student

number of students
return students

The `Course` class is implemented in Listing 7.11. The `Course` class uses an array to store the students for the course. For simplicity, assume that the maximum course enrollment is `100`. The array is created using `new String[100]` in line 3. The `addStudent` method (line 10) adds a student to the array. Whenever a new student is added to the course, `numberOfStudents` is increased (line 11). The `getStudents` method returns the array.

LISTING 7.11 Course.java

```
 1 public class Course {
 2   private String name;
 3   private String[] students = new String[100];
 4   private int numberOfStudents;
 5
 6   public Course(String name) {
 7     this.name = name;
 8   }
 9
10   public void addStudent(String student) {
11     students[numberOfStudents] = student;
12     numberOfStudents++;
13   }
14
15   public String[] getStudents() {
16     return students;
17   }
18
```

create students

add a course

return students

```
19    public int getNumberOfStudents() {                               number of students
20      return numberOfStudents;
21    }
22
23    public String getName() {
24      return name;
25    }
26 }
```

The array size is fixed in Listing 7.11. You can improve it to automatically increase the array size in Exercise 7.8.

Note

When you create a **Course** object, an array object is created. A **Course** object contains a reference to the array. For simplicity, you can say that the **Course** object contains the array.

Note

The user can create a **Course** and manipulate it through the public methods **addStudent**, **getNumberOfStudents**, and **getStudents**. However, the user doesn't need to know how these methods are implemented. The **Course** class encapsulates the internal implementation. This example uses an array to store students. You may use a different data structure to store students. The program that uses **Course** does not need to change as long as the contract of the public methods remains unchanged.

7.17 (Optional) Case Study: The **StackOfIntegers** Class

This section gives another example to demonstrate the creation and use of classes. Let us create a class for stacks.

A *stack* is a data structure that holds objects in a last-in first-out fashion. It has many applications. For example, the compiler uses a stack to process method invocations. When a method is invoked, its parameters and local variables are pushed into a stack. When a method calls another method, the new method's parameters and local variables are pushed into the stack. When a method finishes its work and returns to its caller, its associated space is released from the stack.

For simplicity, assume the stack holds the **int** values and name the stack class **StackOfIntegers**. The UML diagram for the class is shown in Figure 7.26.

stack

StackOfIntegers	
-elements: int[] -size: int	An array to store integers in the stack. The number of integers in the stack.
+StackOfIntegers() +StackOfIntegers(capacity: int) +empty(): boolean +peek(): int +push(value: int): int +pop(): int +getSize(): int	Constructs an empty stack with a default capacity of 16. Constructs an empty stack with a specified capacity. Returns true if the stack is empty. Returns the integer at the top of the stack without removing it from the stack. Stores an integer in the top of the stack. Removes the integer at the top of the stack and returns it. Returns the number of elements in the stack.

FIGURE 7.26 The **StackOfIntegers** class encapsulates the stack storage and provides the operations for manipulating the stack.

Suppose that the class is available. Let us write a test program in Listing 7.12 that uses the class to create a stack (line 3), stores ten integers 0, 1, 2, ..., and 9 (line 6), and displays them in reverse order (line 9).

LISTING 7.12 TestStackOfIntegers.java

```
1 public class TestStackOfIntegers {
2   public static void main(String[] args) {
3     StackOfIntegers stack = new StackOfIntegers();
4
5     for (int i = 0; i < 10; i++)
6       stack.push(i);
7
8     while (!stack.empty())
9       System.out.print(stack.pop() + " ");
10  }
11 }
```

create a stack

push to stack

pop from stack

How do you implement the `StackOfIntegers` class? The elements in the stack are stored in an array named `elements`. When you create a stack, the array is also created. The no-arg constructor creates an array with the default capacity of 16. The variable `size` counts the number of elements in the stack, and `size - 1` is the index of the element at the top of the stack, as shown in Figure 7.27. For an empty stack, `size` is 0.

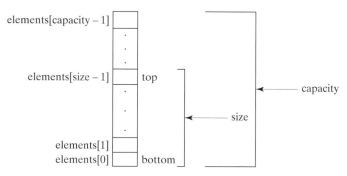

FIGURE 7.27 The `StackOfIntegers` class encapsulates the stack storage and provides the operations for manipulating the stack.

The `StackOfIntegers` class is implemented in Listing 7.13. The methods `empty()`, `peek()`, `pop()`, and `getSize()` are easy to implement. To implement `push(int value)`, assign `value` to `elements[size]` if `size < capacity` (line 24). If the stack is full (i.e., `size >= capacity`), create a new array of twice the current capacity (line 19), copy the contents of the current array to the new array (line 19), and assign the reference of the new array to the current array in the stack (line 20). Now you can add the new value to the array (line 24).

LISTING 7.13 StackOfIntegers.java

```
1 public class StackOfIntegers {
2   private int[] elements;
3   private int size;
4   public static final int DEFAULT_CAPACITY = 16;
5
6   /** Construct a stack with the default capacity 16 */
7   public StackOfIntegers() {
8     this(DEFAULT_CAPACITY);
9   }
```

max capacity 16

```
10
11    /** Construct a stack with the specified maximum capacity */
12    public StackOfIntegers(int capacity) {
13      elements = new int[capacity];
14    }
15
16    /** Push a new integer into the top of the stack */
17    public int push(int value) {
18      if (size >= elements.length) {
19        int[] temp = new int[elements.length * 2];                    double the capacity
20        System.arraycopy(elements, 0, temp, 0, elements.length);
21        elements = temp;
22      }
23
24      return elements[size++] = value;                                add to stack
25    }
26
27    /** Return and remove the top element from the stack */
28    public int pop() {
29      return elements[--size];
30    }
31
32    /** Return the top element from the stack */
33    public int peek() {
34      return elements[size - 1];
35    }
36
37    /** Test whether the stack is empty */
38    public boolean empty() {
39      return size == 0;
40    }
41
42    /** Return the number of elements in the stack */
43    public int getSize() {
44      return size;
45    }
46  }
```

Note

Stacks are frequently used in programming. Java provides the **Stack** class in the `java.util` package, which will be introduced in Chapter 22, "Java Collections Framework."

 # 7.18 (Optional GUI) Creating Windows

When you develop programs to create graphical user interfaces, you will use Java classes such as **JFrame**, **JButton**, **JRadioButton**, **JComboBox**, and **JList** to create frames, buttons, radio buttons, combo boxes, lists, and so on. Listing 7.14 is an example that creates two windows using the **JFrame** class. The output of the program is shown in Figure 7.28.

LISTING 7.14 TestFrame.java (Using Java API Classes)

```
1 import javax.swing.JFrame;
2
3 public class TestFrame {
4   public static void main(String[] args) {
5     JFrame frame1 = new JFrame();                    create an object
6     frame1.setTitle("Window 1");                     invoke a method
```

```
 7        frame1.setSize(200, 150);
 8        frame1.setLocation(200, 100);
 9        frame1.setDefaultCloseOperation(JFrame.EXIT_ON_CLOSE);
10        frame1.setVisible(true);
11
12        JFrame frame2 = new JFrame();
13        frame2.setTitle("Window 2");
14        frame2.setSize(200, 150);
15        frame2.setLocation(410, 100);
16        frame2.setDefaultCloseOperation(JFrame.EXIT_ON_CLOSE);
17        frame2.setVisible(true);
18    }
19 }
```

create an object

invoke a method

FIGURE 7.28 The program creates two windows using the JFrame class.

This program creates two objects of the JFrame class (lines 5, 12) and then uses the methods setTitle, setSize, setLocation, setDefaultCloseOperation, and setVisible to set the properties of the objects. The setTitle method sets a title for the window (lines 6, 13). The setSize method sets the window's width and height (lines 7, 14). The setLocation method specifies the location of the window's upper-left corner (lines 8, 15). The setDefaultCloseOperation method terminates the program when the frame is closed (lines 9, 16). The setVisible method displays the window. You can add graphical user interface components, such as buttons, labels, text fields, combo boxes, lists, and menus, to the window. The components are defined using classes. GUI programming will be introduced in Part 3, "GUI Programming."

KEY TERMS

accessor method (getter)   230
class   214
class abstraction   239
class encapsulation   239
class's contract   239
composition   240
constant   224
constructor   216
data field encapsulation   229
default constructor   216
dot operator (.)   217
immutable class   232
instance   214
instance method   217
instance variable   217
instantiation   214
mutator method (setter)   230

null   220
no-arg constructor   216
object-oriented programming
    (OOP)   214
Unified Modeling Language
    (UML)   215
package-private
    (or package-access)   228
private   228
public   228
reference variable   237
reference type   216
stack   234
static method   224
static variable   224
this keyword   236

CHAPTER SUMMARY

- A class is a template for objects. It defines the generic properties of objects, and provides constructors for creating objects and methods for manipulating them.

- A class is also a data type. You can use it to declare object reference variables. An object reference variable that appears to hold an object actually contains a reference to that object. Strictly speaking, an object reference variable and an object are different, but most of the time the distinction between them can be ignored.

- An object is an instance of a class. You use the `new` operator to create an object, and the dot (`.`) operator to access members of that object through its reference variable.

- An instance variable or method belongs to an instance of a class. Its use is associated with individual instances. A static variable is a variable shared by all instances of the same class. A static method is a method that can be invoked without using instances.

- Every instance of a class can access the class's static variables and methods. However, it is better to invoke static variables and methods using `ClassName.variable` and `ClassName.method` for clarity.

- Modifiers specify how the class, method, and data are accessed. A `public` class, method, or data is accessible to all clients. A `private` method or data is only accessible inside the class.

- You can provide a `get` method or a `set` method to enable clients to see or modify the data. Colloquially, a `get` method is referred to as a *getter* (or *accessor*), and a `set` method is referred to as a *setter* (or *mutator*).

- A `get` method has the signature `public returnType getPropertyName()`. If the `returnType` is `boolean`, the `get` method should be defined as `public boolean isPropertyName()`. A `set` method has the signature `public void setPropertyName(dataType propertyValue)`.

- All parameters are passed to methods using pass-by-value. For a parameter of a primitive type, the actual value is passed; for a parameter of a reference type, the reference for the object is passed.

- The scope of instance and static variables is the entire class, regardless of where the variables are declared. Instance and static variables can be declared anywhere in the class.

- The keyword `this` can be used to refer to the calling object. It can also be used inside a constructor to invoke another constructor of the same class.

- A Java array is an object that can contain primitive type values or object type values. When an array is created, its elements are assigned the default value of `0` for the numeric primitive data types, `'\u0000'` for `char` types, `false` for `boolean` types, and `null` for object types.

REVIEW QUESTIONS

Sections 7.2–7.4

7.1 Describe the relationship between an object and its defining class. How do you declare a class? How do you declare an object reference variable? How do you create an object? How do you declare and create an object in one statement?

7.2 What are the differences between constructors and methods?

7.3 Is an array an object or a primitive type value? Can an array contain elements of an object type as well as a primitive type? Describe the default value for the elements of an array.

7.4 What is wrong with the following program?

```
public class ShowErrors {
  public static void main(String[] args) {
    ShowErrors t = new ShowErrors(5);
  }
}
```

(a)

```
public class ShowErrors {
  public static void main(String[] args) {
    ShowErrors t = new ShowErrors();
    t.x();
  }
}
```

(b)

```
public class ShowErrors {
  public void method1() {
    Circle c;
    System.out.println("What is radius "
      + c.getRadius());
    c = new Circle();
  }
}
```

(c)

```
public class ShowErrors {
  public static void main(String[] args) {
    C c = new C(5.0);
    System.out.println(c.value);
  }
}

class C {
  int value = 2;
}
```

(d)

7.5 What is wrong in the following code?

```
1 class Test {
2   public static void main(String[] args) {
3     A a = new A();
4     a.print();
5   }
6 }
7
8 class A {
9   String s;
10
11   A(String s) {
12     this.s = s;
13   }
14
15   public void print() {
16     System.out.print(s);
17   }
18 }
```

7.6 What is the printout of the following code?

```java
public class Foo {
  private boolean x;

  public static void main(String[] args) {
    Foo foo = new Foo();
    System.out.println(foo.x);
  }
}
```

Sections 7.5 Using Classes from the Java Library

7.7 How do you create a Date for the current time? How do you display the current time?

7.8 How do you create a Random object and obtain a random int value, double value, and boolean value?

7.9 Which packages contain the classes Date, Random, JOptionPane, System, and Math?

Section 7.6 Static Variables, Constants, and Methods

7.10 Suppose that the class Foo is defined in (a). Let f be an instance of Foo. Which of the statements in (b) are correct?

```java
public class Foo {
  int i;
  static String s;

  void imethod() {
  }

  static void smethod() {
  }
}
```

(a)

```java
System.out.println(f.i);
System.out.println(f.s);
f.imethod();
f.smethod();
System.out.println(Foo.i);
System.out.println(Foo.s);
Foo.imethod();
Foo.smethod();
```

(b)

7.11 Add the static keyword in the place of ? if appropriate.

```java
public class Test {
  private int count;

  public ? void main(String[] args) {
    ...
  }

  public ? int getCount() {
    return count;
  }

  public ? int factorial(int n) {
    int result = 1;
    for (int i = 1; i <= n; i++)
      result *= i;

    return result;
  }
}
```

7.12 Can you invoke an instance method or reference an instance variable from a static method? Can you invoke a static method or reference a static variable from an instance method? What is wrong in the following code?

```
1 public class Foo {
2   public static void main(String[] args) {
3     method1();
4   }
5
6   public void method1() {
7     method2();
8   }
9
10  public static void method2() {
11    System.out.println("What is radius " + c.getRadius());
12  }
13
14  Circle c = new Circle();
15 }
```

Sections 7.7–7.9

7.13 What is an accessor method? What is a mutator method? What are the naming conventions for accessor methods and mutator methods?

7.14 What are the benefits of data field encapsulation?

7.15 In the following code, `radius` is private in the `Circle` class, and `myCircle` is an object of the `Circle` class. Does the following highlighted code cause any problems? Explain why.

```
public class Circle {
  private double radius = 1.0;

  /** Find the area of this circle */
  double getArea() {
    return radius * radius * Math.PI;
  }

  public static void main(String[] args) {
    Circle myCircle = new Circle();
    System.out.println("Radius is " + myCircle.radius);
  }
}
```

7.16 If a class contains only private data fields and no set methods, is the class immutable?

7.17 If all the data fields in a class are private and primitive type, and the class contains no set methods, is the class immutable?

Section 7.10 Passing Objects to Methods

7.18 Describe the difference between passing a parameter of a primitive type and passing a parameter of a reference type. Show the output of the following program:

```
public class Test {

  public static void main(String[] args) {
    Count myCount = new Count();
    int times = 0;

    for (int i = 0; i < 100; i++)
      increment(myCount, times);

    System.out.println("count is " + myCount.count);
    System.out.println("times is " + times);
  }

  public static void increment(Count c, int times) {
    c.count++;
    times++;
  }
}
```

```
public class Count {
  public int count;

  Count(int c) {
    count = c;
  }

  Count() {
    count = 1;
  }
}
```

7.19   Show the output of the following program:

```
public class Test {
  public static void main(String[] args) {
    Circle circle1 = new Circle(1);
    Circle circle2 = new Circle(2);

    swap1(circle1, circle2);
    System.out.println("After swap1: circle1 = " +
      circle1.radius + " circle2 = " + circle2.radius);

    swap2(circle1, circle2);
    System.out.println("After swap2: circle1 = " +
      circle1.radius + " circle2 = " + circle2.radius);
  }

  public static void swap1(Circle x, Circle y) {
    Circle temp = x;
    x = y;
    y = temp;
  }

  public static void swap2(Circle x, Circle y) {
    double temp = x.radius;
    x.radius = y.radius;
    y.radius = temp;
  }
}

class Circle {
  double radius;

  Circle(double newRadius) {
    radius = newRadius;
  }
}
```

7.20 Show the printout of the following code:

```
public class Test {
  public static void main(String[] args) {
    int[] a = {1, 2};
    swap(a[0], a[1]);
    System.out.println("a[0] = " + a[0]
      + " a[1] = " + a[1]);
  }

  public static void swap(int n1, int n2) {
    int temp = n1;
    n1 = n2;
    n2 = temp;
  }
}
```

(a)

```
public class Test {
  public static void main(String[] args) {
    int[] a = {1, 2};
    swap(a);
    System.out.println("a[0] = " + a[0]
      + " a[1] = " + a[1]);
  }

  public static void swap(int[] a) {
    int temp = a[0];
    a[0] = a[1];
    a[1] = temp;
  }
}
```

(b)

```
public class Test {
  public static void main(String[] args) {
    T t = new T();
    swap(t);
    System.out.println("e1 = " + t.e1
      + " e2 = " + t.e2);
  }

  public static void swap(T t) {
    int temp = t.e1;
    t.e1 = t.e2;
    t.e2 = temp;
  }
}

class T {
  int e1 = 1;
  int e2 = 2;
}
```

(c)

```
public class Test {
  public static void main(String[] args) {
    T t1 = new T();
    T t2 = new T();
    System.out.println("t1's i = " +
      t1.i + " and j = " + t1.j);
    System.out.println("t2's i = " +
      t2.i + " and j = " + t2.j);
  }
}

class T {
  static int i = 0;
  int j = 0;

  T() {
    i++;
    j = 1;
  }
}
```

(d)

Sections 7.11–7.12

7.21 What is the output of the following program?

```
public class Foo {
  static int i = 0;
  static int j = 0;

  public static void main(String[] args) {
    int i = 2;
    int k = 3;

    {
      int j = 3;
      System.out.println("i + j is " + i + j);
    }
```

```
            k = i + j;
            System.out.println("k is " + k);
            System.out.println("j is " + j);
        }
    }
```

7.22 Describe the role of the `this` keyword. What is wrong in the following code?

```
1 public class C {
2   int p;
3
4   public void setP(int p) {
5     p = p;
6   }
7 }
```

Sections 7.13–7.17

7.23 What is wrong in the following code?

```
1 public class Test {
2   public static void main(String[] args) {
3     java.util.Date[] dates = new java.util.Date[10];
4     System.out.println(dates[0]);
5     System.out.println(dates[0].toString());
6   }
7 }
```

7.24 If you redefine the `Loan` class without set methods, is the class immutable?

7.25 Is the `StackOfIntegers` class immutable?

PROGRAMMING EXERCISES

Pedagogical Note

The exercises in Part 2 achieve *three objectives*:

1. Design and draw UML for classes.
2. Implement classes from the UML.
3. Use classes to develop applications.

three objectives

Solutions for the UML diagrams for the even-numbered exercises can be downloaded from the Student Web Site and all others can be downloaded from the Instructor Web Site.

Sections 7.2–7.11

7.1 (*The Rectangle class*) Design a class named `Rectangle` to represent a rectangle. The class contains:

■ Two `double` data fields named `width` and `height` that specify the width and height of the rectangle. The default values are `1` for both `width` and `height`.
■ A string data field named `color` that specifies the color of a rectangle. Hypothetically, assume that all rectangles have the same color. The default color is white.
■ A no-arg constructor that creates a default rectangle.
■ A constructor that creates a rectangle with the specified `width` and `height`.
■ The accessor and mutator methods for all three data fields.
■ A method named `getArea()` that returns the area of this rectangle.
■ A method named `getPerimeter()` that returns the perimeter.

Draw the UML diagram for the class. Implement the class. Write a test program that creates two `Rectangle` objects. Assign width `4` and height `40` to the first object and width `3.5` and height `35.9` to the second object. Assign color red to all `Rectangle` objects. Display the properties of both objects and find their areas and perimeters.

7.2 (*The Fan class*) Design a class named `Fan` to represent a fan. The class contains:

- Three constants named `SLOW`, `MEDIUM`, and `FAST` with values `1`, `2`, and `3` to denote the fan speed.
- An `int` data field named `speed` that specifies the speed of the fan (default `SLOW`).
- A `boolean` data field named `on` that specifies whether the fan is on (default `false`).
- A `double` data field named `radius` that specifies the radius of the fan (default `5`).
- A string data field named `color` that specifies the color of the fan (default `blue`).
- A no-arg constructor that creates a default fan.
- The accessor and mutator methods for all four data fields.
- A method named `toString()` that returns a string description for the fan. If the fan is on, the method returns the fan speed, color, and radius in one combined string. If the fan is not on, the method returns fan color and radius along with the string `"fan is off"` in one combined string.

Draw the UML diagram for the class. Implement the class. Write a test program that creates two `Fan` objects. Assign maximum speed, radius `10`, color `yellow`, and turn it on to the first object. Assign medium speed, radius `5`, color `blue`, and turn it off to the second object. Display the objects by invoking their `toString` method.

7.3 (*The Account class*) Design a class named `Account` that contains:

- An `int` data field named `id` for the account (default `0`).
- A `double` data field named `balance` for the account (default `0`).
- A `double` data field named `annualInterestRate` that stores the current interest rate (default `0`).
- A `Date` data field named `dateCreated` that stores the date when the account was created.
- A no-arg constructor that creates a default account.
- The accessor and mutator methods for `id`, `balance`, and `annualInterestRate`.
- The accessor method for `dateCreated`.
- A method named `getMonthlyInterestRate()` that returns the monthly interest rate.
- A method named `withDraw` that withdraws a specified amount from the account.
- A method named `deposit` that deposits a specified amount to the account.

Draw the UML diagram for the class. Implement the class. Write a test program that creates an `Account` object with an account ID of `1122`, a balance of `20000`, and an annual interest rate of `4.5%`. Use the `withdraw` method to withdraw $2500, use the `deposit` method to deposit $3000, and print the balance, the monthly interest, and the date when this account was created.

7.4 (*The Stock class*) Design a class named `Stock` that contains:

- A string data field named `symbol` for the stock's symbol.
- A string data field named `name` for the stock's name.
- A `double` data field named `previousClosingPrice` that stores the stock price for the previous day.
- A `double` data field named `currentPrice` that stores the stock price for the current time.
- A constructor that creates a stock with specified symbol and name.
- The accessor methods for all data fields.
- The mutator methods for `previousClosingPrice` and `currentPrice`.
- A method named `changePercent()` that returns the percentage changed from `previousClosingPrice` to `currentPrice`.

Draw the UML diagram for the class. Implement the class. Write a test program that creates a `Stock` object with the stock symbol SUNW, the name Sun Microsystems Inc, and the previous closing price of `100`. Set a new current price to `90` and display the price-change percentage.

7.5* (*Using the GregorianCalendar class*) Java API has the `GregorianCalendar` class in the `java.util` package that can be used to obtain the year, month, and day of a date. The no-arg constructor constructs an instance for the current date, and the methods `get(GregorianCalendar.YEAR)`, `get(GregorianCalendar.MONTH)`, and `get(GregorianCalendar.DAY_OF_MONTH)` return the year, month, and day. Write a program to test this class to display the current year, month, and day.

7.6** (*Displaying calendars*) Rewrite the `PrintCalendar` class in §5.11, "Method Abstraction and Stepwise Refinement," to display calendars in a message dialog box. Since the output is generated from several static methods in the class, you may define a static `String` variable `output` for storing the output and display it in a message dialog box.

7.7* (*The Time class*) Design a class named `Time`. The class contains:

- Data fields `hour`, `minute`, and `second` that represents a time.
- A no-arg constructor that creates a `Time` object for the current time. (The data fields value will represent the current time)
- A constructor that constructs a `Time` object with a specified elapse time since the middle night, January 1, 1970 in milliseconds. (The data fields value will represent this time.)
- Three get methods for the data fields `hour`, `minute`, and `second`, respectively.

Draw the UML diagram for the class. Implement the class. Write a test program that creates two `Time` objects (using `new Time()` and `new Time(555550000)`) and display their hour, minute, and second.

Hint

The No-arg constructor uses the current time. The current time can be obtained using `System.currentTimeMillis()`, as shown in Listing 2.8, ShowCurrentTime.java. The other constructor sets the hour, minute, and second for the specified elapse time. For example, if the elapse time is `555550000` milliseconds, the hour is `10`, the minute is `19`, and the second is `10`.

7.8* (*The Course class*) The array size is fixed in Listing 7.11. Improve it to automatically increase the array size by creating a new larger array and copying the contents of the current array to it.

Sections 7.12–7.16

7.9   (*The MyInteger class*) Design a class named `MyInteger`. The class contains:

- An `int` data field named `value` that stores the `int` value represented by this object.
- A constructor that creates a `MyInteger` object for the specified `int` value.
- A get method that returns the `int` value.
- Methods `isEven()`, `isOdd()`, and `isPrime()` that return `true` if the value is even, odd, or prime, respectively.
- Static methods `isEven(int)`, `isOdd(int)`, and `isPrime(int)` that return `true` if the specified value is even, odd, or prime, respectively.
- Static methods `isEven(MyInteger)`, `isOdd(MyInteger)`, and `isPrime(MyInteger)` that return `true` if the specified value is even, odd, or prime, respectively.
- Methods `equals(int)` and `equals(MyInteger)` that return `true` if the value in the object is equal to the specified value.
- A static method `parseInt(int)` that converts a string to an `int` value.

Draw the UML diagram for the class. Implement the class. Write a client program that tests all methods in the class.

7.10   (*Modifying the Loan class*) Rewrite the `Loan` class to add two static methods for computing monthly payment and total payment, as follows:

```
public static double monthlyPayment(double annualInterestRate,
    int numOfYears, double loanAmount)

public static double totalPayment(double annualInterestRate,
    int numOfYears, double loanAmount)
```

Write a client program to test these two methods.

7.11   (*The MyPoint class*) Design a class named `MyPoint` to represent a point with x and y-coordinates. The class contains:

- Two data fields x and y that represent the coordinates.
- A no-arg constructor that creates a point (0, 0).
- A constructor that constructs a point with specified coordinates.
- Two get methods for data fields x and y, respectively.
- A method named `distance` that returns the distance from this point to another point of the `MyPoint` type.
- A method named `distance` that returns the distance from this point to another point with specified x and y-coordinates.

Draw the UML diagram for the class. Implement the class. Write a test program that creates two points (0, 0) and (10, 30.5) and displays the distance between them.

7.12* (*Displaying the prime factors*) Write a program that receives a positive integer and displays all its smallest factors in decreasing order. For example, if the integer is 120, the smallest factors are displayed as 5, 3, 2, 2, 2. Use the `StackOfIntegers` class to store the factors (e.g., 2, 2, 2, 3, 5) and retrieve and display them in reverse order.

7.13**(*Displaying the prime numbers*) Write a program that displays all the prime numbers less than 120 in decreasing order. Use the `StackOfIntegers` class to store the prime numbers (e.g., 2, 3, 5, ...) and retrieve and display them in reverse order.

7.14***   (*The Tax class*) Design a class named `Tax` to contain the following instance data fields:

- `int filingStatus`: One of the four tax filing statuses: `0` — single filer, `1` — married filing jointly, `2` — married filing separately, and `3` — head of household. Use the public static constants `SINGLE_FILER` (`0`), `MARRIED_JOINTLY` (`1`), `MARRIED_SEPARATELY` (`2`), `HEAD_OF_HOUSEHOLD` (`3`) to represent the status.
- `int[][] brackets`: Stores the tax brackets for each filing status (see Listing 6.11, ComputeTax.java).
- `double[] rates`: Stores tax rates for each bracket (see Listing 6.11).
- `double taxableIncome`: Stores the taxable income.

Provide the get and set methods for each data field and the `getTax()` method that returns the tax. Also provide a no-arg constructor and the constructor `Tax(filingStatus, brackets, rates, taxableIncome)`.

Draw the UML diagram for the class. Implement the class. Write a test program that uses the `Tax` class to print the 2001 and 2002 tax tables for taxable income from $50,000 to $60,000 with intervals of $1,000 for all four statuses. The tax rates for the year 2002 were given in Table 3.7. The tax rates for 2001 are shown in Table 7.1.

TABLE 7.1   2001 United States Federal Personal Tax Rates

Tax rate	Single filers	Married filing jointly or qualifying widow(er)	Married filing separately	Head of household
15%	Up to $27,050	Up to $45,200	Up to $22,600	Up to $36,250
27.5%	$27,051–$65,550	$45,201–$109,250	$22,601–$54,625	$36,251–$93,650
30.5%	$65,551–$136,750	$109,251–$166,500	$54,626–$83,250	$93,651–$151,650
35.5%	$136,751–$297,350	$166,501–$297,350	$83,251–$148,675	$151,651–$297,350
39.1%	$297,351 or more	$297,351 or more	$148,676 or more	$297,351 or more

CHAPTER 8

STRINGS AND TEXT I/O

Objectives

- To use the `String` class to process fixed strings (§8.2).

- To use the `Character` class to process a single character (§8.3).

- To use the `StringBuilder`/`StringBuffer` class to process flexible strings (§8.4).

- To know the differences between the `String`, `StringBuilder`, and `StringBuffer` classes (§§8.2–8.4).

- To learn how to pass strings to the `main` method from the command line (§8.5).

- (Optional) To use the regular expressions to represent patterns for matching, replacing, and splitting strings (§8.6).

- To discover file properties, delete and rename files using the `File` class (§8.7).

- To write data to a file using the `PrintWriter` class (§8.8.1).

- To read data from a file using the `Scanner` class (§8.8.2).

- (Optional GUI) To add components to a frame (§8.9).

8.1 Introduction

Strings are used often in programming. A *string* is a sequence of characters. In many languages, strings are treated as arrays of characters, but in Java a string is an object. Java provides the `String`, `StringBuilder`, and `StringBuffer` classes for storing and processing strings.

In most cases, you use the `String` class to create strings. The `String` class is efficient for storing and processing strings, but strings created with the `String` class cannot be modified. The `StringBuilder` and `StringBuffer` classes enable you to create flexible strings that can be modified.

This chapter also introduces how to process command-line arguments to the `main` method and how to perform simple text input and output using the `Scanner` class and the `PrintWriter` class.

8.2 The `String` Class

The `java.lang.String` class models a sequence of characters as a string. You have already used string literals, such as the parameter in the `println(String s)` method. The Java compiler converts the string literal into a string object and passes it to `println`.

The `String` class has eleven constructors and more than forty methods for examining individual characters in a sequence, comparing strings, searching substrings, obtaining substrings, and creating a copy of a string with all the characters translated to uppercase or lowercase. The most frequently used methods are listed in Figure 8.1.

8.2.1 Constructing a String

You can create a string object from a string value or from an array of characters. To create a string from a string literal, use a syntax like this one:

```
String newString = new String(stringLiteral);
```

The argument `stringLiteral` is a sequence of characters enclosed inside double quotes. The following statement creates a `String` object `message` for the string literal `"Welcome to Java"`:

```
String message = new String("Welcome to Java");
```

string literal object

Since strings are used frequently, Java treats a string literal as a `String` object. So the following statement is valid:

```
String message = "Welcome to Java";
```

You can also create a string from an array of characters. For example, the following statements create the string "Good Day".

```
char[] charArray = {'G', 'o', 'o', 'd', ' ', 'D', 'a', 'y'};
String message = new String(charArray);
```

 Note

string, string variable,
string value

A `String` variable holds a reference to a `String` object that stores a string value. Strictly speaking, the terms `String` *variable*, `String` *object*, and *string value* are different, but the distinctions between them can be ignored most of the time. For simplicity, the term *string* will often be used to refer to `String` variable, `String` object, and string value.

java.lang.String	
+String()	Constructs an empty string.
+String(value: String)	Constructs a string with the specified string literal value.
+String(value: char[])	Constructs a string with the specified character array.
+charAt(index: int): char	Returns the character at the specified index from this string.
+compareTo(anotherString: String): int	Compares this string with another string.
+compareToIgnoreCase(anotherString: String): int	Compares this string with another string ignoring case.
+concat(anotherString: String): String	Concatenate this string with another string.
+endsWith(suffix: String): boolean	Returns true if this string ends with the specified suffix.
+equals(anotherString: String): boolean	Returns true if this string is equal to another string.
+equalsIgnoreCase(anotherString: String): boolean	Checks whether this string equals another string ignoring case.
+getChars(srcBegin: int, srcEnd: int, dst: char[] dstBegin: int): void	Copies characters from this string into the destination character array.
+indexOf(ch: int): int	Returns the index of the first occurrence of ch.
+indexOf(ch: int, fromIndex: int): int	Returns the index of the first occurrence of ch after fromIndex.
+indexOf(str: String): int	Returns the index of the first occurrence of str.
+indexOf(str: String, fromIndex: int): int	Returns the index of the first occurrence of str after fromIndex.
+lastIndexOf(ch: int): int	Returns the index of the last occurrence of ch.
+lastIndexOf(ch: int, fromIndex: int): int	Returns the index of the last occurrence of ch before fromIndex.
+lastIndexOf(str: String): int	Returns the index of the last occurrence of str.
+lastIndexOf(str: String, fromIndex: int): int	Returns the index of the last occurrence of str before fromIndex.
+regionMatches(toffset: int, other: String, offset: int, len: int): boolean	Returns true if the specified subregion of this string exactly. matches the specified subregion of the string argument.
+length(): int	Returns the number of characters in this string.
+replace(oldChar: char, newChar: char): String	Returns a new string with oldChar replaced by newChar.
+replaceFirst(oldString: String, newString: String): String	Replace the first matching substring in this string with the new substring.
+replaceAll(oldString: String, newString: String): String	Replace all matching substrings in this string with the new substring.
+startsWith(prefix: String): boolean	Returns true if this string starts with the specified prefix.
+subString(beginIndex: int): String	Returns the substring from beginIndex.
+subString(beginIndex: int, endIndex: int): String	Returns the substring from beginIndex to endIndex -1.
+toCharArray(): char[]	Returns a char array consisting of characters from this string.
+toLowerCase(): String	Returns a new string with all characters converted to lowercase.
+toString(): String	Returns a new string with itself.
+toUpperCase(): String	Returns a new string with all characters converted to uppercase.
+trim(): String	Returns a string with blank characters trimmed on both sides.
+copyValueOf(data: char[]): String	Returns a new string consisting of the char array data.
+valueOf(c: char): String	Returns a string consisting of the character c.
+valueOf(data: char[]): String	Same as copyValueOf(data: char[]): String.
+valueOf(d: double): String	Returns a string representing the double value.
+valueOf(f: float): String	Returns a string representing the float value.
+valueOf(i: int): String	Returns a string representing the int value.
+valueOf(l: long): String	Returns a string representing the long value.

FIGURE 8.1   The **String** class provides the methods for processing a string.

8.2.2   Immutable Strings and Interned Strings

A **String** *object is immutable; its contents cannot be changed.* Does the following code change the contents of the string?

immutable

```
String s = "Java";
s = "HTML";
```

The answer is no. The first statement creates a **String** object with the content "Java" and assigns its reference to **s**. The second statement creates a new **String** object with the content "HTML" and assigns its reference to **s**. The first **String** object still exists after the assignment, but it can no longer be accessed because variable **s** now points to the new object, as shown in Figure 8.2.

Since strings are immutable and are frequently used, the JVM improves efficiency and saves memory, by using a unique instance for string literals with the same character sequence.

After executing `String s = "Java";`   After executing `s = "HTML";`

FIGURE 8.2 Strings are immutable; their contents cannot be changed once created.

interned string

Such an instance is called *interned*. You can also use a **String** object's **intern** method to return an *interned string*. For example, the following statements:

```java
String s = "Welcome to Java";

String s1 = new String("Welcome to Java");

String s2 = s1.intern();

String s3 = "Welcome to Java";

System.out.println("s1 == s is " + (s1 == s));
System.out.println("s2 == s is " + (s2 == s));
System.out.println("s == s3 is " + (s == s3));
```

display

```
s1 == s is false
s2 == s is true
s == s3 is true
```

In the preceding statements, **s**, **s2**, and **s3** refer to the same interned string **"Welcome to Java"**, therefore **s2 == s** and **s == s3** are **true**. However, **s1 == s** is **false**, because **s** and **s1** are two different string objects even though they have the same contents.

8.2.3 String Comparisons

Often, in a program, you need to compare the contents of two strings. You might attempt to use the == operator, as follows:

==

```java
if (string1 == string2)
  System.out.println("string1 and string2 are the same object");
else
  System.out.println("string1 and string2 are different objects");
```

However, the == operator only checks whether **string1** and **string2** refer to the same object; it does not tell you whether **string1** and **string2** contain the same contents. Therefore, you cannot use the == operator to find out whether two string variables have the same contents. Instead, you should use the **equals** method for an equality comparison of the contents of objects. The code given below, for instance, can be used to compare two strings.

s1.equals(s2)

```java
if (string1.equals(string2))
  System.out.println("string1 and string2 have the same contents");
else
  System.out.println("string1 and string2 are not equal");
```

Note

Strings with the same contents do not always share the same object. For example, the following two variables, s1 and s2, are different even though their contents are identical:

```
String s1 = new String("Welcome to Java");
String s2 = "Welcome to Java";

System.out.println("s1 == s2 is " + (s1 == s2));
System.out.println("s1.equals(s2) is " + (s1.equals(s2)));
```

In this case, s1 == s2 is false since they point to two different objects, but *s1.equals(s2)* is true since the objects have the same contents. For safety and clarity, you should always use the equals method to test whether two strings have the same contents, and the == operator to test whether the two strings have the same references (i.e., point to the same memory location).

Note

For two strings x and y, x.equals(y) if and only if x.intern() == y.intern().

The compareTo method can also be used to compare two strings. For example, consider the following code:

```
s1.compareTo(s2)
```

The method returns the value 0 if s1 is equal to s2, a value less than 0 if s1 is lexicographically less than s2, and a value greater than 0 if s1 is lexicographically greater than s2.

The actual value returned from the compareTo method depends on the offset of the first two distinct characters in s1 and s2 from left to right. For example, suppose s1 is "abc" and s2 is "abg", and s1.compareTo(s2) returns –4. The first two characters (a vs. a) from s1 and s2 are compared. Because they are equal, the second two characters (b vs. b) are compared. Because they are also equal, the third two characters (c vs. g) are compared. Since the character c is 4 less than g, the comparison returns –4.

s1.compareTo(s2)

Caution

Syntax errors will occur if you compare strings by using comparison operators, such as >, >=, <, or <=. Instead, you have to use s1.compareTo(s2).

Note

The equals method returns true if two strings are equal, and false if they are not equal. The compareTo method returns 0, a positive integer, or a negative integer, depending on whether one string is equal to, greater than, or less than the other string.

The **String** class also provides equalsIgnoreCase and regionMatches methods for comparing strings. The equalsIgnoreCase method ignores the case of the letters when determining whether two strings are equal. The regionMatches method compares portions of two strings for equality. You can also use str.startsWith(prefix) to check whether string str starts with a specified prefix, and str.endsWith(suffix) to check whether string str ends with a specified suffix.

8.2.4 String Length and Retrieving Individual Characters

You can get the length of a string by invoking its length() method. For example, message.length() returns the length of the string message.

The s.charAt(index) method can be used to retrieve a specific character in a string s, where the index is between 0 and s.length() – 1. For example, message.charAt(0) returns the character W, as shown in Figure 8.3.

length()
charAt(index)

FIGURE 8.3 A `String` object is represented using an array internally.

string literal

Note
When you use a string, you often know its literal value. For convenience, Java allows you to use the *string literal* to refer directly to strings without creating new variables. Thus, `"Welcome to Java".charAt(0)` is correct and returns `W`.

encapsulating string

Note
A string value is represented using a private array variable internally. The array cannot be accessed outside of the `String` class. The `String` class provides many public methods, such as `length()` and `charAt(index)`, to retrieve the array information. This is a good example of encapsulation: the detailed data structure of the class is hidden from the user through the private modifier, and thus the user cannot directly manipulate the internal data structure. If the array were not private, the user would be able to change the string content by modifying the array. This would violate the tenet that the `String` class is immutable.

string index range

Caution
Accessing characters in a string `s` out of bounds is a common programming error. To avoid it, make sure that you do not use an index beyond `s.length()` – 1. For example, `s.charAt(s.length())` would cause a `StringIndexOutOfBoundsException`.

length()

Caution
`length` is a method in the `String` class but is a property of an array object. So you have to use `s.length()` to get the number of characters in string `s`, and `a.length` to get the number of elements in array `a`.

8.2.5 String Concatenation

You can use the `concat` method to concatenate two strings. The statement shown below, for example, concatenates strings `s1` and `s2` into `s3`:

```
String s3 = s1.concat(s2);
```

Since string concatenation is heavily used in programming, Java provides a convenient way to concatenate strings. You can use the plus (+) sign to concatenate two or more strings. So the above statement is equivalent to

s1 + s2

```
String s3 = s1 + s2;
```

The following code combines the strings `message`, `" and "`, and `"HTML"` into one string:

```
String myString = message + " and " + "HTML";
```

Recall that the + sign can also concatenate a number with a string. In this case, the number is converted into a string and then concatenated. Note that at least one of the operands must be a string in order for concatenation to take place.

8.2.6 Obtaining Substrings

You can obtain a single character from a string using the `charAt` method. You can also obtain a substring from a string using the `substring` method in the `String` class. The `substring` method has two versions:

■ `public String substring(int beginIndex, int endIndex)`
  Returns a new string that is a substring of the string. The substring begins at the specified `beginIndex` and extends to the character at index `endIndex` – `1`, as shown in Figure 8.4. Thus the length of the substring is `endIndex-beginIndex`.

`substring(int, int)`

■ `public String substring(int beginIndex)`
  Returns a new string that is a substring of the string. The substring begins with the character at the specified index and extends to the end of the string, as shown in Figure 8.4.

`substring(int)`

FIGURE 8.4   The `substring` method obtains a substring from a string.

For example,

```
String message = "Welcome to Java".substring(0, 11) + "HTML";
```

The string `message` now becomes `"Welcome to HTML"`.

8.2.7 String Conversions

The contents of a string cannot be changed once the string is created. But you can obtain a new string using the `toLowerCase`, `toUpperCase`, `trim`, and `replace` methods. The `toLowerCase` and `toUpperCase` methods return a new string by converting all the characters in the string to lowercase or uppercase. The `trim` method returns a new string by eliminating blank characters from both ends of the string. The `replace(oldChar, newChar)` method can be used to replace all occurrences of a character in the string with a new character.

For example,

```
"Welcome".toLowerCase()  returns a new string, welcome.
"Welcome".toUpperCase()  returns a new string, WELCOME.
"  Welcome".trim() returns a new string, Welcome.
"Welcome".replace('e', 'A')  returns a new string, WAlcomA.
"Welcome".replaceFirst("e", "A") returns a new string, WAlcome.
"Welcome".replaceAll("e", "A") returns a new string, WAlcomA.
```

`toLowerCase()`
`toUpperCase()`
`trim()`
`replace`

8.2.8 Finding a Character or a Substring in a String

You can use the `indexOf` and `lastIndexOf` methods to find a character or a substring in a string. Four overloaded `indexOf` methods and four overloaded `lastIndexOf` methods are defined in the `String` class.

■ `public int indexOf(int ch)`
  (`public int lastIndexOf(int ch)`)

  Returns the index of the first (*last*) character in the string that matches the specified character `ch`. Returns −1 if the specified character is not in the string. When you pass a character to `ch` (e.g., `indexOf('a')`), the character's Unicode value is passed to the parameter `ch` (e.g., the Unicode value for `'a'` is 97 in decimal).

■ **public int** indexOf(**int** ch, **int** fromIndex)
   (*public int lastIndexOf(int ch, int endIndex)*)

Returns the index of the first (*last*) character in the string starting from (*ending at*) the specified `fromIndex` (`endIndex`) that matches the specified character `ch`. Returns −1 if the specified character is not in the substring beginning at position `fromIndex` (*ending at position* `endIndex`).

■ **public int** indexOf(String str)
   (*public int lastIndexOf(String str)*)

Returns the index of the first character of the (*last*) substring in the string that matches the specified string `str`. Returns −1 if the `str` argument is not in the string.

■ **public int** indexOf(String str, **int** fromIndex)
   (*public int lastIndexOf(String str, int endIndex)*)

Returns the index of the first character of the (*last*) substring in the string starting from (*ending at*) the specified `fromIndex` (`endIndex`) that matches the specified string `str`. Returns −1 if the `str` argument is not in the substring.

For example,

indexOf
```
"Welcome to Java".indexOf('W') returns 0.
"Welcome to Java".indexOf('o') returns 4.
"Welcome to Java".indexOf('o', 5) returns 9.
"Welcome to Java".indexOf("come") returns 3.
"Welcome to Java".indexOf("Java", 5) returns 11.
"Welcome to Java".indexOf("java", 5) returns -1.
```

lastIndexOf
```
"Welcome to Java".lastIndexOf('W') returns 0.
"Welcome to Java".lastIndexOf('o') returns 9.
"Welcome to Java".lastIndexOf('o', 5) returns 4.
"Welcome to Java".lastIndexOf("come") returns 3.
"Welcome to Java".lastIndexOf("Java", 5) returns -1.
"Welcome to Java".lastIndexOf("java", 5) returns -1.
```

8.2.9 Conversion Between Strings and Arrays

Strings are not arrays, but a string can be converted into an array, and vice versa. To convert a string to an array of characters, use the `toCharArray` method. For example, the following statement converts the string `"Java"` to an array:

toCharArray
```
char[] chars = "Java".toCharArray();
```

So `chars[0]` is `'J'`, `chars[1]` is `'a'`, `chars[2]` is `'v'`, and `chars[3]` is `'a'`.

You can also use the `getChars(int srcBegin, int srcEnd, char[] dst, int dstBegin)` method to copy a substring of the string from index `srcBegin` to index `srcEnd-1` into a character array `dst` starting from index `dstBegin`. For example, the following code copies a substring "3720" in "CS3720" from index `2` to index `6 - 1` into the character array `dst` starting from index `4`:

getChars
```
char[] dst = {'J', 'A', 'V', 'A', '1', '3', '0', '1'};
"CS3720".getChars(2, 6, dst, 4);
```

Thus `dst` becomes `{'J', 'A', 'V', 'A', '3', '7', '2', '0'}`.

To convert an array of characters into a string, use the `String(char[])` constructor or the `valueOf(char[])` method. For example, the following statement constructs a string from an array using the `String` constructor:

```
String str = new String(new char[]{'J', 'a', 'v', 'a'});
```

The next statement constructs a string from an array using the `valueOf` method.

```
String str = String.valueOf(new char[]{'J', 'a', 'v', 'a'});
```

valueOf

8.2.10 Converting Characters and Numeric Values to Strings

The `valueOf` method can be used to convert an array of characters into a string. There are several overloaded versions of the `valueOf` method that can be used to convert a character and numeric values to strings with different parameter types, `char`, `double`, `long`, `int`, and `float`. For example, to convert a double value `5.44` to a string, use `String.valueOf(5.44)`. The return value is a string consisting of the characters `'5'`, `'.'`, `'4'`, and `'4'`.

overloaded **valueOf**

Note
Use `Double.parseDouble(str)` or `Integer.parseInt(str)` to convert a string to a `double` value or an `int` value.

Tip
You can use *regular expressions* to parse and validate strings. For more information, see §8.6, "Regular Expressions."

regular expression

8.2.11 Example: Checking Palindromes

This example writes a program that prompts the user to enter a string and reports whether the string is a palindrome, as shown in Figure 8.5. A string is a palindrome if it reads the same forward and backward. The words "mom," "dad," and "noon," for instance, are all palindromes.

FIGURE 8.5 The program checks whether a string is a palindrome.

One solution is to check whether the first character in the string is the same as the last character. If so, check whether the second character is the same as the second-last character. This process continues until a mismatch is found or all the characters in the string are checked, except for the middle character if the string has an odd number of characters.

To implement this idea, use two variables, say `low` and `high`, to denote the position of two characters at the beginning and the end in a string `s`, as shown in Listing 8.1 (lines 24, 27). Initially, `low` is 0 and `high` is `s.length() - 1`. If the two characters at these positions match, increment `low` by 1 and decrement `high` by 1 (lines 33–34). This process continues until (`low >= high`) or a mismatch is found.

LISTING 8.1 CheckPalindrome.java

```
1  import javax.swing.JOptionPane;
2
3  public class CheckPalindrome {
4    /** Main method */
5    public static void main(String[] args) {
6      // Prompt the user to enter a string
7      String s = JOptionPane.showInputDialog("Enter a string:");
8
9      // Declare and initialize output string
10     String output = "";
11
12     if (isPalindrome(s))
13       output = s + " is a palindrome";
14     else
15       output = s + " is not a palindrome";
16
17     // Display the result
18     JOptionPane.showMessageDialog(null, output);
19   }
20
21   /** Check if a string is a palindrome */
22   public static boolean isPalindrome(String s) {
23     // The index of the first character in the string
24     int low = 0;
25
26     // The index of the last character in the string
27     int high = s.length ()- 1;
28
29     while (low < high) {
30       if (s.charAt(low) != s.charAt(high))
31         return false; // Not a palindrome
32
33       low++;
34       high--;
35     }
36
37     return true; // The string is a palindrome
38   }
39 }
```

input string (line 7)

low index (line 24)

high index (line 27)

update indices (line 33)

8.3 The **Character** Class

Java provides a wrapper class for every primitive data type. These classes are `Character`, `Boolean`, `Byte`, `Short`, `Integer`, `Long`, `Float`, and `Double` for `char`, `boolean`, `byte`, `short`, `int`, `long`, `float`, and `double`. All these classes are in the `java.lang` package. They enable the primitive data values to be treated as objects. They also contain useful methods for processing primitive values. This section introduces the `Character` class. The other wrapper classes will be introduced in Chapter 10, "Abstract Classes and Interfaces."

The Character class has a constructor and several methods for determining a character's category (uppercase, lowercase, digit, etc.) and for converting characters from uppercase to lowercase, and vice versa, as shown in Figure 8.6.

java.lang.Character	
+Character(value: char)	Constructs a character object with char value.
+charValue(): char	Returns the char value from this object.
+compareTo(anotherCharacter: Character): int	Compares this character with another.
+equals(anotherCharacter: Character): boolean	Returns true if this character is equal to another.
+isDigit(ch: char): boolean	Returns true if the specified character is a digit.
+isLetter(ch: char): boolean	Returns true if the specified character is a letter.
+isLetterOrDigit(ch: char): boolean	Returns true if the character is a letter or a digit.
+isLowerCase(ch: char): boolean	Returns true if the character is a lowercase letter.
+isUpperCase(ch: char): boolean	Returns true if the character is an uppercase letter.
+toLowerCase(ch: char): char	Returns the lowercase of the specified character.
+toUpperCase(ch: char): char	Returns the uppercase of the specified character.

FIGURE 8.6   The Character class provides the methods for manipulating a character.

You can create a Character object from a char value. For example, the following statement creates a Character object for the character 'a'.

```
Character character = new Character('a');
```

The charValue method returns the character value wrapped in the Character object. The compareTo method compares this character with another character and returns an integer that is the difference between the Unicodes of this character and the other character. The equals method returns true if and only if the two characters are the same. For example, suppose charObject is new Character('b'):

```
charObject.compareTo(new Character('a')) returns 1
charObject.compareTo(new Character('b')) returns 0
charObject.compareTo(new Character('c')) returns -1
charObject.compareTo(new Character('d') returns -2
charObject.equals(new Character('b')) returns true
charObject.equals(new Character('d')) returns false
```

Most of the methods in the Character class are static methods. The isDigit(char ch) method returns true if the character is a digit. The isLetter(char ch) method returns true if the character is a letter. The isLetterOrDigit(char ch) method is true if the character is a letter or a digit. The isLowerCase(char ch) method is true if the character is a lowercase letter. The isUpperCase(char ch) method is true if the character is an uppercase letter. The toLowerCase(char ch) method returns the lowercase letter for the character, and the toUpperCase(char ch) method returns the uppercase letter for the character.

8.3.1   Example: Counting Each Letter in a String

This example presents a program that prompts the user to enter a string and counts the number of occurrences of each letter in the string regardless of case, as shown in Figure 8.7.

FIGURE 8.7 The program counts the number of occurrences for each letter in the string.

Here are the steps to solve this problem:

1. Convert all the uppercase letters in the string to lowercase using the `toLowerCase` method in the `String` class.

2. Create an array, say `counts` of twenty-six `int` values, each of which counts the occurrences of a letter. That is, `counts[0]` counts the number of **a**'s, `counts[1]` counts the number of **b**'s, and so on.

3. For each character in the string, check whether it is a (lowercase) letter. If so, increment the corresponding count in the array.

LISTING 8.2 CountEachLetter.java

```
 1  import javax.swing.JOptionPane;
 2
 3  public class CountEachLetter {
 4    /** Main method */
 5    public static void main(String[] args) {
 6      // Prompt the user to enter a string
 7      String s = JOptionPane.showInputDialog("Enter a string:");
 8
 9      // Invoke the countLetters method to count each letter
10      int[] counts = countLetters(s.toLowerCase());
11
12      // Declare and initialize output string
13      String output = "";
14
15      // Display results
16      for (int i = 0; i < counts.length; i++) {
17        if (counts[i] != 0)
18          output += (char)('a' + i) + " appears   " +
19            counts[i] + ((counts[i] == 1) ? " time\n" : " times\n");
20      }
21
22      // Display the result
23      JOptionPane.showMessageDialog(null, output);
24    }
25
26    // Count each letter in the string
27    public static int[] countLetters(String s) {
28      int[] counts = new int[26];
29
30      for (int i = 0; i < s.length(); i++) {
31        if (Character.isLetter(s.charAt(i)))
32          counts[s.charAt(i) - 'a']++;
33      }
34
35      return counts;
36    }
37  }
```

input string

count letters

count a letter

The `main` method reads a string (line 7) and counts the number of occurrences of each letter in the string by invoking the `countLetters` method (line 10). Since the case of the letters is ignored, the program uses the `toLowerCase` method to convert the string into all lowercase and pass the new string to the `countLetters` method.

The `countLetters` method (lines 27–36) returns an array of twenty-six elements. Each element counts the number of occurrences of a letter in the string `s`. The method processes each character in the string. If the character is a letter, its corresponding count is increased by 1. For example, if the character (`s.charAr(i)`) is `'a'`, the corresponding count is `counts['a' - 'a']` (i.e., `counts[0]`). If the character is `'b'`, the corresponding count is `counts['b' - 'a']` (i.e., `counts[1]`) since the Unicode of `'b'` is `1` more than that of `'a'`. If the character is `'z'`, the corresponding count is `counts['z' - 'a']` (i.e., `counts[25]`) since the Unicode of `'z'` is `25` more than that of `'a'`.

8.4 The **StringBuilder/StringBuffer** Class

The `StringBuilder`/`StringBuffer` class is an alternative to the `String` class. In general, a `StringBuilder`/`StringBuffer` can be used wherever a string is used. `StringBuilder/StringBuffer` is more flexible than `String`. You can add, insert, or append new contents into a string buffer, whereas the value of a `String` object is fixed once the string is created.

The `StringBuilder` class, introduced in JDK 1.5, is similar to `StringBuffer` except that the `update` methods in `StringBuffer` are synchronized. Use `StringBuffer` if it may be accessed by multiple tasks concurrently. Using `StringBuilder` is more efficient if it is accessed by a single task. The constructors and methods in `StringBuffer` and `StringBuilder` are almost the same. This section covers `StringBuffer`. You may replace `StringBuffer` by `StringBuilder`. The program can compile and run without any other changes.

`StringBuilder`

The `StringBuffer` class has three constructors and more than thirty methods for managing the buffer and modifying strings in the buffer. You can create an empty string buffer or a string buffer from a string. The most frequently used methods are listed in Figure 8.8.

java.lang.StringBuffer	
+StringBuffer()	Constructs an empty string buffer with capacity 16.
+StringBuffer(capacity: int)	Constructs a string buffer with the specified capacity.
+StringBuffer(str: String)	Constructs a string buffer with the specified string.
+append(data: char[]): StringBuffer	Appends a char array into this string buffer.
+append(data: char[], offset: int, len: int): StringBuffer	Appends a subarray in data into this string buffer.
+append(v: *aPrimitiveType*): StringBuffer	Appends a primitive type value as a string to this buffer.
+append(str: String): StringBuffer	Appends a string to this string buffer.
+capacity(): int	Returns the capacity of this string buffer.
+charAt(index: int): char	Returns the character at the specified index.
+delete(startIndex: int, endIndex: int): StringBuffer	Deletes characters from startIndex to endIndex-1.
+deleteCharAt(index: int): StringBuffer	Deletes a character at the specified index.
+insert(index: int, data: char[], offset: int, len: int): StringBuffer	Inserts a subarray of the data in the array to the buffer at the specified index.
+insert(offset: int, data: char[]): StringBuffer	Inserts data into this buffer at the position offset.
+insert(offset: int, b: *aPrimitiveType*): StringBuffer	Inserts a value converted to a string into this buffer.
+insert(offset: int, str: String): StringBuffer	Inserts a string into this buffer at the position offset.
+length(): int	Returns the number of characters in this buffer.
+replace(int startIndex, int endIndex, String str): StringBuffer	Replaces the characters in this buffer from startIndex to endIndex-1 with the specified string.
+reverse(): StringBuffer	Reverses the characters in the buffer.
+setCharAt(index: int, ch: char): void	Sets a new character at the specified index in this buffer.
+setLength(newLength: int): void	Sets a new length in this buffer.
+substring(startIndex: int): String	Returns a substring starting at startIndex.
+substring(startIndex: int, endIndex: int): String	Returns a substring from startIndex to endIndex-1.

FIGURE 8.8 The `StringBuffer` class provides the methods for processing a string buffer.

8.4.1 Modifying Strings in the Buffer

You can append new contents at the end of a string buffer, insert new contents at a specified position in a string buffer, and delete or replace characters in a string buffer.

The `StringBuffer` class provides several overloaded methods to append `boolean`, `char`, `char array`, `double`, `float`, `int`, `long`, and `String` into a string buffer. For example, the following code appends strings and characters into `strBuf` to form a new string, `"Welcome to Java"`.

```
StringBuffer strBuf = new StringBuffer();
```

append

```
strBuf.append("Welcome");
strBuf.append(' ');
strBuf.append("to");
strBuf.append(' ');
strBuf.append("Java");
```

The `StringBuffer` class also contains overloaded methods to insert `boolean`, `char`, `char array`, `double`, `float`, `int`, `long`, and `String` into a string buffer. Consider the following code:

insert

```
strBuf.insert(11, "HTML and ");
```

Suppose `strBuf` contains `"Welcome to Java"` before the `insert` method is applied. This code inserts `"HTML and "` at position 11 in `strBuf` (just before J). The new `strBuf` is `"Welcome to HTML and Java"`.

You can also delete characters from a string in the buffer using the two `delete` methods, reverse the string using the `reverse` method, replace characters using the `replace` method, or set a new character in a string using the `setCharAt` method.

For example, suppose `strBuf` contains `"Welcome to Java"` before each of the following methods is applied:

delete

```
strBuf.delete(8, 11)
```
changes the buffer to `Welcome Java`.
```
strBuf.deleteCharAt(8)
```
changes the buffer to `Welcome o Java`.

reverse
replace
setCharAt

```
strBuf.reverse()
```
changes the buffer to `avaJ ot emocleW`.
```
strBuf.replace(11, 15, "HTML")
```
changes the buffer to `Welcome to HTML`.
```
strBuf.setCharAt(0, 'w')
```
sets the buffer to `welcome to Java`.

Note

All these modification methods except `setCharAt` do two things: (1) change the contents of the string buffer, (2) return the reference of the string buffer. For example, the following statement

```
StringBuffer strBuf1 = strBuf.reverse();
```

reverses the string in the buffer and assigns the reference of the buffer to `strBuf1`. Thus `strBuf` and `strBuf1` both point to the same `StringBuffer` object. Recall that a method with nonvoid return value type may be invoked as a statement if you are not interested in the return value of the method. In this case, the return value is simply ignored. For example, in the following statement

```
strBuf.reverse();
```

the return value is ignored.

Tip

If a string does not require any change, use `String` rather than `StringBuffer`. Java can perform some optimizations for `String`, such as sharing interned strings.

8.4.2   The `toString`, `capacity`, `length`, `setLength`, and `charAt` Methods

The `StringBuffer` class provides many other methods for manipulating string buffers.

- The `toString()` method returns the string from the string buffer.   `toString()`

- The `capacity()` method returns the current capacity of the string buffer. The capac-   `capacity()`
  ity is the number of characters it is able to store without having to increase its size.

- The `length()` method returns the number of characters actually stored in the string   `length()`
  buffer.

- The `setLength(newLength)` method sets the length of the string buffer. If the   `setLength(int)`
  `newLength` argument is less than the current length of the string buffer, the string buffer
  is truncated to contain exactly the number of characters given by the `newLength` argument. If the `newLength` argument is greater than or equal to the current length, sufficient
  `null` characters (`'\u0000'`) are appended to the string buffer so that `length` becomes
  the `newLength` argument. The `newLength` argument must be greater than or equal to `0`.

- The `charAt(index)` method returns the character at a specific `index` in the string   `charAt(int)`
  buffer. The first character of a string buffer is at index `0`, the next at index `1`, and so
  on. The `index` argument must be greater than or equal to `0`, and less than the length
  of the string buffer.

Note

The length of the string is always less than or equal to the capacity of the buffer. The length is   length and capacity
the actual size of the string stored in the buffer, and the capacity is the current size of the
buffer. The buffer's capacity is automatically increased if more characters are added to exceed
its capacity. Internally, a string buffer is an array of characters, so the buffer's capacity is the
size of the array. If the buffer's capacity is exceeded, the array is replaced by a new array. The
new array size is `2 * (the previous array size + 1)`.

Tip

You can use `new StringBuffer(initialCapacity)` to create a `StringBuffer` with a
specified *initial capacity*. By carefully choosing the initial capacity, you can make your program   initial capacity
more efficient. If the capacity is always larger than the actual length of the buffer, the JVM will
never need to reallocate memory for the buffer. On the other hand, if the capacity is too large, you
will waste memory space.

8.4.3   Example: Ignoring Nonalphanumeric Characters When Checking Palindromes

Listing 8.1, CheckPalindrome.java, considered all the characters in a string to check whether
it was a palindrome. Write a new program that ignores nonalphanumeric characters in checking whether a string is a palindrome. A sample run of the program is shown in Figure 8.9.
  Here are the steps to solve the problem:

1. Filter the string by removing the nonalphanumeric characters. This can be done by creating an empty string buffer, adding each alphanumeric character in the string to a
   string buffer, and returning the string from the string buffer. You can use the
   `isLetterOrDigit(ch)` method in the `Character` class to check whether character
   `ch` is a letter or a digit.

2. Obtain a new string that is the reversal of the filtered string. Compare the reversed string
   with the filtered string using the `equals` method.

The complete program is shown in Listing 8.3.

LISTING 8.3 PalindromeIgnoreNonAlphanumeric.java

```
1  import javax.swing.JOptionPane;
2
3  public class PalindromeIgnoreNonAlphanumeric {
4    /** Main method */
5    public static void main(String[] args) {
6      // Prompt the user to enter a string
7      String s = JOptionPane.showInputDialog("Enter a string:");
8
9      // Declare and initialize output string
10     String output = "Ignoring nonalphanumeric characters, \nis "
11       + s + " a palindrome? " + isPalindrome(s);
12
13     // Display the result
14     JOptionPane.showMessageDialog(null, output);
15   }
16
17   /** Return true if a string is a palindrome */
18   public static boolean isPalindrome(String s) {
19     // Create a new string by eliminating nonalphanumeric chars
20     String s1 = filter(s);
21
22     // Create a new string that is the reversal of s1
23     String s2 = reverse(s1);
24
25     // Compare if the reversal is the same as the original string
26     return s2.equals(s1);
27   }
28
29   /** Create a new string by eliminating nonalphanumeric chars */
30   public static String filter(String s) {
31     // Create a string buffer
32     StringBuffer strBuf = new StringBuffer();
33
34     // Examine each char in the string to skip alphanumeric char
35     for (int i = 0; i < s.length(); i++) {
36       if (Character.isLetterOrDigit(s.charAt(i))) {
37         strBuf.append(s.charAt(i));
38       }
39     }
40
41     // Return a new filtered string
42     return strBuf.toString();
43   }
44
45   /** Create a new string by reversing a specified string */
46   public static String reverse(String s) {
47     StringBuffer strBuf = new StringBuffer(s);
48     strBuf.reverse(); // Use the reverse method for StringBuffer object
49     return strBuf.toString();
50   }
51 }
```

check palindrome — line 18

add letter or digit — line 37

The `filter(String s)` method (lines 30–43) examines each character in string `s` and copies it to a string buffer if the character is a letter or a numeric character. The `filter` method returns the string in the buffer. The `reverse(String s)` method (lines 46–50)

FIGURE 8.9   The program checks whether a string is a palindrome, ignoring nonalphanumeric characters.

creates a new string that reverses the specified string `s`. The `filter` and `reverse` methods both return a new string. The original string is not changed.

The program in Listing 8.1 checks whether a string is a palindrome by comparing pairs of characters from both ends of the string. Listing 8.3 uses the `reverse` method in the `StringBuffer` class to reverse the string, then compares whether the two strings are equal to determine whether the original string is a palindrome.

8.5 Command-Line Arguments

Perhaps you have already noticed the unusual declarations for the `main` method, which has parameter `args` of `String[]` type. It is clear that `args` is an array of strings. The `main` method is just like a regular method with a parameter. You can call a regular method by passing actual parameters. Can you pass arguments to `main`? Of course, yes. For example, the `main` method in class `B` is invoked by a method in `A`, as shown below.

A `main` method is just a regular method. Furthermore, you can pass arguments from the command line.

```
public class A {
  public static void main(String[] args) {
    String[] strings = {"New York",
      "Boston", "Atlanta"};
    B.main(strings);
  }
}
```

```
class B {
  public static void main(String[] args) {
    for (int i = 0; i < args.length; i++)
      System.out.println(args[i]);
  }
}
```

8.5.1   Passing Strings to the `main` Method

You can pass strings to a `main` method from the command line when you run the program. The following command line, for example, starts the program `TestMain` with three strings: `arg0`, `arg1`, and `arg2`:

```
java TestMain arg0 arg1 arg2
```

`arg0`, `arg1`, and `arg2` are strings, but they don't have to appear in double quotes on the command line. The strings are separated by a space. A string that contains a space must be enclosed in double quotes. Consider the following command line:

```
java TestMain "First num" alpha 53
```

It starts the program with three strings: "First num" and alpha, and 53, a numeric string. Note that 53 is actually treated as a string. You can use "53" instead of 53 in the command line.

When the main method is invoked, the JVM creates an array to hold the command-line arguments and pass the array reference to args. For example, if you invoke a program with n arguments, the Java interpreter creates an array like this one:

```
args = new String[n];
```

The Java interpreter then passes args to invoke the main method.

 Note

If you run the program with no strings passed, the array is created with new String[0]. In this case, the array is empty with length 0. args references to this empty array. Therefore, args is not null, but args.length is 0.

8.5.2 Example: Processing Command-Line Arguments

The strings passed to the main program are stored in args, which is an array of strings. The first string is stored in args[0], and args.length is the number of strings passed.

This example presents a program that performs binary operations on integers. The program receives three arguments: an integer followed by an operator and another integer. For example, to add two integers, use this command:

```
java Calculator 2 + 3
```

The program will display the following output:

```
2 + 3 = 5
```

Figure 8.10 shows sample runs of the program.

```
Command Prompt                                            _ □ ×
c:\book>java Calculator
Usage: java Calculator operand1 operator operand2

c:\book>java Calculator 63 + 40
63 + 40 = 103

c:\book>java Calculator 63 - 40
63 - 40 = 23

c:\book>java Calculator 63 "*" 40
63 * 40 = 2520

c:\book>java Calculator 63 / 40
63 / 40 = 1

c:\book>
```

FIGURE 8.10 The program takes three arguments (operand1 operator operand2) from the command line and displays the expression and the result of the arithmetic operation.

Here are the steps in the program:

1. Use args.length to determine whether three arguments have been provided in the command line. If not, terminate the program using System.exit(0).

2. Perform a binary arithmetic operation on the operands args[0] and args[2] using the operator specified in args[1].

The program is shown in Listing 8.4.

LISTING 8.4 Calculator.java

```
 1 public class Calculator {
 2   /** Main method */
 3   public static void main(String[] args) {
 4     // Check number of strings passed
 5     if (args.length != 3) {
 6       System.out.println(
 7         "Usage: java Calculator operand1 operator operand2");
 8       System.exit(0);
 9     }
10
11     // The result of the operation
12     int result = 0;
13
14     // Determine the operator
15     switch (args[1].charAt(0)) {                              check operator
16       case '+': result = Integer.parseInt(args[0]) +
17                          Integer.parseInt(args[2]);
18              break;
19       case '-': result = Integer.parseInt(args[0]) -
20                          Integer.parseInt(args[2]);
21              break;
22       case '*': result = Integer.parseInt(args[0]) *
23                          Integer.parseInt(args[2]);
24              break;
25       case '/': result = Integer.parseInt(args[0]) /
26                          Integer.parseInt(args[2]);
27     }
28
29     // Display result
30     System.out.println(args[0] + ' ' + args[1] + ' ' + args[2]
31       + " = " + result);
32   }
33 }
```

`Integer.parseInt(args[0])` (line 16) converts a digital string into an integer. The string must consist of digits. If not, the program will terminate abnormally.

In the sample run, "*" had to be used instead of * for the command

```
java Calculator 63 "*" 40
```

In JDK 1.1 and above, the * symbol refers to all the files in the current directory when it is used on a command line. Therefore, in order to specify the multiplication operator, the * must be enclosed in quote marks in the command line. The following program displays all the files in the current directory when issuing the command `java Test *`:

```
public class Test {
  public static void main(String[] args) {
    for (int i = 0; i < args.length; i++)
      System.out.println(args[i]);
  }
}
```

8.6 (Optional) Regular Expressions

A *regular expression* (abbreviated *regex*) is a string that describes a pattern for matching a set of strings. Regular expression is a powerful tool for string manipulations. You can use regular expressions for matching, replacing, and splitting strings.

regular expression
regex

Pedagogical Note

The previous edition of this book introduced the `StringTokenizer` class for extracting tokens from a string. Using regular expressions is more powerful and flexible than `StringTokenizer` for splitting strings. Therefore, `StringTokenizer` is obsolete.

StringTokenizer
obsolete

8.6.1 Matching Strings

Let us begin with the `matches` method in the `String` class. At first glance, the `matches` method is very similar to the `equals` method. For example, the following two statements both evaluate to `true`:

matches(regex)

```
"Java".matches("Java");
"Java".equals("Java");
```

However, the `matches` method is more powerful. It can match not only a fixed string, but also a set of strings that follow a pattern. For example, the following statements all evaluate to `true`:

```
"Java is fun".matches("Java.*")
"Java is cool".matches("Java.*")
"Java is powerful".matches("Java.*")
```

`"Java.*"` in the preceding statements is a regular expression. It describes a string pattern that begins with Java followed by any zero or more characters. Here, the substring `.*` matches any zero or more characters.

8.6.2 Regular Expression Syntax

A regular expression consists of literal characters and special symbols. Table 8.1 lists some frequently used syntax for regular expressions.

Note

backslash (\)

Backslash is a special character that starts an escape sequence in a string. So you need to use `"\\d"` in Java to represent `\d`.

Note

whitespace

Recall that a *whitespace* (or a *whitespace character*) is any character which does not display itself but does take up space. The characters `' '`, `'\t'`, `'\n'`, `'\r'`, `'\f'` are whitespace characters. So `\s` is the same as `[ \t\n\r\f]`, and `\S` is the same as `[^ \t\n\r\f\v]`.

Note

word characters

A *word character* is any letter, digit, or the underscore character. So `\w` is the same as `[a-z[A-Z][0-9]_]` or simply `[a-zA-Z0-9_]`, and `\W` is the same as `[^a-zA-Z0-9_]`.

Note

quantifiers

The last six entries `*`, `+`, `?`, `{n}`, `{n,}`, and `{n, m}` in Table 8.1 are called *quantifiers* that specify how many times the pattern before a quantifier may repeat. For example, `A*` matches zero or more A's, `A+` matches one or more A's, `A?` matches zero or one A's, `A{3}` matches exactly AAA, `A{3,}` matches at least three A's, and `A{3,6}` matches between 3 and 6 A's. `*` is the same as `{0,}`, `+` is the same as `{1,}`, and `?` is the same as `{0,1}`.

Caution

no spaces

Do not use spaces in the repeat quantifiers. For example, `A{3,6}` cannot be written as `A{3, 6}` with a space after the comma.

Note

grouping pattern

You may use parentheses to group patterns. For example, `(ab){3}` matches **ababab**, but `ab{3}` matches **abbb**.

TABLE 8.1   Frequently Used Regular Expressions

Regular Expression	Matches	Example
x	a specified character x	Java matches Java
.	any single character	Java matches J . . a
(ab|cd)	ab or cd	ten matches t(en|im)
[abc]	a, b, or c	Java matches Ja[uvwx]a
[^abc]	any character except a, b, or c	Java matches Ja[^ars]a
[a-z]	a through z	Java matches [A-M]av[a-d]
[^a-z]	any character except a through z	Java matches Jav[^b-d]
[a-e[m-p]]	a through e or m through p	Java matches [A-G[I-M]]av[a-d]
[a-e&&[c-p]]	intersection of a-e with c-p	Java matches [A-P&&[I-M]]av[a-d]
\d	a digit, same as [1-9]	Java2 matches "Java[\\d]"
\D	a non-digit	$Java matches "[\\D][\\D]ava"
\w	a word character	Java matches "[\\w]ava"
\W	a non-word character	$Java matches "[\\W][\\w]ava"
\s	a whitespace character	"Java 2" matches "Java\\s2"
\S	a non-whitespace char	Java matches "[\\S]ava"
p*	zero or more occurrences of pattern p	Java matches "[\w]*"
p+	one or more occurrences of pattern p	Java matches "[\\w]+"
p?	zero or one occurrence of pattern p	Java matches "[\\w]?Java" / Java matches "[\\w]?ava"
p{n}	exactly n occurrences of pattern p	Java matches "[\\w]{4}"
p{n,}	at least n occurrences of pattern p	Java matches "[\\w]{3,}"
p{n, m}	between n and m occurrences (inclusive)	Java matches "[\\w]{1, 9}"

Let us use several examples to demonstrate how to construct regular expressions.

Example 1

The pattern for social security numbers is xxx-xx-xxxx, where x is a digit. A regular expression for social security numbers can be described as

    [\\d]{3}-[\\d]{2}-[\\d]{4}

Example 2

An even number ends with digits 0, 2, 4, 6, or 8. The pattern for even numbers can be described as

    [\\d]*[02468]

Example 3

The pattern for telephone numbers is (xxx) xxx-xxxx, where x is a digit and the first digit cannot be zero. A regular expression for telephone numbers can be described as

```
\\([1-9][\\d]{2}\\) [\\d]{3}-[\\d]{4}
```

Note that the parentheses symbols (and) are special characters in a regular expression for grouping patterns. To represent a literal (or) in a regular expression, you have to use \\(and \\).

Example 4

Suppose the last name consists of at most twenty five letters and the first letter is in uppercase. The pattern for a last name can be described as

```
[A-Z][a-zA-Z]{1,24}
```

Note that you cannot have arbitrary whitespace in a regular expression. For example, [A-Z][\\a-zA-Z]{1, 24} would be wrong.

Example 5

Java identifiers are defined in §2.3, "Identifiers."

- An identifier must start with a letter, an underscore (_), or a dollar sign ($). It cannot start with a digit.

- An identifier is a sequence of characters that consists of letters, digits, underscores (_), and dollar signs ($).

The pattern for identifiers can be described as

```
[a-zA-Z_$][\\w$]*
```

Example 6

What strings are matched by the regular expression "Welcome to (Java|HTML)"? The answer is Welcome to Java or Welcome to HTML.

Example 7

What strings are matched by the regular expression ".*"? The answer is any string.

8.6.3 Replacing and Splitting Strings

The matches method in the String class returns true if the string matches the regular expression. The String class also contains the replaceAll, replaceFirst, and split methods for replacing and splitting strings, as shown in Figure 8.11.

The replaceAll method replaces all matching substring and the replaceFirst method replaces the first matching substring. For example, the following code

replaceAll(regex, string)

```
System.out.println("Java Java Java".replaceAll("v\\w", "wi"));
```

displays

```
Jawi Jawi Jawi
```

java.lang.String	
+matches(regex: String): boolean	Returns true if this string matches the pattern.
+replaceAll(regex: String, replacement: String): String	Returns a new string that replaces all matching substrings with the replacement.
+replaceFirst(regex: String, replacement: String): String	Returns a new string that replaces the first matching substring with the replacement.
+split(regex: String): String[]	Returns an array of strings consisting of the substrings split by the matches.
+split(regex: String, limit: int): String[]	Same as the preceding split method except that the limit parameter controls the number of times the pattern is applied.

FIGURE 8.11   The **String** class contains the methods for matching, replacing, and splitting strings using regular expressions.

The following code

```
System.out.println("Java Java Java".replaceFirst("v\\w", "wi"));
```
replaceFirst(regex, string)

displays

```
Jawi Java Java
```

There are two overloaded **split** methods. The **split(regex)** method splits a string into substrings delimited by the matches. For example, the following statement

```
String[] tokens = "Java1HTML2Perl".split("\\d");
```
split(regex)

splits string **"Java1HTML2Perl"** into **Java**, **HTML**, and **Perl** and saved in **tokens[0]**, **tokens[1]**, and **tokens[2]**.

In the **split(regex, limit)** method, the **limit** parameter determines how many times the pattern is matched. If **limit <= 0**, **split(regex, limit)** is the same as **split(regex)**. If **limit > 0**, the pattern is matched at most **limit − 1** times. Here are some examples:

```
"Java1HTML2Perl".split("\\d", 0); splits into Java, HTML, Perl
"Java1HTML2Perl".split("\\d", 1); splits into Java1HTML2Perl
"Java1HTML2Perl".split("\\d", 2); splits into Java, HTML2Perl
"Java1HTML2Perl".split("\\d", 3); splits into Java, HTML, Perl
"Java1HTML2Perl".split("\\d", 4); splits into Java, HTML, Perl
"Java1HTML2Perl".split("\\d", 5); splits into Java, HTML, Perl
```
split(regex, limit)

 Note

By default, all the quantifiers are *greedy*. This means that they will match as many occurrences as possible. For example, the following statement displays **JRvaa**, since the first match is **aaa**:

greedy match

```
System.out.println("Jaaavaa".replaceFirst("a+",   "R"));
```

You can change a quantifier's default behavior by appending a question mark (**?**) after it. The quantifier becomes *reluctant*, which means that it will match as few occurrences as possible. For example, the following statement displays **JRaavaa**, since the first match is **a**:

reluctant match

```
System.out.println("Jaaavaa".replaceFirst("a+?", "R"));
```

8.7 The **File** Class

Data stored in variables, arrays, and objects is temporary and is lost when the program terminates. To permanently store the data created in a program, you need to save them in a file on a disk or a CD. The file can be transported and can be read later by other programs. Since data are stored in files, this section introduces how to use the `File` class to obtain file properties and to delete and rename files. The next section introduces how to read/write data from/to text files.

absolute file name

Every file is placed in a directory in the file system. An *absolute file* name contains a file name with its complete path and drive letter. For example, `c:\book\Welcome.java` is the absolute file name for the file `Welcome.java` on the Windows operating system. Here

directory path

`c:\book` is referred to as the *directory path* for the file. Absolute file names are machine-dependent. On Unix, the absolute file name may be `/home/liang/book/Welcome.java`, where `/home/liang/book` is the directory path for the file `Welcome.java`.

The `File` class is intended to provide an abstraction that deals with most of the machine-dependent complexities of files and path names in a machine-independent fashion. The `File` class contains the methods for obtaining file properties and for renaming and deleting files, as shown in Figure 8.12. However, the `File` class does not contain the methods for reading and writing file contents.

java.io.File	
`+File(pathname: String)`	Creates a File object for the specified pathname. The pathname may be a directory or a file.
`+File(parent: String, child: String)`	Creates a File object for the child under the directory parent. The child may be a filename or a subdirectory.
`+File(parent: File, child: String)`	Creates a File object for the child under the directory parent. The parent is a File object. In the preceding constructor, the parent is a string.
`+exists(): boolean`	Returns true if the file or the directory represented by the File object exists.
`+canRead(): boolean`	Returns true if the file represented by the File object exists and can be read.
`+canWrite(): boolean`	Returns true if the file represented by the File object exists and can be written.
`+isDirectory(): boolean`	Returns true if the File object represents a directory.
`+isFile(): boolean`	Returns true if the File object represents a file.
`+isAbsolute(): boolean`	Returns true if the File object is created using an absolute path name.
`+isHidden(): boolean`	Returns true if the file represented in the File object is hidden. The exact definition of *hidden* is system-dependent. On Windows, you can mark a file hidden in the File Properties dialog box. On Unix systems, a file is hidden if its name begins with a period character '.'.
`+getAbsolutePath(): String`	Returns the complete absolute file or directory name represented by the File object.
`+getCanonicalPath(): String`	Returns the same as getAbsolutePath() except that it removes redundant names, such as "." and "..", from the pathname, resolves symbolic links (on Unix platforms), and converts drive letters to standard uppercase (on Win32 platforms).
`+getName(): String`	Returns the last name of the complete directory and file name represented by the File object. For example, newFile("c:\\book\\test.dat").getName() returns test.dat.
`+getPath(): String`	Returns the complete directory and file name represented by the File object. For example, new File("c:\\book\\test.dat").getPath() returns c:\book\test.dat.
`+getParent(): String`	Returns the complete parent directory of the current directory or the file represented by the File object. For example, new File("c:\\book\\test.dat").getParent() returns c:\book.
`+lastModified(): long`	Returns the time that the file was last modified.
`+delete(): boolean`	Deletes this file. The method returns true if the deletion succeeds.
`+renameTo(dest: File): boolean`	Renames this file. The method returns true if the operation succeeds.

FIGURE 8.12 The `File` class can be used to obtain file and directory properties and to delete and rename files.

The filename is a string. The `File` class is a wrapper class for the file name and its directory path. For example, `new File("c:\\book")` creates a `File` object for the directory `c:\book`, and `new File("c:\\book\\test.dat")` creates a `File` object for the file `c:\\book\\test.dat`, both on Windows. You can use the `File` class's `isDirectory()` method to check whether the object represents a directory, and the `isFile()` method to check whether the object represents a file name.

Caution

The directory separator for Windows is a backslash (\). The backslash is a special character in Java and should be written as \\ in a string literal (see Table 2.5).

\ in file names

Note

Constructing a `File` instance does not create a file on the machine. You can create a `File` instance for any filename regardless of whether it exists or not. You can invoke the `exists()` method on a `File` instance to check whether the file exists.

Do not use absolute file names in your program. If you use a file name such as `"c:\\book\\Welcome.java"`, it will work on Windows but not on other platforms. You should use a file name relative to the current directory. For example, you may create a `File` object using `new File("Welcome.java")` for the file `Welcome.java` in the current directory. You may create a `File` object using `new File("image/us.gif")` for the file `us.gif` under the image directory in the current directory. The forward slash (/) is the Java directory separator, which is the same as on Unix. The statement `new File("image/us.gif")` works on Windows, Unix, or any other platform.

relative file name

Java directory separator (/)

Listing 8.5 demonstrates how to create a `File` object and use the methods in the `File` class to obtain its properties. The program creates a `File` object for the file `us.gif`. This file is stored under the `image` directory in the current directory.

LISTING 8.5 TestFileClass.java

```java
 1 public class TestFileClass {
 2   public static void main(String[] args) {
 3     java.io.File file = new java.io.File("image/us.gif");
 4     System.out.println("Does it exist? " + file.exists());
 5     System.out.println("Can it be read? " + file.canRead());
 6     System.out.println("Can it be written? " + file.canWrite());
 7     System.out.println("Is it a directory? " + file.isDirectory());
 8     System.out.println("Is it a file? " + file.isFile());
 9     System.out.println("Is it absolute? " + file.isAbsolute());
10     System.out.println("Is it hidden? " + file.isHidden());
11     System.out.println("Absolute path is " +
12       file.getAbsolutePath());
13     System.out.println("Last modified on " +
14       new java.util.Date(file.lastModified()));
15   }
16 }
```

create a **File**
file exist?
can read?
can write?
is directory?
is file?
is absolute name?
is hidden?

The `lastModified()` method returns the date and time when the file was last modified, measured in milliseconds since the Unix time (00:00:00 GMT, January 1, 1970). The `Date` class is used to display it in a readable format in lines 13–14.

Figure 8.13(a) shows a sample run of the program on Windows, and Figure 8.13(b), a sample run on Unix. As shown in the figures, the path-naming conventions on Windows are different from those on Unix.

(a) On Windows   (b) On Unix

FIGURE 8.13 The program creates a `File` object and displays file properties.

8.8 Text I/O

A `File` object encapsulates the properties of a file or a path, but does not contain the methods for reading/writing data from/to a file. In order to perform I/O, you need to create objects using appropriate Java I/O classes. The objects contain the methods for reading/writing data from/to a file. This section introduces how to read/write strings and numeric values from/to a text file using the `Scanner` and `PrintWriter` classes.

8.8.1 Writing Data Using `PrintWriter`

The `java.io.PrintWriter` class can be used to write data to a text file. First, you have to create a `PrintWriter` object for a text file as follows:

```
PrintWriter output = new PrintWriter(filename);
```

Then, you can invoke the `print`, `println`, and `printf` methods on the `PrintWriter` object to write data to a file. Figure 8.14 summarizes frequently used methods in `PrintWriter`.

Listing 8.6 gives an example that creates an instance of `PrintWriter` and writes two lines to the file "scores.txt". Each line consists of first name (a string), middle name initial (a character), last name (a string), and score (an integer).

java.io.PrintWriter	
+PrintWriter(filename: String)	Creates a PrintWriter object for the specified file.
+print(s: String): void	Writes a string.
+print(c: char): void	Writes a character.
+print(cArray: char[]): void	Writes an array of character.
+print(i: int): void	Writes an int value.
+print(l: long): void	Writes a long value.
+print(f: float): void	Writes a float value.
+print(d: double): void	Writes a double value.
+print(b: boolean): void	Writes a boolean value.
Also contains the overloaded println methods.	A println method acts like a print method; additionally it prints a line separator. The line separator string is defined by the system. It is \r\n on Windows and \n on Unix.
Also contains the overloaded printf methods.	The printf method was introduced in §3.6, "Formatting Console Output and Strings."

FIGURE 8.14 The `PrintWriter` class contains the methods for writing data to a text file.

LISTING 8.6 `WriteData.java`

```
1 public class WriteData {
2   public static void main(String[] args) throws Exception {
3     java.io.File file = new java.io.File("scores.txt");
```

throws an exception

create `File` object

```
4      if (file.exists()) {                                      file exist?
5        System.out.println("File already exists");
6        System.exit(0);
7      }
8
9      // Create a file
10     java.io.PrintWriter output = new java.io.PrintWriter(file);    create PrintWriter
11
12     // Write formatted output to the file
13     output.print("John T Smith ");
14     output.println(90);
15     output.print("Eric K Jones ");
16     output.println(85);
17
18     // Close the file                                          print data
19     output.close();                                           close file
20   }
21 }
```

```
John T Smith 90   scores.txt
Eric K Jones 85
```

Lines 3–7 check whether the file scores.txt exists. If so, exit the program (line 6).

Invoking the constructor `new PrintWriter(String filename)` will create a new file if the file does not exist. If the file already exists, the current content in the file will be discarded.

create a file

Invoking the constructor `new PrintWriter(String filename)` may throw an I/O exception. Java forces you to write the code to deal with this type of exception. You will learn how to handle it in Chapter 17, "Exceptions and Assertions." For now, simply declare `throws Exception` in the method declaration (line 2).

throws Exception

You have used the `System.out.print` and `System.out.println` methods to write text to the console. `System.out` is a standard Java object for the console. You can create objects for writing text to any file using `print`, `println`, and `printf` (lines 13–16).

print method

The `close()` method must be used to close the file. If this method is not invoked, the data may not be saved properly in the file.

close file

8.8.2 Reading Data Using Scanner

The `java.util.Scanner` class was used to read strings and primitive values from the console in §2.13, "Console Input using the Scanner Class." A Scanner breaks its input into tokens delimited by whitespace characters. To read from the keyboard, you create a Scanner for `System.in`, as follows:

```
Scanner input = new Scanner(System.in);
```

To read from a file, create a Scanner for a file, as follows:

```
Scanner input = new Scanner(new File(filename));
```

Figure 8.15 summarizes frequently used methods in Scanner.

Listing 8.7 gives an example that creates an instance of Scanner and reads data from the file "scores.txt".

LISTING 8.7 ReadData.java

```
1 public class ReadData {
2   public static void main(String[] args) throws Exception {
3     // Create a File instance
4     java.io.File file = new java.io.File("scores.txt");          create a File
5
6     // Create a Scanner for the file
7     java.util.Scanner input = new java.util.Scanner(file);       create a Scanner
8
```

has next?
read items

```
 9    // Read data from a file
10    while (input.hasNext()) {
11      String firstName = input.next();
12      String mi = input.next();
13      String lastName = input.next();
14      int score = input.nextInt();
15      System.out.println(
16        firstName + " " + mi + " " + lastName + " " + score);
17    }
18
19    // Close the file
20    input.close();
21  }
22 }
```

close file (line 20 annotation)

John T Smith 90
Eric K Jones 85

java.util.Scanner	
+Scanner(source: File)	Creates a Scanner that produces values scanned from the specified file.
+Scanner(source: String)	Creates a Scanner that produces values scanned from the specified string.
+close()	Closes this scanner.
+hasNext(): boolean	Returns true if this scanner has another token in its input.
+next(): String	Returns next token as a string.
+nextByte(): byte	Returns next token as a byte.
+nextShort(): short	Returns next token as a short.
+nextInt(): int	Returns next token as an int.
+nextLong(): long	Returns next token as a long.
+nextFloat(): float	Returns next token as a float.
+nextDouble(): double	Returns next token as a double.
+useDelimiter(pattern: String): Scanner	Sets this scanner's delimiting pattern.

FIGURE 8.15 The Scanner class contains the methods for scanning data.

File class

Note that new Scanner(String) creates a Scanner for a given string. To create a Scanner to read data from a file, you have to use the java.io.File class to create an instance of the File using the constructor new File(filename) (line 4), and use new Scanner(File) to create a Scanner for the file (line 7).

throws Exception

Invoking the constructor new Scanner(File) may throw an I/O exception. So the main method declares throws Exception in line 2.

Each iteration in the while loop reads first name, mi, last name, and score from the text file (lines 10–17). The file is closed in line 20.

close file

It is not necessary to close the input file (line 20), but it is a good practice to do so to release the resources occupied by the file.

Note

set delimiter

By default, the delimiters for separating tokens in a Scanner are whitespace. You can use the useDelimiter(String regex) method to set a new pattern for delimiters.

8.8.3 Example: Replacing Text

Write a class named ReplaceText that replaces a string in a text file with a new string. The filename and strings are passed as command-line arguments as follows:

```
java ReplaceText sourceFile targetFile oldString newString
```

For example, invoking

```
java ReplaceText FormatString.java t.txt StringBuilder StringBuffer
```

replaces all the occurrences of `StringBuilder` by `StringBuffer` in `FormatString.java` and saves the new file in `t.txt`.

Listing 8.8 gives the solution to the problem. The program checks the number of arguments passed to the `main` method (lines 7–11), checks whether the source and target files exist (lines 14–25), creates a `Scanner` for the source file (line 28), creates a `PrintWriter` for the target file, and repeatedly reads a line from the source file (line 32), replaces the text (line 33), and writes a new line to the target file (line 34). You must close the output file (line 38) to ensure that data is saved to the file properly.

LISTING 8.8   ReplaceText.java

```java
 1 import java.io.*;
 2 import java.util.*;
 3
 4 public class ReplaceText {
 5   public static void main(String[] args) throws Exception {
 6     // Check command line parameter usage
 7     if (args.length != 4) {                                          check command usage
 8       System.out.println(
 9         "Usage: java ReplaceText sourceFile targetFile oldStr newStr");
10       System.exit(0);
11     }
12
13     // Check if source file exists
14     File sourceFile = new File(args[0]);
15     if (!sourceFile.exists()) {                                      source file exists?
16       System.out.println("Source file " + args[0] + " does not exist");
17       System.exit(0);
18     }
19
20     // Check if target file exists
21     File targetFile = new File(args[1]);
22     if (targetFile.exists()) {                                       target file exists?
23       System.out.println("Target file " + args[1] + " already exists");
24       System.exit(0);
25     }
26
27     // Create input and output files
28     Scanner input = new Scanner(sourceFile);                         create a Scanner
29     PrintWriter output = new PrintWriter(targetFile);                create a PrintWriter
30
31     while (input.hasNext()) {                                        has next?
32       String s1 = input.nextline();                                 read a line
33       String s2 = s1.replaceAll(args[2], args[3]);
34       output.println(s2);
35     }
36
37     input.close();                                                   close file
38     output.close();
39   }
40 }
```

Pedagogical Note

The previous edition of this book introduced text I/O using many subclasses of `java.io.Writer` and `java.io.Reader`. These classes are lower-level and difficult to learn. The new features in `java.io.PrinterWriter` and `java.util.Scanner` classes are sufficient for all text I/O needs. For this reason, the old-style text I/O is now moved to Supplement VI.B, "Text I/O Using `Reader` and `Writer`."   simplifying text I/O

8.9 (Optional GUI) Containers and Layout Managers

container

JFrame is a *container* that can hold other components. You can add GUI components such as labels, buttons, checkboxes, radio buttons, and combo boxes to a GUI container. Listing 8.9 gives an example that adds a button to a **JFrame**, as shown in Figure 8.16(a).

LISTING 8.9 HoldComponents.java

```
1  import javax.swing.*;
2
3  public class HoldComponents {
4    public static void main(String[] args) {
5      JFrame frame = new JFrame();
6
7      // Add a button to frame
8      JButton jbtOK = new JButton("OK");
9      frame.add(jbtOK);
10
11     frame.setTitle("Window 1");
12     frame.setSize(200, 150);
13     frame.setLocation(200, 100);
14     frame.setDefaultCloseOperation(JFrame.EXIT_ON_CLOSE);
15     frame.setVisible(true);
16   }
17 }
```

create a frame

create a button
add button

display frame

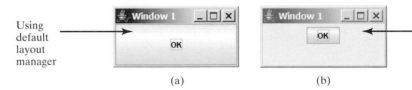

Using default layout manager

Using default FlowLayout manager

(a)   (b)

FIGURE 8.16 The frame holds a button using a default layout manager in (a) and using a **FlowLayout** manager in (b).

layout manager

The program creates a **JFrame** in line 5 and a **JButton** in line 8. The button is added to the frame in line 9. Line 14 displays the frame. Each container uses a *layout manager* object to automatically arrange the components in a container. If you don't specify a layout manager, the default layout manager is used. In this case, the button is placed in the center of the frame and occupies the whole frame, as shown in Figure 8.16(a). To display a button in its preferred size as shown in Figure 8.16(b), use a **FlowLayout** manager as shown in Listing 8.10.

FlowLayout manager

LISTING 8.10 UseFlowLayout.java

```
1  import javax.swing.*;
2  import java.awt.*;
3
4  public class UseFlowLayout {
5    public static void main(String[] args) {
6      JFrame frame = new JFrame();
7
8      // Set FlowLayout for the frame
9      FlowLayout layout = new FlowLayout();
10     frame.setLayout(layout);
11
12     // Add a button to frame
13     JButton jbtOK = new JButton("OK");
14     frame.add(jbtOK);
15
```

import package

create a frame

create **FlowLayout**
set layout

```
16      frame.setTitle("Window 1");
17      frame.setSize(200, 150);
18      frame.setLocation(200, 100);
19      frame.setDefaultCloseOperation(JFrame.EXIT_ON_CLOSE);
20      frame.setVisible(true);                                    display frame
21   }
22 }
```

The `FlowLayout` class is in the `java.awt` package, which is imported in line 2. A `FlowLayout` manager is created in line 9 and is set to the frame in line 10. The frame will use the `FlowLayout` to place the components. Listing 8.11 gives another example that adds two buttons in a frame of `FlowLayout`, as shown in Figure 8.17.

LISTING 8.11   TwoButtons.java

```
1 import javax.swing.*;
2 import java.awt.*;
3
4 public class TwoButtons {
5   public static void main(String[] args) {
6     JFrame frame = new JFrame();                                 create a frame
7
8     // Set FlowLayout for the frame
9     FlowLayout layout = new FlowLayout();                        create FlowLayout
10    frame.setLayout(layout);                                     set layout
11
12    // Add two buttons to frame
13    JButton jbtOK = new JButton("OK");                           OK button
14    JButton jbtCancel = new JButton("Cancel");                   Cancel button
15    frame.add(jbtOK);                                            add button
16    frame.add(jbtCancel);                                        add button
17
18    frame.setTitle("Window 1");
19    frame.setSize(200, 150);
20    frame.setLocation(200, 100);
21    frame.setDefaultCloseOperation(JFrame.EXIT_ON_CLOSE);
22    frame.setVisible(true);                                      display frame
23   }
24 }
```

FIGURE 8.17   The frame holds two buttons using a `FlowLayout` manager.

KEY TERMS

interned string   263   regular expression   269

CHAPTER SUMMARY

■ Strings are objects encapsulated in the `String` class. A string can be constructed using one of the eleven constructors or using a string literal shorthand initializer.

■ A `String` object is immutable; its contents cannot be changed. To improve efficiency and save memory, the JVM stores string literals in a unique object if two literal strings have the same character sequence. This unique object is called an interned string object.

■ You can get the length of a string by invoking its `length()` method, and retrieve a character at the specified `index` in the string using the `charAt(index)` method.

■ You can use the `concat` method to concatenate two strings, or the plus (+) sign to concatenate two or more strings.

■ You can use the `substring` method to obtain a substring from the string.

■ You can use the `equals` and `compareTo` methods to compare strings. The `equals` method returns `true` if two strings are equal, and `false` if they are not equal. The `compareTo` method returns `0`, a positive integer, or a negative integer, depending on whether one string is equal to, greater than, or less than the other string.

■ The `Character` class is a wrapper class for a single character. The `Character` class provides useful static methods to determine whether a character is a letter (`isLetter(char)`), a digit (`isDigit(char)`), uppercase (`isUpperCase(char)`), or lowercase (`isLowerCase(char)`).

■ The `StringBuilder`/`StringBuffer` class can be used to replace the `String` class. The `String` object is immutable, but you can add, insert, or append new contents into a `StringBuilder`/`StringBuffer` object. Use `String` if the string contents do not require any change, and use `StringBuilder`/`StringBuffer` if they change.

■ You can pass strings to the `main` method from the command line. Strings passed to the `main` program are stored in `args`, which is an array of strings. The first string is represented by `args[0]`, and `args.length` is the number of strings passed.

■ The `File` class is used to obtain file properties and manipulate files. It does not contain the methods for reading/writing data from/to a file.

■ You can use `Scanner` to read string and primitive data value from a text file and use `PrintWriter` to write data to a text file.

■ You can use the regular expressions to represent patterns for matching, replacing, and splitting strings.

REVIEW QUESTIONS

Section 8.2 The `String` Class

8.1   Suppose that `s1`, `s2`, `s3`, and `s4` are four strings, given as follows:

```java
String s1 = "Welcome to Java";
String s2 = s1;
String s3 = new String("Welcome to Java");
String s4 = s3.intern();
```

What are the results of the following expressions?

(1) `s1 == s2`   (3) `s1.equals(s2)`
(2) `s1 == s3`   (4) `s2.equals(s3)`

(5)	s1.compareTo(s2)	(15)	s1.substring(5, 11)
(6)	s2.compareTo(s3)	(16)	s1.startsWith("Wel")
(7)	s1 == s4	(17)	s1.endsWith("Java")
(8)	s1.charAt(0)	(18)	s1.toLowerCase()
(9)	s1.indexOf('j')	(19)	s1.toUpperCase()
(10)	s1.indexOf("to")	(20)	" Welcome ".trim()
(11)	s1.lastIndexOf('a')	(21)	s1.replace('o', 'T')
(12)	s1.lastIndexOf("o", 15)	(22)	s1.replaceAll("o", "T")
(13)	s1.length()	(23)	s1.replaceFirst("o", "T")
(14)	s1.substring(5)	(24)	s1.toCharArray()

8.2   Suppose that `s1` and `s2` are two strings. Which of the following statements or expressions are incorrect?

```
String s = new String("new string");
String s3 = s1 + s2;
String s3 = s1 - s2;
s1 == s2;
s1 >= s2;
s1.compareTo(s2);
int i = s1.length();
char c = s1(0);
char c = s1.charAt(s1.length());
```

8.3   What is the printout of the following code?

```
String s1 = "Welcome to Java";
String s2 = "Welcome to Java";
System.out.println("s1 == s2 is " + s1 == s2);
System.out.println("s1 == s2 is " + (s1 == s2));
```

8.4   How do you compare whether two strings are equal without considering cases? How do you convert all the letters in a string to uppercase? How do you convert all the letters in a string to lowercase? Do the conversion methods (**toLowerCase**, **toUpperCase**, **trim**, **replace**) change the contents of the string that invokes them?

8.5   Suppose string `s` is created using `new String()`; what is `s.length()`?

8.6   How do you convert a `char`, an array of characters, or a number to a string?

8.7   Why does the following code cause a `NullPointerException`?

```
1 public class Test {
2   private String text;
3
4   public Test(String s) {
5     String text = s;
6   }
7
8   public static void main(String[] args) {
9     Test test = new Test("ABC");
10     System.out.println(test.text.toLowerCase());
11   }
12 }
```

8.8   What is wrong in the following program?

```
1 public class Test {
2   String text;
3
```

```
4    public void Test(String s) {
5      this.text  = s;
6    }
7
8    public static void main(String[] args) {
9      Test test = new Test("ABC");
10     System.out.println(test);
11   }
12 }
```

Section 8.3 The **Character** Class

8.9   How do you determine whether a character is in lowercase or uppercase?

8.10   How do you determine whether a character is alphanumeric?

Section 8.4 The **StringBuilder/StringBuffer** Class

8.11   What is the difference between **StringBuilder** and **StringBuffer**?

8.12   How do you create a string buffer for a string? How do you get the string from a string buffer?

8.13   Write three statements to reverse a string **s** using the **reverse** method in the **StringBuffer** class.

8.14   Write three statements to delete a substring from a string **s** of twenty characters, starting at index 4 and ending with index 10. Use the **delete** method in the **StringBuffer** class.

8.15   What is the internal structure of a string and a string buffer?

8.16   Suppose that **s1** and **s2** are given as follows:

```
StringBuffer s1 = new StringBuffer("Java");
StringBuffer s2 = new StringBuffer("HTML");
```

Show the results of the following expressions of **s1** after each statement. Assume that the expressions are independent.

```
(1) s1.append(" is fun");    (7)  s1.deleteCharAt(3);
(2) s1.append(s2);           (8)  s1.delete(1, 3);
(3) s1.insert(2, "is fun");  (9)  s1.reverse();
(4) s1.insert(1, s2);        (10) s1.replace(1, 3, "Computer");
(5) s1.charAt(2);            (11) s1.substring(1, 3);
(6) s1.length();             (12) s1.substring(2);
```

8.17   Show the output of the following program:

```
public class Test {
  public static void main(String[] args) {
    String s = "Java";
    StringBuffer buffer = new StringBuffer(s);
    change(s, buffer);

    System.out.println(s);
    System.out.println(buffer);
  }

  private static void change(String s, StringBuffer buffer) {
    s = s + " and HTML";
    buffer.append(" and HTML");
  }
}
```

Section 8.5 Command-Line Arguments

8.18 This book declares the `main` method as

```
public static void main(String[] args)
```

Can it be replaced by one of the following lines?

```
public static void main(String args[])
public static void main(String[] x)
public static void main(String x[])
static void main(String x[])
```

8.19 Show the output of the following program when invoked using

(1) java Test I have a dream
(2) java Test "1 2 3"
(3) java Test
(4) java Test "*"
(5) java Test *

```java
public class Test {
  public static void main(String[] args) {
    System.out.println("Number of strings is " + args.length);
    for (int i = 0; i < args.length; i++)
      System.out.println(args[i]);
  }
}
```

Section 8.6 Regular Expressions

8.20 Describe whitespace characters, word characters, quantifiers, and grouping patterns in regular expressions.

8.21 Show the output of the following statements:

```java
System.out.println("abc".matches("a[\\w]c"));
System.out.println("12Java".matches("[\\d]{2}[\\w]{4}"));
System.out.println("12Java".matches("[\\w]*"));
System.out.println("12Java".matches("[\\W]*"));
System.out.println("12Java".matches("[\\d]*"));
System.out.println("12Java".matches("[\\d]{2}[\\w]"));
System.out.println("12Java".matches("[\\d]{2}[\\W]*"));
System.out.println("12Java".matches("[\\D]{2}[\\w]+"));
System.out.println("12Java".matches("[\\d]{1}[\\w]"));
System.out.println("12Java".matches("[\\d]{1}[\\w]*"));
System.out.println("12_Java".matches("[\\d]{2}[\\w]{5}"));
System.out.println("12Java".matches("[\\d]{2}[\\w]{1,15}"));
System.out.println("12#Java".matches("[\\d]{2}[\\w]{1,15}"));
```

8.22 Show the output of the following statements:

```java
System.out.println("Java".replaceAll("[av]", "RX"));
System.out.println("Java".replaceAll("av", "RX"));
System.out.println("Java".replaceAll("[a][v]", "RX"));
System.out.println("Java".replaceFirst("\\w", "RX"));
System.out.println("Java".replaceFirst("\\w*", "RX"));
System.out.println("Java12".replaceAll("\\d", "RX"));
System.out.println("Java".replaceAll("\\d", "RX"));
System.out.println("Java".replaceAll("\\W", "RX"));
System.out.println("Java".replaceAll("\\D", "RX"));
System.out.println("Java".replaceAll("\\w*", "RX"));
```

```
System.out.println("Java".replaceAll("\\w+", "RX"));
System.out.println("Java".replaceAll("\\w+?", "RX"));
System.out.println("Java".replaceFirst("\\w+?", "RX"));
```

8.23 The following methods split a string into substrings. Show the substrings for each method.

```
"Java".split("[a]")
"Java".split("[av]")
"Java#HTML#PHP".split("#")
"JavaTOHTMLToPHP".split("TO|To")
"JavaTOHTMLToPHP".split("TH")
"JavaTOHTMLToPHP".split("T|H")
"JavaTOHTMLToPHP".split("J")
```

8.24 How do you check whether a string contains all numeric digits?

Section 8.7 The File Class

8.25 What is wrong about creating a File object using the following statement?

```
new File("c:\book\test.dat");
```

8.26 How do you check whether a file already exists? How do you delete a file? How do you rename a file? Can you find the file size (the number of bytes) using the File class?

8.27 Can you use the File class for I/O?

Section 8.8 Text I/O

8.28 How do you create a PrintWriter to write data to a file? What is the reason to declare throws Exception in the main method in Listing 8.6, WriteData.java. What would happen if the close() method is not invoked in Listing 8.6.

8.29 Show the contents of the file temp.txt after the following program is executed:

```
public class Test {
  public static void main(String[] args) throws Exception {
    java.io.PrintWriter output = new java.io.PrintWriter("temp.txt");
    output.printf("amount is %f %e\r\n", 32.32, 32.32);
    output.printf("amount is %5.4f %5.4e\r\n", 32.32, 32.32);
    output.printf("%6b\r\n", (1 > 2));
    output.printf("%6s\r\n", "Java");
    output.close();
  }
}
```

8.30 How do you create a Scanner to read data from a file? What is the reason to declare throws Exception in the main method in Listing 8.7, ReadData.java. What would happen if the close() method is not invoked in Listing 8.7.

8.31 What will happen if you attempt to create a Scanner for a nonexistent file? What will happen if you attempt to create a PrintWriter for an existing file?

PROGRAMMING EXERCISES

Section 8.2 The String Class

8.1* (*Revising Listing 8.1 CheckPalindrome.java*) Rewrite Listing 8.1 by creating a new string that is a reversal of the string and compare the two to determine whether the string is a palindrome. Write your own `reverse` method using the following header:

```
public static String reverse(String s)
```

8.2* (*Revising Listing 8.1 CheckPalindrome.java*) Rewrite Listing 8.1 to ignore cases.

8.3** (*Checking substrings*) You can check whether a string is a substring of another string by using the `indexOf` method in the `String` class. Write your own method for this function. Write a program that prompts the user to enter two strings, and check whether the first string is a substring of the second.

8.4* (*Occurrences of a specified character*) Write a method that finds the number of occurrences of a specified character in the string using the following header:

```
public static int count(String str, char a)
```

For example, `count("Welcome", 'e')` returns 2.

Section 8.3 The Character Class

8.5** (*Occurrences of each digit in a string*) Write a method that counts the occurrences of each digit in a string using the following header:

```
public static int[] count(String s)
```

The method counts how many times a digit appears in the string. The return value is an array of ten elements, each of which holds the count for a digit. For example, after executing `int[] counts = count("12203AB3")`, `counts[0]` is 1, `counts[1]` is 1, `counts[2]` is 2, `counts[3]` is 2.

Write a `main` method to display the count for `"SSN is 343 32 4545 and ID is 434 34 4323"`.

8.6* (*Counting the letters in a string*) Write a method that counts the number of letters in the string using the following header:

```
public static int countLetters(String s)
```

Write a `main` method to invoke `countLetters("Java in 2008")` and display its return value.

8.7* (*Hex to decimal*) Write a method that parses a hex number as a string into a decimal integer. The method header is as follows:

```
public static int parseHex(String hexString)
```

For example, `hexString` A5 is 165 ($10 \times 16 + 5 = 165$) and FAA is 4129 ($15 \times 16^2 + 10 \times 16 + 10 = 4129$). So `parseHex("A5")` returns 165, and `parseHex("FAA")` returns `4129`. Use hex strings `ABC` and `10A` to test the method. Note that `Integer.parseInt("FAA", 16)` parses a hex string to a decimal value. Do not use this method in this exercise.

8.8* (*Binary to decimal*) Write a method that parses a binary number as a string into a decimal integer. The method header is as follows:

```java
public static int parseBinary(String binaryString)
```

For example, `binaryString` 10001 is 17 ($1 \times 2^4 + 0 \times 2^3 + 0 \times 2^2 + 0 \times 2 + 1 = 17$) So, `parseBinary("10001")` returns `17`. Use binary string `11111111` to test the method. Note that `Integer.parseInt("10001", 2)` parses a binary string to a decimal value. Do not use this method in this exercise.

Section 8.4 The `StringBuilder/StringBuffer` Class

8.9** (*Decimal to hex*) Write a method that parses a decimal number into a hex number as a string. The method header is as follows:

```java
public static String convertDecimalToHex(int value)
```

See §1.5, "Number Systems," for converting a decimal into a hex. Use decimal `298` and `9123` to test the method.

8.10** (*Decimal to binary*) Write a method that parses a decimal number into a binary number as a string. The method header is as follows:

```java
public static String convertDecimalToBinary(int value)
```

See §1.5, "Number Systems," for converting a decimal into a binary. Use decimal `298` and `9123` to test the method.

8.11** (*Sorting characters in a string*) Write a method that returns a sorted string using the following header:

```java
public static String sort(String s)
```

For example, `sort("acb")` returns `abc`.

8.12** (*Anagrams*) Write a method that checks whether two words are anagrams. Two words are anagrams if they contain the same letters in any order. For example, "silent" and "listen" are anagrams. The header of the method is as follows:

```java
public static boolean isAnagram(String s1, String s2)
```

Write a `main` method to invoke `isAnagram("silent", "listen")`, `isAnagram("garden", "ranged")`, and `isAnagram("split", "lisp")`.

Section 8.5 Command-Line Arguments

8.13* (*Passing a string to check palindromes*) Rewrite Example 8.1, "Checking Palindromes," by passing the string as a command-line argument.

8.14* (*Summing integers*) Write two programs. The first program passes an unspecified number of integers as separate strings to the `main` method and displays their total. The second program passes an unspecified number of integers in one string to the `main` method and displays their total. Name the two programs `Exercise8_14a` and `Exercise8_14b`, as shown in Figure 8.18.

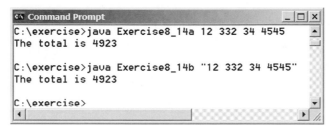

Figure 8.18
The program adds all the numbers passed from the command line.

8.15* (*Finding the number of uppercase letters in a string*) Write a program that passes a string to the `main` method and displays the number of uppercase letters in a string.

Section 8.6 Regular Expressions

8.16* (*Monetary units*) Rewrite Listing 2.7, ComputeChange.java, to receive the input as a string, and extract the dollars and cents using the split method in the `String` class.

8.17* (*Extracting words*) Write a program that extracts words from a string using the spaces and punctuation marks as delimiters. Enter the string from an input dialog box.

8.18* (*Summing values*) Write a program that reads a string from an input dialog box. The string consists of double values separated by spaces. Display the sum of the values.

Sections 8.7–8.8

8.19**(*Reformatting Java source code*) Write a program that converts the Java source code from the next-line brace style to the end-of-line brace style. For example, the following Java source in (a) uses the next-line brace style. Your program converts it to the end-of-line brace style in (b).

```
public class Test
{
  public static void main(String[] args)
  {
    // Some statements
  }
}
```

```
public class Test {
  public static void main(String[] args) {
    // Some statements
  }
}
```

(a) Next-line brace style   (b) End-of-line brace style

Your program can be invoked from the command line with the Java source code file as the argument. It converts the Java source code to a new format. For example, the following command converts the Java source code file Test.java to the end-of-line brace style.

```
java Exercise8_19 Test.java
```

8.20* (*Counting characters, words, and lines in a file*) Write a program that will count the number of characters (excluding control characters `'\r'` and `'\n'`), words, and lines, in a file. Words are separated by spaces, tabs, carriage-returns, or line-feed characters. The filename should be passed as a command-line argument, as shown in Figure 8.19.

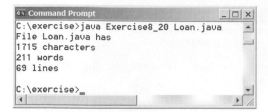

FIGURE 8.19 The program displays the number of characters, words, and lines in a given file.

8.21* *(Processing scores in a text file)* Suppose that a text file named `Exercise8_21.txt` contains an unspecified number of scores. Write a program that reads the scores from the file and displays their total and average. Scores are separated by blanks.

8.22* *(Writing/Reading data)* Write a program to create a file named `Exercise8_22.txt` if it does not exist. Write one hundred integers created randomly into the file using text I/O. Integers are separated by spaces in the file. Read the data back from the file and display the sorted data.

8.23* *(Replacing text)* Listing 8.8, ReplaceText.java, gives a program that replaces text in a source file and saves the change into a new file. Revise the program to save the change into the original file. For example, invoking

```
java Exercise8_23 file oldString newString
```

replaces `oldString` in the source file with `newString`.

 Hint

Read each line from the file, replace all the occurrences of `oldString` with `newString`, and append it into a string builder. Finally write the string builder to the original file.

8.24* *(Removing text)* Write a program that removes all the occurrences of a specified string from a text file. For example, invoking

```
java Exercise8_24 John filename
```

removes string `John` from the specified file.

 Hint

Read each line from the file, remove all the occurrences of the text in the line, and append the line into a string builder. Finally write the string builder to the source file.

CHAPTER 9

INHERITANCE AND POLYMORPHISM

Objectives

- To develop a subclass from a superclass through inheritance (§9.2).

- To invoke the superclass's constructors and methods using the `super` keyword (§9.3).

- To override methods in the subclass (§9.4).

- To distinguish differences between overriding and overloading (§9.5).

- To explore the useful methods (`equals(Object)`, `hashCode()`, `toString()`, `finalize()`, `clone()`, and `getClass()`) in the `Object` class (§9.6, §9.13 Optional).

- To comprehend polymorphism, dynamic binding, and generic programming (§9.7).

- To describe casting and explain why explicit downcasting is necessary (§9.8).

- To store, retrieve, and manipulate objects in an `ArrayList` (§9.9).

- To implement a `Stack` class using `ArrayList` (§9.10).

- To restrict access to data and methods using the `protected` visibility modifier (§9.11).

- To declare constants, unmodifiable methods, and nonextendable classes using the `final` modifier (§9.12).

- (Optional) To understand the effect of hiding data fields and static methods (§9.14).

- (Optional) To initialize data using initialization blocks and to distinguish between instance initialization and static initialization blocks (§9.15).

- (Optional GUI) To use inheritance in GUI programming (§9.16).

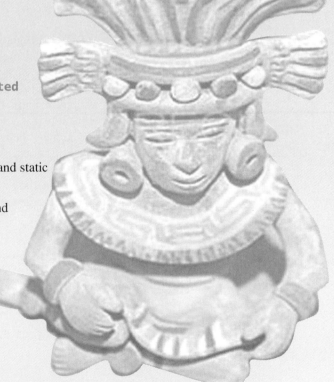

9.1 Introduction

inheritance

Object-oriented programming allows you to derive new classes from existing classes. This is called *inheritance*. Inheritance is an important and powerful concept in Java. In fact, every class you define in Java is inherited from an existing class, either explicitly or implicitly. The classes you created in the preceding chapters were all extended implicitly from the `java.lang.Object` class.

This chapter introduces the concept of inheritance. Specifically, it discusses superclasses and subclasses, the use of the keyword `super`, and the `Object` class, explores polymorphism and dynamic binding, generic programming, and casting objects, and introduces the modifiers `protected` and `final`.

9.2 Superclasses and Subclasses

subclass
superclass
supertype
subtype

In Java terminology, a class `C1` extended from another class `C2` is called a *subclass*, and `C2` is called a *superclass*. A superclass is also referred to as a *supertype*, a *parent class,* or a *base class*, and a subclass as a *subtype*, a *child class*, an *extended class*, or a *derived class*. A subclass inherits accessible data fields and methods from its superclass, and may also add new data fields and methods.

Consider geometric objects. Suppose you want to design the classes to model geometric objects like circles and rectangles. Geometric objects have many common properties and behaviors. They can be drawn in a certain color, filled or unfilled. Thus a general class `GeometricObject` can be used to model all geometric objects. This class contains the properties `color` and `filled` and their appropriate get and set methods. Assume that this class also contains the `dateCreated` property and the `getDateCreated()` and `toString()` methods. The `toString()` method returns a string representation for the object. Since a circle is a special type of geometric object, it shares common properties and methods with other geometric objects. Thus it makes sense to define the `Circle` class that extends the `GeometricObject` class. Likewise, `Rectangle` can also be declared as a subclass of `GeometricObject`. Figure 9.1 shows the relationship among these classes. An arrow pointing to the superclass is used to denote the inheritance relationship between the two classes involved.

The `Circle` class inherits all accessible data fields and methods from the `GeometricObject` class. In addition, it has a new data field, `radius`, and its associated get and set methods. It also contains the `getArea()`, `getPerimeter()`, and `getDiameter()` methods for returning the area, perimeter, and diameter of the circle.

The `Rectangle` class inherits all accessible data fields and methods from the `GeometricObject` class. In addition, it has the data fields `width` and `height`, and the associated get and set methods. It also contains the `getArea()` and `getPerimeter()` methods for returning the area and perimeter of the rectangle.

 Note

To avoid naming conflict with improved versions of the `GeometricObject`, `Circle`, and `Rectangle` classes introduced in the next chapter, put classes `GeometricObject`, `Circle`, and `Rectangle` into a package named `chapter9`. The package name must be mapped to the file system directory structure, so, place the files `GeometricObject.java`, `Circle.java`, and `Rectangle.java` into `c:\book\chapter9`.

package **chapter9**

The `GeometricObject`, `Circle`, and `Rectangle` classes are shown in Listings 9.1, 9.2, and 9.3.

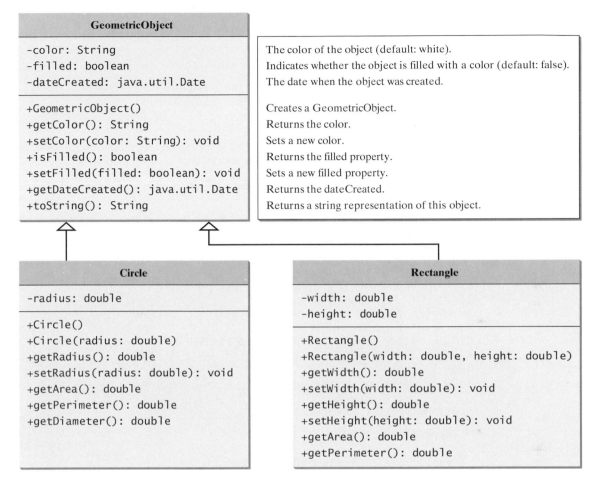

FIGURE 9.1   The `GeometricObject` class is the superclass for `Circle` and `Rectangle`.

LISTING 9.1   GeometricObject.java

```
1  package chapter9;                                                package
2
3  public class GeometricObject {
4    private String color = "white";                               data fields
5    private boolean filled;
6    private java.util.Date dateCreated;
7
8    /** Construct a default geometric object */
9    public GeometricObject() {                                     constructor
10     dateCreated = new java.util.Date();                          date constructed
11   }
12
13   /** Return color */
14   public String getColor() {                                     methods
15     return color;
16   }
17
```

```
18    /** Set a new color */
19    public void setColor(String color) {
20      this.color = color;
21    }
22
23    /** Return filled. Since filled is boolean,
24      so, the get method name is isFilled */
25    public boolean isFilled() {
26      return filled;
27    }
28
29    /** Set a new filled */
30    public void setFilled(boolean filled) {
31      this.filled = filled;
32    }
33
34    /** Get dateCreated */
35    public java.util.Date getDateCreated() {
36      return dateCreated;
37    }
38
39    /** Return a string representation of this object */
40    public String toString() {
41      return "created on " + dateCreated + "\ncolor: " + color +
42        " and filled: " + filled;
43    }
44  }
```

LISTING 9.2 Circle.java

```
1  package chapter9;
2
3  public class Circle extends GeometricObject {
4    private double radius;
5
6    public Circle() {
7    }
8
9    public Circle(double radius) {
10      this.radius = radius;
11    }
12
13    /** Return radius */
14    public double getRadius() {
15      return radius;
16    }
17
18    /** Set a new radius */
19    public void setRadius(double radius) {
20      this.radius = radius;
21    }
22
23    /** Return area */
24    public double getArea() {
25      return radius * radius * Math.PI;
26    }
27
28    /** Return diameter */
29    public double getDiameter() {
30      return 2 * radius;
31    }
32
```

package

data fields

constructor

methods

```
33    /** Return perimeter */
34    public double getPerimeter() {
35      return 2 * radius * Math.PI;
36    }
37
38    /* Print the circle info */
39    public void printCircle() {
40      System.out.println("The circle is created " + getDateCreated() +
41        " and the radius is " + radius);
42    }
43 }
```

LISTING 9.3 Rectangle.java

```
1 package chapter9;                                              package
2
3 public class Rectangle extends GeometricObject {
4    private double width;                                       data fields
5    private double height;
6
7    public Rectangle() {                                        constructor
8    }
9
10   public Rectangle(double width, double height) {
11     this.width = width;
12     this.height = height;
13   }
14
15   /** Return width */                                         methods
16   public double getWidth() {
17     return width;
18   }
19
20   /** Set a new width */
21   public void setWidth(double width) {
22     this.width = width;
23   }
24
25   /** Return height */
26   public double getHeight() {
27     return height;
28   }
29
30   /** Set a new height */
31   public void setHeight(double height) {
32     this.height = height;
33   }
34
35   /** Return area */
36   public double getArea() {
37     return width * height;
38   }
39
40   /** Return perimeter */
41   public double getPerimeter() {
42     return 2 * (width + height);
43   }
44 }
```

The classes **Circle** and **Rectangle** extend the **GeometricObject** class. The reserved word **extends** tells the compiler that these classes extend the **GeometricObject** class, thus inheriting the methods **getColor**, **setColor**, **isFilled**, **setFilled**, and **toString**.

The following code in Listing 9.4 creates objects of **Circle** and **Rectangle**, and invokes the methods on these objects.

LISTING 9.4 TestCircleRectangle.java

package

```
 1  package chapter9;
 2
 3  public class TestCircleRectangle {
 4    public static void main(String[] args) {
 5      Circle circle = new Circle(1);
 6      System.out.println("A circle " + circle.toString());
 7      System.out.println(circle.getRadius());
 8      System.out.println("The radius is " + circle.getRadius());
 9      System.out.println("The area is " + circle.getArea());
10      System.out.println("The diameter is " + circle.getDiameter());
11
12      Rectangle rectangle = new Rectangle(2, 4);
13      System.out.println("\nA rectanlge " + rectangle.toString());
14      System.out.println("The area is " + rectangle.getArea());
15      System.out.println("The perimeter is " +
16        rectangle.getPerimeter());
17    }
18  }
```

Circle object
invoke **toString**

Rectangle object
invoke **toString**

```
C:\book>java chapter9.TestCircleRectangle
A circle created on Thu Sep 01 12:24:24 EDT 2005
color: white and filled: false
1.0
The radius is 1.0
The area is 3.141592653589793
The diameter is 2.0

A rectanlge created on Thu Sep 01 12:24:24 EDT 2005
color: white and filled: false
The area is 8.0
The perimeter is 12.0

C:\book>
```

FIGURE 9.2 The methods in **GeometricObject** are inherited in **Circle** and **Rectangle**.

Since **radius** is **1**, **color** is **white**, and **filled** is **false** by default, the output is as shown in Figure 9.2. Note that **TestCircleRectangle.java** is stored in **c:\book\chapter9** and the **TestCircleRectangle** class is in package **chapter9**. Thus you have to run it from **c:\book** using the command **java chapter9.TestCircleRectangle** with the complete class name.

Note

more in subclass

Contrary to the conventional interpretation, a subclass is not a subset of its superclass. In fact, a subclass usually contains more information and functions than its superclass.

Caution

no blind extension

Inheritance is used to model the *is-a* relationship. Do not blindly extend a class just for the sake of reusing methods. For example, it makes no sense for a **Tree** class to extend a **Person** class. A subclass and its superclass must have the is-a relationship.

9.3 Using the **super** Keyword

A subclass inherits accessible data fields and methods from its superclass. Does it inherit constructors? Can superclass constructors be invoked from subclasses? This section addresses these questions and their ramification.

The discussion in §7.12, "The **this** Keyword," introduced the use of the keyword **this** as a surrogate to refer to the calling object. The keyword **super** refers to the superclass of the class in which **super** appears. It can be used in two ways:

- To call a superclass constructor.

- To call a superclass method.

9.3.1 Calling Superclass Constructors

The syntax to call a superclass constructor is:

super(), or **super**(parameters);

The statement **super**() invokes the no-arg constructor of its superclass, and the statement **super(arguments)** invokes the superclass constructor that matches the **arguments**. The statement **super**() or **super(arguments)** must appear in the first line of the subclass constructor and is the only way to invoke a superclass constructor.

Caution

You must use the keyword **super** to call the superclass constructor, and the call must be the first statement in the constructor. Invoking a superclass constructor's name in a subclass causes a syntax error.

Note

A constructor is used to construct an instance of a class. Unlike properties and methods, the constructors of a superclass are not inherited in the subclass. They can only be invoked from the constructors of the subclasses, using the keyword **super**.

9.3.2 Constructor Chaining

A constructor may invoke an overloaded constructor or its superclass's constructor. If neither of them is invoked explicitly, the compiler puts **super**() as the first statement in the constructor. For example,

```
public A() {
}
```
is equivalent to
```
public A() {
   super();
}
```

```
public A(double d) {
   // some statements
}
```
is equivalent to
```
public A(double d) {
   super();
   // some statements
}
```

In any case, constructing an instance of a class invokes the constructors of all the superclasses along the inheritance chain. A superclass's constructor is called before the subclass's constructor. This is called *constructor chaining*. Consider the following code:

constructor chaining

```
1  public class Faculty extends Employee {
2    public static void main(String[] args) {
3      new Faculty();
4    }
```

```
 5
 6    public Faculty() {
 7       System.out.println("(4) Faculty's no-arg constructor is invoked");
 8    }
 9 }
10
11 class Employee extends Person {
12    public Employee() {
13       this("(2) Invoke Employee's overloaded constructor");
14       System.out.println("(3) Employee's no-arg constructor is invoked");
15    }
16
17    public Employee(String s) {
18       System.out.println(s);
19    }
20 }
21
22 class Person {
23    public Person() {
24       System.out.println("(1) Person's no-arg constructor is invoked");
25    }
26 }
```

invoke overloaded
constructor

In line 3, `new Faculty()` invokes `Faculty`'s no-arg constructor. Since `Faculty` is a subclass of `Employee`, `Employee`'s no-arg constructor is invoked before any statements in `Faculty`'s constructor are executed. `Employee`'s no-arg constructor invokes `Employee`'s second constructor (line 12). Since `Employee` is a subclass of `Person`, `Person`'s no-arg constructor is invoked before any statements in `Employee`'s second constructor are executed. Therefore, the output of creating an instance of `Faculty` is:

```
(1) Person's no-arg constructor is invoked
(2) Invoke Employee's overloaded constructor
(3) Employee's no-arg constructor is invoked
(4) Faculty's no-arg constructor is invoked
```

no-arg constructor

Caution

If a class is designed to be extended, it is better to provide a no-arg constructor to avoid programming errors. Consider the following code:

```
1 public class Apple extends Fruit {
2 }
3
4 class Fruit {
5    public Fruit(String name) {
6       System.out.println("Fruit's constructor is invoked");
7    }
8 }
```

Since no constructor is explicitly defined in `Apple`, `Apple`'s default no-arg constructor is declared implicitly. Since `Apple` is a subclass of `Fruit`, `Apple`'s default constructor automatically invokes `Fruit`'s no-arg constructor. However, `Fruit` does not have a no-arg constructor because `Fruit` has an explicit constructor defined. Therefore, the program cannot be compiled.

9.3.3 Calling Superclass Methods

The keyword **super** can also be used to reference a method other than the constructor in the superclass. The syntax is like this:

```
super.method(parameters);
```

You could rewrite the `printCircle()` method in the `Circle` class as follows:

```java
public void printCircle() {
  System.out.println("The circle is created " +
    super.getDateCreated() + " and the radius is " + radius);
}
```

It is not necessary to put `super` before `getDateCreated()` in this case, however, because `getDateCreated` is a method in the `GeometricObject` class and is inherited by the `Circle` class. Nevertheless, in some cases, as shown in the next section, the keyword `super` is needed.

Caution
You can use `super.p()` to invoke the method `p()` defined in the superclass. Suppose A extends B, and B extends C, and a method `p()` is defined in C. Can you invoke `super.super.p()` from A? The answer is no. It is illegal to have such a chain of `super`s in Java.

no multiple **super**s

9.4 Overriding Methods

A subclass inherits methods from a superclass. Sometimes it is necessary for the subclass to modify the implementation of a method defined in the superclass. This is referred to as *method overriding*.

method overriding

The `toString` method in the `GeometricObject` class returns the string representation for a geometric object. This method can be overridden to return the string representation for a circle. To override it, add the following new method in Listing 9.2, Circle.java:

```java
public class Circle extends GeometricObject {
  // Other methods are omitted

  /** Override the toString method defined in GeometricObject */
  public String toString() {
    return super.toString() + "\nradius is " + radius;
  }
}
```

The `toString()` method is defined in the `GeometricObeject` class and modified in the `Circle` class. Both methods can be used in the `Circle` class. To invoke the `toString` method defined in the `GeometricObject` class, use `super.toString()`. Can a subclass of `Circle` access the `toString` method defined in the `GeometricObject` class using a syntax such as `super.super.toString()`? No. This is a syntax error. Can an instance of `Circle` invoke the `toString` method defined in the `GeometricObject` class? No, not any more, since `toString()` in `GeometricObject` has been overridden in `Circle`.

Note
Private data fields and methods in a superclass are not accessible outside of the class. Therefore, they are not inherited in a subclass.

private members

Note
An instance method can be overridden only if it is accessible. Thus a private method cannot be overridden, because it is not accessible outside its own class. If a method defined in a subclass is private in its superclass, the two methods are completely unrelated.

override accessible instance method

Note
Like an instance method, a static method can be inherited. However, a static method cannot be overridden. If a static method defined in the superclass is redefined in a subclass, the method defined in the superclass is hidden. Hiding static methods will be further discussed in §9.14, "Hiding Data Fields and Static Methods."

cannot override static method

9.5 Overriding vs. Overloading

You have learned about overloading methods in §5.6, "Overloading Methods." Overloading a method is a way to provide more than one method with the same name but with different signatures to distinguish them. To override a method, the method must be defined in the subclass

same signature
same return type

using the same signature and same return type as in its superclass.

Let us use an example to show the differences between overriding and overloading. In (a), the method `p(int i)` in class **A** overrides the same method defined in class **B**. However, in (b), the method `p(double i)` in class **A** and the method `p(int i)` in class **B** are two overloaded methods. The method `p(int i)` in class **B** is inherited in **A**.

```java
public class Test {
  public static void main(String[] args) {
    A a = new A();
    a.p(10);
  }
}

class B {
  public void p(int i) {
  }
}

class A extends B {
  // This method overrides the method in B
  public void p(int i) {
    System.out.println(i);
  }
}
```

(a)

```java
public class Test {
  public static void main(String[] args) {
    A a = new A();
    a.p(10);
  }
}

class B {
  public void p(int i) {
  }
}

class A extends B {
  // This method overloads the method in B
  public void p(double i) {
    System.out.println(i);
  }
}
```

(b)

When you run the **Test** class in (a), `a.p(10)` invokes the `p(int i)` method defined in class **A**, so the program displays 10. When you run the **Test** class in (b), `a.p(10)` invokes the `p(int i)` method defined in class **B**, so nothing is printed.

9.6 The `Object` Class and Its `toString()` Method

Every class in Java is descended from the `java.lang.Object` class. If no inheritance is specified when a class is defined, the superclass of the class is `Object` by default. For example, the following two class declarations are the same:

```java
public class Circle {
  ...
}
```

Equivalent

```java
public class Circle extends Object {
  ...
}
```

Classes like **String**, **StringBuffer**, **Loan**, and **GeometricObject** are implicitly subclasses of **Object** (as are all the main classes you have seen in this book so far). It is important to be familiar with the methods provided by the **Object** class so that you can use them in your classes. This section introduces the **toString()** method. Other methods will be introduced in §9.13.

The signature of the **toString()** method is

```java
public String toString()
```

Invoking `toString()` on an object returns a string that represents the object. By default, it returns a string consisting of a class name of which the object is an instance, an at sign (@), and the object's hash code in hexadecimal. For example, consider the following code for the `Loan` class defined in Listing 7.9:

string representation

```
Loan loan = new Loan();
System.out.println(loan.toString());
```

The code displays something like **Loan@15037e5**. This message is not very helpful or informative. Usually you should override the **toString** method so that it returns a descriptive string representation of the object. For example, the **toString** method in the `GeometricObject` class in Listing 9.1 was overridden as follows:

```
public String toString() {
  return "color: " + color + "and is filled: " + filled;
}
```

 Note

You can also pass an object to invoke `System.out.println(object)` or `System.out.print(object)`. This is equivalent to invoking `System.out.println(object.toString())` or `System.out.print(object.toString())`. So you could replace `System.out.println(loan.toString())` with `System.out.println(loan)`.

print object

9.7 Polymorphism, Dynamic Binding, and Generic Programming

The inheritance relationship enables a subclass to inherit features from its superclass with additional new features. A subclass is a specialization of its superclass; every instance of a subclass is an instance of its superclass, but not vice versa. For example, every circle is an object, but not every object is a circle. Therefore, you can always pass an instance of a subclass to a parameter of its superclass type. Consider the code in Listing 9.5.

LISTING 9.5   PolymorphismDemo.java

```
 1 package chapter9;
 2
 3 public class PolymorphismDemo {
 4   public static void main(String[] args) {
 5     m(new GraduateStudent());
 6     m(new Student());
 7     m(new Person());
 8     m(new Object());
 9   }
10
11   public static void m(Object x) {
12     System.out.println(x.toString());
13   }
14 }
15
16 class GraduateStudent extends Student {
17 }
18
19 class Student extends Person {
20   public String toString() {
21     return "Student";
22   }
23 }
24
```

package

polymorphic call

dynamic binding

override **toString()**

override **toString()**

```
25 class Person extends Object {
26   public String toString() {
27     return "Person";
28   }
29 }
```

It produces the output shown in Figure 9.3. Why? Let us discuss the reason. Method m (line 11) takes a parameter of the **Object** type. You can invoke m with any object (e.g., **new GraduateStudent()**, **new Student()**, **new Person()**, and **new Object()**) in lines 5–8). An object of a subtype can be used wherever its supertype value is required.

FIGURE 9.3 An instance of a subclass is also an instance of its superclass.

When the method **m(Object x)** is executed, the argument x's **toString** method is invoked. x may be an instance of **GraduateStudent**, **Student**, **Person**, or **Object**. Classes **GraduateStudent**, **Student**, **Person**, and **Object** have their own implementations of the **toString** method. Which implementation is used will be determined dynamically by the Java Virtual Machine at runtime. This capability is known as *dynamic binding*. It is also known as *polymorphism* (from a Greek word meaning "many forms") because one method has many implementations.

dynamic binding
polymorphism

Dynamic binding works as follows: Suppose an object o is an instance of classes C_1, C_2, ..., C_{n-1}, and C_n, where C_1 is a subclass of C_2, C_2 is a subclass of C_3, ..., and C_{n-1} is a subclass of C_n, as shown in Figure 9.4. That is, C_n is the most general class, and C_1 is the most specific class. In Java, C_n is the **Object** class. If o invokes a method p, the JVM searches the implementation for the method p in C_1, C_2, ..., C_{n-1}, and C_n, in this order, until it is found. Once an implementation is found, the search stops and the first-found implementation is invoked. For example, when **m(new GraduateStudent())** is invoked in line 5, the **toString** method defined in the **Student** class is used.

java.lang.Object

If o is an instance of C_1, o is also an instance of C_2, C_3, ..., C_{n-1}, and C_n

FIGURE 9.4 The method to be invoked is dynamically bound at runtime.

Note

matching vs. binding

Matching a method signature and binding a method implementation are two separate issues. The *declared type* of the reference variable decides which method to match at compile time. The compiler finds a matching method according to parameter type, number of parameters, and order of the parameters at compile time. A method may be implemented in several subclasses. The Java Virtual Machine dynamically binds the implementation of the method at runtime, decided by the *actual class* of the object referenced by the variable.

Note

Dynamic binding enables new classes to be loaded on the fly without recompilation. There is no need for developers to create, and for users to install, major new software versions. New features can be incorporated transparently as needed. For example, suppose you have placed the classes Test, GraduateStudent, Student, Person in four separate files. If you change Graduate-Student as follows:

benefits of dynamic binding

```
class GraduateStudent extends Student {
  public String toString() {
    return "Graduate Student";
  }
}
```

You have a new version of GraduateStudent with a new toString method, but you don't have to recompile the classes Test, Student, and Person. When you run Test, the JVM dynamically binds the new toString method for the object of GraduateStudent when executing m(new GraduateStudent()).

Polymorphism allows methods to be used generically for a wide range of object arguments. This is known as *generic programming*. If a method's parameter type is a superclass (e.g., Object), you may pass an object to this method of any of the parameter's subclasses (e.g., Student or String). When an object (e.g., a Student object or a String object) is used in the method, the particular implementation of the method of the object invoked (e.g., toString) is determined dynamically.

generic programming

9.8 Casting Objects and the **instanceof** Operator

You have already used the casting operator to convert variables of one primitive type to another. Casting can also be used to convert an object of one class type to another within an inheritance hierarchy. In the preceding section, the statement

```
m(new Student());
```

assigns the object new Student() to a parameter of the Object type. This statement is equivalent to

```
Object o = new Student(); // Implicit casting
m(o);
```

The statement Object o = new Student(), known as *implicit casting*, is legal because an instance of Student is automatically an instance of Object.

implicit casting

Suppose you want to assign the object reference o to a variable of the Student type using the following statement:

```
Student b = o;
```

A compilation error would occur. Why does the statement Object o = new Student() work and the statement Student b = o doesn't? Because a Student object is always an instance of Object, but an Object is not necessarily an instance of Student. Even though you can see that o is really a Student object, the compiler is not clever enough to know it. To tell the compiler that o is a Student object, use an *explicit casting*. The syntax is similar to the one used for casting among primitive data types. Enclose the target object type in parentheses and place it before the object to be cast, as follows:

explicit casting

```
Student b = (Student)o; // Explicit casting
```

It is always possible to cast an instance of a subclass to a variable of a superclass (known as *upcasting*), because an instance of a subclass is *always* an instance of its superclass. When

upcasting

downcasting

casting an instance of a superclass to a variable of its subclass (known as *downcasting*), explicit casting must be used to confirm your intention to the compiler with the (SubclassName) cast notation. For the casting to be successful, you must make sure that the object to be cast is an instance of the subclass. If the superclass object is not an instance of the subclass, a runtime

ClassCastException

ClassCastException occurs. For example, if an object is not an instance of Student, it cannot be cast into a variable of Student. It is a good practice, therefore, to ensure that the object is an instance of another object before attempting a casting. This can be accomplished

instanceof

by using the instanceof operator. Consider the following code:

```
Object myObject = new Circle();
... // Some lines of code
/** Perform casting if myObject is an instance of Circle */
if (myObject instanceof Circle) {
  System.out.println("The circle diameter is " +
    ((Circle)myObject).getDiameter());
  ...
}
```

You may be wondering why casting is necessary. Variable myObject is declared Object. The *declared type* decides which method to match at compile time. Using myObject.getDiameter() would cause a compilation error because the Object class does not have the getDiameter method. The compiler cannot find a match for myObject.getDiameter(). It is necessary to cast myObject into the Circle type to tell the compiler that myObject is also an instance of Circle.

Why not declare myObject as a Circle type in the first place? To enable generic programming, it is a good practice to declare a variable with a supertype, which can accept a value of any subtype.

lowercase keywords

Note

instanceof is a Java keyword. Every letter in a Java keyword is in lowercase.

casting analogy

Tip

To help understand casting, you may also consider the analogy of fruit, apple, and orange, with the Fruit class as the superclass for Apple and Orange. An apple is a fruit, so you can always safely assign an instance of Apple to a variable for Fruit. However, a fruit is not necessarily an apple, so you have to use explicit casting to assign an instance of Fruit to a variable of Apple.

9.8.1 Example: Demonstrating Polymorphism and Casting

Listing 9.6 is an example that demonstrates polymorphism and casting. The program creates two objects (lines 7–8), a circle and a rectangle, and invokes the displayObject method to display them (lines 11–12). The displayObject method displays the area and diameter if the object is a circle (line 17), and the area if the object is a rectangle (line 23). Figure 9.5 shows the output of the program.

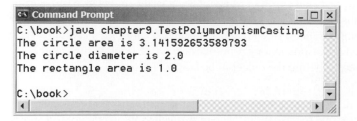

FIGURE 9.5 The program demonstrates polymorphism and casting.

LISTING **9.6** TestPolymorphismCasting.java

```java
1 package chapter9;
2
3 public class TestPolymorphismCasting {
4   /** Main method */
5   public static void main(String[] args) {
6     // Declare and initialize two objects
7     Object object1 = new Circle(1);
8     Object object2 = new Rectangle(1, 1);
9
10    // Display circle and rectangle
11    displayObject(object1);
12    displayObject(object2);
13  }
14
15  /** A method for displaying an object */
16  public static void displayObject(Object object) {
17    if (object instanceof Circle) {
18      System.out.println("The circle area is " +
19        ((Circle)object).getArea());
20      System.out.println("The circle diameter is " +
21        ((Circle)object).getDiameter());
22    }
23    else if (object instanceof Rectangle) {
24      System.out.println("The rectangle area is " +
25        ((Rectangle)object).getArea());
26    }
27  }
28 }
```

The `displayObject(Object object)` method is an example of generic programming. It can be invoked by passing any instance of `Object`.

The program uses implicit casting to assign a `Circle` object to `object1` and a `Rectangle` object to `object2` (lines 7–8), and then invokes the `displayObject` method to display the information on these objects (lines 11–12).

In the `displayObject` method (lines 16–27), explicit casting is used to cast the object to `Circle` if the object is an instance of `Circle`, and the methods `getArea` and `getDiameter` are used to display the area and diameter of the circle.

Casting can only be done when the source object is an instance of the target class. The program uses the `instanceof` operator to ensure that the source object is an instance of the target class before performing a casting (line 17).

Explicit casting to `Circle` (lines 19, 21) and to `Rectangle` (line 25) is necessary because the `getArea` and `getDiameter` methods are not available in the `Object` class.

Caution

The object member access operator (.) precedes the casting operator. Use parentheses to ensure that casting is done before the . operator, as in

. precedes casting

```java
((Circle)object).getArea();
```

9.9 The **ArrayList** Class

You can create an array to store objects. But the array's size is fixed once the array is created. Java provides the `ArrayList` class that can be used to store an unlimited number of objects. Figure 9.6 shows some methods in `ArrayList`.

java.util.ArrayList	
+ArrayList()	Creates an empty list.
+add(o: Object): void	Appends a new element o at the end of this list.
+add(index: int, o: Object): void	Adds a new element o at the specified index in this list.
+clear(): void	Removes all the elements from this list.
+contains(o: Object): boolean	Returns true if this list contains the element o.
+get(index: int): Object	Returns the element from this list at the specified index.
+indexOf(o: Object):int	Returns the index of the first matching element in this list.
+isEmpty(): boolean	Returns true if this list contains no elements.
+lastIndexOf(o: Object): int	Returns the index of the last matching element in this list.
+remove(o: Object): boolean	Removes the element o from this list.
+size(): int	Returns the number of elements in this list.
+remove(index: int): boolean	Removes the element at the specified index.
+set(index: int, o: Object): Object	Sets the element at the specified index.

FIGURE 9.6 An `ArrayList` stores an unlimited number of objects.

Listing 9.7 is an example of using `ArrayList`. The program creates an `ArrayList` using its no-arg constructor (line 4). The **add** method adds any instance of **Object** into the list. Since **String** is a subclass of **Object**, strings can be added to the list in lines 7–17. The **add** method (lines 7–17) adds an object to the end of list. So, after `cityList.add("London")` (line 7), the list contains

[London]

After `cityList.add("New York")` (line 9), the list contains

[London, New York]

After adding Paris, Toronto, Hong Kong, and Singapore (lines 11–17), the list would contain

[London, New York, Paris, Toronto, Hong Kong, Singapore]

Invoking `size()` (line 21) returns the size of the list, which is currently 6. Invoking `contains("Toronto")` (line 23) checks whether the object is in the list. In this case, it returns **true**, since **Toronto** is in the list. Invoking `indexOf("New York")` (line 25) returns the index of the object in the list, which is 1 in this case. If the object is not in the list, it returns −1. The `isEmpty()` method (line 27) checks whether the list is empty. It returns **false**, since the list is not empty.

The statement `cityList.add(2, "Beijing")` (line 30) inserts an object to the list at the specified index. After this statement, the list becomes

[London, New York, Beijing, Paris, Toronto, Hong Kong, Singapore]

The statement `cityList.remove("Toronto")` (line 35) removes the object from the list. After this statement, the list becomes

[London, New York, Beijing, Paris, Hong Kong, Singapore]

The statement `cityList.remove(1)` (line 40) removes the object at the specified index from the list. After this statement, the list becomes

[London, Beijing, Paris, Hong Kong, Singapore]

The `get(index)` method (line 45) returns the object at the specified index. Figure 9.7 shows the output of the program.

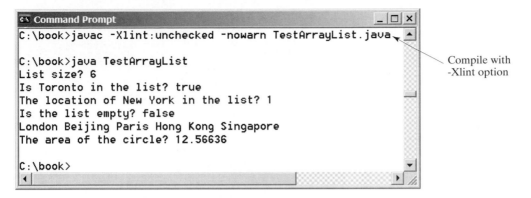

Compile with -Xlint option

FIGURE 9.7   The program demonstrates how to use `ArrayList`.

LISTING 9.7   TestArrayList.java

```
 1 public class TestArrayList {
 2   public static void main(String[] args) {
 3     // Create a list to store cities
 4     java.util.ArrayList cityList = new java.util.ArrayList();
 5
 6     // Add some cities in the list
 7     cityList.add("London");
 8     // cityList now contains [London]
 9     cityList.add("New York");
10     // cityList now contains [London, New York]
11     cityList.add("Paris");
12     // cityList now contains [London, New York, Paris]
13     cityList.add("Toronto");
14     // cityList now contains [London, New York, Paris, Toronto]
15     cityList.add("Hong Kong");
16     // contains [London, New York, Paris, Toronto, Hong Kong]
17     cityList.add("Singapore");
18     // contains [London, New York, Paris, Toronto,
19     //           Hong Kong, Singapore]
20
21     System.out.println("List size? " + cityList.size());
22     System.out.println("Is Toronto in the list? " +
23       cityList.contains("Toronto"));
24     System.out.println("The location of New York in the list? "
25       + cityList.indexOf("New York"));
26     System.out.println("Is the list empty? " +
27       cityList.isEmpty()); // Print false
28
29     // Insert a new city at index 2
30     cityList.add(2, "Beijing");
31     // contains [London, New York, Beijing, Paris, Toronto,
32     //           Hong Kong, Singapore]
33
34     // Remove a city from the list
35     cityList.remove("Toronto");
36     // contains [London, New York, Beijing, Paris,
37     //           Hong Kong, Singapore]
38
39     // Remove a city at index 1
40     cityList.remove(1);
41     // contains [London, Beijing, Paris, Hong Kong, Singapore]
42
```

create **ArrayList**

add element

list size

contains element?

element index

is empty?

remove element

remove element

get element

```
43      // Display London Beijing Paris Hong Kong Singapore
44      for (int i = 0; i < cityList.size(); i++)
45        System.out.print(cityList.get(i) + " ");
46      System.out.println();
47
48      // Create a list to store two circles
49      java.util.ArrayList list = new java.util.ArrayList();
50
51      // Add two circles
52      list.add(new Circle(2));
53      list.add(new Circle(3));
54
55      // Display the area of the first circle in the list
56      System.out.println("The area of the circle? " +
57        ((Circle)list.get(0)).getArea());
58    }
59 }
```

create **ArrayList**

Note

compile with **–Xlint** opiton

You will get a compilation warning "unchecked operation" in JDK 1.5 when compiling this program. Ignore it and recompile it with the –**Xlint** option, as shown in Figure 9.5. This warning can be fixed using generic types in Chapter 21, "Generics."

array vs. **ArrayList**

ArrayList objects can be used like arrays, but there are many differences. Table 9.1 lists their similarities and differences.

TABLE 9.1 Differences and Similarity between Arrays and **ArrayList**

	Array	ArrayList
Creating an array/ArrayList	Object[] a = new Object[10]	ArrayList list = new ArrayList()
Accessing an element	a [index]	list.get(index)
Updating an element	a [index] = "London";	list.set(index, "London");
Returning size	a.length	list.size()
Adding a new element		list.add("London")
Inserting a new element		list.add(index, "London")
Removing an element		list.remove(index)
Removing an element		list.remove(Object)
Removing all elements		list.clear()

Once an array is created, its size is fixed. You can access an array element using the square bracket notation (e.g., **a[index]**). When an **ArrayList** is created, its size is 0. You cannot use the **get** and **set** method if the element is not in the list. It is easy to add, insert, and remove elements in a list, but it is rather complex to add, insert, and remove elements in an array. You have to write the code to manipulate the array in order to perform these operations.

Note

java.util.Vector is also a class for storing objects, which is very similar to the **ArrayList** class. All the methods in **ArrayList** are also available in **Vector**. The **Vector** class was introduced in JDK 1.1. The **ArrayList** class introduced in JDK 1.2 was intended to replace the **Vector** class.

Vector class

9.10 A Custom Stack Class

"Case Study: The StackOfIntegers Class," in §7.17, presented a stack class for storing int values. This section introduces a stack class to store objects. Recall that a stack is a data structure that holds objects in a last-in first-out fashion. You can use an ArrayList to implement Stack, as shown in Listing 9.8. The UML diagram for the class is shown in Figure 9.8.

MyStack	
-list: ArrayList	A list to store elements.
+isEmpty(): boolean	Returns true if this stack is empty.
+getSize(): int	Returns the number of elements in this stack.
+peek(): Object	Returns the top element in this stack.
+pop(): Object	Returns and removes the top element in this stack.
+push(o: Object): Object	Adds a new element to the top of this stack.
+search(o: Object): int	Returns the position of the first element in the stack from the top that matches the specified element.

FIGURE 9.8 The MyStack class encapsulates the stack storage and provides the operations for manipulating the stack.

LISTING 9.8 MyStack.java

```java
1  public class MyStack {
2    private java.util.ArrayList list = new java.util.ArrayList();    array list
3
4    public boolean isEmpty() {                                        stack empty?
5      return list.isEmpty();
6    }
7
8    public int getSize() {                                           get stack size
9      return list.size();
10   }
11
12   public Object peek() {                                           peek stack
13     return list.get(getSize() - 1);
14   }
15
16   public Object pop() {                                            remove
17     Object o = list.get(getSize() - 1);
18     list.remove(getSize() - 1);
19     return o;
20   }
21
22   public Object push(Object o) {                                   add
23     list.add(o);
24     return o;
25   }
26
27   public int search(Object o) {                                    search
28     return list.lastIndexOf(o);
29   }
30
```

```
31  /** Override the toString in the Object class */
32  public String toString() {
33    return "stack: " + list.toString();
34  }
35 }
```

An array list is created to store the elements in the stack (line 2). The `isEmpty()` method (lines 4–6) returns `list.isEmpty()`. The `getSize()` method (lines 8–10) returns `list.size()`. The `peek()` method (lines 12–14) looks at the element at the top of the stack without removing it. The end of the list is the top of the stack. The `pop()` method (lines 16–20) removes the top element from the stack and returns it. The `push(Object element)` method (lines 22–25) adds the specified element to the stack. The `search(Object element)` method checks whether the specified element is in the stack, and returns the index of first-matching element in the stack from the top by invoking `list.lastIndexOf(o)`. The `toString()` method defined in the `Object` class is overridden to display the contents of the stack by invoking `list.toString()`.

Note

composition
is-a
has-a

In Listing 9.8, `MyStack` contains `ArrayList`. The relationship between `MyStack` and `ArrayList` is called *composition*. While inheritance models an *is-a* relationship, composition models a *has-a* relationship. You may also implement `MyStack` as a subclass of `ArrayList`. Relationships will be discussed in detail in Chapter 11, "Object-Oriented Design."

9.11 The **protected** Data and Methods

The modifier `protected` can be applied to data and methods in a class. A protected datum or a protected method in a public class can be accessed *by any class in the same package or its subclasses*, even if the subclasses are in different packages.

The modifiers `private`, `protected`, and `public` are known as *visibility* or *accessibility modifiers* because they specify how class and class members are accessed. The visibility of these modifiers increases in this order:

Visibility increases
⟶
private, none (if no modifier is used), protected, public

Table 9.2 summarizes the accessibility of the members in a class. Figure 9.9 illustrates how a public, protected, default, and private datum or method in class `C1` can be accessed from a class `C2` in the same package, from a subclass `C3` in the same package, from a subclass `C4` in a different package, and from a class `C5` in a different package.

Use the `private` modifier to hide the members of the class completely so that they cannot be accessed directly from outside the class. Use no modifiers to allow the members of the

TABLE 9.2 Data and Methods Visibility

Modifier on members in a class	Accessed from the same class	Accessed from the same package	Accessed from a subclass	Accessed from a different package
public	✓	✓	✓	✓
protected	✓	✓	✓	–
(default)	✓	✓	–	–
private	✓	–	–	–

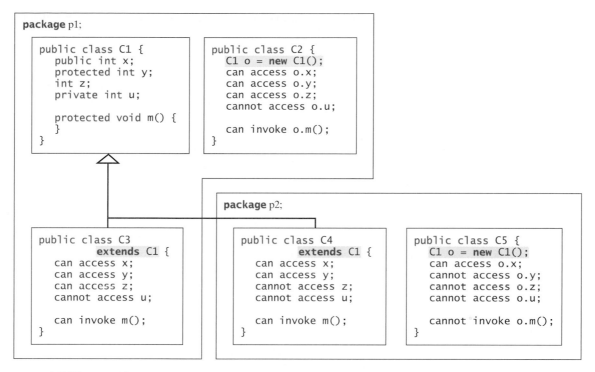

FIGURE 9.9   Visibility modifiers are used to control how data and methods are accessed.

class to be accessed directly from any class within the same package but not from other packages. Use the **protected** modifier to enable the members of the class to be accessed by the subclasses in any package or classes in the same package. Use the **public** modifier to enable the members of the class to be accessed by any class.

Your class can be used in two ways: for creating instances of the class, and for creating subclasses by extending the class. Make the members **private** if they are not intended for use from outside the class. Make the members **public** if they are intended for the users of the class. Make the fields or methods **protected** if they are intended for the extenders of the class but not the users of the class.

The **private** and **protected** modifiers can only be used for members of the class. The **public** modifier and the default modifier (i.e., no modifier) can be used on members of the class as well on the class. A class with no modifier (i.e., not a public class) is not accessible by classes from other packages.

 Note
A subclass may override a protected method in its superclass and change its visibility to public. However, a subclass cannot weaken the accessibility of a method defined in the superclass. For example, if a method is defined as public in the superclass, it must be defined as public in the subclass.

9.12 The **final** Classes, Methods, and Variables

You have already seen the **final** modifier used in declaring constants. You may occasionally want to prevent classes from being extended. In such cases, use the **final** modifier to indicate that a class is final and cannot be a parent class. The **Math** class, introduced in Chapter 5, "Methods," is a final class. The **String** and **StringBuffer** classes, introduced in Chapter 8, "Strings," are also final classes.

You also can define a method to be final; a final method cannot be overridden by its subclasses.

final local variable

Note

The modifiers are used on classes and class members (data and methods), except that the `final` modifier can also be used on local variables in a method. A final local variable is a constant inside a method.

9.13 (Optional) Methods in the `Object` Class

The discussion in §9.6 introduced the `toString` method in the `Object` class. Other useful methods are as follows:

- **public boolean** equals(Object object)
- **public int** hashCode()
- **protected void** finalize() **throws** Throwable
- **protected native** Object clone() **throws** CloneNotSupportedException
- **public final native** Class getClass()

native method

Note

A `native` method is implemented using a programming language other than Java. Some methods, such as `clone`, need to access hardware using the native machine language or the C language. These methods are marked `native`. A native method can be `final`, `public`, `private`, `protected`, overloaded, or overridden.

Note

A `finalize` method may throw `Throwable`, and the `clone` method may throw `CloneNot-SupportedException`. Exception handling will be introduced in Chapter 17, "Exceptions and Assertions." (*Chapter 17 can be covered after this chapter.*) For now, you need to know that `throws Throwable` and `throws CloneNotSupportedException` are part of the method declarations for the `finalize` and `clone` methods.

9.13.1 The `equals` Method

The `equals` method tests whether two objects are equal. The syntax for invoking it is:

```
object1.equals(object2);
```

The default implementation of the `equals` method in the `Object` class is:

```
public boolean equals(Object obj) {
   return (this == obj);
}
```

Thus, using the `equals` method is equivalent to the `==` operator in the `Object` class, but it is really intended for the subclasses of the `Object` class to modify the `equals` method to test whether two distinct objects have the same content.

You have already used the `equals` method to compare two strings in §8.2, "The `String` Class." The `equals` method in the `String` class is inherited from the `Object` class and is modified in the `String` class to test whether two strings are identical in content. You can override the `equals` method in the `Circle` class to compare whether two circles are equal based on their radius, as follows:

```
public boolean equals(Object o) {
   if (o instanceof Circle) {
```

```
      return radius == ((Circle)o).radius;
    }
    else
      return false;
  }
```

Note

The == comparison operator is used for comparing two primitive data type values or for determining whether two objects have the same references. The **equals** method is intended to test whether two objects have the same contents, provided that the method is modified in the defining class of the objects. The == operator is stronger than the **equals** method, in that the == operator checks whether the two reference variables refer to the same object.

== vs. **equals**

Caution

Using the signature **equals(SomeClassName obj)** (e.g., **equals(Circle c)**) to override the **equals** method in a subclass is a common mistake. You should use **equals(Object obj)**). See Review Question 9.16.

equals(Object)

9.13.2 The **hashCode** Method

Invoking **hashCode()** on an object returns the object's hash code. *Hash code* is an integer that can be used to store the object in a hash set so that it can be located quickly. Hash sets will be introduced in Chapter 22, "Java Collections Framework." The **hashCode** implemented in the **Object** class returns the internal memory address of the object in hexadecimal. Your class should override the **hashCode** method whenever the **equals** method is overridden. By contract, if two objects are equal, their hash codes must be same. Two unequal objects may have the same hash code, but you should implement the **hashCode** method to avoid too many such cases. Additionally, invoking the **hashCode** method multiple times must return the same integer during one execution of the program. The integer need not be the same in different executions. For example, the **hashCode** method is overridden in the **String** class by returning $s_0*31^{(n-1)} + s_1*31^{(n-2)} + \cdots + s_{n-1}$ as the hash code, where s_i is **s.charAt(i)**.

hash code

If you override the **equals** method in a class, you should also override the **hashCode** method in the same class to ensure that two equal **Circle** objects have the same **hashCode**. For example, you may override the **hashCode** method in the **Circle** class as follows:

```
public int hashCode() {
  return (int)(radius * 1999711);
}
```

9.13.3 The **finalize** Method

The **finalize** method is invoked on an object by the garbage collector when the object becomes garbage. An object becomes garbage if it is no longer accessed. By default, the **finalize** method does nothing. A subclass should override the **finalize** method to dispose of system resources or to perform other cleanup, if necessary.

Note

The **finalize** method is invoked by the JVM. You should never write the code to invoke it in your program. For this reason, the protected modifier is appropriate.

Listing 9.9 demonstrates the effect of overriding the **finalize()** method.

LISTING 9.9 FinalizationDemo.java

```
1 public class FinalizationDemo {
2   public static void main(String[] args) {
3     Cake a1 = new Cake(1);
```

garbage collecting

```
 4        Cake a2 = new Cake(2);
 5        Cake a3 = new Cake(3);
 6
 7        // To dispose the objects a2 and a3
 8        a2 = a3 = null;
 9        System.gc(); // Invoke the Java garbage collector
10      }
11 }
12
13 class Cake extends Object {
14    private int id;
15
16    public Cake(int id) {
17      this.id = id;
18      System.out.println("Cake object " + id + " is created");
19    }
20
21    protected void finalize() throws java.lang.Throwable {
22      super.finalize();
23      System.out.println("Cake object " + id + " is disposed");
24    }
25 }
```

override finalize

The following is the output of this program:

```
Cake object 1 is created
Cake object 2 is created
Cake object 3 is created
Cake object 2 is disposed
Cake object 3 is disposed
```

Line 8 assigns `null` to `a2` and `a3`. The objects previously referenced by `a2` and `a3` are no longer accessible. Therefore, they are garbage. `System.gc()` in line 9 requests the garbage collector to be invoked to reclaim space from all discarded objects. Normally you don't need to invoke this method explicitly, because the JVM automatically invokes it whenever necessary. The `finalize` method on the objects `a2` and `a3` are invoked by the garbage collector. When the program terminates, `a1` also becomes garbage, and `a1`'s `finalize` method is then invoked. Since the program has already exited, no message is displayed on the console.

Line 22 invokes the `finalize()` method in the superclass. This is a good practice to ensure that the finalization operations defined in the superclass are carried out.

9.13.4 The `clone` Method

Sometimes you need to make a copy of an object. Mistakenly, you might use the assignment statement, as follows:

```
newObject = someObject;
```

This statement does not create a duplicate object. It simply assigns the reference of `someObject` to `newObject`. To create a new object with separate memory space, use the `clone()` method:

```
newObject = someObject.clone();
```

This statement copies `someObject` to a new memory location and assigns the reference of the new object to `newObject`. For example,

```
java.util.Date date = new java.util.Date();
java.util.Date date1 = (java.util.Date)(date.clone());
```

creates a new `Date` object, `date`, and its clone `date1`. Note that `date.equals(date1)` is `true`, but `date == date1` is `false`.

Note

Not all objects can be cloned. For an object to be cloneable, its class must implement the `java.lang.Cloneable` interface, which is introduced in §10.4.4, "The `Cloneable` Interface."

Tip

An array is treated as an object in Java and is an instance of the `Object` class. The `clone` method can also be used to copy arrays. The following statement uses the `clone` method to copy the `sourceArray` of the `int[]` type to the `targetArray`:

```
int[] targetArray = (int[])sourceArray.clone();
```

Since the return type of the `clone` method is `Object`, `(int[])` is used to cast it to the `int[]` type.

9.13.5   The `getClass` Method

A class must be loaded in order to be used. When the JVM loads the class, it creates an object that contains the information about the class, such as class name, constructors, and methods. This object is an instance of `java.lang.Class`. It is referred to as a *meta-object* in this book, because it describes the information about the class.

meta-object

Through the meta-object, you can discover the information about the class at runtime. Every object can use the `getClass()` method to return its meta-object. For example, the following code

```
Object obj = new Object();
Class metaObject = obj.getClass();
System.out.println("Object obj's class is "
  + metaObject.getName());
```

displays

```
Object obj's class is java.lang.Object
```

Note

There is only one meta-object for a class. Every object has a meta-object. If two objects were created from the same class, their meta-objects are the same.

9.14 (Optional) Hiding Data Fields and Static Methods

This section is marked optional because hidden instance/static data fields and static methods are rarely useful, and they should not be used, for the sake of simplicity and clarity. You may skip this section now and consult it for reference in the future.

You can override an instance method, but you cannot override a data field (instance or static) or a static method. If you declare a data field or a static method in a subclass with the same name as one in the superclass, the one in the superclass is hidden, but it still exists. The two data fields or static methods are independent. You can reference the hidden data field or static method using the keyword **super** in the subclass. The hidden field or method can also be accessed via a reference variable of the superclass's type.

When invoking an instance method from a reference variable, the *actual class of the object* referenced by the variable decides which implementation of the method is used *at runtime*. When accessing a data field or a static method, the *declared type* of the reference variable decides which field or static method is used *at compile time*. This is the key difference between invoking an instance method and accessing a data field or a static method.

Listing 9.10 demonstrates the effect of hiding data fields and static methods.

LISTING 9.10 HidingDemo.java

```
1 public class HidingDemo {
2   public static void main(String[] args) {
3     A x = new B();
4
5     // Access instance data field i
6     System.out.println("(1) x.i is " + x.i);
7     System.out.println("(2) (B)x.i is " + ((B)x).i);
8
9     // Access static data field j
10    System.out.println("(3) x.j is " + x.j);
11    System.out.println("(4) ((B)x).j is " + ((B)x).j);
12
13    // Invoke static method m1
14    System.out.println("(5) x.m1() is " + x.m1());
15    System.out.println("(6) ((B)x).m1() is " + ((B)x).m1());
16
17    // Invoke instance method m2
18    System.out.println("(7) x.m2() is " + x.m2());
19    System.out.println("(8) x.m3() is " + x.m3());
20  }
21 }
22
23 class A {
24   public int i = 1;
25   public static int j = 11;
26
27   public static String m1() {
28     return "A's static m1";
29   }
30
31   public String m2() {
32     return "A's instance m2";
33   }
34
35   public String m3() {
36     return "A's instance m3";
37   }
38 }
39
40 class B extends A {
41   public int i = 2;
42   public static int j = 12;
43
44   public static String m1() {
45     return "B's static m1";
46   }
47
48   public String m2() {
49     return "B's instance m2";
50   }
51 }
```

Margin notes:

- same as A.j (line 10)
- same as B.j (line 11)
- same as A.m1() (line 14)
- same as B.m1() (line 15)
- dynamic binding (line 18)
- dynamic binding (line 19)
- hiding data field (line 41)
- hiding data field (line 42)
- hiding static method (lines 44–45)
- override instance method (lines 48–49)

The printout of the program is:

```
(1) x.i is 1
(2) (B)x.i is 2
(3) x.j is 11
```

```
(4) ((B)x).j is 12
(5) x.m1() is A's static m1
(6) ((B)x).m1() is B's static m1
(7) x.m2() is B's instance m2
(8) x.m3() is A's instance m3
```

Here are the explanations:

1. `x.i` is 1 because `x`'s declared type is class `A`.

2. To use `i` in class `B`, you need to cast `x` to `B` using `((B)x).i`.

3. `x.j` is 11 because `x`'s declared type is class `A`. `x.j` is better written as `A.j`.

4. To use `j` in class `B`, you need to cast `x` to `B` using `((B)x).j`. `((B)x).j` is better written as `B.j`.

5. `x.m1()` invokes the static `m1` method in `A` because `x`'s declared type is `A`. `x.m1()` is better written as `A.m1()`.

6. `((B)x).m1()` invokes the static `m1` method in `B` because the type for `(B)x` is `B`. `((B)x).m1()` is better written as `B.m1()`.

7. `x.m2()` invokes the `m2` method in `B` at runtime because `x` actually references to the object of class `B`.

8. `x.m3()` invokes the `m3` method in `A` at runtime because `m3` is implemented in `A`.

Note

A static method or a static field can always be accessed using its declared class name, regardless of whether it is hidden or not.

9.15 (Optional) Initialization Blocks

Initialization blocks can be used to initialize objects along with the constructors. An *initialization block* is a block of statements enclosed inside a pair of braces. An initialization block appears within the class declaration, but not inside methods or constructors. It is executed as if it were placed at the beginning of every constructor in the class.

Initialization blocks can simplify the classes if you have multiple constructors sharing a common code and none of them can invoke other constructors. The common code can be placed in an initialization block, as shown in the example in Figure 9.10(a). In this example, none of the constructors can invoke any of the others using the syntax `this(...)`. When an instance is created using a constructor of the `Book` class, the initialization block is executed to increase the object count by 1. The program is equivalent to Figure 9.10(b).

Note

A class may have multiple initialization blocks. In such cases, the blocks are executed in the order they appear in the class.

The initialization block in Figure 9.10(a) is referred to as an *instance initialization block* because it is executed whenever an instance of the class is created. A *static initialization block* is much like an instance initialization block except that it is declared **static**, can only refer to static members of the class, and is executed when the class is loaded. The JVM loads the class dynamically when it is needed. A superclass is loaded before its subclasses. The order of the execution can be summarized as follows:

instance initialization block

static initialization block

loading a class

1. When a class is used for the first time, it needs to be loaded. Loading involves two phases:

   1.1. Load superclasses. Before loading any class, its superclass must be loaded if it is not already loaded. This is a recursive process until a superclass along the inheritance chain is already loaded.

```
public class Book {
  private static int numOfObjects;
  private String title
  private int id;

  public Book(String title) {
    this.title = title;
  }

  public Book(int id) {
    this.id = id;
  }

  {
    numOfObjects++;
  }
}
```

Equivalent

```
public class Book {
  private static int numOfObjects;
  private String title;
  private int id;

  public Book(String title) {
    numOfObjects++;
    this.title = title;
  }

  public Book(int id) {
    numOfObjects++;
    this.id = id;
  }
}
```

(a) A class with initialization blocks

(b) An equivalent class

FIGURE 9.10 An initialization block can simplify coding for constructors.

1.2. After a class is loaded to the memory, its static data fields and static initialization block are executed in the order they appear in the class.

2. Invoking a constructor of the class involves three phases:

2.1. Invoke a constructor of the superclass. This is a recursive process until the superclass is `java.lang.Object`.

2.2. Initialize instance data fields and execute initialization blocks in the order they appear in the class.

2.3. Execute the body of the constructor.

Listing 9.11 demonstrates the execution order of initialization blocks.

LISTING 9.11   InitializationDemo.java

```
 1 public class InitializationDemo {
 2   public static void main(String[] args) {
 3     new InitializationDemo();
 4   }
 5
 6   public InitializationDemo() {
 7     new M();
 8   }
 9
10   {
11     System.out.println("(2) InitializationDemo's instance block");
12   }
13
14   static {
15     System.out.println("(1) InitializationDemo's static block");
16   }
17 }
18
19 class M extends N {
20   M() {
```

instance
  initialization
  block

static
  initialization
  block

```
21        System.out.println("(8) M's constructor body");
22    }
23
24    {                                                                    instance initialization
25        System.out.println("(7) M's instance initialization block");     block
26    }
27
28    static {                                                             static initialization
29        System.out.println("(4) M's static initialization block");       block
30    }
31 }
32
33 class N {
34    N() {
35        System.out.println("(6) N's constructor body");
36    }
37
38    {                                                                    instance initialization
39        System.out.println("(5) N's instance initialization block");     block
40    }
41
42    static {                                                             static initialization
43        System.out.println("(3) N's static initialization block");       block
44    }
45 }
```

The output of this program is:

```
(1) InitializationDemo's static block
(2) InitializationDemo's instance block
(3) N's static initialization block
(4) M's static initialization block
(5) N's instance initialization block
(6) N's constructor body
(7) M's instance initialization block
(8) M's constructor body
```

The program is executed in the following order:

1. The superclass of `InitializationDemo`, `java.lang.Object` is loaded first. Then class `InitializationDemo` is loaded, so `InitializationDemo`'s static initialization block is executed.

2. `InitializationDemo`'s constructor is invoked (line 3), so `InitializationDemo`'s instance initialization block is executed.

3. When executing `new M()` (line 7), class `M` needs to be loaded, which causes class `M`'s superclass (i.e., `N`) to be loaded first. So `N`'s static initialization block is executed. (Note that `N`'s superclass `java.lang.Object` has already been loaded in (1)).

4. Class `M` is now loaded. So `M`'s static initialization block is executed.

5. When invoking `M`'s constructor, the no-arg constructor of `M`'s superclass is invoked first; therefore, `N`'s instance initialization block is executed.

6. The regular code in `N`'s no-arg constructor is invoked after `N`'s instance initialization block is executed.

7. After N's no-arg constructor is invoked, M's no-arg constructor is invoked, which causes M's instance initialization block to be executed first.

8. The regular code in M's no-arg constructor is invoked after M's instance initialization block is executed.

Note

instance variable

static variable

If an *instance variable* is declared with an initial value (e.g., **double radius = 5**), the variable is initialized just as in an initialization block. That is, it is initialized when the constructor of the class is executed. If a *static variable* is declared with an initial value (e.g., **static double radius = 5**), the variable is initialized just as in a static initialization block. That is, it is initialized when the class is loaded.

 ## 9.16 (Optional GUI) Inheriting GUI Components

You learned how to create frames in the optional GUI sections in the preceding two chapters. The frames were created in the **main** method. A frame created in this way cannot be reused. It is better to declare a custom frame class by extending the **JFrame** class. To demonstrate, let us rewrite Listing 8.11, TwoButtons.java, using a custom frame class, as shown in Listing 9.12.

LISTING 9.12 CustomFrame.java

custom frame class
frame constructor

set layout

create a button

add button
display frame

```
1  import javax.swing.*;
2  import java.awt.*;
3
4  public class CustomFrame extends JFrame {
5    public CustomFrame() {
6      // Set FlowLayout for the frame
7      FlowLayout layout = new FlowLayout();
8      setLayout(layout);
9
10     // Add two buttons to frame
11     JButton jbtOK = new JButton("OK");
12     JButton jbtCancel = new JButton("Cancel");
13     add(jbtOK);
14     add(jbtCancel);
15   }
16
17   public static void main(String[] args) {
18     JFrame frame = new CustomFrame();
19     frame.setTitle("Window 1");
20     frame.setSize(200, 150);
21     frame.setLocation(200, 100);
22     frame.setDefaultCloseOperation(JFrame.EXIT_ON_CLOSE);
23     frame.setVisible(true);
24   }
25 }
```

The **CustomFrame** class extends **JFrame** to inherit all accessible methods from **JFrame**. Invoking **new CustomFrame()** in line 18 creates an instance of **CustomFrame**, which is also an instance of **JFrame**. The constructor of **CustomFrame** sets a **FlowLayout** for the frame in line 8 and adds two buttons in lines 13–14. The **CustomFrame** class can now be reused, as shown in Listing 9.13.

LISTING 9.13 UseCustomFrame.java

```
1  import javax.swing.*;
2
3  public class UseCustomFrame {
```

```
 4   public static void main(String[] args) {
 5     JFrame frame = new CustomFrame();                                        create a frame
 6     frame.setTitle("Use CustomFrame");
 7     frame.setSize(200, 150);
 8     frame.setLocation(200, 100);
 9     frame.setDefaultCloseOperation(JFrame.EXIT_ON_CLOSE);
10     frame.setVisible(true);                                                  display frame
11   }
12 }
```

KEY TERMS

array list 315	is-a relationship 320
casting objects 313	meta-object 325
constructor chaining 307	override 309
dynamic binding 311	polymorphism 311
final 301	protected 320
generic programming 313	subclass 302
has-a relationship 320	subtype 302
inheritance 302	superclass 302
initialization block 327	supertype 302
instanceof 314	

CHAPTER SUMMARY

■ You can derive a new class from an existing class. This is known as *class inheritance*. The new class is called a *subclass*, *child class*, or *extended class*. The existing class is called a *superclass*, *parent class*, or *base class*.

■ A constructor is used to construct an instance of a class. Unlike properties and methods, the constructors of a superclass are not inherited in the subclass. They can only be invoked from the constructors of the subclasses, using the keyword **super**.

■ A constructor may invoke an overloaded constructor or its superclass's constructor. If none of them is invoked explicitly, the compiler puts **super()** as the first statement in the constructor.

■ To override a method, the method must be defined in the subclass using the same signature as in its superclass.

■ An instance method can be overridden only if it is accessible. Thus a private method cannot be overridden, because it is not accessible outside its own class. If a method defined in a subclass is private in its superclass, the two methods are completely unrelated.

■ Like an instance method, a static method can be inherited. However, a static method cannot be overridden. If a static method defined in the superclass is redefined in a subclass, the method defined in the superclass is hidden.

■ Every class in Java is descended from the **java.lang.Object** class. If no inheritance is specified when a class is defined, the superclass of the class is **Object**.

■ If a method's parameter type is a superclass (e.g., **Object**), you may pass an object to this method of any of the parameter's subclasses (e.g., **Circle** or **String**). When an object (e.g., a `Circle` object or a `String` object) is used in the method, the particular implementation of the method of the object that is invoked (e.g., `toString`) is determined dynamically.

■ It is always possible to cast an instance of a subclass to a variable of a superclass, because an instance of a subclass is *always* an instance of its superclass. When casting an instance of a superclass to a variable of its subclass, explicit casting must be used to confirm your intention to the compiler with the (`SubclassName`) cast notation.

■ You can override an instance method, but you cannot override a field (instance or static) or a static method. If you declare a field or a static method in a subclass with the same name as one in the superclass, the one in the superclass is hidden, but it still exists. The two fields or static methods are independent. You can reference the hidden field or static method using the `super` keyword in the subclass. The hidden field or method can also be accessed via a reference variable of the superclass's type.

■ When invoking an instance method from a reference variable, the *actual class of the object* referenced by the variable decides which implementation of the method is used *at runtime*. When accessing a field or a static method, the *declared type* of the reference variable decides which method is used *at compile time*.

■ You can use `obj instanceof AClass` to check whether an object is an instance of a class.

■ You can use the `protected` modifier to prevent the data and methods from being accessed by non-subclasses from a different package.

■ You can use the `final` modifier to indicate that a class is final and cannot be a parent class.

REVIEW QUESTIONS

Sections 9.2–9.5

9.1 What is the printout of running the class `C` in (a)? What problem arises in compiling the program in (b)?

```
class A {
  public A() {
    System.out.println(
      "A's no-arg constructor is invoked");
  }
}

class B extends A {
}

public class C {
  public static void main(String[] args) {
    B b = new B();
  }
}
```

(a)

```
class A {
  public A(int x) {
  }
}

class B extends A {
  public B() {
  }
}

public class C {
  public static void main(String[] args) {
    B b = new B();
  }
}
```

(b)

9.2 True or false? (1) A subclass is a subset of a superclass. (2) When invoking a constructor from a subclass, its superclass's no-arg constructor is always invoked. (3) You can override a private method defined in a superclass. (4) You can override a static method defined in a superclass.

9.3 Identify the problems in the following classes:

```java
 1 public class Circle {
 2   private double radius;
 3
 4   public Circle (double radius) {
 5     radius = radius;
 6   }
 7
 8   public double getRadius() {
 9     return radius;
10   }
11
12   public double getArea() {
13     return radius * radius * Math.PI;
14   }
15 }
16
17 class B extends Circle {
18   private double length;
19
20   B(double radius, double length) {
21     Circle(radius);
22     length = length;
23   }
24
25   /** Override getArea() */
26   public double getArea() {
27     return getArea() * length;
28   }
29 }
```

9.4 Explain the difference between method overloading and method overriding.

Section 9.6 The `Object` class and Its `toString()` Method

9.5 Does every class have a `toString` method? Where does it come from? How is it used? Is it appropriate to override this method?

9.6 Show the output of following program:

```java
 1 public class Test {
 2   public static void main(String[] args) {
 3     A a = new A(3);
 4   }
 5 }
 6
 7 class A extends B {
 8   public A(int t) {
 9     System.out.println("A's constructor is invoked");
10   }
11 }
12
```

```
13 class B {
14   public B() {
15     System.out.println("B's constructor is invoked");
16   }
17 }
```

Is the no-arg constructor of `Object` invoked when `new A(3)` is invoked?

Sections 9.6–9.7

9.7 For the `GeometricObject` and `Circle` classes in Listings 9.1 and 9.2, answer the following questions:

(a) Assume that `circle` is a `Circle` object and `object1` is a `GeometricObject`, are the following Boolean expressions true or false?

```
(circle instanceof GeometricObject)
(object1 instanceof GeometricObject)
(circle instanceof Circle)
(object1 instanceof Circle)
```

(b) Are the following statements correct?

```
Circle circle = new Circle(5);
GeometricObject object = circle;
```

(c) Are the following statements correct?

```
GeometricObject object = new GeometricObject();
Circle circle = (Circle)object;
```

9.8 Suppose that `Fruit`, `Apple`, `Orange`, `Golden Delicious Apple`, and `Macintosh Apple` are declared, as shown in Figure 9.11. Assume that `fruit` is an instance of `GoldenDelicious` and `orange` is an instance of `Orange`. Answer the following questions:

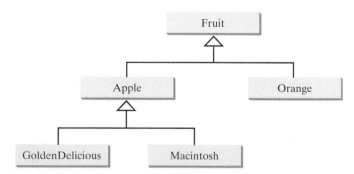

FIGURE 9.11 `GoldenDelicious` and `Macintosh` are subclasses of `Apple`, `Apple` and `Orange` are subclasses of `Fruit`.

(1) Is `fruit instanceof Orange`?
(2) Is `fruit instanceof Apple`?
(3) Is `fruit instanceof GoldenDelicious`?
(4) Is `fruit instanceof Macintosh`?
(5) Is `orange instanceof Orange`?
(6) Is `orange instanceof Fruit`?
(7) Is `orange instanceof Apple`?

(8) Suppose the method `makeApple` is defined in the `Apple` class. Can `fruit` invoke this method? Can `orange` invoke this method?

(9) Suppose the method `makeOrangeJuice` is defined in the `Orange` class. Can `orange` invoke this method? Can `fruit` invoke this method?

9.9 What is wrong in the following code?

```
 1 public class Test {
 2   public static void main(String[] args) {
 3     Object fruit = new Fruit();
 4     Object apple = (Apple)fruit;
 5   }
 6 }
 7
 8 class Apple extends Fruit {
 9 }
10
11 class Fruit {
12 }
```

Section 9.9 The `ArrayList` Class

9.10 How do you create an `ArrayList`? How do you append an object to a list? How do you insert an object at the beginning of a list? How do you find the number of objects in a list? How do you remove a given object from a list? How do you remove the last object from the list? How do you check whether a given object is in a list? How do you retrieve an object at a specified index from a list?

9.11 Identify three errors in the following code:

```
ArrayList list = new ArrayList();
list.add("New York");
list.add("Austin");
list.add(new java.util.Date());
String city = list.get(0);
list.set(3, "Dallas");
System.out.println(list.get(3));
```

Section 9.11 The `protected` Data and Methods

9.12 What modifier should you use on a class so that a class in the same package can access it, but a class in a different package cannot access it?

9.13 What modifier should you use so that a class in a different package cannot access the class, but its subclasses in any package can access it?

9.14 In the following code, classes `A` and `B` are in the same package. If the question marks are replaced by blanks, can class `B` be compiled? If the question marks are replaced by `private`, can class `B` be compiled? If the question marks are replaced by `protected`, can class `B` be compiled?

```
package p1;

public class A {
  ?   int i;

  ?   void m() {
    ...
  }
}
```

```
package p1;

public class B extends A {
  public void m1(String[] args) {
    System.out.println(i);
    m();
  }
}
```

(a)   (b)

9.15 In the following code, classes **A** and **B** are in different packages. If the question marks are replaced by blanks, can class **B** be compiled? If the question marks are replaced by `private`, can class **B** be compiled? If the question marks are replaced by `protected`, can class **B** be compiled?

```
package p1;

public class A {
    ?    int i;
    ?    void m() {
        ...
    }
}
```
(a)

```
package p2;

public class B extends A {
    public void m1(String[] args) {
        System.out.println(i);
        m();
    }
}
```
(b)

Section 9.13 The Methods in the **Object** Class

9.16 When overriding the `equals` method, a common mistake is mistyping its signature in the subclass. For example, the `equals` method is incorrectly written as `equals(Circle circle)`, as shown in (a) in the following code, instead, it should be `equals(Object circle)`, as shown in (b). Show the output of running class **Test** with the **Circle** class in (a) and in (b).

```
public class Test {
    public static void main(String[] args) {
        Object circle1 = new Circle();
        Object circle2 = new Circle();
        System.out.println(circle1.equals(circle2));
    }
}
```

```
class Circle {
    double radius;

    public boolean equals(Circle circle) {
        return this.radius == circle.radius;
    }
}
```
(a)

```
class Circle {
    double radius;

    public boolean equals(Object circle) {
        return this.radius ==
            ((Circle)circle).radius;
    }
}
```
(b)

9.17 Where are the `equals`, `hashCode`, `finalize`, `clone`, and `getClass` methods defined? When is the `finalize` method invoked?

9.18 Since the `clone` method is defined in `Object`, every object can invoke this method. Is it true?

9.19 What is the return type of the `getClass` method? If two objects o1 and o2 have the same class type, is `o1.getClass()` same as `o2.getClass()`?

Section 9.14 Hiding Fields and Static Methods

9.20 Show the output of running class **Test**.

```
class A {
  int i = 1;
  static int j = 3;

  void m() {
    i = 5;
  }

  static void m1() {
    j = 7;
  }
}
```
(a)

```
class B extend A {
  int i = 2;
  static int j = 4;

  void m() {
    i = 6;
  }

  static void m1() {
    j = 8;
  }
}
```
(b)

```
public class Test {
  public static void main
      (String[] args) {
    B b = new B();
    System.out.println(b.i);
    System.out.println(b.j);

    A a = new B();
    System.out.println(a.i);
    System.out.println(a.j);

    a.m();
    a.m1();
    System.out.println(a.i);
    System.out.println(a.j);
  }
}
```
(c)

9.21 For the `HidingDemo` class in Listing 9.10, what is the output if line 3 is replaced by `B x = new B()`? What error would occur if line 3 is replaced by `A x = new A()`?

Section 9.15 Initialization Blocks

9.22 Show the output of following program:

```
public class Test {
  public static void main(String[] args) {
    A a = new A();
  }
}

class A {
  int i = 1;
  static int j = 2;

  {
    System.out.println("i is " + i);
  }

  static {
    System.out.println("j is " + j);
  }
}
```
(a)

```
public class Test {
  public static void main(String[] args) {
    A a = new A();
  }
}

class A extends B {
  int i = 5;
  static int j = 4;

  A() {
    System.out.println("i is " + i);
    System.out.println("j is " + j);
  }

  void m() {
    System.out.println("i is " + i);
    System.out.println("j is " + j);
  }
}

class B {
  B() {
    m();
  }

  void m() {
  }
}
```
(b)

9.23 For the `InitializationDemo` class in Listing 9.11, what is the output if line 3 is deleted? What is the output if line 3 is replaced by `new N()`? What is the output if line 3 is replaced by `N object = new M()`?

Comprehensive

9.24 Define the following terms: inheritance, superclass, subclass, the keywords `super` and `this`, casting objects, the modifiers `protected` and `final`.

9.25 Indicate true or false for the following statements:

- A protected datum or method can be accessed by any class in the same package.
- A protected datum or method can be accessed by any class in different packages.
- A protected datum or method can be accessed by its subclasses in any package.
- A final class can have instances.
- A final class can be extended.
- A final method can be overridden.
- You can always successfully cast an instance of a subclass to a superclass.
- You can always successfully cast an instance of a superclass to a subclass.
- The order in which modifiers appear before a method is important.

9.26 Describe the difference between method matching and method binding.

9.27 What are advantages of dynamic binding?

PROGRAMMING EXERCISES

Sections 9.2–9.4

9.1 (*The `Triangle` class*) Design a class named `Triangle` that extends `Geometric-Object`. The class contains:

- Three `double` data fields named `side1`, `side2`, and `side3` with default values `1.0` to denote three sides of the triangle.
- A no-arg constructor that creates a default triangle.
- A constructor that creates a rectangle with the specified `side1`, `side2`, and `side3`.
- The accessor methods for all three data fields.
- A method named `getArea()` that returns the area of this triangle.
- A method named `getPerimeter()` that returns the perimeter of this triangle.
- A method named `toString()` that returns a string description for the triangle.

For the formula to compute the area of a triangle, see Exercise 5.19. The `toString()` method is implemented as follows:

```
return "Triangle: side1 = " + side1 + " side2 = " + side2 +
  " side3 = " + side3;
```

Draw the UML diagram that involves the classes `Triangle` and `GeometricObject`. Implement the class. Write a test program that creates a `Triangle` object with sides 1, 1.5, 1, sets color `yellow` and filled `true`, and displays the area, perimeter, color, and whether filled or not.

Sections 9.5–9.9

9.2 (*The `Person`, `Student`, `Employee`, `Faculty`, and `Staff` classes*) Design a class named `Person` and its two subclasses named `Student` and `Employee`. Make `Faculty` and `Staff` subclasses of `Employee`. A person has a name, address, phone number, and email address. A student has a class status (freshman, sophomore, junior, or senior). Define the status as a constant. An employee has an office, salary, and date-hired. Define a class named `MyDate` that contains the fields `year`, `month`, and `day`. A faculty member has office hours and a rank. A staff member has a title. Override the `toString` method in each class to display the class name and the person's name.

Draw the UML diagram for the classes. Implement the classes. Write a test program that creates a `Person`, `Student`, `Employee`, `Faculty`, and `Staff`, and invokes their `toString()` methods.

9.3 (*Subclasses of Account*) In Exercise 7.3, the `Account` class was created to model a bank account. An account has the properties account number, balance, annual interest rate, and date created, and methods to deposit and withdraw. Create two subclasses for checking and saving accounts. A checking account has an overdraft limit, but a savings account cannot be overdrawn.

Draw the UML diagram for the classes. Implement the classes. Write a test program that creates objects of `Account`, `SavingsAccount`, and `CheckingAccount`, and invokes their `toString()` methods.

9.4 (*Implementing MyStack using inheritance*) In Listing 9.8, `MyStack` is implemented using composition. Create a new stack class that extends `MyArrayList`.

Draw the UML diagram for the classes. Implement `MyStack`.

9.5 (*The Course class*) Rewrite the `Course` class in Listing 7.11. Use an `ArrayList` to replace an array to store students.

9.6 (*Using ArrayList*) Write a program that creates an `ArrayList`, adds a `Loan` object, a `Date` object, a string, a `JFrame` object, and a `Circle` object to the list, and uses a loop to display all the elements in the list by invoking the object's `toString()` method.

CHAPTER 10

ABSTRACT CLASSES AND INTERFACES

Objectives

- To design and use abstract classes (§10.2).

- To process a calendar using the `Calendar` and `GregorianCalendar` classes (§10.3).

- To declare interfaces to model weak inheritance relationships (§10.4).

- To define a natural order using the `Comparable` interface (§10.4.1).

- To know the similarities and differences between an abstract class and an interface (§10.4.2).

- To declare custom interfaces (§10.4.3).

- (Optional) To make objects cloneable using the `Cloneable` interface (§10.4.4).

- To use wrapper classes (`Byte`, `Short`, `Integer`, `Long`, `Float`, `Double`, `Character`, and `Boolean`) to wrap primitive data values into objects (§10.5).

- (Optional) To use the `BigInteger` and `BigDecimal` classes for computing very large numbers with arbitrary precisions (§10.5.6).

- To create a generic sort method (§10.5).

- To simplify programming using JDK 1.5 automatic conversion between primitive types and wrapper class types (§10.6).

- (Optional GUI) To handle GUI events (§10.7).

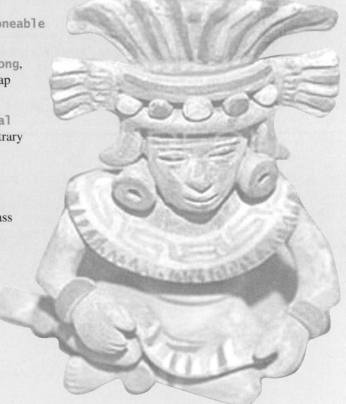

10.1 Introduction

In the inheritance hierarchy, classes become more specific and concrete *with each new sub-class*. If you move from a subclass back up to a superclass, the classes become more general and less specific. Class design should ensure that a superclass contains common features of its subclasses. Sometimes a superclass is so abstract that it cannot have any specific instances. Such a class is referred to as an *abstract class*.

Sometimes it is necessary to derive a subclass from several classes. This capability is known as *multiple inheritance*. Java, however, does not allow multiple inheritance. A Java class may inherit directly from only one superclass. This restriction is known as *single inheritance*. If you use the **extends** keyword to define a subclass, it allows only one parent class. With interfaces, you can obtain the effect of multiple inheritance.

This chapter introduces abstract classes and interfaces, and discusses how to use wrapper classes for primitive data type values.

10.2 Abstract Classes

`GeometricObject` was declared as the superclass for `Circle` and `Rectangle` in the preceding chapter. `GeometricObject` models common features of geometric objects. Both `Circle` and `Rectangle` contain the `getArea()` and `getPerimeter()` methods for computing the area and perimeter of a circle and a rectangle. Since you can compute areas and perimeters for all geometric objects, it is better to declare the `getArea()` and `getPerimeter()` methods in the `GeometricObject` class. However, these methods cannot be implemented in the `GeometricObject` class because their implementation is dependent on the specific type of geometric object. Such methods are referred to as *abstract methods*. After you declare the methods in `GeometricObject`, `GeometricObject` becomes an abstract class. The new `GeometricObject` class is shown in Figure 10.1. In UML graphic notation, the names of abstract classes and their abstract methods are italicized, as shown in Figure 10.1. Listing 10.1 gives the source code for the new `GeometricObject` class.

LISTING 10.1 GeometricObject.java

```java
 1  public abstract class GeometricObject {
 2    private String color = "white";
 3    private boolean filled;
 4    private java.util.Date dateCreated;
 5
 6    /** Construct a default geometric object */
 7    protected GeometricObject() {
 8      dateCreated = new java.util.Date();
 9    }
10
11    /** Return color */
12    public String getColor() {
13      return color;
14    }
15
16    /** Set a new color */
17    public void setColor(String color) {
18      this.color = color;
19    }
20
21    /** Return filled. Since filled is boolean,
22        so, the get method name is isFilled */
```

Margin notes: abstract class • multiple inheritance • single inheritance • abstract method • **abstract** class

```
23   public boolean isFilled() {
24     return filled;
25   }
26
27   /** Set a new filled */
28   public void setFilled(boolean filled) {
29     this.filled = filled;
30   }
31
32   /** Get dateCreated */
33   public java.util.Date getDateCreated() {
34     return dateCreated;
35   }
36
37   /** Return a string representation of this object */
38   public String toString() {
39     return "created on " + dateCreated + "\ncolor: " + color +
40       " and filled: " + filled;
41   }
42
43   /** Abstract method getArea */
44   public abstract double getArea();                       abstract method
45
46   /** Abstract method getPerimeter */
47   public abstract double getPerimeter();                  abstract method
48 }
```

The # sign indicates protected modifer

GeometricObject

-color: String
-filled: boolean
-dateCreated: java.util.Date

#GeometricObject()
+getColor(): String
+setColor(color: String): void
+isFilled(): boolean
+setFilled(filled: boolean): void
+getDateCreated(): java.util.Date
+toString(): String
+getArea(): double
+getPerimeter(): double

Circle

-radius: double

+Circle()
+Circle(radius: double)
+getRadius(): double
+setRadius(radius: double): void
+getDiameter(): double

Rectangle

-width: double
-height: double

+Rectangle()
+Rectangle(width: double, height: double)
+getWidth(): double
+setWidth(width: double): void
+getHeight(): double
+setHeight(height: double): void

FIGURE 10.1 The new `GeometricObject` class contains abstract methods.

Abstract classes are like regular classes with data and methods, but you cannot create instances of abstract classes using the `new` operator. An abstract method is a method signature without implementation. Its implementation is provided by the subclasses. A class that contains abstract methods must be declared abstract.

The `GeometricObject` abstract class provides the common features (data and methods) for geometric objects. Because you don't know how to compute areas and perimeters of geometric objects, `getArea` and `getPerimeter` are defined as abstract methods. These methods are implemented in the subclasses. The implementation of `Circle` and `Rectangle` is the same as in Listings 9.2 and 9.3 except that they don't have the `package` statements. The new `GeometricObject.java`, `Circle.java`, and `Rectangle.java` are stored in `c:\book`. Note that the `GeometricObject`, `Circle`, and `Rectangle` classes in the preceding chapter are placed in a package named *chapter9* to avoid naming conflicts with the classes in this chapter.

abstract method in abstract class

Note
An abstract method cannot be contained in a nonabstract class. If a subclass of an abstract superclass does not implement all the abstract methods, the subclass must be declared abstract. In other words, in a nonabstract subclass extended from an abstract class, all the abstract methods must be implemented, even if they are not used in the subclass. Also note that abstract methods are non-static.

object cannot be created from abstract class

Note
An abstract class cannot be instantiated using the `new` operator, but you can still define its constructors, which are invoked in the constructors of its subclasses. For instance, the constructors of `GeometricObject` are invoked in the `Circle` class and the `Rectangle` class.

abstract class without abstract method

Note
A class that contains abstract methods must be abstract. However, it is possible to declare an abstract class that contains no abstract methods. In this case, you cannot create instances of the class using the `new` operator. This class is used as a base class for defining a new subclass.

superclass of abstract class may be concrete

Note
A subclass can be abstract even if its superclass is concrete. For example, the `Object` class is concrete, but its subclasses, such as `GeometricObject`, may be abstract.

concrete method overridden to be abstract

Note
A subclass can override a method from its superclass to declare it **abstract**. This is *very unusual*, but is useful when the implementation of the method in the superclass becomes invalid in the subclass. In this case, the subclass must be declared abstract.

abstract class as type

Note
You cannot create an instance from an abstract class using the `new` operator, but an abstract class can be used as a data type. Therefore, the following statement, which creates an array whose elements are of `GeometricObject` type, is correct.

```
GeometricObject[] objects = new GeometricObject[10];
```

You may be wondering whether the abstract methods `getArea` and `getPerimeter` should be removed from the `GeometricObject` class. The following example shows the benefits of retaining them in the `GeometricObject` class.

10.2.1 Example: Using the `GeometricObject` Class

This example presents a program that creates two geometric objects, a circle and a rectangle, invokes the `equalArea` method to check whether the two objects have equal areas, and invokes the `displayGeometricObject` method to display the objects.

Listing 10.2 gives the solution to the problem. A sample run of the program is shown in Figure 10.2.

LISTING 10.2 TestGeometricObject.java

```java
1 public class TestGeometricObject {
2   /** Main method */
3   public static void main(String[] args) {
4     // Declare and initialize two geometric objects
5     GeometricObject geoObject1 = new Circle(5);
6     GeometricObject geoObject2 = new Rectangle(5, 3);
7
8     System.out.println("The two objects have the same area? " +
9       equalArea(geoObject1, geoObject2));
10
11     // Display circle
12     displayGeometricObject(geoObject1);
13
14     // Display rectangle
15     displayGeometricObject(geoObject2);
16   }
17
18   /** A method for comparing the areas of two geometric objects */
19   public static boolean equalArea(GeometricObject object1,
20       GeometricObject object2) {
21     return object1.getArea() == object2.getArea();
22   }
23
24   /** A method for displaying a geometric object */
25   public static void displayGeometricObject(GeometricObject object) {
26     System.out.println();
27     System.out.println("The area is " + object.getArea());
28     System.out.println("The perimeter is " + object.getPerimeter());
29   }
30 }
```

FIGURE 10.2   The program compares the areas of the objects and displays their properties.

The methods `getArea()` and `getPerimeter()` defined in the `GeometricObject` class are overridden in the `Circle` class and the `Rectangle` class. The statements (lines 5–6)

```java
GeometricObject geoObject1 = new Circle(5);
GeometricObject geoObject2 = new Rectangle(5, 3);
```

create a new circle and rectangle, and assign them to the variables `geoObject1` and `geoObject2`. These two variables are of the `GeometricObject` type.

When invoking `equalArea(geoObject1, geoObject2)` (line 9), the `getArea` method defined in the `Circle` class is used for `object1.getArea()`, since `geoObject1` is a circle, and the `getArea` method defined in the `Rectangle` class is used for `object2.getArea()`, since `geoObject2` is a rectangle.

Similarly, when invoking `displayGeometricObject(geoObject1)` (line 12), the methods `getArea` and `getPerimeter` defined in the `Circle` class are used, and when invoking `displayGeometricObject(geoObject2)` (line 15), the methods `getArea` and `getPerimeter` defined in the `Rectangle` class are used. The JVM dynamically determines which of these methods to invoke at runtime, depending on the type of object.

Note that if the `getArea` and `getPerimeter` methods were not defined in `GeometricObject`, you cannot define the `equalArea` and `displayObject` methods in this program. So, you now see the benefits of defining the abstract methods in `GeometricObject`.

10.3 The `Calendar` and `GregorianCalendar` Classes

java.util.Calendar

An instance of `java.util.Date` represents a specific instant in time with millisecond precision. `java.util.Calendar` is an abstract base class for extracting detailed calendar information, such as year, month, date, hour, minute, and second. Subclasses of `Calendar` can implement specific calendar systems, such as the Gregorian calendar, the lunar calendar, and the Jewish calendar. Currently, `java.util.GregorianCalendar` for the Gregorian calendar is supported in Java, as shown in Figure 10.3.

java.util.Gregorian
Calendar

You can use `new GregorianCalendar()` to construct a default `GregorianCalendar` with the current time and `new GregorianCalendar(year, month, date)` to construct a `GregorianCalendar` with the specified `year`, `month`, and `date`. The `month` parameter is `0`-based, that is, `0` is for January.

constructing calendar

java.util.Calendar	
`#Calendar()`	Constructs a default calendar.
`+get(field: int): int`	Returns the value of the given calendar field.
`+set(field: int, value: int): void`	Sets the calendar field with the specified value.
`+set(year: int, month: int, dayOfMonth: int): void`	Sets the calendar with the specified year, month, and date. The month parameter is 0-based, that is, 0 is for January.
`+getActualMaximum(field: int): int`	Returns the maximum value that the specified calendar field could have.
`+add(field: int, amount: int): void`	Adds or subtracts the specified amount of time to the given calendar field.
`+getTime(): java.util.Date`	Returns a Date object representing this calendar's time value (million-second offset from the Unix epoch).
`+setTime(date: java.util.Date): void`	Sets this calendar's time with the given Date object.

java.util.GregorianCalendar	
`+GregorianCalendar()`	Constructs a GregorianCalendar for the current time.
`+GregorianCalendar(year: int, month: int, dayOfMonth: int)`	Constructs a GregorianCalendar for the specified year, month, and day of month.
`+GregorianCalendar(year: int, month: int, dayOfMonth: int, hour:int, minute: int, second: int)`	Constructs a GregorianCalendar for the specified year, month, day of month, hour, minute, and second. The month parameter is 0-based, that is, 0 is for January.

FIGURE 10.3 The abstract `Calendar` class defines common features of various calendars.

The `get(int field)` method defined in the `Calendar` class is useful to extract the value for a given time field. The time fields are defined as constants, such as `YEAR`, `MONTH`, `DATE`, `HOUR` (for the twelve-hour clock), `HOUR_OF_DAY` (for the twenty-four-hour clock), `MINUTE`, `SECOND`, `DAY_OF_WEEK` (the day number within the current week, with 1 for Sunday), `DAY_OF_MONTH` (the day in the current month), `DAY_OF_YEAR` (the day number in the current year with 1 for the first day of the year), `WEEK_OF_MONTH` (the week number within the current month), and `WEEK_OF_YEAR` (the week number within the current year). For example, the following code

```java
// Construct a Gregorian calendar for the current date and time
java.util.Calendar calendar = new java.util.GregorianCalendar();
System.out.println("Year\tMonth\tDate\tHour\tHour24\tMinute\tSecond");
System.out.println(calendar.get(Calendar.YEAR) + "\t" +
  calendar.get(Calendar.MONTH) + "\t" + calendar.get(Calendar.DATE)
  + "\t" + calendar.get(Calendar.HOUR) + "\t" +
  calendar.get(Calendar.HOUR_OF_DAY) + "\t" +
  calendar.get(Calendar.MINUTE) + "\t" +
  calendar.get(Calendar.SECOND));
System.out.print("Day of week: " +
  calendar.get(Calendar.DAY_OF_WEEK) + "\t");
System.out.print("Day of month: " +
  calendar.get(Calendar.DAY_OF_MONTH) + "\t");
System.out.println("Day of year: " +
  calendar.get(Calendar.DAY_OF_YEAR));
System.out.print("Week of month: " +
  calendar.get(Calendar.WEEK_OF_MONTH) + "\t");
System.out.print("Week of year: " +
  calendar.get(Calendar.WEEK_OF_YEAR));
```

displays the information for the current date and time, as follows:

```
Year Month  Date  Hour  Hour24  Minute  Second
2003 2      9     8     20      17      39
Day of week: 1     Day of month: 9      Day of year: 68
Week of month: 3  Week of year: 11
```

The `set(int field, value)` method defined in the `Calendar` class can be used to set a field. For example, you can use `calendar.set(Calendar.DAY_OF_MONTH, 1)` to set the `calendar` to the first day of the month.

The `add(field, value)` method adds or subtracts the specified amount to a given field. For example, to subtract five days from the current time of the calendar, you must call `add(Calendar.DAY_OF_MONTH, -5)`.

To obtain the number of days in a month, use `calendar.getActualMaximum (Calendar.DAY_OF_MONTH)`. For example, if the `calendar` were for March, this method would return 31.

You can set a time represented in a `Date` object for the `calendar` by invoking `calendar.setTime(date)` and retrieve the time by invoking `calendar.getTime()`.

10.4 Interfaces

An *interface* is a classlike construct that contains only constants and abstract methods. In many ways, an interface is similar to an abstract class, but an abstract class can contain variables and concrete methods as well as constants and abstract methods.

get(field)

set(field, value)

add(field, amount)

getActualMaximum (field)

setTime(Date)
getTime()

interface

To distinguish an interface from a class, Java uses the following syntax to declare an interface:

```
modifier interface InterfaceName {
  /** Constant declarations */
  /** Method signatures */
}
```

An interface is treated like a special class in Java. Each interface is compiled into a separate bytecode file, just like a regular class. As with an abstract class, you cannot create an instance from an interface using the **new** operator, but in most cases you can use an interface more or less the same way you use an abstract class. For example, you can use an interface as a data type for a variable, as the result of casting, and so on.

Suppose you want to design a generic method to find the larger of two objects. The objects can be students, circles, or rectangles. Since compare methods are different for different types of objects, you need to define a generic compare method to determine the order of the two objects. Then you can tailor the method to compare students, circles, or rectangles. For example, you can use student ID as the key for comparing students, radius as the key for comparing circles, and area as the key for comparing rectangles. You can use an interface to define a generic **compareTo** method, as follows:

java.lang.
 Comparable

```
// Interface for comparing objects, defined in java.lang
package java.lang;

public interface Comparable {
  public int compareTo(Object o);
}
```

The **compareTo** method determines the order of this object with the specified object **o**, and returns a negative integer, zero, or a positive integer if this object is less than, equal to, or greater than the specified object **o**.

Note

The `Comparable` interface has been available since JDK 1.2, and is included in the `java.lang` package.

Many classes in the Java library (e.g., **String** and **Date**) implement **Comparable** to define a natural order for the objects. If you examine the source code of these classes, you will see the keyword **implements** used in the classes, as shown below:

```
public class String extends Object
    implements Comparable {
  // class body omitted
}
```

```
public class Date extends Object
    implements Comparable {
  // class body omitted
}
```

Thus strings are comparable, and so are dates. Let **s** be a **String** object and **d** be a **Date** object. All the following expressions are all true:

```
s instanceof String
s instanceof Object
s instanceof Comparable
```

```
d instanceof java.util.Date
d instanceof Object
d instanceof Comparable
```

A generic **max** method for finding the larger of two objects can be declared, as shown in (a) or (b):

```
// Max.java: Find a maximum object
public class Max {
  /** Return the maximum of two objects */
  public static Comparable max
     (Comparable o1, Comparable o2 ) {
    if (o1.compareTo(o2) > 0)
      return o1;
    else
      return o2;
  }
}
```

(a)

```
// Max.java: Find a maximum object
public class Max {
  /** Return the maximum of two objects */
  public static Object max
     (Object o1, Object o2 ) {

    if (((Comparable)o1).compareTo(o2) > 0)
      return o1;
    else
      return o2;
  }
}
```

(b)

The `max` method in (a) *is simpler* than the one in (b). In the `Max` class in (b), `o1` is declared as `Object`, and `(Comparable)o1` tells the compiler to cast `o1` into `Comparable` so that the `compareTo` method can be invoked from `o1`. However, no casting is needed in the `Max` class in (a), since `o1` is declared as `Comparable`.

(a) is simpler

The `max` method in (a) *is more robust* than the one in (b). You must invoke the `max` method with two comparable objects. Suppose you invoke `max` with two noncomparable objects

(a) is more robust

```
Max.max(anyObject1, anyObject2);
```

The compiler will detect the error using the `max` method in (a), because `anyObject1` is not an instance of `Comparable`. Using the `max` method in (b), this line of code will compile fine, but will have a runtime `ClassCastException`, because `anyObject1` is not an instance of `Comparable` and cannot be cast into `Comparable`.

From now on, assume that the `max` method in (a) is in the text. Since strings are comparable and dates are comparable, you can use the `max` method to find the larger of two instances of `String` or `Date`. Here is an example:

```
String s1 = "abcdef";
String s2 = "abcdee";
String s3 = (String)Max.max(s1, s2);
```

```
Date d1 = new Date();
Date d2 = new Date();
Date d3 = (Date)Max.max(d1, d2);
```

The `return` value from the `max` method is of the `Comparable` type. So you need to cast it to `String` or `Date` explicitly.

10.4.1 Declaring Classes to Implement `Comparable`

You cannot use the `max` method to find the larger of two instances of `Rectangle`, because `Rectangle` does not implement `Comparable`. However, you can declare a new rectangle class that implements `Comparable`. The instances of this new class are comparable. Let this new class be named `ComparableRectangle`, as shown in Listing 10.3.

LISTING 10.3 ComparableRectangle.java

```
1  public class ComparableRectangle extends Rectangle
2     implements Comparable {
3    /** Construct a ComparableRectangle with specified properties */
4    public ComparableRectangle(double width, double height) {
5      super(width, height);
6    }
7
```

```
 8     /** Implement the compareTo method defined in Comparable */
 9     public int compareTo(Object o) {
10       if (getArea() > ((ComparableRectangle)o).getArea())
11         return 1;
12       else if (getArea() < ((ComparableRectangle)o).getArea())
13         return -1;
14       else
15         return 0;
16     }
17   }
```

`ComparableRectangle` extends `Rectangle` and implements `Comparable`, as shown in Figure 10.4. The keyword `implements` indicates that `ComparableRectangle` inherits all the constants from the `Comparable` interface and implements the methods in the interface. The `compareTo` method compares the areas of two rectangles. An instance of `CompareRectangle` is also an instance of `Rectangle`, `GeometricObject`, `Object`, and `Comparable`.

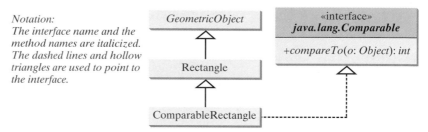

Notation:
The interface name and the method names are italicized. The dashed lines and hollow triangles are used to point to the interface.

FIGURE 10.4 `ComparableRectangle` extends `Rectangle` and implements `Comparable`.

You can now use the `max` method to find the larger of two objects of `CompareRectangle`. Here is an example:

```
ComparableRectangle rectangle1 = new ComparableRectangle(4, 5);
ComparableRectangle rectangle2 = new ComparableRectangle(3, 6);
System.out.println(Max.max(rectangle1, rectangle2));
```

An interface provides another form of generic programming. It would be difficult to use a generic `max` method to find the maximum of the objects without using an interface in this example, because multiple inheritance would be necessary to inherit `Comparable` and another class, such as `Rectangle`, at the same time.

The `Object` class contains the `equals` method, which is intended for the subclasses of the `Object` class to override in order to compare whether the contents of the objects are the same. Suppose that the `Object` class contains the `compareTo` method, as defined in the `Comparable` interface; the new `max` method can be used to compare a list of *any* objects. Whether a `compareTo` method should be included in the `Object` class is debatable. Since the `compareTo` method is not defined in the `Object` class, the `Comparable` interface is created in Java 2 to enable objects to be compared if they are instances of the `Comparable` interface. It is strongly recommended (though not required) that `compareTo` should be consistent with `equals`. That is, for two objects o1 and o2, `o1.compareTo(o2) == 0` if and only if `o1.equals(o2)` is `true`.

10.4.2 Interfaces vs. Abstract Classes

An interface can be used the same way as an abstract class, but declaring an interface is different from declaring an abstract class. Table 10.1 summarizes the differences.

TABLE 10.1 Interfaces vs. Abstract Classes

	Variables	*Constructors*	*Methods*
Abstract class	No restrictions	Constructors are invoked by subclasses through constructor chaining. An abstract class cannot be instantiated using the new operator.	No restrictions
Interface	All variables must be `public static final`	No constructors. An interface cannot be instantiated using the new operator.	All methods must be public abstract instance methods

Note

Since all data fields are `public final static` and all methods are `public abstract` in an interface, Java allows these modifiers to be omitted. Therefore the following declarations are equivalent:

omitting modifiers

```
public interface T1 {
  public static final int K = 1;

  public abstract void p();
}
```

Equivalent

```
public interface T1 {
  int K = 1;

  void p();
}
```

Tip

A constant defined in an interface can be accessed using the syntax `Interface-Name.CONSTANT_NAME` (e.g., `T1.K`).

accessing constants

Java allows only single inheritance for class extension, but multiple extensions for interfaces. For example,

```
public class NewClass extends BaseClass
    implements Interface1, ..., InterfaceN {
  ...
}
```

An interface can inherit other interfaces using the **extends** keyword. Such an interface is called a *subinterface*. For example, `NewInterface` in the following code is a subinterface of `Interface1`, ..., and `InterfaceN`:

subinterface

```
public interface NewInterface extends Interface1, ..., InterfaceN {
  // constants and abstract methods
}
```

A class implementing `NewInterface` must implement the abstract methods defined in `NewInterface`, `Interface1`, ..., and `InterfaceN`. An interface can only extend other interfaces, not classes. A class can extend its superclass and implement multiple interfaces.

All classes share a single root, the `Object` class, but there is no single root for interfaces. Like a class, an interface also defines a type. A variable of an interface type can reference any instance of the class that implements the interface. If a class implements an interface, the interface is like a superclass for the class. You can use an interface as a data type and cast a variable of an interface type to its subclass, and vice versa. For example, suppose that `c` is an instance of `Class2` in Figure 10.5. `c` is also an instance of `Object`, `Class1`, `Interface1`, `Interface1_1`, `Interface1_2`, `Interface2_1`, and `Interface2_2`.

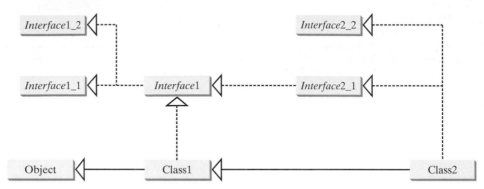

FIGURE 10.5 Abstract class *Class1* implements *Interface1*, *Interface1* extends *Interface1_1* and *Interface1_2*. *Class2* extends *Class1* and implements *Interface2_1* and *Interface2_2*.

Caution

conflict interfaces

On rare occasions, a class may implement two interfaces with conflict information (e.g., two identical constants with different values or two methods with the same signature but different return types). This type of error will be detected by the compiler.

Abstract classes and interfaces can both be used to model common features. How do you
is-a relationship
decide whether to use an interface or a class? In general, a *strong is-a relationship* that clearly describes a parent–child relationship should be modeled using classes. For example, a staff member is a person, so the relationship between them should be modeled using class inheritance. A *weak is-a relationship*, also known as *an is-kind-of relationship*, indicates that an object possesses a certain property. A weak is-a relationship can be modeled using interfaces. For example, all strings are comparable, so the `String` class implements the `Comparable` interface. You can also use interfaces to circumvent the single-inheritance restriction if multiple inheritance is desired. In the case of multiple inheritance, you have to design one as a superclass and others as interfaces. See Chapter 11, "Object-Oriented Design," for more discussion.

is-kind-of relationship

Note

Class names are nouns. Interface names may be adjectives or nouns. For example, both `java.lang.Comparable` and `java.awt.event.ActionListener` are interfaces. `Comparable` is an adjective, and `ActionListener` is a noun. `ActionListener` will be introduced in Chapter 14, "Event-Driven Programming."

10.4.3 Creating Custom Interfaces

An example of implementing the `Comparable` interface is given in §10.4.1, "Declaring Classes to Implement Comparable". This section creates a custom interface. Suppose you want to describe whether an object is edible. You can declare the `Edible` interface:

```java
public interface Edible {
  /** Describe how to eat */
  public String howToEat();
}
```

To denote that an object is edible, the class for the object must implement `Edible`. Let us create the following two sets of classes:

- Create a class named `Animal` and its subclasses `Tiger`, `Chicken`, and `Elephant`. Since chicken is edible, implement the `Edible` interface for the `Chicken` class, as follows:

```java
class Animal {
}
```

```
class Chicken extends Animal implements Edible, Comparable {
  int weight;

  public Chicken(int weight) {
    this.weight = weight;
  }

  public String howToEat() {
    return "Fry it";
  }

  public int compareTo(Object o) {
    return weight - ((Chicken)o).weight;
  }
}

class Tiger extends Animal {
}
```

A class may implement several interfaces. The `Chicken` class also implements the `Comparable` interface to compare two chickens according to their weight.

■ Create a class named `Fruit` and its subclasses `Apple` and `Orange`. Since all fruits are edible, implement the `Edible` interface for the `Fruit` class. The `Fruit` class is abstract, because you cannot implement the `howToEat` method without knowing exactly what the fruit is. In the `Apple` class and the `Orange` class, implement the `howToEat` method, as follows:

```
abstract class Fruit implements Edible {
}

class Apple extends Fruit {
  public String howToEat() {
    return "Make apple cider";
  }
}

class Orange extends Fruit {
  public String howToEat() {
    return "Make orange juice";
  }
}
```

To demonstrate how the `Edible` interface may be used, create the following program that creates an array with three objects. The `showObject` method invokes the `howToEat()` method if the object is edible.

```
public class TestEdible {
  public static void main(String[] args) {
    Object[] objects = {new Tiger(), new Chicken(), new Apple()};
    for (int i = 0; i < objects.length; i++)
      showObject(objects[i]);
  }

  public static void showObject(Object object) {
    if (object instanceof Edible)
      System.out.println(((Edible)object).howToEat());
  }
}
```

The program displays

```
Fry it
Make apple cider
```

10.4.4 (Optional) The `Cloneable` Interface

An interface contains constants and abstract methods, but the `Cloneable` interface is a special case. The `Cloneable` interface in the `java.lang` package is defined as follows:

java.lang.Cloneable

```
package java.lang;

public interface Cloneable {
}
```

marker interface

This interface is empty. An interface with an empty body is referred to as a *marker interface*. A marker interface does not contain constants or methods. It is used to denote that a class possesses certain desirable properties. A class that implements the `Cloneable` interface is marked cloneable, and its objects can be cloned using the `clone()` method defined in the `Object` class.

Many classes in the Java library (e.g., `Date`, `Calendar`, and `ArrayList`) implement `Cloneable`. Thus, the instances of these classes can be cloned. For example, the following code

```
Calendar calendar = new GregorianCalendar(2003, 2, 1);
Calendar calendarCopy = (Calendar)calendar.clone();
System.out.println("calendar == calendarCopy is " +
  (calendar == calendarCopy));
System.out.println("calendar.equals(calendarCopy) is " +
  calendar.equals(calendarCopy));
```

displays

```
calendar == calendarCopy is false
calendar.equals(calendarCopy) is true
```

how to implement
`Cloneable`

To declare a custom class that implements the `Cloneable` interface, the class must override the `clone()` method in the `Object` class. Listing 10.4 declares a class named `House` that implements `Cloneable` and `Comparable`.

LISTING 10.4 House.java

```
 1 public class House implements Cloneable, Comparable {
 2   private int id;
 3   private double area;
 4   private java.util.Date whenBuilt;
 5
 6   public House(int id, double area) {
 7     this.id = id;
 8     this.area = area;
 9     whenBuilt = new java.util.Date();
10   }
11
12   public double getId() {
13     return id;
14   }
15
16   public double getArea() {
17     return area;
18   }
19
20   public java.util.Date getWhenBuilt() {
21     return whenBuilt;
22   }
23
```

```
24    /** Override the protected clone method defined in the Object
25       class, and strengthen its accessibility */
26    public Object clone() {
27      try {
28        return super.clone();
29      }
30      catch (CloneNotSupportedException ex) {
31        return null;
32      }
33    }
34
35    /** Implement the compareTo method defined in Comparable */
36    public int compareTo(Object o) {
37      if (area > ((House)o).area)
38        return 1;
39      else if (area < ((House)o).area)
40        return -1;
41      else
42        return 0;
43    }
44 }
```

This exception is thrown if House does not implement **Cloneable**

The **House** class overrides the **clone** method (lines 26–33) defined in the **Object** class. The **clone** method in the **Object** class is defined as follows:

protected native Object clone() **throws** CloneNotSupportedException;

The keyword **native** indicates that this method is not written in Java, but is implemented in the JVM for the native platform. The keyword **protected** restricts the method to be accessed in the same package or in a subclass. For this reason, the **Cloneable** class must override the method and change the visibility modifier to **public** so that the method can be used in any package. Since the **clone** method implemented for the native platform in the **Object** class performs the task of cloning objects, the **clone** method in the **House** class simply invokes **super.clone()**. The **clone** method defined in the **Object** class may throw **CloneNotSupportedException**. Thus, **super.clone()** must be placed in a **try-catch** block. Exceptions and the **try-catch** block are introduced in Chapter 17, "Exceptions and Assertions."

CloneNotSupported-Exception

The **House** class overrides the **compareTo** method (lines 36–43) defined in the **Comparable** interface. The method compares the areas of two houses.

You can now create an object of the **House** class and create an identical copy from it, as follows:

```
House house1 = new House(1, 1750.50);
House house2 = (House)house1.clone();
```

house1 and **house2** are two different objects with identical contents. The **clone** method in the **Object** class copies each field from the original object to the target object. If the field is of a primitive type, its value is copied. For example, the value of **area** (**double** type) is copied from **house1** to **house2**. If the field is of an object, the reference of the field is copied. For example, the field **whenBuilt** is of the **Date** class, so its reference is copied into **house2**, as shown in Figure 10.6. Therefore, **house1.whenBuilt == house2.whenBuilt** is **true**, although **house1 == house2** is **false**. This is referred to as a *shallow copy* rather than a *deep copy*, meaning that if the field is of an object, the reference of the field is copied rather than its contents.

shallow copy
deep copy

If you want to perform a deep copy, you can override the **clone** method with custom cloning operations instead of invoking **super.clone()**. See Exercise 10.4.

FIGURE 10.6 The `clone` method copies the values of primitive type fields and the references of object type fields.

Note

You learned how to use the `arraycopy` method to copy arrays in Chapter 6, "Arrays." This method provides shallow copies. It works fine for arrays of primitive data type elements, but not for arrays of object type elements. To support a deep copy, you have to deal with how to copy individual object elements in the array.

Caution

If the `House` class does not override the `clone()` method, the program will receive a syntax error because `clone()` is protected in `java.lang.Object`. If `House` does not implement `java.lang.Cloneable`, invoking `super.clone()` (line 28) in House.java would cause a `CloneNotSupportedException`. Thus, to enable cloning an object, the class for the object must override the `clone()` method and implement `Cloneable`.

10.5 Processing Primitive Data Type Values as Objects

Primitive data types are not used as objects in Java due to performance considerations. Because of the overhead of processing objects, the language's performance would be adversely affected if primitive data types were treated as objects. However, many Java methods require the use of objects as arguments. For example, the `add(object)` method in the `ArrayList` class adds an object to an `ArrayList`. Java offers a convenient way to incorporate, or wrap, a primitive data type into an object (e.g., wrapping `int` into the `Integer` class, and wrapping `double` into the `Double` class). The corresponding class is called a *wrapper class*. By using a wrapper object instead of a primitive data type variable, you can take advantage of generic programming.

wrapper class

Java provides `Boolean`, `Character`, `Double`, `Float`, `Byte`, `Short`, `Integer`, and `Long` wrapper classes for primitive data types. These classes are grouped in the `java.lang` package. Their inheritance hierarchy is shown in Figure 10.7.

Note

The wrapper class name for a primitive type is the same as the primitive data type name with the first letter capitalized. The exceptions are `Integer` and `Character`.

Each numeric wrapper class extends the abstract `Number` class, which contains the methods `doubleValue()`, `floatValue()`, `intValue()`, `longValue()`, `shortValue()`, and

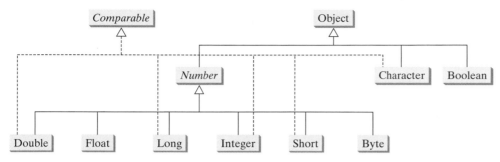

FIGURE 10.7 The Number class is an abstract superclass for Double, Float, Long, Integer, Short, and Byte.

byteValue(). These methods "convert" objects into primitive type values. The methods doubleValue(), floatValue(), intValue(), and longValue() are abstract. The methods byteValue() and shortValue() are not abstract; they simply return (byte)intValue() and (short)intValue(), respectively.

Each wrapper class overrides the toString, equals, and hashCode methods defined in the Object class. Since all the numeric wrapper classes and the Character class implement the Comparable interface, the compareTo method is implemented in these classes.

Wrapper classes are very similar. The Character class was introduced in Chapter 8, "Strings and Text I/O." The Boolean class is rarely used. The following sections use Integer and Double as examples to introduce the numeric wrapper classes. The key features of Integer and Double are shown in Figure 10.8.

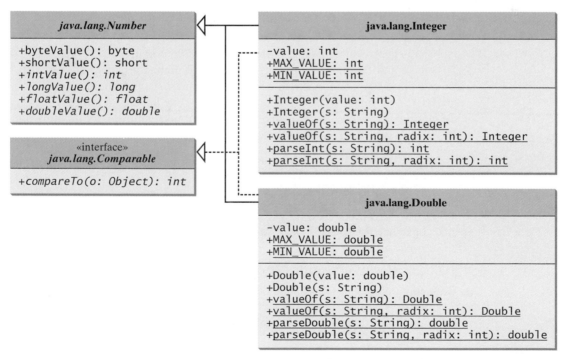

FIGURE 10.8 The wrapper classes provide constructors, constants, and conversion methods for manipulating various data types.

10.5.1 Numeric Wrapper Class Constructors

You can construct a wrapper object either from a primitive data type value or from a string representing the numeric value. The constructors for `Integer` and `Double` are:

```
public Integer(int value)
public Integer(String s)
public Double(double value)
public Double(String s)
```

For example, you can construct a wrapper object for `double` value `5.0` using either

```
Double doubleObject = new Double(5.0);
```

or

```
Double doubleObject = new Double("5.0");
```

You can construct a wrapper object for `int` value `5` using either

```
Integer integerObject = new Integer(5);
```

or

```
Integer integerObject = new Integer("5");
```

Note

no no-arg constructor
immutable

(1) The wrapper classes do not have no-arg constructors. (2) The instances of all wrapper classes are *immutable*; this means that their internal values cannot be changed once the objects are created.

10.5.2 Numeric Wrapper Class Constants

Each numeric wrapper class has the constants `MAX_VALUE` and `MIN_VALUE`. `MAX_VALUE` represents the maximum value of the corresponding primitive data type. For `Byte`, `Short`, `Integer`, and `Long`, `MIN_VALUE` represents the minimum `byte`, `short`, `int`, and `long` values. For `Float` and `Double`, `MIN_VALUE` represents the minimum *positive* `float` and `double` values. The following statements display the maximum integer (2, 147, 483, 647), the minimum positive float (1.4E−45), and the maximum double floating-point number (1.79769313486231570e+308d):

```
System.out.println("The maximum integer is " + Integer.MAX_VALUE);
System.out.println("The minimum positive float is " +
  Float.MIN_VALUE);
System.out.println(
  "The maximum double precision floating-point number is " +
  Double.MAX_VALUE);
```

10.5.3 Conversion Methods

Each numeric wrapper class implements the abstract methods `doubleValue`, `floatValue`, `intValue`, `longValue`, and `shortValue`, which are defined in the `Number` class. These methods "convert" objects into primitive type values.

For example,

```
long l = doubleObject.longValue(); // Note it truncates
```

This converts `doubleObject`'s double value to a `long` variable `l`

```
int i = integerObject.intValue();
```

This assigns the `int` value of `integerObject` to `i`

```
double d = 5.9;
Double doubleObject = new Double(d);
String s = doubleObject.toString();
```

This converts `double d` to a string `s`.

10.5.4   The Static `valueOf` Methods

The numeric wrapper classes have a useful class method, `valueOf(String s)`. This method creates a new object initialized to the value represented by the specified string. For example,

```
Double doubleObject = Double.valueOf("12.4");
Integer integerObject = Integer.valueOf("12");
```

10.5.5   The Methods for Parsing Strings into Numbers

You have used the `parseInt` method in the `Integer` class to parse a numeric string into an `int` value and the `parseDouble` method in the `Double` class to parse a numeric string into a double value. Each numeric wrapper class has two overloaded parsing methods to parse a numeric string into an appropriate numeric value based on 10 (decimal) or any specified radix (e.g., 2 for binary, 8 for octal, and 16 for hexadecimal). These methods are shown below:

```
// These two methods are in the Byte class
public static byte parseByte(String s)
public static byte parseByte(String s, int radix)

// These two methods are in the Short class
public static short parseShort(String s)
public static short parseShort(String s, int radix)

// These two methods are in the Integer class
public static int parseInt(String s)
public static int parseInt(String s, int radix)

// These two methods are in the Long class
public static long parseLong(String s)
public static long parseLong(String s, int radix)

// These two methods are in the Float class
public static float parseFloat(String s)
public static float parseFloat(String s, int radix)

// These two methods are in the Double class
public static double parseDouble(String s)
public static double parseDouble(String s, int radix)
```

For example,

```
Integer.parseInt("11", 2) returns 3;
Integer.parseInt("12", 8) returns 10;
Integer.parseInt("13", 10) returns 13;
Integer.parseInt("1A", 16) returns 26;
```

`Integer.parseInt("12", 2)` would raise a runtime exception because 12 is not a binary number.

10.5.6   (Optional) `BigInteger` and `BigDecimal` Classes

If you need to compute with very large numbers and high precision, you can use the `BigInteger` and `BigDecimal` classes in the `java.math` package. They are wrapper classes for integer and decimal values. Both are *immutable*. Both extend the `Number` class and   immutable implement the `Comparable` interface. The largest integer of the `long` type is 9223372036854775807. An instance of `BigInteger` can represent an integer of any size. You can use new `BigInteger(String)` and new `BigDecimal(String)` to create an instance of `BigInteger` and `BigDecimal` and use the `add`, `subtract`, `multiple`, and `divide` methods to perform numeric operations. For example, the following code creates two `BigInteger` objects and multiplies them:

```
BigInteger a = new BigInteger("9223372036854775807");
BigInteger b = new BigInteger("10000000");
BigInteger c = a.multiply(b);
System.out.println(c);
```

The output is 92233720368547758070000000.

There is no limit to the precision of a `BigDecimal` object. The `divide` method may throw an `ArithmeticException` if the result cannot be terminated. However, you can use the overloaded `divide(BigDecimal d, int scale, int roundingMode)` method to specify a scale and a rounding mode to avoid this exception. For example, the following code created two `BigDecimal` objects and performs division with scale 20 and rounding mode `BigDecimal.ROUND_UP`:

```
BigDecimal a = new BigDecimal(1.0);
BigDecimal b = new BigDecimal(3);
BigDecimal c = a.divide(b, 20, BigDecimal.ROUND_UP);
System.out.println(c);
```

The output is 0.33333333333333333334.

10.5.7 Example: Sorting an Array of Objects

This example presents a static generic method for sorting an array of comparable objects. The objects are instances of the `Comparable` interface, and they are compared using the `compareTo` method. The method can be used to sort an array of any objects as long as their classes implement the `Comparable` interface.

To test the method, the program sorts an array of integers, an array of double numbers, an array of characters, and an array of strings. The program is shown in Listing 10.5. Figure 10.9 shows a sample run of the code.

FIGURE 10.9 The program uses a generic sort method to sort an array of comparable objects.

LISTING 10.5 `GenericSort.java`

```
1  public class GenericSort {
2    public static void main(String[] args) {
3      // Create an Integer array
4      Integer[] intArray = {new Integer(2), new Integer(4),
5        new Integer(3)};
6
```

```java
 7    // Create a Double array
 8    Double[] doubleArray = {new Double(3.4), new Double(1.3),
 9      new Double(-22.1)};
10
11    // Create a Character array
12    Character[] charArray = {new Character('a'),
13      new Character('J'), new Character('r')};
14
15    // Create a String array
16    String[] stringArray = {"Tom", "John", "Fred"};
17
18    // Sort the arrays
19    sort(intArray);                                          sort Integer objects
20    sort(doubleArray);                                       sort Double objects
21    sort(charArray);                                         sort Character objects
22    sort(stringArray);                                       sort String objects
23
24    // Display the sorted arrays
25    System.out.print("Sorted Integer objects: ");
26    printList(intArray);
27    System.out.print("Sorted Double objects: ");
28    printList(doubleArray);
29    System.out.print("Sorted Character objects: ");
30    printList(charArray);
31    System.out.print("Sorted String objects: ");
32    printList(stringArray);
33  }
34
35  /** Sort an array of comparable objects */
36  public static void sort(Object[] list) {                  generic sort method
37    Object currentMax;
38    int currentMaxIndex;
39
40    for (int i = list.length - 1; i >= 1; i--) {
41      // Find the maximum in the list[0..i]
42      currentMax = list[i];
43      currentMaxIndex = i;
44
45      for (int j = i - 1; j >= 0; j--) {
46        if (((Comparable)currentMax).compareTo(list[j]) < 0) {   compareTo
47          currentMax = list[j];
48          currentMaxIndex = j;
49        }
50      }
51
52      // Swap list[i] with list[currentMaxIndex] if necessary;
53      if (currentMaxIndex != i) {
54        list[currentMaxIndex] = list[i];
55        list[i] = currentMax;
56      }
57    }
58  }
59
60  /** Print an array of objects */
61  public static void printList(Object[] list) {
62    for (int i = 0; i < list.length; i++)
63      System.out.print(list[i] + " ");
64    System.out.println();
65  }
66 }
```

The algorithm for the `sort` method is the same as in §6.8.1, "Selection Sort." The sort method in §6.8.1 sorts an array of double values. The sort method in this example can sort an array of any object type, provided that the objects are also instances of the `Comparable` interface. This is another example of *generic programming*, a subject discussed in §9.7, "Polymorphism, Dynamic Binding, and Generic Programming." Generic programming enables a method to operate on arguments of generic types, making it reusable with multiple types.

`Integer`, `Double`, `Character`, and `String` implement `Comparable`, so the objects of these classes can be compared using the `compareTo` method. The sort method uses the `compareTo` method to determine the order of the objects in the array.

 Tip

`Arrays.sort` method

Java provides a static `sort` method for sorting an array of any object type in the `java.util.Arrays` class, provided that the elements in the array are comparable. Thus you can use the following code to sort arrays in this example:

```
java.util.Arrays.sort(intArray);
java.util.Arrays.sort(doubleArray);
java.util.Arrays.sort(charArray);
java.util.Arrays.sort(stringArray);
```

 Note

Arrays are objects. An array is an instance of the `Object` class. Furthermore, if `A` is a subtype of `B`, every instance of `A[]` is an instance of `B[]`. Therefore, the following statements are all true:

```
new int[10]     instanceof Object
new Integer[10] instanceof Object
new Integer[10] instanceof Comparable[]
new Integer[10] instanceof Number[]
new Number[10]  instanceof Object[]
```

 Caution

Although an `int` value can be assigned to a `double` type variable, `int[]` and `double[]` are two incompatible types. Therefore, you cannot assign an `int[]` array to a variable of `double[]` or `Object[]` type.

10.6 Automatic Conversion Between Primitive Types and Wrapper Class Types

JDK 1.5 allows primitive types and wrapper classes to be converted automatically. For example, the following statement in (a) can be simplified as in (b) due to autoboxing:

```
Integer intObject = new Integer(2);
```
Equivalent
```
Integer intObject = 2;
```

(a)

New JDK 1.5 autoboxing   (b)

boxing
unboxing

Converting a primitive value to a wrapper object is called *boxing*. The reverse conversion is called *unboxing*. The JDK 1.5 compiler will automatically box a primitive value that appears in a context requiring an object, and will unbox an object that appears in a context requiring a primitive value. Consider the following example:

```
1 Integer[] intArray = {1, 2, 3};
2 System.out.println(intArray[0] + intArray[1] + intArray[2]);
```

In line 1, primitive values 1, 2, and 3 are automatically boxed into objects `new Integer(1)`, `new Integer(2)`, and `new Integer(3)`. In line 2, objects `intArray[0]`, `intArray[1]`, and `intArray[2]` are automatically converted into `int` values that are added together.

 ## 10.7 (Optional GUI) Handling GUI Events

When you run the program in Listing 9.12, it displays two buttons. If you click a button, there is no response. To respond, you need to write the code to process the clicking button action. The button is a *source object* where the action originates. You need to create an object capable of handling the action event on a button. This object is called a *listener*. Not all objects can be listeners for an action event. To be a listener, two requirements must be met:

source object
listener object

1. The object must be an instance of the `ActionListener` interface. The `Action-Listener` interface contains the `actionPerformed` method for processing the event.

ActionListener interface

2. The `ActionListener` object `listener` must be registered with the source using the method `source.addActionListener(listener)`.

**addActionListener-
(listener)**

Listing 10.6 gives the code that processes the `ActionEvent` on the two buttons. When you click the OK button, the message "OK button clicked" is displayed. When you click the Cancel button, the message "Cancel button clicked" is displayed, as shown in Figure 10.10.

FIGURE 10.10   The program responds to button-clicking action events.

LISTING 10.6   HandleEvent.java

```java
1 import javax.swing.*;
2 import java.awt.*;
3 import java.awt.event.*;
4
5 public class HandleEvent extends JFrame {
6   public HandleEvent() {
7     // Set FlowLayout for the frame
8     FlowLayout layout = new FlowLayout();
9     setLayout(layout);
10
11     // Add two buttons to frame
12     JButton jbtOK = new JButton("OK");
13     JButton jbtCancel = new JButton("Cancel");
14     add(jbtOK);
15     add(jbtCancel);
16
17     // Register listeners
18     OKListenerClass listener1 = new OKListenerClass();
19     CancelListenerClass listener2 = new CancelListenerClass();
20     jbtOK.addActionListener(listener1);
21     jbtCancel.addActionListener(listener2);
22   }
23
```

create listener

register listener

```
24    public static void main(String[] args) {
25      JFrame frame = new HandleEvent();
26      frame.setTitle("Handle Event");
27      frame.setSize(200, 150);
28      frame.setLocation(200, 100);
29      frame.setDefaultCloseOperation(JFrame.EXIT_ON_CLOSE);
30      frame.setVisible(true);
31    }
32  }
33
34  class OKListenerClass implements ActionListener {
35    public void actionPerformed(ActionEvent e) {
36      System.out.println("OK button clicked");
37    }
38  }
39
40  class CancelListenerClass implements ActionListener {
41    public void actionPerformed(ActionEvent e) {
42      System.out.println("Cancel button clicked");
43    }
44  }
```

listener class
process event

listener class
process event

Two listener classes are declared in lines 34–44. Each listener class implements `ActionListener` to process `ActionEvent`. The object `listener1` is an instance of `OKListenerClass` (line 18), which is registered with the button `jbtOK` in line 20. When the OK button is clicked, the `actionPerformed(ActionEvent)` method (line 36) in `OKListenerClass` is invoked to process the event. The object `listener2` is an instance of `CancelListenerClass` (line 19), which is registered with the button `jbtCancel` in line 21. When the OK button is clicked, the `actionPerformed(ActionEvent)` method (line 42) in `CancelListenerClass` is invoked to process the event.

KEY TERMS

abstract class 342	multiple inheritance 342
abstract method 342	subinterface 351
deep copy 355	shallow copy 355
interface 347	single inheritance 342
marker interface 354	wrapper class 356

CHAPTER SUMMARY

■ Abstract classes are like regular classes with data and methods, but you cannot create instances of abstract classes using the `new` operator.

■ An abstract method cannot be contained in a nonabstract class. If a subclass of an abstract superclass does not implement all the inherited abstract methods of the superclass, the subclass must be declared abstract.

■ A class that contains abstract methods must be abstract. However, it is possible to declare an abstract class that contains no abstract methods.

■ A subclass can be abstract even if its superclass is concrete.

- An interface is a classlike construct that contains only constants and abstract methods. In many ways, an interface is similar to an abstract class, but an abstract class can contain constants and abstract methods as well as variables and concrete methods.

- An interface is treated like a special class in Java. Each interface is compiled into a separate bytecode file, just like a regular class.

- The `java.lang.Comparable` interface defines the `compareTo` method. Many classes in the Java library implement `Comparable`.

- The `java.lang.Cloneable` interface is a marker interface. An object of the class that implements the `Cloneable` interface is cloneable.

- A class can extend only one superclass but can implement one or more interfaces.

- An interface can extend one or more interfaces.

- Many Java methods require the use of objects as arguments. Java offers a convenient way to incorporate, or wrap, a primitive data type into an object (e.g., wrapping `int` into the `Integer` class, and wrapping double into the `Double` class). The corresponding class is called a *wrapper class*. By using a wrapper object instead of a primitive data type variable, you can take advantage of generic programming.

- The wrapper class for `byte` is `Byte`, for `short` is `Short`, for `int` is `Integer`, for `long` is `Long`, for `float` is `Float`, for `double` is `Double`, for `char` is `Character`, and for `boolean` is `Boolean`.

- The numeric wrapper classes extend the abstract `java.lang.Number` class and implement the `java.lang.Comparable` interface. The `Character` class also implements `java.lang.Comparable`.

REVIEW QUESTIONS

Section 10.2 Abstract Classes

10.1   Which of the following class definitions defines a legal abstract class?

```
class A {
  abstract void unfinished() {
  }
}
```
(a)

```
public class abstract A {
  abstract void unfinished();
}
```
(d)

```
class A {
  abstract void unfinished();
}
```
(b)

```
abstract class A {
  protected void unfinished();
}
```
(e)

```
abstract class A {
  abstract void unfinished();
}
```
(c)

```
abstract class A {
  abstract int unfinished();
}
```
(f)

10.2 The getArea and getPerimeter methods may be removed from the GeometricObject class. What are the benefits of defining getArea and getPerimeter as abstract methods in the GeometricObject class?

Section 10.4 Interfaces

10.3 Which of the following is a correct interface?

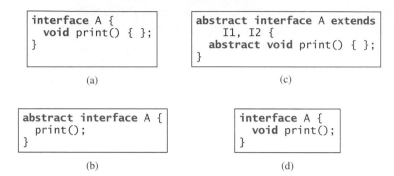

```
interface A {
  void print() { };
}
```
(a)

```
abstract interface A extends
    I1, I2 {
  abstract void print() { };
}
```
(c)

```
abstract interface A {
  print();
}
```
(b)

```
interface A {
  void print();
}
```
(d)

10.4 Two max methods are defined in §10.4. Explain why the max with the signature max(Comparable, Comparable) is better than the one with the signature max(Object, Object).

Are these statements correct?

```
String s = Max.max("abc", "efg");
Date date = Max.max(new Date(), new Date());
```

10.5 You can define the compareTo method in a class without implementing the Comparable interface. What are the benefits of implementing the Comparable interface?

10.6 What would happen if the House class (defined in Listing 10.4) does not override the clone() method or if House does not implement java.lang.Cloneable?

10.7 Show the printout of the following code:

```
java.util.Date date = new java.util.Date();
java.util.Date date1 = (java.util.Date)(date.clone());
System.out.println(date == date1);
System.out.println(date.equals(date1));
```

10.8 Show the printout of the following code:

```
java.util.ArrayList list = new java.util.ArrayList();
list.add("New York"); list.add(new java.util.Date());
java.util.ArrayList list1 =
  (java.util.ArrayList)(list.clone());
System.out.println(list == list1);
System.out.println(list.get(0) == list1.get(0));
System.out.println(list.get(1) == list1.get(1));
```

10.9 What is wrong in the following code?

```
public class Test {
  public static void main(String[] args) {
    GeometricObject x = new Circle(3);
    GeometricObject y = x.clone();
    System.out.println(x == y);
  }
}
```

Section 10.5 Processing Primitive Data Type Values as Objects

10.10 Can you assign `new int[10]`, `new String[100]`, `new Object[50]`, or `new Calendar[20]` into a variable of `Object[]` type?

10.11 Describe primitive-type wrapper classes. Why do you need these wrapper classes?

10.12 Are the following statements correct?

```java
Integer i = new Integer("23");
Integer i = new Integer(23);
Integer i = Integer.valueOf("23");
Integer i = Integer.parseInt("23", 8);
Double d = new Double();
Double d = Double.valueOf("23.45");
int i = (Integer.valueOf("23")).intValue();
double d = (Double.valueOf("23.4")).doubleValue();
int i = (Double.valueOf("23.4")).intValue();
String s = (Double.valueOf("23.4")).toString();
```

10.13 How do you convert an integer into a string? How do you convert a numeric string into an integer? How do you convert a double number into a string? How do you convert a numeric string into a double value?

10.14 Why do the following two lines of code compile but cause a runtime error?

```java
Number numberRef = new Integer(0);
Double doubleRef = (Double)numberRef;
```

10.15 Why do the following two lines of code compile but cause a runtime error?

```java
Number[] numberArray = new Integer[2];
numberArray[0] = new Double(1.5);
```

10.16 What is wrong in the following code?

```java
public class Test {
  public static void main(String[] args) {
    Number x = new Integer(3);
    System.out.println(x.intValue());
    System.out.println(x.compareTo(new Integer(4)));
  }
}
```

10.17 What is wrong in the following code?

```java
public class Test {
  public static void main(String[] args) {
    Number x = new Integer(3);
    System.out.println(x.intValue());
    System.out.println((Integer)x.compareTo(new Integer(4)));
  }
}
```

10.18 What is the output of the following code?

```java
public class Test {
  public static void main(String[] args) {
    java.math.BigInteger x = new java.math.BigInteger("3");
    java.math.BigInteger y = new java.math.BigInteger("7");
    x.add(y);
    System.out.println(x);
  }
}
```

Section 10.6 Automatic Conversion Between Primitive Types and Wrapper Classes

10.19 Describe the boxing and unboxing features in JDK 1.5. Are the following statements correct in JDK 1.5?

```
Number x = 3;
Integer x = 3;
Double x = 3;
Double x = 3.0;
int x = new Integer(3);
int x = new Integer(3) + new Integer(4);
double y = 3.4;
y.intValue();

JOptionPane.showMessageDialog(null, 45.5);
```

Comprehensive

10.20 Define the following terms: abstract classes, interfaces. What are the similarities and differences between abstract classes and interfaces?

10.21 Indicate true or false for the following statements:

■ An abstract class can have instances created using the constructor of the abstract class.
■ An abstract class can be extended.
■ An interface is compiled into a separate bytecode file.
■ A subclass of a nonabstract superclass cannot be abstract.
■ A subclass cannot override a concrete method in a superclass to declare it abstract.
■ An abstract method must be non-static
■ An interface can have static methods.
■ An interface can extend one or more interfaces.
■ An interface can extend an abstract class.
■ An abstract class can extend an interface.

PROGRAMMING EXERCISES

Comprehensive

10.1* (*Enabling GeometricObject comparable*) Modify the GeometricObject class to implement the Comparable interface, and define a static max method in the GeometricObject class for finding the larger of two GeometricObject objects. Draw the UML diagram and implement the new GeometricObject class. Write a test program that uses the max method to find the larger of two circles and the larger of two rectangles.

10.2* (*The ComparableRectangle class*) Create a class named ComparableRectangle that extends Rectangle and implements Comparable. Draw the UML diagram and implement the compareTo method to compare the rectangles on the basis of area. Write a test class to find the larger of two instances of - ComparableRectangle objects.

10.3* (*The Colorable interface*) Design an interface named Colorable with a void method named howToColor(). Every class of a colorable object must implement the Colorable interface. Design a class named Square that extends GeometricObject and implements Colorable. Implement howToColor to display a message on how to color the square.

Draw a UML diagram that involves `Colorable`, `Square`, and `Geometric-Object`. Write a test program that creates an array of five `Geometric-Objects`. For each object in the array, invoke its `howToColor` method if it is colorable.

10.4* (*Revising the House class*) Rewrite the `House` class in Listing 10.4 to perform a deep copy on the `whenBuilt` field.

10.5* (*Enabling Circle comparable*) Rewrite the `Circle` class in Listing 9.2 to extend `GeometricObject` and implement the `Comparable` interface. Override the `equals` and `hashCode` methods in the `Object` class. Two `Circle` objects are equal if their radii are the same. Draw the UML diagram that involves `Circle`, `GeometricObject`, and `Comparable`.

10.6* (*Enabling Rectangle comparable*) Rewrite the `Rectangle` class in Listing 9.3 to extend `GeometricObject` and implement the `Comparable` interface. Override the `equals` and `hashCode` methods in the `Object` class. Two `Rectangle` objects are equal if their areas are the same. Draw the UML diagram that involves `Rectangle`, `GeometricObject`, and `Comparable`.

10.7* (*The Octagon class*) Write a class named `Octagon` that extends `Geometric-Object` and implements the `Comparable` and `Cloneable` interfaces. Assume that all eight sides of the octagon are of equal size. The area can be computed using the following formula:

$$\text{area} = \left(2 + 4/\sqrt{2}\right) * \text{side} * \text{side}$$

Draw the UML diagram that involves `Octagon`, `GeometricObject`, `Comparable`, and `Cloneable`. Write a test program that creates an `Octagon` object with side value 5 and displays its area and perimeter. Create a new object using the `clone` method and compare the two objects using the `compareTo` method.

10.8* (*Summing the areas of geometric objects*) Write a method that sums the areas of all the geometric objects in an array. The method signature is:

```
public static double sumArea(GeometricObject[] a)
```

Write a test program that creates an array of three objects (a circle and a rectangle) and computes their total area using the `sumArea` method.

10.9* (*Finding the largest object*) Write a method that returns the largest object in an array of objects. The method signature is:

```
public static Object max(Object[] a)
```

All the objects are instances of the `Comparable` interface. The order of the objects in the array is determined using the `compareTo` method.

Write a test program that creates an array of ten strings, an array of ten integers, and an array of ten dates, and finds the largest string, integer, and date in the arrays.

10.10** (*Displaying calendars*) Rewrite the `PrintCalendar` class in Listing 5.8 to display a calendar for a specified month using the `Calendar` and `Gregorian-Calendar` classes. Your program receives the month and year from the command line. For example:

```
java Exercise10_10 6 2005
```

This displays the calendar shown in Figure 10.11.

FIGURE 10.11 The program displays a calendar for June 2005.

You also can run the program without the year. In this case, the year is the current year. If you run the program without specifying a month and a year, the month is the current month.

CHAPTER 11

OBJECT-ORIENTED DESIGN

Objectives

- To become familiar with the process of program development (§11.2).

- To learn the relationship types: association, aggregation, composition, dependency, strong inheritance, and weak inheritance (§11.3).

- To declare classes to represent the relationships among them (§11.3).

- To design systems by identifying the classes and discovering the relationships among these classes (§11.4).

- To implement the `Rational` class and process rational numbers using this class (§11.5).

- To design classes that follow the class-design guidelines (§11.6).

- To model dynamic behavior using sequence diagrams and statechart diagrams (§11.7 optional)

- To know the concept of framework-based programming using the Java API (§11.8).

11.1 Introduction

The preceding chapters introduced objects, classes, class inheritance, and interfaces. You learned the concepts of object-oriented programming. This chapter focuses on the development of software systems using the object-oriented approach, and introduces class modeling using the Unified Modeling Language (UML). You will learn class-design guidelines, and the techniques for designing reusable classes through the `Rational` class.

11.2 The Software Development Process

Developing a software project is an engineering process. Software products, no matter how large or how small, have the same developmental phases: requirements specification, analysis, design, implementation, testing, deployment, and maintenance, as shown in Figure 11.1.

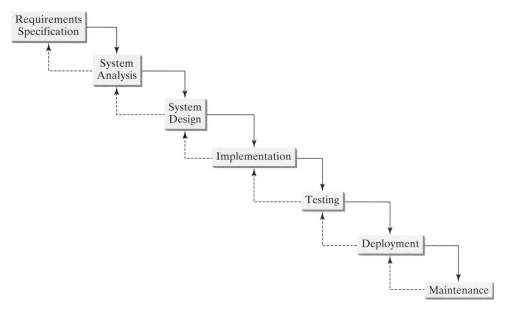

FIGURE 11.1 Developing a project involves requirements specification, system analysis, system design, implementation, testing, deployment, and maintenance.

requirements specification

Requirements specification is a formal process that seeks to understand the problem and document in detail what the software system needs to do. This phase involves close interaction between users and developers. Most of the examples in this book are simple, and their requirements are clearly stated. In the real world, however, problems are not well defined. You need to work closely with your customer and study a problem carefully to identify its requirements.

system analysis

System analysis seeks to analyze the business process in terms of data flow, and to identify the system's input and output. Part of the analysis entails modeling the system's behavior. The model is intended to capture the essential elements of the system and to define services to the system.

system design

System design is the process of designing the system's components. This phase involves the use of many levels of abstraction to decompose the problem into manageable components, identify classes and interfaces, and establish relationships among the classes and interfaces.

implementation

Implementation is translating the system design into programs. Separate programs are written for each component and put to work together. This phase requires the use of a programming language like Java. The implementation involves coding, testing, and debugging.

testing

Testing ensures that the code meets the requirements specification and weeds out bugs. An independent team of software engineers not involved in the design and implementation of the project usually conducts such testing.

Deployment makes the project available for use. For a Java applet, this means installing it on a Web server; for a Java application, installing it on the client's computer. A project usually consists of many classes. An effective approach for deployment is to package all the classes into a Java archive file, as will be introduced in §16.12, "Packaging and Deploying Java Projects."

deployment

Maintenance is concerned with changing and improving the product. A software product must continue to perform and improve in a changing environment. This requires periodic upgrades of the product to fix newly discovered bugs and incorporate changes.

maintenance

This chapter is mainly concerned with object-oriented design. While there are many object-oriented methodologies, UML has become the industry-standard notation for object-oriented modeling, and itself leads to a methodology. The process of designing classes calls for identifying the classes and discovering the relationships among them.

11.3 Discovering Class Relationships

The common relationships among classes are: *association*, *aggregation*, *composition*, *dependency*, and *inheritance*.

11.3.1 Association

Association is a general binary relationship that describes an activity between two classes. For example, a student taking a course is an association between the `Student` class and the `Course` class, and a faculty member teaching a course is an association between the `Faculty` class and the `Course` class. These associations can be represented in UML graphical notations, as shown in Figure 11.2.

association

An association is illustrated by a solid line between two classes with an optional label that describes the relationship. In Figure 11.2, the labels are *Take* and *Teach*. Each relationship may have an optional small black triangle that indicates the direction of the relationship. In Figure 11.2, the direction indicates that a student takes a course, as opposed to a course taking a student.

FIGURE 11.2 A student may take any number of courses, and a faculty member teaches at most three courses. A course may have from five to sixty students and is taught by only one faculty member.

Each class involved in the relationship may have a role name that describes the role it plays in the relationship. In Figure 11.2, *teacher* is the role name for `Faculty`.

Each class involved in an association may specify a *multiplicity*. A multiplicity could be a number or an interval that specifies how many objects of the class are involved in the relationship. The character `*` means unlimited number of objects, and the interval `m..n` means that the number of objects should be between `m` and `n`, inclusive. In Figure 11.2, each student may take any number of courses, and each course must have at least five students and at most sixty students. Each course is taught by only one faculty member, and a faculty member may teach from zero to three courses per semester.

Association may exist between objects of the same class. For example, a person may have a supervisor. This is illustrated in Figure 11.3.

FIGURE 11.3 A person may have a supervisor.

In Java code, an association can be implemented using data fields and methods. The method in one class contains a parameter of the other class. For example, the relationships in Figure 11.2 may be implemented in the following classes:

```java
public class Student {
  private Course[]
    courseList;

  public void addCourse(
    Course s)
}
```

```java
public class Course {
  private Student[]
    classList;
  private Faculty faculty;

  public void addStudent(
    Student s)

  public void setFaculty(
    Faculty faculty)
}
```

```java
public class Faculty {
  private Course[]
    courseList;

  public void addCourse(
    Course c)
}
```

 Note

If you don't need to know the courses a student takes or a faculty member teaches, the data field **courseList** and the **addCourse** method in **Student** or **Faculty** can be omitted.

11.3.2 Aggregation and Composition

aggregation

Aggregation is a special form of association that represents an ownership relationship between two objects. Aggregation models *has-a* relationships. The owner object is called an *aggregating object*, and its class, an *aggregating class*. The subject object is called an *aggregated object*, and its class, an *aggregated class*. The association "a person has a supervisor" in Figure 11.3 is actually an aggregation.

aggregating object
aggregated object

composition

An object may be owned by several other aggregating objects. If an object is exclusively owned by an aggregating object, the relationship between the object and its aggregating object is referred to as *composition*. For example, "a student has a name" is a composition relationship between the **Student** class and the **Name** class, whereas "a student has an address" is an aggregation relationship between the **Student** class and the **Address** class, since an address may be shared by several students. In UML, a filled diamond is attached to an aggregating class (e.g., **Student**) to denote the composition relationship with an aggregated class (e.g., **Name**), and an empty diamond is attached to an aggregating class (e.g., **Student**) to denote the aggregation relationship with an aggregated class (e.g., **Address**), as shown in Figure 11.4.

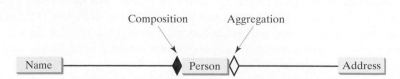

FIGURE 11.4 A student has a name and an address.

An aggregation relationship is usually represented as a data field in the aggregating class. For example, the relationship in Figure 11.4 can be represented as follows:

Aggregated class   Aggregating class   Aggregated class

In the relationship "a person has a supervisor," as shown in Figure 11.3, a supervisor can be represented as a data field in the **Person** class, as follows:

```
public class Person {
  private Person supervisor;
  ...
}
```

If a person has several supervisors, as shown in Figure 11.5, you may use an array or an **ArrayList** to store the supervisors.

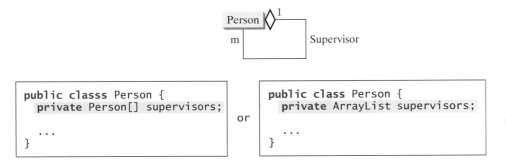

FIGURE 11.5   A person may have several supervisors.

 Note

Since aggregation and composition relationships are translated into the same class template, for simplicity, both are called composition.

aggregation or composition

11.3.3   Dependency

A *dependency* describes a relationship between two classes where one (called **client**) uses the other (called *supplier*). In UML, draw a dashed line with an arrow from the client class to the supplier class. For example, the **ArrayList** class uses **Object** because you can add objects to an **ArrayList**. The relationship between **ArrayList** and **Object** can be described using dependency, as shown in Figure 11.6(a). The **Calendar** class uses **Date** because you can set a calendar with a specified **Date** object. The relationship between **Calendar** and **Date** can be described using dependency, as shown in Figure 11.6(b).

client
supplier

ArrayList ┤------→ Object   *Calendar* ┤------→ Date

(a)   (b)

FIGURE 11.6   (a) **ArrayList** uses **Object**. (b) **Calendar** uses **Date**.

In Java code, a dependency can be implemented using a method in the client class. The method contains a parameter of the supplier class type. For example, the `ArrayList` class has the `add(Object)` method that adds an object to the `ArrayList`. The `Calendar` class has the `setTime(Date)` method that sets a new time in the calendar.

```
public class ArrayList {
    public void add(Object o)


    ...
}
```

```
public abstract class Calendar {
    public void setTime(Date d)


    ...
}
```

 Note

dependency vs. association

Both association and dependency describe one class as depending on another. Association is stronger than dependency. In association, the state of the object changes when its associated object changes. In dependency, the client object and the supplier object are loosely coupled. The association relationship is implemented using data fields and methods. There is a strong connection between the two classes. The dependency relationship is implemented using methods.

11.3.4 Inheritance

strong is-a
weak is-a

Inheritance models the *is-a* relationship between two classes. A *strong is-a* relationship describes a direct inheritance relationship between two classes. A *weak is-a* relationship describes that a class has certain properties. A strong is-a relationship can be represented using class inheritance. For example, the relationship "a faculty member is a person" (shown in Figure 11.7(a)) is a strong is-a relationship and can be represented using the class in Figure 11.7(b).

Person ◁——— Faculty

```
public class Faculty extends Person {
    ...
}
```

(a)   (b)

FIGURE 11.7   `Faculty` extends `Person`.

A weak is-a relationship can be represented using interfaces. For example, the weak is-a relationship "students are comparable based on their grades" (shown in Figure 11.8(a)) can be represented by implementing the `Comparable` interface, as shown in Figure 11.8(b).

```
public class Student extends Person
    implements Comparable {
    ...

    /** Implement the compareTo method */
    public int compareTo(Object object) {
        ...
    }
}
```

(a)   (b)

FIGURE 11.8   `Student` extends `Person` and implements `Comparable`.

Note

Not all is-a relationships should be modeled using inheritance. For example, a square is a rectangle, but you should not declare a `Square` class to extend a `Rectangle` class, because there is nothing to extend (or supplement) from a rectangle to a square. For class `A` to extend class `B`, `A` should contain more detailed information than `B`.

nonextensible is-a

11.4 Case Study: Object-Oriented Design

The key to object-oriented programming is to model the application in terms of cooperative objects. Carefully designed classes are critical when a project is being developed. There are many levels of abstraction in system design. You have learned method abstraction and have applied it to the development of large programs. Methods are means to group statements. Classes extend abstraction to a higher level and provide a means of grouping methods. Classes do more than just group methods, however; they also contain data fields. Methods and data fields together describe the properties and behaviors of classes.

The power of classes is further extended by inheritance. Inheritance enables a class to extend the contract and the implementation of an existing class without knowing the details of the existing class. In the development of a Java program, class abstraction is applied to decompose the problem into a set of related classes, and method abstraction is applied to design individual classes.

This case study models borrowing loans to demonstrate how to identify classes, discover the relationships between classes, and apply class abstraction in object-oriented program development.

For simplicity, the example does not attempt to build a complete system for storing, processing, and manipulating loans for borrowers; instead it focuses on modeling borrowers and the loans for the borrowers. The following steps are usually involved in building an object-oriented system:

1. Identify classes for the system.

2. Establish relationships among classes.

3. Describe the attributes and methods in each class.

4. Implement the classes.

The first step is to *identify classes* for the system. There are many strategies for identifying classes in a system, one of which is to study how the system works and select a number of use cases, or scenarios. Since a borrower is a person who obtains a loan, and a person has a name and an address, you can identify the following classes: `Person`, `Name`, `Address`, `Borrower`, and `Loan`.

identify classes

Identifying objects is not easy for novice programmers. How do you find the right objects? There is no unique solution even for simple problems. Software development is more an art than a science. The quality of a program ultimately depends on the programmer's intuition, experience, and knowledge. This example identifies five classes: `Name`, `Address`, `Person`, `Borrower`, and `Loan`. There are several alternatives. One would combine `Name`, `Address`, `Person`, and `Borrower` into one class. This design is not clear because it puts too many entities into one class.

The second step is to *establish relationships* among the classes. The relationship is derived from the system analysis. The first two steps are intertwined. When you identify classes, you also think about the relationships among them. Establishing relationships among objects helps you understand the interactions among objects. An object-oriented system consists of a collection of interrelated cooperative objects. The relationships for the classes in this example are illustrated in Figure 11.9.

establish relationships

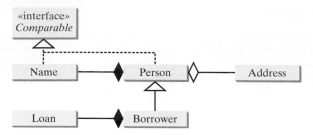

FIGURE 11.9 A borrower is a person who has a loan.

The third step is to describe the attributes and methods in each of the classes you have identified. The `Name` class has the properties `firstName`, `mi`, and `lastName`, their associated get and set methods, and the `getFullName` method for returning the full name. You can compare names in alphabetical order of their last name, first name, and mi. The `Address` class has the properties `street`, `city`, `state`, and `zip`, their associated `get` and `set` methods, and the `getAddress` method for returning the full address. The `Loan` class, presented in Listing 7.9, Loan.java, has the properties `annualInterestRate`, `numberOfYears`, and `loanAmount`, their associated property `get` and `set` methods, and `getMonthlyPayment` and `getTotalPayment` methods. The `Person` class has the properties `name` and `address`, their associated get and set methods, and the `toString` method for displaying complete information about the person. `Borrower` is a subclass of `Person`. Additionally, `Borrower` has the `loan` property and its associated `get` and `set` methods, and the `toString` method for displaying the person and the loan payments. You can compare persons according to their names. Figure 11.9 is expanded to Figure 11.10.

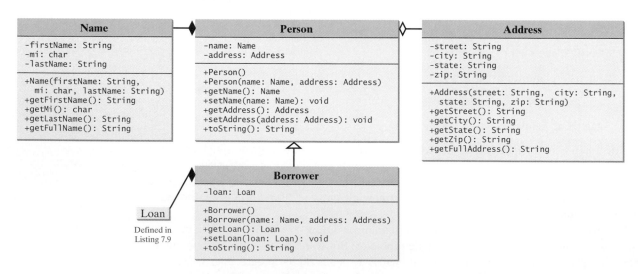

FIGURE 11.10 A borrower has a name, an address, and a loan.

The fourth step is to write the code for the classes. The program is long, but most of the *coding* is for the `get` and `set` methods. Once an object is identified, its properties and methods can be defined by analyzing the requirements and scenarios of the system. It is a good practice to provide complete `get` and `set` methods. These may not be needed for your current project, but will be useful in other projects, because your classes are designed for reuse in future projects. Listings 11.1, 11.2, 11.3, and 11.4 give the `Name`, `Address`, `Person`, and `Borrower` classes.

LISTING 11.1   Name.java

```java
 1 public final class Name implements Comparable {
 2   private String firstName;
 3   private char mi;
 4   private String lastName;
 5
 6   /** Construct a name with firstName, mi, and lastName */
 7   public Name(String firstName, char mi, String lastName) {
 8     this.firstName = firstName;
 9     this.mi = mi;
10     this.lastName = lastName;
11   }
12
13   /** Return firstName */
14   public String getFirstName() {
15     return firstName;
16   }
17
18   /** Return middle name initial */
19   public char getMi() {
20     return mi;
21   }
22
23   /** Return lastName */
24   public String getLastname() {
25     return lastName;
26   }
27
28   /** Obtain full name */
29   public String getFullName() {
30     return firstName + ' ' + mi + ' ' + lastName;
31   }
32
33   /** Implement compareTo in the Comparable interface */
34   public int compareTo(Object o) {
35     if (!lastName.equals(((Name)o).lastName)) {
36       return lastName.compareTo(((Name)o).lastName);
37     }
38     else if (!firstName.equals(((Name)o).firstName)) {
39       return firstName.compareTo(((Name)o).firstName);
40     }
41     else {
42       return mi - ((Name)o).mi;
43     }
44   }
45 }
```

LISTING 11.2   Address.java

```java
1 public final class Address {
2   private String street;
3   private String city;
4   private String state;
5   private String zip;
6
```

```
 7    /** Create an address with street, city, state, and zip */
 8    public Address(String street, String city,
 9      String state, String zip) {
10      this.street = street;
11      this.city = city;
12      this.state = state;
13      this.zip = zip;
14    }
15
16    /** Return street */
17    public String getStreet() {
18      return street;
19    }
20
21    /** Return city */
22    public String getCity() {
23      return city;
24    }
25
26    /** Return state */
27    public String getState() {
28      return state;
29    }
30
31    /** Return zip */
32    public String getZip() {
33      return zip;
34    }
35
36    /** Get full address */
37    public String getFullAddress() {
38      return street + '\n' + city + ", " + state + ' ' + zip + '\n';
39    }
40  }
```

LISTING 11.3 Person.java

```
 1  public class Person {
 2    private Name name;
 3    private Address address;
 4
 5    /** Construct a person with default properties */
 6    public Person() {
 7      this(new Name("Jill", 'S', "Barr"),
 8        new Address("100 Main", "Savannah", "GA", "31411"));
 9    }
10
11    /** Construct a person with specified name and address */
12    public Person(Name name, Address address) {
13      this.name = name;
14      this.address = address;
15    }
16
17    /** Return name */
18    public Name getName() {
19      return name;
20    }
21
```

```
22   /** Set a new name */
23   public void setName(Name name) {
24     this.name = name;
25   }
26
27   /** Return address */
28   public Address getAddress() {
29     return address;
30   }
31
32   /** Set a new address */
33   public void setAddress(Address address) {
34     this.address = address;
35   }
36
37   /** Override the toString method */
38   public String toString() {
39     return '\n' + name.getFullName() + '\n' +
40       address.getFullAddress() + '\n';
41   }
42
43   /** Implement compareTo in the Comparable interface */
44   public int compareTo(Object o) {
45     return name.compareTo(((Person)o).name);
46   }
47 }
```

LISTING 11.4   Borrower.java

```
1 public class Borrower extends Person {
2    private Loan loan;
3
4    /** Construct a borrower with default properties */
5    public Borrower() {
6      super();
7    }
8
9    /** Create a borrower with specified name and address */
10   public Borrower(Name name, Address address) {
11     super(name, address);
12   }
13
14   /** Return loan */
15   public Loan getLoan() {
16     return loan;
17   }
18
19   /** Set a new loan */
20   public void setLoan(Loan loan) {
21     this.loan = loan;
22   }
23
24   /** String representation for borrower */
25   public String toString() {
26     return super.toString() +
27       "Monthly payment is " + loan.getMonthlyPayment() + '\n' +
28       "Total payment is " + loan.getTotalPayment();
29   }
30 }
```

Listing 11.5 is a test program that uses the classes Name, Address, Borrower, and Loan. The output of the program is shown in Figure 11.11.

Listing 11.5 BorrowLoan.java

```java
1 import javax.swing.JOptionPane;
2
3 public class BorrowLoan {
4   /** Main method */
5   public static void main(String[] args) {
6     // Create a name
7     Name name = new Name("John", 'D', "Smith");
8
9     // Create an address
10     Address address = new Address("100 Main Street", "Savannah",
11       "GA", "31419");
12
13     // Create a loan
14     Loan loan = new Loan(5.5, 15, 250000);
15
16     // Create a borrower
17     Borrower borrower = new Borrower(name, address);
18
19     borrower.setLoan(loan);
20
21     // Display loan information
22     JOptionPane.showMessageDialog(null, borrower.toString());
23   }
24 }
```

Figure 11.11 The program creates name, address, and loan, stores the information in a Borrower object, and displays the information with the loan payment.

11.5 Case Study: The Rational Class

A rational number is a number with a numerator and a denominator in the form a/b, where a is the numerator and b is the denominator. For example, 1/3, 3/4, and 10/4 are rational numbers.

A rational number cannot have a denominator of 0, but a numerator of 0 is fine. Every integer a is equivalent to a rational number a/1. Rational numbers are used in exact computations involving fractions; for example, 1/3 = 0.33333 . . . . This number cannot be precisely represented in floating-point format using data type **double** or **float**. To obtain the exact result, it is necessary to use rational numbers.

Java provides data types for integers and floating-point numbers, but not for rational numbers. This section shows how to design a class to represent rational numbers.

Since rational numbers share many common features with integers and floating-point numbers, and `Number` is the base class for numeric wrapper classes, it is appropriate to define `Rational` as a subclass of `Number`. Since rational numbers are comparable, the `Rational` class should also implement the `Comparable` interface. Figure 11.12 illustrates the `Rational` class and its relationship to the `Number` class and the `Comparable` interface.

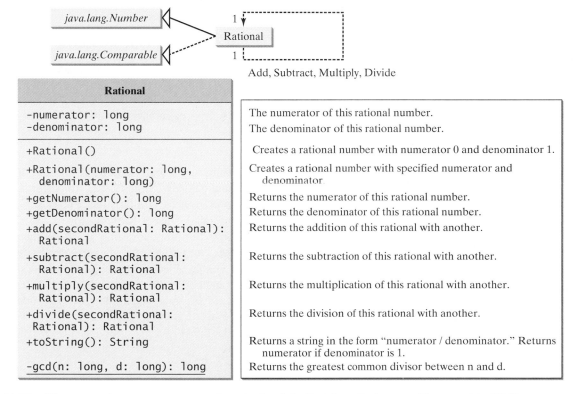

FIGURE 11.12   The properties, constructors, and methods of the `Rational` class are illustrated in UML.

A rational number consists of a numerator and a denominator. There are many equivalent rational numbers; for example, $1/3 = 2/6 = 3/9 = 4/12$. For convenience, $1/3$ is used in this example to represent all rational numbers that are equivalent to $1/3$. The numerator and the denominator of $1/3$ have no common divisor except 1, so $1/3$ is said to be in lowest terms.

To reduce a rational number to its lowest terms, you need to find the greatest common divisor (GCD) of the absolute values of its numerator and denominator, and then divide both numerator and denominator by this value. You can use the method for computing the GCD of two integers `n` and `d`, as suggested in Listing 4.6, GreatestCommonDivisor.java. The numerator and denominator in a `Rational` object are reduced to their lowest terms.

As usual, let us first write a test program to create two `Rational` objects and test its methods. Listing 11.6 is a test program. Its output is shown in Figure 11.13.

```
C:\book>java TestRationalClass
2 + 2/3 = 8/3
2 - 2/3 = 4/3
2 * 2/3 = 4/3
2 / 2/3 = 3
2/3 is 0.6666666666666666

C:\book>_
```

FIGURE 11.13   The program creates two `Rational` objects and displays their addition, subtraction, multiplication, and division.

LISTING 11.6 TestRationalClass.java

```
1 public class TestRationalClass {
2   /** Main method */
3   public static void main(String[] args) {
4     // Create and initialize two rational numbers r1 and r2.
5     Rational r1 = new Rational(4, 2);
6     Rational r2 = new Rational(2, 3);
7
8     // Display results
9     System.out.println(r1 + " + " + r2 + " = " + r1.add(r2));
10    System.out.println(r1 + " - " + r2 + " = " + r1.subtract(r2));
11    System.out.println(r1 + " * " + r2 + " = " + r1.multiply(r2));
12    System.out.println(r1 + " / " + r2 + " = " + r1.divide(r2));
13    System.out.println(r2 + " is " + r2.doubleValue());
14  }
15 }
```

The `main` method creates two rational numbers, `r1` and `r2` (lines 5–6), and displays the results of `r1 + r2`, `r1 - r2`, `r1 * r2`, and `r1 / r2` (lines 9–12). To perform `r1 + r2`, invoke `r1.add(r2)` to return a new `Rational` object. Similarly, `r1.subtract(r2)` is for `r1 - r2`, `r1.multiply(r2)` for `r1 * r2`, and `r1.divide(r2)` for `r1 / r2`.

The `doubleValue()` method displays the double value of `r2` (line 13). The `doubleValue()` method is defined in `java.lang.Number` and overridden in `Rational`.

Note that when a string is concatenated with an object using the plus sign (+), the object's string representation from the `toString()` method is used to concatenate with the string. So `r1 + " + " + r2 + " = " + r1.add(r2)` is equivalent to `r1.toString() + " + " + r2.toString() + " = " + r1.add(r2).toString()`.

The `Rational` class is implemented in Listing 11.7.

LISTING 11.7 Rational.java

```
1 public class Rational extends Number implements Comparable {
2   // Data fields for numerator and denominator
3   private long numerator = 0;
4   private long denominator = 1;
5
6   /** Construct a rational with default properties */
7   public Rational() {
8     this(0, 1);
9   }
10
11  /** Construct a rational with specified numerator and denominator */
12  public Rational(long numerator, long denominator) {
13    long gcd = gcd(numerator, denominator);
14    this.numerator = ((denominator > 0) ? 1 : -1) * numerator / gcd;
15    this.denominator = Math.abs(denominator) / gcd;
16  }
17
18  /** Find GCD of two numbers */
19  private static long gcd(long n, long d) {
20    long n1 = Math.abs(n);
21    long n2 = Math.abs(d);
22    int gcd = 1;
23
```

```
24      for (int k = 1; k <= n1 && k <= n2; k++) {
25        if (n1 % k == 0 && n2 % k == 0)
26          gcd = k;
27      }
28
29      return gcd;
30    }
31
32    /** Return numerator */
33    public long getNumerator() {
34      return numerator;
35    }
36
37    /** Return denominator */
38    public long getDenominator() {
39      return denominator;
40    }
41
42    /** Add a rational number to this rational */
43    public Rational add(Rational secondRational) {
44      long n = numerator * secondRational.getDenominator() +
45        denominator * secondRational.getNumerator();
46      long d = denominator * secondRational.getDenominator();
47      return new Rational(n, d);
48    }
49
50    /** Subtract a rational number from this rational */
51    public Rational subtract(Rational secondRational) {
52      long n = numerator * secondRational.getDenominator()
53        - denominator * secondRational.getNumerator();
54      long d = denominator * secondRational.getDenominator();
55      return new Rational(n, d);
56    }
57
58    /** Multiply a rational number to this rational */
59    public Rational multiply(Rational secondRational) {
60      long n = numerator * secondRational.getNumerator();
61      long d = denominator * secondRational.getDenominator();
62      return new Rational(n, d);
63    }
64
65    /** Divide a rational number from this rational */
66    public Rational divide(Rational secondRational) {
67      long n = numerator * secondRational.getDenominator();
68      long d = denominator * secondRational.numerator;
69      return new Rational(n, d);
70    }
71
72    /** Override the toString() method */
73    public String toString() {
74      if (denominator == 1)
75        return numerator + "";
76      else
77        return numerator + "/" + denominator;
78    }
79
80    /** Override the equals method in the Object class */
81    public boolean equals(Object parm1) {
```

$\frac{a}{b} + \frac{c}{d} = \frac{ad + bc}{bd}$

$\frac{a}{b} - \frac{c}{d} = \frac{ad - bc}{bd}$

$\frac{a}{b} \times \frac{c}{d} = \frac{ac}{bd}$

$\frac{a}{b} \div \frac{c}{d} = \frac{ad}{bc}$

```
82      if ((this.subtract((Rational)(parm1))).getNumerator() == 0)
83        return true;
84      else
85        return false;
86    }
87
88    /** Override the hashCode method in the Object class */
89    public int hashCode() {
90      return new Double(this.doubleValue()).hashCode();
91    }
92
93    /** Override the abstract intValue method in java.lang.Number */
94    public int intValue() {
95      return (int)doubleValue();
96    }
97
98    /** Override the abstract floatValue method in java.lang.Number */
99    public float floatValue() {
100     return (float)doubleValue();
101   }
102
103   /** Override the doubleValue method in java.lang.Number */
104   public double doubleValue() {
105     return numerator * 1.0 / denominator;
106   }
107
108   /** Override the abstract longValue method in java.lang.Number */
109   public long longValue() {
110     return (long)doubleValue();
111   }
112
113   /** Override the compareTo method in java.lang.Comparable */
114   public int compareTo(Object o) {
115     if ((this.subtract((Rational)o)).getNumerator() > 0)
116       return 1;
117     else if ((this.subtract((Rational)o)).getNumerator() < 0)
118       return -1;
119     else
120       return 0;
121   }
122 }
```

The rational number is encapsulated in a `Rational` object. Internally, a rational number is represented in its lowest terms (line 13), and the numerator determines its sign (line 14). The denominator is always positive (line 15).

The `gcd()` method (lines 19–30 in the `Rational` class) is private; it is not intended for use by clients. The `gcd()` method is only for internal use by the `Rational` class. The `gcd()` method is also static, since it is not dependent on any particular `Rational` object.

The `abs(x)` method (lines 20–21 in the `Rational` class) is defined in the `Math` class that returns the absolute value of `x`.

Two `Rational` objects can interact with each other to perform add, subtract, multiply, and divide operations. These methods return a new `Rational` object (lines 43–70).

The methods `toString`, `equals`, and `hashCode` in the `Object` class are overridden in the `Rational` class (lines 73–91). The `toString()` method returns a string representation of a `Rational` object in the form `numerator/denominator`, or simply `numerator` if `denominator` is 1. The `equals(Object other)` method returns `true` if this rational number is equal to the other rational number. By contract, if two objects are equal, their hash codes must be the same. For this reason, you should override `hashCode` whenever the `equals` method is overridden.

The abstract methods `intValue`, `longValue`, `floatValue`, and `doubleValue` in the `Number` class are implemented in the `Rational` class (lines 94–111). These methods return `int`, `long`, `float`, and `double` value for this rational number.

The `compareTo(Object other)` method in the `Comparable` interface is implemented in the `Rational` class (lines 114–121) to compare this rational number to the other rational number.

> **Tip**
>
> The get methods for the properties `numerator` and `denominator` are provided in the `Rational` class, but the set methods are not provided, so the contents of a `Rational` object cannot be changed once the object is created. The `Rational` class is *immutable*. A well-known example of an immutable class is the `String` class. The wrapper classes introduced in §10.5, "Processing Primitive Data Type Values as Objects," are also immutable.

immutable

> **Tip**
>
> The numerator and denominator are represented using two variables. It is possible to use an array of two integers to represent the numerator and denominator. See Exercise 11.2. The signatures of the public methods in the `Rational` class are not changed, although the internal representation of a rational number is changed. This is a good example to illustrate the idea that the data fields of a class should be kept private so as to encapsulate the implementation of the class from the use of the class.

encapsulation

11.6 Class Design Guidelines

You have learned how to design classes from the preceding two examples and from many other examples in the preceding chapters. Here are some guidelines.

11.6.1   Cohesion

A class should describe a single entity, and all the class operations should logically fit together to support a *coherent purpose*. You can use a class for students, for example, but you should not combine students and staff in the same class, because students and staff have different operations.

coherent purpose

A single entity with too many responsibilities can be broken into several classes to separate responsibilities. The classes `String`, `StringBuffer`, and `StringBuilder` all deal with strings, for example, but have different responsibilities. The `String` class deals with immutable strings, the `StringBuilder` class is for creating mutable strings, and the `StringBuffer` class is similar to `StringBuilder` except that `StringBuffer` contains synchronized methods for updating strings.

separating responsibilities

The `Date`, `Calendar`, and `GregorianCalendar` classes all deal with date and time, but have different responsibilities. The `Date` class represents a specific time. `Calendar` is an abstract class for extracting detailed calendar information from a specific time. `GregorianCalendar` implements a concrete calendar system.

11.6.2   Consistency

Follow standard Java programming style and naming conventions. Choose informative names for classes, data fields, and methods. A popular style is to place the data declaration before the constructor, and place constructors before methods.

naming conventions

Choose names consistently. It is not a good practice to choose different names for similar operations. For example, the `length()` method returns the size of a `String`, a `StringBuilder`, and a `StringBuffer`. But the `size()` method is used to return the size of a `Collection` and a `Map`. It is better to use the same name for consistency.

naming consistency

no-arg constructor

In general, you should consistently provide a public no-arg constructor for constructing a default instance. If a class does not support a no-arg constructor, document the reason. A public default no-arg constructor is assumed if no constructors are defined explicitly. A constructor invokes its superclass no-arg constructor by default if a constructor does not invoke an overloaded constructor or its superclass's constructor.

private constructor
protected constructor

If you want to prevent users from creating an object for a class, you may declare a private constructor in the class, as is the case for the `Math` class. The constructors in abstract classes should always be declared `protected`.

11.6.3 Encapsulation

encapsulating data fields

A class should use the `private` modifier to hide its data from direct access by clients. This makes the class easy to maintain.

Provide a `get` method only if you want the field to be readable, and provide a `set` method only if you want the field to be updateable. For example, the `Rational` class provides get methods for numerator and denominator, but no set methods, because `Rational` is an immutable class.

A class should also hide methods not intended for client use. The `gcd` method in the `Rational` class in the preceding section is private, for example, because it is only for internal use within the class.

private vs. protected

A class can present two contracts: one for the users of the class, and one for the extenders of the class. Make the fields `private` and the accessor and mutator methods `public` if they are intended for the users of the class. Make the fields or methods `protected` if they are intended for extenders of the class. The contract for extenders encompasses the contract for users. The extended class may increase the visibility of an instance method from `protected` to `public`, or may change its implementation, but you should never change the implementation in a way that violates the contract.

11.6.4 Clarity

Cohesion, consistency, and encapsulation are good guidelines for achieving design clarity. Additionally, a class should have a clear contract that is easy to explain and easy to understand.

easy to explain

Users can incorporate classes in many different combinations, orders, and environments. Therefore, you should design a class that imposes no restrictions on what or when the user can do with it, design the properties in a way that lets the user set them in any order and with any combination of values, and design methods that function independently of their order of occur-

independent methods

rence. For example, the `Loan` class contains the properties `loanAmount`, `numberOfYears`, and `annualInterestRate`. The values of these properties can be set in any order.

intuitive meaning

Methods should be defined intuitively without generating confusion. For example, the `substring(int beginIndex, int endIndex)` method in the `String` class is somehow confusing. The method returns a substring from `beginIndex` to `endIndex` $-$ `1`, rather than `endIndex`.

You should not declare a data field that can be derived from other data fields. For example, the following `Person` class has two data fields: `birthDate` and `age`. Since `age` can be

independent properties

derived from `birthDate`, age should not be declared as a data field.

```java
public class Person {
  private java.util.Date birthDate;
  int age;

  ...
}
```

11.6.5 Completeness

Classes are designed for use by many different customers. In order to be useful in a wide range of applications, a class should provide a variety of ways for customization through properties and methods. For example, the `String` class contains more than fifty methods that are useful for a variety of applications. The `Calendar` class defines many time fields as constants, such as `YEAR`, `MONTH`, `DATE`, `HOUR`, `HOUR_OF_DAY`, `MINUTE`, `SECOND`, and `DAY_OF_WEEK`, and provides many methods for extracting date and time, and for setting a new date and time in the calendar.

11.6.6 Instance vs. Static

A variable or method that is dependent on a specific instance of the class should be an instance variable or method. A variable that is shared by all the instances of a class should be declared `static`. For example, the variable `numberOfObjects` in `Circle2` in Listing 7.3, Circle2.java, is shared by all the objects of the `Circle2` class, and therefore is declared static. A method that is not dependent on a specific instance should be declared as a static method. For instance, the `getNumberOfObjects` method in `Circle2` and the `gcd` method in `Rational` are not tied to any specific instance, and therefore are declared as static methods.

Always reference static variables and methods from a class name (rather than a reference variable) to improve readability and avoid errors.

Do not pass a parameter from a constructor to initialize a static data field. It is better to use a set method to change the static data field. The following class in (a) is better replaced by (b).

```
public class SomeThing {
  int t1;
  static int t2;

  public SomeThing(int t1, int t2) {
    ...
  }
}
```

(a)

```
public class SomeThing {
  int t1;
  static int t2;

  public SomeThing(int t1) {
    ...
  }
  public static void setT2(int t2) {
    SomeThing.t2 = t2;
  }
}
```

(b)

Instance and static are integral parts of object-oriented programming. A data field or method is either instance or static. Do not mistakenly overlook static data fields or methods. It is a common design error to declare an instance method that should have been declared static. For example, the `factorial(int n)` method for computing the factorial of `n` should be declared static, because it is independent of any specific instance.

common design error

A constructor is always instance, because it is used to create a specific instance. A static variable or method can be invoked from an instance method, but an instance variable or method cannot be invoked from a static method.

11.6.7 Inheritance vs. Aggregation

The difference between inheritance and aggregation is the difference between an is-a relationship and a has-a relationship. For example, an apple is a fruit; thus, you would use inheritance to model the relationship between the classes `Apple` and `Fruit`. A person has a name; thus you would use aggregation to model the relationship between the classes `Person` and `Name`.

11.6.8 Interfaces vs. Abstract Classes

Both interfaces and abstract classes can be used to generalize common features. How do you decide whether to use an interface or a class? In general, a *strong is-a relationship* that clearly describes a parent–child relationship should be modeled using classes. For example, since an orange is a fruit, their relationship should be modeled using class inheritance. A *weak is-a relationship*, also known as an *is-kind-of relationship*, indicates that an object possesses a certain property. A weak is-a relationship can be modeled using interfaces. For example, all strings are comparable, so the `String` class implements the `Comparable` interface. A circle or a rectangle is a geometric object, so `Circle` can be designed as a subclass of `GeometricObject`. Circles are different and comparable based on their radii, so `Circle` can implement the `Comparable` interface.

Interfaces are more flexible than abstract classes, because a subclass can extend only one superclass but can implement any number of interfaces. However, interfaces cannot contain concrete methods. The virtues of interfaces and abstract classes can be combined by creating an interface with an abstract class that implements it. Then you can use the interface or the abstract class, whichever is convenient. For this reason, such classes are known as *convenience classes*. For example, in the Java Collections Framework, which is introduced in Chapter 22, "Java Collections Framework," the `AbstractCollection` class is a convenience class for the `Collection` interface, and the `AbstractSet` class is a convenience class for the `Set` interface.

 ## 11.7 (Optional) Modeling Dynamic Behavior Using Sequence Diagrams and Statecharts

The UML diagrams presented so far describe the properties and methods of a class or the static relationships among classes. This section introduces the sequence diagrams and statechart diagrams that model the dynamic behaviors of objects.

11.7.1 Sequence Diagrams

Sequence diagrams describe interactions among objects by depicting the time-ordering of method invocations. A sequence diagram consists of the following elements, as shown in Figure 11.14:

- **Class role** represents the roles the object plays. The objects at the top of the diagram represent class roles.

- **Lifeline** represents the existence of an object over a period of time. A vertical dotted line extending from the object is used to denote a lifeline.

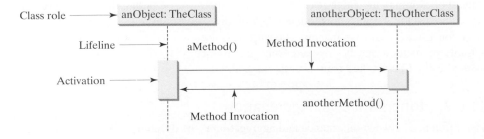

FIGURE 11.14 Sequence diagrams describe interactions between objects.

- **Activation** represents the time during which an object is performing an operation. Thin rectangles placed on lifelines are used to denote activations.

- **Method invocation** represents communication between objects. Horizontal arrows labeled with method calls are used to denote method invocations.

The interactions among the objects in the BorrowLoan class on page in Listing 11.5 are illustrated in Figure 11.15.

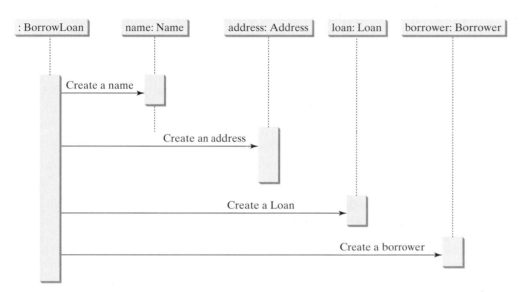

FIGURE 11.15 The BorrowLoan object invokes the methods in the Name, Address, Loan, and Borrower objects.

11.7.2 Statechart Diagrams

Statechart diagrams describe the flow of control of an object. A statechart diagram contains the following elements, as shown in Figure 11.16:

- **State** represents a situation during the life of an object in which it satisfies some condition, performs some action, or waits for some event to occur. All states have names. States are denoted by rectangles with rounded corners, except for the initial state, which is denoted by a small filled circle.

- **Transition** represents the relationship between two states, indicating that an object will perform some action to transfer from one state to the other. A solid arrow with appropriate method invocation denotes a transition.

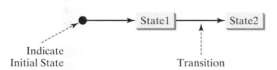

FIGURE 11.16 Statechart diagrams describe the flow of control of an object.

The life cycle of an object can be illustrated using a statechart diagram, as shown in Figure 11.17.

FIGURE 11.17   The life cycle of an object can be described using a statechart diagram.

11.8 Framework-Based Programming Using Java API

API

The Java API (*Application Program Interface*) consists of numerous classes and interfaces grouped into more than a dozen packages. You have used classes and interfaces in the `java.lang`, `javax.swing`, and `java.util` packages.

- `java.lang` contains core Java classes (e.g., `System`, `Math`, `Object`, `String`, `StringBuffer`, `Number`, `Character`, `Boolean`, `Byte`, `Short`, `Integer`, `Long`, `Float`, `Double`, `Comparable`, and `Cloneable`). This package is implicitly imported to every Java program.

- `javax.swing` contains the graphical user interface components for developing Swing GUI programs.

- `java.util` contains many utilities, such as `Arrays`, `ArrayList`, `Vector`, `Date`, `Calendar`, and `GregorianCalendar`.

These are just a few of the classes and interfaces you have learned. To create comprehensive projects, you have to use more classes and interfaces in the Java API. The classes and interfaces in the Java API establish a framework for programmers to develop applications using Java. For example, the classes and interfaces in the Java GUI API establish a framework for developing GUI programs. You have to use these classes and interfaces and follow their conventions and rules to create applications. This is referred to as *framework-based programming*.

framework-based programming

Once you understand the concept of Java and object-oriented programming, the most important lesson from now on is learning how to use the API to develop useful programs. The most effective way to achieve this is to imitate good examples. The book provides many carefully designed examples to demonstrate the concept of framework-based programming using the Java API. You will learn the Java GUI programming framework in Chapters 12–16, the Java exception-handling framework in Chapter 17, and the Java I/O framework in Chapter 18.

KEY TERMS

aggregated object   374
aggregating object   374
aggregation   374
Application Program Interface (API)
   392
association   373

composition   374
dependency   375
framework-based programming   392
sequence diagram   390
statechart   391

CHAPTER SUMMARY

- Developing a project involves *requirements specification, system analysis, system design, implementation, testing, deployment,* and *maintenance.* The process of designing classes calls for identifying the classes and discovering the relationships among them.

- The common relationships among classes are *association*, *aggregation*, *composition*, *dependency*, and *inheritance*.

- Some guidelines for class design are *cohesion*, *consistency*, *encapsulation*, *clarity*, and *completeness*.

- A property shared by all the instances of a class should be declared as a static property.

- Don't mistakenly overlook static data fields or methods. A method not tied to a specific instance should be declared static.

- The difference between inheritance and aggregation is the difference between an is-a relationship and a has-a relationship.

- Both interfaces and abstract classes can be used to generalize common features. How do you decide whether to use an interface or a class? In general, a *strong is-a relationship* that clearly describes a parent–child relationship should be modeled using classes.

- Interfaces are more flexible than abstract classes, because a subclass can extend only one superclass but can implement any number of interfaces. However, interfaces cannot contain concrete methods.

- Sequence diagrams describe interactions among objects by depicting the time-ordering of method invocations. Statechart diagrams describe the flow of control of an object.

REVIEW QUESTIONS

Section 11.3 Discovering Relationships Among Objects

11.1 What are the common types of relationships among classes? Describe the graphical notations for modeling the relationships among classes.

11.2 What relationship is appropriate for the following classes? Draw the relationships using UML diagrams.

- Company and Employee
- Course and Faculty
- Student and Person
- House and Window
- Account and Savings Account
- The JOptionPane class and the String class
- The Loan class and the Date class (§7.15)

Section 11.5 The Rational Class

11.3 Show the output of the following code:

```java
public class Test {
  public static void main(String[] args) {
    Rational r1 = new Rational(1, 3);
    Rational r2 = new Rational(2, 4);
    System.out.println(r1 + " + " + r2 + " = " + r1.add(r2));
    System.out.println(r2 + " + " + r1 + " = " + r2.add(r1));
    System.out.println(r1 + " - " + r2 + " = " + r1.subtract(r2));
    System.out.println(r2 + " - " + r1 + " = " + r2.subtract(r1));
```

```
        System.out.println(r1 + " * " + r2 + " = " + r1.multiply(r2));
        System.out.println(r2 + " * " + r1 + " = " + r2.multiply(r1));
        System.out.println(r1 + " / " + r2 + " = " + r1.divide(r2));
        System.out.println(r2 + " / " + r1 + " = " + r2.divide(r1));
        System.out.println(r1 + " = " + r1.doubleValue());
        System.out.println(r2 + " = " + r2.doubleValue());
    }
}
```

11.4 What is wrong in the following code?

```
Number r = new Rational();
System.out.println(r);
System.out.println(r.doubleValue());
System.out.println(r.add(new Rational()));
System.out.println((Rational)r.add(new Rational()));
System.out.println(((Rational)r).add(new Rational()));
```

11.5 What is wrong in the following code?

```
Number r = new Number();
System.out.println(r);
```

11.6 Is the following code correct?

```
Comparable r = new Rational();
System.out.println(r);
```

```
Comparable r = new Rational();
System.out.println(
    r.compareTo(new Rational()));
```

(a)   (b)

Section 11.6 Class Design Guidelines

11.7 What is cohesion? Give examples of cohesive class design.

11.8 What is consistency? Give examples of nonconsistent class design.

11.9 What is encapsulation? What are the benefits of data field encapsulation?

11.10 When is it appropriate to use the `protected` modifier?

11.11 Which of the following is poor design?

- A data field is derived from other data fields in the same class.
- A method must be invoked after/before invoking another method in the same class.
- A method is an instance method, but it does not reference any instance data fields or invoke instance methods.
- A parameter is passed from a constructor to initialize a static data field.

11.12 Which of the following is incorrect?

- A static method may reference instance data fields or invoke instance methods.
- An instance method may reference static data fields or invoke static methods.
- A constructor may be static.
- A constructor may be private.
- A constructor may invoke a static method.
- A constructor may invoke an overloaded constructor.
- A constructor invokes its superclass no-arg constructor by default if it does not invoke an overloaded constructor or its superclass's constructor.

- An abstract class contains constructors.
- The constructors in an abstract class are public.
- The constructors in an abstract class are private.
- You may declare a final abstract class.
- An interface may contain constructors.
- An interface may contain instance data fields.
- An interface may contain static methods.

PROGRAMMING EXERCISES

Section 11.5 The `Rational` Class

11.1 (*Using the Rational class*) Write a program that will compute the following summation series using the `Rational` class:

$$\frac{1}{2} + \frac{2}{3} + \frac{3}{4} + \cdots + \frac{98}{99} + \frac{99}{100}$$

11.2* (*Demonstrating the benefits of encapsulation*) Rewrite the `Rational` class in Section 11.5 using a new internal representation for numerator and denominator. Declare an array of two integers as follows:

```
private long[] r = new long[2];
```

Use `r[0]` to represent the numerator and `r[1]` to represent the denominator. The signatures of the methods in the `Rational` class are not changed, so a client application that uses the previous `Rational` class can continue to use this new `Rational` class without being recompiled.

11.3* (*Creating a rational number calculator*) Write a program similar to Listing 8.4, Calculator.java. Instead of using integers, use rationals, as shown in Figure 11.18. You will need to use the `split` method in the `String` class, introduced in §8.6.3, "Replacing and Splitting Strings," to retrieve the numerator string and denominator string, and convert strings into integers using the `Integer.parseInt` method.

```
 19  20  21  22  23  24  25
 26  27  28  29  30

C:\exercise>java Exercise11_3 1/2 + 1/3
1/2 + 1/3 = 5/6

C:\exercise>java Exercise11_3 1/2 - 1/3
```

FIGURE 11.18 The program takes three arguments (operand1, operator, and operand2) from the command line and displays the expression and the result of the arithmetic operation.

Comprehensive

11.4** (*The Person and Student classes*) Design the `Student` class that extends `Person`. Implement the `compareTo` method in the `Person` class to compare persons in alphabetical order of their last name. Implement the `compareTo` method to compare students in alphabetical order of their major and last name. Draw a UML diagram that involves `Person`, `Student`, `Comparable`, and `Name`.

Write a test program with the following four methods:

```
/** Sort an array of comparable objects  */
public static void sort(Object[] list)

/** Print an array of objects */
public static void printList(Object[] object)

/** Return the max object in an array of comparable objects */
public static Object max(Object[] list)
```

`main` method: Test the `sort`, `printList`, and `max` methods using an array of four students, an array of four strings, an array of one hundred random rationals, and an array of one hundred random integers.

PART 3

GUI PROGRAMMING

Part 1, "Fundamentals of Programming," introduced basic programming concepts that are supported in all programming languages. Part 2, "Object-Oriented Programming," introduced object-oriented programming concepts, principles, and practices that are common in the object-oriented programming languages. Java is not simply a programming language. It is also a development and deployment platform with an extensive set of classes and interfaces in the API. You have to use the classes and interfaces in the API and follow their conventions and rules to develop your own projects. The design of the API for Java GUI programming is an excellent example of how the object-oriented principle is applied. In the chapters that follow, you will learn the framework of Java GUI API and use the GUI components to develop user-friendly interfaces for applications and applets.

Chapter 12

Getting Started with GUI Programming

Chapter 13

Graphics

Chapter 14

Event-Driven Programming

Chapter 15

Creating User Interfaces

Chapter 16

Applets and Multimedia

Prerequisites for Part 3

Part 3, "GUI Programming," may be intertwined with Part 2, "Object-Oriented Programming." You can cover GUI programming in Chapters 12 and 13, "Getting Started with GUI Programming" and "Graphics," after you have covered abstract classes in Chapter 10, "Abstract Classes and Interfaces."

GUI early

Interfaces in Chapter 10, "Abstract Classes and Interfaces," can be covered just before Chapter 14, *Event-Driven Programming*.

event-driven programming

applets early

The concept and simple examples of using applets can be covered earlier after Chapter 12, "GUI Basics."

GETTING STARTED WITH GUI PROGRAMMING

Objectives

- To get a glimpse of simple GUI components (§12.2).

- To describe the Java GUI API hierarchy (§12.3).

- To create user interfaces using frames, panels, and simple GUI components (§12.4).

- To understand the role of layout managers (§12.5).

- To use the `FlowLayout`, `GridLayout`, and `BorderLayout` managers to layout components in a container (§12.5).

- To specify colors and fonts using the `Color` and `Font` classes (§§12.6–12.7).

- To use `JPanel` as subcontainers (§12.8).

- To apply common features such as borders, tool tips, fonts, and colors on Swing components (§12.9).

- To use borders to visually group user-interface components (§12.9).

- To create image icons using the `ImageIcon` class (§12.10).

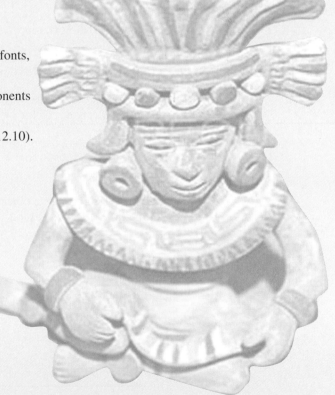

12.1   Introduction

Until now, you have only used dialog boxes and the command window for input and output. You used `JOptionPane.showInputDialog` to obtain input, and `JOptionPane.showMessageDialog` and `System.out.println` to display results. These approaches have limitations and are inconvenient. For example, to read ten numbers, you have to open ten input dialog boxes. Starting with this chapter, you will learn Java GUI programming. You will create custom graphical user interfaces (GUI, pronounced *goo-ee*) to obtain input and display output in the same user interface.

This chapter introduces the basics of Java GUI programming. Specifically, it discusses GUI components and their relationships, containers and layout managers, colors, fonts, borders, and tool tips.

12.2   GUI Components

You create graphical user interfaces using GUI objects such as buttons, labels, text fields, check boxes, radio buttons, and combo boxes. Each type of GUI object is defined in a class, such as `JButton`, `JLabel`, `JTextField`, `JCheckBox`, `JRadioButton`, and `JComboBox`. Each GUI component class provides several constructors that you can use to create GUI component objects. The following are examples to create buttons, labels, text fields, check boxes, radio buttons, and combo boxes:

```java
// Create a button with text OK
JButton jbtOK = new JButton("OK");

// Create a label with text "Enter your name: "
JLabel jlblName = new JLabel("Enter your name: ");

// Create a text field with text "Type Name Here"
JTextField jtfName = new JTextField("Type Name Here");

// Create a check box with text bold
JCheckBox jchkBold = new JCheckBox("Bold");

// Create a radio button with text red
JRadioButton jrbRed = new JRadioButton("Red");

// Create a combo box with choices red, green, and blue
JComboBox jcboColor = new JComboBox(new String[]{"Red",
  "Green", "Blue"});
```

Figure 12.1 shows these objects displayed in a frame. How to add components into a frame will be introduced in §12.4.2.

FIGURE 12.1   The GUI component objects can be displayed.

12.2.1 Swing vs. AWT

Why do the GUI component classes have the prefix *J*? Instead of `JButton`, why not name it simply `Button`? In fact, there is a class already named `Button` in the `java.awt` package.

When Java was introduced, the GUI classes were bundled in a library known as the Abstract Windows Toolkit (AWT). For every platform on which Java runs, the AWT components are automatically mapped to the platform-specific components through their respective agents, known as *peers*. AWT is fine for developing simple graphical user interfaces, but not for developing comprehensive GUI projects. Besides, AWT is prone to platform-specific bugs because its peer-based approach relies heavily on the underlying platform. With the release of Java 2, the AWT user-interface components were replaced by a more robust, versatile, and flexible library known as *Swing components*. Swing components are painted directly on canvases using Java code, except for components that are subclasses of `java.awt.Window` or `java.awt.Panel`, which must be drawn using native GUI on a specific platform. Swing components are less dependent on the target platform and use less of the native GUI resource. For this reason, Swing components that don't rely on native GUI are referred to as *lightweight components,* and AWT components are referred to as *heavyweight components*.

lightweight
heavyweight

To distinguish new Swing component classes from their AWT counterparts, the names of Swing GUI component classes begin with a prefixed *J*. Although AWT components are still supported in Java 2, it is better to learn to how program using Swing components, because the AWT user-interface components will eventually fade away. This book uses Swing GUI components exclusively.

why prefix J?

12.3 The Java GUI API

The design of the Java API for GUI programming is an excellent example of the use of classes, inheritance, and interfaces. The API contains the essential classes listed below. Their hierarchical relationships are shown in Figures 12.2 and 12.3.

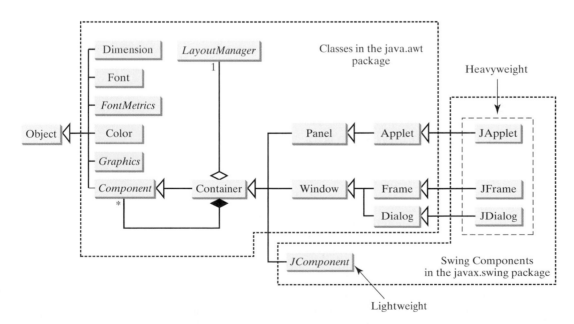

FIGURE 12.2 Java GUI programming utilizes the classes shown in this hierarchical diagram.

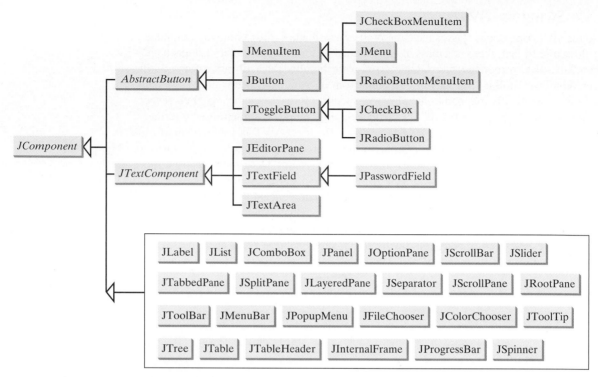

FIGURE 12.3 JComponent and its subclasses are the basic elements for building graphical user interfaces.

The GUI classes can be classified into three groups: *container classes*, *helper classes*, and *component classes*. The container classes, such as JFrame, JPanel, and JApplet, are used to contain other components. The helper classes, such as Graphics, Color, Font, FontMetrics, and Dimension, are used by components and containers to draw and place objects. The GUI component classes, such as JButton, JTextField, JTextArea, JComboBox, JList, JRadioButton, and JMenu, are subclasses of JComponent.

 Note

The JFrame, JApplet, JDialog, and JComponent classes and their subclasses are grouped in the javax.swing package. All the other classes in Figure 12.2 are grouped in the java.awt package.

12.3.1 Swing GUI Components

Component is a superclass of all the user-interface classes, and JComponent is a superclass of all the lightweight Swing components, Since JComponent is an abstract class, you cannot use new JComponent() to create an instance of JComponent. However, you can use the constructors of concrete subclasses of JComponent to create JComponent instances. It is important to become familiar with the class inheritance hierarchy. For example, the following statements all display true:

```
JButton jbtOK = new JButton("OK");
System.out.println(jbtOK instanceof JButton);
System.out.println(jbtOK instanceof AbstractButton);
System.out.println(jbtOK instanceof JComponent);
System.out.println(jbtOK instanceof Container);
System.out.println(jbtOK instanceof Component);
System.out.println(jbtOK instanceof Object);
```

12.3.2 Container Classes

Container classes are GUI components that are used as containers to contain other GUI components. `Window`, `Panel`, `Applet`, `Frame`, and `Dialog` are the container classes for AWT components. To work with Swing components, use `Component`, `Container`, `JFrame`, `JDialog`, `JApplet`, and `JPanel`.

- `Container` is used to group components. Frames, panels, and applets are examples of containers.

- `JFrame` is a window not contained inside another window. It is the container that holds other Swing user-interface components in Java GUI applications.

- `JDialog` is a popup window or message box generally used as a temporary window to receive additional information from the user or to provide notification that an event has occurred.

- `JApplet` is a subclass of `Applet`. You must extend `JApplet` to create a Swing-based Java applet.

- `JPanel` is an invisible container that holds user-interface components. Panels can be nested. You can place panels inside a container that includes a panel. `JPanel` can also be used as a canvas to draw graphics.

12.3.3 GUI Helper Classes

The helper classes, such as `Graphics`, `Color`, `Font`, `FontMetrics`, `Dimension`, and `LayoutManager`, are not subclasses of `Component`. They are used to describe the properties of GUI components, such as graphics context, colors, fonts, and dimension.

- `Graphics` is an abstract class that provides a graphical context for drawing strings, lines, and simple shapes.

- `Color` deals with the colors of GUI components. For example, you can specify background or foreground colors in components like `JFrame` and `JPanel`, or you can specify colors of lines, shapes, and strings in drawings.

- `Font` specifies fonts for the text and drawings on GUI components. For example, you can specify the font type (e.g., SansSerif), style (e.g., bold), and size (e.g., 24 points) for the text on a button.

- `FontMetrics` is an abstract class used to get the properties of the fonts.

- `Dimension` encapsulates the width and height of a component (in integer precision) in a single object.

- `LayoutManager` is an interface whose instances specify how components are arranged in a container.

 Note
The helper classes are in the `java.awt` package. The Swing components do not replace all the classes in AWT, only the AWT GUI component classes (e.g., `Button`, `TextField`, `TextArea`). The AWT helper classes remain unchanged.

12.4 Frames

To create a user interface, you need to create either a frame or an applet to hold the user-interface components. Creating Java applets will be introduced in Chapter 16, "Applets and Multimedia." This section introduces frames.

12.4.1 Creating a Frame

To create a frame, use the `JFrame` class, as shown in Figure 12.4.

javax.swing.JFrame	
+JFrame()	Creates a default frame with no title.
+JFrame(title: String)	Creates a frame with the specified title.
+setSize(width: int, height: int): void	Specifies the size of the frame.
+setLocation(x: int, y: int): void	Specifies the upper-left-corner location of the frame.
+setVisible(visible: boolean): void	Sets true to display the frame.
+setDefaultCloseOperation(mode: int): void	Specifies the operation when the frame is closed.
+setLocationRelativeTo (c: Component): void	Sets the location of the frame relative to the specified component. If the component is null, the frame is centered on the screen.

FIGURE 12.4 `Frame` is a top-level container to hold GUI components.

The program in Listing 12.1 creates a frame.

LISTING 12.1 MyFrame.java

import package

create frame
set size
center frame
close upon exit
display the frame

```
1  import javax.swing.*;
2
3  public class MyFrame {
4    public static void main(String[] args) {
5      JFrame frame = new JFrame("MyFrame"); // Create a frame
6      frame.setSize(400, 300); // Set the frame size
7      frame.setLocationRelativeTo(null); // New since JDK 1.4
8      frame.setDefaultCloseOperation(JFrame.EXIT_ON_CLOSE);
9      frame.setVisible(true); // Display the frame
10   }
11 }
```

The frame is not displayed *until* the `frame.setVisible(true)` method is invoked. `frame.setSize(400, 300)` specifies that the frame is 400 pixels wide and 300 pixels high. If the `setSize` method is not used, the frame will be sized to display just the title bar. Since the `setSize` and `setVisible` methods are both defined in the `Component` class, they are inherited by the `JFrame` class. Later you will see that these methods are also useful in many other subclasses of `Component`.

When you run the `MyFrame` program, a window will be displayed on-screen (see Figure 12.5(a)).

FIGURE 12.5 (a) The program creates and displays a frame with the title `MyFrame`. (b) An OK button is added to the frame.

Invoking `setLocationRelativeTo(null)` (line 7) centers the frame on the screen. Invoking `setDefaultCloseOperation(JFrame.EXIT ON CLOSE)` (line 8) tells the program to terminate when the frame is closed. If this statement is not used, the program does not terminate when the frame is closed. In that case, you have to stop the program by pressing Ctrl+C at the DOS prompt window in Windows or use the kill command to stop the process in Unix.

 Note
Recall that a pixel is the smallest unit of space for drawing on the screen. You can think of a pixel as a small rectangle and think of the screen as paved with pixels. The *resolution* specifies the number of pixels per square inch. The more pixels the screen has, the higher the screen's resolution. The higher the resolution, the more fine detail you can see.

pixel and resolution

12.4.2 Adding Components to a Frame

The frame shown in Figure 12.5(a) is empty. Using the **add** method, you can add components into the frame, as in Listing 12.2.

LISTING 12.2 MyFrameWithComponents.java

```
 1 import javax.swing.*;
 2
 3 public class MyFrameWithComponents {
 4   public static void main(String[] args) {
 5     JFrame frame = new JFrame("MyFrameWithComponents");
 6
 7     // Add a button into the frame
 8     JButton jbtOK = new JButton("OK");
 9     frame.add(jbtOK);
10
11     frame.setSize(400, 300);
12     frame.setDefaultCloseOperation(JFrame.EXIT_ON_CLOSE);
13     frame.setLocationRelativeTo(null); // Center the frame
14     frame.setVisible(true);
15   }
16 }
```

create a button
add to frame

set size
exit upon closing window
center the frame
set visible

Each `JFrame` contains a content pane. A content pane is an instance of `java.awt.Container`. The GUI components such as buttons are placed in the content pane in a frame. Prior to JDK 1.5, you have to use the `getContentPane` method in the `JFrame` class to return the content pane of the frame, and then invoke the content pane's `add` method to place a component into the content pane. This was cumbersome. JDK 1.5 allows you to place components to the content pane by invoking a frame's `add` method. This new feature is called *content pane delegation*. Strictly speaking, a component is added into the content pane of a frame. But for simplicity we say that a component is added to a frame.

content pane delegation

An object of `JButton` was created using `new JButton("OK")`, and this object was added to the content pane of the frame (line 9).

The `add(Component comp)` method defined in the `Container` class adds an instance of `Component` to the container. Since `JButton` is a subclass of `Component`, an instance of `JButton` is also an instance of `Component`. To remove a component from a container, use the `remove` method. The following statement removes the button from the container:

```
container.remove(jbtOK);
```

When you run the program `MyFrameWithComponents`, the window will be displayed as in Figure 12.5(b). The button is always centered in the frame and occupies the entire frame no matter how you resize it. This is because components are put in the frame by the content pane's layout manager, and the default layout manager for the content pane places the button in the center. In the next section, you will use several different layout managers to place components in other locations as desired.

12.5 Layout Managers

In many other window systems, the user-interface components are arranged by using hard-coded pixel measurements. For example, put a button at location (**10, 10**) in the window. Using hard-coded pixel measurements, the user interface might look fine on one system but be unusable on another. Java's layout managers provide a level of abstraction that automatically maps your user interface on all window systems.

Note

Java also supports hard-coded fixed layout, which will be covered in Chapter 28, "Containers, Layout Managers, and Borders." Since it is platform-dependent, it is rarely used in practice.

The Java GUI components are placed in containers, where they are arranged by the container's layout manager. In the preceding program, you did not specify where to place the OK button in the frame, but Java knows where to place it because the layout manager works behind the scenes to place components in the correct locations. A layout manager is created using a layout manager class. Every layout manager class implements the **LayoutManager** interface.

Layout managers are set in containers using the **setLayout(LayoutManager)** method. For example, you can use the following statements to create an instance of *XLayout* and set it in a container:

```
LayoutManager layoutManager = new XLayout();
container.setLayout(layoutManager);
```

This section introduces three basic layout managers: **FlowLayout**, **GridLayout**, and **BorderLayout**. More layout managers will be introduced in Chapter 28, "Containers, Layout Managers, and Borders."

12.5.1 FlowLayout

FlowLayout is the simplest layout manager. The components are arranged in the container from left to right in the order in which they were added. When one row is filled, a new row is started. You can specify the way the components are aligned by using one of three constants: **FlowLayout.RIGHT**, **FlowLayout.CENTER**, or **FlowLayout.LEFT**. You can also specify the gap between components in pixels. The constructors and methods in **FlowLayout** are shown in Figure 12.6.

FIGURE 12.6 FlowLayout lays out components row by row.

Listing 12.3 gives a program that demonstrates flow layout. The program adds three labels and text fields into the frame with a **FlowLayout** manager. If you resize the frame, the components may be rearranged. In Figure 12.7(a), the first row has three components, but in Figure 12.7(b), the first row has four components, because the width has been increased.

(a)   (b)

FIGURE 12.7   The components are added by the `FlowLayout` manager to fill in the rows in the container one after another.

LISTING 12.3   ShowFlowLayout.java

```
 1 import javax.swing.JLabel;
 2 import javax.swing.JTextField;
 3 import javax.swing.JFrame;
 4 import java.awt.FlowLayout;
 5
 6 public class ShowFlowLayout extends JFrame {          extends JFrame
 7   public ShowFlowLayout() {
 8     // Set FlowLayout, aligned left with horizontal gap 10
 9     // and vertical gap 20 between components
10     setLayout (new FlowLayout(FlowLayout.LEFT, 10, 20));   set layout
11
12     // Add labels and text fields to the frame
13     add(new JLabel("First Name"));                    add label
14     add(new JTextField(8));                           add text field
15     add(new JLabel("MI"));
16     add(new JTextField(1));
17     add(new JLabel("Last Name"));
18     add(new JTextField(8));
19   }
20
21   /** Main method */
22   public static void main(String[] args) {
23     ShowFlowLayout frame = new ShowFlowLayout();       create frame
24     frame.setTitle("ShowFlowLayout");
25     frame.setLocationRelativeTo(null); // Center the frame
26     frame.setDefaultCloseOperation(JFrame.EXIT_ON_CLOSE);
27     frame.setSize(200, 200);
28     frame.setVisible(true);                           set visible
29   }
30 }
```

This example creates a program using a style different from the programs in the preceding section, where frames were created using the `JFrame` class. This example creates a class named `ShowFlowLayout` that extends the `JFrame` class (line 6). The `main` method in this program creates an instance of `ShowFlowLayout` (line 23). The constructor of `ShowFlowLayout` constructs and places the components in the frame. This is the preferred style of creating GUI applications for three reasons:

1. Creating a GUI application means creating a frame, so it is natural to define a frame to extend `JFrame`.

2. The frame may be further extended to add new components or functions.

3. The class can be easily reused. For example, you can create multiple frames by creating multiple instances of the class.

Using one style consistently makes programs easy to read. From now on, most of the GUI main classes will extend the `JFrame` class. The constructor of the main class constructs the user interface. The `main` method creates an instance of the main class and then displays the frame.

In this example, the `FlowLayout` manager is used to place components in a frame. If you resize the frame, the components are automatically rearranged to fit in it, as shown in Figure 12.7(b).

If you replace the `setLayout` statement (line 10) with `setLayout(new FlowLayout (FlowLayout.RIGHT, 0, 0))`, all the rows of buttons will be right-aligned with no gaps.

An anonymous `FlowLayout` object was created in the statement (line 10):

```
setLayout(new FlowLayout(FlowLayout.LEFT, 10, 20));
```

which is equivalent to:

```
FlowLayout layout = new FlowLayout(FlowLayout.LEFT, 10, 20);
setLayout(layout);
```

This code creates an explicit reference to the object `layout` of the `FlowLayout` class. The explicit reference is not necessary, because the object is not directly referenced in the `ShowFlowLayout` class.

The `setTitle` method (line 24) is defined in the `java.awt.Frame` class. Since `JFrame` is a subclass of `Frame`, you can use it to set a title for an object of `JFrame`.

Suppose you add the same button into the container ten times, will ten buttons appear in the container? No, only the last one will be displayed.

Caution
Do not forget to put the `new` operator before a layout manager class when setting a layout style; for example, `setLayout(new FlowLayout())`.

Note
The constructor `ShowFlowLayout()` does not explicitly invoke the constructor `JFrame()`, but the constructor `JFrame()` is invoked implicitly. See §9.3.2, "Constructor Chaining."

12.5.2 GridLayout

The `GridLayout` manager arranges components in a grid (matrix) formation with the number of rows and columns defined by the constructor. The components are placed in the grid from left to right, starting with the first row, then the second, and so on, in the order in which they are added. The constructors and methods in `GridLayout` are shown in Figure 12.8.

The get and set methods for these data fields are provided in the class, but omitted in the UML diagram for brevity.

java.awt.GridLayout	
-rows: int	The number of rows in this layout manager (default: 1).
-columns: int	The number of columns in this layout manager (default: 1).
-hgap: int	The horizontal gap of this layout manager (default: 0).
-vgap: int	The vertical gap of this layout manager (default: 0).
+GridLayout()	Creates a default GridLayout manager.
+GridLayout(rows: int, columns: int)	Creates a GridLayout with a specified number of rows and columns.
+GridLayout(rows: int, columns: int, hgap: int, vgap: int)	Creates a GridLayout manager with a specified number of rows and columns, horizontal gap, and vertical gap.

FIGURE 12.8 `GridLayout` lays out components in equal-sized cells on a grid.

You can specify the number of rows and columns in the grid. The basic rules are as follows:

- The number of rows or the number of columns can be zero, but not both. If one is zero and the other is nonzero, the nonzero dimension is fixed, while the zero dimension is determined dynamically by the layout manager. For example, if you specify zero rows and three columns for a grid that has ten components, GridLayout creates three fixed columns of four rows, with the last row containing one component. If you specify three rows and zero columns for a grid that has ten components, GridLayout creates three fixed rows of four columns, with the last row containing two components.

- If both the number of rows and the number of columns are nonzero, the number of rows is the dominating parameter; that is, the number of rows is fixed, and the layout manager dynamically calculates the number of columns. For example, if you specify three rows and three columns for a grid that has ten components, GridLayout creates three fixed rows of four columns, with the last row containing two components.

Listing 12.4 gives a program that demonstrates grid layout. The program is similar to the one in Listing 12.3. It adds three labels and three text fields to the frame of GridLayout instead of FlowLayout, as shown in Figure 12.9.

FIGURE 12.9 The GridLayout manager divides the container into grids, then the components are added to fill in the cells row by row.

LISTING 12.4 ShowGridLayout.java

```java
 1 import javax.swing.JLabel;
 2 import javax.swing.JTextField;
 3 import javax.swing.JFrame;
 4 import java.awt.GridLayout;
 5
 6 public class ShowGridLayout extends JFrame {
 7   public ShowGridLayout() {
 8     // Set GridLayout, 3 rows, 2 columns, and gaps 5 between
 9     // components horizontally and vertically
10     setLayout(new GridLayout(3, 2, 5, 5));            set layout
11
12     // Add labels and text fields to the frame
13     add(new JLabel("First Name"));                    add label
14     add(new JTextField(8));                           add text field
15     add(new JLabel("MI"));
16     add(new JTextField(1));
17     add(new JLabel("Last Name"));
18     add(new JTextField(8));
19   }
20
21   /** Main method */
22   public static void main(String[] args) {
23     ShowGridLayout frame = new ShowGridLayout();      create a frame
24     frame.setTitle("ShowGridLayout");
25     frame.setLocationRelativeTo(null); // Center the frame
26     frame.setDefaultCloseOperation(JFrame.EXIT_ON_CLOSE);
```

set visible

```
27      frame.setSize(200, 125);
28      frame.setVisible(true);
29   }
30 }
```

If you resize the frame, the layout of the buttons remains unchanged (i.e., the number of rows and columns does not change, and the gaps don't change either).

All components are given equal size in the container of `GridLayout`.

Replacing the `setLayout` statement (line 10) with `setLayout(new GridLayout(3, 10))` would still yield three rows and *two* columns. The columns parameter is ignored because the rows parameter is nonzero. The actual number of columns is calculated by the layout manager.

What would happen if the `setLayout` statement (line 10) is replaced with `setLayout (new GridLayout(4, 2))` or with `setLayout(new GridLayout(2, 2))`? Please try it yourself.

Note

In `FlowLayout` and `GridLayout`, the order in which the components are added to the container is important. It determines the location of the components in the container.

12.5.3   BorderLayout

The `BorderLayout` manager divides the window into five areas: East, South, West, North, and Center. Components are added to a `BorderLayout` by using **add(Component, index)**, where **index** is a constant `BorderLayout.EAST`, `BorderLayout.SOUTH`, `Border-Layout.WEST`, `BorderLayout.NORTH`, or `BorderLayout.CENTER`. The constructors and methods in `BorderLayout` are shown in Figure 12.10.

FIGURE 12.10   `BorderLayout` lays out components in five areas.

The components are laid out according to their preferred sizes and where they are placed in the container. The North and South components can stretch horizontally; the East and West components can stretch vertically; the Center component can stretch both horizontally and vertically to fill any empty space.

Listing 12.5 gives a program that demonstrates border layout. The program adds five buttons labeled `East`, `South`, `West`, `North`, and `Center` into the frame with a `BorderLayout` manager, as shown in Figure 12.11.

LISTING 12.5   ShowBorderLayout.java

```
1 import javax.swing.JButton;
2 import javax.swing.JFrame;
3 import java.awt.BorderLayout;
4
```

```
 5  public class ShowBorderLayout extends JFrame {
 6    public ShowBorderLayout() {
 7      // Set BorderLayout with horizontal gap 5 and vertical gap 10
 8      setLayout(new BorderLayout(5, 10));                              set layout
 9
10      // Add buttons to the frame
11      add(new JButton("East"), BorderLayout.EAST);                    add buttons
12      add(new JButton("South"), BorderLayout.SOUTH);
13      add(new JButton("West"), BorderLayout.WEST);
14      add(new JButton("North"), BorderLayout.NORTH);
15      add(new JButton("Center"), BorderLayout.CENTER);
16    }
17
18    /** Main method */
19    public static void main(String[] args) {
20      ShowBorderLayout frame = new ShowBorderLayout();                create a frame
21      frame.setTitle("ShowBorderLayout");
22      frame.setLocationRelativeTo(null); // Center the frame
23      frame.setDefaultCloseOperation(JFrame.EXIT_ON_CLOSE);
24      frame.setSize(300, 200);                                        set visible
25      frame.setVisible(true);
26    }
27  }
```

FIGURE 12.11 `BorderLayout` divides the container into five areas, each of which can hold a component.

The buttons are added to the frame (lines 11–15). Note that the `add` method for `BorderLayout` is different from the one for `FlowLayout` and `GridLayout`. With `BorderLayout` you specify where to put the components.

It is unnecessary to place components to occupy all the areas. If you remove the East button from the program and rerun it, you will see that the center stretches rightward to occupy the East area.

 Note

For convenience, `BorderLayout` interprets the absence of an index specification as `BorderLayout.CENTER`. For example, `add(component)` is the same as `add(Component, BorderLayout.CENTER)`. If you add two components into a container of `BorderLayout`, as follows,

```
container.add(component1);
container.add(component2);
```

only the last component is displayed.

12.5.4 Properties of Layout Managers

Layout managers have properties that can be changed dynamically. `FlowLayout` has `alignment`, `hgap`, and `vgap` properties. You can use the `setAlignment`, `setHgap`, and setVgap methods to specify the alignment and the horizontal and vertical gaps. GridLayout has the rows, columns, hgap, and vgap properties. You can use the setRows, setColumns, setHgap, and setVgap methods to specify the number of rows, the number of columns, and the horizontal and vertical gaps. BorderLayout has the hgap and vgap properties. You can use the setHgap and setVgap methods to specify the horizontal and vertical gaps.

In the preceding sections, an anonymous layout manager is used because the properties of a layout manager do not change once it is created. If you have to change the properties of a layout manager dynamically, the layout manager must be explicitly referenced by a variable. You can then change the properties of the layout manager through the variable. For example, the following code creates a layout manager and sets its properties:

```
// Create a layout manager
FlowLayout flowLayout = new FlowLayout();

// Set layout properties
flowLayout.setAlignment(FlowLayout.RIGHT);
flowLayout.setHgap(10);
flowLayout.setVgap(20);
```

 ### 12.5.5 (Optional) The validate and doLayout Methods

validate()

A container can have only one layout manager at a time. You can change its layout manager by using the setLayout(aNewLayout) method and then use the validate() method to force the container to again layout the components in the container using the new layout manager.

doLayout()

If you use the same layout manager but change its properties, you need to use the doLayout() method to force the container to re-layout the components using the new properties of the layout manager.

12.6 The **Color** Class

You can set colors for GUI components by using the java.awt.Color class. Colors are made of red, green, and blue components, each of which is represented by an unsigned byte value that describes its intensity, ranging from 0 (darkest shade) to 255 (lightest shade). This is known as the *RGB model*.

You can create a color using the following constructor:

public Color(**int** r, **int** g, **int** b);

in which r, g, and b specify a color by its red, green, and blue components. For example,

Color color = **new** Color(128, 100, 100);

 Note

The arguments r, g, b are between 0 and 255. If a value beyond this range is passed to the argument, an IllegalArgumentException would throw.

IllegalArgument-
Exception

You can use the setBackground(Color c) and setForeground(Color c) methods defined in the java.awt.Component class to set a component's background and foreground colors. Here is an example of setting the background and foreground of a button:

```
JButton jbtOK = new JButton();
jbtOK.setBackground(color);
jbtOK.setForeground(new Color(100, 1, 1));
```

Alternatively, you can use one of the thirteen standard colors (black, blue, cyan, darkGray, gray, green, lightGray, magenta, orange, pink, red, white, yellow)

defined as constants in `java.awt.Color`. The following code, for instance, sets the foreground color of a button to red:

```
jbtOK.setForeground(Color.red);
```

Note

The standard color names are constants, but they are named as variables with lowercase for the first word and uppercase for the first letters of subsequent words. Thus the color names violate the Java naming convention. Since JDK 1.4, you can also use the new constants BLACK, BLUE, CYAN, DARK_GRAY, GRAY, GREEN, LIGHT_GRAY, MAGENTA, ORANGE, PINK, RED, WHITE, and YELLOW.

color constants

12.7 The **Font** Class

You can create a font using the `java.awt.Font` class and set fonts for the components using the `setFont` method in the `Component` class.

The constructor for `Font` is:

```
public Font(String name, int style, int size);
```

You can choose a font name from `SansSerif`, `Serif`, `Monospaced`, `Dialog`, or `DialogInput`, choose a style from `Font.PLAIN` (0), `Font.BOLD` (1), `Font.ITALIC` (2), and `Font.BOLD + Font.ITALIC` (3), and specify a font size of any positive integer. For example, the following statements create two fonts and set one font to a button:

```
Font font1 = new Font("SansSerif", Font.BOLD, 16);
Font font2 = new Font("Serif", Font.BOLD + Font.ITALIC, 12);

JButton jbtOK = new JButton("OK");
jbtOK.setFont(font1);
```

Tip (Optional)

If your system supports other fonts, such as "Times New Roman," you can use it to create a `Font` object. To find the fonts available on your system, you need to create an instance of `java.awt.GraphicsEnvironment` using its static method `getLocalGraphicsEnvironment()`. `GraphicsEnvironment` is an abstract class that describes the graphics environment on a particular system. You can use its `getAllFonts()` method to obtain all the available fonts on the system, and its `getAvailableFontFamilyNames()` method to obtain the names of all the available fonts. For example, the following statements print all the available font names in the system:

find available fonts

```
GraphicsEnvironment e =
  GraphicsEnvironment.getLocalGraphicsEnvironment();
String[] fontnames = e.getAvailableFontFamilyNames();

for (int i = 0; i < fontnames.length; i++)
  System.out.println(fontnames[i]);
```

12.8 Using Panels as Subcontainers

Suppose that you want to place ten buttons and a text field on a frame. The buttons are placed in grid formation, but the text field is placed on a separate row. It is difficult to achieve the desired look by placing all the components in a single container. With Java GUI programming, you can divide a window into panels. Panels act as subcontainers to group user-interface components. You add the buttons in one panel, and then add the panel into the frame. The Swing version of panel is `JPanel`. You can use `new JPanel()` to create a panel with a default `FlowLayout` manager or `new JPanel(LayoutManager)` to create a panel with the specified layout manager. Use the **add(Component)** method to add a component to the panel. For example, the following code creates a panel and adds a button to it:

```
JPanel p = new JPanel();
p.add(new JButton("OK"));
```

Panels can be placed inside a frame or inside another panel. The following statement places panel **p** into frame **f**:

```
f.add(p);
```

Listing 12.6 gives an example that demonstrates using panels as subcontainers. The program creates a user interface for a microwave oven, as shown in Figure 12.12.

FIGURE 12.12 The program uses panels to organize components.

LISTING 12.6 TestPanels.java

panel p1

panel p2

add p2 to frame

```
 1 import java.awt.*;
 2 import javax.swing.*;
 3
 4 public class TestPanels extends JFrame {
 5   public TestPanels() {
 6     // Create panel p1 for the buttons and set GridLayout
 7     JPanel p1 = new JPanel();
 8     p1.setLayout(new GridLayout(4, 3));
 9
10     // Add buttons to the panel
11     for (int i = 1; i <= 9; i++) {
12       p1.add (new JButton("" + i));
13     }
14
15     p1.add(new JButton("" + 0));
16     p1.add(new JButton("Start"));
17     p1.add(new JButton("Stop"));
18
19     // Create panel p2 to hold a text field and p1
20     JPanel p2 = new JPanel(new BorderLayout());
21     p2.add (new JTextField("Time to be displayed here"),
22       BorderLayout.NORTH);
23     p2.add (p1, BorderLayout.CENTER);
24
25     // add contents into the frame
26     add(p2, BorderLayout.EAST);
27     add(new JButton("Food to be placed here"),
```

```
28        BorderLayout.CENTER);
29    }
30
31    /** Main method */
32    public static void main(String[] args) {
33      TestPanels frame = new TestPanels();
34      frame.setTitle("The Front View of a Microwave Oven");
35      frame.setLocationRelativeTo(null); // Center the frame
36      frame.setDefaultCloseOperation(JFrame.EXIT_ON_CLOSE);
37      frame.setSize(400, 250);
38      frame.setVisible(true);
39    }
40 }
```

The `setLayout` method is defined in `java.awt.Container`. Since `JPanel` is a subclass of `Container`, you can use `setLayout` to set a new layout manager in the panel (line 8). Lines 7–8 can be replaced by `JPanel p1 = new JPanel(new GridLayout(4, 3))`.

To achieve the desired layout, the program uses panel `p1` of `GridLayout` to group the number buttons, the Stop button, and the Start button, and panel `p2` of `BorderLayout` to hold a text field in the north and `p1` in the center. The button representing the food is placed in the center of the frame, and `p2` is placed in the east of the frame.

The statement (lines 21–22)

```
p2.add(new JTextField("Time to be displayed here"),
  BorderLayout.NORTH);
```

creates an instance of `JTextField` and adds it to `p2`. `JTextField` is a GUI component that can be used for user input as well as to display values.

Note

The `Container` class is the superclass for Swing GUI component classes, such as `JButton`. In theory, you could use the `setLayout` method to set the layout in a button and add components into a button, because all the public methods in the `Container` class are inherited into `JButton`, but for practical reasons you should not use buttons as containers.

12.9 Common Features of Swing GUI Components

You have used several GUI components (e.g., `JFrame`, `Container`, `JPanel`, `JButton`, `JLabel`, `JTextField`) in this chapter. Many more GUI components will be introduced in this book. It is important to understand the common features of Swing GUI components. The `Component` class is the root for all GUI components and containers. All Swing GUI components (except `JFrame`, `JApplet`, and `JDialog`) are subclasses of `JComponent`, as shown in Figures 12.2 and 12.3. Figure 12.13 lists some frequently used methods in `Component`, `Container`, and `JComponent` for manipulating properties like font, color, size, tool tip text, and border.

Component
Container
JComponent

A *tool tip* is a text displayed on a component when you move the mouse on the component. It is often used to describe the function of a component.

You can set a border on any object of the `JComponent` class. Swing has several types of borders. To create a titled border, use `new TitledBorder(String title)`. To create a line border, use `new LineBorder(Color color, int width)`, where `width` specifies the thickness of the line.

Listing 12.7 is an example to demonstrate Swing common features. The example creates a panel `p1` to hold three buttons (line 8) and a panel `p2` to hold two labels (line 25). The background of the button `jbtLeft` is set to `white` (line 12), and the foreground of the button `jbtCenter` is set to `green` (line 13). The tool tip of the button `jbtRight` is set in line 14.

FIGURE 12.13 All the Swing GUI components inherit the public methods from `Component`, `Container`, and `JComponent`.

Titled borders are set on panels **p1** and **p2** (lines 18, 36), and line borders are set on the labels (lines 32–33).

LISTING 12.7 TestSwingCommonFeatures.java

```
1 import java.awt.*;
2 import javax.swing.*;
3 import javax.swing.border.*;
4
5 public class TestSwingCommonFeatures extends JFrame {
6   public TestSwingCommonFeatures() {
7     // Create a panel to group three buttons
8     JPanel p1 = new JPanel(new FlowLayout(FlowLayout.LEFT, 2, 2));
9     JButton jbtLeft = new JButton("Left");
10    JButton jbtCenter = new JButton("Center");
11    JButton jbtRight = new JButton("Right");
12    jbtLeft.setBackground(Color.WHITE);
13    jbtCenter.setForeground(Color.GREEN);
14    jbtRight.setToolTipText("This is the Right button");
15    p1.add(jbtLeft);
16    p1.add(jbtCenter);
17    p1.add(jbtRight);
18    p1.setBorder(new TitledBorder("Three Buttons"));
```

set background
set foreground
set tool tip text

set titled border

```
19
20      // Create a font and a line border
21      Font largeFont = new Font("TimesRoman", Font.BOLD, 20);        create a font
22      Border lineBorder = new LineBorder(Color.BLACK, 2);            create a border
23
24      // Create a panel to group two labels
25      JPanel p2 = new JPanel(new GridLayout(1, 2, 5, 5));
26      JLabel jlblRed = new JLabel("Red");
27      JLabel jlblOrange = new JLabel("Orange");
28      jlblRed.setForeground(Color.RED);                              set foreground
29      jlblOrange.setForeground(Color.ORANGE);
30      jlblRed.setFont(largeFont);                                    set font
31      jlblOrange.setFont(largeFont);
32      jlblRed.setBorder(lineBorder);                                 set line border
33      jlblOrange.setBorder(lineBorder);
34      p2.add(jlblRed);
35      p2.add(jlblOrange);
36      p2.setBorder(new TitledBorder("Two Labels"));                  set titled border
37
38      // Add two panels to the frame
39      setLayout(new GridLayout(2, 1, 5, 5));
40      add(p1);
41      add(p2);
42    }
43
44    public static void main(String[] args) {
45      // Create a frame and set its properties
46      JFrame frame = new TestSwingCommonFeatures();
47      frame.setTitle("TestSwingCommonFeatures");
48      frame.setSize(300, 150);
49      frame.setLocationRelativeTo(null); // Center the frame
50      frame.setDefaultCloseOperation(JFrame.EXIT_ON_CLOSE);
51      frame.setVisible(true);
52    }
53 }
```

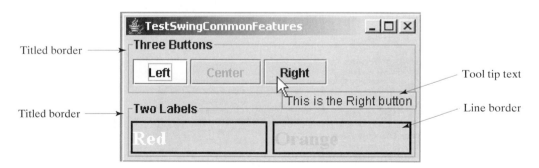

FIGURE 12.14 The font, color, border, and tool tip text are set in the message panel.

 Note

The same property may have different default values in different components. For example, the   property default values
`visible` property in `JFrame` is `false` by default, but it is `true` in every instance of
`JComponent` (e.g., `JButton` and `JLabel`) by default. To display a `JFrame`, you have to
invoke `setVisible(true)` to set the `visible` property `true`, but you don't have to set this
property for a `JButton` or a `JLabel`, because it is already `true`. To make a `JButton` or a

JLabel invisible, you may invoke setVisible(false) on. Please run the program and see the effect after inserting the following two statements in line 37:

```
jbtLeft.setVisible(false);
jlblRed.setVisible(false);
```

12.10 Image Icons

Java uses the javax.swing.ImageIcon class to represent an icon. An icon is a fixed-size picture; typically it is small and used to decorate components. Images are normally stored in image files. You can use new ImageIcon(filename) to construct an image icon. For example, the following statement creates an icon from an image file us.gif in the image directory under the current class path:

create **ImageIcon**

```
ImageIcon icon = new ImageIcon("image/us.gif");
```

Note

"image/us.gif" is located in "c:\book\image\us.gif." The back slash (\) is the Windows file path notation. On Unix, the forward slash (/) should be used. In Java, the forward slash (/) is used to denote a relative file path under the Java classpath (e.g., image/left.gif, as in this example).

file path character

Note

Java currently supports three image formats: GIF (Graphics Interchange Format), JPEG (Joint Photographic Experts Group), and PNG (Portable Network Graphics). The image filenames for these types end with .gif, .jpg, and .png, respectively. If you have a bitmap file or image files in other formats, you can use image-processing utilities to convert them into GIF, JPEG, or PNG format for use in Java.

image file format

Note

File names are not case sensitive on Windows, but are case sensitive on Unix. To enable your programs to run on all platforms, name all the image files consistently, using lowercase.

naming files consistently

An image icon can be displayed in a label or a button using new JLabel(imageIcon) or new JButton(imageIcon). Listing 12.8 demonstrates displaying icons in a label and a button. The example creates two labels and two buttons with icons, as shown in Figure 12.15.

FIGURE 12.15 The image icons are displayed in labels and buttons.

LISTING 12.8 TestImageIcon.java

```
1  import javax.swing.*;
2  import java.awt.*;
3
4  public class TestImageIcon extends JFrame {
5    private ImageIcon usIcon = new ImageIcon("image/us.gif");
6    private ImageIcon myIcon = new ImageIcon("image/my.jpg");
```

create image icons

```
 7    private ImageIcon frIcon = new ImageIcon("image/fr.gif");
 8    private ImageIcon ukIcon = new ImageIcon("image/uk.gif");
 9
10    public TestImageIcon() {
11      setLayout(new GridLayout(1, 4, 5, 5));
12      add(new JLabel(usIcon));
13      add(new JLabel(myIcon));
14      add(new JButton(frIcon));
15      add(new JButton(ukIcon));
16    }
17
18    /** Main method */
19    public static void main(String[] args) {
20      TestImageIcon frame = new TestImageIcon();
21      frame.setTitle("TestImageIcon");
22      frame.setLocationRelativeTo(null); // Center the frame
23      frame.setDefaultCloseOperation(JFrame.EXIT_ON_CLOSE);
24      frame.setSize(200, 200);
25      frame.setVisible(true);
26    }
27  }
```

a label with image

a button with image

Note

GUI components cannot be shared by containers because a GUI component can appear in only one container at a time. Therefore, the relationship between a component and a container is the composition denoted by a solid diamond, as shown in Figure 12.2.

Note

Borders and icons can be shared. Thus you can create a border or icon and use it to set the **border** or **icon** property for any GUI component. For example, the following statements set a border **b** for two panels **p1** and **p2**:

sharing borders and icons

```
p1.setBorder(b);
p2.setBorder(b);
```

The following statements set an icon in two buttons **jbt1** and **jbt2**:

```
jbt1.setIcon(icon);
jbt2.setIcon(icon);
```

KEY TERMS

AWT 401	lightweight component 401
heavyweight component 401	Swing 401

CHAPTER SUMMARY

- Every container has a layout manager that is used to position and place components in the container in the desired locations. Three simple and useful layout managers are **FlowLayout**, **GridLayout**, and **BorderLayout**.

- You can use a **JPanel** as a subcontainer to group components to achieve a desired layout.

- Use the **add** method to place components to a **JFrame** or a **JPanel**. By default, the frame's layout is **BorderLayout**, and the **JPanel**'s layout is **FlowLayout**.

■ You can set colors for GUI components by using the `java.awt.Color` class. Colors are made of red, green, and blue components, each of which is represented by an unsigned byte value that describes its intensity, ranging from 0 (darkest shade) to 255 (lightest shade). This is known as the *RGB model*.

■ The syntax to create a `Color` object is `Color color = new Color(r, g, b)`, in which `r`, `g`, and `b` specify a color by its red, green, and blue components. Alternatively, you can use one of the thirteen standard colors (`black`, `blue`, `cyan`, `darkGray`, `gray`, `green`, `lightGray`, `magenta`, `orange`, `pink`, `red`, `white`, `yellow`) defined as constants in `java.awt.Color`.

■ Every Swing GUI component is a subclass of `javax.swing.JComponent`, and `JComponent` is a subclass of `java.awt.Component`. The properties `font`, `background`, `foreground`, `height`, `width`, and `preferredSize` in `Component` are inherited in these subclasses, as are `toolTipText` and `border` in `JComponent`.

■ You can use borders on any Swing components. You can create an image icon using the `ImageIcon` class and display it in a label and a button. Icons and borders can be shared.

REVIEW QUESTIONS

Sections 12.3–12.4

12.1   Which class is the root of the Java GUI component classes? Is a container class a subclass of `Component`? Which class is the root of the Swing GUI component classes?

12.2   Explain the difference between AWT GUI components, such as `java.awt.Button`, and Swing components, such as `javax.swing.JButton`.

12.3   How do you create a frame? How do you set the size for a frame? How do you get the size of a frame? How do you add components to a frame? What would happen if the statements `frame.setSize(400, 300)` and `frame.setVisible(true)` were swapped in the `MyFrameWithComponents` class in Section 12.4.2, "Adding Components to a Frame"?

12.4   Determine whether the following statements are true or false:

■ You can add a button to a frame.
■ You can add a frame to a panel.
■ You can add a panel to a frame.
■ You can add any number of components to a panel or a frame.
■ You can derive a class from `JButton`, `JPanel`, `JFrame`, or `JApplet`.

12.5   The following program is supposed to display a button in a frame, but nothing is displayed. What is the problem?

```
 1 public class Test extends javax.swing.JFrame {
 2   public Test() {
 3     add(new javax.swing.JButton("OK"));
 4   }
 5
 6   public static void main(String[] args) {
 7     javax.swing.JFrame frame = new javax.swing.JFrame();
 8     frame.setSize(100, 200);
 9     frame.setVisible(true);
10   }
11 }
```

12.6 Which of the following statements have syntax errors?

```
Component c1 = new Component();
JComponent c2 = new JComponent();
Component c3 = new JButton();
JComponent c4 = new JButton();
Container c5 = new JButton();
c5.add(c4);
Object c6 = new JButton();
c5.add(c6);
```

Section 12.5 Layout Managers

12.7 Why do you need to use layout managers? What is the default layout manager for a frame? How do you add a component to a frame?

12.8 Describe FlowLayout. How do you create a FlowLayout manager? How do you add a component to a FlowLayout container? Is there a limit to the number of components that can be added to a FlowLayout container?

12.9 Describe GridLayout. How do you create a GridLayout manager? How do you add a component to a GridLayout container? Is there a limit to the number of components that can be added to a GridLayout container?

12.10 Describe BorderLayout. How do you create a BorderLayout manager? How do you add a component to a BorderLayout container? Can you add multiple components in the same section?

Sections 12.6–12.7

12.11 How do you create a color? What is wrong about creating a Color using new Color(400, 200, 300)? Which of the following two colors are darker, new Color(10, 0, 0) or new Color(200, 0, 0)?

12.12 How do you create a font? How do you find all the available fonts on your system?

Section 12.8 Using Panels as Subcontainers

12.13 How do you create a panel with a specified layout manager?

12.14 What is the default layout manager for a JPanel? How do you add a component to a JPanel?

12.15 Can you use the setTitle method in a panel? What is the purpose of using a panel?

12.16 Since a GUI component class such as JButton is a subclass of Container, can you add components into a button?

Sections 12.9–12.10

12.17 How do you set background color, foreground color, font, and tool tip text on a Swing GUI component? Why is the tool tip text not displayed in the following code?

```
1  import javax.swing.*;
2
3  public class Test extends JFrame {
4    private JButton jbtOK = new JButton("OK");
5
6    public static void main(String[] args) {
7      // Create a frame and set its properties
8      JFrame frame = new Test();
9      frame.setTitle("Logic Error");
```

```
10      frame.setSize(200, 100);
11      frame.setDefaultCloseOperation(JFrame.EXIT_ON_CLOSE);
12      frame.setVisible(true);
13    }
14
15    public Test() {
16      jbtOK.setToolTipText("This is a button");
17      add(new JButton("OK"));
18    }
19  }
```

12.18 Show the output of the following code:

```
import javax.swing.*;

public class Test {
  public static void main(String[] args) {
    JButton jbtOK = new JButton("OK");
    System.out.println(jbtOK.isVisible());

    JFrame frame = new JFrame();
    System.out.println(frame.isVisible());
  }
}
```

12.19 How do you create an `ImageIcon` from the file image/us.gif in the class directory?

12.20 What happens if you add a button to a container several times, as shown below? Does it cause syntax errors? Does it cause runtime errors?

```
JButton jbt = new JButton();
JPanel panel = new JPanel();
panel.add(jbt);
panel.add(jbt);
panel.add(jbt);
```

12.21 Will the following code display three buttons? Will the buttons display the same icon?

```
1 import javax.swing.*;
2 import java.awt.*;
3
4 public class Test extends JFrame  {
5   public static void main(String[] args) {
6     // Create a frame and set its properties
7     JFrame frame = new Test();
8     frame.setTitle("ButtonIcons");
9     frame.setSize(200, 100);
10    frame.setDefaultCloseOperation(JFrame.EXIT_ON_CLOSE);
11    frame.setVisible(true);
12  }
13
14  public Test() {
15    ImageIcon usIcon = new ImageIcon("image/usIcon.gif");
16    JButton jbt1 = new JButton(usIcon);
17    JButton jbt2 = new JButton(usIcon);
18
19    JPanel p1 = new JPanel();
20    p1.add(jbt1);
```

```
21
22     JPanel p2 = new JPanel();
23     p2.add(jbt2);
24
25     JPanel p3 = new JPanel();
26     p2.add(jbt1);
27
28     add(p1, BorderLayout.NORTH);
29     add(p2, BorderLayout.SOUTH);
30     add(p3, BorderLayout.CENTER);
31   }
32 }
```

12.22 Can a border or an icon be shared by GUI components?

PROGRAMMING EXERCISES

Section 12.5 Layout Managers

12.1 (*Using the* FlowLayout *manager*) Write a program that meets the following requirements (see Figure 12.16):

■ Create a frame and set its layout to FlowLayout.
■ Create two panels and add them to the frame.
■ Each panel contains three buttons. The panel uses FlowLayout.

FIGURE 12.16 Exercise 12.1 places three buttons in one panel and three buttons in another panel.

12.2 (*Using the* BorderLayout *manager*) Rewrite the preceding program to create the same user interface, but instead of using FlowLayout for the frame, use BorderLayout. Place one panel in the south of the frame and the other panel in the center.

12.3 (*Using the* GridLayout *manager*) Rewrite the preceding program to create the same user interface. Instead of using FlowLayout for the panels, use a GridLayout of two rows and three columns.

12.4 (*Using* JPanel *to group buttons*) Rewrite the preceding program to create the same user interface. Instead of creating buttons and panels separately, define a class that extends the JPanel class. Place three buttons in your panel class, and create two panels from the user-defined panel class.

12.5 (*Displaying labels*) Write a program that displays four lines of text in four labels, as shown in Figure 12.17(a). Add a line border on each label.

12.6 (*Displaying icons*) Write a program that displays four icons in four labels, as shown in Figure 12.17(b). Add a line border on each label. (Use any images of your choice or the ones in the book, which can be obtained along with the book's source code).

(a)   (b)

FIGURE 12.17 (a) Exercise 12.5 displays four labels. (b) Exercise 12.6 displays four icons.

12.7**(*Displaying a TicTacToe board*) Display a frame that contains nine labels. A label may display a cross image icon, a not image icon, or nothing, as shown in Figure 12.18(a). What to display is randomly decided. Use the `Math.random()` method to generate an integer 0, 1, or 2, which corresponds to displaying a cross image icon, a not image icon, or nothing. The cross and not images can be obtained from the `cross.gif` and `not.gif` files in the `image` directory on the Companion Website.

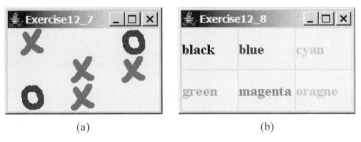

(a)   (b)

FIGURE 12.18 (a) A TicTacToe board is displayed with image icons in labels. (b) Six labels are placed in the frame.

12.8* (*Swing common features*) Display a frame that contains six labels. Set the background of the labels to white. Set the foreground of the labels to black, blue, cyan, green, magenta, and orange, respectively, as shown in Figure 12.18(b). Set the border of each label to a line border with the yellow color. Set the font of each label to TimesRoman, bold, and 20 pixels. Set the text and tool tip text of each label to the name of its foreground color.

CHAPTER 13

GRAPHICS

Objectives

- To understand Java coordinate systems (§13.2).

- To draw things using the methods in the `Graphics` class (§13.3).

- To understand how and when a `Graphics` object is created (§13.3).

- To override the `paintComponent` method to draw things on a GUI component (§13.4).

- To use a panel as a canvas to draw things (§13.5).

- To draw strings, lines, rectangles, ovals, arcs, and polygons (§§13.6, 13.8–13.9).

- To obtain font properties using `FontMetrics` and know how to center a message (§13.10).

- (Optional) To display image in a GUI component (§13.13).

- To develop reusable GUI components `FigurePanel`, `MessagePanel`, `StillClock`, and `ImageViewer` (§§13.7, 13.11, 13.12 Optional, 13.14 Optional).

13.1 Introduction

The preceding chapter introduced GUI components and their relationships, containers and layout managers, colors, fonts, and image icons. This chapter introduces how to paint graphics on GUI components. You will learn how to draw strings, lines, rectangles, ovals, arcs, polygons, and images, and how to develop reusable GUI components.

13.2 Graphical Coordinate Systems

To paint, you need to know where to paint. Each component has its own coordinate system with the origin (0, 0) at the upper-left corner of the component. The *x* coordinate increases to the right, and the *y* coordinate increases downward. Note that the Java coordinate system is different from the conventional coordinate system, as shown in Figure 13.1. The location of the upper-left corner of a component c1 (e.g., a button) inside its parent component c2 (e.g., a panel) can be located using c1.getX() and c1.getY(), as shown in Figure 13.2.

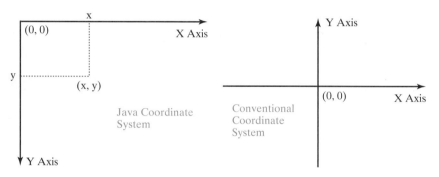

FIGURE 13.1 The Java coordinate system is measured in pixels, with (0, 0) at its upper-left corner.

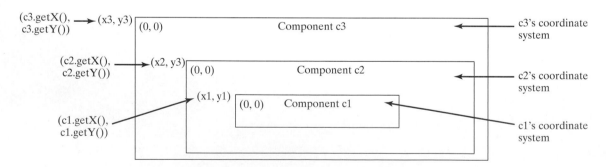

FIGURE 13.2 Each GUI component has its own coordinate system.

13.3 The **Graphics** Class

You can draw strings, lines, rectangles, ovals, arcs, polygons, and polylines, using the methods in the **Graphics** class, as shown in Figure 13.3.

The **Graphics** class is an abstract class that provides a device-independent graphics interface for displaying figures and images on the screen on different platforms. Whenever a component (e.g., a button, a label, a panel) is displayed, the JVM automatically creates a

java.awt.Graphics	
+setColor(color: Color): void	Sets a new color for subsequent drawings.
+setFont(font: Font): void	Sets a new font for subsequent drawings.
+drawString(s: String, x: int, y: int): void	Draws a string starting at point (x, y).
+drawLine(x1: int, y1: int, x2: int, y2: int): void	Draws a line from (x1, y1) to (x2, y2).
+drawRect(x:int, y: int, w: int, h: int): void	Draws a rectangle with specified upper-left-corner point at (x, y) and width w and height h.
+fillRect(x: int, y: int, w: int, h: int): void	Draws a filled rectangle with specified upper-left-corner point at (x, y) and width w and height h.
+drawRoundRect(x: int, y: int, w: int, h: int, aw: int, ah: int): void	Draws a round-cornered rectangle with specified arc width aw and arc height ah.
+fillRoundRect(x: int, y: int, w: int, h: int, aw: int, ah: int): void	Draws a filled round-cornered rectangle with specified arc width aw and arc height ah.
+draw3DRect(x: int, y: int, w: int, h: int, raised: boolean): void	Draws a 3-D rectangle raised above the surface or sunk into the surface.
+fill3DRect(x: int, y: int, w: int, h: int, raised: boolean): void	Draws a filled 3-D rectangle raised above the surface or sunk into the surface.
+drawOval(x: int, y: int, w: int, h: int): void	Draws an oval bounded by the rectangle specified by the parameters x, y, w, and h.
+fillOval(x: int, y: int, w: int, h: int): void	Draws a filled oval bounded by the rectangle specified by the parameters x, y, w, and h.
+drawArc(x: int, y: int, w: int, h: int, startAngle: int, arcAngle: int): void	Draws an arc conceived as part of an oval bounded by the rectangle specified by the parameters x, y, w, and h.
+fillArc(x: int, y: int, w: int, h: int, startAngle: int, arcAngle: int): void	Draws a filled arc conceived as part of an oval bounded by the rectangle specified by the parameters x, y, w, and h.
+drawPolygon(xPoints: int[], yPoints: int[], nPoints: int): void	Draws a closed polygon defined by arrays of x and y coordinates. Each pair of (x[i], y[i]) coordinates is a point.
+fillPolygon(xPoints: int[], yPoints: int[], nPoints: int): void	Draws a filled polygon defined by arrays of x and y coordinates. Each pair of (x[i], y[i]) coordinates is a point.
+drawPolygon(g: Polygon): void	Draws a closed polygon defined by a Polygon object.
+fillPolygon(g: Polygon): void	Draws a filled polygon defined by a Polygon object.
+drawPolyline(xPoints: int[], yPoints: int[], nPoints: int): void	Draws a polyline defined by arrays of x and y coordinates. Each pair of (x[i], y[i]) coordinates is a point.

FIGURE 13.3 The `Graphics` class contains the methods for drawing strings and shapes.

`Graphics` object for the component on the native platform. This object can be obtained using the `getGraphics()` method. For example, the `Graphics` object for a label `jlblBanner` can be obtained using

```
Graphics graphics = jlblBanner.getGraphics();
```

Think of a GUI component as a piece of paper and the `Graphics` object as a pencil or paintbrush. You can apply the methods in the `Graphics` class to draw things on a GUI component.

To fully understand the Graphics class, we first present an intuitive, but not practical example in Listing 13.1. The program creates a label in line 5. When the `main` method is executed, the constructor `TestGetGraphics` is executed (line 13) and the label is added to the frame (line 8). At this time, the `Graphics` object for the label has not been created because the label has not been displayed. Therefore, `jlblBanner.getGraphics()` returns `null` (line 9). After the frame is displayed in line 18, all the components in the frame are also displayed. The `Graphics` object for the label is obtained in line 21. A line is drawn from (0, 0) to (50, 50) on the label, as shown in Figure 13.4.

FIGURE 13.4 A line is drawn on a label, and the label is placed inside the frame.

LISTING 13.1 TestGetGraphics.java

```
 1  import javax.swing.*;
 2  import java.awt.Graphics;
 3
 4  public class TestGetGraphics extends JFrame {
 5    private JLabel jlblBanner = new JLabel("Banner");
 6
 7    public TestGetGraphics() {
 8      add(jlblBanner);
 9      System.out.println(jlblBanner.getGraphics());
10    }
11
12    public static void main(String[] args) {
13      TestGetGraphics frame = new TestGetGraphics();
14      frame.setTitle("TestGetGraphics");
15      frame.setLocationRelativeTo(null); // Center the frame
16      frame.setDefaultCloseOperation(JFrame.EXIT_ON_CLOSE);
17      frame.setSize(200, 100);
18      frame.setVisible(true);
19      JOptionPane.showMessageDialog(null,
20        "Delay on purpose\nClick OK to dismiss the dialog");
21      Graphics graphics = frame.jlblBanner.getGraphics();
22      graphics.drawLine(0, 0, 50, 50);
23    }
24  }
```

Margin notes:
create a label (line 5)
add a label (line 8)
create a frame (line 13)
display frame / for delay purpose (lines 18–19)
get graphics (line 21)
draw line (line 22)

When you run this program, the frame is displayed (line 18), then a message dialog box is displayed (line 19). What is the purpose of having a message dialog box in this program? The purpose is to delay the execution of lines 21 and 22. Without the delay, you might not see the line (line 22). The reason will be discussed in the next section.

When you create a label with a text such as new JLabel("Banner"), you see the text on the label when the label is displayed. The text is actually painted on the label using the drawString method in the Graphics class internally.

Every GUI component has a Graphics object that can be obtained using getGraphics() after the component is displayed. You may rewrite this example using a button, a text field, or a text area rather a label. Note that jlblBanner.getGraphics() returns null in line 9, because jlblBanner has not been displayed yet. It is displayed when the frame is set visible in line 18.

In line 9, jlblBanner.getGraphics() is used to return a Graphics object. In line 21, why do you have to use frame.jlblBanner.getGraphics() in the main method? This is because jlblBanner is an instance variable, and it cannot be referenced directly in a static method.

13.4 The **paintComponent** Method

The program in Listing 13.1 has two problems:

1. If you resize the frame, the line disappears.

2. It is awkward to program because you have to make sure that the component is displayed before obtaining its `Graphics` object using the `getGraphics()` method. For this reason, lines 21 and 22 are placed after the frame is displayed in line 18.

Because of these two problems, you should avoid programming using the `getGraphics()` method. To fix the first problem, you need to know its cause. When you resize the frame, the JVM automatically invokes the `paintComponent` method of a Swing component (e.g., a `JLabel`) to redisplay the graphics on the component. Since you did not draw a line in the `paintComponent` method, the line is gone when the frame is resized. To permanently display the line, you need to draw the line in the `paintComponent` method. The signature of the `paintComponent` method is as follows:

```
protected void paintComponent(Graphics g)
```

This method, defined in the `JComponent` class, is invoked whenever a component is first displayed or redisplayed. The `Graphics` object `g` is created automatically by the JVM for every visible GUI component. The JVM obtains the `Graphics` object and passes it to invoke `paintComponent`.

In order to draw things on a component (e.g., a `JLabel`) consistently, you need to declare a class that extends a Swing GUI component class and overrides its `paintComponent` method to specify what to draw. The program in Listing 13.1 can be rewritten as shown in Listing 13.2. The output is the same as shown in Figure 13.4. When you resize the frame, the JVM invokes the `paintComponent` method to repaint the line and the text.

LISTING 13.2 TestPaintComponent.java

```
 1 import javax.swing.*;
 2 import java.awt.Graphics;
 3
 4 public class TestPaintComponent extends JFrame {
 5   public TestPaintComponent() {
 6     add(new NewLabel("Banner"));                          create a label
 7   }
 8
 9   public static void main(String[] args) {
10     TestPaintComponent frame = new TestPaintComponent();
11     frame.setTitle("TestPaintComponent");
12     frame.setLocationRelativeTo(null); // Center the frame
13     frame.setDefaultCloseOperation(JFrame.EXIT_ON_CLOSE);
14     frame.setSize(200, 100);
15     frame.setVisible(true);
16   }
17 }
18
19 class NewLabel extends JLabel {
20   public NewLabel(String text) {                          new label class
21     super(text);
22   }
23
```

override
  paintComponent
draw things in the
   superclass **drawline**

```
24   protected void paintComponent(Graphics g) {
25     super.paintComponent(g);
26     g.drawLine(0, 0, 50, 50);
27   }
28 }
```

The `paintComponent` method is automatically invoked to paint graphics when the component is first displayed or whenever the component needs to be redisplayed. The text "banner" is drawn in the `paintComponent` method defined in the `JLabel` class. Invoking `super.paintComponent(g)` (line 25) displays the text in the label, and invoking the `drawLine` method (line 26) draws a line.

super.paintComponent-
  (g)

The JVM invokes `paintComponent` to draw things on a component. The user should never invoke `paintComponent` directly. For this reason, the protected visibility is sufficient for `paintComponent`.

protected
  paintComponent

13.5 Drawing Graphics on Panels

Panels are invisible and are used as small containers that group components to achieve a desired layout. Another important use of `JPanel` is for drawing. You can draw things on any Swing GUI component, but normally you should use a `JPanel` as a canvas to draw things.

To draw in a `JPanel`, you create a new class that extends `JPanel` and overrides the `paintComponent` method to tell the panel how to draw things. Listing 13.3 is an example to demonstrate drawings on a panel. The example declares the `NewPanel` class, which extends `JPanel` and overrides the `paintComponent` method to draw a line (line 22) and a string (line 23), as shown in Figure 13.5.

FIGURE 13.5 A line and a string are drawn on a panel.

LISTING 13.3 `TestPanelDrawing.java`

create a label

```
1  import javax.swing.*;
2  import java.awt.Graphics;
3
4  public class TestPanelDrawing extends JFrame {
5    public TestPanelDrawing() {
6      add(new NewPanel());
7    }
8
9    public static void main(String[] args) {
10     TestPanelDrawing frame = new TestPanelDrawing();
11     frame.setTitle("TestPanelDrawing");
12     frame.setLocationRelativeTo(null); // Center the frame
13     frame.setDefaultCloseOperation(JFrame.EXIT_ON_CLOSE);
14     frame.setSize(200, 100);
15     frame.setVisible(true);
16   }
17 }
18
```

```
19 class NewPanel extends JPanel {
20   protected void paintComponent(Graphics g) {
21     super.paintComponent(g);
22     g.drawLine(0, 0, 50, 50);
23     g.drawString("Banner", 0, 40);
24   }
25 }
```

new panel class

override
paintComponent
draw things in the
superclass

draw a line

All the drawing methods have parameters that specify the locations of the subjects to be drawn. All measurements in Java are made in pixels. The string "Banner" is drawn at location (0, 40).

Note

Invoking `super.paintComponent(g)` (line 21) is necessary to ensure that the viewing area is cleared before a new drawing is displayed.

**super.paint-
Component(g)**

Tip

Some textbooks declare a canvas class by subclassing **JComponent**. The problem is that you have to write the code to paint the background color if you wish to set a background in the canvas. A simple `setBackground(Color color)` method will not set a background color in a **JComponent**.

extends **JComponent?**

13.6 Drawing Strings, Lines, Rectangles, and Ovals

The **drawString(String s, int x, int y)** method draws a string starting at the point (x, y), as shown in Figure 13.6(a).

drawString

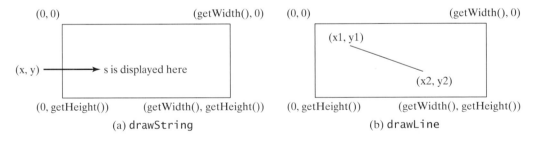

(a) drawString   (b) drawLine

FIGURE 13.6   (a) The **drawString(s, x, y)** method draws a string starting at (x, y). (b) The **drawLine(x1, y1, x2, y2)** method draws a line between two specified points.

The **drawLine(int x1, int y1, int x2, int y2)** method draws a straight line from point (x1, y1) to point (x2, y2), as shown in Figure 13.6(b).

drawLine

Java provides six methods for drawing rectangles in outline or filled with color. You can draw plain rectangles, round-cornered rectangles, or three-dimensional rectangles.

The **drawRect(int x, int y, int w, int h)** method draws a plain rectangle, and the **fillRect(int x, int y, int w, int h)** method draws a filled rectangle. The parameters x and y represent the upper-left corner of the rectangle, and w and h are its width and height (see Figure 13.7).

drawRect
fillRect

The **drawRoundRect(int x, int y, int w, int h, int aw, int ah)** method draws a round-cornered rectangle, and the **fillRoundRect(int x, int y, int w, int h, int aw, int ah)** method draws a filled round-cornered rectangle. Parameters x, y, w, and h are the same as in the **drawRect** method, parameter aw is the horizontal diameter

drawRoundRect

fillRoundRect

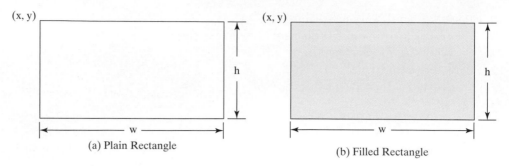

FIGURE 13.7 (a) The `drawRect(x, y, w, h)` method draws a rectangle. (b) The `fillRect(x, y, w, h)` method draws a filled rectangle.

of the arcs at the corner, and `ah` is the vertical diameter of the arcs at the corner (see Figure 13.8(a)). In other words, `aw` and `ah` are the width and the height of the oval that produces a quarter-circle at each corner.

draw3DRect

The `draw3DRect(int x, int y, int w, int h, boolean raised)` method draws a 3D rectangle and the `fill3DRect(int x, int y, int w, int h, boolean raised)`

fill3DRect

method draws a filled 3D rectangle. The parameters `x`, `y`, `w`, and `h` are the same as in the `drawRect` method. The last parameter, a Boolean value, indicates whether the rectangle is raised above the surface or sunk into the surface.

Depending on whether you wish to draw an oval in outline or filled solid, you can use either

drawOval

the `drawOval(int x, int y, int w, int h)` method or the `fillOval(int x, int y,`

fillOval

`int w, int h)` method. An oval is drawn based on its bounding rectangle. Parameters `x` and `y` indicate the top-left corner of the bounding rectangle, and `w` and `h` indicate the width and height, respectively, of the bounding rectangle, as shown in Figure 13.8(b).

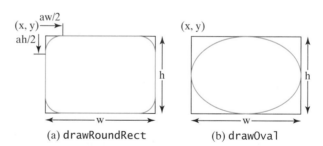

FIGURE 13.8 (a) The `drawRoundRect(x, y, w, h, aw, ah)` method draws a round-cornered rectangle. (b) The `drawOval(x, y, w, h)` method draws an oval based on its bounding rectangle.

13.7 Case Study: The **FigurePanel** Class

This example develops a useful class for displaying various figures. The class enables the user to set the figure type and specify whether the figure is filled, and displays the figure on a panel. The UML diagram for the class is shown in Figure 13.9. The panel can display lines, rectangles, round-cornered rectangles, and ovals. Which figure to display is decided by the `type` property. If the `filled` property is `true`, the rectangle, round-cornered rectangle, and oval are filled in the panel.

The UML diagram serves as the contract for the `FigurePanel` class. The user can use the class without knowing how the class is implemented. Let us begin by writing a program in Listing 13.4 that uses the class to display six figure panels, as shown in Figure 13.10.

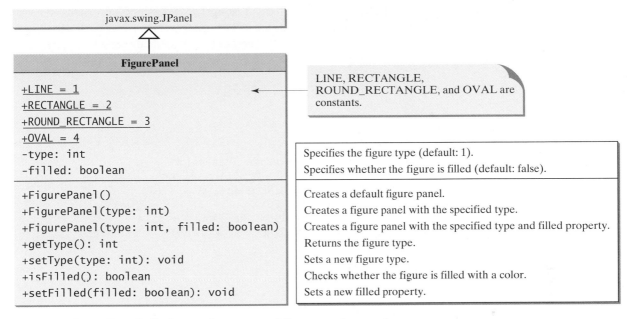

FIGURE 13.9   FigurePanel displays various types of figures on the panel.

LISTING 13.4   TestFigurePanel.java

```
1  import java.awt.*;
2  import javax.swing.*;
3
4  public class TestFigurePanel extends JFrame {
5    public TestFigurePanel() {
6      setLayout(new GridLayout(2, 3, 5, 5));
7      add(new FigurePanel(FigurePanel.LINE));              display lines
8      add(new FigurePanel(FigurePanel.RECTANGLE));         display a rectangle
9      add(new FigurePanel(FigurePanel.ROUND_RECTANGLE));   round-cornered
                                                              rectangle
10     add(new FigurePanel(FigurePanel.OVAL));              display an oval
11     add(new FigurePanel(FigurePanel.RECTANGLE, true));   filled rectangle
12     add(new FigurePanel(FigurePanel.ROUND_RECTANGLE, true)); filled round-
                                                              cornered rectangle
13   }
14
15   public static void main(String[] args) {
16     TestFigurePanel frame = new TestFigurePanel();
17     frame.setSize(400, 200);
18     frame.setTitle("TestFigurePanel");
19     frame.setLocationRelativeTo(null); // Center the frame
20     frame.setDefaultCloseOperation(JFrame.EXIT_ON_CLOSE);
21     frame.setVisible(true);
22   }
23 }
```

FIGURE 13.10   Six FigurePanel objects are created to display six figures.

The `FigurePanel` class is implemented in Listing 13.5. Four constants, `LINE`, `RECTANGLE`, `ROUND_RECTANGLE`, and `OVAL`, are declared in lines 6–9. Four types of figures are drawn according to the **type** property (line 37). The **setColor** method (lines 39, 44, 53, 62) sets a new color for the drawing.

LISTING 13.5 FigurePanel.java

```java
1  import java.awt.*;
2  import javax.swing.JPanel;
3
4  public class FigurePanel extends JPanel {
5    // Define constants
6    public static final int LINE = 1;
7    public static final int RECTANGLE = 2;
8    public static final int ROUND_RECTANGLE = 3;
9    public static final int OVAL = 4;
10
11   private int type = 1;
12   private boolean filled;
13
14   /** Construct a default FigurePanel */
15   public FigurePanel() {
16   }
17
18   /** Construct a FigurePanel with the specified type */
19   public FigurePanel(int type) {
20     this.type = type;
21   }
22
23   /** Construct a FigurePanel with the specified type and filled */
24   public FigurePanel(int type, boolean filled) {
25     this.type = type;
26     this.filled = filled;
27   }
28
29   /** Draw a figure on the panel */
30   public void paintComponent(Graphics g) {
31     super.paintComponent(g);
32
33     // Get the appropriate size for the figure
34     int width = getSize().width;
35     int height = getSize().height;
36
37     switch (type) {
38       case LINE: // Display two cross lines
39         g.setColor(Color.BLACK);
40         g.drawLine(10, 10, width - 10, height - 10);
41         g.drawLine(width - 10, 10, 10, height - 10);
42         break;
43       case RECTANGLE: // Display a rectangle
44         g.setColor(Color.BLUE);
45         if (filled)
46           g.fillRect((int)(0.1 * width), (int)(0.1 * height),
47             (int)(0.8 * width), (int)(0.8 * height));
48         else
49           g.drawRect((int)(0.1 * width), (int)(0.1 * height),
50             (int)(0.8 * width), (int)(0.8 * height));
51         break;
```

constants

override
  paintComponent(g)

check type

draw lines

fill a rectangle

draw a rectangle

```
52        case ROUND_RECTANGLE: // Display a round-cornered rectangle
53          g.setColor(Color.RED);
54          if (filled)
55            g.fillRoundRect((int)(0.1 * width), (int)(0.1 * height),
56              (int)(0.8 * width), (int)(0.8 * height), 20, 20);
57          else
58            g.drawRoundRect((int)(0.1 * width), (int)(0.1 * height),
59              (int)(0.8 * width), (int)(0.8 * height), 20, 20);
60          break;
61        case OVAL: // Display an oval
62          g.setColor(Color.BLACK);
63          if (filled)
64            g.fillOval((int)(0.1 * width), (int)(0.1 * height),
65              (int)(0.8 * width), (int)(0.8 * height));
66          else
67            g.drawOval((int)(0.1 * width), (int)(0.1 * height),
68              (int)(0.8 * width), (int)(0.8 * height));
69      }
70    }
71
72    /** Set a new figure type */
73    public void setType(int type) {
74      this.type = type;
75      repaint();
76    }
77
78    /** Return figure type */
79    public int getType() {
80      return type;
81    }
82
83    /** Set a new filled property */
84    public void setFilled(boolean filled) {
85      this.filled = filled;
86      repaint();
87    }
88
89    /** Check if the figure is filled */
90    public boolean isFilled() {
91      return filled;
92    }
93
94    /** Specify preferred size */
95    public Dimension getPreferredSize() {
96      return new Dimension(80, 80);
97    }
98  }
```

fill round-cornered rect

draw round-cornered rect

fill an oval

draw an oval

repaint panel

repaint panel

override
getPreferredSize()

The `repaint` method (lines 75, 86) is defined in the `Component` class. Invoking `repaint` causes the `paintComponent` method to be called. The `repaint` method is invoked to refresh the viewing area. Typically, you call it if you have new things to display.

Caution

The `paintComponent` method should never be invoked directly. It is invoked either by the JVM whenever the viewing area changes or by the `repaint` method. You should override the `paintComponent` method to tell the system how to paint the viewing area, but never override the `repaint` method.

don't invoke
paintComponent

request repaint using
repaint()

 Note

The `repaint` method lodges a request to update the viewing area and returns immediately. Its effect is asynchronous, and if several requests are outstanding, it is likely that only the last `paintComponent` will be done.

getPreferredSize()

The `getPreferredSize()` method (lines 95–97), defined in `Component`, is overridden in `FigurePanel` to specify the preferred size for the layout manager to consider when laying out a `FigurePanel` object. This property may or may not be considered by the layout manager, depending on its rules. For example, a component uses its preferred size in a container with a `FlowLayout` manager, but its preferred size may be ignored if it is placed in a container with a `GridLayout` manager. It is a good practice to override `getPreferredSize()` in a subclass of `JPanel` to specify a preferred size, because the default preferred size for a `JPanel` is 0 by 0.

13.8 Drawing Arcs

An arc is conceived as part of an oval bounded by a rectangle. The methods to draw or fill an arc are as follows:

```
drawArc(int x, int y, int w, int h, int startAngle, int arcAngle);
fillArc(int x, int y, int w, int h, int startAngle, int arcAngle);
```

Parameters x, y, w, and h are the same as in the `drawOval` method; parameter `startAngle` is the starting angle; `arcAngle` is the spanning angle (i.e., the angle covered by the arc). Angles are measured in degrees and follow the usual mathematical conventions (i.e., 0 degrees is in the easterly direction, and positive angles indicate counterclockwise rotation from the easterly direction); see Figure 13.11.

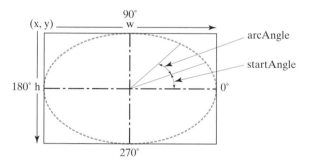

FIGURE 13.11 The `drawArc` method draws an arc based on an oval with specified angles.

Listing 13.6 is an example of how to draw arcs; the output is shown in Figure 13.12.

LISTING 13.6 DrawArcs.java

```java
1  import javax.swing.JFrame;
2  import javax.swing.JPanel;
3  import java.awt.Graphics;
4
5  public class DrawArcs extends JFrame {
6    public DrawArcs() {
7      setTitle("DrawArcs");
```

```
 8        add(new ArcsPanel());
 9      }
10
11    /** Main method */
12    public static void main(String[] args) {
13      DrawArcs frame = new DrawArcs();
14      frame.setLocationRelativeTo(null); // Center the frame
15      frame.setDefaultCloseOperation(JFrame.EXIT_ON_CLOSE);
16      frame.setSize(250, 300);
17      frame.setVisible(true);
18    }
19  }
20
21  // The class for drawing arcs on a panel
22  class ArcsPanel extends JPanel {
23    // Draw four blazes of a fan
24    protected void paintComponent(Graphics g) {
25      super.paintComponent(g);
26
27      int xCenter = getWidth() / 2;
28      int yCenter = getHeight() / 2;
29      int radius = (int)(Math.min(getWidth(), getHeight()) * 0.4);
30
31      int x = xCenter - radius;
32      int y = yCenter - radius;
33
34      g.fillArc(x, y, 2 * radius, 2 * radius, 0, 30);
35      g.fillArc(x, y, 2 * radius, 2 * radius, 90, 30);
36      g.fillArc(x, y, 2 * radius, 2 * radius, 180, 30);
37      g.fillArc(x, y, 2 * radius, 2 * radius, 270, 30);
38    }
39  }
```

add a panel

override
  paintComponent

30° arc from 0°
30° arc from 90°
30° arc from 180°
30° arc from 270°

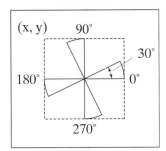

FIGURE 13.12   The program draws four filled arcs.

Note

Angles may be negative. A negative starting angle sweeps clockwise from the easterly direction, as shown in Figure 13.13. A negative spanning angle sweeps clockwise from the starting angle. The following two statements draw the same arc:

negative degrees

```
g.fillArc(x, y, 2 * radius, 2 * radius, -30, -20);
g.fillArc(x, y, 2 * radius, 2 * radius, -50, 20);
```

The first statement uses negative starting angle −30 and negative spanning angle −20, as shown in Figure 13.13(a). The second statement uses negative starting angle −50 and positive spanning angle 20, as shown in Figure 13.13(b).

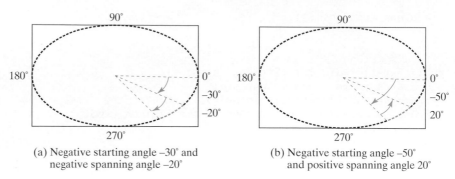

(a) Negative starting angle –30° and   (b) Negative starting angle –50°
negative spanning angle –20°   and positive spanning angle 20°

FIGURE 13.13   Angles may be negative.

13.9 The **Polygon** Class and Drawing Polygons and Polylines

The `Polygon` class encapsulates a description of a closed two-dimensional region within a coordinate space. This region is bounded by an arbitrary number of line segments, each of which is one side (or edge) of the polygon. Internally, a polygon comprises a list of (x, y) coordinate pairs in which each pair defines a vertex of the polygon, and two successive pairs are the endpoints of a line that is a side of the polygon. The first and final pairs of (x, y) points are joined by a line segment that closes the polygon.

The two constructors given below are used to create a `Polygon` object.

- **public** Polygon()
  Constructs an empty polygon.

- **public** Polygon(**int**[] xpoints, **int**[] ypoints, **int** npoints)
  Constructs and initializes a `Polygon` with specified points. Parameters `xpoints` and `ypoints` are arrays representing x-coordinates and y-coordinates, and `npoints` indicates the number of points.

To append a point to the polygon, use the `addPoint(int x, int y)` method. The `Polygon` class has the public data fields `xpoints`, `ypoints`, and `npoints`, which represent the array of x-coordinates and y-coordinates, and the total number of points.

Here is an example of creating a polygon and adding points into it:

```
Polygon polygon = new Polygon();
polygon.addPoint(40, 20);
polygon.addPoint(70, 40);
polygon.addPoint(60, 80);
polygon.addPoint(45, 45);
polygon.addPoint(20, 60);
```

To draw or fill a polygon, use one of the following methods:

```
drawPolygon(Polygon polygon);

fillPolygon(Polygon polygon);

drawPolygon(int[] xpoints, int[] ypoints, int npoints);

fillPolygon(int[] xpoints, int[] ypoints, int npoints);
```

For example:

```
int x[] = {40, 70, 60, 45, 20};
int y[] = {20, 40, 80, 45, 60};
g.drawPolygon(x, y, x.length);
```

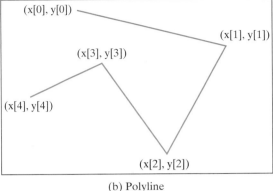

(a) Polygon   (b) Polyline

FIGURE 13.14   The **drawPolygon** method draws a polygon, and the **polyLine** method draws a polyline.

The drawing method opens the polygon by drawing lines between point (x[i], y[i]) and point (x[i+1], y[i+1]) for i = 0, ... , x.length-1; it closes the polygon by drawing a line between the first and last points (see Figure 13.14(a)).

To draw a polyline, use the **drawPolyline(int[] x, int[] y, int nPoints)** method, which draws a sequence of connected lines defined by arrays of x and y coordinates. For example, the following code draws the polyline, as shown in Figure 13.14(b):

```
int x[] = {40, 70, 60, 45, 20};
int y[] = {20, 40, 80, 45, 60};
g.drawPolygon(x, y, x.length);
```

Listing 13.7 is an example of how to draw a hexagon, with the output shown in Figure 13.15.

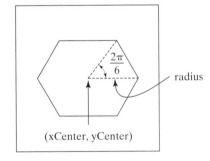

FIGURE 13.15   The program uses the **drawPolygon** method to draw a polygon.

LISTING 13.7 DrawPolygon.java

```
 1  import javax.swing.JFrame;
 2  import javax.swing.JPanel;
 3  import java.awt.Graphics;
 4  import java.awt.Polygon;
 5
 6  public class DrawPolygon extends JFrame {
 7    public DrawPolygon() {
 8      setTitle("DrawPolygon");
 9      add(new PolygonsPanel());                          add a panel
10    }
11
12    /** Main method */
13    public static void main(String[] args) {
14      DrawPolygon frame = new DrawPolygon();
```

```
15        frame.setLocationRelativeTo(null); // Center the frame
16        frame.setDefaultCloseOperation(JFrame.EXIT_ON_CLOSE);
17        frame.setSize(200, 250);
18        frame.setVisible(true);
19    }
20 }
21
22 // Draw a polygon in the panel
23 class PolygonsPanel extends JPanel {
24    protected void paintComponent(Graphics g) {
25      super.paintComponent(g);
26
27      int xCenter = getWidth() / 2;
28      int yCenter = getHeight() / 2;
29      int radius = (int)(Math.min(getWidth(), getHeight()) * 0.4);
30
31      // Create a Polygon object
32      Polygon polygon = new Polygon();
33
34      // Add points to the polygon
35      polygon.addPoint)(xCenter + radius, yCenter);
36      polygon.addPoint)((int)(xCenter + radius *
37        Math.cos(2 * Math.PI / 6)), (int)(yCenter - radius *
38        Math.sin(2 * Math.PI / 6)));
39      polygon.addPoint((int)(xCenter + radius *
40        Math.cos(2 * 2 * Math.PI / 6)), (int)(yCenter - radius *
41        Math.sin(2 * 2 * Math.PI / 6)));
42      polygon.addPoint((int)(xCenter + radius *
43        Math.cos(3 * 2 * Math.PI / 6)), (int)(yCenter - radius *
44        Math.sin(3 * 2 * Math.PI / 6)));
45      polygon.addPoint((int)(xCenter + radius *
46        Math.cos(4 * 2 * Math.PI / 6)), (int)(yCenter - radius *
47        Math.sin(4 * 2 * Math.PI / 6)));
48      polygon.addPoint((int)(xCenter + radius *
49        Math.cos(5 * 2 * Math.PI / 6)), (int)(yCenter - radius *
50        Math.sin(5 * 2 * Math.PI / 6)));
51
52      // Draw the polygon
53      g.drawPolygon(polygon);
54    }
55 }
```

override
paintComponent

add a point

draw polygon

13.10 Centering a Display Using the **FontMetrics** Class

You can display a string at any location in a panel. Can you display it centered? To do so, you need to use the FontMetrics class to measure the exact width and height of the string for a particular font. FontMetrics can measure the following attributes for a given font (see Figure 13.16):

- **Leading**, pronounced *ledding*, is the amount of space between lines of text.

- **Ascent** is the distance from the baseline to the ascent line. The top of most characters in the font will be under the ascent line, but some may extend above the ascent line.

- **Descent** is the distance from the baseline to the descent line. The bottom of most descending characters (e.g., *j*, *y*, and *g*) in the font will be above the descending line, but some may extend below the descending line.

- **Height** is the sum of leading, ascent, and descent.

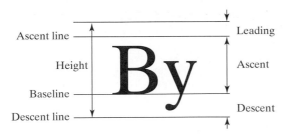

FIGURE 13.16 The FontMetrics class can be used to determine the font properties of characters for a given font.

FontMetrics is an abstract class. To get a FontMetrics object for a specific font, use the following getFontMetrics methods defined in the Graphics class:

- **public** FontMetrics getFontMetrics(Font font)
  Returns the font metrics of the specified font.

- **public** FontMetrics getFontMetrics()
  Returns the font metrics of the current font.

You can use the following instance methods in the FontMetrics class to obtain the attributes of a font and the width of a string when it is drawn using the font:

```
public int getAscent() // Return the ascent
public int getDescent() // Return the descent
public int getLeading() // Return the leading
public int getHeight() // Return the height
public int stringWidth(String str) // Return the width of the string
```

Listing 13.8 gives an example that displays a message in the center of the panel, as shown in Figure 13.17.

FIGURE 13.17 The program uses the FontMetrics class to measure the string width and height, and displays it at the center of the panel.

LISTING 13.8 TestCenterMessage.java

```
1 import javax.swing.*;
2 import java.awt.*;
3
4 public class TestCenterMessage extends JFrame {
5   public TestCenterMessage() {
6     CenterMessage messagePanel = new CenterMessage();
7     add(messagePanel);
8     messagePanel.setBackground(Color.WHITE);
```

create a message panel
add a message panel
set background

set font
```
 9       messagePanel.setFont(new Font("Californian FB", Font.BOLD, 30));
10     }
11
12     /** Main method */
13     public static void main(String[] args) {
14       TestCenterMessage frame = new TestCenterMessage();
15       frame.setLocationRelativeTo(null); // Center the frame
16       frame.setDefaultCloseOperation(JFrame.EXIT_ON_CLOSE);
17       frame.setSize(300, 150);
18       frame.setVisible(true);
19     }
20   }
21
22   class CenterMessage extends JPanel {
23     /** Paint the message */
```
override **paintComponent**
```
24     protected void paintComponent(Graphics g) {
25       super.paintComponent(g);
26
```
get **FontMetrics**
```
27       // Get font metrics for the current font
28       FontMetrics fm = g.getFontMetrics();
29
30       // Find the center location to display
31       int stringWidth = fm.stringWidth("Welcome to Java");
32       int stringAscent = fm.getAscent();
33
34       // Get the position of the leftmost character in the baseline
35       int xCoordinate = getWidth() / 2 - stringWidth / 2;
36       int yCoordinate = getHeight() / 2 + stringAscent / 2;
37
38       g.drawString("Welcome to Java", xCoordinate, yCoordinate);
39     }
40   }
```

The methods `getWidth()` and `getHeight()` (lines 35–36), defined in the `Component` class, return the component's width and height, respectively.

`yCoordinate` is the height of the baseline for the first character of the string to be displayed. When `centered` is `true`, `yCoordinate` should be `getHeight() / 2 + h / 2`, where `h` is the ascent of the string.

`xCoordinate` is the width of the baseline for the first character of the string to be displayed. When `centered` is `true`, `xCoordinate` should be `getWidth() / 2 - stringWidth / 2`.

13.11 Case Study: The **MessagePanel** Class

This case study develops a useful class that displays a message in a panel. The class enables the user to set the location of the message, center the message, and move the message with the specified interval. The contract of the class is shown in Figure 13.18.

Let us first write a test program in Listing 13.9 that uses the `MessagePanel` class to display four message panels, as shown in Figure 13.19.

LISTING 13.9 TestMessagePanel.java

```
1 import java.awt.*;
2 import javax.swing.*;
3
4 public class TestMessagePanel extends JFrame {
5   public TestMessagePanel() {
```

```
 6     MessagePanel messagePanel1 = new MessagePanel("Wecome to Java");     create message panel
 7     MessagePanel messagePanel2 = new MessagePanel("Java is fun");
 8     MessagePanel messagePanel3 = new MessagePanel("Java is cool");
 9     MessagePanel messagePanel4 = new MessagePanel("I love Java");
10     messagePanel1.setFont(new Font("SansSerif", Font.ITALIC, 20));       set font
11     messagePanel2.setFont(new Font("Courier", Font.BOLD, 20));
12     messagePanel3.setFont(new Font("Times", Font.ITALIC, 20));
13     messagePanel4.setFont(new Font("Californian FB", Font.PLAIN, 20));
14     messagePanel1.setBackground(Color.red);                              set background
15     messagePanel2.setBackground(Color.cyan);
16     messagePanel3.setBackground(Color.green);
17     messagePanel4.setBackground(Color.white);
18     messagePanel1.setCentered(true);
19
20     setLayout(new GridLayout(2, 2));
21     add(messagePanel1);                                                  add message panel
22     add(messagePanel2);
23     add(messagePanel3);
24     add(messagePanel4);
25   }
26
27   public static void main(String[] args) {
28     TestMessagePanel frame = new TestMessagePanel();
29     frame.setSize(300, 200);
30     frame.setTitle("TestMessagePanel");
31     frame.setLocationRelativeTo(null); // Center the frame
32     frame.setDefaultCloseOperation(JFrame.EXIT_ON_CLOSE);
33     frame.setVisible(true);
34   }
35 }
```

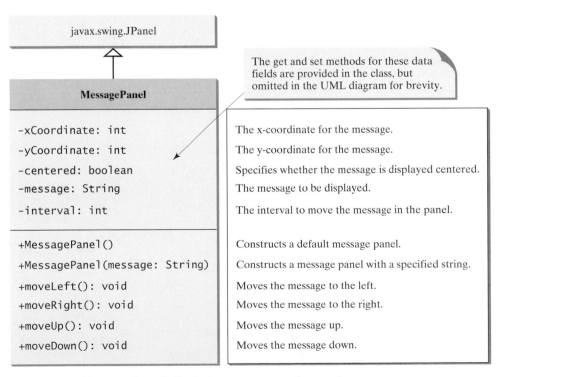

FIGURE 13.18 MessagePanel displays a message on the panel.

FIGURE 13.19 `TestMessagePanel` uses `MessagePanel` to display four message panels.

The `MessagePanel` class is implemented in Listing 13.10. The program seems long but is actually simple, because most of the methods are `get` and `set` methods, and each method is relatively short and easy to read.

LISTING 13.10 MessagePanel.java

```
 1 import java.awt.FontMetrics;
 2 import java.awt.Dimension;
 3 import java.awt.Graphics;
 4 import javax.swing.JPanel;
 5
 6 public class MessagePanel extends JPanel {
 7   /** The message to be displayed */
 8   private String message = "Welcome to Java";
 9
10   /** The x coordinate where the message is displayed */
11   private int xCoordinate = 20;
12
13   /** The y coordinate where the message is displayed */
14   private int yCoordinate = 20;
15
16   /** Indicate whether the message is displayed in the center */
17   private boolean centered;
18
19   /** The interval for moving the message horizontally and vertically */
20   private int interval = 10;
21
22   /** Construct with default properties */
23   public MessagePanel() {
24   }
25
26   /** Construct a message panel with a specified message */
27   public MessagePanel(String message) {
28     this.message = message;
29   }
30
31   /** Return message */
32   public String getMessage() {
33     return message;
34   }
35
36   /** Set a new message */
37   public void setMessage(String message) {
38     this.message = message;
39     repaint();
40   }
41
```

repaint panel

```
42    /** Return xCoordinator */
43    public int getXCoordinate() {
44      return xCoordinate;
45    }
46
47    /** Set a new xCoordinator */
48    public void setXCoordinate(int x) {
49      this.xCoordinate = x;
50      repaint();                                                    repaint panel
51    }
52
53    /** Return yCoordinator */
54    public int getYCoordinate() {
55      return yCoordinate;
56    }
57
58    /** Set a new yCoordinator */
59    public void setYCoordinate(int y) {
60      this.yCoordinate = y;
61      repaint();                                                    repaint panel
62    }
63
64    /** Return centered */
65    public boolean isCentered() {
66      return centered;
67    }
68
69    /** Set a new centered */
70    public void setCentered(boolean centered) {
71      this.centered = centered;
72      repaint();                                                    repaint panel
73    }
74
75    /** Return interval */
76    public int getInterval() {
77      return interval;
78    }
79
80    /** Set a new interval */
81    public void setInterval(int interval) {
82      this.interval = interval;
83      repaint();                                                    repaint panel
84    }
85
86    /** Paint the message */
87    protected void paintComponent(Graphics g) {                    override
88      super.paintComponent(g);                                       paintComponent
89
90      if (centered) {                                              check centered
91        // Get font metrics for the current font
92        FontMetrics fm = g.getFontMetrics();
93
94        // Find the center location to display
95        int stringWidth = fm.stringWidth(message);
96        int stringAscent = fm.getAscent();
97        // Get the position of the leftmost character in the baseline
98        xCoordinate = getWidth() / 2 - stringWidth / 2;
99        yCoordinate = getHeight() / 2 + stringAscent / 2;
100     }
101
```

```
102        g.drawString(message, xCoordinate, yCoordinate);
103    }
104
105    /** Move the message left */
106    public void moveLeft() {
107      xCoordinate -= interval;
108      repaint();
109    }
110
111    /** Move the message right */
112    public void moveRight() {
113      xCoordinate += interval;
114      repaint();
115    }
116
117    /** Move the message up */
118    public void moveUp() {
119      yCoordinate -= interval;
120      repaint();
121    }
122
123    /** Move the message down */
124    public void moveDown() {
125      yCoordinate += interval;
126      repaint();
127    }
128
129    /** Override get method for preferredSize */
130    public Dimension getPreferredSize() {
131      return new Dimension(200, 30);
132    }
133 }
```

override
getPreferredSize

The `paintComponent` method displays the message centered, if the `centered` property is `true` (line 90). `message` is initialized to `"Welcome to Java"` in line 8. If it is not initialized, a `NullPointerException` runtime error would occur when you create a `MessagePanel` using the no-arg constructor, because `message` would be `null` in line 102.

Caution

The `MessagePanel` class uses the properties `xCoordinate` and `yCoordinate` to specify the position of the message displayed on the panel. Do not use the property names `x` and `y`, because they are already defined in the `Component` class to return the position of the component in the parent's coordinate system using `getX()` and `getY()`.

Note

The `Component` class has the `setBackground`, `setForeground`, and `setFont` methods. These methods are for setting colors and fonts for the entire component. Suppose you want to draw several messages in a panel with different colors and fonts; you have to use the `setColor` and `setFont` methods in the `Graphics` class to set the color and font for the current drawing.

Note

design classes for reuse

One of the key features of Java programming is the reuse of classes. Throughout the book, reusable classes are developed and later reused. `MessagePanel` is an example of this, as are `Loan` in §7.15 and `FigurePanel` in §13.7. It can be reused whenever you need to display a message on a panel. To make your class reusable in a wide range of applications, you should provide a variety of ways to use it. `MessagePanel` provides many properties and methods that will be used in several examples in the book.

13.12 (Optional) Case Study: The **StillClock** Class

This case study develops a class that displays a clock on a panel. The contract of the class is shown in Figure 13.20.

FIGURE 13.20 StillClock displays an analog clock.

Let us first write a test program in Listing 13.11 that uses the StillClock class to display an analog clock and uses the MessagePanel class to display the hour, minute, and second in a panel, as shown in Figure 13.21(a).

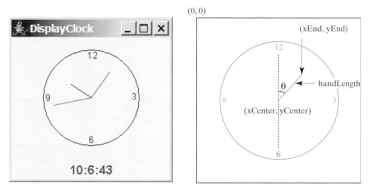

FIGURE 13.21 (a) The DisplayClock program displays a clock that shows the current time. (b) The end-point of a clock hand can be determined given the spanning angle, the hand length, and the center point.

LISTING 13.11 DisplayClock.java

```
1 import java.awt.*;
2 import javax.swing.*;
3
4 public class DisplayClock extends JFrame {
5   public DisplayClock() {
6     // Create an analog clock for the current time
7     StillClock clock = new StillClock();          create a clock
8
```

create a message
panel

```
 9     // Display hour, minute, and seconds in the message panel
10     MessagePanel messagePanel = new MessagePanel(clock.getHour() +
11       ":"+ clock.getMinute() + ":"+ clock.getSecond());
12     messagePanel.setCentered(true);
13     messagePanel.setForeground(Color.blue);
14     messagePanel.setFont(new Font("Courier", Font.BOLD, 16));
15
16     // Add the clock and message panel to the frame
17     add(clock);
18     add(messagePanel, BorderLayout.SOUTH);
19   }
20
21   public static void main(String[] args) {
22     DisplayClock frame = new DisplayClock();
23     frame.setTitle("DisplayClock");
24     frame.setLocationRelativeTo(null); // Center the frame
25     frame.setDefaultCloseOperation(JFrame.EXIT_ON_CLOSE);
26     frame.setSize(300, 350);
27     frame.setVisible(true);
28   }
29 }
```

add a clock
add a message panel

skip implementation?

implementation

The rest of this section explains how to implement the StillClock class. Since you can use the class without knowing how it is implemented, you can skip the implementation if you wish.

To draw a clock, you need to draw a circle and three hands for second, minute, and hour. To draw a hand, you need to specify the two ends of the line. As shown in Figure 13.21(b), one end is the center of the clock at (xCenter, yCenter); the other end, at (xEnd, yEnd), is determined by the following formula:

```
xEnd = xCenter + handLength x sin(θ)
yEnd = yCenter - handLength x cos(θ)
```

Since there are sixty seconds in one minute, the angle for the second hand is

```
second x (2π/60)
```

The position of the minute hand is determined by the minute and second. The exact minute value combined with seconds is minute + second/60. For example, if the time is 3 minutes and 30 seconds, the total minutes are 3.5. Since there are sixty minutes in one hour, the angle for the minute hand is

```
(minute + second/60) x (2π/60)
```

Since one circle is divided into twelve hours, the angle for the hour hand is

```
(hour + minute/60 + second/(60 x 60))) x (2π/12)
```

For simplicity, you can omit the seconds in computing the angles of the minute hand and the hour hand, because they are very small and can be neglected. Therefore, the end-points for the second hand, minute hand, and hour hand can be computed as:

```
xSecond = xCenter + secondHandLength x sin(second x (2π/60))
ySecond = yCenter - secondHandLength x cos(second x (2π/60))
xMinute = xCenter + minuteHandLength x sin(minute x (2π/60))
yMinute = yCenter - minuteHandLength x cos(minute x (2π/60))
xHour = xCenter + hourHandLength x sin((hour + minute/60) x (2π/60)))
yHour = yCenter - hourHandLength x cos((hour + minute/60) x (2π/60)))
```

The StillClock class is implemented in Listing 13.12.

LISTING 13.12 StillClock.java

```
1  import java.awt.*;
2  import javax.swing.*;
3  import java.util.*;
4
5  public class StillClock extends JPanel {
6    private int hour;
7    private int minute;
8    private int second;
9
10   /** Construct a default clock with the current time */
11   public StillClock() {
12     setCurrentTime();
13   }
14
15   /** Construct a clock with specified hour, minute, and second */
16   public StillClock(int hour, int minute, int second) {
17     this.hour = hour;
18     this.minute = minute;
19     this.second = second;
20   }
21
22   /** Return hour */
23   public int getHour() {
24     return hour;
25   }
26
27   /** Set a new hour */
28   public void setHour(int hour) {
29     this.hour = hour;
30     repaint();                                                      repaint panel
31   }
32
33   /** Return minute */
34   public int getMinute() {
35     return minute;
36   }
37
38   /** Set a new minute */
39   public void setMinute(int minute) {
40     this.minute = minute;
41     repaint();                                                      repaint panel
42   }
43
44   /** Return second */
45   public int getSecond() {
46     return second;
47   }
48
49   /** Set a new second */
50   public void setSecond(int second) {
51     this.second = second;
52     repaint();                                                      repaint panel
53   }
54
55   /** Draw the clock */
56   protected void paintComponent(Graphics g) {
57     super.paintComponent(g);                                       override
58                                                                     paintComponent
```

```
59      // Initialize clock parameters
60      int clockRadius =
61        (int)(Math.min(getWidth(), getHeight()) * 0.8 * 0.5);
62      int xCenter = getWidth() / 2;
63      int yCenter = getHeight() / 2;
64
65      // Draw circle
66      g.setColor(Color.black);
67      g.drawOval(xCenter - clockRadius, yCenter - clockRadius,
68        2 * clockRadius, 2 * clockRadius);
69      g.drawString("12", xCenter - 5, yCenter - clockRadius + 12);
70      g.drawString("9", xCenter - clockRadius + 3, yCenter + 5);
71      g.drawString("3", xCenter + clockRadius - 10, yCenter + 3);
72      g.drawString("6", xCenter - 3, yCenter + clockRadius - 3);
73
74      // Draw second hand
75      int sLength = (int)(clockRadius * 0.8);
76      int xSecond = (int)(xCenter + sLength *
77        Math.sin(second * (2 * Math.PI / 60)));
78      int ySecond = (int)(yCenter - sLength *
79        Math.cos(second * (2 * Math.PI / 60)));
80      g.setColor(Color.red);
81      g.drawLine(xCenter, yCenter, xSecond, ySecond);
82
83      // Draw minute hand
84      int mLength = (int)(clockRadius * 0.65);
85      int xMinute = (int)(xCenter + mLength *
86        Math.sin(minute * (2 * Math.PI / 60)));
87      int yMinute = (int)(yCenter - mLength *
88        Math.cos(minute * (2 * Math.PI / 60)));
89      g.setColor(Color.blue);
90      g.drawLine(xCenter, yCenter, xMinute, yMinute);
91
92      // Draw hour hand
93      int hLength = (int)(clockRadius * 0.5);
94      int xHour = (int)(xCenter + hLength *
95        Math.sin((hour % 12 + minute / 60.0) * (2 * Math.PI / 12)));
96      int yHour = (int)(yCenter - hLength *
97        Math.cos((hour % 12 + minute / 60.0) * (2 * Math.PI / 12)));
98      g.setColor(Color.green);
99      g.drawLine(xCenter, yCenter, xHour, yHour);
100   }
101
102   public void setCurrentTime() {
103     // Construct a calendar for the current date and time
104     Calendar calendar = new GregorianCalendar();
105
106     // Set current hour, minute, and second
107     this.hour = calendar.get(Calendar.HOUR_OF_DAY);
108     this.minute = calendar.get(Calendar.MINUTE);
109     this.second = calendar.get(Calendar.SECOND);
110   }
111
112   public Dimension getPreferredSize() {
113     return new Dimension(200, 200);
114   }
115 }
```

get current time (line 104)

override *getPreferredSize* (lines 112–113)

The program enables the clock size to adjust as the frame resizes. Every time you resize the frame, the `paintComponent` method is automatically invoked to paint the new frame. The `paintComponent` method displays the clock in proportion to the panel width (`getWidth()`) and height (`getHeight()`) (lines 60–63 in `StillClock`).

Note

Like the `MessagePanel` class, the `StillClock` class is an example of a reusable class. `StillClock` will be used throughout the book. `StillClock` provides many properties and methods that enable it to be used in a wide range of applications.

design classes for reuse

13.13 (Optional) Displaying Images

You learned how to create image icons and display them in labels and buttons in §12.10, "Image Icons." For example, the following statements create an image icon and display it in a label:

```
ImageIcon icon = new ImageIcon("image/us.gif");
JLabel jlblImage = new JLabel(imageIcon);
```

An image icon displays a fixed-size image. To display an image in a flexible size, you need to use the `java.awt.Image` class. An image can be created from an image icon using the `getImage()` method as follows:

```
Image image = imageIcon.getImage();
```

Using a label as an area for displaying images is simple and convenient, but you don't have much control over how the image is displayed. A more flexible way to display images is to use the `drawImage` method of the `Graphics` class on a panel. Four versions of the `drawImage` method are shown in Figure 13.22.

java.awt.Graphics	
+drawImage(image: Image, x: int, y: int, bgcolor: Color, observer: ImageObserver): void	Draws the image in a specified location. The image's top-left corner is at (x, y) in the graphics context's coordinate space. Transparent pixels in the image are drawn in the specified color bgcolor. The observer is the object on which the image is displayed. The image is cut off if it is larger than the area it is being drawn on.
+drawImage(image: Image, x: int, y: int, observer: ImageObserver): void	Same as the preceding method except that it does not specify a background color.
+drawImage(image: Image, x: int, y: int, width: int, height: int, observer: ImageObserver): void	Draws a scaled version of the image that can fill all of the available space in the specified rectangle.
+drawImage(image: Image, x: int, y: int, width: int, height: int, bgcolor: Color, observer: ImageObserver): void	Same as the preceding method except that it provides a solid background color behind the image being drawn.

FIGURE 13.22 You can apply the `drawImage` method on a `Graphics` object to display an image in a GUI component.

`ImageObserver` is an asynchronous update interface that receives notifications of image information as the image is constructed. The `Component` class implements `ImageObserver`. Therefore, every GUI component is an instance of `ImageObserver`. To draw images using the `drawImage` method in a Swing component, such as `JPanel`, override the `paintComponent` method to tell the component how to display the image in the panel.

Note

You can also create an `ImageIcon` from an `Image` object using `new ImageIcon(image)`.

Listing 13.13 gives the code that displays an image from **image/us.gif**. The file **image/us.gif** (line 12) is under the **class** directory. The **Image** from the file is created in lines 11–14. The **drawImage** method displays the image to fill in the whole panel, as shown in Figure 13.23.

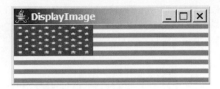

FIGURE 13.23 An image is displayed in a panel.

LISTING 13.13 DisplayImage.java

```
 1  import java.awt.*;
 2  import javax.swing.*;
 3
 4  public class DisplayImage extends JFrame {
 5    public DisplayImage() {
 6      add(new ImageCanvas());
 7    }
 8
 9    public static void main(String[] args) {
10      JFrame frame = new DisplayImage();
11      frame.setTitle("DisplayImage");
12      frame.setSize(300, 300);
13      frame.setLocationRelativeTo(null); // Center the frame
14      frame.setDefaultCloseOperation(JFrame.EXIT_ON_CLOSE);
15      frame.setVisible(true);
16    }
17  }
18
19  class ImageCanvas extends JPanel {
20    ImageIcon imageIcon = new ImageIcon("image/us.gif");
21    Image image = imageIcon.getImage();
22
23    /** Draw image on the panel */
24    public void paintComponent(Graphics g) {
25      super.paintComponent(g);
26
27      if (image != null)
28        g.drawImage(image, 0, 0, getWidth(), getHeight(), this);
29    }
30  }
```

add panel (line 6)

create image icon (line 20)
get image (line 21)

override
 paintComponent (line 24)

draw image (line 28)

13.14 (Optional) Case Study: The **ImageViewer** Class

Displaying an image is a common task in Java programming. This case study develops a reusable component named **ImageViewer** that displays an image on a panel. The class contains the properties **image**, **stretched**, **xCoordinate**, and **yCoordinate**, with associated accessor and mutator methods, as shown in Figure 13.24.

You can use images in Swing components like **JLabel** and **JButton**, but these images are not stretchable. The image in an **ImageViewer** can be stretched.

stretchable image

Let us write a test program in Listing 13.14 that displays six images using the **ImageViewer** class. Figure 13.25 shows a sample run of the program.

FIGURE 13.24   The ImageViewer class displays an image on a panel.

LISTING 13.14   SixFlags.java

```
1 import javax.swing.*;
2 import java.awt.*;
3
4 public class SixFlags extends JFrame {
5   public SixFlags() {
6     Image image1 = new ImageIcon("image/us.gif").getImage();
7     Image image2 = new ImageIcon("image/ca.gif").getImage();
8     Image image3 = new ImageIcon("image/india.gif").getImage();
9     Image image4 = new ImageIcon("image/uk.gif").getImage();
10    Image image5 = new ImageIcon("image/china.gif").getImage();
11    Image image6 = new ImageIcon("image/norway.gif").getImage();
12
13    setLayout(new GridLayout(2, 0, 5, 5));
14    add(new ImageViewer(image1));
15    add(new ImageViewer(image2));
16    add(new ImageViewer(image3));
17    add(new ImageViewer(image4));
18    add(new ImageViewer(image5));
19    add(new ImageViewer(image6));
20  }
21
22  public static void main(String[] args) {
23    SixFlags frame = new SixFlags();
24    frame.setTitle("SixFlags");
25    frame.setLocationRelativeTo(null); // Center the frame
26    frame.setDefaultCloseOperation(JFrame.EXIT_ON_CLOSE);
27    frame.setSize(400, 320);
28    frame.setVisible(true);
29  }
30 }
```

create image

create image viewer

FIGURE 13.25   Six images are displayed in six ImageViewer components.

implementation

skip implementation?

The `ImageViewer` class is implemented in Listing 13.15. (*Note: You may skip the implementation.*) The accessor and mutator methods for the properties `image`, `stretched`, `xCoordinate`, and `yCoordinate` are easy to implement. The `paintComponent` method (lines 26–35) displays the image on the panel. Line 29 ensures that the image is not null before displaying it. Line 30 checks whether the image is stretched or not.

LISTING 13.15 `ImageViewer.java`

```java
1  import java.awt.*;
2  import javax.swing.*;
3
4  public class ImageViewer extends JPanel {
5    /** Hold value of property image. */
6    private java.awt.Image image;
7
8    /** Hold value of property stretched. */
9    private boolean stretched = true;
10
11   /** Hold value of property xCoordinate. */
12   private int xCoordinate;
13
14   /** Hold value of property yCoordinate. */
15   private int yCoordinate;
16
17   /** Construct an empty image viewer */
18   public ImageViewer() {
19   }
20
21   /** Construct an image viewer for a specified Image object */
22   public ImageViewer(Image image) {
23     this.image = image;
24   }
25
26   protected void paintComponent(Graphics g)  {
27     super.paintComponent(g);
28
29     if(image != null)
30       if (isStretched())
31         g.drawImage(image, xCoordinate, yCoordinate,
32           getSize().width, getSize().height, this);
33       else
34         g.drawImage(image, xCoordinate, yCoordinate, this);
35   }
36
37   /** Return value of property image */
38   public java.awt.Image getImage() {
39     return image;
40   }
41
42   /** Set a new value for property image */
43   public void setImage(java.awt.Image image) {
44     this.image = image;
45     repaint();
46   }
47
48   /** Return value of property stretched */
49   public boolean isStretched() {
50     return stretched;
51   }
52
```

properties

constructor

constructor

image null?

stretched

non-stretched

```
53   /** Set a new value for property stretched */
54   public void setStretched(boolean stretched) {
55     this.stretched = stretched;
56     repaint();
57   }
58
59   /** Return value of property xCoordinate */
60   public int getXCoordinate() {
61     return xCoordinate;
62   }
63
64   /** Set a new value for property xCoordinate */
65   public void setXCoordinate(int xCoordinate) {
66     this.xCoordinate = xCoordinate;
67     repaint();
68   }
69
70   /** Return value of property yCoordinate */
71   public int getYCoordinate() {
72     return yCoordinate;
73   }
74
75   /** Set a new value for property yCoordinate */
76   public void setYCoordinate(int yCoordinate) {
77     this.yCoordinate = yCoordinate;
78     repaint();
79   }
80 }
```

CHAPTER SUMMARY

- Each component has its own coordinate system with the origin (`0, 0`) at the upper-left corner of the window. The *x*-coordinate increases to the right, and the *y*-coordinate increases downward.

- The `Graphics` class is an abstract class for displaying figures and images on the screen on different platforms. The `Graphics` class is implemented on the native platform in the JVM. When you use the `paintComponent(g)` method to paint on a GUI component, this `g` is an instance of a concrete subclass of the abstract `Graphics` class for the specific platform. The `Graphics` class encapsulates the platform details and enables you to draw things uniformly without concern for the specific platform.

- Invoking `super.paintComponent(g)` is necessary to ensure that the viewing area is cleared before a new drawing is displayed. The user can request the component to be redisplayed by invoking the `repaint()` method defined in the `Component` class. Invoking `repaint()` causes `paintComponent` to be invoked by the JVM. The user should never invoke `paintComponent` directly. For this reason, the protected visibility is sufficient for `paintComponent`.

- Normally you use `JPanel` as a canvas. To draw on a `JPanel`, you create a new class that extends `JPanel` and overrides the `paintComponent` method to tell the panel how to draw things.

- You can set fonts for the components or subjects you draw, and use font metrics to measure font size. Fonts and font metrics are encapsulated in the classes `Font` and

FontMetrics. FontMetrics can be used to compute the exact length and width of a string, which is helpful for measuring the size of a string in order to display it in the right position.

■ The Component class has the setBackground, setForeground, and setFont methods. These methods are used to set colors and fonts for the entire component. Suppose you want to draw several messages in a panel with different colors and fonts; you have to use the setColor and setFont methods in the Graphics class to set the color and font for the current drawing.

■ To display an image, first create an image icon. You can then use ImageIcon's getImage() method to get an Image object for the image and draw the image using the drawImage method in the java.awt.Graphics class.

REVIEW QUESTIONS

Sections 13.2–13.3

13.1 Suppose that you want to draw a new message below an existing message. Should the x, y coordinate increase or decrease?

13.2 Why does jlblBanner.getGraphics() in line 9 in Listing 13.1 return null? What is the reason for showing the message dialog box in line 19 in Listing 13.1? In line 9, jlblBanner.getGraphics() is used to return a Graphics object. In line 21, why do you have to use frame.jlblBanner.getGraphics() in the main method?

Sections 13.4–13.5

13.3 Describe the paintComponent method. Where is it defined? How is it invoked? Can it be directly invoked? Can the program cause this method to be invoked?

13.4 Why is the paintComponent method protected? What happens if you change it to public or private in a subclass? Why is super.paintComponent(g) invoked in line 25 in Listing 13.2 and in line 21 in Listing 13.3?

13.5 Can you draw things on any Swing GUI component? Why should you use a panel as a canvas for drawings rather than a label or a button?

Sections 13.6–13.9

13.6 Describe the methods for drawing strings, lines, rectangles, round-cornered rectangles, 3D rectangles, ovals, arcs, polygons, and polylines.

13.7 Describe the methods for filling rectangles, round-cornered rectangle, ovals, arcs, and polygons.

13.8 How do you get and set colors and fonts in a Graphics object?

13.9 Write a statement to draw the following shapes:
   ■ Draw a thick line from (10, 10) to (70, 30). You can draw several lines next to each other to create the effect of one thick line.
   ■ Draw/fill a rectangle of width 100 and height 50 with the upper-left corner at (10, 10).
   ■ Draw/fill a round-cornered rectangle with width 100, height 200, corner horizontal diameter 40, and corner vertical diameter 20.
   ■ Draw/fill a circle with radius 30.

- Draw/fill an oval with width 50 and height 100.
- Draw the upper half of a circle with radius 50.
- Draw/fill a polygon connecting the following points: (20, 40), (30, 50), (40, 90), (90, 10), (10, 30).
- Draw a 3-D cube like the one in Figure 13.26.

FIGURE 13.26   Use the drawLine method to draw a 3-D cube.

Sections 13.10–13.12

13.10   How do you find the leading, ascent, descent, and height of a font? How do you find the exact length of a string in a Graphics object?

13.11   If message is not initialized in line 8 in Listing 13.9, MessagePanel.java, what would happen when you create a MessagePanel using its no-arg constructor?

13.12   The following program is supposed to display a message on the panel, but nothing is displayed. There are problems in lines 2 and 14. Identify them.

```
1 public class TestDrawMessage extends javax.swing.JFrame {
2   public void TestDrawMessage() {
3     add(new DrawMessage());
4   }
5
6   public static void main(String[] args) {
7     javax.swing.JFrame frame = new TestDrawMessage();
8     frame.setSize(100, 200);
9     frame.setVisible(true);
10   }
11 }
12
13 class DrawMessage extends javax.swing.JPanel {
14   protected void PaintComponent(java.awt.Graphics g) {
15     super.paintComponent(g);
16     g.drawString("Welcome to Java", 20, 20);
17   }
18 }
```

Sections 13.13–13.14

13.13   How do you create an Image object from the ImageIcon object?

13.14   How do you create an ImageIcon object from an Image object?

13.15   Describe the drawImage method in the Graphics class.

13.16   Explain the differences between displaying images in a JLabel and in a JPanel.

13.17   Which package contains ImageIcon, and which contains Image?

PROGRAMMING EXERCISES

Sections 13.2–13.9

13.1* (*Displaying a 3 × 3 grid*) Write a program that displays a 3 × 3 grid, as shown in Figure 13.27(a). Use red color for vertical lines and blue color for horizontal lines.

FIGURE 13.27 (a) Exercise 13.1 displays a grid. (b) Exercise 13.2 displays two objects of `OvalButton`. (c) Exercise 13.3 displays a checkerboard.

13.2** (*Creating a custom button class*) Develop a custom button class named `OvalButton` that extends `JButton` and displays the button text inside an oval. Figure 13.27(b) shows two buttons created using the `OvalButton` class.

13.3* (*Displaying a checkerboard*) Write a program that displays a checkerboard, as shown in Figure 13.27(c).

13.4* (*Displaying a multiplication table*) Write a program that displays a multiplication table in a panel using the drawing methods, as shown in Figure 13.28(a).

 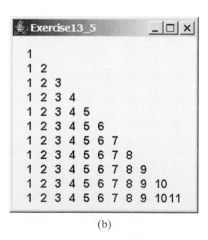

(a)   (b)

FIGURE 13.28 (a) Exercise 13.4 displays a multiplication table. (b) Exercise 13.5 displays numbers in a triangle formation.

13.5** (*Displaying numbers in a triangular pattern*) Write a program that displays numbers in a triangular pattern, as shown in Figure 13.28(b). The number of lines in the display changes to fit the window as the window resizes.

13.6** (*Improving FigurePanel*) The `FigurePanel` class in Listing 13.5 can display lines, rectangles, round-cornered rectangles, and ovals. Add appropriate new code in the class to display arcs and polygons. Write a test program to display the shapes as shown in Figure 13.29(a), using the new `FigurePanel` class.

(a)   (b)   (c)

FIGURE 13.29   (a) Four panels of geometric figures are displayed in a frame of `GridLayout`. (b) `TicTacToe` cells display X, O, or nothing randomly. (c) Exercise 13.8 draws an octagon.

13.7** (*Displaying a TicTacToe board*) Create a custom panel that displays X, O, or nothing. What to display is randomly decided whenever a panel is repainted. Use the `Math.random()` method to generate an integer 0, 1, or 2, which corresponds to displaying X, O, or nothing. Create a frame that contains nine custom panels, as shown in Figure 13.29(b).

13.8** (*Drawing an octagon*) Write a program that draws an octagon, as shown in Figure 13.29(c).

13.9* (*Creating four fans*) Write a program that places four fans in a frame of `GridLayout` with two rows and two columns, as shown in Figure 13.30(a).

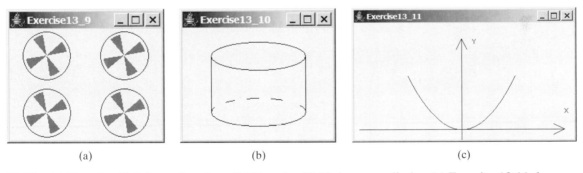

(a)   (b)   (c)

FIGURE 13.30   (a) Exercise 13.9 draws four fans. (b) Exercise 13.10 draws a cylinder. (c) Exercise 13.11 draws a diagram for function $f(x) = x^2$.

13.10* (*Creating a cylinder*) Write a program that draws a cylinder, as shown in Figure 13.30(b).

13.11** (*Plotting the square function*) Write a program that draws a diagram for the function $f(x) = x^2$ (see Figure 13.30(c)).

 Hint

Add points to a polygon `p` using the following loop:

```
double scaleFactor = 0.1;
for (int x = -100; x <= 100; x++) {
  p.addPoint(x + 200, 200 - (int)(scaleFactor * x * x));
}
```

Connect the points using **g.drawPolyline(p.xpoints, p.ypoints, p.npoints)** for a **Graphics** object **g**. **p.xpoints** returns an array of **x** coordinates, **p.ypoints** returns an array of **y** coordinates, and **p.npoints** returns the number of points in **Polygon** object **p**.

13.12**(*Plotting the sine function*) Write a program that draws a diagram for the sine function, as shown in Figure 13.31(a).

 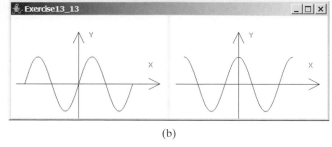

(a) (b)

FIGURE 13.31 (a) Exercise 13.12 draws a diagram for function $f(x) = sin(x)$. (b) Exercise 13.13 draws the sine and cosine functions.

 Hint

The Unicode for π is \u03c0. To display -2π use **g.drawString("-2\u03c0", x, y)**. For a trigonometric function like **sin(x)**, x is in radians. Use the following loop to add the points to a polygon **p**:

```
for (int x = -100; x <= 100; x++) {
  p.addPoint(x + 200,
    100 - (int)(50 * Math.sin((x / 100.0) * 2 * Math.PI)));
}
```

-2π is at (100, 100), the center of the axis is at (200, 100), and 2π is at (300, 100). Use the **drawPolyline** method in the **Graphics** class to connect the points.

13.13**(*Plotting functions using generic methods*) Write a generic class that draws the diagram for a function. The class is defined as follows:

```
public abstract class AbstractDrawFunction extends JPanel {
  /** Polygon to hold the points */
  private Polygon p = new Polygon();

  protected AbstractDrawFunction () {
    drawFunction();
  }

  /** Return the y coordinate */
  abstract double f(double x);

  /** Obtain points for x coordinates 100, 101, ..., 300 */
  public void drawFunction() {
    for (int x = -100; x <= 100; x++) {
      p.addPoint(x + 200, 200 - (int)f(x));
    }
  }

  /** Implement paintComponent to draw axes, labels, and
   *  connecting points
   */
```

```
    protected void paintComponent(Graphics g) {
      // To be completed by you
    }
  }
```

Test the class with the following functions:

```
  f(x) = x²;
  f(x) = sin(x);
  f(x) = cos(x);
  f(x) = tan(x);
  f(x) = cos(x) + 5sin(x);
  f(x) = cos(x) + 5sin(x);
  f(x) = log(x) + x²;
```

For each function, create a class that extends the `AbstractDrawFunction` class and implements the `f` method. Figure 13.31(b) displays the drawings for the sine function and the cosine function.

13.14** (*Displaying a bar chart*) Write a program that uses a bar chart to display the percentages of the overall grade represented by projects, quizzes, midterm exams, and the final exam, as shown in Figure 13.32(a). Suppose that projects take **20** percent and are displayed in red, quizzes take **10** percent and are displayed in blue, midterm exams take **30** percent and are displayed in green, and the final exam takes **40** percent and is displayed in orange.

(a)   (b)

FIGURE 13.32   Exercise 13.14 and Exercise 13.15 use a bar chart and a pie chart to show the percentages of projects, quizzes, midterm exams, and final exam in the overall grade.

13.15** (*Displaying a pie chart*) Write a program that uses a pie chart to display the percentages of the overall grade represented by projects, quizzes, midterm exams, and the final exam, as shown in Figure 13.32(b). Suppose that projects take **20** percent and are displayed in red, quizzes take **10** percent and are displayed in blue, midterm exams take **30** percent and are displayed in green, and the final exam takes **40** percent and is displayed in orange.

13.16   (*Obtaining font information*) Write a program that displays the message "Java is fun" in a panel. Set the panel's font to TimesRoman, bold, and 20-pixel. Display the font's leading, ascent, descent, height, and the string width as a tool tip text for the panel, as shown in Figure 13.33(a).

(a)   (b)

FIGURE 13.33   (a) Exercise 13.16 displays font properties in a tool tip text. (b) Exercise 13.17 uses `MessagePanel` to display four strings.

13.17 (*Using the `MessagePanel` class*) Write a program that displays four messages, as shown in Figure 13.33(b).

13.18 (*Using the `StillClock` class*) Write a program that displays two clocks. The hour, minute, and second values are **4**, **20**, **45** for the first clock, and **22**, **46**, **15** for the second clock, as shown in Figure 13.34(a).

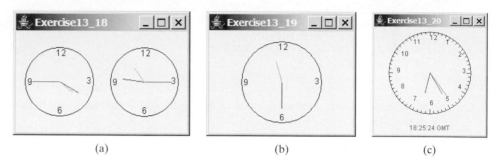

(a)   (b)   (c)

FIGURE 13.34   (a) Exercise 13.18 displays two clocks. (b) Exercise 13.19 displays a clock with random hour and minute values. (c) Exercise 13.20 displays a detailed clock.

13.19* (*Random time*) Modify the `StillClock` class with three new Boolean properties: `hourHandVisible`, `minuteHandVisible`, and `secondHandVisible`, and their associated accessor and mutator methods. You can use the set methods to make a hand visible or invisible. Write a test program that displays only the hour and minute hands. The hour and minute values are randomly generated. The hour is between **0** and **11**, and the minute is either **0** or **30**, as shown in Figure 13.34(b).

13.20** (*Drawing a detailed clock*) Modify the `StillClock` class in §13.12, "Case Study: The `StillClock` Class," to draw the clock with more details on the hours and minutes, as shown in Figure 13.34(c).

13.21** (*Displaying a TicTacToe board with images*) Rewrite Exercise 12.7 to display an image in a `JPanel` instead of displaying an image icon in a `JLabel`.

CHAPTER 14

EVENT-DRIVEN PROGRAMMING

Objectives

- To start learning about event-driven programming with a simple example (§14.1).

- To explain the concept of event-driven programming (§14.2).

- To understand events, event sources, and event classes (§14.2).

- To declare listener classes and write the code to handle events (§14.3).

- To register listener objects in the source object (§14.3).

- To declare inner classes and anonymous inner classes (§§14.3.1–14.3.2).

- To create listeners using inner classes and anonymous inner classes (§14.3.2).

- To understand how an event is handled (§14.3).

- To write programs to deal with `ActionEvent` (§14.3).

- To write programs to deal with `MouseEvent` (§14.4).

- To write programs to deal with `KeyEvent` (§14.5).

- (Optional) To use the `Timer` class to control animations (§14.6).

14.1 Introduction

event-driven programming

All the programs so far execute in a procedural order. This chapter introduces event-driven programming. In *event-driven programming*, code is executed when an event occurs (e.g., a button click or a mouse movement).

Before delving into event-driven programming, it is helpful to get a taste using a simple example. The example displays a button in the frame. A message is displayed on the console when a button is clicked, as shown in Figure 14.1.

FIGURE 14.1 A message is displayed when clicking the button.

The program is given in Listing 14.1. When a button is clicked, an event is fired from the button. The button is the source of the event. A listener object is created in line 11 and is registered with the button in line 12. When an action event occurs on the button, the button notifies the listener by invoking the listener's `actionPerformed` method (line 27).

LISTING 14.1 SimpleEventdemo.java

```
1  import javax.swing.*;
2  import java.awt.event.*;
3  import java.awt.*;
4
5  public class SimpleEventDemo extends JFrame {
6    public SimpleEventDemo() {
7      JButton jbtOK = new JButton("OK");
8      setLayout(new FlowLayout());
9      add(jbtOK);
10
11     ActionListener listener = new OKListener();
12     jbtOK.addActionListener(listener);
13   }
14
15   /** Main method */
16   public static void main(String[] args) {
17     JFrame frame = new SimpleEventDemo();
18     frame.setTitle("SimpleEventDemo");
19     frame.setLocationRelativeTo(null); // Center the frame
20     frame.setDefaultCloseOperation(JFrame.EXIT_ON_CLOSE);
21     frame.setSize(220, 80);
22     frame.setVisible(true);
23   }
24 }
25
26 class OKListener implements ActionListener {
27   public void actionPerformed(ActionEvent e) {
28     System.out.println("It is OK");
29   }
30 }
```

create listener
register listener

listener class
handle event

Now that you have had a taste of event-driven programming, you probably have many questions, such as why a listener class is declared to implement the `ActionListener` interface. This chapter will give you all the answers.

14.2 Event and Event Source

When you run Java GUI programs, the program interacts with the user and the events drive its execution. An *event* can be defined as a signal to the program that something has happened. Events are triggered either by external user actions, such as mouse movements, button clicks, and keystrokes, or by internal program activities, such as a timer. The program can choose to respond to or ignore an event.

event

The component on which an event is *fired* or *generated* is called the *source object* or *source component*. For example, a button is the source object for a button-clicking action event. An event is an instance of an event class. The root class of the event classes is `java.util.EventObject`. The hierarchical relationships of some event classes are shown in Figure 14.2.

source object

fire event

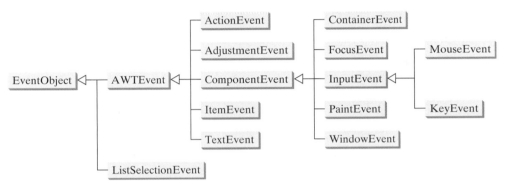

FIGURE 14.2   An event is an object of the `EventObject` class.

An event object contains whatever properties are pertinent to the event. You can identify the source object of an event using the `getSource()` instance method in the `EventObject` class. The subclasses of `EventObject` deal with special types of events, such as action events, window events, component events, mouse events, and key events. Table 14.1 lists external user actions, source objects, and event types fired.

`getSource()`

 Note
If a component can fire an event, any subclass of the component can fire the same type of event. For example, every GUI component can fire `MouseEvent`, `KeyEvent`, `FocusEvent`, and `ComponentEvent`, since `Component` is the superclass of all GUI components.

 Note
All the event classes in Figure 14.2 are included in the `java.awt.event` package except `ListSelectionEvent`, which is in the `javax.swing.event` package. AWT events were originally designed for AWT components, but many Swing components fire them.

14.3 Listeners, Registrations, and Handling Events

Java uses a delegation-based model for event handling: a source object fires an event, and an object interested in the event handles the event. The latter object is called a *listener*. Two things are needed for an object to be a listener for an event on a source object, as shown in Figure 14.3.

listener

TABLE 14.1 User Action, Source Object, and Event Type

User Action	Source Object	Event Type Fired
Click a button	`JButton`	`ActionEvent`
Press return on a text field	`JTextField`	`ActionEvent`
Select a new item	`JComboBox`	`ItemEvent, ActionEvent`
Select item(s)	`JList`	`ListSelectionEvent`
Click a check box	`JCheckBox`	`ItemEvent, ActionEvent`
Click a radio button	`JRadioButton`	`ItemEvent, ActionEvent`
Select a menu item	`JMenuItem`	`ActionEvent`
Move the scroll bar	`JScrollBar`	`AdjustmentEvent`
Window opened, closed, iconified, deiconified, or closing	`Window`	`WindowEvent`
Mouse pressed, released, clicked, entered, or exited	`Component`	`MouseEvent`
Mouse moved or dragged	`Component`	`MouseEvent`
Key released or pressed	`Component`	`KeyEvent`
Component added or removed from the container	`Container`	`ContainerEvent`
Component moved, resized, hidden, or shown	`Component`	`ComponentEvent`
Component gained or lost focus	`Component`	`FocusEvent`

(a) A generic source component with a generic listener

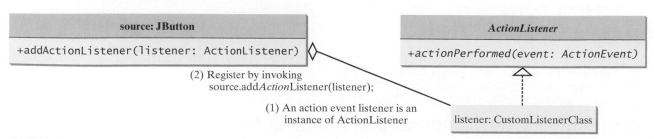

(b) A JButton source component with an ActionListener

FIGURE 14.3 A listener must be an instance of a listener interface and must be registered with a source component.

1. The listener object must be an instance of the corresponding event-listener interface to ensure that the listener has the correct method for processing the event. Java provides a *listener interface* for every type of GUI event. The listener interface is usually named *X*`Listener` for *X*`Event`, with the exception of `MouseMotionListener`. For example, the corresponding listener interface for `ActionEvent` is `ActionListener`; each listener for `ActionEvent` should implement the `ActionListener` interface. Table 14.2 lists event types, the corresponding listener interfaces, and the methods defined in the listener interfaces. The listener interface contains the method(s), known as the *handler(s)*, invoked by the source object to process the event.

listener interface
X`Event`/*X*`Listener`
`ActionEvent`/`Action-`
`    Listener`

handler

TABLE 14.2   Events, Event Listeners, and Listener Methods

Event Class (Handlers)	Listener Interface	Listener Methods
`ActionEvent`	`ActionListener`	`actionPerformed(ActionEvent)`
`ItemEvent`	`ItemListener`	`itemStateChanged(ItemEvent)`
`MouseEvent`	`MouseListener`	`mousePressed(MouseEvent)`
		`mouseReleased(MouseEvent)`
		`mouseEntered(MouseEvent)`
		`mouseExited(MouseEvent)`
		`mouseClicked(MouseEvent)`
	`MouseMotionListener`	`mouseDragged(MouseEvent)`
		`mouseMoved(MouseEvent)`
`KeyEvent`	`KeyListener`	`keyPressed(KeyEvent)`
		`keyReleased(KeyEvent)`
		`keyTyped(KeyEvent)`
`WindowEvent`	`WindowListener`	`windowClosing(WindowEvent)`
		`windowOpened(WindowEvent)`
		`windowIconified(WindowEvent)`
		`windowDeiconified(WindowEvent)`
		`windowClosed(WindowEvent)`
		`windowActivated(WindowEvent)`
		`windowDeactivated(WindowEvent)`
`ContainerEvent`	`ContainerListener`	`componentAdded(ContainerEvent)`
		`componentRemoved(ContainerEvent)`
`ComponentEvent`	`ComponentListener`	`componentMoved(ComponentEvent)`
		`componentHidden(ComponentEvent)`
		`componentResized(ComponentEvent)`
		`componentShown(ComponentEvent)`
`FocusEvent`	`FocusListener`	`focusGained(FocusEvent)`
		`focusLost(FocusEvent)`
`AdjustmentEvent`	`AdjustmentListener`	`adjustmentValueChanged (AdjustmentEvent)`

2. The listener object must be registered by the source object. Registration methods are dependent on the event type. For **ActionEvent**, the method is **addActionListener**. In general, the method is named **addXListener** for *XEvent*. A source object may fire several types of events. For each event, the source object maintains a list of listeners and notifies all the registered listeners by invoking the *handler* on the listener object to respond to the event, as shown in Figure 14.4. (Figure 14.4 shows the internal implementation of a source class. It addresses the question how a handler is invoked.)

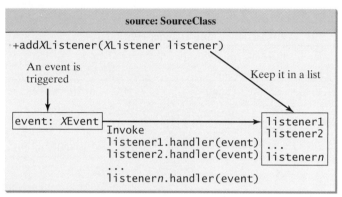

(a) Internal function of a generic source object

(b) Internal function of a JButton object

FIGURE 14.4 The source object notifies the listeners of the event by invoking the handler of the listener object.

Now you have the answers to all your questions about the simple example in Listing 14.1. Since a **JButton** object fires **ActionEvent**, a listener object for **ActionEvent** must be an instance of **ActionListener**, so the listener class implements **ActionListener** in line 26. The source object invokes **addActionListener(listener)** to register a listner, as follows:

```
JButton jbt = new JButton("OK"); // Line 7 in Listing 14.1
ActionListener listener = new OKListener(); // Line 11 in Listing 14.1
jbt.addActionListener(listener ); // Line 12 in Listing 14.1
```

When you click the button, the **JButton** object fires an **ActionEvent** and passes it to invoke the listener's **actionPerformed** method to handle the event.

The event object contains information pertinent to the event, which can be obtained using the methods, as shown in Figure 14.5. For example, you can use **e.getSource()** to obtain

java.util.EventObject	
+getSource(): Object	Returns the source object for the event.

java.awt.event.AWTEvent

java.awt.event.ActionEvent	
+getActionCommand(): String	Returns the command string associated with this action. For a button, its text is the command string.
+getModifiers(): int	Returns the modifier keys held down during this action event.
+getWhen(): long	Returns the timestamp when this event occurred. The time is the number of milliseconds since January 1, 1970, 00:00:00 GMT.

FIGURE 14.5 You can obtain useful information from an event object.

the source object in order to determine whether it is a button, a check box, or a radio button. For an action event, you can use `e.getWhen()` to obtain the time when the event occurs.

14.3.1   Inner Class Listeners

A listener class is designed specifically to create a listener object for a GUI component (e.g., a button). The listener class will not be shared by other applications and therefore is appropriately defined inside the frame class as an inner class.

An *inner class*, or *nested class*, is a class defined within the scope of another class. The   inner class
code in Figure 14.6(a) declares two separate classes, `Test` and `A`. The code in Figure 14.6(b) declares `A` as an inner class in `Test`.

```
public class Test {
    ...
}

public class A {
    ...
}
```
(a)

```
public class Test {
    ...

    // Inner class
    public class A {
        ...
    }
}
```
(b)

```
// OuterClass.java: inner class demo
public class OuterClass {
    private int data;

    /** A method in the outer class */
    public void m() {
        // Do something
    }

    // An inner class
    class InnerClass {
        /** A method in the inner class */
        public void mi() {
            // Directly reference data and method
            // defined in its outer class
            data++;
            m();
        }
    }
}
```
(c)

FIGURE 14.6 Inner classes combine dependent classes into the primary class.

The class `InnerClass` defined inside `OuterClass` in Figure 14.6(c) is another example of an inner class. An inner class may be used just like a regular class. Normally, you declare a class an inner class if it is only used by its outer class. An inner class has the following features:

- An inner class is compiled into a class named *OuterClassName$InnerClassName*.class. For example, the inner class **A** in **Test** is compiled into *Test$A*.class in Figure 14.6(b).

- An inner class can reference the data and methods defined in the outer class in which it nests, so you do not need to pass the reference of an object of the outer class to the constructor of the inner class. For this reason, inner classes can make programs simple and concise.

- An inner class can be declared with a visibility modifier subject to the same visibility rules applied to a member of the class.

- An inner class can be declared **static**. A **static** inner class can be accessed using the outer class name. A **static** inner class cannot access non-static members of the outer class.

- Objects of an inner class are often created in the outer class. But you can also create an object of an inner class from another class. If the inner class is non-static, you must first create an instance of the outer class, then use the following syntax to create an object for the inner class:

```
OuterClass.InnerClass innerObject = outerObject.new InnerClass();
```

- If the inner class is static, use the following syntax to create an object for it:

```
OuterClass.InnerClass innerObject = new OuterClass.InnerClass();
```

Tip
A simple use of inner classes is to combine dependent classes into a primary class. This reduces the number of source files. It also makes class files easy to organize, since all the class files are named with the primary class as the prefix. For example, rather than creating two source files, Test.java and A.java, in Figure 14.6(a), you can combine class **A** into class **Test** and create just one source file, Test.java, in Figure 14.6(b). The resulting class files are Test.class and Test$A.class.

Listing 14.1 can now be modified using an inner class.

LISTING 14.2 SimpleEventDemoInnerClass.java

```
 1  import javax.swing.*;
 2  import java.awt.event.*;
 3  import java.awt.*;
 4
 5  public class SimpleEventDemoInnerClass extends JFrame {
 6    public SimpleEventDemoInnerClass() {
 7      JButton jbtOK = new JButton("OK");
 8      setLayout(new FlowLayout());
 9      add(jbtOK);
10
11      ActionListener listener = new OKListener();
12      jbtOK.addActionListener(listener);
13    }
14
15    /** Main method */
16    public static void main(String[] args) {
17      JFrame frame = new SimpleEventDemoInnerClass();
18      frame.setTitle("SimpleEventDemoInnerClass");
```

create listener
register listener

```
19      frame.setLocationRelativeTo(null); // Center the frame
20      frame.setDefaultCloseOperation(JFrame.EXIT_ON_CLOSE);
21      frame.setSize(220, 80);
22      frame.setVisible(true);
23    }
24
25    private class OKListener implements ActionListener {
26      public void actionPerformed(ActionEvent e) {
27        System.out.println("It is OK");
28      }
29    }
30  }
```

Inner class

listener class
handle event

Listing 14.2 is the same as Listing 14.1 except that the `OKListener` class is now an inner class. As an inner class, it can conveniently reference data and methods in the frame class. Since the listener class will not be used by applications outside the frame class, it is declared `private`.

The interaction between the source and the listener is shown in Figure 14.7.

1. **jbtOK** registers `listener` by invoking `addActionListener(listener)`.

2. **jbtOK** invokes `listener`'s `actionPerformed` method to process an `ActionEvent`.

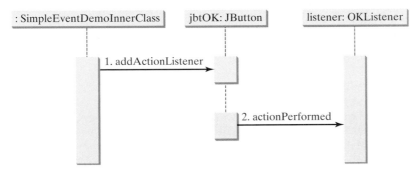

FIGURE 14.7   The source invokes `actionPerformed` in the listener (`OKListener`) to handle an `ActionEvent`.

14.3.2   Anonymous Inner Class Listeners

Inner class listeners can be shortened using anonymous inner classes. An *anonymous inner class* is an inner class without a name. It combines declaring an inner class and creating an instance of the class in one step. An anonymous inner class is declared as follows:

anonymous inner class

```
new SuperClassName/InterfaceName() {
    // Implement or override methods in superclass or interface
    // Other methods if necessary
}
```

Since an anonymous inner class is a special kind of inner class, it is treated like an inner class in many ways. In addition, it has the following features:

■ An anonymous inner class must always extend a superclass or implement an interface, but it cannot have an explicit **extends** or **implements** clause.

■ An anonymous inner class must implement all the abstract methods in the superclass or in the interface.

■ An anonymous inner class always uses the no-arg constructor from its superclass to create an instance. If an anonymous inner class implements an interface, the constructor is `Object()`.

■ An anonymous inner class is compiled into a class named OuterClassName$*n*.class. For example, if the outer class `Test` has two anonymous inner classes, they are compiled into Test$1.class and Test$2.class.

Listing 14.3 is an example of rewriting the preceding example using anonymous inner classes.

LISTING 14.3 `SimpleEventDemoAnonymousInnerClass.java`

```
1  import javax.swing.*;
2  import java.awt.event.*;
3  import java.awt.*;
4
5  public class SimpleEventDemoAnonymousInnerClass extends JFrame {
6    public SimpleEventDemoAnonymousInnerClass() {
7      JButton jbtOK = new JButton("OK");
8      setLayout(new FlowLayout());
9      add(jbtOK);
10
11     // Create and register anonymous inner class listener
12     jbtOK.addActionListener(new ActionListener() {
13       public void actionPerformed(ActionEvent e) {
14         System.out.println("It is OK");
15       }
16     });
17   }
18
19   /** Main method */
20   public static void main(String[] args) {
21     JFrame frame = new SimpleEventDemoAnonymousInnerClass();
22     frame.setTitle("SimpleEventDemoAnonymousInnerClass");
23     frame.setLocationRelativeTo(null); // Center the frame
24     frame.setDefaultCloseOperation(JFrame.EXIT_ON_CLOSE);
25     frame.setSize(220, 80);
26     frame.setVisible(true);
27   }
28 }
```

anonymous listener
handle event

The anonymous listener (lines 12–16) in this example works the same way as the inner class listener in the preceding example. The program is condensed using an anonymous inner class.

Anonymous inner classes are compiled into `OuterClassName$#.class`, where # starts at 1 and is incremented for each anonymous class encountered by the compiler. In this example, the anonymous inner class is compiled into `SimpleEventDemoAnonymous InnerClass$1.class`.

Pedagogical Note
Anonymous adapters make programs simple and concise, and enable handlers to access data and methods in the outer class. From here on, this book will use anonymous inner class event adapters to implement listeners.

anonymous adapter
advantages

14.3.3 Example: Handling Simple Action Events

This example writes a program that displays two buttons, OK and Cancel, in a frame. A message is displayed on the console to indicate which button and when it is clicked, as shown in Figure 14.8. The program is given in Listing 14.4.

FIGURE 14.8 The program responds to the button action events.

LISTING 14.4 TestActionEvent.java

```
1  import javax.swing.*;
2  import java.awt.*;
3  import java.awt.event.*;
4
5  public class TestActionEvent extends JFrame {
6    private JButton jbtOK = new JButton("OK");                          create buttons
7    private JButton jbtCancel = new JButton("Cancel");
8
9    public TestActionEvent() {
10     setLayout(new FlowLayout());                                      set FlowLayout
11
12     add(jbtOK);                                                       add components
13     add(jbtCancel);
14
15     jbtOK.addActionListener(new ActionListener() {                    create a listener
16       public void actionPerformed(ActionEvent e) {
17         System.out.println("The " + e.getActionCommand() + " button "
18           + "is clicked at\n  " + new java.util.Date(e.getWhen()));
19       }
20     });
21
22     jbtCancel.addActionListener(new ActionListener() {                create a listener
23       public void actionPerformed(ActionEvent e) {
24         System.out.println("The " + e.getActionCommand() + " button "
25           + "is clicked at\n  " + new java.util.Date(e.getWhen()));
26       }
27     });
28   }
29
30   /** Main method */
31   public static void main(String[] args) {
32     TestActionEvent frame = new TestActionEvent();
33     frame.setTitle("TestActionEvent");
34     frame.setDefaultCloseOperation(JFrame.EXIT_ON_CLOSE);
35     frame.setSize(220, 80);
36     frame.setVisible(true);
37   }
38 }
```

The button objects **jbtOK** and **jbtCancel** are the source of **ActionEvent**. Anonymous inner class listeners are used to create listeners for **jbtOK** and **jbtCancel** in lines 15 and 22.

Clicking a button causes the **actionPerformed** method in the listener to be invoked. The **e.getActionCommand()** method returns the action command from the button (line 17). By default, a button's action command is the text of the button.

The **e.getWhen()** method returns the time of the action in milliseconds since January 1, 1970, 00:00:00 GMT. The **Date** class converts the time to year, month, date, hours, minutes, and seconds (line 18).

14.3.4 Example: Handling Window Events

This example writes a program that demonstrates handling window events. Any subclass of the `Window` class can fire the following window events: window opened, closing, closed, activated, deactivated, iconified, and deiconified. The program in Listing 14.5 creates a frame, listens to the window events, and displays a message to indicate the occurring event. Figure 14.9 shows a sample run of the program.

FIGURE 14.9   The window events are displayed on the console when you run the program from a DOS prompt.

LISTING 14.5 TestWindowEvent.java

```
1  import java.awt.event.*;
2  import javax.swing.JFrame;
3
4  public class TestWindowEvent extends JFrame {
5    public static void main(String[] args) {
6      TestWindowEvent frame = new TestWindowEvent();
7      frame.setLocationRelativeTo(null); // Center the frame
8      frame.setDefaultCloseOperation(JFrame.EXIT_ON_CLOSE);
9      frame.setTitle("TestWindowEvent");
10     frame.setSize(220, 80);
11     frame.setVisible(true);
12   }
13
14   public TestWindowEvent() {
15     addWindowListener(new WindowListener() {
16       /**
17        * Handler for window deiconified event
18        * Invoked when a window is changed from a minimized
19        * to a normal state.
20        */
21       public void windowDeiconified(WindowEvent event) {
22         System.out.println("Window deiconified");
23       }
24
25       /**
26        * Handler for window iconified event
27        * Invoked when a window is changed from a normal to a
28        * minimized state. For many platforms, a minimized window
29        * is displayed as the icon specified in the window's
30        * iconImage property.
31        */
32       public void windowIconified(WindowEvent event) {
33         System.out.println("Window iconified");
34       }
35
36       /**
37        * Handler for window activated event
38        * Invoked when the window is set to be the user's
39        * active window, which means the window (or one of its
```

(margin notes) anonymous listener — line 15; override handler — line 21; override handler — line 32

```
40          * subcomponents) will receive keyboard events.
41          */
42         public void windowActivated(WindowEvent event) {        override handler
43           System.out.println("Window activated");
44         }
45
46         /**
47          * Handler for window deactivated event
48          * Invoked when a window is no longer the user's active
49          * window, which means that keyboard events will no longer
50          * be delivered to the window or its subcomponents.
51          */
52         public void windowDeactivated(WindowEvent event) {       override handler
53           System.out.println("Window deactivated");
54         }
55
56         /**
57          * Handler for window opened event
58          * Invoked the first time a window is made visible.
59          */
60         public void windowOpened(WindowEvent event) {
61           System.out.println("Window opened");
62         }
63
64         /**
65          * Handler for window closing event
66          * Invoked when the user attempts to close the window
67          * from the window's system menu.  If the program does not
68          * explicitly hide or dispose the window while processing
69          * this event, the window close operation will be cancelled.
70          */
71         public void windowClosing(WindowEvent event) {           override handler
72           System.out.println("Window closing");
73         }
74
75         /**
76          * Handler for window closed event
77          * Invoked when a window has been closed as the result
78          * of calling dispose on the window.
79          */
80         public void windowClosed(WindowEvent event) {            override handler
81           System.out.println("Window closed");
82         }
83       });
84   }
85 }
```

The `WindowEvent` can be fired by the `Window` class or by any subclass of `Window`. Since `JFrame` is a subclass of `Window`, it can fire `WindowEvent`.

`TestWindowEvent` extends `JFrame` and implements `WindowListener`. The `WindowListener` interface defines several abstract methods (`windowActivated`, `windowClosed`, `windowClosing`, `windowDeactivated`, `windowDeiconified`, `windowIconified`, `windowOpened`) for handling window events when the window is activated, closed, closing, deactivated, deiconified, iconified, or opened.

When a window event, such as activation, occurs, the `windowActivated` method is triggered. Implement the `windowActivated` method with a concrete response if you want the event to be processed.

14.3.5 Listener Interface Adapters

convenience adapter

Because the methods in the `WindowListener` interface are abstract, you must implement all of them even if your program does not care about some of the events. For convenience, Java provides support classes, called *convenience adapters*, which provide default implementations for all the methods in the listener interface. The default implementation is simply an empty body. Java provides convenience listener adapters for every AWT listener interface with multiple handlers. A convenience listener adapter is named *X*Adapter for *X*Listener. For example, `WindowAdapter` is a convenience listener adapter for `WindowListener`. Table 14.3 lists the convenience adapters.

TABLE 14.3 Convenience Adapters

Adapter	Interface
WindowAdapter	WindowListener
MouseAdapter	MouseListener
MouseMotionAdapter	MouseMotionListener
KeyAdapter	KeyListener
ContainerAdapter	ContainerListener
ComponentAdapter	ComponentListener
FocusAdapter	FocusListener

Using `WindowAdapter`, the preceding example can be simplified as shown in Listing 14.6 if you are only interested in the window activated event. The `WindowAdapter` class is used to create an anonymous listener instead of `WindowListener` (line 15). The `windowActivated` handler is implemented in line 16.

LISTING 14.6 TestWindowEvent.java

```
1  import java.awt.event.*;
2  import javax.swing.JFrame;
3
4  public class AdapterDemo extends JFrame {
5    public static void main(String[] args) {
6      AdapterDemo frame = new AdapterDemo();
7      frame.setLocationRelativeTo(null); // Center the frame
8      frame.setDefaultCloseOperation(JFrame.EXIT_ON_CLOSE);
9      frame.setTitle("AdapterDemo");
10     frame.setSize(220, 80);
11     frame.setVisible(true);
12   }
13
14   public AdapterDemo() {
15     addWindowListener(new WindowAdapter() {
16       public void windowActivated(WindowEvent event) {
17         System.out.println("Window activated");
18       }
19     });
20   }
21 }
```

register listener
override handler

14.4 Mouse Events

A mouse event is fired whenever a mouse is pressed, released, clicked, moved, or dragged on a component. The mouse event object captures the event, such as the number of clicks associated with it or the location (x and y coordinates) of the mouse, as shown in Figure 14.10.

java.awt.event.InputEvent	
+getWhen(): long	Returns the timestamp when this event occurred.
+isAltDown(): boolean	Returns true if the Alt modifier is down on this event.
+isControlDown(): boolean	Returns true if the Control modifier is down on this event.
+isMetaDown(): boolean	Returns true if the Meta modifier is down on this event.
+isShiftDown(): boolean	Returns true if the Shift modifier is down on this event.

java.awt.event.MouseEvent	
+getButton(): int	Indicates which mouse button has been clicked.
+getClickCount(): int	Returns the number of mouse clicks associated with this event.
+getPoint():java.awt.Point	Returns a Point object containing the x and y coordinates.
+getX(): int	Returns the x-coordinate of the mouse point.
+getY(): int	Returns the y-coordinate of the mouse point.

FIGURE 14.10 The MouseEvent class encapsulates information for mouse events.

Since the MouseEvent class inherits InputEvent, you can use the methods defined in the InputEvent class on a MouseEvent object.

The java.awt.Point class represents a point on a component. The class contains two   **Point** class
public variables, x and y, for coordinates. To create a Point, use the following constructor:

```
Point(int x, int y)
```

This constructs a Point object with the specified x and y coordinates. Normally, the data fields in a class should be private. This class has two public data fields, which is not a good practice.

Java provides two listener interfaces, MouseListener and MouseMotionListener, to handle mouse events, as shown in Figure 14.11. Implement the MouseListener interface to listen for such actions as pressing, releasing, entering, exiting, or clicking the mouse, and implement the MouseMotionListener interface to listen for such actions as dragging or moving the mouse.

14.4.1 Example: Moving a Message on a Panel Using a Mouse

This example writes a program that displays a message in a panel, as shown in Listing 14.7. You can use the mouse to move the message. The message moves as the mouse drags and is always displayed at the mouse point. A sample run of the program is shown in Figure 14.12.

java.awt.event.MouseListener	
+mousePressed(e: MouseEvent): void	Invoked after the mouse button has been pressed on the source component.
+mouseReleased(e: MouseEvent): void	Invoked after the mouse button has been released on the source component.
+mouseClicked(e: MouseEvent): void	Invoked after the mouse button has been clicked (pressed and released) on the source component.
+mouseEntered(e: MouseEvent): void	Invoked after the mouse enters the source component.
+mouseExited(e: MouseEvent): void	Invoked after the mouse exits the source component.

java.awt.event.MouseMotionListener	
+mouseDragged(e: MouseEvent): void	Invoked after a mouse button is moved with a button pressed.
+mouseMoved(e: MouseEvent): void	Invoked after a mouse button is moved without a button pressed.

FIGURE 14.11 The `MouseListener` interface handles mouse pressed, released, clicked, entered, and exited events. The `MouseMotionListener` interface handles mouse dragged and moved events.

FIGURE 14.12 You can move the message by dragging the mouse.

LISTING 14.7 MoveMessageDemo.java

```
1  import java.awt.*;
2  import java.awt.event.*;
3  import javax.swing.*;
4
5  public class MoveMessageDemo extends JFrame {
6    public MoveMessageDemo() {
7      // Create a MovableMessagePanel instance for moving a message
8      MovableMessagePanel p = new MovableMessagePanel("Welcome to Java");
9
10     // Place the message panel in the frame
11     getContentPane().setLayout(new BorderLayout());
12     getContentPane().add(p);
13   }
14
15   /** Main method */
16   public static void main(String[] args) {
17     MoveMessageDemo frame = new MoveMessageDemo();
18     frame.setTitle("MoveMessageDemo");
19     frame.setLocationRelativeTo(null); // Center the frame
20     frame.setDefaultCloseOperation(JFrame.EXIT_ON_CLOSE);
21     frame.setSize(200, 100);
22     frame.setVisible(true);
23   }
24
```

create a panel

```
25  // Inner class: MovableMessagePanel draws a message
26  static class MovableMessagePanel extends JPanel {                          inner class
27    private String message = "Welcome to Java";
28    private int x = 20;
29    private int y = 20;
30
31    /** Construct a panel to draw string s */
32    public MovableMessagePanel(String s) {
33      message = s;                                                           set a new message
34      addMouseMotionListener(new MouseMotionAdapter() {                      anonymous listener
35        /** Handle mouse dragged event */
36        public void mouseDragged(MouseEvent e) {                             override handler
37          // Get the new location and repaint the screen
38          x = e.getX();                                                      new location
39          y = e.getY();
40          repaint();                                                         repaint
41        }
42      });
43    }
44
45    /** Paint the component */
46    protected void paintComponent(Graphics g) {
47      super.paintComponent(g);
48      g.drawString(message, x, y);
49    }
50  }
51 }
```

The MovableMessagePanel class extends JPanel to draw a message (line 26). Additionally, it handles redisplaying the message when the mouse is dragged. This class is declared as an inner class inside the main class because it is only used in this class. Furthermore, the inner class is declared static because it does not reference any instance members of the main class.

The MouseMotionListener interface contains two handlers, mouseMoved and mouseDragged, for handling mouse-motion events. When you move the mouse with the button pressed, the mouseDragged method is invoked to repaint the viewing area and display the message at the mouse point. When you move the mouse without pressing the button, the mouseMoved method is invoked.

Because the listener is only interested in the mouse dragged event, the anonymous inner class listener extends MouseMotionAdapter to override the mouseDragged method. If the inner class implements the MouseMotionListener interface, you would have to implement all of the handlers even if your listener does not care about some of the events.

The mouseDragged method is invoked when you move the mouse with a button pressed. This method obtains the mouse location using getX and getY methods (lines 38–39) in the MouseEvent class. This becomes the new location for the message. Invoking the repaint() method (line 40) causes paintComponent to be invoked (line 46), which displays the message in a new location.

14.5 Key Events

Key events enable the use of the keys to control and perform actions or get input from the keyboard. A key event is fired whenever a key is pressed, released, or typed on a component. The KeyEvent object describes the nature of the event (namely, that a key has been pressed, released, or typed) and the value of the key, as shown in Figure 14.13. Java provides the KeyListener to handle key events, as shown in Figure 14.14.

The keyPressed handler is invoked when a key is pressed, the keyReleased handler is invoked when a key is released, and the keyTyped handler is invoked when a Unicode

```
  ┌──────────────────────────────────┐
  │   java.awt.event.InputEvent       │
  └──────────────────────────────────┘
                  △
  ┌──────────────────────────────────┐
  │   java.awt.event.KeyEvent         │
  ├──────────────────────────────────┤
  │ +getKeyChar(): char               │    Returns the character associated with the key in this event.
  │ +getKeyCode(): int                │    Returns the integer key code associated with the key in this event.
  └──────────────────────────────────┘
```

FIGURE 14.13 The KeyEvent class encapsulates information about key events.

```
  ┌──────────────────────────────────────┐
  │      java.awt.event.KeyListener       │
  ├──────────────────────────────────────┤
  │ +keyPressed(e: KeyEvent): void        │    Invoked after a key is pressed on the source component.
  │ +keyReleased(e: KeyEvent): void       │    Invoked after a key is released on the source component.
  │ +keyTyped(e: KeyEvent): void          │    Invoked after a key is pressed and then released on the source component.
  └──────────────────────────────────────┘
```

FIGURE 14.14 The KeyListener interface handles key pressed, released, and typed events.

character is entered. If a key does not have a Unicode (e.g., function keys, modifier keys, action keys, and control keys), the keyTyped handler will be not be invoked.

Every key event has an associated key character or key code that is returned by the getKeyChar() or getKeyCode() method in KeyEvent. The key codes are constants defined in Table 14.4. For a key of the Unicode character, the key code is the same as the Unicode value. For the key pressed and key released events, getKeyCode() returns the value as defined in the table. For the key typed event, getKeyCode() returns VK_UNDEFINED.

TABLE 14.4 Key Constants

Constant	Description	Constant	Description
VK_HOME	The Home key	VK_SHIFT	The Shift key
VK_END	The End key	VK_BACK_SPACE	The Backspace key
VK_PGUP	The Page Up key	VK_CAPS_LOCK	The Caps Lock key
VK_PGDN	The Page Down key	VK_NUM_LOCK	The Num Lock key
VK_UP	The up-arrow key	VK_ENTER	The Enter key
VK_DOWN	The down-arrow key	VK_UNDEFINED	The keyCode unknown
VK_LEFT	The left-arrow key	VK_F1 to VK_F12	The function keys from F1 to F12
VK_RIGHT	The right-arrow key		
VK_ESCAPE	The Esc key	VK_0 to VK_9	The number keys from 0 to 9
VK_TAB	The Tab key	VK_A to VK_Z	The letter keys from A to Z
VK_CONTROL	The Control key		

The program in Listing 14.8 displays a user-input character. The user can move the character up, down, left, and right, using the arrow keys VK_UP, VK_DOWN, VK_LEFT, and VK_RIGHT. Figure 14.15 contains a sample run of the program.

LISTING 14.8 KeyEventDemo.java

```java
1 import java.awt.*;
2 import java.awt.event.*;
3 import javax.swing.*;
```

```
 4
 5  public class KeyEventDemo extends JFrame {
 6    private KeyboardPanel keyboardPanel = new KeyboardPanel();          create a panel
 7
 8    /** Initialize UI */
 9    public KeyEventDemo() {
10      // Add the keyboard panel to accept and display user input
11      add(keyboardPanel);
12
13      // Set focus
14      keyboardPanel.setFocusable(true);                                 focusable
15    }
16
17    /** Main method */
18    public static void main(String[] args) {
19      KeyEventDemo frame = new KeyEventDemo();
20      frame.setTitle("KeyEventDemo");
21      frame.setLocationRelativeTo(null); // Center the frame
22      frame.setDefaultCloseOperation(JFrame.EXIT_ON_CLOSE);
23      frame.setSize(300, 300);
24      frame.setVisible(true);
25    }
26
27    // Inner class: KeyboardPanel for receiving key input
28    static class KeyboardPanel extends JPanel {                         inner class
29      private int x = 100;
30      private int y = 100;
31      private char keyChar = 'A'; // Default key
32
33      public KeyboardPanel() {
34        addKeyListener(new KeyAdapter() {                               register listener
35          public void keyPressed(KeyEvent e) {                          override handler
36            switch (e.getKeyCode()) {
37              case KeyEvent.VK_DOWN: y += 10; break;
38              case KeyEvent.VK_UP: y -= 10; break;
39              case KeyEvent.VK_LEFT: x -= 10; break;
40              case KeyEvent.VK_RIGHT: x += 10; break;
41              default: keyChar = e.getKeyChar();                        get the key pressed
42            }
43
44            repaint();                                                  repaint
45          }
46        });
47      }
48
49      /** Draw the character */
50      protected void paintComponent(Graphics g) {
51        super.paintComponent(g);
52
53        g.setFont(new Font("TimesRoman", Font.PLAIN, 24));
54        g.drawString(String.valueOf(keyChar), x, y);                    redraw character
55      }
56    }
57  }
```

The **KeyboardPanel** class extends **JPanel** to display a character (line 28). This class is declared as an inner class inside the main class because it is only used in this class. Furthermore, the inner class is declared static because it does not reference any instance members of the main class.

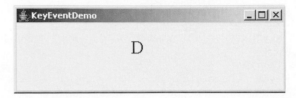

FIGURE 14.15 The program responds to key events by displaying a character and moving it up, down, left, or right.

Because the program gets input from the keyboard, it listens for `KeyEvent` and extends `KeyAdapter` to handle key input (line 34).

When a key is pressed, the `keyPressed` handler is invoked. The program uses `e.getKeyCode()` to obtain the key code and `e.getKeyChar()` to get the character for the key. When a non-arrow key is pressed, the key is displayed (line 41). When an arrow key is pressed, the character moves in the direction indicated by the arrow key (lines 37–40).

focusable

Only a focused component can receive `KeyEvent`. To make a component *focusable*, set its `isFocusable` property to `true` (line 14).

efficient?

Every time the component is repainted, a new font is created for the `Graphics` object in line 53. This is not efficient. It is better to create the font one time as a data field.

14.6 (Optional) Animation Using the `Timer` Class

Not all source objects are GUI components. The `javax.swing.Timer` class is a source component that fires an `ActionEvent` at a predefined rate. Figure 14.16 lists some of the methods in the class.

javax.swing.Timer	
+Timer(delay: int, listener: ActionListener)	Creates a Timer object with a specified delay in milliseconds and an ActionListener.
+addActionListener(listener: ActionListener): void	Adds an ActionListener to the timer.
+start(): void	Starts this timer.
+stop(): void	Stops this timer.
+setDelay(delay: int): void	Sets a new delay value for this timer.

FIGURE 14.16 A `Timer` object fires an `ActionEvent` at a fixed rate.

A `Timer` object serves as the source of an `ActionEvent`. The listeners must be instances of `ActionListener` and registered with a `Timer` object. You create a `Timer` object using its sole constructor with a delay and a listener, where `delay` specifies the number of milliseconds between two action events. You can add additional listeners using the `addActionListener` method, and adjust the `delay` using the `setDelay` method . To start the timer, invoke the `start()` method. To stop the timer, invoke the `stop()` method.

The `Timer` class can be used to control animations. For example, you can use it to display a moving message, as shown in Figure 14.17, with the code in Listing 14.9.

FIGURE 14.17 A message moves in the panel.

LISTING 14.9   AnimationDemo.java

```
1 import java.awt.*;
2 import java.awt.event.*;
3 import javax.swing.*;
4
5 public class AnimationDemo extends JFrame {
6   public AnimationDemo() {
7     // Create a MovingMessagePanel for displaying a moving message
8     add(new MovingMessagePanel("message moving?"));                    create panel
9   }
10
11  /** Main method */
12  public static void main(String[] args) {
13    AnimationDemo frame = new AnimationDemo();
14    frame.setTitle("AnimationDemo");
15    frame.setLocationRelativeTo(null); // Center the frame
16    frame.setDefaultCloseOperation(JFrame.EXIT_ON_CLOSE);
17    frame.setSize(280, 100);
18    frame.setVisible(true);
19  }
20
21  //Inner class: Displaying a moving message
22  static class MovingMessagePanel extends JPanel {
23    private String message = "Welcome to Java";
24    private int xCoordinate = 0;
25    private int yCoordinate = 20;
26
27    public MovingMessagePanel(String message) {
28      this.message = message;                                          set message
29
30      // Create a timer
31      Timer timer = new Timer(1000, new TimerListener());              create timer
32      timer.start();                                                   start timer
33    }
34
35    /** Paint message */
36    public void paintComponent(Graphics g) {
37      super.paintComponent(g);
38
39      if (xCoordinate > getWidth()) {
40        xCoordinate = -20;                                             reset x-coordinate
41      }
42      xCoordinate += 5;
43      g.drawString(message, xCoordinate, yCoordinate);                 move message
44    }
45
46    class TimerListener implements ActionListener {                    listener class
47      /** Handle ActionEvent */                                        event handler
48      public void actionPerformed(ActionEvent e) {
49        repaint();                                                     repaint
50      }
51    }
52  }
53 }
```

The `MovingMessagePanel` class extends `JPanel` to display a message (line 22). This class
is declared as an inner class inside the main class because it is only used in this class.

Furthermore, the inner class is declared static because it does not reference any instance members of the main class.

An inner class listener is declared in line 46 to listener for `ActionEvent`. Line 31 creates a `Timer` for the listener. The timer is started in line 32. The timer fires an `ActionEvent` every second, and the listener responds in line 49 to repaint the panel. When a panel is painted, its *x* coordinate is increased (line 42), so the message is displayed to the right. When the x coordinate exceeds the bound of the panel, it is reset to −20 (line 40), so the message continues moving from left to right.

In §13.12, "Case Study: The `StillClock` Class," you drew a `StillClock` to show the current time. The clock does not tick after it is displayed. What can you do to make the clock display a new current time every second? The key to making the clock tick is to repaint it every second with a new current time. You can use a timer to control the repainting of the clock with the code in Listing 14.10.

LISTING 14.10 ClockAnimation.java

```
 1  import java.awt.event.*;
 2  import javax.swing.*;
 3
 4  public class ClockAnimation extends StillClock {
 5    public ClockAnimation() {
 6      // Create a timer with delay 1000 ms
 7      Timer timer = new Timer(1000, new TimerListener());
 8      timer.start();
 9    }
10
11    private class TimerListener implements ActionListener {
12      /** Handle the action event */
13      public void actionPerformed(ActionEvent e) {
14        // Set new time and repaint the clock to display current time
15        setCurrentTime();
16        repaint();
17      }
18    }
19
20    /** Main method */
21    public static void main(String[] args) {
22      JFrame frame = new JFrame("ClockAnimation");
23      ClockAnimation clock = new ClockAnimation();
24      frame.add(clock);
25      frame.setLocationRelativeTo(null); // Center the frame
26      frame.setDefaultCloseOperation(JFrame.EXIT_ON_CLOSE);
27      frame.setSize(200, 200);
28      frame.setVisible(true);
29    }
30  }
```

create timer
start timer

listener class

implement handler

set new time
repaint

The program displays a running clock, as shown in Figure 14.18. `ClockAnimation` extends `StillClock` and repaints the clock every 1 second triggered by a timer. Line 7 creates a `Timer` for a `ClockAnimation`. The timer is started in line 8 when a `ClockAnimation` is constructed. The timer fires an `ActionEvent` every second, and the listener responds in line 15 to set a new time and repaint the clock. The `setCurrentTime()` method defined in `StillClock` sets the current time in the clock.

FIGURE 14.18   A live clock is displayed in the panel.

KEY TERMS

anonymous inner class 471	event listener interface 467
convenience listener adapter 476	event object 465
event 465	event registration 467
event delegation 465	event source (source object) 465
event handler 467	event-driven programming 464
event listener 464	inner class? 469

CHAPTER SUMMARY

■ The root class of the event classes is `java.util.EventObject`. The subclasses of `EventObject` deal with special types of events, such as action events, window events, component events, mouse events, and key events. You can identify the source object of an event using the `getSource()` instance method in the `EventObject` class. If a component can fire an event, any subclass of the component can fire the same type of event.

■ The listener object's class must implement the corresponding event-listener interface. Java provides a listener interface for every event class. The listener interface is usually named *X*`Listener` for *X*`Event`, with the exception of `MouseMotionListener`. For example, the corresponding listener interface for `ActionEvent` is `ActionListener`; each listener for `ActionEvent` should implement the `ActionListener` interface. The listener interface contains the method(s), known as the *handler(s)*, which process the events.

■ The listener object must be registered by the source object. Registration methods are dependent on the event type. For `ActionEvent`, the method is `addActionListener`. In general, the method is named `addXListener` for *X*`Event`.

■ An *inner class*, or *nested class*, is a class defined within the scope of another class. An inner class can reference the data and methods defined in the outer class in which it nests, so you do not need to pass the reference of the outer class to the constructor of the inner class.

■ Convenience adapters are support classes that provide default implementations for all the methods in the listener interface. Java provides convenience listener adapters for every AWT listener interface with multiple handlers. A convenience listener adapter is named *X*Adapter for *X*Listener.

■ A source object may fire several types of events. For each event, the source object maintains a list of listeners and notifies all the registered listeners by invoking the *handler* on the listener object to process the event.

■ A mouse event is fired whenever a mouse is clicked, released, moved, or dragged on a component. The mouse-event object captures the event, such as the number of clicks associated with it or the location (x- and y-coordinates) of the mouse point.

■ Java provides two listener interfaces, `MouseListener` and `MouseMotionListener`, to handle mouse events, implement the `MouseListener` interface to listen for such actions as mouse pressed, released, clicked, entered, or exited, and implement the `MouseMotionListener` interface to listen for such actions as mouse dragged or moved.

■ A `KeyEvent` object describes the nature of the event (namely, that a key has been pressed, released, or typed) and the value of the key.

■ The `keyPressed` handler is invoked when a key is pressed, the `keyReleased` handler is invoked when a key is released, and the `keyTyped` handler is invoked when a Unicode character is entered. If a key does not have a Unicode (e.g., function keys, modifier keys, action keys, and control keys), the `keyTyped` handler will be not be invoked.

■ You can use the `Timer` class to control Java animations. A timer fires an `ActionEvent` at a fixed rate. The listener updates the painting to simulate an animation.

REVIEW QUESTIONS

Sections 14.2–14.3

14.1 Can a button fire a `WindowEvent`? Can a button fire a `MouseEvent`? Can a button fire an `ActionEvent`?

14.2 Why must a listener be an instance of an appropriate listener interface? Explain how to register a listener object and how to implement a listener interface.

14.3 Can a source have multiple listeners? Can a listener listen on multiple sources? Can a source be a listener for itself?

14.4 How do you override a method defined in the listener interface? Do you need to override all the methods defined in the listener interface?

14.5 Can an inner class be used in a class other than the class in which it nests?

14.6 Can the modifiers `public`, `private`, and `static` be used on inner classes?

14.7 If class A is an inner class in class B, what is the `.class` file for A? If class B contains two anonymous inner classes, what are the `.class` file names for these two classes?

14.8 What is wrong in the following code?

```
import java.swing.*;
import java.awt.*;

public class Test extends JFrame {
  public Test() {
    JButton jbtOK = new JButton("OK");
    add(jbtOK);
  }

  private class Listener
      implements ActionListener {
    public void actionPerform
        (ActionEvent e) {
      System.out.println
        (jbtOK.getActionCommand());
    }
  }

  /** Main method omitted */
}
```
(a)

```
import java.awt.event.*;
import javax.swing.*;

public class Test extends JFrame {
  public Test() {
    JButton jbtOK = new JButton("OK");
    add(jbtOK);
    jbtOK.addActionListener(
      new ActionListener() {
        public void actionPerformed
            (ActionEvent e) {
          System.out.println
            (jbtOK.getActionCommand());
        }
    } // Something missing here
  }

  /** Main method omitted */
}
```
(b)

Sections 14.4–14.5

14.9 What method do you use to get the source of an event? What method do you use to get the timestamp for an action event, a mouse event or a key event? What method do you use to get the mouse point position for a mouse event? What method do you use to get the key character for a key event?

14.10 What is the listener interface for mouse pressed, released, clicked, entered, and exited? What is the listener interface for mouse moved and dragged?

14.11 Does every key in the keyboard have a Unicode? Is a key code in the KeyEvent class equivalent to a Unicode?

14.12 Is the keyPressed handler invoked after a key is pressed? Is the keyReleased handler invoked after a key is released? Is the keyTyped handler invoked after *any* key is typed?

Section 14.6 (Optional) Animation Using the Timer Class

14.13 How do you create a timer? How do you start a timer? How do you stop a timer?

14.14 Does the Timer class have a no-arg constructor? Can you add multiple listeners to a timer?

PROGRAMMING EXERCISES

Sections 14.2–14.3

14.1 (*Finding which button has been clicked on the console*) Add the code to Exercise 12.1 that will display a message on the console indicating which button has been clicked.

14.2 (*Using ComponentEvent*) Any GUI component can fire a ComponentEvent. The ComponentListener defines the componentMoved, componentResized, componentShown, and componentHidden methods for processing component events. Write a test program to demonstrate ComponentEvent.

14.3* (*Finding which button has been clicked on a panel*) Write a program that creates a user interface with two buttons named OK and Cancel and a message panel for displaying a message. When you click the OK button, a message "The OK button has been clicked" is displayed. When you click the Cancel button, a message "The Cancel button has been clicked" is displayed, as shown in Figure 14.19(a).

(a)

(b)

(c)

FIGURE 14.19 (a) Exercise 14.3 displays which button is clicked on a message panel. (b) Exercise 14.4 displays the mouse position. (c) Exercise 14.9 uses the arrow keys to draw the lines.

Section 14.4 Mouse Events

14.4* (*Displaying the mouse position*) Write two programs, one displays the mouse position when the mouse is clicked (see Figure 14.19(b)), and the other displays the mouse position when the mouse is pressed and the display disappears when the mouse is released.

14.5* (*Setting background color using a mouse*) Write a program that displays the background color of a panel as black when the mouse is pressed and as white when the mouse is released.

14.6** (*Alternating two messages*) Write a program to rotate two messages "Java is fun" and "Java is powerful" displayed on a panel with a mouse click.

Section 14.5 Key Events

14.7** (*Entering and displaying a string*) Write a program that receives a string from the keyboard and displays it on a panel. The Enter key signals the end of a string. Whenever a new string is entered, it is displayed on the panel.

14.8* (*Displaying a character*) Write a program to get a character input from the keyboard and display the character where the mouse points.

14.9* (*Drawing lines using the arrow keys*) Write a program that draws line segments using the arrow keys. The line starts from the center of the frame and draws toward east, north, west, or south when the right-arrow key, up-arrow key, left-arrow key, or down-arrow key is clicked, as shown in Figure 14.19(c).

Section 14.6 (Optional) Animation Using the Timer Class

14.10* (*Displaying a flashing label*) Write a program that displays a flashing label.

Hint

To make the label flash, you need to repaint the panel alternately with the label and without the label (blank screen) at a fixed rate. Use a boolean variable to control the alternation.

14.11* (*Controlling a moving label*) Modify Listing 14.9, AnimationDemo.java, to control a moving label using the mouse. The label freezes when the mouse is pressed, and moves again when the button is released.

14.12**(*Displaying a running fan*) Listing 13.6, DrawArcs.java, displays a motionless fan. Write a program that displays a running fan.

14.13**(*Slides show*) Twenty-five slides are stored as image files (slide0.jpg, slide1.jpg, ..., slide24.jpg) in the image directory downloadable along with the source code in the book. The size of each image is 800 × 600 pixels. Write a Java application that automatically displays the slides repeatedly. Each slide is shown for a second. The slides are displayed in order. When the last slide finishes, the first slide is redisplayed, and so on. (Hint: place a label in the frame and set a slide as an image icon in the label.)

14.14**(*Raising flag*) Write a Java program that animates raising a flag, as shown in Figure 14.20. (See §13.13, "Displaying Images," on how to display images.)

FIGURE 14.20 A flag is rising upward.

14.15**(*Racing car*) Write a Java program that simulates car racing, as shown in Figure 14.21(a). The car moves from left to right. When it hits the right end, it restarts from the left and continues the same process. You can use a timer to control the animation. Redraw the car with new base coordinates (x, y), as shown in Figure 14.21(b).

 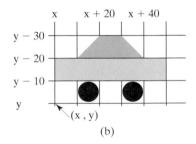

(a)   (b)

FIGURE 14.21 (a) Exercise 14.15 displays a moving car. (b) You can redraw a car with a new base point.

CHAPTER 15

CREATING USER INTERFACES

Objectives

■ To create graphical user interfaces with various user-interface components: `JButton`, `JCheckBox`, `JRadioButton`, `JLabel`, `JTextField`, `JTextArea`, `JComboBox`, `JList`, `JScrollBar`, and `JSlider` (§§15.2–15.11).

■ To create listeners for various types of events (§§15.2–15.11).

■ To display multiple windows in an application (§15.12).

15.1 Introduction

GUI

A graphical user interface (*GUI*) makes a system user-friendly and easy to use. Creating a GUI requires creativity and knowledge of how GUI components work. Since the GUI components in Java are very flexible and versatile, you can create a wide assortment of useful user interfaces.

Many Java IDEs provide tools for visually designing and developing GUI interfaces. This enables you to rapidly assemble the elements of a user interface (UI) for a Java application or applet with minimum coding. Tools, however, cannot do everything. You have to modify the programs they produce. Consequently, before you begin to use the visual tools, it is imperative that you understand the basic concepts of Java GUI programming.

Previous chapters briefly introduced several GUI components. This chapter introduces the frequently used GUI components in detail (see Figure 15.1).

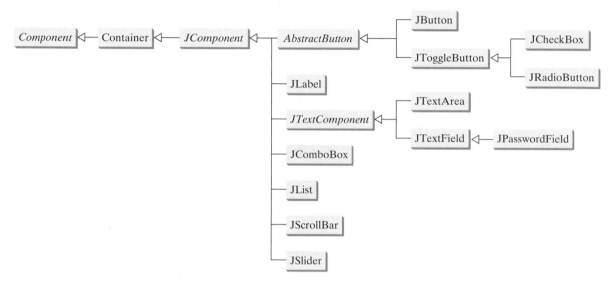

FIGURE 15.1   These Swing GUI components are frequently used to create user interfaces.

 Note

naming convention for components

Throughout this book, the prefixes `jbt`, `jchk`, `jrb`, `jlbl`, `jtf`, `jpf`, `jta`, `jcbo`, `jlst`, `jscb`, and `jsld` are used to name reference variables for `JButton`, `JCheckBox`, `JRadioButton`, `JLabel`, `JTextField`, `JPasswordField`, `JTextArea`, `JComboBox`, `JList`, `JScrollBar`, and `JSlider`.

15.2 Buttons

A *button* is a component that triggers an action event when clicked. Swing provides regular buttons, toggle buttons, check box buttons, and radio buttons. The common features of these buttons are represented in `javax.swing.AbstractButton`, as shown in Figure 15.2.

AbstractButton
JButton

This section introduces the regular buttons defined in the `JButton` class. `JButton` inherits `AbstractButton` and provides several constructors to create buttons, as shown in Figure 15.3.

15.2.1   Icons, Pressed Icons, and Rollover Icons

A regular button has a default icon, pressed icon, and rollover icon. Normally, you use the default icon. The other icons are for special effects. A pressed icon is displayed when a button is pressed, and a rollover icon is displayed when the mouse is over the button but not

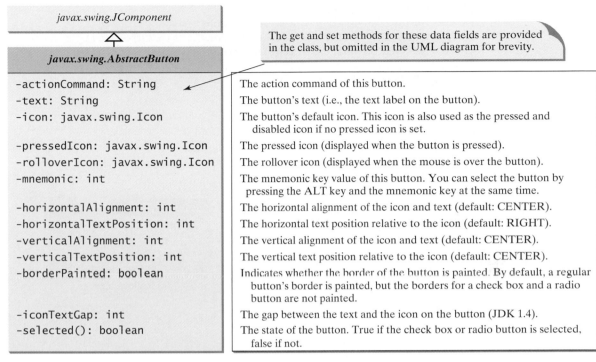

FIGURE 15.2 `AbstractButton` defines common features of different types of buttons.

FIGURE 15.3 `JButton` defines a regular push button.

pressed. For example, Listing 15.1 displays the American flag as a regular icon, the Canadian flag as a pressed icon, and the British flag as a rollover icon, as shown in Figure 15.4.

LISTING 15.1 TestButtonIcons.java

```java
1 import javax.swing.*;
2
3 public class TestButtonIcons extends JFrame  {
4   public static void main(String[] args) {
5     // Create a frame and set its properties
6     JFrame frame = new TestButtonIcons();
7     frame.setTitle("ButtonIcons");
8     frame.setSize(200, 100);
9     frame.setLocationRelativeTo(null); // Center the frame
10    frame.setDefaultCloseOperation(JFrame.EXIT_ON_CLOSE);
11    frame.setVisible(true);
12  }
13
```

```
          14    public TestButtonIcons() {
          15      ImageIcon usIcon = new ImageIcon("image/usIcon.gif");
          16      ImageIcon caIcon = new ImageIcon("image/caIcon.gif");
          17      ImageIcon ukIcon = new ImageIcon("image/ukIcon.gif");
          18
          19      JButton jbt = new JButton("Click it", usIcon);
          20      jbt.setPressedIcon(caIcon);
          21      jbt.setRolloverIcon(ukIcon);
          22
          23      add(jbt);
          24    }
          25  }
```

create icons (lines 15–17)
regular icon (line 19)
pressed icon (line 20)
rollover icon (line 21)
add a button (line 23)

(a) Default icon   (b) Pressed icon   (c) Rollover icon

FIGURE 15.4 A button can have several types of icons.

15.2.2 Alignments

horizontal alignment

Horizontal alignment specifies how the icon and text are placed horizontally on a button. You can set the horizontal alignment using `setHorizontalAlignment(int)` with one of the five constants `LEADING`, `LEFT`, `CENTER`, `RIGHT`, `TRAILING`, as shown in Figure 15.5. At present, `LEADING` and `LEFT` are the same, and `TRAILING` and `RIGHT` are the same. Future implementation may distinquish them. The default horizontal alignment is `Swing-Constants.TRAILING`.

Horizontally left   Horizontally center   Horizontally right

FIGURE 15.5 You can specify how the icon and text are placed on a button horizontally.

vertical alignment

Vertical alignment specifies how the icon and text are placed vertically on a button. You can set the vertical alignment using `setVerticalAlignment(int)` with one of the three constants `TOP`, `CENTER`, `BOTTOM`, as shown in Figure 15.6. The default vertical alignment is `SwingConstants.CENTER`.

Vertically top   vertically center   Vertically bottom

FIGURE 15.6 You can specify how the icon and text are placed on a button vertically.

15.2.3 Text Positions

Horizontal text position specifies the horizontal position of the text relative to the icon. You can set the horizontal text position using `setHorizontalTextPosition(int)` with one of the five constants `LEADING`, `LEFT`, `CENTER`, `RIGHT`, `TRAILING`, as shown in Figure 15.7. At present, `LEADING` and `LEFT` are the same, and `TRAILING` and `RIGHT` are the same. Future implementation may distinquish them. The default horizontal text position is `SwingConstants.RIGHT`.

horizontal text position

  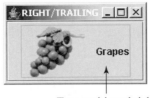

Text positioned left   Text positioned center   Text positioned right

FIGURE 15.7 You can specify the horizontal position of the text relative to the icon.

Vertical text position specifies the vertical position of the text relative to the icon. You can set the vertical text position using `setVerticalTextPosition(int)` with one of the three constants `TOP`, `CENTER`, `BOTTOM`, as shown in Figure 15.8. The default vertical text position is `SwingConstants.CENTER`.

vertical text position

Text positioned top   Text positioned   Text positioned bottom

FIGURE 15.8 You can specify the vertical position of the text relative to the icon.

Note

The constants `LEFT`, `CENTER`, `RIGHT`, `LEADING`, `TRAILING`, `TOP`, and `BOTTOM` used in `AbstractButton` are also used in many other Swing components. These constants are centrally defined in the `javax.swing.SwingConstants` interface. Since all Swing GUI components implement `SwingConstants`, you can reference the constants through `SwingConstants` or a GUI component. For example, `SwingConstants.CENTER` is the same as `JButton.CENTER`.

`SwingConstants`

`JButton` can generate many types of events, but often you need to respond to an `ActionEvent`. When a button is pressed, it generates an `ActionEvent`.

15.2.4 Example: Using Buttons

This example presents a program, shown in Listing 15.2, that displays a message on a panel and uses two buttons, <= and =>, to move the message on the panel to the left or right. The layout of the UI and the output of the program are shown in Figure 15.9.

Here are the major steps in the program:

1. Create the user interface.
   Create a `MessagePanel` object to display the message. The `MessagePanel` class was created in §13.11, "Case Study: The `MessagePanel` Class." Place it in the center of the frame. Create two buttons, <= and =>, on a panel. Place the panel in the south of the frame.

MessagePanel

JPanel with
FlowLayout

FIGURE 15.9 Clicking the <= and => buttons causes the message on the panel to move to the left and right, respectively.

2. Process the event.
   Create and register listeners for processing the action event to move the message left or right according to whether the left or right button was clicked.

LISTING 15.2 ButtonDemo.java

```java
 1 import java.awt.*;
 2 import java.awt.event.ActionListener;
 3 import java.awt.event.ActionEvent;
 4 import javax.swing.*;
 5
 6 public class ButtonDemo extends JFrame {
 7   // Create a panel for displaying message
 8   protected MessagePanel messagePanel
 9     = new MessagePanel("Welcome to Java");
10
11   // Declare two buttons to move the message left and right
12   private JButton jbtLeft = new JButton("<=");
13   private JButton jbtRight = new JButton("=>");
14
15   public static void main(String[] args) {
16     ButtonDemo frame = new ButtonDemo();
17     frame.setTitle("ButtonDemo");
18     frame.setLocationRelativeTo(null); // Center the frame
19     frame.setDefaultCloseOperation(JFrame.EXIT_ON_CLOSE);
20     frame.setSize(250, 100);
21     frame.setVisible(true);
22   }
23
24   public ButtonDemo() {
25     // Set the background color of messagePanel
26     messagePanel.setBackground(Color.white);
27
28     // Create Panel jpButtons to hold two Buttons "<=" and "right =>"
29     JPanel jpButtons = new JPanel();
30     jpButtons.setLayout(new FlowLayout());
31     jpButtons.add(jbtLeft);
32     jpButtons.add(jbtRight);
33
34     // Set keyboard mnemonics
35     jbtLeft.setMnemonic('L');
36     jbtRight.setMnemonic('R');
37
38     // Set icons and remove text
39     // jbtLeft.setIcon(new ImageIcon("image/left.gif"));
40     // jbtRight.setIcon(new ImageIcon("image/right.gif"));
```

create frame

create UI

mnemonic

```
41       // jbtLeft.setText(null);
42       // jbtRight.setText(null);
43
44       // Set tool tip text on the buttons
45       jbtLeft.setToolTipText("Move message to left");          tool tip
46       jbtRight.setToolTipText("Move message to right");
47
48       // Place panels in the frame
49       setLayout(new BorderLayout());
50       add(messagePanel, BorderLayout.CENTER);
51       add(jpButtons, BorderLayout.SOUTH);
52
53       // Register listeners with the buttons
54       jbtLeft.addActionListener(new ActionListener() {         register listener
55         public void actionPerformed(ActionEvent e) {
56           messagePanel.moveLeft();
57         }
58       });
59       jbtRight.addActionListener(new ActionListener() {        register listener
60         public void actionPerformed(ActionEvent e) {
61           messagePanel.moveRight();
62         }
63       });
64     }
65 }
```

`messagePanel` (line 8) is deliberately declared `protected` so that it can be referenced by a subclass in future examples.

You can set an icon image on the button by using the `setIcon` method. If you uncomment the following code in lines 39–42:

```
// jbtLeft.setIcon(new ImageIcon("image/left.gif"));
// jbtRight.setIcon(new ImageIcon("image/right.gif"));
// jbtLeft.setText(null);
// jbtRight.setText(null);
```

the texts are replaced by the icons, as shown in Figure 15.10(a). `"image/left.gif"` is located in `"c:\book\image\left.gif"`. Note that the back slash is the Windows file path notation. In Java, the forward slash should be used.

(a)   (b)   (c)

FIGURE 15.10 You can set an icon on a `JButton` and access a button using mnemonic keys.

You can set text and an icon on a button at the same time, if you wish, as shown in Figure 15.10(b). By default, the text and icon are centered horizontally and vertically.

The button can also be accessed by using the keyboard mnemonics. Pressing ALT+L is equivalent to clicking the <= button, since you set the mnemonic property to `'L'` in the left button (line 35). If you change the left button text to "Left" and the right button to "Right," the L and R in the captions of these buttons will be underlined, as shown in Figure 15.10(b).

Chapter 15   Creating User Interfaces

Each button has a tool-tip text (lines 45–46), which appears when the mouse is set on the button without clicking, as shown in Figure 15.10(c).

 Note

locating **MessagePanel**

Since **MessagePanel** is not in the Java API, you should place MessagePanel.java in the same directory with ButtonDemo.java.

15.3 Check Boxes

toggle button

A *toggle button* is a two-state button like a light switch. **JToggleButton** inherits **Abstract-Button** and implements a toggle button. Often **JToggleButton**'s subclasses **JCheckBox** and **JRadioButton** are used to enable the user to toggle a choice on or off. This section introduces **JCheckBox**. **JRadioButton** will be introduced in the next section.

JCheckBox inherits all the properties from **AbstractButton**, such as **text**, **icon**, **mnemonic**, **verticalAlignment**, **horizontalAlignment**, **horizontalTextPosition**, **verticalTextPosition**, and **selected**, and provides several constructors to create check boxes, as shown in Figure 15.11.

FIGURE 15.11   **JCheckBox** defines a check box button.

Here is an example of a check box with text Student, red foreground, white background, mnemonic key 'S', and initially selected.

```
JCheckBox jchk = new JCheckBox("Student", true);
jchk.setForeground(Color.red);
jchk.setBackground(Color.white);
jchk.setMnemonic('S');
```

When a check box is clicked (checked or unchecked), it fires an **ItemEvent** and then an **ActionEvent**. To see if a check box is selected, use the **isSelected()** method.

Listing 15.3 gives a program that adds three check boxes named *Centered*, *Bold*, and *Italic* into the preceding example to let the user specify whether the message is centered, bold, or italic, as shown in Figure 15.12.

There are at least two approaches to writing this program. The first is to revise the preceding **ButtonDemo** class to insert the code for adding the check boxes and processing their events. The second is to create a subclass that extends **ButtonDemo**. Please implement the first approach as an exercise. Listing 15.3 gives the code to implement the second approach.

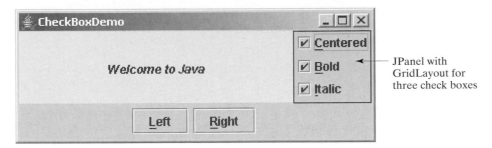

FIGURE 15.12   Three check boxes are added to specify how the message is displayed.

LISTING 15.3   CheckBoxDemo.java

```
1  import java.awt.*;
2  import java.awt.event.*;
3  import javax.swing.*;
4
5  public class CheckBoxDemo extends ButtonDemo {
6    // Create three check boxes to control the display of message
7    private JCheckBox jchkCentered = new JCheckBox("Centered");
8    private JCheckBox jchkBold = new JCheckBox("Bold");
9    private JCheckBox jchkItalic = new JCheckBox("Italic");
10
11   public static void main(String[] args) {
12     CheckBoxDemo frame = new CheckBoxDemo();
13     frame.setTitle("CheckBoxDemo");
14     frame.setLocationRelativeTo(null); // Center the frame
15     frame.setDefaultCloseOperation(JFrame.EXIT_ON_CLOSE);
16     frame.setSize(500, 200);
17     frame.setVisible(true);
18   }
19
20   public CheckBoxDemo() {
21     // Set mnemonic keys
22     jchkCentered.setMnemonic('C');
23     jchkBold.setMnemonic('B');
24     jchkItalic.setMnemonic('I');
25
26     // Create a new panel to hold check boxes
27     JPanel jpCheckBoxes = new JPanel();
28     jpCheckBoxes.setLayout(new GridLayout(3, 1));
29     jpCheckBoxes.add(jchkCentered);
30     jpCheckBoxes.add(jchkBold);
31     jpCheckBoxes.add(jchkItalic);
32     add(jpCheckBoxes, BorderLayout.EAST);
33
34     // Register listeners with the check boxes
35     jchkCentered.addActionListener(new ActionListener() {
36       public void actionPerformed(ActionEvent e) {
37         messagePanel.setCentered(jchkCentered.isSelected());
38       }
39     });
40     jchkBold.addActionListener(new ActionListener() {
41       public void actionPerformed(ActionEvent e) {
42         setNewFont();
43       }
44     });
```

create frame

create UI

register listener

register listener

register listener

```
45    jchkItalic.addActionListener(new ActionListener() {
46      public void actionPerformed(ActionEvent e) {
47        setNewFont();
48      }
49    });
50  }
51
```

set a new font

```
52  private void setNewFont() {
53    // Determine a font style
54    int fontStyle = Font.PLAIN;
55    fontStyle += (jchkBold.isSelected() ? Font.BOLD : Font.PLAIN);
56    fontStyle += (jchkItalic.isSelected() ? Font.ITALIC : Font.PLAIN);
57
58    // Set font for the message
59    Font font = messagePanel.getFont();
60    messagePanel.setFont(
61      new Font(font.getName(), fontStyle, font.getSize()));
62  }
63 }
```

CheckBoxDemo extends ButtonDemo and adds three check boxes to control how the message is displayed. When a CheckBoxDemo is constructed (line 12), its superclass's no-arg constructor is invoked, so you don't have to rewrite the code that is already in the constructor of ButtonDemo.

When a check box is checked or unchecked, the listener's actionPerformed method is invoked to process the event. When the "Centered" check box is checked or unchecked, the centered property of the MessagePanel class is set to true or false.

The current font name and size used in MessagePanel are obtained from messagePanel.getFont() using the getName() and getSize() methods. The font styles (Font.BOLD and Font.ITALIC) are specified in the check boxes. If no font style is selected, the font style is Font.PLAIN. Font styles are combined by adding together the selected integers representing the fonts.

The keyboard mnemonics 'C', 'B', and 'I' are set on the check boxes "Centered," "Bold," and "Italic," respectively (lines 22–24). You can use a mouse gesture or a shortcut key to select a check box.

The setFont method (line 60) defined in the Component class is inherited in the MessagePanel class. This method automatically invokes the repaint method. Invoking setFont in messagePanel automatically repaints the message.

A check box fires an ActionEvent and an ItemEvent when it is clicked. You could process either the ActionEvent or the ItemEvent to redisplay the message. The example processes the ActionEvent. If you wish to process the ItemEvent, you could create a listener for ItemEvent and register it with a check box, as shown below:

```
public class CheckBoxDemoUsingItemEvent extends ButtonDemo {
    ... // Same as in CheckBoxDemo.java, so omitted

  public CheckBoxDemoUsingItemEvent() {
      ... // Same as in CheckBoxDemo.java, so omitted

    // To listen for ItemEvent
    jchkCentered.addItemListener(newItemListener() {
      /** Handle ItemEvent */
      public void itemStateChanged(ItemEvent e) {
        messagePanel.setCentered(jchkCentered.isSelected());
      }
    });
  }
}
```

15.4 Radio Buttons

Radio buttons, also known as *option buttons*, enable you to choose a single item from a group of choices. In appearance radio buttons resemble check boxes, but check boxes display a square that is either checked or blank, whereas radio buttons display a circle that is either filled (if selected) or blank (if not selected).

JRadioButton inherits `AbstractButton` and provides several constructors to create radio buttons, as shown in Figure 15.13. These constructors are similar to the constructors for JCheckBox.

javax.swing.JRadioButton	
+JRadioButton()	Creates a default radio button with no text and icon.
+JRadioButton(text: String)	Creates a radio button with text.
+JRadioButton(text: String, selected: boolean)	Creates a radio button with text and specifies whether the radio button is initially selected.
+JRadioButton(icon: Icon)	Creates a radio button with an icon.
+JRadioButton(text: String, icon: Icon)	Creates a radio button with text and an icon.
+JRadioButton(text: String, icon: Icon, selected: boolean)	Creates a radio button with text and an icon, and specifies whether the radio button is initially selected.

FIGURE 15.13 `JRadioButton` defines a radio button.

Here is an example of a radio button with text Student, red foreground, white background, mnemonic key 'S', and initially selected.

```
JRadioButton jrb = new JRadioButton("Student", true);
jrb.setForeground(Color.red);
jrb.setBackground(Color.white);
jrb.setMnemonic('S');
```

To group radio buttons, you need to create an instance of `java.swing.ButtonGroup` and use the `add` method to add them to it, as follows:

```
ButtonGroup group = new ButtonGroup();
group.add(jrb1);
group.add(jrb2);
```

This code creates a radio button group for radio buttons `jrb1` and `jrb2` so that `jrb1` and `jrb2` are selected mutually exclusively. Without grouping, `jrb1` and `jrb2` would be independent.

Note

ButtonGroup is not a subclass of `java.awt.Component`, so a ButtonGroup object cannot be added to a container.

When a radio button is clicked (selected or deselected), it fires an `ItemEvent` and then an `ActionEvent`. To see if a radio button is selected, use the `isSelected()` method.

Listing 15.4 gives a program that adds three radio buttons named *Red*, *Green*, and *Blue* into the preceding example to let the user choose the color of the message, as shown in Figure 15.14.

Again there are at least two approaches to writing this program. The first is to revise the preceding CheckBoxDemo class to insert the code for adding the radio buttons and processing

GUI helper class

JPanel with
GridLayout
for three
radio buttons

FIGURE 15.14 Three radio buttons are added to specify the color of the message.

their events. The second is to create a subclass that extends CheckBoxDemo. Listing 15.4 gives
the code to implement the second approach.

LISTING 15.4 RadioButtonDemo.java

```
1  import java.awt.*;
2  import java.awt.event.*;
3  import javax.swing.*;
4
5  public class RadioButtonDemo extends CheckBoxDemo {
6    // Declare radio buttons
7    private JRadioButton jrbRed, jrbGreen, jrbBlue;
8
9    public static void main(String[] args) {
10     RadioButtonDemo frame = new RadioButtonDemo();
11     frame.setLocationRelativeTo(null); // Center the frame
12     frame.setDefaultCloseOperation(JFrame.EXIT_ON_CLOSE);
13     frame.setTitle("RadioButtonDemo");
14     frame.setSize(500, 200);
15     frame.setVisible(true);
16   }
17
18   public RadioButtonDemo() {
19     // Create a new panel to hold check boxes
20     JPanel jpRadioButtons = new JPanel();
21     jpRadioButtons.setLayout(new GridLayout(3, 1));
22     jpRadioButtons.add(jrbRed = new JRadioButton("Red"));
23     jpRadioButtons.add(jrbGreen = new JRadioButton("Green"));
24     jpRadioButtons.add(jrbBlue = new JRadioButton("Blue"));
25     add(jpRadioButtons, BorderLayout.WEST);
26
27     // Create a radio button group to group three buttons
28     ButtonGroup group = new ButtonGroup();
29     group.add(jrbRed);
30     group.add(jrbGreen);
31     group.add(jrbBlue);
32
33     // Set keyboard mnemonics
34     jrbRed.setMnemonic('E');
35     jrbGreen.setMnemonic('G');
36     jrbBlue.setMnemonic('U');
37
38     // Register listeners for check boxes
39     jrbRed.addActionListener(new ActionListener() {
40       public void actionPerformed(ActionEvent e) {
41         messagePanel.setForeground(Color.red);
42       }
43     });
```

create frame

create UI

group buttons

register listener

```
44      jrbGreen.addActionListener(new ActionListener() {          register listener
45        public void actionPerformed(ActionEvent e) {
46          messagePanel.setForeground(Color.green);
47        }
48      });
49      jrbBlue.addActionListener(new ActionListener() {           register listener
50        public void actionPerformed(ActionEvent e) {
51          messagePanel.setForeground(Color.blue);
52        }
53      });
54
55      // Set initial message color to blue
56      jrbBlue.setSelected(true);
57      messagePanel.setForeground(Color.blue);
58    }
59  }
```

RadioButtonDemo extends CheckBoxDemo and adds three radio buttons to specify the message color. When a radio button is clicked, the radio button's action event listener sets the corresponding foreground color in messagePanel.

The keyboard mnemonics 'R' and 'B' are already set for the Right button and Bold check box. To avoid conflict, the keyboard mnemonics 'E', 'G', and 'U' are set on the radio buttons "Red", "Green", and "Blue", respectively (lines 34–36).

The program creates a ButtonGroup group and puts three JRadioButton instances (jrbRed, jrbGreen, and jrbBlue) in the group (lines 28–31).

A radio button fires an ActionEvent and an ItemEvent when it is selected or deselected. You could process either the ActionEvent or the ItemEvent to choose a color. The example processes the ActionEvent. Please rewrite the code using the ItemEvent as an exercise.

15.5 Labels

A *label* is a display area for a short text, an image, or both. It is often used to label other components (usually text fields). Figure 15.15 lists the constructors and methods in JLabel.

javax.swing.JComponent	

The get and set methods for these data fields are provided in the class, but omitted in the UML diagram for brevity.

javax.swing.JLabel	
-text: String	The label's text.
-icon: javax.swing.Icon	The label's image icon.
-horizontalAlignment: int	The horizontal alignment of the text and icon on the label.
-horizontalTextPosition: int	The horizontal text position relative to the icon on the label.
-verticalAlignment: int	The vertical alignment of the text and icon on the label.
-verticalTextPosition: int	The vertical text position relative to the icon on the label.
-iconTextGap: int	The gap between the text and the icon on the label (JDK 1.4).
+JLabel()	Creates a default label with no text and icon.
+JLabel(icon: javax.swing.Icon)	Creates a label with an icon.
+JLabel(icon: Icon, hAlignment: int)	Creates a label with an icon and the specified horizontal alignment.
+JLabel(text: String)	Creates a label with text.
+JLabel(text: String, icon: Icon, hAlignment: int)	Creates a label with text, an icon, and the specified horizontal alignment.
+JLabel(text: String, hAlignment: int)	Creates a label with text and the specified horizontal alignment.

FIGURE 15.15   JLabel displays text or an icon, or both.

JLabel inherits all the properties from JComponent and has many properties similar to the ones in JButton, such as text, icon, horizontalAlignment, verticalAlignment, horizontalTextPosition, verticalTextPosition, and iconTextGap. For example, the following code displays a label with text and an icon:

```
// Create an image icon from an image file
ImageIcon icon = new ImageIcon("image/grapes.gif");

// Create a label with text, an icon,
// with centered horizontal alignment
JLabel jlbl = new JLabel("Grapes", icon, SwingConstants.CENTER);

// Set label's text alignment and gap between text and icon
jlbl.setHorizontalTextPosition(SwingConstants.CENTER);
jlbl.setVerticalTextPosition(SwingConstants.BOTTOM);
jlbl.setIconTextGap(5);
```

15.6 Text Fields

A *text field* can be used to enter or display a string. JTextField is a subclass of JTextComponent. Figure 15.16 lists the constructors and methods in JTextField.

FIGURE 15.16 JTextField enables you to enter or display a string.

JTextField inherits JTextComponent, which inherits JComponent. Here is an example of creating a non-editable text field with red foreground color and right horizontal alignment:

```
JTextField jtfMessage = new JTextField("T-Strom");
jtfMessage.setEditable(false);
jtfMessage.setForeground(Color.red);
jtfMessage.setHorizontalAlignment(SwingConstants.RIGHT);
```

When you move the cursor in the text field and press the Enter key, it fires an ActionEvent.

Listing 15.5 gives a program that adds a text field to the preceding example to let the user set a new message, as shown in Figure 15.17.

Listing 15.5 creates a subclass that extends RadioButtonDemo.

LISTING 15.5 TextFieldDemo.java

```
1 import java.awt.*;
2 import java.awt.event.*;
3 import javax.swing.*;
4
```

```
5  public class TextFieldDemo extends RadioButtonDemo {
6    private JTextField jtfMessage = new JTextField(10);
7
8    /** Main method */
9    public static void main(String[] args) {
10     TextFieldDemo frame = new TextFieldDemo();
11     frame.pack();
12     frame.setTitle("TextFieldDemo");
13     frame.setLocationRelativeTo(null); // Center the frame
14     frame.setDefaultCloseOperation(JFrame.EXIT_ON_CLOSE);
15     frame.setVisible(true);
16   }
17
18   public TextFieldDemo() {
19     // Create a new panel to hold label and text field
20     JPanel jpTextField = new JPanel();
21     jpTextField.setLayout(new BorderLayout(5, 0));
22     jpTextField.add(
23       new JLabel("Enter a new message"), BorderLayout.WEST);
24     jpTextField.add(jtfMessage, BorderLayout.CENTER);
25     add(jpTextField, BorderLayout.NORTH);
26
27     jtfMessage.setHorizontalAlignment(JTextField.RIGHT);
28
29     // Register listener
30     jtfMessage.addActionListener(new ActionListener() {
31       /** Handle ActionEvent */
32       public void actionPerformed(ActionEvent e) {
33         messagePanel.setMessage(jtfMessage.getText());
34         jtfMessage.requestFocusInWindow();
35       }
36     });
37   }
38 }
```

create frame
pack frame

create UI

listener

FIGURE 15.17 A label and a text field are added to set a new message.

TextFieldDemo extends RadioButtonDemo and adds a label and a text field to let the user enter a new message. After you set a new message in the text field and press the Enter key, a new message is displayed. Pressing the Enter key on the text field triggers an action event. The listener sets a new message in messagePanel (line 33).

Instead of using the setSize method to set the size for the frame, the program uses the pack() method (line 11), which automatically sizes up the frame according to the size of the components placed in it.

The requestFocusInWindow() method (line 34) defined in the Component class requests the component to receive input focus. Thus, jtfMessage.request-FocusInWindow() (line 34) requests the input focus on jtfMessage. You will see the cursor on jtfMessage after the actionPerformed method is invoked.

pack()

requestFocus-InWindow()

JPasswordField

Note

If a text field is used for entering a password, use `JPasswordField` to replace `JTextField`. `JPasswordField` extends `JTextField` and hides the input text with echo characters (e.g., `******`). By default, the echo character is `*`. You can specify a new echo character using the `setEchoChar(char)` method.

15.7 Text Areas

If you want to let the user enter multiple lines of text, you have to create several instances of `JTextField`. A better alternative is to use `JTextArea`, which enables the user to enter multiple lines of text. Figure 15.18 lists the constructors and methods in `JTextArea`.

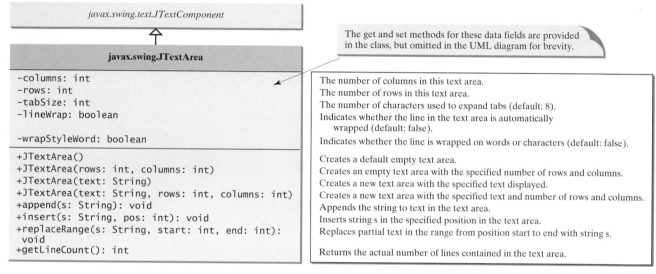

FIGURE 15.18 `JTextArea` enables you to enter or display multiple lines of characters.

Like `JTextField`, `JTextArea` inherits `JTextComponent`, which contains the methods `getText`, `setText`, `isEditable`, and `setEditable`. Here is an example of creating a text area with five rows and twenty columns, line-wrapped on words, red foreground color, and Courier font, bold, 20 pixels.

wrap line
wrap word

```
JTextArea jtaNote = new JTextArea("This is a text area", 5, 20);
jtaNote.setLineWrap(true);
jtaNote.setWrapStyleWord(true);
jtaNote.setForeground(Color.red);
jtaNote.setFont(new Font("Courier", Font.BOLD, 20));
```

`JTextArea` does not handle scrolling, but you can create a `JScrollPane` object to hold an instance of `JTextArea` and let `JScrollPane` handle scrolling for `JTextArea`, as follows:

```
// Create a scroll pane to hold text area
JScrollPane scrollPane = new JScrollPane(jta = new JTextArea());
add(scrollPane, BorderLayout.CENTER);
```

Listing 15.6 gives a program that displays an image and a text in a label, and a text in a text area, as shown in Figure 15.19.

Here are the major steps in the program:

1. Create a class named `DescriptionPanel` that extends `JPanel`. This class contains a text area inside a scroll pane, a label for displaying an image icon, and a title. This class is used in the present example and will be reused in later examples.

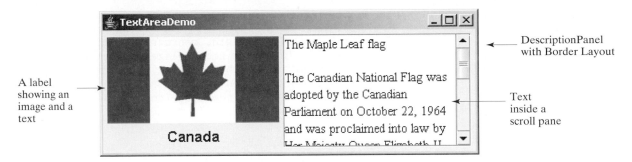

FIGURE 15.19   The program displays an image in a label, a title in a label, and a text in the text area.

2. Create a class named `TextAreaDemo` that extends `JFrame`. Create an instance of `DescriptionPanel` and add it to the center of the frame. The relationship between `DescriptionPanel` and `TextAreaDemo` is shown in Figure 15.20.

FIGURE 15.20   `TextAreaDemo` uses `DescriptionPanel` to display an image, title, and text description of a national flag.

LISTING 15.6   TextAreaDemo.java

```java
1  import java.awt.*;
2  import javax.swing.*;
3
4  public class TextAreaDemo extends JFrame {
5    // Declare and create a description panel
6    private DescriptionPanel descriptionPanel = new DescriptionPanel();
7
8    public static void main(String[] args) {
9      TextAreaDemo frame = new TextAreaDemo();                          create frame
10     frame.pack();
11     frame.setLocationRelativeTo(null); // Center the frame
12     frame.setDefaultCloseOperation(JFrame.EXIT_ON_CLOSE);
13     frame.setTitle("TextAreaDemo");
14     frame.setVisible(true);
15   }
16
17   public TextAreaDemo() {
18     // Set title, text and image in the description panel          create UI
19     descriptionPanel.setTitle("Canada");
20     String description = "The Maple Leaf flag \n\n" +
21       "The Canadian National Flag was adopted by the Canadian " +
22       "Parliament on October 22, 1964 and was proclaimed into law " +
23       "by Her Majesty Queen Elizabeth II (the Queen of Canada) on " +
```

```
24          "February 15, 1965. The Canadian Flag (colloquially known " +
25          "as The Maple Leaf Flag) is a red flag of the proportions " +
26          "two by length and one by width, containing in its center a " +
27          "white square, with a single red stylized eleven-point " +
28          "mapleleaf centered in the white square.";
29        descriptionPanel.setDescription(description);
30        descriptionPanel.setImageIcon(new ImageIcon("image/ca.gif"));
31
32        // Add the description panel to the frame
33        setLayout(new BorderLayout());
34        add(descriptionPanel, BorderLayout.CENTER);
35      }
36    }
37
38    // Define a panel for displaying image and text
39    class DescriptionPanel extends JPanel {
40      /** Label for displaying an image icon and a text */
41      private JLabel jlblImageTitle = new JLabel();
42
43      /** Text area for displaying text */
44      private JTextArea jtaDescription = new JTextArea();
45
46      public DescriptionPanel() {
47        // Center the icon and text and place the text under the icon
48        jlblImageTitle.setHorizontalAlignment(JLabel.CENTER);
49        jlblImageTitle.setHorizontalTextPosition(JLabel.CENTER);
50        jlblImageTitle.setVerticalTextPosition(JLabel.BOTTOM);
51
52        // Set the font in the label and the text field
53        jlblImageTitle.setFont(new Font("SansSerif", Font.BOLD, 16));
54        jtaDescription.setFont(new Font("Serif", Font.PLAIN, 14));
55
56        // Set lineWrap and wrapStyleWord true for the text area
57        jtaDescription.setLineWrap(true);
58        jtaDescription.setWrapStyleWord(true);
59        jtaDescription.setEditable(false);
60
61        // Create a scroll pane to hold the text area
62        JScrollPane scrollPane = new JScrollPane(jtaDescription);
63
64        // Set BorderLayout for the panel, add label and scrollpane
65        setLayout(new BorderLayout(5, 5));
66        add(scrollPane, BorderLayout.CENTER);
67        add(jlblImageTitle, BorderLayout.WEST);
68      }
69
70      /** Set the title */
71      public void setTitle(String title) {
72        jlblImageTitle.setText(title);
73      }
74
75      /** Set the image icon */
76      public void setImageIcon(ImageIcon icon) {
77        jlblImageTitle.setIcon(icon);
78      }
79
80      /** Set the text description */
81      public void setDescription(String text) {
82        jtaDescription.setText(text);
83      }
84    }
```

Marginal labels:

label — line 41
text area — line 44
wrap line — line 57
wrap word — line 58
read only — line 59
scroll pane — line 62

`TextAreaDemo` simply creates an instance of `DescriptionPanel` (line 6), and sets the title (line 19), image (line 30), and text in the description panel (line 29). `DescriptionPanel` is a subclass of `JPanel`. `DescriptionPanel` contains a label for displaying an image icon and a text title, and a text area for displaying a description of the image.

It is not necessary to create a separate class for `DescriptionPanel` in this example. Nevertheless, this class was created for reuse in the next example, where you will use it to display a description panel for various images.

The text area is inside a `JScrollPane` (line 62), which provides scrolling functions for the text area. Scroll bars automatically appear if there is more text than the physical size of the text area, and disappear if the text is deleted and the remaining text does not exceed the text area size.

The `lineWrap` property is set to `true` (line 57) so that the line is automatically wrapped when the text cannot fit in one line. The `wrapStyleWord` property is set to `true` (line 58) so that the line is wrapped on words rather than characters. The text area is set non-editable (line 59), so you cannot edit the description in the text area.

15.8 Combo Boxes

A *combo box*, also known as a *choice list* or *drop-down list*, contains a list of items from which the user can choose. It is useful in limiting a user's range of choices and avoids the cumbersome validation of data input. Figure 15.21 lists several frequently used constructors and methods in `JComboBox`.

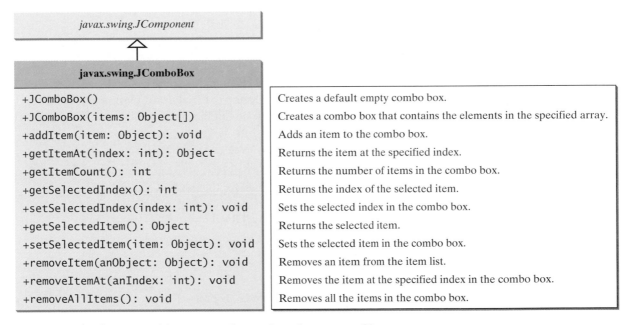

FIGURE 15.21   `JComboBox` enables you to select an item from a set of items.

The following statements create a combo box with four items, red foreground, white background, and the second item selected:

```
JComboBox jcb = new JComboBox(new Object[]
  {"Item 1", "Item 2", "Item 3", "Item 4"});
jcb.setForeground(Color.red);
jcb.setBackground(Color.white);
jcb.setSelectedItem("Item 2");
```

`JComboBox` can generate `ActionEvent` and `ItemEvent`, among many other events. Whenever an item is selected, an `ActionEvent` is fired. Whenever a new item is selected,

JComboBox generates `ItemEvent` twice, once for deselecting the previously selected item, and the other for selecting the currently selected item. Note that no `ItemEvent` is fired if the current item is reselected. To respond to an `ItemEvent`, you need to implement the `itemStateChanged(ItemEvent e)` handler for processing a choice. To get data from a JComboBox menu, you can use `getSelectedItem()` to return the currently selected item, or `e.getItem()` method to get the item from the `itemStateChanged(ItemEvent e)` handler.

Listing 15.7 gives a program that lets users view an image and a description of a country's flag by selecting the country from a combo box, as shown in Figure 15.22.

FIGURE 15.22 A country's info, including a flag image and a description of the flag, is displayed when the country is selected in the combo box.

Here are the major steps in the program:

1. Create the user interface.
   Create a combo box with country names as its selection values. Create a `DescriptionPanel` object. The `DescriptionPanel` class was introduced in the preceding example. Place the combo box in the north of the frame and the description panel in the center of the frame.

2. Process the event.
   Create a listener to implement the `itemStateChanged` handler to set the flag title, image, and text in the description panel for the selected country name.

LISTING 15.7 ComboBoxDemo.java

```
1  import java.awt.*;
2  import java.awt.event.*;
3  import javax.swing.*;
4
5  public class ComboBoxDemo extends JFrame {
6    // Declare an array of Strings for flag titles
7    private String[] flagTitles = {"Canada", "China", "Denmark",
8      "France", "Germany", "India", "Norway", "United Kingdom",
9      "United States of America"};
10
11   // Declare an ImageIcon array for the national flags of 9 countries
12   private ImageIcon[] flagImage = {
13     new ImageIcon("image/ca.gif"),
14     new ImageIcon("image/china.gif"),
15     new ImageIcon("image/denmark.gif"),
16     new ImageIcon("image/fr.gif"),
17     new ImageIcon("image/germany.gif"),
18     new ImageIcon("image/india.gif"),
```

country

image icon

```
19      new ImageIcon("image/norway.gif"),
20      new ImageIcon("image/uk.gif"),
21      new ImageIcon("image/us.gif")
22    };
23
24    // Declare an array of strings for flag descriptions
25    private String[] flagDescription = new String[9];                      description
26
27    // Declare and create a description panel
28    private DescriptionPanel descriptionPanel = new DescriptionPanel();
29
30    // Create a combo box for selecting countries
31    private JComboBox jcbo = new JComboBox(flagTitles);                     combo box
32
33    public static void main(String[] args) {
34      ComboBoxDemo frame = new ComboBoxDemo();
35      frame.pack();
36      frame.setTitle("ComboBoxDemo");
37      frame.setLocationRelativeTo(null); // Center the frame
38      frame.setDefaultCloseOperation(JFrame.EXIT_ON_CLOSE);
39      frame.setVisible(true);
40    }
41
42    public ComboBoxDemo() {                                                 create UI
43      // Set text description
44      flagDescription[0] = "The Maple Leaf flag \n\n" +
45        "The Canadian National Flag was adopted by the Canadian " +
46        "Parliament on October 22, 1964 and was proclaimed into law " +
47        "by Her Majesty Queen Elizabeth II (the Queen of Canada) on " +
48        "February 15, 1965. The Canadian Flag (colloquially known " +
49        "as The Maple Leaf Flag) is a red flag of the proportions " +
50        "two by length and one by width, containing in its center a " +
51        "white square, with a single red stylized eleven-point " +
52        "mapleleaf centered in the white square.";
53      flagDescription[1] = "Description for China ... ";
54      flagDescription[2] = "Description for Denmark ... ";
55      flagDescription[3] = "Description for France ... ";
56      flagDescription[4] = "Description for Germany ... ";
57      flagDescription[5] = "Description for India ... ";
58      flagDescription[6] = "Description for Norway ... ";
59      flagDescription[7] = "Description for UK ... ";
60      flagDescription[8] = "Description for US ... ";
61
62      // Set the first country (Canada) for display
63      setDisplay(0);
64
65      // Add combo box and description panel to the list
66      add(jcbo, BorderLayout.NORTH);
67      add(descriptionPanel, BorderLayout.CENTER);
68
69      // Register listener
70      jcbo.addItemListener(new ItemListener() {                            listener
71        /** Handle item selection */
72        public void itemStateChanged(ItemEvent e) {
73          setDisplay(jcbo.getSelectedIndex());
74        }
75      });
76    }
77
```

```
78    /** Set display information on the description panel */
79    public void setDisplay(int index) {
80      descriptionPanel.setTitle(flagTitles[index]);
81      descriptionPanel.setImageIcon(flagImage[index]);
82      descriptionPanel.setDescription(flagDescription[index]);
83    }
84 }
```

The listener listens to `ItemEvent` from the combo box and implements `ItemListener` (lines 70–75). Instead of using `ItemEvent`, you may rewrite the program to use `ActionEvent` for handling combo box item selection.

The program stores the flag information in three arrays: `flagTitles`, `flagImage`, and `flagDescription` (lines 7–25). The array `flagTitles` contains the names of nine countries, the array `flagImage` contains images of the nine countries' flags, and the array `flagDescription` contains descriptions of the flags.

The program creates an instance of `DescriptionPanel` (line 28), which was presented in Listing 15.6, TextAreaDemo.java. The program creates a combo box with initial values from `flagTitles` (line 31). When the user selects an item in the combo box, the `ItemStateChanged` handler is executed, finds the selected index, and sets its corresponding flag title, flag image, and flag description on the panel.

15.9 Lists

A *list* is a component that basically performs the same function as a combo box but enables the user to choose a single value or multiple values. The Swing `JList` is very versatile. Figure 15.23 lists several frequently used constructors and methods in `JList`.

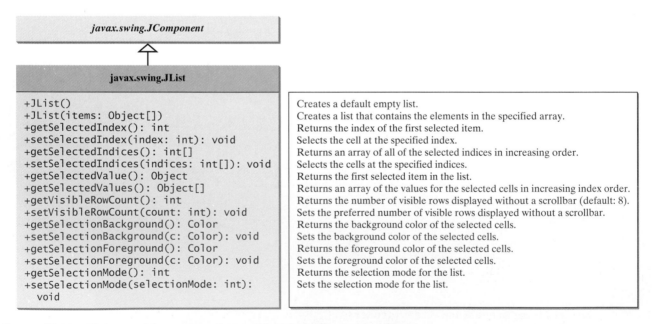

FIGURE 15.23 `JList` enables you to select multiple items from a set of items.

`selectionMode` is one of the three values (`SINGLE_SELECTION`, `SINGLE_INTERVAL_SELECTION`, `MULTIPLE_INTERVAL_SELECTION`) defined in `javax.swing.SelectionModel` that indicate whether a single item, single-interval item, or multiple-interval item can be selected. Single selection allows only one item to be selected. Single-interval selection allows multiple selections, but the selected items must be contiguous. Multiple-interval selection allows selections of multiple contiguous items without restrictions, as shown in Figure 15.24. The default value is MULTIPLE_INTERVAL_SELECTION.

(a) Single selection   (b) Single-interval selection   (c) Multiple-interval selection

FIGURE 15.24 JList has three selection modes: single selection, single-interval selection, and multiple-interval selection.

The following statements create a list with six items, red foreground, white background, pink selection foreground, black selection background, and visible row count 4:

```
JList jlst = new JList(new Object[]
    {"Item 1", "Item 2", "Item 3", "Item 4", "Item 5", "Item 6"});
jlst.setForeground(Color.red);
jlst.setBackground(Color.white);
jlst.setSelectionForeground(Color.pink);
jlst.setSelectionBackground(Color.black);
jlst.setVisibleRowCount(4);
```

Lists do not scroll automatically. To make a list scrollable, create a scroll pane and add the list to it. Text areas are made scrollable in the same way.

JList generates javax.swing.event.ListSelectionEvent to notify the listeners of the selections. The listener must implement the valueChanged handler in the javax.swing.event.ListSelectionListener interface to process the event.

Listing 15.8 gives a program that lets users select countries in a list and display the flags of the selected countries in the labels. Figure 15.25 shows a sample run of the program.

JList inside a scroll pane

JPanel with GridLayout

An image is displayed on a JLabel

FIGURE 15.25 When the countries in the list are selected, corresponding images of their flags are displayed in the labels.

Here are the major steps in the program:

1. Create the user interface.
   Create a list with nine country names as selection values, and place the list inside a scroll pane. Place the scroll pane in the west of the frame. Create nine labels to be used to display the countries' flag images. Place the labels in the panel, and place the panel in the center of the frame.

2. Process the event.
   Create a listener to implement the **valueChanged** method in the **ListSelection-Listener** interface to set the selected countries' flag images in the labels.

LISTING 15.8 `ListDemo.java`

```java
 1 import java.awt.*;
 2 import javax.swing.*;
 3 import javax.swing.event.*;
 4
 5 public class ListDemo extends JFrame {
 6   final int NUMBER_OF_FLAGS = 9;
 7
 8   // Declare an array of Strings for flag titles
 9   private String[] flagTitles = {"Canada", "China", "Denmark",
10     "France", "Germany", "India", "Norway", "United Kingdom",
11     "United States of America"};
12
13   // The list for selecting countries
14   private JList jlst = new JList(flagTitles);
15
16   // Declare an ImageIcon array for the national flags of 9 countries
17   private ImageIcon[] imageIcons = {
18     new ImageIcon("image/ca.gif"),
19     new ImageIcon("image/china.gif"),
20     new ImageIcon("image/denmark.gif"),
21     new ImageIcon("image/fr.gif"),
22     new ImageIcon("image/germany.gif"),
23     new ImageIcon("image/india.gif"),
24     new ImageIcon("image/norway.gif"),
25     new ImageIcon("image/uk.gif"),
26     new ImageIcon("image/us.gif")
27   };
28
29   // Arrays of labels for displaying images
30   private JLabel[] jlblImageViewer = new JLabel[NUMBER_OF_FLAGS];
31
32   public static void main(String[] args) {
33     ListDemo frame = new ListDemo();
34     frame.setSize(650, 500);
35     frame.setTitle("ListDemo");
36     frame.setLocationRelativeTo(null); // Center the frame
37     frame.setDefaultCloseOperation(JFrame.EXIT_ON_CLOSE);
38     frame.setVisible(true);
39   }
40
41   public ListDemo() {
42     // Create a panel to hold nine labels
43     JPanel p = new JPanel(new GridLayout(3, 3, 5, 5));
44
45     for (int i = 0; i < NUMBER_OF_FLAGS; i++) {
46       p.add(jlblImageViewer[i] = new JLabel());
47       jlblImageViewer[i].setHorizontalAlignment
48         (SwingConstants.CENTER);
49     }
50
51     // Add p and the list to the frame
52     add(p, BorderLayout.CENTER);
53     add(new JScrollPane(jlst), BorderLayout.WEST);
54
```

create frame

create UI

```
55        // Register listeners
56        jlst.addListSelectionListener(new ListSelectionListener() {
57          /** Handle list selection */
58          public void valueChanged(ListSelectionEvent e) {
59            // Get selected indices
60            int[] indices = jlst.getSelectedIndices();
61
62            int i;
63            // Set icons in the labels
64            for (i = 0; i < indices.length; i++) {
65              jlblImageViewer[i].setIcon(imageIcons[indices[i]]);
66            }
67
68            // Remove icons from the rest of the labels
69            for (; i < NUMBER_OF_FLAGS; i++) {
70              jlblImageViewer[i].setIcon(null);
71            }
72          }
73        });
74    }
75  }
```

`handler`

The anonymous inner class listener listens to `ListSelectionEvent` for handling the selection of country names in the list (lines 56–73). `ListSelectionEvent` and `ListSelection Listener` are defined in the `javax.swing.event` package, so this package is imported in the program (line 3).

The program creates an array of nine labels for displaying flag images for nine countries. The program loads the images of the nine countries into an image array (lines 17–27) and creates a list of the nine countries in the same order as in the image array (lines 9–11). Thus the index `0` of the image array corresponds to the first country in the list.

The list is placed in a scroll pane (line 53) so that it can be scrolled when the number of items in the list extends beyond the viewing area.

By default, the selection mode of the list is multiple-interval, which allows the user to select multiple items from different blocks in the list. When the user selects countries in the list, the `valueChanged` handler (lines 58–72) is executed, which gets the indices of the selected item and sets their corresponding image icons in the label to display the flags.

15.10 Scroll Bars

`JScrollBar` is a component that enables the user to select from a range of values, as shown in Figure 15.26.

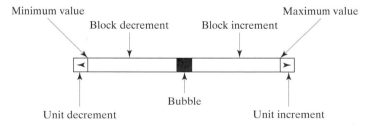

FIGURE 15.26 A scroll bar represents a range of values graphically.

Normally, the user changes the value of the scroll bar by making a gesture with the mouse. For example, the user can drag the scroll bar's bubble up and down, or click in the scroll bar's unit-increment or block-increment areas. Keyboard gestures can also be mapped to the scroll bar. By convention, the Page Up and Page Down keys are equivalent to clicking in the scroll bar's block-increment and block-decrement areas.

 Note

The width of the scroll bar's track corresponds to `maximum + visibleAmount`. When a scroll bar is set to its maximum value, the left side of the bubble is at `maximum`, and the right side is at `maximum + visibleAmount`.

`JScrollBar` has the following properties, as shown in Figure 15.27.

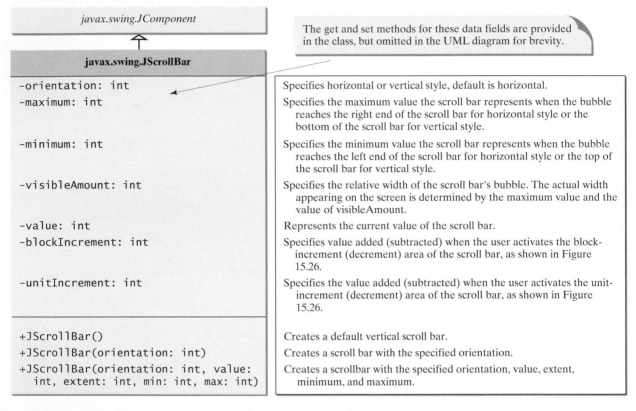

FIGURE 15.27 `JScrollBar` enables you to select from a range of values.

Normally, a program changes a scroll bar's value by calling the `setValue` method. The `setValue` method simultaneously and synchronously sets the minimum, maximum, visible amount, and value properties of a scroll bar, so that they are mutually consistent.

When the user changes the value of the scroll bar, the scroll bar generates an instance of `AdjustmentEvent`, which is passed to every registered listener. An object that wishes to be notified of changes to the scroll bar's value must implement the `adjustmentValueChanged` method in the `AdjustmentListener` interface defined in the package `java.awt.event`.

Listing 15.9 gives a program that uses horizontal and vertical scroll bars to control a message displayed on a panel. The horizontal scroll bar is used to move the message to the left or the right, and the vertical scroll bar to move it up and down. A sample run of the program is shown in Figure 15.28.

Here are the major steps in the program:

1. Create the user interface.

   Create a `MessagePanel` object and place it in the center of the frame. Create a vertical scroll bar and place it in the east of the frame. Create a horizontal scroll bar and place it in the south of the frame.

Message panel

Vertical scroll bar

Horizontal scroll bar

FIGURE 15.28 The scroll bars move the message on a panel horizontally and vertically.

2. Process the event.
   Create a listener to implement the `adjustmentValueChanged` handler to move the message according to the bar movement in the scroll bars.

LISTING 15.9 ScrollBarDemo.java

```
1 import java.awt.*;
2 import java.awt.event.*;
3 import javax.swing.*;
4
5 public class ScrollBarDemo extends JFrame {
6   // Create horizontal and vertical scroll bars
7   private JScrollBar jscbHort =
8     new JScrollBar(JScrollBar.HORIZONTAL);          horizontal scroll bar
9   private JScrollBar jscbVert =                     vertical scroll bar
10    new JScrollBar(JScrollBar.VERTICAL);
11
12  // Create a MessagePanel
13  private MessagePanel messagePanel =
14    new MessagePanel("Welcome to Java");
15
16  public static void main(String[] args) {
17    ScrollBarDemo frame = new ScrollBarDemo();      create frame
18    frame.setTitle("ScrollBarDemo");
19    frame.setLocationRelativeTo(null); // Center the frame
20    frame.setDefaultCloseOperation(JFrame.EXIT_ON_CLOSE);
21    frame.pack();
22    frame.setVisible(true);
23  }
24
25  public ScrollBarDemo() {                           create UI
26    // Add scroll bars and message panel to the frame
27    setLayout(new BorderLayout());
28    add(messagePanel, BorderLayout.CENTER);
29    add(jscbVert, BorderLayout.EAST);               add scroll bar vertical
30    add(jscbHort, BorderLayout.SOUTH);
31
32    // Register listener for the scroll bars
33    jscbHort.addAdjustmentListener(new AdjustmentListener() {   adjustment listener
34      public void adjustmentValueChanged(AdjustmentEvent e) {
35        // getValue() and getMaximumValue() return int, but for better
36        // precision, use double
37        double value = jscbHort.getValue();
38        double maximumValue = jscbHort.getMaximum();
39        double newX = (value * messagePanel.getWidth()
40          / maximumValue);
41        messagePanel.setXCoordinate((int) newX);
42      }
43    });
```

adjustment listener

```
44    jscbVert.addAdjustmentListener(new AdjustmentListener() {
45      public void adjustmentValueChanged(AdjustmentEvent e) {
46        // getValue() and getMaximumValue() return int, but for better
47        // precision, use double
48        double value = jscbVert.getValue();
49        double maximumValue = jscbVert.getMaximum();
50        double newY = (value * messagePanel.getHeight()
51          / maximumValue);
52        messagePanel.setYCoordinate((int)newY);
53      }
54    });
55  }
56 }
```

The program creates two scroll bars (`jscbVert` and `jscbHort`) (lines 7–10) and an instance of `MessagePanel` (`messagePanel`) (lines 13–14). `messagePanel` is placed in the center of the frame; `jscbVert` and `jscbHort` are placed in the east and south sections of the frame (lines 29–30), respectively.

You can specify the orientation of the scroll bar in the constructor or use the `set-Orientation` method. By default, the property value is `100` for `maximum`, `0` for `minimum`, `10` for `blockIncrement`, and `10` for `visibleAmount`.

When the user drags the bubble, or clicks the increment or decrement unit, the value of the scroll bar changes. An instance of `AdjustmentEvent` is generated and passed to the listener by invoking the `adjustmentValueChanged` handler. The listener for the vertical scroll bar moves the message up and down (lines 34–42), and the listener for the horizontal bar moves the message to right and left (lines 43–53).

The maximum value of the vertical scroll bar corresponds to the height of the panel, and the maximum value of the horizontal scroll bar corresponds to the width of the panel. The ratio between the current and maximum values of the horizontal scroll bar is the same as the ratio between the x value and the width of the message panel. Similarly, the ratio between the current and maximum values of the vertical scroll bar is the same as the ratio between the y value and the height of the message panel. The x-coordinate and y-coordinate are set in response to the scroll bar adjustments (lines 39, 50).

15.11 Sliders

`JSlider` is similar to `JScrollBar`, but `JSlider` has more properties and can appear in many forms. Figure 15.29 shows two sliders.

FIGURE 15.29 The sliders move the message on a panel horizontally and vertically.

`JSlider` lets the user graphically select a value by sliding a knob within a bounded interval. The slider can show both major tick marks and minor tick marks between them. The number of pixels between the tick marks is controlled by the `majorTickSpacing` and `minorTickSpacing` properties. Sliders can be displayed horizontally or vertically, with or without ticks, and with or without labels. The frequently used constructors and properties in JSlider are shown in Figure 15.30.

FIGURE 15.30 JSlider enables you to select from a range of values.

 Note

The values of a vertical scroll bar increase from top to bottom, but the values of a vertical slider decrease from top to bottom.

 Note

All the properties listed in Figure 15.30 have the associated get and set methods, which are omitted for brevity. By convention, the get method for a Boolean property is named *is\<PropertyName\>()*. In the JSlider class, the get methods for **paintLabels**, **paintTicks()**, **paintTrack()**, and **inverted** are **getPaintLabels()**, **getPaintTicks()**, **getPaintTrack()**, and **getInverted()**, which violate the naming convention.

When the user changes the value of the slider, the slider generates an instance of **javax.swing.event.ChangeEvent**, which is passed to any registered listeners. Any object that wishes to be notified of changes to the slider's value must implement **stateChanged** method in the **ChangeListener** interface defined in the package **javax.swing.event**.

Listing 15.10 writes a program that uses the sliders to control a message displayed on a panel, as shown in Figure 15.29. Here are the major steps in the program:

1. Create the user interface.
   Create a MessagePanel object and place it in the center of the frame. Create a vertical slider and place it in the east of the frame. Create a horizontal slider and place it in the south of the frame.

2. Process the event.
   Create a listener to implement the **stateChanged** handler in the **ChangeListener** interface to move the message according to the knot movement in the slider.

LISTING 15.10 SliderBarDemo.java

```
 1 import java.awt.*;
 2 import javax.swing.*;
 3 import javax.swing.event.*;
 4
 5 public class SliderDemo extends JFrame {
 6   // Create horizontal and vertical sliders
 7   private JSlider jsldHort = new JSlider(JSlider.HORIZONTAL);
 8   private JSlider jsldVert = new JSlider(JSlider.VERTICAL);
 9
10   // Create a MessagePanel
11   private MessagePanel messagePanel =
12    new MessagePanel("Welcome to Java");
13
14   public static void main(String[] args) {
15     SliderDemo frame = new SliderDemo();
16     frame.setTitle("SliderDemo");
17     frame.setLocationRelativeTo(null); // Center the frame
18     frame.setDefaultCloseOperation(JFrame.EXIT_ON_CLOSE);
19     frame.pack();
20     frame.setVisible(true);
21   }
22
23   public SliderDemo() {
24     // Add sliders and message panel to the frame
25     setLayout(new BorderLayout(5, 5));
26     add(messagePanel, BorderLayout.CENTER);
27     add(jsldVert, BorderLayout.EAST);
28     add(jsldHort, BorderLayout.SOUTH);
29
30     // Set properties for sliders
31     jsldHort.setMaximum(50);
32     jsldHort.setPaintLabels(true);
33     jsldHort.setPaintTicks(true);
34     jsldHort.setMajorTickSpacing(10);
35     jsldHort.setMinorTickSpacing(1);
36     jsldHort.setPaintTrack(false);
37     jsldVert.setInverted(true);
38     jsldVert.setMaximum(10);
39     jsldVert.setPaintLabels(true);
40     jsldVert.setPaintTicks(true);
41     jsldVert.setMajorTickSpacing(10);
42     jsldVert.setMinorTickSpacing(1);
43
44     // Register listener for the sliders
45     jsldHort.addChangeListener(new ChangeListener() {
46       /** Handle scroll bar adjustment actions */
47       public void stateChanged(ChangeEvent e) {
48         // getValue() and getMaximumValue() return int, but for better
49         // precision, use double
50         double value = jsldHort.getValue();
51         double maximumValue = jsldHort.getMaximum();
52         double newX = (value * messagePanel.getWidth()
53           / maximumValue);
54         messagePanel.setXCoordinate((int)newX);
55       }
56     });
57     jsldVert.addChangeListener(new ChangeListener() {
```

horizontal slider
vertical slider

create frame

create UI

slider properties

listener

listener

```
58        /** Handle scroll bar adjustment actions */
59        public void stateChanged(ChangeEvent e) {
60          // getValue() and getMaximumValue() return int, but for better
61          // precision, use double
62          double value = jsldVert.getValue();
63          double maximumValue = jsldVert.getMaximum();
64          double newY = (value * messagePanel.getHeight()
65            / maximumValue);
66          messagePanel.setYCoordinate((int)newY);
67        }
68      });
69  }
70 }
```

JSlider is similar to JScrollBar, but JSlider has more features. As shown in this example, you can specify maximum, labels, major ticks, and minor ticks on a JSlider (lines 31–35). You can also choose to hide the track (line 36). Since the values of a vertical slider decrease from top to bottom, the setInverted method reverses the order (line 37).

JSlider fires ChangeEvent when the slider is changed. The listener needs to implement the stateChanged handler in ChangeListener (lines 45–69). Note that JScrollBar fires AdjustmentEvent when the scroll bar is adjusted.

15.12 Creating Multiple Windows

Occasionally, you may want to create multiple windows in an application. The application opens a new window to perform the specified task. The new windows are called *subwindows*, and the main frame is called the *main window*.

To create a subwindow from an application, you need to create a subclass of JFrame that defines the task and tells the new window what to do. You can then create an instance of this subclass in the application and launch the new window by setting the frame instance to be visible.

Listing 15.11 gives a program that creates a main window with a text area in the scroll pane and a button named "Show Histogram." When the user clicks the button, a new window appears that displays a histogram to show the occurrences of the letters in the text area. Figure 15.31 contains a sample run of the program.

FIGURE 15.31   The histogram is displayed in a separate frame.

Here are the major steps in the program:

1. Create a main class for the frame named MultipleWindowsDemo in Listing 15.11. Add a text area inside a scroll pane, and place the scroll pane in the center of the frame. Create a button "Show Histogram" and place it in the south of the frame.

2. Create a subclass of `JPanel` named `Histogram` in Listing 15.12. The class contains a data field named `count` of the `int[]` type, which counts the occurrences of twenty-six letters. The values in `count` are displayed in the histogram.

3. Implement the `actionPerformed` handler in `MultipleWindowsDemo`, as follows:

   a. Create an instance of `Histogram`. Count the letters in the text area and pass the count to the `Histogram` object.

   b. Create a new frame and place the `Histogram` object in the center of frame. Display the frame.

LISTING 15.11 MultipleWindowsDemo.java

```java
 1 import java.awt.*;
 2 import java.awt.event.*;
 3 import javax.swing.*;
 4
 5 public class MultipleWindowsDemo extends JFrame {
 6   private JTextArea jta;
 7   private JButton jbtShowHistogram = new JButton("Show Histogram");
 8   private Histogram histogram = new Histogram();
 9
10   // Create a new frame to hold the histogram panel
11   private JFrame histogramFrame = new JFrame();
12
13   public MultipleWindowsDemo() {
14     // Store text area in a scroll pane
15     JScrollPane scrollPane = new JScrollPane(jta = new JTextArea());
16     scrollPane.setPreferredSize(new Dimension(300, 200));
17     jta.setWrapStyleWord(true);
18     jta.setLineWrap(true);
19
20     // Place scroll pane and button in the frame
21     add(scrollPane, BorderLayout.CENTER);
22     add(jbtShowHistogram, BorderLayout.SOUTH);
23
24     // Register listener
25     jbtShowHistogram.addActionListener(new ActionListener() {
26       /** Handle the button action */
27       public void actionPerformed(ActionEvent e) {
28         // Count the letters in the text area
29         int[] count = countLetters();
30
31         // Set the letter count to histogram for display
32         histogram.showHistogram(count);
33
34         // Show the frame
35         histogramFrame.setVisible(true);
36       }
37     });
38
39     // Create a new frame to hold the histogram panel
40     histogramFrame.add(histogram);
41     histogramFrame.pack();
42     histogramFrame.setTitle("Histogram");
43   }
44
```

create subframe (line 8)

create subframe (line 11)

create UI (line 13)

display subframe (line 35)

```
45   /** Count the letters in the text area */
46   private int[] countLetters() {
47     // Count for 26 letters
48     int[] count = new int[26];
49
50     // Get contents from the text area
51     String text = jta.getText();
52
53     // Count occurrence of each letter (case insensitive)
54     for (int i = 0; i < text.length(); i++) {
55       char character = text.charAt(i);
56
57       if ((character >= 'A') && (character <= 'Z')) {
58         count[(int)character - 65]++; // The ASCII for 'A' is 65
59       }
60       else if ((character >= 'a') && (character <= 'z')) {
61         count[(int)character - 97]++; // The ASCII for 'a' is 97
62       }
63     }
64
65     return count; // Return the count array
66   }
67
68   public static void main(String[] args) {
69     MultipleWindowsDemo frame = new MultipleWindowsDemo();                create main frame
70     frame.setLocationRelativeTo(null); // Center the frame
71     frame.setDefaultCloseOperation(JFrame.EXIT_ON_CLOSE);
72     frame.setTitle("MultipleWindowsDemo");
73     frame.pack();
74     frame.setVisible(true);
75   }
76 }
```

LISTING 15.12   Histogram.java

```
 1 import javax.swing.*;
 2 import java.awt.*;
 3
 4 public class Histogram extends JPanel {
 5   // Count the occurrence of 26 letters
 6   private int[] count;
 7
 8   /** Set the count and display histogram */
 9   public void showHistogram(int[] count) {
10     this.count = count;
11     repaint();
12   }
13
14   /** Paint the histogram */
15   protected void paintComponent(Graphics g) {
16     if (count == null) return; // No display if count is null           paint histogram
17
18     super.paintComponent(g);
19
20     // Find the panel size and bar width and interval dynamically
21     int width = getWidth();
22     int height = getHeight();
```

```
23      int interval = (width - 40) / count.length;
24      int individualWidth = (int)(((width - 40) / 24) * 0.60);
25
26      // Find the maximum count. The maximum count has the highest bar
27      int maxCount = 0;
28      for (int i = 0; i < count.length; i++) {
29        if (maxCount < count[i])
30          maxCount = count[i];
31      }
32
33      // x is the start position for the first bar in the histogram
34      int x = 30;
35
36      // Draw a horizontal base line
37      g.drawLine(10, height - 45, width - 10, height - 45);
38      for (int i = 0; i < count.length; i++) {
39        // Find the bar height
40        int barHeight =
41          (int)(((double)count[i] / (double)maxCount) * (height - 55));
42
43        // Display a bar (i.e., rectangle)
44        g.drawRect(x, height - 45 - barHeight, individualWidth,
45          barHeight);
46
47        // Display a letter under the base line
48        g.drawString((char)(65 + i) + " ", x, height - 30);
49
50        // Move x for displaying the next character
51        x += interval;
52      }
53    }
54
55    /** Override getPreferredSize */
56    public Dimension getPreferredSize() {
57      return new Dimension(300, 300);
58    }
59  }
```

`preferredSize` (line 56 margin note)

The program contains two classes: `MultipleWindowsDemo` and `Histogram`. Their relationship is shown in Figure 15.32.

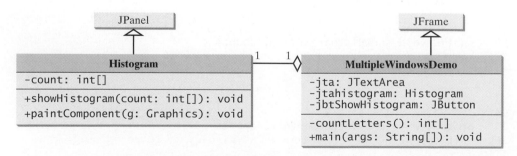

FIGURE 15.32 `MultipleWindowsDemo` uses `Histogram` to display a histogram of the occurrences of the letters in a text area in the frame.

`MultipleWindowsDemo` is a frame that holds a text area in a scroll pane and a button. `Histogram` is a subclass of `JPanel` that displays a histogram for the occurrences of letters in the text area.

When the user clicks the "Show Histogram" button, the handler counts the occurrences of letters in the text area. Letters are counted regardless of their case. Nonletter characters are not counted. The count is stored in an `int` array of twenty-six elements. The first element stores the count for letter '*a*' or '*A*,' and the last element in the array stores the count for letter '*z*' or 'Z.' The count array is passed to the histogram for display.

The `MultipleWindowsDemo` class contains a `main` method. The `main` method creates an instance of `MultipleWindowsDemo` and displays the frame. The `MultipleWindowsDemo` class also contains an instance of `JFrame`, named `histogramFrame`, which holds an instance of `Histogram`. When the user clicks the "Show Histogram" button, `histogramFrame` is set visible to display the histogram.

The height and width of the bars in the histogram are determined dynamically according to the window size of the histogram.

You cannot add an instance of `JFrame` to a container. For example, adding `histogramFrame` to the main frame would cause a runtime exception. However, you can create a frame instance and set it visible to launch a new window.

CHAPTER SUMMARY

■   You learned how to create graphical user interfaces using Swing GUI components `JButton`, `JCheckBox`, `JRadioButton`, `JLabel`, `JTextField`, `JTextArea`, `JComboBox`, `JList`, `JScrollBar`, and `JSlider`. You also learned how to handle events on these components.

■   You can display a text and icon on buttons (`JButton`, `JCheckBox`, `JRadioButton`) and labels.

REVIEW QUESTIONS

Sections 15.2–15.4

15.1   How do you create a button labeled "OK"? How do you change text on a button? How do you set an icon, pressed icon, and rollover icon in a button?

15.2   Given a `JButton` object `jbtOK`, write statements to set the button's foreground to red, background to yellow, mnemonic to 'K', tool tip text to "Click OK to proceed", horizontal alignment to RIGHT, vertical alignment to BOTTOM, horizontal text position to LEFT, vertical text position to TOP, and icon text gap to 5.

15.3   How do you create a check box? How do you create a check box with the box checked initially? How do you determine whether a check box is selected?

15.4   What is wrong if the statement `super.actionPerformed(e)` in `CheckBoxDemo` is omitted?

15.5   How do you create a radio button? How do you create a radio button with the button selected initially? How do you group the radio buttons together? How do you determine whether a radio button is selected?

Sections 15.5–15.9

15.6   How do you create a label named "Address"? How do you change the name on a label? How do you set an icon in a label?

15.7   Given a `JLabel` object `jlblMap`, write statements to set label's foreground to red, background to yellow, mnemonic to 'K', tool tip text to "Click OK to proceed", horizontal alignment to RIGHT, vertical alignment to BOTTOM, horizontal text position to LEFT, vertical text position to TOP, and icon text gap to 5.

15.8 How do you create a text field with ten columns and the default text "Welcome to Java"? How do you write the code to check whether a text field is empty?

15.9 How do you create a text area with ten rows and twenty columns? How do you insert three lines into the text area? How do you create a scrollable text area?

15.10 How do you create a combo box, add three items to it, and retrieve a selected item?

15.11 How do you create a list with an array of strings?

Sections 15.10–15.12

15.12 How do you create a horizontal scroll bar? What event can a scroll bar generate?

15.13 How do you create a vertical slider? What event can a slider generate?

15.14 Explain how to create and show multiple frames in an application.

PROGRAMMING EXERCISES

Sections 15.2–15.5

15.1* (*Revising Listing 15.2, ButtonDemo.java*) Rewrite Listing 15.2 to add a group of radio buttons to select background colors. The available colors are red, yellow, white, gray, and green (see Figure 15.33).

FIGURE 15.33 The $<=$ and $=>$ buttons move the message on the panel, and you can also set the background color for the message.

15.2* (*Selecting geometric figures*) Write a program that draws various figures, as shown in Figure 15.34. The user selects a figure from a radio button and specifies whether it is filled in a check box. (Hint: Use the `FigurePanel` class introduced in §13.7 to display a figure.)

FigurePanel

Panel with
FlowLayout

FIGURE 15.34 The program displays lines, rectangles, and ovals when you select a shape type.

15.3**(*Traffic lights*) Write a program that simulates a traffic light. The program lets the user select one of three lights: red, yellow, or green. When a radio button is selected, the light is turned on, and only one light can be on at a time (see Figure 15.35). No light is on when the program starts.

FIGURE 15.35 The radio buttons are grouped to let you select only one color in the group to control a traffic light.

Sections 15.6–15.10

15.4* (*Creating a simple calculator*) Write a program to perform add, subtract, multiply, and divide operations (see Figure 15.36).

FIGURE 15.36 The program does addition, subtraction, multiplication, and division on double numbers.

15.5* (*Creating a miles/kilometers converter*) Write a program that converts miles and kilometers, as shown in Figure 15.37. If you enter a value in the Mile text field and press the Enter key, the corresponding kilometer is displayed in the Kilometer text field. Likewise, if you enter a value in the Kilometer text field and press the Enter key, the corresponding mile is displayed in the Mile text field.

FIGURE 15.37 The program converts miles to kilometers, and vice versa.

15.6* (*Creating an investment value calculator*) Write a program that calculates the future value of an investment at a given interest rate for a specified number of years. The formula for the calculation is as follows:

$$\text{futureValue} = \text{investmentAmount} * (1 + \text{monthlyInterestRate})^{\text{years}*12}$$

Use text fields for interest rate, investment amount, and years. Display the future amount in a text field when the user clicks the Calculate button, as shown in Figure 15.38.

FIGURE 15.38 The user enters the investment amount, years, and interest rate to compute future value.

15.7* (*Setting clock time*) Write a program that displays a clock time and sets the clock time with the input from three text fields, as shown in Figure 15.39. Use the StillClock in §13.12, "Case Study: The StillClock Class."

FIGURE 15.39 The program displays the time specified in the text fields.

15.8** (*Selecting a font*) Write a program that can dynamically change the font of a message to be displayed on a panel. The message can be displayed in bold and italic at the same time, or can be displayed in the center of the panel. You can select the font name or font size from combo boxes, as shown in Figure 15.40. The available font names can be obtained using getAvailableFontFamilyNames() in GraphicsEnvironment (§12.7, "The Font Class"). The combo box for font size is initialized with numbers from 1 to 100.

FIGURE 15.40 You can dynamically set the font for the message.

15.9** (*Demonstrating JLabel properties*) Write a program to let the user dynamically set the properties horizontalAlignment, verticalAlignment, horizontalTextAlignment, and verticalTextAlignment, as shown in Figure 15.41.

FIGURE 15.41 You can set the alignment and text-position properties of a button dynamically.

15.10* (*Adding new features into Listing 15.2, ButtonDemo.java, incrementally*) Improve Listing 15.2 incrementally, as follows (see Figure 15.42):

1. Add a text field labeled "Enter a new message" in the same panel with the buttons. Upon typing a new message in the text field and pressing the Enter key, the new message is displayed in the message panel.

2. Add a combo box labeled "Select an interval" in the same panel with the buttons. The combo box enables the user to select a new interval for moving the message. The selection values range from 5 to 100 with interval 5. The user can also type a new interval in the combo box.

3. Add three radio buttons that enable the user to select the foreground color for the message as Red, Green, and Blue. The radio buttons are grouped in a panel, and the panel is placed in the north of the frame's content pane.

4. Add three check boxes that enable the user to center the message and display it in italic or bold. Place the check boxes in the same panel with the radio buttons.

5. Add a border titled "Message Panel" on the message panel, add a border titled "South Panel" on the panel for buttons, and add a border titled "North Panel" on the panel for radio buttons and check boxes.

FIGURE 15.42 The program uses buttons, labels, text fields, combo boxes, radio buttons, check boxes, and borders.

15.11* (*Demonstrating JTextField properties*) Write a program that sets the horizontal-alignment and column-size properties of a text field dynamically, as shown in Figure 15.43.

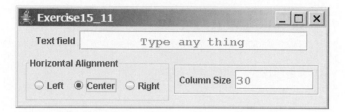

FIGURE 15.43 You can set the horizontal-alignment and column-size properties of a text field dynamically.

15.12* (*Demonstrating* **JTextArea** *properties*) Write a program that demonstrates the wrapping styles of the text area. The program uses a check box to indicate whether the text area is wrapped. In the case where the text area is wrapped, you need to specify whether it is wrapped by characters or by words, as shown in Figure 15.44.

FIGURE 15.44 You can set the options to wrap a text area by characters or by words dynamically.

15.13* (*Comparing loans with various interest rates*) Rewrite Exercise 4.21 to create a user interface, as shown in Figure 15.45. Your program should let the user enter the loan amount and loan period in number of years from a text field, and should display the monthly and total payments for each interest rate starting from 5 percent to 8 percent, with increments of one-eighth, in a text area.

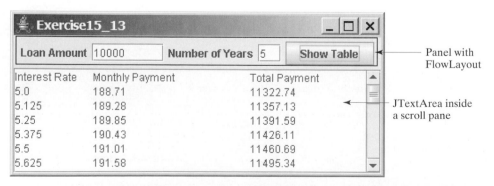

FIGURE 15.45 The program displays a table for monthly payments and total payments on a given loan based on various interest rates.

15.14* (*Using* **JComboBox** *and* **JList**) Write a program that demonstrates selecting items in a list. The program uses a combo box to specify a selection mode, as shown in Figure 15.46. When you select items, they are displayed in a label below the list.

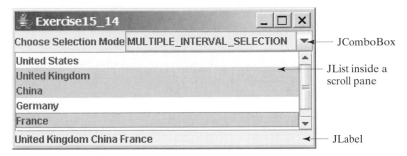

FIGURE 15.46 You can choose single selection, single-interval selection, or multiple-interval selection in a list.

Sections 15.11–15.13

15.15** (*Using JScrollBar*) Write a program that uses scroll bars to select the foreground color for a label, as shown in Figure 15.47. Three horizontal scroll bars are used for selecting the red, green, and blue components of the color. Use a title border on the panel that holds the scroll bars.

FIGURE 15.47 The foreground color changes in the label as you adjust the scroll bars.

15.16** (*Using JSlider*) Revise the preceding exercise using sliders.

15.17*** (*Displaying a calendar*) Write a program that displays the calendar for the current month, as shown in Figure 15.48. Use labels, and set texts on the labels to display the calendar. Use the GregorianCalendar class in §10.3, "The

FIGURE 15.48 The program displays the calendar for the current month.

`Calendar` and `GregorianCalendar` classes," to obtain the information about month, year, first day of the month, and number of days in the month.

15.18* (*Revising Listing 15.11, MultipleWindowsDemo.java*) Instead of displaying the occurrences of the letters using the `Histogram` component in Listing 15.11, use a bar chart, so that the display is as shown in Figure 15.49.

FIGURE 15.49 The number of occurrences of each letter is displayed in a bar chart.

Three exercises involving text I/O using Scanner

15.19** (*Text Viewer*) Write a program that displays a text file in a text area, as shown in Figure 15.50. The user enters a filename in a text field and clicks the View button; the file is then displayed in a text area.

FIGURE 15.50 The program displays a histogram that shows the occurrences of each letter in the file.

15.20** (*Displaying country flag and flag description*) Listing 15.7, ComboBoxDemo.java, gives a program that lets users view a country's flag image and description by selecting the country from a combo box. The description is a string coded in the program. Rewrite the program to read the text description from a file. Suppose that the descriptions are stored in the file `description0.txt`, ..., and `description8.txt` under the text directory for the nine countries Canada, China, Denmark, France, Germany, India, Norway, the United Kingdom, and the United States, in this order.

15.21** (*Creating a histogram for occurrences of letters*) In Listing 15.11, MultipleWindowsDemo.java, you developed a program that displays a histogram to show the occurrences of each letter in a text area. Reuse the `Histogram` class created in Listing 15.12 to write a program that will display a histogram on a panel. The histogram should show the occurrences of each letter in a text file, as shown in Figure 15.51. Assume that the letters are not case-sensitive.

- Place a panel that will display the histogram in the center of the frame.
- Place a label and a text field in a panel, and put the panel in the south side of the frame. The text file will be entered from this text field.
- Pressing the Enter key on the text field causes the program to count the occurrences of each letter and display the count in a histogram.

FIGURE 15.51   The program displays a histogram that shows the occurrences of each letter in the file.

15.22** *(Slideshow)* Exercise 14.13 developed a slideshow using images. Rewrite Exercise 14.13 to develop a slideshow using text files. Suppose ten text files named `slide0.txt`, `slide1.txt`, ..., and `slide9.txt` are stored in the `text` directory downloadable along with the source code in the book. Each slide displays the text from one file. Each slide is shown for a second. The slides are displayed in order. When the last slide finishes, the first slide is redisplayed, and so on. Use a text area to display the slide.

CHAPTER 16

APPLETS AND MULTIMEDIA

Objectives

- To explain how the Web browser controls and executes applets (§16.2).

- To describe the `init`, `start`, `stop`, and `destroy` methods in the `Applet` class (§§16.2.1–16.2.4).

- To develop Swing applets using the `JApplet` class (§16.3).

- To know how to embed applets in Web pages (§16.4).

- To run applets from the appletviewer and from Web browsers (§§16.4.1–16.4.2).

- To write a Java program that can run as both an application and an applet (§16.5).

- To pass string values to applets from HTML (§16.6).

- (Optional) To locate resource (images and audio) using the `URL` class (§16.9).

- (Optional) To play audio (§16.10).

- (Optional) To package and deploy Java projects using Java archive files (§16.12).

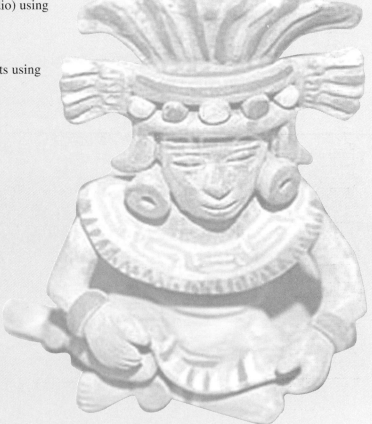

16.1 Introduction

Java's early success has been attributed to applets. Running from a Java-enabled Web browser, applets bring dynamic interaction and live animation to an otherwise static HTML page. It is safe to say that Java would be nowhere today without applets. They made Java instantly appealing, attractive, and popular during its infancy. Java is now used not only for applets, but also for standalone applications and as a programming language for developing server-side applications and for mobile devices.

In this book so far, you have only used Java applications. Everything you have learned about writing applications, however, also applies to writing applets. Applications and applets share many common programming features, although they differ slightly in some respects. For example, every application must have a `main` method, which is invoked by the Java interpreter. Java applets, on the other hand, do not need a `main` method. They run in the Web browser environment. Because applets are invoked from a Web page, Java provides special features that enable applets to run from a Web browser.

In this chapter, you will learn how to write Java applets, discover the relationship between applets and the Web browser, and explore the similarities and differences between applications and applets. You will also learn how to create multimedia applets with images and audio.

16.2 The `Applet` Class

The `Applet` class provides the essential framework that enables applets to be run from a Web browser. While every Java application has a `main` method that is executed, when the application starts, applets do not have a `main` method. Instead they depend on the browser to call the methods in the `Applet` class. Every applet is a subclass of `java.applet.Applet`, as outlined below:

subclass of `Applet`

```
public class MyApplet extends java.applet.Applet {
  ...
  /** The no-arg constructor is called by the browser when the Web
   *  page containing this applet is initially loaded, or reloaded
   */
  public MyApplet() {
    ...
  }

  /** Called by the browser after the applet is loaded
   */
  public void init() {
    ...
  }

  /** Called by the browser after the init() method, or
   *  every time the Web page is visited
   */
  public void start() {
    ...
  }

  /** Called by the browser when the page containing this
   *  applet becomes inactive
   */
  public void stop() {
    ...
  }

  /** Called by the browser when the Web browser exits */
  public void destroy() {
    ...
  }

  /** Other methods if necessary... */
}
```

no-arg constructor required

When the applet is loaded, the Web browser creates an instance of the applet by invoking the applet's *no-arg constructor*. So the applet must have a no-arg constructor declared either explicitly or implicitly. The browser uses the `init`, `start`, `stop`, and `destroy` methods to control the applet. By default, these methods do nothing. To perform specific functions, they need to be modified in the user's applet so that the browser can call your code properly. Figure 16.1(a) shows how the browser calls these methods, and Figure 16.1(b) illustrates the flow of control of an applet using a statechart diagram.

no-arg constructor

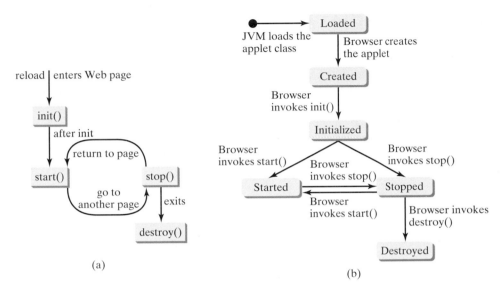

FIGURE 16.1   The Web browser uses the `init`, `start`, `stop`, and `destroy` methods to control the applet.

16.2.1 The `init` Method

The `init` method is invoked after the applet is created. A subclass of `Applet` should override this method if the subclass has an initialization to perform. The functions usually implemented in this method include setting up user-interface components, loading resources such as images and audio, and getting string parameter values from the `<applet>` tag in the HTML page.

`init()`

16.2.2 The `start` Method

The `start` method is invoked after the `init` method. It is also called when the user returns to the Web page containing the applet after surfing other pages.

`start()`

A subclass of `Applet` overrides this method if it has any operation that needs to be performed whenever the Web page containing the applet is visited. An applet with animation, for example, might start the timer to resume animation.

16.2.3 The `stop` Method

The `stop` method is the opposite of the `start` method. The `start` method is called when the user moves back to the page that contains the applet. The `stop` method is invoked when the user leaves the page.

`stop()`

A subclass of `Applet` overrides this method if it has any operation that needs to be performed each time the Web page containing the applet is no longer visible. An applet with animation, for example, might stop the timer to pause animation.

16.2.4 The `destroy` Method

destroy()

The `destroy` method is invoked when the browser exits normally to inform the applet that it is no longer needed and should release any resources it has allocated. The `stop` method is always called before the `destroy` method.

A subclass of `Applet` overrides this method if it has any operation that needs to be performed before it is destroyed. Usually, you won't need to override this method unless you wish to release specific resources that the applet created.

16.3 The `JApplet` Class

The `Applet` class is an AWT class and is not designed to work with Swing components. To use Swing components in Java applets, it is necessary to create a Java applet that extends `javax.swing.JApplet`, which is a subclass of `java.applet.Applet`. `JApplet` inherits all the methods from the `Applet` class. In addition, it provides support for laying out Swing components.

To add a component to an applet, you add it to the content pane of an applet, which is similar to adding a component to the content pane of a frame. By default, the content pane of `JApplet` uses `BorderLayout`. Here is an example of a simple applet that uses `JLabel` to display a message.

add a label in applet

```
// WelcomeApplet.java: Applet for displaying a message
import javax.swing.*;

public class WelcomeApplet extends JApplet {
  /** Initialize the applet */
  public void init() {
    add(new JLabel("Welcome to Java", JLabel.CENTER));
  }
}
```

content pane delegation

Note

The *content pane delegation* feature in JDK 1.5 allows you to invoke the **add** method from an applet to place components to the content pane of an applet. Strictly speaking, a component is added into the content pane of an applet. But for simplicity we say that a component is added to an applet.

You cannot run this applet standalone, because it does not have a `main` method. To run this applet, you have to create an HTML file with the applet tag that references the applet. When you write Java GUI applications, you must create a frame to hold graphical components, set the frame size, and make the frame visible. Applets are run from the Web browser. The Web browser automatically places the applet inside it and makes it visible. The following section shows how to create HTML files for applets.

alternative coding

Note

You may rewrite the `WelcomeApplet` by moving the code in the `init` method to the no-arg constructor, as follows:

```
// WelcomeApplet.java: Applet for displaying a message
import javax.swing.*;

public class WelcomeApplet extends JApplet {
  /** Construct the applet */
  public WelcomeApplet() {
    add(new JLabel("Welcome to Java", JLabel.CENTER));
  }
}
```

16.4 The HTML File and the `<applet>` Tag

HTML is a markup language that presents static documents on the Web. It uses tags to instruct the Web browser how to render a Web page and contains a tag called `<applet>` that incorporates applets into a Web page.

The following HTML file named WelcomeApplet.html invokes the WelcomeApplet.class:

```html
<html>
  <head>
    <title>Welcome Java Applet</title>
  </head>
  <body>
    <applet
      code = "WelcomeApplet.class"
      width = 350
      height = 200>
    </applet>
  </body>
</html>
```

applet class

A *tag* is an instruction to the Web browser. The browser interprets the tag and decides how to display or otherwise treat the subsequent contents of the HTML document. Tags are enclosed inside brackets. The first word in a tag, called the *tag name*, describes tag functions. Tags can have additional attributes, sometimes with values after an equals sign, which further define the tag's action. For example, in the preceding HTML file, `<applet>` is the tag name, and `code`, `width`, and `height` are the attributes. The `width` and `height` attributes specify the rectangular viewing area of the applet.

Most tags have a *start tag* and a corresponding *end tag*. The tag has a specific effect on the region between the start tag and the end tag. For example, `<applet...>...</applet>` tells the browser to display an applet. An end tag is always the start tag's name preceded by a slash.

An HTML document begins with the `<html>` tag, which declares that the document is written in HTML. Each document has two parts, a *head* and a *body*, defined by `<head>` and `<body>` tags, respectively. The head part contains the document title, using the `<title>` tag and other information the browser can use when rendering the document, and the body part contains the actual contents of the document. The header is optional. For more information, refer to Supplement VI.A, "HTML and XHTML Tutorial."

HTML tag

The complete syntax of the `<applet>` tag is as follows:

`<applet>` tag

```html
<applet
  [codebase = applet_url]
  code = classfilename.class
  width = applet_viewing_width_in_pixels
  height = applet_viewing_height_in_pixels
  [archive = archivefile]
  [vspace = vertical_margin]
  [hspace = horizontal_margin]
  [align = applet_alignment]
  [alt = alternative_text]
>
<param name = param_name1 value = param_value1>
<param name = param_name2 value = param_value2>
...
<param name = param_name3 value = param_value3>
</applet>
```

`<param>` tag

The `code`, `width`, and `height` attributes are required; all the others are optional. The `<param>` tag is introduced in §16.6, "Passing Strings to Applets." The other attributes are explained below.

codebase attribute

- **codebase** specifies a base where your classes are loaded. If this attribute is not used, the Web browser loads the applet from the directory in which the HTML page is located. If your applet is located in a different directory from the HTML page, you must specify the `applet_url` for the browser to load the applet. This attribute enables you to load the class from anywhere on the Internet. The classes used by the applet are dynamically loaded when needed.

archive attribute

- **archive** instructs the browser to load an archive file that contains all the class files needed to run the applet. Archiving allows the Web browser to load all the classes from a single compressed file at one time, thus reducing loading time and improving performance. To create archives, see §16.12, "Packaging and Deploying Java Projects."

- **vspace** and **hspace** specify the size, in pixels, of the blank margin to pad around the applet vertically and horizontally.

- **align** specifies how the applet will be aligned in the browser. One of nine values is used: `left`, `right`, `top`, `texttop`, `middle`, `absmiddle`, `baseline`, `bottom`, or `absbottom`.

- **alt** specifies the text to be displayed in case the browser cannot run Java.

16.4.1 Viewing Applets Using the Applet Viewer Utility

appletviewer

You can test the applet using the applet viewer utility, which can be invoked from the DOS prompt using the *appletviewer* command from `c:\book`, as shown in Figure 16.2. Its output is shown in Figure 16.3.

FIGURE 16.2 The appletviewer command runs a Java applet in the applet viewer utility.

FIGURE 16.3 The WelcomeApplet program is running from the applet viewer.

16.4.2 Viewing Applets from a Web Browser

Applets are eventually displayed in a Web browser. Using the applet viewer, you do not need to start a Web browser. The applet viewer functions as a browser. It is convenient for testing applets during development. However, you should also test the applets from a Web browser before deploying them on a Web site. To display an applet from a Web browser, open the applet's HTML file (e.g., WelcomeApplet.html). Its output is shown in Figure 16.4.

FIGURE 16.4   The WelcomeApplet program is displayed in Internet Explorer.

To make your applet accessible on the Web, you need to store the WelcomeApplet.class and WelcomeApplet.html on a Web server. You can view the applet from an appropriate URL. For cxample, I have uploaded these two files on Web server www.cs.armstrong.edu/. As shown in Figure 16.5, you can access the applet from www.cs.armstrong.edu/liang/intro6e/book/WelcomeApplet.html.

FIGURE 16.5   The `WelcomeApplet` program is downloaded from the Web server.

16.4.3   Example: The Loan Applet

This example writes an applet that computes loan payments. The applet enables the user to enter the interest rate, the number of years, and the loan amount. Clicking the Compute Payment button displays the monthly payment and the total payment, as shown in Figure 16.6. The applet is given in Listing 16.1.

FIGURE 16.6   The applet computes the monthly payment and the total payment when provided with the interest rate, number of years, and loan amount.

LISTING 16.1 LoanApplet.java

```java
1  import java.awt.*;
2  import java.awt.event.*;
3  import javax.swing.*;
4  import javax.swing.border.TitledBorder;
5
6  public class LoanApplet extends JApplet {
7    // Declare and create text fields for interest rate
8    // year, loan amount, monthly payment, and total payment
9    private JTextField jtfAnnualInterestRate = new JTextField();
10   private JTextField jtfNumberOfYears = new JTextField();
11   private JTextField jtfLoanAmount = new JTextField();
12   private JTextField jtfMonthlyPayment = new JTextField();
13   private JTextField jtfTotalPayment = new JTextField();
14
15   // Declare and create a Compute Payment button
16   private JButton jbtComputeLoan = new JButton("Compute Payment");
17
18   /** Initialize user interface */
19   public void init() {
20     // Set properties on the text fields
21     jtfMonthlyPayment.setEditable(false);
22     jtfTotalPayment.setEditable(false);
23
24     // Right align text fields
25     jtfAnnualInterestRate.setHorizontalAlignment(JTextField.RIGHT);
26     jtfNumberOfYears.setHorizontalAlignment(JTextField.RIGHT);
27     jtfLoanAmount.setHorizontalAlignment(JTextField.RIGHT);
28     jtfMonthlyPayment.setHorizontalAlignment(JTextField.RIGHT);
29     jtfTotalPayment.setHorizontalAlignment(JTextField.RIGHT);
30
31     // Panel p1 to hold labels and text fields
32     JPanel p1 = new JPanel(new GridLayout(5, 2));
33     p1.add(new JLabel("Annual Interest Rate"));
34     p1.add(jtfAnnualInterestRate);
35     p1.add(new JLabel("Number of Years"));
36     p1.add(jtfNumberOfYears);
37     p1.add(new JLabel("Loan Amount"));
38     p1.add(jtfLoanAmount);
39     p1.add(new JLabel("Monthly Payment"));
40     p1.add(jtfMonthlyPayment);
41     p1.add(new JLabel("Total Payment"));
42     p1.add(jtfTotalPayment);
43     p1.setBorder(new
44       TitledBorder("Enter interest rate, year and loan amount"));
45
46     // Panel p2 to hold the button
47     JPanel p2 = new JPanel(new FlowLayout(FlowLayout.RIGHT));
48     p2.add(jbtComputeLoan);
49
50     // Add the components to the applet
51     add(p1, BorderLayout.CENTER);
52     add(p2, BorderLayout.SOUTH);
53
54     // Register listener
55     jbtComputeLoan.addActionListener(new ButtonListener());
56   }
57
```

(margin notes, top to bottom:)
create text fields

create a button

create UI

titled border

add to applet

```
58   /** Handle the Compute Payment button */
59   private class ButtonListener implements ActionListener {          listener class
60     public void actionPerformed(ActionEvent e) {
61       // Get values from text fields
62       double interest =
63         Double.parseDouble(jtfAnnualInterestRate.getText());
64       int year =
65         Integer.parseInt(jtfNumberOfYears.getText());
66       double loanAmount =
67         Double.parseDouble(jtfLoanAmount.getText());
68
69       // Create a loan object
70       Loan loan = new Loan(interest, year, loanAmount);              create Loan object
71
72       // Display monthly payment and total payment
73       jtfMonthlyPayment.setText(String.format("%.2f",
74         loan.getMonthlyPayment()));
75       jtfTotalPayment.setText(String.format("%.2f",
76         loan.getTotalPayment()));
77     }
78   }
79 }
```

You need to use the `public` modifier for the `LoanApplet`; otherwise, the Web browser   public applet
cannot load it (line 6).

The `init` method initializes the user interface (lines 19–56). The program overrides this
method to create user-interface components (labels, text fields, and a button), and places them
in the applet.

The only event handled is the Compute Payment button. When this button is clicked, the
`actionPerformed` method gets the interest rate, number of years, and loan amount from the
text fields. It then creates a `Loan` object (line 70) to obtain the monthly payment and the total
payment. Finally, it displays the monthly and total payments in their respective text fields.
The `Loan` class is responsible for computing the payments. This class was introduced in
§7.15, "Case Study: The `Loan` Class."

To run the applet, embed it in the HTML file, as shown in Listing 16.2.

LISTING 16.2 LoanApplet.html

```
<!-- HTML code, this code is separated from the preceding Java code -->
<html>
  <head>
    <title>Loan Applet</title>
  </head>
  <body>
    This is a loan calculator. Enter your input for interest, year,
    and loan amount. Click the "Compute Payment" button, you will
    get the payment information. <p>
    <applet
      code = "LoanApplet.class"
      width = 300
      height = 150
      alt = "You must have a Java 2-enabled browser to view the applet">
    </applet>
  </body>
</html>
```

Applet demos

Tip

Many interesting applets are included in the JDK demo. To run them, change the directory to

c:\Program Files\Java\jdk1.**5.0**\demo\applets

Use the **dir** command to list the contents in the directory, as shown in Figure 16.7(a). Change to a subdirectory (e.g., using the command **cd Animator**). There are one or several .html files in that directory for executing applets (e.g., **example1.html**). In the command window, type the following to run the applet, as shown in Figure 16.7(b):

appletviewer example1.html

(a)

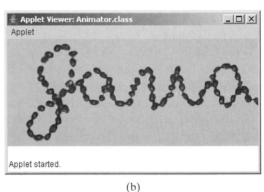

(b)

FIGURE 16.7 You can find applet examples in the JDK demo directory.

16.5 Enabling Applets to Run as Applications

The **JFrame** class and the **JApplet** class have a lot in common despite some differences. Since they both are subclasses of the **Container** class, all their user-interface components, layout managers, and event-handling features are the same. Applications, however, are invoked from the static **main** method by the Java interpreter JVM, and applets are run by the Web browser. The Web browser creates an instance of the applet using the applet's no-arg constructor and controls and executes the applet through the **init**, **start**, **stop**, and **destroy** methods.

For security reasons, the restrictions listed below are imposed on applets to prevent destructive programs from damaging the system on which the browser is running.

- Applets are not allowed to read from, or write to, the file system of the computer. Otherwise, they could damage the files and spread viruses.

- Applets are not allowed to run programs on the browser's computer. Otherwise, they might call destructive local programs and damage the local system on the user's computer.

- Applets are not allowed to establish connections between the user's computer and any other computer, except for the server where the applets are stored. This restriction prevents the applet from connecting the user's computer to another computer without the user's knowledge.

Note

A new security protocol was introduced in Java 2 to allow *trusted applets* to circumvent the secu-   trusted applet
rity restrictions. See http://www.developer.com/java/ent/article.php/3303561 for detailed instructions on
how to create trusted applets.

In general, an applet can be converted to an application without loss of functionality. An
application can be converted to an applet as long as it does not violate the security restrictions
imposed on applets. You can implement a `main` method in an applet to enable the applet to
run as an application. This feature has both theoretical and practical implications. Theoretically,
it blurs the difference between applets and applications. You can write a class that is both an
applet and an application. From the standpoint of practicality, it is convenient to be able to
run a program in two ways.

It is not difficult to write such programs on your own. Suppose you have an applet named
`MyApplet`. To enable it to run as an application, all you need to do is add a `main` method in
the applet with the implementation, as follows:

```
 1 public static void main(String[] args) {
 2     // Create a frame
 3     JFrame frame = new JFrame("Applet is in the frame");                create frame
 4
 5     // Create an instance of the applet
 6     MyApplet applet = new MyApplet();                                   create applet
 7
 8     // Add the applet to the frame
 9     frame.add(applet, BorderLayout.CENTER);                             add applet
10
11     // Invoke init and start
12     applet.init();                                                      init()
13     applet.start();                                                     start()
14
15     // Display the frame                                                show frame
16     frame.setLocationRelativeTo(null); // Center the frame
17     frame.setDefaultCloseOperation(JFrame.EXIT_ON_CLOSE);
18     frame.setSize(300, 300);
19     frame.setVisible(true);
20 }
```

The `main` method creates a frame to hold an applet (line 13). When the applet is run from
a Web browser, the Web browser invokes the `init` and `start` methods of the applet. When
the applet is run standalone, you have to manually invoke the `init` and `start` methods in
order to perform the operations in these methods (lines 12–13).

You can revise the `LoanApplet` class in Listing 16.1 to enable `LoanApplet` to run standalone by adding a `main` method in Listing 16.3.

LISTING 16.3   New LoanApplet.java with a **main** Method

```
 1 import java.awt.*;
 2 import java.awt.event.*;
 3 import javax.swing.*;
 4 import javax.swing.border.TitledBorder;
 5
 6 public class LoanApplet extends JApplet {
 7     // Same code in Listing 16.1 from line 7 to line 78
 8     ...                                                                  code omitted
 9
10     public static void main(String[] args) {
11         // Create a frame                                               new main method
12         JFrame frame = new JFrame("Applet is in the frame");
```

```
13
14      // Create an instance of the applet
15      LoanApplet applet = new LoanApplet();
16
17      // Add the applet to the frame
18      frame.add(applet, BorderLayout.CENTER);
19
20      // Invoke applet's init method
21      applet.init();
22
23      // Display the frame
24      frame.setLocationRelativeTo(null); // Center the frame
25      frame.setDefaultCloseOperation(JFrame.EXIT_ON_CLOSE);
26      frame.setSize(300, 300);
27      frame.setVisible(true);
28   }
29 }
```

16.6 Passing Strings to Applets

In §8.5, "Command-Line Arguments," you learned how to pass strings to Java applications from a command line. Strings are passed to the `main` method as an array of strings. When the application starts, the `main` method can use these strings. There is no `main` method in an applet, however, and applets are not run from the command line by the Java interpreter.

How, then, can applets accept arguments? In this section, you will learn how to pass strings to Java applets. To be passed to an applet, a parameter must be declared in the HTML file, and must be read by the applet when it is initialized. Parameters are declared using the `<param>` tag. The `<param>` tag must be embedded in the `<applet>` tag and has no end tag. The syntax for the `<param>` tag is given below:

```
<param name = parametername value = stringvalue />
```

This tag specifies a parameter and its corresponding string value.

 Note
There is no comma separating the parameter name from the parameter value in the HTML code. The HTML parameter names are not case sensitive.

Suppose you want to write an applet to display a message. The message is passed as a parameter. In addition, you want the message to be displayed at a specific location with x-coordinate and y-coordinate, which are passed as two parameters. The parameters and their values are listed in Table 16.1.

TABLE 16.1 Parameter Names and Values for the `DisplayMessage` Applet

Parameter Name	Parameter Value
MESSAGE	"Welcome to Java"
X	20
Y	30

The HTML source file is given in Listing 16.4.

LISTING 16.4 DisplayMessage.html

```html
<html>
  <head>
    <title>Passing Strings to Java Applets</title>
  </head>
  <body>
    <p>This applet gets a message from the HTML
       page and displays it.</p>
    <applet
      code = "DisplayMessage.class"
      width = 200
      height = 50
      alt = "You must have a Java 2-enabled browser to view the applet"
    >
      <param name = MESSAGE value = "Welcome to Java" />
      <param name = X value = 20 />
      <param name = Y value = 30 />
    </applet>
  </body>
</html>
```

To read the parameter from the applet, use the following method defined in the `Applet` class:

```
public String getParameter(String parametername);
```

This returns the value of the specified parameter.

The applet is given in Listing 16.5. A sample run of the applet is shown in Figure 16.8.

FIGURE 16.8 The applet displays the message `Welcome to Java` passed from the HTML page.

LISTING 16.5 DisplayMessage.java

```java
 1 import javax.swing.*;
 2
 3 public class DisplayMessage extends JApplet {
 4   /** Initialize the applet */
 5   public void init() {
 6     // Get parameter values from the HTML file
 7     String message = getParameter("MESSAGE");                          getParameter
 8     int x = Integer.parseInt(getParameter("X"));
 9     int y = Integer.parseInt(getParameter("Y"));
10
11     // Create a message panel
12     MessagePanel messagePanel = new MessagePanel(message);
13     messagePanel.setXCoordinate(x);
14     messagePanel.setYCoordinate(y);
15
```

add to applet

```
16       // Add the message panel to the applet
17       add(messagePanel);
18     }
19 }
```

The program gets the parameter values from the HTML in the `init` method. The values are strings obtained using the **getParameter** method (lines 7–9). Because **x** and **y** are `int`, the program uses **Integer.parseInt(string)** to parse a digital string into an `int` value.

If you change `Welcome to Java` in the HTML file to `Welcome to HTML`, and reload the HTML file in the Web browser, you should see `Welcome to HTML` displayed. Similarly, the **x** and **y** values can be changed to display the message in a desired location.

 Caution

The **Applet**'s **getParameter** method can be invoked only after an instance of the applet is created. Therefore, this method cannot be invoked in the constructor of the applet class. You should invoke it from the `init` method.

You can add a **main** method to enable this applet to run standalone. The applet takes the parameters from the HTML file when it runs as an applet and takes the parameters from the command line when it runs standalone. The program, as shown in Listing 16.6, is identical to **DisplayMessage** except for the addition of a new **main** method and of a variable named **isStandalone** to indicate whether it is running as an applet or as an application.

LISTING 16.6 DisplayMessageApp.java

```
1 import javax.swing.*;
2 import java.awt.Font;
3 import java.awt.BorderLayout;
4
5 public class DisplayMessageApp extends JApplet {
6   private String message = "A default message"; // Message to display
7   private int x = 20; // Default x coordinate
8   private int y = 20; // Default y coordinate
9
10   /** Determine if it is application */
```

isStandalone

```
11   private boolean isStandalone = false;
12
13   /** Initialize the applet */
14   public void init() {
15     if (!isStandalone) {
16       // Get parameter values from the HTML file
```

applet params

```
17       message = getParameter("MESSAGE");
18       x = Integer.parseInt(getParameter("X"));
19       y = Integer.parseInt(getParameter("Y"));
20     }
21
22     // Create a message panel
23     MessagePanel messagePanel = new MessagePanel(message);
24     messagePanel.setFont(new Font("SansSerif", Font.BOLD, 20));
25     messagePanel.setXCoordinate(x);
26     messagePanel.setYCoordinate(y);
27
28     // Add the message panel to the applet
29     add(messagePanel);
30   }
31
32   /** Main method to display a message
33     @param args [0] x coordinate
```

```
34        @param args [1] y coordinate
35        @param args [2] message
36      */
37    public static void main(String[] args) {
38      // Create a frame
39      JFrame frame = new JFrame("DisplayMessageApp");
40
41      // Create an instance of the applet
42      DisplayMessageApp applet = new DisplayMessageApp();
43
44      // It runs as an application
45      applet.isStandalone = true;                                   standalone
46
47      // Get parameters from the command line
48      applet.getCommandLineParameters(args);                        command params
49
50      // Add the applet instance to the frame
51      frame.add(applet, BorderLayout.CENTER);
52
53      // Invoke applet's init method
54      applet.init();
55      applet.start();
56
57      // Display the frame
58      frame.setSize(300, 300);
59      frame.setLocationRelativeTo(null); // Center the frame
60      frame.setDefaultCloseOperation(JFrame.EXIT_ON_CLOSE);
61      frame.setVisible(true);
62    }
63
64    /** Get command line parameters */
65    private void getCommandLineParameters(String[] args) {
66      // Check usage and get x, y and message
67      if (args.length != 3) {
68        System.out.println(
69          "Usage: java DisplayMessageApp x y message");
70        System.exit(0);
71      }
72      else {
73        x = Integer.parseInt(args[0]);
74        y = Integer.parseInt(args[1]);
75        message = args[2];
76      }
77    }
78 }
```

When you run the program as an applet, the main method is ignored. When you run it as an application, the main method is invoked. A sample run of the program as an application and as an applet is shown in Figure 16.9.

Figure 16.9 The DisplayMessageApp class can run as an application and as an applet.

The **main** method creates a **JFrame** object **frame** and creates a **JApplet** object **applet**, then places the applet **applet** into the frame **frame** and invokes its **init** method. The application runs just like an applet.

The **main** method sets **isStandalone true** (line 45) so that it does not attempt to retrieve HTML parameters when the **init** method is invoked.

The **setVisible(true)** method (line 61) is invoked *after* the components are added to the applet, and the applet is added to the frame to ensure that the components will be visible. Otherwise, the components are not shown when the frame starts.

omitting **main** method

Important Pedagogical Note

From now on, all the GUI examples will be created as applets with a **main** method. Thus you will be able to run the program either as an applet or as an application. For brevity, the **main** method is not listed in the text.

 ## 16.7 (Optional) Case Study: TicTacToe

You have learned about objects, classes, arrays, class inheritance, GUI, event-driven programming, and applets from the many examples in this chapter and the preceding chapters. Now it is time to put what you have learned to work in developing comprehensive projects. In this section, you will develop a Java applet with which to play the popular game of TicTacToe.

In a game of TicTacToe, two players take turns marking an available cell in a 3 × 3 grid with their respective tokens (either X or O). When one player has placed three tokens in a horizontal, vertical, or diagonal row on the grid, the game is over and that player has won. A draw (no winner) occurs when all the cells on the grid have been filled with tokens and neither player has achieved a win. Figure 16.10 shows two representative sample runs of the example.

 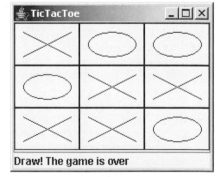

(a) The x player won the game

(b) Draw—no game winners

FIGURE 16.10 Two players play a TicTacToe game.

All the examples you have seen so far show simple behaviors that are easy to model with classes. The behavior of the TicTacToe game is somewhat more complex. To create classes that model the behavior, you need to study and understand the game.

Assume that all the cells are initially empty, and that the first player takes the X token, and the second player takes the O token. To mark a cell, the player points the mouse to the cell and clicks it. If the cell is empty, the token (X or O) is displayed. If the cell is already filled, the player's action is ignored.

From the preceding description, it is obvious that a cell is a GUI object that handles the mouse-click event and displays tokens. Such an object could be either a button or a panel. Drawing on panels is more flexible than on buttons, because the token (X or O) can be drawn on a panel in any size, but on a button it can only be displayed as a text label. Therefore, a panel should be used to model a cell. How do you know the state of the cell (empty, X, or O)? You use a property named `token` of `char` type in the `Cell` class. The `Cell` class is responsible for drawing the token when an empty cell is clicked. So you need to write the code for listening to the `MouseEvent` and for painting the shapes for tokens X and O. The `Cell` class can be defined as shown in Figure 16.11.

FIGURE 16.11   The `Cell` class paints the token on a cell.

The TicTacToe board consists of nine cells, declared using `new Cell[3][3]`. To determine which player's turn it is, you can introduce a variable named `whoseTurn` of `char` type. `whoseTurn` is initially X, then changes to O, and subsequently changes between X and O whenever a new cell is occupied. When the game is over, set `whoseTurn` to `' '`.

How do you know whether the game is over, whether there is a winner, and who the winner, if any, is? You can create a method named `isWon(char token)` to check whether a specified token has won and a method named `isFull()` to check whether all the cells are occupied.

Clearly, two classes emerge from the foregoing analysis. One is the `Cell` class, which handles operations for a single cell; and the other is the `TicTacToe` class, which plays the whole game and deals with all the cells. The relationship between these two classes is shown in Figure 16.12.

FIGURE 16.12   The `TicTacToe` class contains nine cells.

Since the `Cell` class is only to support the `TicTacToe` class, it can be defined as an inner class in `TicTacToe`. The complete program is given in Listing 16.7.

LISTING 16.7 TicTacToe.java

```java
import java.awt.*;
import java.awt.event.*;
import javax.swing.*;
import javax.swing.border.LineBorder;

public class TicTacToe extends JApplet {
  // Indicate which player has a turn, initially it is the X player
  private char whoseTurn = 'X';

  // Create and initialize cells
  private Cell[][] cells = new Cell[3][3];

  // Create and initialize a status label
  private JLabel jlblStatus = new JLabel("X's turn to play");

  /** Initialize UI */
  public TicTacToe() {
    // Panel p to hold cells
    JPanel p = new JPanel(new GridLayout(3, 3, 0, 0));
    for (int i = 0; i < 3; i++)
      for (int j = 0; j < 3; j++)
        p.add(cells[i][j] = new Cell());

    // Set line borders on the cells panel and the status label
    p.setBorder(new LineBorder(Color.red, 1));
    jlblStatus.setBorder(new LineBorder(Color.yellow, 1));

    // Place the panel and the label to the applet
    add(p, BorderLayout.CENTER);
    add(jlblStatus, BorderLayout.SOUTH);
  }

  /** Determine if the cells are all occupied */
  public boolean isFull() {
    for (int i = 0; i < 3; i++)
      for (int j = 0; j < 3; j++)
        if (cells[i][j].getToken() == ' ')
          return false;

    return true;
  }

  /** Determine if the player with the specified token wins */
  public boolean isWon(char token) {
    for (int i = 0; i < 3; i++)
      if ((cells[i][0].getToken() == token)
          && (cells[i][1].getToken() == token)
          && (cells[i][2].getToken() == token)) {
        return true;
      }

    for (int j = 0; j < 3; j++)
      if ((cells[0][j].getToken() == token)
          && (cells[1][j].getToken() == token)
          && (cells[2][j].getToken() == token)) {
        return true;
      }

```

Margin notes: main class **TicTacToe**, check **isFull**, check rows, check columns

```
59      if ((cells[0][0].getToken() == token)                          check major diagonal
60          && (cells[1][1].getToken() == token)
61          && (cells[2][2].getToken() == token)) {
62        return true;
63      }
64
65      if ((cells[0][2].getToken() == token)                          check subdiagonal
66          && (cells[1][1].getToken() == token)
67          && (cells[2][0].getToken() == token)) {
68        return true;
69      }
70
71      return false;
72    }
73
74    // An inner class for a cell
75    public class Cell extends JPanel {                               inner class Cell
76      // Token used for this cell
77      private char token = ' ';
78
79      public Cell() {
80        setBorder(new LineBorder(Color.black, 1)); // Set cell's border
81        addMouseListener(new MouseListener()); // Register listener    register listener
82      }
83
84      /** Return token */
85      public char getToken() {
86        return token;
87      }
88
89      /** Set a new token */
90      public void setToken(char c) {
91        token = c;
92        repaint();
93      }
94
95      /** Paint the cell */
96      protected void paintComponent(Graphics g) {                    paint cell
97        super.paintComponent(g);
98
99        if (token == 'X') {
100         g.drawLine(10, 10, getWidth() - 10, getHeight() - 10);
101         g.drawLine(getWidth() - 10, 10, 10, getHeight() - 10);
102       }
103       else if (token == 'O') {
104         g.drawOval(10, 10, getWidth() - 20, getHeight() - 20);
105       }
106     }
107
108     private class MouseListener extends MouseAdapter {             listener class
109       /** Handle mouse click on a cell */
110       public void mouseClicked(MouseEvent e) {
111         // If cell is empty and game is not over
112         if (token == ' ' && whoseTurn != ' ') {
113           setToken(whoseTurn); // Set token in the cell
114
115           // Check game status
116           if (isWon(whoseTurn)) {
117             jlblStatus.setText(whoseTurn + " won! The game is over");
118             whoseTurn = ' '; // Game is over
```

```
119              }
120              else if (isFull()) {
121                jlblStatus.setText("Draw! The game is over");
122                whoseTurn = ' '; // Game is over
123              }
124              else {
125                whoseTurn = (whoseTurn == 'X') ? 'O': 'X';
126                jlblStatus.setText(whoseTurn + "'s turn");
127              }
128            }
129          }
130        }
131      }
```
main method omitted
```
132 }
```

The **TicTacToe** class initializes the user interface with nine cells placed in a panel of **GridLayout** (lines 19–22). A label named **jlblStatus** is used to show the status of the game (line 14). The variable **whoseTurn** (line 8) is used to track the next type of token to be placed in a cell. The methods **isFull** (lines 34–41) and **isWon** (lines 44–72) are for checking the status of the game.

Since **Cell** is an inner class in **TicTacToe**, the variable (**whoseTurn**) and methods (**isFull** and **isWon**) defined in **TicTacToe** can be referenced from the **Cell** class. The inner class makes programs simple and concise. If **Cell** were not declared as an inner class of **TicTacToe**, you would have to pass an object of **TicTacToe** to **Cell** in order for the variables and methods in **TicTacToe** to be used in **Cell**. You will rewrite the program without using an inner class in Exercise 16.6.

The listener for **MouseEvent** is registered for the cell (line 81). If an empty cell is clicked and the game is not over, a token is set in the cell (line 113). If the game is over, **whoseTurn** is set to ' ' (lines 118, 122). Otherwise, **whoseTurn** is alternated to a new turn (line 125).

Tip

incremental development
and testing

Use an incremental approach in developing and testing a Java project of this kind. The foregoing program can be divided into five steps.

1.   Lay out the user interface and display a fixed token X on a cell.

2.   Enable the cell to display a fixed token X upon a mouse click.

3.   Coordinate between the two players so as to display tokens X and O alternately.

4.   Check whether a player wins, or whether all the cells are occupied without a winner.

5.   Implement displaying a message on the label upon each move by a player.

 ## 16.8 (Optional) Case Study: Bouncing Ball

This section presents an applet that displays a ball bouncing in a panel. Use two buttons to suspend and resume the movement, and use a scroll bar to control the bouncing speed, as shown in Figure 16.13.

FIGURE 16.13   The ball's movement is controlled by the Suspend and Resume buttons and the scroll bar.

Here are the major steps to complete this example.

1. Create a subclass of **JPanel** named **Ball** to display a ball bouncing, as shown in Listing 16.8.

2. Create a subclass of **JPanel** named **BallControl** to contain the ball with a scroll bar and two control buttons *Suspend* and *Resume*, as shown in Listing 16.9.

3. Create an applet named **BounceBallApp** to contain an instance of **BallControl** and enable the applet to run standalone, as shown in Listing 16.10.

The relationship among these classes is shown in Figure 16.14.

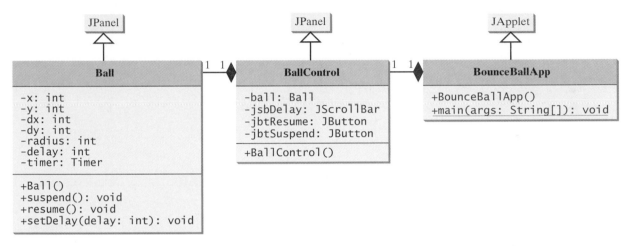

FIGURE 16.14   **BounceBallApp** contains **BallControl**, and **BallControl** contains **Ball**.

LISTING 16.8 Ball.java

```
1  import javax.swing.Timer;
2  import java.awt.*;
3  import javax.swing.*;
4  import java.awt.event.*;
5
6  public class Ball extends JPanel {
7    private int delay = 10;                                            timer delay
8
9    // Create a timer with delay 1000 ms
10   protected Timer timer = new Timer(delay, new TimerListener());      create timer
11
12   private int x = 0; private int y = 0; // Current ball position
13   private int radius = 5; // Ball radius
14   private int dx = 2; // Increment on ball's x-coordinate
15   private int dy = 2; // Increment on ball's y-coordinate
16
17   public Ball() {
18     timer.start();                                                   start timer
19   }
20
21   private class TimerListener implements ActionListener {             timer listener
22     /** Handle the action event */
23     public void actionPerformed(ActionEvent e) {
24       repaint();                                                     repaint ball
25     }
26   }
```

paint ball

```
27
28  protected void paintComponent(Graphics g) {
29    super.paintComponent(g);
30
31    g.setColor(Color.red);
32
33    // Check boundaries
34    if (x < radius) dx = Math.abs(dx);
35    if (x > getWidth() - radius) dx = -Math.abs(dx);
36    if (y < radius) dy = Math.abs(dy);
37    if (y > getHeight() - radius) dy = -Math.abs(dy);
38
39    // Adjust ball position
40    x += dx;
41    y += dy;
42    g.fillOval(x - radius, y - radius, radius * 2, radius * 2);
43  }
44
45  public void suspend() {
46    timer.stop(); // Suspend timer
47  }
48
49  public void resume() {
50    timer.start(); // Resume timer
51  }
52
53  public void setDelay(int delay) {
54    this.delay = delay;
55    timer.setDelay(delay);
56  }
57 }
```

Using `Timer` to control animation was introduced in §14.6, "Animation Using the `Timer` Class." `Ball` extends `JPanel` to display a moving ball. The timer listener implements `ActionListener` to listen for `ActionEvent` (line 21). Line 10 creates a `Timer` for a `Ball`. The timer is started in line 18 when a `Ball` is constructed. The timer fires an `ActionEvent` at a fixed rate. The listener responds in line 24 to repaint the ball to animate ball movement. The center of the ball is at (x, y), which changes to (x + dx, y + dy) on the next display. The `suspend` and `resume` methods (lines 45–51) can be used to stop and start the timer. The `setDelay(int)` method (lines 53–56) sets a new delay.

LISTING 16.9 BallControl.java

button

scroll bar

create UI

```
1 import javax.swing.*;
2 import java.awt.event.*;
3 import java.awt.*;
4
5 public class BallControl extends JPanel {
6   private Ball ball = new Ball();
7   private JButton jbtSuspend = new JButton("Suspend");
8   private JButton jbtResume = new JButton("Resume");
9   private JScrollBar jsbDelay = new JScrollBar();
10
11  public BallControl() {
12    // Group buttons in a panel
13    JPanel panel = new JPanel();
14    panel.add(jbtSuspend);
15    panel.add(jbtResume);
```

```
16
17      // Add ball and buttons to the panel
18      ball.setBorder(new javax.swing.border.LineBorder(Color.red));
19      jsbDelay.setOrientation(JScrollBar.HORIZONTAL);
20      ball.setDelay(jsbDelay.getMaximum());
21      setLayout(new BorderLayout());
22      add(jsbDelay, BorderLayout.NORTH);
23      add(ball, BorderLayout.CENTER);
24      add(panel, BorderLayout.SOUTH);
25
26      // Register listeners
27      jbtSuspend.addActionListener(new ActionListener() {          register listener
28        public void actionPerformed(ActionEvent e) {
29          ball.suspend();                                          suspend
30        }
31      });
32      jbtResume.addActionListener(new ActionListener() {           register listener
33        public void actionPerformed(ActionEvent e) {
34          ball.resume();                                           resume
35        }
36      });
37      jsbDelay.addAdjustmentListener(new AdjustmentListener() {     register listener
38        public void adjustmentValueChanged(AdjustmentEvent e) {
39          ball.setDelay(jsbDelay.getMaximum() - e.getValue());     new delay
40        }
41      });
42    }
43 }
```

The `BallControl` class extends `JPanel` to display the ball with a scroll bar and two control buttons. When the *Suspend* button is clicked, the ball's `suspend()` method is invoked to suspend the ball movement (line 29). When the *Resume* button is clicked, the ball's `resume()` method is invoked to resume the ball movement (line 34). The bouncing speed can be changed using the scroll bar.

LISTING 16.10 BounceBallApp.java

```
1 import java.awt.*;
2 import java.awt.event.*;
3 import java.applet.*;
4 import javax.swing.*;
5
6 public class BounceBallApp extends JApplet {
7    public BounceBallApp() {
8      add(new BallControl());                         add BallControl
9    }
10 }                                                    main method omitted
```

The `BounceBallApp` class simply places an instance of `BallControl` in the applet. The `main` method is provided in the applet (not displayed in the listing for brevity) so that you can also run it standalone.

16.9 (Optional) Locating Resource Using the **URL** Class

You have used the `ImageIcon` class to create an icon from an image file and used the `setIcon` method or the constructor to place the icon in a GUI component, such as a button or a label. For example, the following statements create an `ImageIcon` and set it on a `JLabel` object `jlbl`:

```
ImageIcon imageIcon = new ImageIcon("c:\\book\\image\\us.gif");
jlbl.setIcon(imageIcon);
```

This approach presents a problem. The file location is fixed, because it uses the absolute file path on Windows. As a result, the program cannot run on other platforms and cannot run as an applet. Assume that **image/us.gif** is under the class directory. You can circumvent this problem by using a relative path, as follows:

```
ImageIcon imageIcon = new ImageIcon("image/us.gif");
```

This works fine with Java applications on all platforms, but does not work with Java applets because applets cannot load local files. To make it to work with both applications and applets, you need to locate the file using the **URL** class.

why **URL** class?

The **java.net.URL** class can be used to identify files (image, audio, text, etc.) on the Internet. In general, a URL (Uniform Resource Locator) is a pointer to a "resource" on the World Wide Web on a local machine or a remote host. A resource can be something as simple as a file or a directory.

An URL for a file can also be accessed by class code in a way that is independent of the location of the file as long as the file is located in the class directory. Recall that the class directory is where the class (i.e., the .class file) is stored. For example, all the classes in this book are stored in c:\book. So the class directory is **c:\book**.

As discussed in §9.13.5, "The **getClass** Method," when a class is loaded, the JVM creates a meta-object for the class, which can be obtained using

```
java.lang.Class metaObject = this.getClass();
```

The **Class** class provides access to useful information about the class, such as the data fields, constructors, and methods. It also contains the **getResource(filename)** method, which can be used to obtain the URL of a given file name in the class directory.

To obtain the URL of a file in the class directory, use

```
URL url = metaObject.getResource(filename);
```

For example, if the class directory is **c:\book**, the following statements create a URL for **c:\book\image\us.gif**:

```
Class metaObject = this.getClass();
URL url = metaObject.getResource("image/us.gif");
```

You can now create an **ImageIcon** using

```
ImageIcon imageIcon = new ImageIcon(url);
```

Listing 16.11 gives the code that displays an image from **image/us.gif** in the class directory. The file **image/us.gif** is under the class directory, and its URL is obtained using the **getResource** method (line 5). A label with an image icon is created in line 6. The image icon is obtained from the URL.

LISTING 16.11 DisplayImageWithURL.java

```
1  import javax.swing.*;
2
3  public class DisplayImageWithURL extends JApplet {
4    public DisplayImageWithURL() {
5      java.net.URL url = this.getClass().getResource("image/us.gif");
6      add(new JLabel(new ImageIcon(url)));
7    }
8  }
```

get image URL
create a label

main method omitted

If you replace the code in lines 5–6 with the following code,

```
add(new JLabel(new ImageIcon("image/us.gif")));
```

you can still run the program standalone, but not from a browser.

16.10 (Optional) Playing Audio

There are several formats for audio files. Prior to Java 2, sound files in the AU format used on the UNIX operating system were the only ones Java was able to play. With Java 2, you can play sound files in the WAV, AIFF, MIDI, AU, and RMF formats, with better sound quality.

To play an audio file in an applet, first create an *audio clip object* for the audio file. The audio clip is created once and can be played repeatedly without reloading the file. To create an audio clip, use the static method `newAudioClip()` in the `java.applet.Applet` class:

```
AudioClip audioClip = Applet.newAudioClip(url);
```

Audio was originally used with Java applets. For this reason, the `AudioClip` interface is in the `java.applet` package.

The following statements, for example, create an `AudioClip` for the `beep.au` audio file in the class directory:

```
Class metaObject = this.getClass();
URL url = metaObject.getResource("beep.au");
AudioClip audioClip = Applet.newAudioClip(url);
```

To manipulate a sound for an audio clip, use the `play()`, `loop()`, and `stop()` methods in `java.applet.AudioClip`, as shown in Figure 16.15.

«interface» *java.applet.AudioClip*	
+*play()*	Starts playing this audio clip. Each time this method is called, the clip is restarted from the beginning.
+*loop()*	Plays the clip repeatedly.
+*stop()*	Stops playing the clip.

FIGURE 16.15 The `AudioClip` interface provides the methods for playing sound.

Listing 16.12 gives the code that displays the Danish flag and plays the Danish national anthem repeatedly. The image file `image/denmark.gif` and audio file `audio/denmark.mid` are stored under the class directory. Line 12 obtains the audio file URL. Line 13 creates an audio clip for the file. Line 14 repeatedly plays the audio.

LISTING 16.12 `DisplayImagePlayAudio.java`

```
 1 import javax.swing.*;
 2 import java.net.URL;
 3 import java.applet.*;
 4
 5 public class DisplayImagePlayAudio extends JApplet {
 6   private AudioClip audioClip;
 7
 8   public DisplayImagePlayAudio() {
 9     URL urlForImage = getClass().getResource("image/denmark.gif");    get image URL
10     add(new JLabel(new ImageIcon(urlForImage)));                      create a label
```

```
11
12    URL urlForAudio = getClass().getResource("audio/denmark.mid");
13    audioClip = Applet.newAudioClip(urlForAudio);
14    audioClip.loop();
15  }
16
17    public void start() {
18      if (audioClip != null) audioClip.loop();
19    }
20
21    public void stop() {
22      if (audioClip != null) audioClip.stop();
23    }
24  }
```

get audio URL *(line 12)*
create an audio clip *(line 13)*
play audio repeatedly *(line 14)*

start audio *(line 18)*

stop audio *(line 22)*

main method omitted *(line 24)*

The `stop` method (lines 21–23) stops the audio when the applet is not displayed, and the `start` method (lines 17–19) restarts the audio when the applet is redisplayed. Please try to run this applet from a browser and observe the effect without the `stop` and `start` methods.

16.11 (Optional) Case Study: Multimedia Animations

This case study presents a multimedia animation with images and audio. The images are for seven national flags, named `flag0.gif`, `flag1.gif`, ..., `flag6.gif` for Denmark, Germany, China, India, Norway, the UK, and the US. They are stored under the `image` directory in the class path. The audio consists of national anthems for these seven nations, named `anthem0.mid`, `anthem1.mid`, ..., and `anthem6.mid`. They are stored under the `audio` directory in the class path.

The program presents the nations, starting from the first one. For each nation, it displays its flag and plays its anthem. When the audio finishes, the next nation is presented, and so on. When the last nation is presented, the program starts to present all the nations again. You may suspend animation by clicking the Suspend button and resume it by clicking the Resume button, as shown in Figure 16.16. You can also directly select a nation from a combo box.

FIGURE 16.16 The applet displays a sequence of images and plays audio.

The program is given in Listing 16.13. A timer is created to control the animation (line 15). The timer delay for each presentation is the play time for the anthem. You can find the play time for an audio file using RealPlayer or Windows Media on Windows. The delay times are stored in an array named `delays` (lines 13–14). The delay time for the first audio file (the Danish anthem) is 48 seconds.

LISTING 16.13 `ImageAudioAnimation.java`

```java
1  import java.awt.*;
2  import java.awt.event.*;
3  import javax.swing.*;
4  import java.applet.*;
5
6  public class ImageAudioAnimation extends JApplet {
7    private final static int NUMBER_OF_NATIONS = 7;
8    private int current = 0;
9    private ImageIcon[] icons = new ImageIcon[NUMBER_OF_NATIONS];          image icons
10   private AudioClip[] audioClips = new AudioClip[NUMBER_OF_NATIONS];     audio clips
11   private AudioClip currentAudioClip;                                   current audio clip
12
13   private int[] delays =                                                audio play time
14     {48000, 54000, 59000, 54000, 59000, 31000, 68000};
15   private Timer timer = new Timer(delays[0], new TimerListener());       timer
16
17   private JLabel jlblImageLabel = new JLabel();                         GUI components
18   private JButton jbtResume = new JButton("Resume");
19   private JButton jbtSuspend = new JButton("Suspend");
20   private JComboBox jcboNations = new JComboBox(new Object[]
21     {"Denmark", "Germany", "China", "India", "Norway", "UK", "US"});
22
23   public ImageAudioAnimation() {
24     // Load image icons and audio clips
25     for (int i = 0; i < NUMBER_OF_NATIONS; i++) {
26       icons[i] = new ImageIcon(getClass().getResource(                  create icons
27         "image/flag" + i + ".gif"));
28       audioClips[i] = Applet.newAudioClip(                              create audio clips
29         getClass().getResource("audio/anthem" + i + ".mid"));
30     }
31
32     JPanel panel = new JPanel();                                        create UI
33     panel.add(jbtResume);
34     panel.add(jbtSuspend);
35     panel.add(new JLabel("Select"));
36     panel.add(jcboNations);
37     this.getContentPane().add(jlblImageLabel, BorderLayout.CENTER);
38     this.getContentPane().add(panel, BorderLayout.SOUTH);
39
40     jbtResume.addActionListener(new ActionListener() {                  register listener
41       public void actionPerformed(ActionEvent e) {
42         start();                                                        start animation
43       }
44     });
45     jbtSuspend.addActionListener(new ActionListener() {                 register listener
46       public void actionPerformed(ActionEvent e) {
47         stop();                                                         stop animation
48       }
49     });
50     jcboNations.addActionListener(new ActionListener() {                register listener
51       public void actionPerformed(ActionEvent e) {
52         stop();
53         current = jcboNations.getSelectedIndex();                      select a nation
54         presentNation(current);                                        present a nation
55         timer.start();
56       }
57     });
58
```

```
59       timer.start();
60       jlblImageLabel.setIcon(icons[0]);
61       jlblImageLabel.setHorizontalAlignment(JLabel.CENTER);
62       currentAudioClip = audioClips[0];
63       currentAudioClip.play();
64     }
65
66     private class TimerListener implements ActionListener {
67       public void actionPerformed(ActionEvent e) {
68         current = (current + 1) % NUMBER_OF_NATIONS;
69         presentNation(current);
70       }
71     }
72
73     private void presentNation(int index) {
74       jlblImageLabel.setIcon(icons[index]);
75       jcboNations.setSelectedIndex(index);
76       currentAudioClip = audioClips[index];
77       currentAudioClip.play();
78       timer.setDelay(delays[index]);
79     }
80
81     public void start() {
82       timer.start();
83       currentAudioClip.play();
84     }
85
86     public void stop() {
87       timer.stop();
88       currentAudioClip.stop();
89     }
90   }
```

set a new delay (line 78)

stop audio clip (line 88)

main method omitted (line 90)

A label is created in line 17 to display a flag image. An array of flag images for seven nations is created in lines 26–27. An array of audio clips is created in lines 28–29. Each audio clip is created for an audio file through the URL of the current class. The audio files are stored in the same directory with the applet class file.

The combo box for country names is created in lines 20–21. When a new country name in the combo box is selected, the current presentation is stopped and a new selected nation is presented (line 52–55).

The **presentNation(index)** method (lines 73–79) presents a nation with the specified index. It sets a new image in the label (line 74), synchronizes with the combo box by setting the selected index (line 75), plays the new audio, and sets a new delay time (line 78).

The applet's **start** and **stop** methods are overridden to resume and suspend the animation (lines 81–89).

16.12 (Optional) Packaging and Deploying Java Projects

Your project may consist of many classes and supporting files, such as image files and audio files. To make your programs run on the end-user side, you need to provide end-users with all these files. For convenience, Java supports an archive file that can be used to group all the project files in a compressed file.

Archiving makes it possible for Java applications, applets, and their requisite components (.class files, images, and sounds) to be transported in a single file. This single file can be deployed on an end-user's machine as an application. It also can be downloaded to a browser in a single HTTP transaction, rather than opening a new connection for each piece. This greatly simplifies application deployment and improves the speed with which an applet can be loaded onto a web page and begin functioning.

You can use the JDK **jar** command to create an archive file. The following command creates an archive file named TicTacToe.jar for classes TicTacToe.class and TicTacToe$Cell.class (inner class).

```
jar -cf TicTacToe.jar TicTacToe.class TicTacToe$Cell.class
```

The **-c** option is for creating a new archive file, and the **-f** option specifies the archive file's name.

Note

The Java archive file format (JAR) is based on the popular ZIP file format. You can view the contents of a .jar file using WinZip, a popular compression utility for Windows, as shown in Figure 16.17.

viewing .jar contents

FIGURE 16.17 You can view the files contained in the archive file using the WinZip utility.

16.12.1 The Manifest File

As shown in Figure 16.17, a manifest file was created with the path name `meta-inf\`. The manifest is a special file that contains information about the files packaged in a JAR file. For instance, the manifest file in Figure 16.17 contains the following information:

```
Manifest-Version: 1.0

Name: TicTacToe.class
Java-Bean: True

Name: TicTacToe$Cell.class
Java-Bean: True
```

You can modify the information contained in the manifest file to enable the JAR file to be used for a variety of purposes. For example, you can add information to specify a `main` class to run an application using the .jar file.

16.12.2 Running Archived Projects

You can package all the class files and dependent resource files in an archive file for distribution to the end-user. If the project is a Java application, the user should have a Java-running environment already installed. If it is not installed, the user can download the Java Runtime Environment (JRE) from java.sun.com and install it.

Note

The Java Runtime Environment is the minimum standard Java platform for running Java programs. It contains the Java interpreter, Java core classes, and supporting files. The JRE does not contain any development tools (such as Applet Viewer or javac) or classes that pertain only to a development environment. The JRE is a subset of JDK.

JRE

To run `TicTacToe` as an application, take the following steps:

1. Update the manifest file to insert an entry for the main class. You need to create a text file containing the following two lines:

   ```
   Main-Class: TicTacToe
   ```

   ```
   Sealed: true
   ```

   The first line specifies the main class. The second line is necessary to ensure that the first line can be inserted into an existing manifest file in a jar. Assume that these two lines are contained in the file temp.mf.

2. Execute the `jar` command to insert the main class line into the manifest file in TicTac-Toe.jar, as follows:

   ```
   jar -uvmf temp.mf TicTacToe.jar
   ```

   The **-u** option is for updating an existing jar file, the **-v** option is for displaying command output, the **-m** option is for appending the contents in temp.mf to the manifest file in the archive, and the **-f** option specifies the archive file's name.

3. Run the .jar file using the java command from the directory that contains TicTacToe.jar, as follows:

   ```
   java -jar TicTacToe.jar
   ```

 Note

You can write an installation procedure that creates the necessary directories and subdirectories on the end-user's computer. The installation can also create an icon that the end-user can double-click to start the program. For information on creating Windows desktop icons, please see Supplement I.E, "Creating Shortcuts for Java Applications on Windows."

To run `TicTacToe` as an applet, modify the `<applet>` tag in the HTML file to include an archive attribute. The archive attribute specifies the archive file in which the applet is contained. For example, the HTML file for running `TicTacToe` can be modified as shown below:

```
<applet
  code     = "TicTacToe.class"
  archive  = "TicTacToe.jar"
  width    = 400
  height   = 300
  hspace   = 0
  vspace   = 0
  align    = middle
>
</applet>
```

KEY TERMS

CHAPTER SUMMARY

■   The Web browser controls and executes applets through the `init`, `start`, `stop`, and `destroy` methods in the `Applet` class. Applets always extend the `Applet` class and implement these methods, if applicable, so that they can be run by a Web browser.

- `JApplet` is a subclass of `Applet`. It should be used for developing Java applets with Swing components.

- The applet bytecode must be specified, using the `<applet>` tag in an HTML file to tell the Web browser where to find the applet. The applet can accept string parameters from HTML using the `<param>` tag.

- When an applet is loaded, the Web browser creates an instance of the applet by invoking its no-arg constructor. The `init` method is invoked after the applet is created. The `start` method is invoked after the `init` method. It is also called whenever the applet becomes active again after the page containing the applet is revisited. The `stop` method is invoked when the applet becomes inactive.

- The `destroy` method is invoked when the browser exits normally to inform the applet that it is no longer needed and should release any resources it has allocated. The `stop` method is always called before the `destroy` method.

- The procedures for writing applications and writing applets are very similar. An applet can easily be converted into an application, and vice versa. Moreover, an applet can be written with the additional capability of running as an application.

- You can pass arguments to an applet using the `param` attribute in the applet's tag in HTML. To retrieve the value of the parameter, invoke the `getParameter(paramName)` method.

- The `Applet`'s `getParameter` method can be invoked only after an instance of the applet is created. Therefore, this method cannot be invoked in the constructor of the applet class. You should invoke this method from the `init` method.

- You learned how to incorporate images and audio in Java applications and applets. To load audio and images for Java applications and applets, you have to create a URL for the audio and image. You can create a `URL` from a file under the class directory or from an Internet source.

- To play an audio, create an audio clip from the `URL` for the audio source. You can use the `AudioClip`'s `play()` method to play it once, the `loop()` method to play it repeatedly, and the `stop()` method to stop it.

REVIEW QUESTIONS

Sections 16.2–16.4

16.1 Is every applet an instance of `java.applet.Applet`? Is every applet an instance of `javax.swing.JApplet`?

16.2 Describe the `init()`, `start()`, `stop()`, and `destroy()` methods in the `Applet` class.

16.3 How do you add components to a `JApplet`? What is the default layout manager of the content pane of `JApplet`?

16.4 Why does the applet in (a) display nothing? Why does the applet in (b) have a run-time `NullPointerException` on line 12?

```
import javax.swing.*;

public class WelcomeApplet extends JApplet {
  public void WelcomeApplet() {
    JLabel jlblMessage =
      new JLabel("It is Java");
  }
}
```

```
import javax.swing.*;

public class WelcomeApplet extends JApplet {
  private JLabel jlblMessage;

  public WelcomeApplet() {
    JLabel jlblMessage =
      new JLabel("It is Java");
  }

  public void init() {
    getContentPane().add(jlblMessage);
  }
}
```

(a)   (b)

Sections 16.5–16.6

16.5   Describe the `<applet>` HTML tag. How do you pass parameters to an applet?

16.6   Where is the `getParameter` method defined?

16.7   What is wrong if the `DisplayMessage` applet is revised as follows?

```
public class DisplayMessage extends JApplet {
  /** Initialize the applet */
  public DisplayMessage() {
    // Get parameter values from the HTML file
    String message = getParameter("MESSAGE");
    int x =
      Integer.parseInt(getParameter("X"));
    int y =
      Integer.parseInt(getParameter("Y"));

    // Create a message panel
    MessagePanel messagePanel =
      new MessagePanel(message);
    messagePanel.setXCoordinate(x);
    messagePanel.setYCoordinate(y);

    // Add the message panel to the applet
    getContentPane().add(messagePanel);
  }
}
```

```
public class DisplayMessage extends JApplet {
  private String message;
  private int x;
  private int y;

  /** Initialize the applet */
  public void init() {
    // Get parameter values from the HTML file
    message = getParameter("MESSAGE");
    x = Integer.parseInt(getParameter("X"));
    y = Integer.parseInt(getParameter("Y"));
  }

  public DisplayMessage() {
    // Create a message panel
    MessagePanel messagePanel =
      new MessagePanel(message);
    messagePanel.setXCoordinate(x);
    messagePanel.setYCoordinate(y);

    // Add the message panel to the applet
    getContentPane().add(messagePanel);
  }
}
```

(a) Revision 1   (b) Revision 2

16.8   What are the differences between applications and applets? How do you run an application, and how do you run an applet? Is the compilation process different for applications and applets? List some security restrictions on applets.

16.9   Can you place a frame in an applet?

16.10   Can you place an applet in a frame?

16.11   Delete `super.paintComponent(g)` on line 97 in TicTacToe.java in Listing 16.7 and run the program to see what happens.

Sections 16.9 Locating Resource Using the URL Class

16.12 How do you create a **URL** object for the file http://www.cs.armstrong.edu/
liang/intro6e/book/audio/us.mid on the Internet? How do you create a **URL** object for
the file http://www.cs.armstrong.edu/liang/audio/us.mid in the class directory?

16.13 How do you create an **ImageIcon** from the file image/us.gif in the class directory? How do you create an **ImageIcon** from www.cs.armstrong.edu/liang/intro6e/
book/image/us.gif?

Section 16.10 Playing Audio

16.14 What types of audio files are used in Java?

16.15 How do you create an audio clip from a file anthem/us.mid in the class directory?
How do you create an audio clip from http://www.cs.armstrong.edu/liang/
intro6e/book/audio/us.mid?

16.16 How do you play, repeatedly play, and stop an audio clip?

PROGRAMMING EXERCISES

Sections 16.2–16.4

16.1 (*Converting applications to applets*) Convert Listing 15.2, ButtonDemo.java, into
an applet.

Sections 16.5–16.6

16.2* (*Passing strings to applets*) Rewrite Listing 16.5, DisplayMessage.java, to display
a message with a standard color, font, and size. The **message**, **x**, **y**, **color**,
fontname, and **fontsize** are parameters in the **<applet>** tag, as shown below:

```
<applet
  code = "Exercise16_2.class"
  width = 200
  height = 50
  alt = "You must have a Java-enabled browser to view the applet"
>
  <param name = MESSAGE value = "Welcome to Java" />
  <param name = X value = 40 />
  <param name = Y value = 50 />
  <param name = COLOR value = "red" />
  <param name = FONTNAME value = "Monospaced" />
  <param name = FONTSIZE value = 20 />
</applet>
```

16.3 (*Enabling applets to run standalone*) Rewrite the **LoanApplet** in Listing 16.1,
LoanApplet.Java, to enable it to run as an application as well as an applet.

16.4* (*Creating multiple windows from an applet*) Write an applet that contains two
buttons called *Investment Calculator* and *Loan Calculator*. When you click
Investment Calculator, a frame appears in a new window for calculating future
investment values. When you click *Loan Calculator*, a frame appears in a separate new window for computing loan payments (see Figure 16.18).

FIGURE 16.18 You can show frames in the applets.

16.5**(*A clock learning tool*) Develop a clock applet to show a first-grade student how to read a clock. Modify Exercise 13.20 to display a detailed clock with an hour hand and minute hand in an applet, as shown in Figure 16.19(a). The hour and minute values are randomly generated. The hour is between 0 and 11, and the minute is 0, 15, 30, or 45. A new random time is displayed upon a mouse click on the clock. Enable the applet to run standalone.

(a)   (b)

FIGURE 16.19 (a) Upon a mouse click on the clock, the clock time is randomly displayed. (b) The New Game button starts a new game.

16.6**(*TicTacToe*) Rewrite the program in Listing 16.7, TicTacToe.java, with the following modifications:

- Declare `Cell` as a separate class rather than an inner class.
- Add a button named *New Game*, as shown in Figure 16.19(b). The New Game button starts a new game.

16.7**(*Tax calculator*) Create an applet to compute tax, as shown in Figure 16.20. The applet lets the user select the tax status and enter the taxable income to compute

FIGURE 16.20 The tax calculator computes the tax for the specified taxable income and tax status.

the tax based on the 2001 federal tax rates, as shown in Exercise 7.14. Enable it to run standalone.

16.8***(*Creating a calculator*) Use various panels of `FlowLayout`, `GridLayout`, and `BorderLayout` to lay out the following calculator and to implement addition (+), subtraction (−), division (/), square root (sqrt), and modulus (%) functions (see Figure 16.21(a)). Enable it to run standalone.

(a)   (b)

FIGURE 16.21   (a) Exercise 16.8 is a Java implementation of a popular calculator. (b) Exercise 16.9 converts between decimal, hex, and binary numbers.

16.9*   (*Converting numbers*) Write an applet that converts between decimal, hex, and binary numbers, as shown in Figure 16.21(b). When you enter a decimal value on the decimal value text field and press the Enter key, its corresponding hex and binary numbers are displayed in the other two text fields. Likewise, you can enter values in the other fields and convert them accordingly. Enable it to run standalone.

16.10**(*Repainting a partial area*) When you repaint the entire viewing area of a panel, sometimes only a tiny portion of the viewing area is changed. You can improve the performance by only repainting the affected area, but do not invoke `super.paintComponent(g)` when repainting the panel, because this will cause the entire viewing area to be cleared. Use this approach to write an applet to display the temperatures of each hour during the last twenty-four hours in a histogram. Suppose that the temperatures between 50 and 90 degrees Fahrenheit are obtained randomly and are updated every hour. The temperature of the current hour needs to be redisplayed, while the others remain unchanged. Use a unique color to highlight the temperature for the current hour (see Figure 16.22).

FIGURE 16.22   The histogram displays the average temperature of every hour in the last twenty-four hours.

16.11**(*Showing a running fan*) Write a Java applet that simulates a running fan, as shown in Figure 16.23. The buttons Start, Stop, and Reverse control the fan.

The scrollbar controls the fan's speed. Create a class named **Fan**, a subclass of **JPanel**, to display the fan. This class also contains the methods to suspend and resume the fan, set its speed, and reverse its direction. Create a class named **FanControl** that contains a fan, and three buttons and a scroll bar to control the fan. Create a Java applet that contains an instance of **FanControl**. Enable the applet to run standalone.

FIGURE 16.23 The program simulates a running fan.

16.12***(Controlling a group of fans)* Write a Java applet that displays three fans in a group, with control buttons to start and stop all of them, as shown in Figure 16.24. Use the **FanControl** to control and display a single fan. Enable the applet to run standalone.

FIGURE 16.24 The program runs and controls a group of fans.

16.13****(Creating an elevator simulator)* Write an applet that simulates an elevator going up and down (see Figure 16.25). The buttons on the left indicate the floor where the passenger is now located. The passenger must click a button on the left to request that the elevator come to his or her floor. On entering the elevator, the passenger clicks a button on the right to request that it go to the specified floor. Enable the applet to run standalone.

FIGURE 16.25 The program simulates elevator operations.

16.14* (*Controlling a group of clocks*) Write a Java applet that displays three clocks in a group, with control buttons to start and stop all of them, as shown in Figure 16.26. Use the `ClockControl` to control and display a single clock. Enable the applet to run standalone.

FIGURE 16.26   Three clocks run independently with individual control and group control.

Section 16.9 Displaying Images

16.15* (*Enlarging and shrinking an image*) Write an applet that will display a sequence of images from a single image file in different sizes. Initially, the viewing area for this image has a width of 300 and a height of 300. Your program should continuously shrink the viewing area by 1 in width and 1 in height until it reaches a width of 50 and a height of 50. At that point, the viewing area should continuously enlarge by 1 in width and 1 in height until it reaches a width of 300 and a height of 300. The viewing area should shrink and enlarge (alternately) to create animation for the single image. Enable the applet to run standalone.

16.16*** (*Simulating a stock ticker*) Write a Java applet that displays a stock index ticker (see Figure 16.27). The stock index information is passed from the `<param>` tag in the HTML file. Each index has four parameters: Index Name (e.g., S&P 500), Current Time (e.g., 15:54), the index from the previous day (e.g., 919.01), and Change (e.g., 4.54). Enable the applet to run standalone.

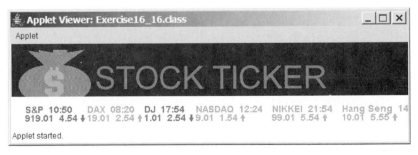

FIGURE 16.27   The program displays a stock index ticker.

Use at least five indexes, such as Dow Jones, S&P 500, NASDAQ, NIKKEI, and Gold & Silver Index. Display positive changes in green, and negative changes in red. The indexes move from right to left in the applet's viewing area. The applet freezes the ticker when the mouse button is pressed; it moves again when the mouse button is released.

16.17** (*Racing cars*) Write an applet that simulates four cars racing, as shown in Figure 16.28. You can set the speed for each car with 1 the highest.

FIGURE 16.28 You can set speed for each car.

16.18** (*Showing national flags*) Write an applet that introduces national flags, one after the other, by presenting each one's image, name, and description (see Figure 16.29) along with audio that reads the description.

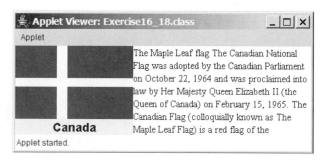

FIGURE 16.29 This applet shows each country's flag, name, and description, one after another, and reads the description that is currently shown.

Suppose your applet displays the flags of eight countries. Assume that the photo image files, named flag0.gif, flag1.gif, and so on, up to flag7.gif, are stored in a subdirectory named image in the applet's directory. The length of each audio is less than 10 seconds. Assume that the name and description of each country's flag are passed from the HTML using the parameter **name0**, **name1**, ..., **name7**, and **description0**, **description1**, ..., and **description7**. Pass the number of countries as an HTML parameter using **numberOfCountries**. Here is an example:

```
<param name="numberOfCountries" value=8>
<param name="name0" value="Canada">
<param name="description0" value=
"The Maple Leaf flag
The Canadian National Flag was adopted by the Canadian
Parliament on October 22, 1964 and was proclaimed into law
by Her Majesty Queen Elizabeth II (the Queen of Canada) on
February 15, 1965. The Canadian Flag (colloquially known
as The Maple Leaf Flag) is a red flag of the proportions
two by length and one by width, containing in its center a
white square, with a single red stylized eleven-point
mapleleaf centered in the white square.">
```

Hint

Use the **DescriptionPanel** class to display the image, name, and the text. The **DescriptionPanel** class was introduced in Listing 15.6, TextAreaDemo.java.

16.19* (*Bouncing balls*) The example in §16.8 simulates a bouncing ball. Extend the example to allow multiple balls, as shown in Figure 16.30. You may use the +*1* or −*1* button to increase or decrease the number of the balls, and use the *Suspend* and *Resume* buttons to freeze the balls or resume bouncing.

FIGURE 16.30   The applet allows you to add or remove bouncing balls.

Section 16.12 Playing Audio

16.20* (*Playing, looping, and stopping a sound clip*) Write an applet that meets the following requirements:

- Get an audio file. The file is in the class directory.
- Place three buttons labeled Play, Loop, and Stop, as shown in Figure 16.31.
- If you click the Play button, the audio file is played once. If you click the Loop button, the audio file keeps playing repeatedly. If you click the Stop button, the playing stops.
- The applet can run as an application.

FIGURE 16.31   Click Play to play an audio clip once, click Loop to play an audio repeatedly, and click Stop to terminate playing.

16.21** (*Creating an alarm clock*) Write an applet that will display a digital clock with a large display panel that shows hour, minute, and second. This clock should allow the user to set an alarm. Figure 16.32(a) shows an example of such a clock. To turn on the alarm, check the Alarm check box. To specify the alarm time, click the "Set alarm" button to display a new frame, as shown in Figure 16.32(b). You can set the alarm time in the frame. Enable the applet to run standalone.

(a)   (b)

FIGURE 16.32   The program displays current hour, minute, and second, and enables you to set an alarm.

16.22**(*Creating an image animator with audio*) Create animation using the applet (see Figure 16.33) to meet the following requirements:

- Allow the user to specify the animation speed. The user can enter the speed in a text field.
- Get the number of frames and the image filename prefix from the user. For example, if the user enters **n** for the number of frames and **L** for the image prefix, then the files are **L1**, **L2**, and so on, to **L**n. Assume that the images are stored in the **image** directory, a subdirectory of the applet's directory.
- Allow the user to specify an audio filename. The audio file is stored in the same directory as the applet. The sound is played while the animation runs.
- Enable the applet to run standalone.

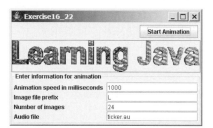

FIGURE 16.33   This applet lets the user select image files, audio file, and animation speed.

16.23**(*Raising flag and playing anthem*) Create an applet that displays a flag rising up, as shown in Figure 14.20. As the national flag rises, play the national anthem. (You may use a flag image and anthem audio file from Listing 16.13.)

PART 4

EXCEPTION HANDLING, I/O, AND RECURSION

This part introduces the use of exception handling and assertions to make your programs robust and correct, the use of input and output to manage and process a large quantity of binary data, and the use of recursion to write methods for solving inherently recursive problems.

Chapter 17
Exceptions and Assertions

Chapter 18
Binary I/O

Chapter 19
Recursion

Prerequisites for Part 4

flexible ordering

All the chapters after Chapter 17 are designed to minimize dependencies so that they can be reordered flexibly.

Chapter 17, "Exceptions and Assertions," can be covered after Chapter 9, "Inheritance and Polymorphism." Chapter 18, "Binary I/O," is usually covered after Chapter 17.

Chapter 19

The concept of recursion and how to write simple recursive programs in §§19.1–19.3 can be covered after Chapter 6, "Arrays."

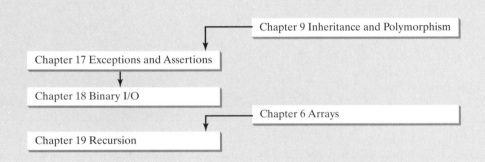

EXCEPTIONS AND ASSERTIONS

Objectives

- To understand exceptions and exception handling (§§17.2–17.3).

- To distinguish exception types: `Error` (fatal) vs. `Exception` (non-fatal), and checked vs. unchecked (§17.3).

- To declare exceptions in a method header (§17.4.1).

- To throw exceptions in a method (§17.4.2).

- To write a `try-catch` block to handle exceptions (§17.4.3).

- To explain how an exception is propagated (§17.4.3).

- To use the `finally` clause in a `try-catch` block (§17.5).

- To know when to use exceptions (§17.6).

- To rethrow exceptions in a `try-catch` block (§17.7).

- To create chained exceptions (§17.8).

- (Optional) To declare custom exception classes (§17.9).

- (Optional) To apply assertions to help ensure program correctness (§17.10).

17.1 Introduction

Three categories of errors (syntax errors, runtime errors, and logic errors) were introduced in §2.15, "Programming Errors." *Syntax errors* arise because the rules of the language have not been followed. They are detected by the compiler. *Runtime errors* occur while the program is running if the environment detects an operation that is impossible to carry out. *Logic errors* occur when a program doesn't perform the way it was intended to. In general, syntax errors are easy to find and easy to correct because the compiler indicates where they came from and why they occurred. You can use the debugging techniques introduced in §2.16, "Debugging," to find logic errors. This chapter introduces using exception handling to deal with runtime errors and using assertions to help ensure program correctness.

17.2 Exception-Handling Overview

An exception is a runtime error. A program that does not provide code for *catching* and *handling* exceptions will terminate abnormally, and may cause serious problems. For example, if your program attempts to transfer money from a savings account to a checking account, but because of a runtime error is terminated *after* the money is drawn from the savings account and *before* the money is deposited in the checking account, the customer will lose money.

Exceptions occur for various reasons. The user may enter an invalid input, for example, or the program may attempt to open a file that doesn't exist, or the network connection may hang up, or the program may attempt to access an out-of-bounds array element.

You have already been briefly introduced to exceptions in earlier chapters. In Chapter 6, "Arrays," you learned that an `ArrayIndexOutOfBoundsException` occurs if you access an element past the end of an array. In Chapter 7, "Objects and Classes," you learned that a `NullPointerException` occurs when you invoke a method on a reference variable with `null` value. In Chapter 8, "Strings and Text I/O," you learned that a `StringIndexOutOfBoundsException` occurs when you access a character in a string using an out-of-bound index. You also learned that text I/O operations may throw exceptions.

When an exception occurs, the normal execution flow of the program will be interrupted. Java provides programmers with the capability to handle runtime exceptions. With this exception handling capability, referred to as *exception handling*, you can develop robust programs for mission-critical computing.

Here is an example. The program in Listing 17.1 terminates abnormally if you enter a floating-point value instead of an integer, as shown in Figure 17.1.

LISTING 17.1 ExceptionDemo.java

```
1    import java.util.Scanner;
2
3    public class ExceptionDemo {
4      public static void main(String[] args) {
5        Scanner scanner = new Scanner(System.in);
6        System.out.print("Enter an integer: ");
7        int number = scanner.nextInt();
8
9        // Display the result
10       System.out.println(
11         "The number entered is " + number);
12     }
13   }
```

If an exception occurs on this line, the rest of the lines in the method are skipped and the program is terminated.

↓ Terminated.

FIGURE 17.1 An exception occurs when you enter an invalid input.

Note that several lines of information are displayed in Figure 17.1 in response to this invalid input. This information, known as the *stack trace*, includes the name of the exception (`java.util.InputMismatchException`) followed by the method call stack at the time the exception occurred. The stack trace helps in debugging a program. Starting from the last line of the stack trace, you see that the exception was detected in line 7 of the `main` method. Each line of the stack trace contains the class name and method (`ExceptionDemo.main`) along with the file name and line number (`ExceptionDemo.java: 7`). Moving up the stack trace, you see that the exception occurred in line 2000 in the `nextInt` method of the `Scanner` class, the exception occurred in line 2040 in the overloaded `nextInt` method of the `Scanner` class, the exception occurred in line 1431 in the `next` method of the `Scanner` class, the exception occurred in line 819 in the `throwFor` method of the `Scanner` class. The last method in the call chain actually threw an `InputMismatchException`.

Java allows the program to catch and process exceptions. You can revise Listing 17.1 to handle the `InputMismatchException` using a new construct called the **try-catch** *block*, as shown in Listing 17.2.

stack trace

try-catch block

LISTING 17.2 HandleExceptionDemo.java

```java
1   import java.util.*;
2
3   public class HandleExceptionDemo {
4     public static void main(String[] args) {
5       Scanner scanner = new Scanner(System.in);
6       boolean continueInput = true;
7
8       do {
9         try{
10          System.out.print("Enter an integer: ");
11          int number = scanner.nextInt();
12
13          // Display the result
14          System.out.println(
15            "The number entered is " + number);
16
17          continueInput = false;
18        }
19        catch (InputMismatchException ex) {
20          System.out.println("Try again. (" +
21            "Incorrect input: an integer is required)");
22          scanner.nextLine(); // discard input
23        }
24      } while (continueInput);
25    }
```

If an exception occurs on this line, the rest of lines in the try block are skipped and the control is transferred to the catch block.

A `try` block begins with the keyword `try` followed by a block of statements in curly braces (`{}`). A `try` block contains the statements that might throw exceptions. A `catch` block begins with the keyword `catch` followed by an exception parameter in parentheses and a block of statements for handling the exception in curly braces. When a statement in a `try` block throws an exception, the rest of the statements in the `try` block are skipped and control is transferred to the `catch` block.

Suppose you enter `3.5` when executing line 11, as shown in Figure 17.2. An `InputMismatchException` occurs and the control is transferred to the `catch` block. The statements in the `catch` block are now executed. The statement `scanner.nextLine()` in line 22 discards the current input line so that the user can enter a new line of input. The variable `continueInput` controls the loop. Its initial value is `true` (line 6), and it is changed to `false` (line 17) when a valid input is received.

FIGURE 17.2 An exception is caught and handled in the program.

17.3 Exceptions and Exception Types

A Java exception is an instance of a class derived from `Throwable`. The `Throwable` class is contained in the `java.lang` package, and subclasses of `Throwable` are contained in various packages. Errors related to GUI components are included in the `java.awt` package; numeric exceptions are included in the `java.lang` package because they are related to the `java.lang.Number` class. You can create your own exception classes by extending `Throwable` or a subclass of `Throwable`. Figure 17.3 shows some of Java's predefined exception classes.

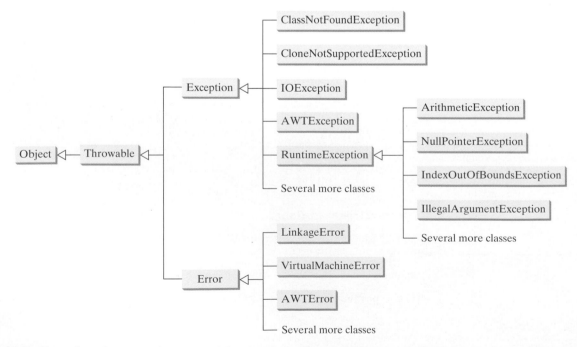

FIGURE 17.3 Exceptions thrown are instances of the classes shown in this diagram, or of subclasses of one of these classes.

Note

The class names `Error`, `Exception`, and `RuntimeException` are somewhat confusing. All three of these classes are exceptions, and all of the errors discussed here occur at runtime.

The exception classes can be classified into three major types: system errors, exceptions, and runtime exceptions.

■ *System errors* are thrown by the JVM and represented in the `Error` class. The `Error` class describes internal system errors. Such errors rarely occur. If one does, there is little you can do beyond notifying the user and trying to terminate the program gracefully. Examples of subclasses of `Error` are listed in Table 17.1.

system error

TABLE 17.1   Examples of Subclasses of `Error`

Class	Possible Reason for Exception
LinkageError	A class has some dependency on another class, but the latter class has changed incompatibly after the compilation of the former class.
VirtualMachineError	The JVM is broken or has run out of the resources necessary for it to continue operating.
AWTError	A fatal error in the GUI runtime system.
AssertionError	An assertion has failed. Assertions will be introduced in §17.8, "Assertions."

■ *Exceptions* are represented in the `Exception` class, which describes errors caused by your program and by external circumstances. These errors can be caught and handled by your program. Examples of subclasses of `Exception` are listed in Table 17.2.

exception

TABLE 17.2   Examples of Subclasses of `Exception`

Class	Possible Reason for Exception
ClassNotFoundException	Attempt to use a class that does not exist. This exception would occur, for example, if you tried to run a nonexistent class using the **java** command, or if your program was composed of, say, three class files, only two of which could be found.
CloneNotSupported Exception	Attempt to clone an object whose defining class does not implement the `Cloneable` interface. Cloning objects were introduced in Chapter 10, "Abstract Classes and Interfaces."
IOException	Related to input/output operations, such as invalid input, reading past the end of a file, and opening a nonexistent file. Examples of subclasses of `IOException` are `InterruptedIOException`, `EOFException` (EOF is short for End Of File), and `FileNotFound Exception`.
AWTException	Exceptions in GUI components.

■ *Runtime exceptions* are represented in the `RuntimeException` class, which describes programming errors, such as bad casting, accessing an out-of-bounds array, and numeric errors. Runtime exceptions are generally thrown by the JVM. Examples of subclasses are listed in Table 17.3.

runtime exception

TABLE 17.3 Examples of Subclasses of **RuntimeException**

Class	Possible Reason for Exception
ArithmeticException	Dividing an integer by zero. Note that floating-point arithmetic does not throw exceptions. See Appendix E, "Special Floating-Point Values."
NullPointerException	Attempt to access an object through a **null** reference variable.
IndexOutOfBoundsException	Index to an array is out of range.
IllegalArgumentException	A method is passed an argument that is illegal or inappropriate.

unchecked exception
checked exception

RuntimeException, **Error**, and their subclasses are known as *unchecked exceptions*. All other exceptions are known as *checked exceptions*, meaning that the compiler forces the programmer to check and deal with them.

In most cases, unchecked exceptions reflect programming logic errors that are not recoverable. For example, a **NullPointerException** is thrown if you access an object through a reference variable before an object is assigned to it; an **IndexOutOfBoundsException** is thrown if you access an element in an array outside the bounds of the array. These are logic errors that should be corrected in the program. Unchecked exceptions can occur anywhere in a program. To avoid cumbersome overuse of **try-catch** blocks, Java does not mandate that you write code to catch or declare unchecked exceptions.

Caution

integer overflow

At present, Java does not throw *integer overflow* exceptions. The following statement adds 1 to the maximum integer.

```
int number = Integer.MAX_VALUE + 1;
System.out.println(number);
```

It displays −2147483648, which is logically incorrect. The cause of this problem is overflow, that is, the result exceeds the maximum for an **int** value.

A future version of Java may fix this problem by throwing an overflow exception.

Tip

BigInteger

For processing large integral values, use the **BigInteger** class, introduced in §10.5.6, "**BigInteger** and **BigDecimal** Classes."

17.4 Understanding Exception Handling

Java's exception-handling model is based on three operations: *declaring an exception*, *throwing an exception*, and *catching an exception*, as shown in Figure 17.4.

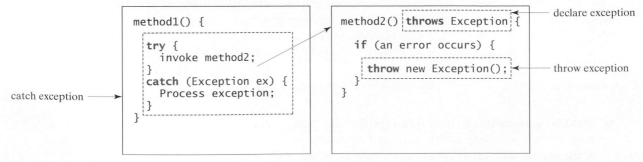

FIGURE 17.4 Exception handling in Java consists of declaring exceptions, throwing exceptions, and catching and processing exceptions.

17.4.1   Declaring Exceptions

In Java, the statement currently being executed belongs to a method. The Java interpreter invokes the `main` method for a Java application, and the Web browser invokes the applet's no-arg constructor and then the `init` method for a Java applet. Every method must state the types of checked exceptions it might throw. This is known as *declaring exceptions*. Because system errors and runtime errors can happen to any code, Java does not require that you declare `Error` and `RuntimeException` (unchecked exceptions) explicitly in the method. However, all other exceptions thrown by the method must be explicitly declared in the method declaration so that the caller of the method is informed of the exception.

declare exception

To declare an exception in a method, use the `throws` keyword in the method declaration, as in this example:

```
public void myMethod() throws IOException
```

The `throws` keyword indicates that `myMethod` might throw an `IOException`. If the method might throw multiple exceptions, add a list of the exceptions, separated by commas, after `throws`:

```
public void myMethod()
   throws Exception1, Exception2, ..., ExceptionN
```

Note

If a method does not declare exceptions in the superclass, you cannot override it to declare exceptions in the subclass.

17.4.2   Throwing Exceptions

A program that detects an error can create an instance of an appropriate exception type and throw it. This is known as *throwing an exception*. Here is an example: Suppose the program detected that an argument passed to the method violates the method contract (e.g., the argument must be non-negative, but a negative argument is passed); the program can create an instance of `IllegalArgumentException` and throw it, as follows:

throw exception

```
IllegalArgumentException ex =
   new IllegalArgumentException("Wrong Argument");
throw ex;
```

Or if you prefer, you can use the following:

```
throw new IllegalArgumentException("Wrong Argument");
```

Note

`IllegalArgumentException` is an exception class in the Java API. In general, each exception class in the Java API has at least two constructors: a no-arg constructor, and a constructor with a `String` argument that describes the exception. This argument is called the *exception message*, which can be obtained using `getMessage()`.

exception message

Tip

The keyword to declare an exception is `throws`, and the keyword to throw an exception is `throw`.

`throws` and `throw`

17.4.3   Catching Exceptions

You now know how to declare an exception and how to throw an exception. When an exception is thrown, it can be caught and handled in a `try-catch` block, as follows:

catch exception

```
try {
  statements;  // Statements that may throw exceptions
}
```

```
      catch (Exception1 exVar1) {
        handler for exception1;
      }
      catch (Exception2 exVar2) {
        handler for exception2;
      }
      ...
      catch (ExceptionN exVar3) {
        handler for exceptionN;
      }
```

If no exceptions arise during the execution of the **try** block, the **catch** blocks are skipped.

If one of the statements inside the **try** block throws an exception, Java skips the remaining statements in the **try** block and starts the process of finding the code to handle the exception. The code that handles the exception is called the *exception handler*; it is found by propagating the exception backward through a chain of method calls, starting from the current method. Each **catch** block is examined in turn, from first to last, to see whether the type of the exception object is an instance of the exception class in the **catch** block. If so, the exception object is assigned to the variable declared and the code in the **catch** block is executed. If no handler is found, Java exits this method, passes the exception to the method that invoked the method, and continues the same process to find a handler. If no handler is found in the chain of methods being invoked, the program terminates and prints an error message on the console. The process of finding a handler is called *catching an exception*.

exception handler

Suppose the **main** method invokes **method1**, **method1** invokes **method2**, **method2** invokes **method3**, and an exception occurs in **method3**, as shown in Figure 17.5. Consider the following scenario:

- If **method3** cannot handle the exception, **method3** is aborted and the control is returned to **method2**. If the exception type is **Exception3**, it is caught by the **catch** block for handling exception **ex3** in **method2**. **statement5** is skipped, and **statement6** is executed.

- If the exception type is **Exception2**, **method2** is aborted, the control is returned to **method1**, and the exception is caught by the **catch** block for handling exception **ex2** in **method1**. **statement3** is skipped, and **statement4** is executed.

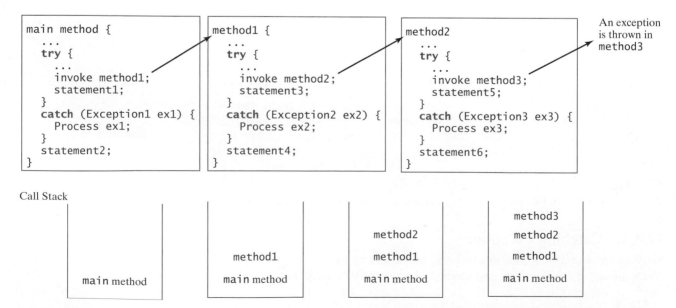

FIGURE 17.5 If an exception is not caught in the current method, it is passed to its caller. The process is repeated until the exception is caught or passed to the **main** method.

■ If the exception type is `Exception1`, `method1` is aborted, the control is returned to the `main` method, and the exception is caught by the `catch` block for handling exception `ex1` in the `main` method. `statement1` is skipped, and `statement2` is executed.

■ If the exception type is not `Exception1`, `Exception2`, or `Exception3`, the exception is not caught and the program terminates. `statement1` and `statement2` are not executed.

Note

Various exception classes can be derived from a common superclass. If a `catch` block catches exception objects of a superclass, it can catch all the exception objects of the subclasses of that superclass.

catch block

Note

The order in which exceptions are specified in `catch` blocks is important. A compilation error will result if a `catch` block for a superclass type appears before a `catch` block for a subclass type. For example, the ordering in (a) is erroneous, because `RuntimeException` is a subclass of `Exception`. The correct ordering should be as shown in (b).

order of exception handlers

```
try {
    ...
}
catch (Exception ex) {
    ...
}
catch (RuntimeException ex) {
    ...
}
```
(a) Wrong order

```
try {
    ...
}
catch (RuntimeException ex) {
    ...
}
catch (Exception ex) {
    ...
}
```
(b) Correct order

Note

Java forces you to deal with checked exceptions. If a method declares a checked exception (i.e., an exception other than `Error` or `RuntimeException`), you must invoke it in a `try-catch` block or declare to throw the exception in the calling method. For example, suppose that method `p1` invokes method `p2`, and `p2` may throw a checked exception (e.g., `IOException`), you have to write the code as shown in (a) or (b).

catch or declare checked exceptions

```
void p1() {
    try {
        p2();
    }
    catch (IOException ex) {
        ...
    }
}
```
(a) catch exception

```
void p1() throws IOException {

    p2();

}
```
(b) throw exception

17.4.4 Getting Information from Exceptions

An exception object contains valuable information about the exception. You may use the following instance methods in the `java.lang.Throwable` class to get information regarding the exception, as shown in Figure 17.6. The `printStackTrace()` method prints stack trace information on the console. The `getStackTrace()` method provides programmatic access to the stack trace information printed by `printStackTrace()`.

methods in **Throwable**

java.lang.Throwable	
+getMessage(): String	Returns the message of this object.
+toString(): String	Returns the concatenation of three strings: (1) the full name of the exception class; (2) ":" (a colon and a space); (3) the getMessage() method.
+printStackTrace(): void	Prints the Throwable object and its call stack trace information on the console.
+getStackTrace(): StackTraceElement[]	Returns an array of stack trace elements representing the stack trace pertaining to this throwable.

FIGURE 17.6   `Throwable` is the root class for all exception objects.

Listing 17.3 gives an example that uses the methods in `Throwable` to display exception information. Line 4 invokes the sum method to return the sum of all the elements in the array. There is an error in line 23 that causes the `ArrayIndexOutOfBoundsException`, a subclass of `IndexOutOfBoundsException`. This exception is caught in the `try-catch` block. Lines 7, 8, 9 display the stack trace, exception message, and exception object and message using the `printStackTrace()`, `getMessage()`, and `toString()` methods, as shown in Figure 17.7. Line 12 obtains stack trace elements into an array. Each element represents a method call. You can obtain the method (line 14), class name (line 15), and exception line number (line 16) for each element.

FIGURE 17.7   You can use the `printStackTrace()`, `getMessage()`, `toString()`, and `getStackTrace()` methods to obtain information from exception objects.

LISTING 17.3 `TestException.java`

```
 1 public class TestException  {
 2   public static void main(String[] args) {
 3     try {
 4       System.out.println(sum(new int[] {1, 2, 3, 4, 5}));
 5     }
 6     catch (Exception ex) {
 7       ex.printStackTrace();
 8       System.out.println("\n" + ex.getMessage());
 9       System.out.println("\n" + ex.toString());
10
11       System.out.println("\nTrace Info Obtained from getStackTrace");
12       StackTraceElement[] traceElements = ex.getStackTrace();
```

invoke sum   (line 4)

printStackTrace()   (line 7)
getMessage()   (line 8)
toString()   (line 9)

```
13        for (int i = 0; i < traceElements.length; i++) {
14          System.out.print("method " + traceElements[i].getMethodName());
15          System.out.print("(" + traceElements[i].getClassName() + ":");      error
16          System.out.println(traceElements[i].getLineNumber() + ")");
17        }
18      }
19    }
20
21    private static int sum(int[] list) {
22      int result = 0;
23      for (int i = 0; i <= list.length; i++)
24        result += list[i];
25      return result;
26    }
27 }
```

17.4.5 Example: Declaring, Throwing, and Catching Exceptions

This example demonstrates declaring, throwing, and catching exceptions by modifying the
setRadius method in the Circle2 class in Listing 7.3. The new setRadius method throws
an exception if the radius is negative.

Rename the circle class given in Listing 17.4 as CircleWithException, which is the
same as Circle2 except that the setRadius(double newRadius) method throws an
IllegalArgumentException if the argument newRadius is negative.

LISTING 17.4 CircleWithException.java

```
 1 public class CircleWithException {
 2   /** The radius of the circle */
 3   private double radius;
 4
 5   /** The number of the objects created */
 6   private static int numberOfObjects = 0;
 7
 8   /** Construct a circle with radius 1 */
 9   public CircleWithException() {
10     this(1.0);
11   }
12
13   /** Construct a circle with a specified radius */
14   public CircleWithException(double newRadius) {
15     setRadius(newRadius);
16     numberOfObjects++;
17   }
18
19   /** Return radius */
20   public double getRadius() {
21     return radius;
22   }
23
24   /** Set a new radius */
25   public void setRadius(double newRadius)
26       throws IllegalArgumentException {                         declare exception
27     if (newRadius >= 0)
28       radius = newRadius;
29     else
30       throw new IllegalArgumentException(                       throw exception
```

```
31               "Radius cannot be negative");
32     }
33
34     /** Return numberOfObjects */
35     public static int getNumberOfObjects() {
36       return numberOfObjects;
37     }
38
39     /** Return the area of this circle */
40     public double findArea() {
41       return radius * radius * 3.14159;
42     }
43 }
```

A test program that uses the new `Circle` class is given in Listing 17.5. Figure 17.8 shows a sample run of the test program.

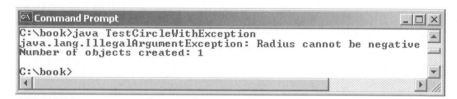

FIGURE 17.8 The exception is thrown when the radius is negative.

LISTING 17.5 TestCircleWithException.java

```
 1 public class TestCircleWithException {
 2   /** Main method */
 3   public static void main(String[] args) {
 4     try {
 5       CircleWithException c1 = new CircleWithException(5);
 6       CircleWithException c2 = new CircleWithException(-5);
 7       CircleWithException c3 = new CircleWithException(0);
 8     }
 9     catch (IllegalArgumentException ex) {
10       System.out.println(ex);
11     }
12
13     System.out.println("Number of objects created: " +
14       CircleWithException.getNumberOfObjects());
15   }
16 }
```

try

catch

The original `Circle2` class remains intact except that the class name is changed to `CircleWithException`, a new constructor `CircleWithException(newRadius)` is added, and the `setRadius` method now declares an exception and throws it if the radius is negative.

The `setRadius` method declares to throw `IllegalArgumentException` in the method declaration (lines 25–26 in CircleWithException.java). The `CircleWithException` class would still compile if the `throws IllegalArgumentException` clause were removed from the method declaration, since it is a subclass of `RuntimeException` and every method can throw `RuntimeException` (unchecked exception) regardless of whether it is declared in the method header.

The test program creates three `CircleWithException` objects, `c1`, `c2`, and `c3`, to test how to handle exceptions. Invoking `new CircleWithException(-5)` (line 6 in Listing 17.5) causes the `setRadius` method to be invoked, which throws an `IllegalArgumentException`, because the radius is negative. In the `catch` block, the type of the object `ex` is `IllegalArgumentException`, which matches the exception object thrown by the `setRadius` method. So this exception is caught by the `catch` block.

The exception handler prints a short message, `ex.toString()` (line 10), about the exception, using `System.out.println(ex)`.

Note that the execution continues in the event of the exception. If the handlers had not caught the exception, the program would have abruptly terminated.

The test program would still compile if the `try` statement were not used, because the method throws an instance of `IllegalArgumentException`, a subclass of `RuntimeException` (unchecked exception). If a method throws an exception other than `RuntimeException` and `Error`, the method must be invoked within a `try-catch` block.

 Note

As you will learn in Chapter 24, "Multithreading" Java supports multithreading. One program can have many threads. Methods are executed on threads. If an exception occurs on a thread, the thread is terminated if the exception is not caught. If a program has only one thread, an uncaught exception will cause the program to terminate. If a program has *multiple threads*, an uncaught exception will terminate only the thread where the exception occurred. However, since certain threads may rely on the terminated thread, terminating a thread may affect the rest of the program.

multiple threads

17.5 The **finally** Clause

Occasionally, you may want some code to be executed regardless of whether an exception occurs or is caught. Java has a `finally` clause that can be used to accomplish this objective. The syntax for the `finally` clause might look like this:

```
try {
  statements;
}
catch (TheException ex) {
  handling ex;
}
finally {
  finalStatements;
}
```

The code in the `finally` block is executed under all circumstances, regardless of whether an exception occurs in the `try` block or is caught. Consider three possible cases:

- If no exception arises in the `try` block, `finalStatements` is executed, and the next statement after the `try` statement is executed.

- If one of the statements causes an exception in the `try` block that is caught in a `catch` block, the other statements in the `try` block are skipped, the `catch` block is executed, and the `finally` clause is executed. If the `catch` block does not rethrow an exception, the next statement after the `try` statement is executed. If it does, the exception is passed to the caller of this method.

- If one of the statements causes an exception that is not caught in any `catch` block, the other statements in the `try` block are skipped, the `finally` clause is executed, and the exception is passed to the caller of this method.

- The `finally` block executes even if there is a `return` statement prior to reaching the `finally` block.

omitting **catch** block

 Note

The **catch** block may be omitted when the **finally** clause is used.

A common use of the **finally** clause is in I/O programming. To ensure that a file is closed under all circumstances, you may place a file closing statement in the **finally** block, as shown in Listing 17.6.

LISTING 17.6 FinallyDemo.java

```
 1 public class FinallyDemo {
 2   public static void main(String[] args) {
 3     java.io.PrintWriter output = null;
 4
 5     try {
 6       // Create a file
 7       output = new java.io.Printwriter("text.txt");
 8
 9       // Write formatted output to the file
10       output.println("Welcome to Java");
11     }
12   catch (java.io.IOException ex) {
13       ex.printStackTrace();
14     }
15   finally {
16       // Close the file
17       if (output != null) output.close();
18     }
19   }
20 }
```

try

catch

finally

The statements in lines 7 and 10 may throw an IOException, so they are placed inside a **try** block. The statement **output.close()** closes the PrintWriter object output in the **finally** block. This statement is executed regardless of whether an exception occurs in the **try** block or is caught.

17.6 When to Use Exceptions

The **try** block contains the code that are executed in normal circumstances. The **catch** block contains the code that are executed in exceptional circumstances. Exception handling separates error-handling code from normal programming tasks, thus making programs easier to read and to modify. Be aware, however, that exception handling usually requires more time and resources because it requires instantiating a new exception object, rolling back the call stack, and propagating the exception through the chain of methods invoked to search for the handler.

An exception occurs in a method. If you want the exception to be processed by its caller, you should create an exception object and throw it. If you can handle the exception in the method where it occurs, there is no need to throw or use exceptions.

In general, common exceptions that may occur in multiple classes in a project are candidates for exception classes. Simple errors that may occur in individual methods are best handled locally without throwing exceptions.

When should you use a **try-catch** block in the code? Use it when you have to deal with unexpected error conditions. Do not use a **try-catch** block to deal with simple, expected situations. For example, the following code

```
try {
  System.out.println(refVar.toString());
}
```

```
catch (NullPointerException ex) {
  System.out.println("refVar is null");
}
```

is better replaced by

```
if (refVar != null)
  System.out.println(refVar.toString());
else
  System.out.println("refVar is null");
```

Which situations are exceptional and which are expected is sometimes difficult to decide. The point is not to abuse exception handling as a way to deal with a simple logic test.

17.7 Rethrowing Exceptions

Java allows an exception handler to rethrow the exception if the handler cannot process the exception or the handler simply wants to let its caller be notified of the exception. The syntax may look like this:

```
try {
  statements;
}
catch (TheException ex) {
  perform operations before exits;
  throw ex;
}
```

The statement `throw ex` rethrows the exception so that other handlers get a chance to process the exception `ex`.

17.8 (Optional) Chained Exceptions

In the preceding section, the `catch` block rethrows the original exception. Sometimes, you may need to throw a new exception (with additional information) along with the original exception. This is called *chained exceptions*. Listing 17.7 gives an example that demonstrates how to create and throw chained exceptions.

LISTING 17.7 ChainedExceptionDemo.java

```
 1 public class ChainedExceptionDemo {
 2   public static void main(String[] args) {
 3     try {
 4       method1();
 5     }
 6     catch (Exception ex) {
 7       ex.printStackTrace();                              stack trace
 8     }
 9   }
10
11   public static void method1() throws Exception {
12     try {
13       method2();
14     }
15     catch (Exception ex) {
16       throw new Exception("New info from method1", ex);   chained exception
17     }
18   }
19
20   public static void method2() throws Exception {
```

```
21        throw new Exception("New info from method2");
22    }
23 }
```

The main method invokes method1 (line 4), method1 invokes method2 (line 13), and method2 throws an exception (line 21). This exception is caught in the catch block in method1 and is wrapped in a new exception in line 16. The new exception is thrown and caught in the catch block in the main method in line 6. Figure 17.9 shows the output from the printStackTrace() method in line 7. The new exception thrown from method1 is displayed first, followed by the original exception thrown from method2.

```
Command Prompt                                                    _ □ ×
C:\book>java ChainedExceptionDemo
java.lang.Exception: New info from method1
        at ChainedExceptionDemo.method1(ChainedExceptionDemo.java:16)
        at ChainedExceptionDemo.main(ChainedExceptionDemo.java:4)
Caused by: java.lang.Exception: New info from method2
        at ChainedExceptionDemo.method2(ChainedExceptionDemo.java:21)
        at ChainedExceptionDemo.method1(ChainedExceptionDemo.java:13)
        ... 1 more

C:\book>
```

FIGURE 17.9   The stack trace displayed the chained exceptions.

17.9 (Optional) Creating Custom Exception Classes

Java provides quite a few exception classes. Use them whenever possible instead of creating your own exception classes. However, if you run into a problem that cannot be adequately described by the predefined exception classes, you can create your own exception class, derived from Exception or from a subclass of Exception, such as IOException.

In Listing 17.4, CircleWithException.java, the setRadius method throws an exception if the radius is negative. Suppose you wish to pass the radius to the handler. In that case, you may create a custom exception class, as shown in Listing 17.8.

LISTING 17.8   InvalidRadiusException.java

```
1 public class InvalidRadiusException extends Exception {
2    private double radius;
3
4    /** Construct an exception */
5    public InvalidRadiusException(double radius) {
6      super("Invalid radius " + radius);
7      this.radius = radius;
8    }
9
10   /** Return the radius */
11   public double getRadius() {
12     return radius;
13   }
14 }
```

This custom exception class extends java.lang.Exception (line 1). The Exception class extends java.lang.Throwable. All the methods (e.g., getMessage(), toString(), and printStackTrace()) in Exception are inherited from Throwable. The Exception class contains four constructors. Among them, the following two constructors are often used:

■ **public** Exception() Constructs an exception with no message.

■ **public** Exception(String message) Constructs an exception with the specified message.

Line 6 invokes the superclass's constructor with a message. This message will be set in the exception object and can be obtained by invoking `getMessage()` on the object.

Tip
Most exception classes in the Java API contain two constructors: a no-arg constructor and a constructor with a message parameter.

To create an `InvalidRadiusException`, you have to pass a radius. So the `setRadius` method in Listing 17.4 can be modified as follows:

```java
/** Set a new radius */
public void setRadius(double newRadius)
    throws InvalidRadiusException {
  if (newRadius >= 0)
    radius = newRadius;
  else
    throw new InvalidRadiusException(newRadius);
}
```

The following code creates a circle object and sets its radius to -5:

```java
try {
  CircleWithException1 c = new CircleWithException1(4);
  c.setRadius(-5);
}
catch (InvalidRadiusException ex) {
  System.out.println("The invalid radius is " + ex.getRadius());
}
```

Invoking `setRadius(-5)` throws an `InvalidRadiusException`, which is caught by the handler. The handler displays the radius in the exception object `ex`.

Tip
Can you declare a custom exception class by extending `RuntimeException`? Yes, but it is not good, because it makes your custom exception unchecked. It is better to make a custom exception checked so that the complier can force these exceptions to be caught in your program.   checked custom exception

17.10 (Optional) Assertions

An *assertion* is a Java statement that enables you to assert an assumption about your program.   assertion
An assertion contains a Boolean expression that should be true during program execution.
Assertions can be used to ensure program correctness and avoid logic errors.

17.10.1   Declaring Assertions

An *assertion* is declared using the new Java keyword `assert` in JDK 1.4, as follows:

```java
assert assertion;
```

or

```java
assert assertion : detailMessage;
```

where *assertion* is a Boolean expression and *detailMessage* is a primitive-type or an `Object` value.

When an assertion statement is executed, Java evaluates the `assertion`. If it is `false`, an `AssertionError` will be thrown. The `AssertionError` class has a no-arg constructor and seven overloaded single-parameter constructors of type `int`, `long`, `float`, `double`, `boolean`, `char`, and `Object`. For the first `assert` statement with no detailed message, the no-arg constructor of `AssertionError` is used. For the second `assert` statement with a detailed message, an appropriate `AssertionError` constructor is used to match the data type of the message. `AssertionError` is a subclass of `Error`, so when an assertion becomes false, the program displays a message on the console and exits.

Here is an example of using assertions:

```
 1  public class AssertionDemo {
 2    public static void main(String[] args) {
 3      int i; int sum = 0;
 4      for (i = 0; i < 10; i++) {
 5        sum += i;
 6      }
 7      assert i == 10;
 8      assert sum > 10 && sum < 5 * 10 : "sum is " + sum;
 9    }
10  }
```

The statement `assert i == 10` asserts that `i` is 10 when the statement is executed. If `i` is not 10, an `AssertionError` is thrown. The statement `assert sum > 10 && sum < 5 * 10 : "sum is " + sum` asserts that `sum > 10` and `sum < 5 * 10`. If `false`, an `AssertionError` with the message `"sum is " + sum` is thrown.

Suppose you typed `i < 100` instead of `i < 10` by mistake in line 4, the following `AssertionError` would be thrown:

```
Exception in thread "main" java.lang.AssertionError
        at AssertionDemo.main(AssertionDemo.java:7)
```

Suppose you typed `sum += 1` instead of `sum += i` by mistake in line 5, the following `AssertionError` would be thrown:

```
Exception in thread "main" java.lang.AssertionError: sum is 10
        at AssertionDemo.main(AssertionDemo.java:8)
```

17.10.2 Running Programs with Assertions

By default, assertions are disabled at runtime. To enable them, use the switch –enableassertions, or –ea for short, as follows:

java –ea AssertionDemo

Assertions can be selectively enabled or disabled at the class level or the package level. The disable switch is –disableassertions, or –da for short. For example, the following command enables assertions in package `package1` and disables assertions in class `Class1`:

java –ea:package1 –da:Class1 AssertionDemo

17.10.3 Using Exception Handling or Assertions

Assertion should not be used to replace exception handling. Exception handling deals with unusual circumstances during program execution. Assertions are intended to ensure the correctness of the program. Exception handling addresses robustness, whereas assertion addresses correctness. Like exception handling, assertions are not used for normal tests, but for internal consistency and validity checks. Assertions are checked at runtime and can be turned on or off at startup time.

Do not use assertions for argument checking in public methods. Valid arguments that may be passed to a public method are considered to be part of the method's contract. The contract must always be obeyed whether assertions are enabled or disabled. For example, the following code in (a) should be rewritten using exception handling, as shown in (b):

```java
public void setRadius(double newRadius) {
  assert newRadius >= 0;
  radius = newRadius;
}
```

```java
public void setRadius(double newRadius) {
  if (newRadius >= 0)
    radius = newRadius;
  else
    throw new IllegalArgumentException(
      "Radius cannot be negative");
}
```

(a)   (b)

Use assertions to reaffirm assumptions. This will increase your confidence in the program's correctness. A common use of assertions is to replace assumptions with assertions in the code. For example, the following code in (a) can be replaced by (b):

```java
if (even) {
  ...
}
else { // even is false
  ...
}
```

```java
if (even) {
  ...
}
else {
  assert !even;
  ...
}
```

(a)   (b)

Similarly, the following code in (a) can also be replaced by (b):

```java
if (numberOfDollars > 1) {
  ...
}
else if (numberOfDollars == 1) {
  ...
}
```

```java
if (numberOfDollars > 1) {
  ...
}
else if (numberOfDollars == 1) {
  ...
}
else
    assert false : numberOfDollars;
```

(a)   (b)

Another good use of assertions is to place them in a `switch` statement without a default case. For example,

```java
switch (month) {
  case 1: ... ; break;
  case 2: ... ; break;
  ...
  case 12: ... ; break;
  default: assert false : "Invalid month: " + month
}
```

KEY TERMS

CHAPTER SUMMARY

■ When an exception occurs, Java creates an object that contains the information for the exception. You can use the information to handle the exception.

■ A Java exception is an instance of a class derived from `java.lang.Throwable`. Java provides a number of predefined exception classes, such as `Error`, `Exception`, `RuntimeException`, `ClassNotFoundException`, `NullPointerException`, and `ArithmeticException`. You can also define your own exception class by extending `Exception`.

■ Exceptions occur during the execution of a method. `RuntimeException` and `Error` are unchecked exceptions; all other exceptions are checked exceptions.

■ When declaring a method, you have to declare a checked exception if the method might throw that checked exception, thus telling the compiler what can go wrong.

■ The keyword for declaring an exception is `throws`, and the keyword for throwing an exception is `throw`.

■ To invoke the method that declares checked exceptions, you must enclose the method call in a `try` statement. When an exception occurs during the execution of the method, the `catch` block catches and handles the exception.

■ If an exception is not caught in the current method, it is passed to its caller. The process is repeated until the exception is caught or passed to the `main` method.

■ If an exception of a subclass of `Exception` occurs in a GUI component, Java prints the error message on the console, but the program goes back to its user-interface-processing loop to run continuously. The exception is ignored.

■ Various exception classes can be derived from a common superclass. If a `catch` block catches the exception objects of a superclass, it can also catch all the exception objects of the subclasses of that superclass.

■ The order in which exceptions are specified in a `catch` block is important. A compilation error will result if you do not specify an exception object of a class before an exception object of the superclass of that class.

■ When an exception occurs in a method, the method exits immediately if it does not catch the exception. If the method is required to perform some task before exiting, you can catch the exception in the method and then rethrow it to the real handler.

■ The code in the `finally` block is executed under all circumstances, regardless of whether an exception occurs in the `try` block or is caught.

■ Exception handling separates error-handling code from normal programming tasks, thus making programs easier to read and to modify.

■ Exception handling should not be used to replace simple tests. You should test simple exceptions whenever possible, and reserve exception handling for dealing with situations that cannot be handled with `if` statements.

■ Exceptions address robustness, whereas assertions address correctness. Exceptions and assertions are not meant to substitute for simple tests. Avoid using exception handling if a simple `if` statement is sufficient. Never use assertions to check normal conditions.

REVIEW QUESTIONS

Sections 17.2–17.3

17.1   Describe the Java `Throwable` class, its subclasses, and the types of exceptions. What `RunTimeException` will the following programs throw, if any?

```java
public class Test {
  public static void main(String[] args) {
    System.out.println(1 / 0);
  }
}
```
(a)

```java
public class Test {
  public static void main(String[] args) {
    int[] list = new int[5];
    System.out.println(list[5]);
  }
}
```
(b)

```java
public class Test {
  public static void main(String[] args) {
    String s = "abc";
    System.out.println(s.charAt(3));
  }
}
```
(c)

```java
public class Test {
  public static void main(String[] args) {
    Object o = new Object();
    String d = (String)o;
  }
}
```
(d)

```java
public class Test {
  public static void main(String[] args) {
    Object o = null;
    System.out.println(o.toString());
  }
}
```
(e)

```java
public class Test {
  public static void main(String[] args) {
    System.out.println(1.0 / 0);
  }
}
```
(f)

17.2   Show the output of the following code:

```java
public class Test {
  public static void main(String[] args) {
    for (int i = 0; i < 2; i++) {
      System.out.print(i + " ");
      try {
        System.out.println(1 / 0);
      }
      catch (Exception ex) {
      }
    }
  }
}
```
(a)

```java
public class Test {
  public static void main(String[] args) {
    try {
      for (int i = 0; i < 2; i++) {
        System.out.print(i + " ");
        System.out.println(1 / 0);
      }
    }
    catch (Exception ex) {
    }
  }
}
```
(b)

17.3   Point out the problem in the following code. Does the code throw any exceptions?

```java
long value = Long.MAX_VALUE + 1;
System.out.println(value);
```

17.4   What is the purpose of declaring exceptions? How do you declare an exception, and where? Can you declare multiple exceptions in a method declaration?

17.5 What is a checked exception, and what is an unchecked exception?

17.6 How do you throw an exception? Can you throw multiple exceptions in one `throw` statement?

17.7 What is the keyword `throw` used for? What is the keyword `throws` used for?

17.8 What does the JVM do when an exception occurs? How do you catch an exception?

17.9 What is the printout of the following code?

```
public class Test {
  public static void main(String[] args) {
    try {
      int value = 30;
      if (value < 40)
        throw new Exception("value is too small");
    }
    catch (Exception ex) {
      System.out.println(ex.getMessage());
    }
    System.out.println("Continue after the catch block");
  }
}
```

What would be the printout if the line

```
int value = 30;
```

is changed to

```
int value = 50;
```

17.10 Suppose that `statement2` causes an exception in the following `try-catch` block:

```
try {
  statement1;
  statement2;
  statement3;
}
catch (Exception1 ex1) {
}
catch (Exception2 ex2) {
}
statement4;
```

Answer the following questions:

- Will `statement3` be executed?
- If the exception is not caught, will `statement4` be executed?
- If the exception is caught in the `catch` block, will `statement4` be executed?
- If the exception is passed to the caller, will `statement4` be executed?

17.11 What is displayed when the following program is run?

```
public class Test {
  public static void main(String[] args) {
    try {
      int [] list = new int [10];
      System.out.println("list[10] is " + list[10]);
    }
```

```java
      catch (ArithmeticException ex) {
        System.out.println("ArithmeticException");
      }
      catch (RuntimeException ex) {
        System.out.println("RuntimeException");
      }
      catch (Exception ex) {
        System.out.println("Exception");
      }
    }
  }
```

17.12 What is displayed when the following program is run?

```java
public class Test {
  public static void main(String[] args) {
    try {
      method();
      System.out.println("After the method call");
    }
    catch (ArithmeticException ex) {
      System.out.println("ArithmeticException");
    }
    catch (RuntimeException ex) {
      System.out.println("RuntimeException");
    }
    catch (Exception e) {
      System.out.println("Exception");
    }
  }

  static void method() throws Exception {
    System.out.println(1 / 0);
  }
}
```

17.13 What is displayed when the following program is run?

```java
public class Test {
  public static void main(String[] args) {
    try {
      method();
      System.out.println("After the method call");
    }
    catch (RuntimeException ex) {
      System.out.println("RuntimeException in main");
    }
    catch (Exception ex) {
      System.out.println("Exception in main");
    }
  }

  static void method() throws Exception {
    try {
      String s = "abc";
      System.out.println(s.charAt(3));
    }
    catch (RuntimeException ex) {
      System.out.println("RuntimeException in method()");
    }
```

```
      catch (Exception ex) {
        System.out.println("Exception in method()");
      }
    }
  }
```

17.14 If an exception is not caught in a non-GUI application, what will happen? If an exception is not caught in a GUI application, what will happen?

17.15 What does the method `printStackTrace` do?

17.16 Does the presence of a `try-catch` block impose overhead when no exception occurs?

17.17 Correct a compilation error in the following code:

```
public void m(int value) {
  if (value < 40)
    throw new Exception("value is too small");
}
```

Sections 17.4–17.7

17.18 Suppose that `statement2` causes an exception in the following statement:

```
try {
  statement1;
  statement2;
  statement3;
}
catch (Exception1 ex1) {
}
catch (Exception2 ex2) {
}
catch (Exception3 ex3) {
  throw ex3;
}
finally {
  statement4;
};
statement5;
```

Answer the following questions:

■ Will `statement5` be executed if the exception is not caught?
■ If the exception is of type `Exception3`, will `statement4` be executed, and will `statement5` be executed?

17.19 Suppose the `setRadius` method throws the `RadiusException` declared in §17.7. What is displayed when the following program is run?

```
public class Test {
  public static void main(String[] args) {
    try {
      method();
      System.out.println("After the method call");
    }
    catch (RuntimeException ex) {
      System.out.println("RuntimeException in main");
    }
    catch (Exception ex) {
      System.out.println("Exception in main");
    }
  }
```

```
static void method() throws Exception {
  try {
    Circle c1 = new Circle(1);
    c1.setRadius(-1);
    System.out.println(c1.getRadius());
  }
  catch (RuntimeException ex) {
    System.out.println("RuntimeException in method()");
  }
  catch (Exception ex) {
    System.out.println("Exception in method()");
    throw ex;
  }
}
}
```

Section 17.10 Assertions

17.20 What is assertion for? How do you declare assertions? How do you compile code with assertions? How do you run programs with assertions?

17.21 What happens when you run the following code?

```
public class Test {
  public static void main(String[] args) {
    int i; int sum = 0;
    for (i = 0; i < 11; i++) {
      sum += i;
    }
    assert i == 10: "i is " + i;
  }
}
```

Comprehensive

17.22 A student wrote a method that checks whether a string is a numeric string, as follows:

```
public static boolean isNumeric(String token) {
  try {
    Double.parseDouble(token);
    return true;
  }
  catch (java.lang.NumberFormatException ex) {
    return false;
  }
}
```

Is it correct? Rewrite it without using exceptions.

PROGRAMMING EXERCISES

Sections 17.2–17.4

17.1* (*NumberFormatException*) Listing 8.4, Calculator.java, is a simple command-line calculator. Note that the program terminates if any operand is non-numeric. Write a program with an exception handler that deals with non-numeric operands; then write another program without using an exception handler to achieve the same objective. Your program should display a message that informs the user of the wrong operand type before exiting (see Figure 17.10).

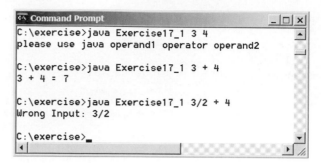

FIGURE 17.10 The program performs arithmetic operations and detects input errors.

17.2* (*ArithmeticException* and *NumberFormatException*) Write a program that creates a user interface to perform integer divisions, as shown in Figure 17.11. The user enters two numbers in the text fields, Number 1 and Number 2. The division of Number 1 and Number 2 is displayed in the Result field when the Divide button is clicked. If Number 1 or Number 2 were not an integer, the program would throw a NumberFormatException. If Number 2 were zero, the program would throw an ArithmeticException. Display the exception in a message dialog box, as shown in Figure 17.11.

FIGURE 17.11 The program displays an error message in the dialog box if the number is not well formatted.

17.3* (*ArrayIndexOutBoundsException*) Write a program that meets the following requirements:

- Create an array with one hundred randomly chosen integers.
- Create a text field to enter an array index and another text field to display the array element at the specified index (see Figure 17.12).
- Create a Show Element button to cause the array element to be displayed. If the specified index is out of bounds, display the message **Out of Bound**.

FIGURE 17.12 The program displays the array element at the specified index or displays the message *Out of Bound* if the index is out of bounds.

17.4* (*IllegalArgumentException*) Modify the Loan class in §7.15, "Case Study: The Loan Class," to throw IllegalArgumentException if the loan amount, interest rate, or number of years is less than or equal to zero.

17.5* (*IllegalTriangleException*) Exercise 9.1 defined the Triangle class with three sides. In a triangle, the sum of any two sides is greater than the other side. The Triangle class must adhere to this rule. Create the IllegalTriangleException class, and modify the constructor of the Triangle class to throw an `IllegalTriangleException` object if a triangle is created with sides that violate the rule, as follows:

```
/** Construct a triangle with the specified sides */
public Triangle(double side1, double side2, double side3)
    throws IllegalTriangleException {
    // Implement it
}
```

17.6* (*NumberFormatException*) Exercise 8.7 specifies the `parseHex(String hexString)` method, which converts a hex string into a decimal number. Implement the `parseHex` method to throw a `NumberFormatException` if the string is not a hex string.

17.7* (*NumberFormatException*) Exercise 8.8 specifies the `parseBinary(String binaryString)` method, which converts a binary string into a decimal number. Implement the `parseBinary` method to throw a `NumberFormatException` if the string is not a binary string.

17.8* (*HexFormatException*) Exercise 17.6 implements the `parseHex` method to throw a `NumberFormatException` if the string is not a hex string. Define a custom exception called `HexFormatException`. Implement the `parseHex` method to throw a `HexFormatException` if the string is not a hex string.

17.9* (*BinaryFormatException*) Exercise 17.7 implements the `parseBinary` method to throw a `BinaryFormatException` if the string is not a binary string. Define a custom exception called `BinaryFormatException`. Implement the `parseBinary` method to throw a `BinaryFormatException` if the string is not a binary string.

CHAPTER 18

BINARY I/O

Objectives

- To understand how I/O is processed in Java (§18.2).

- To distinguish between text I/O and binary I/O (§18.3).

- To read and write bytes using `FileInputStream` and `FileOutputStream` (§18.4.1).

- To read and write primitive values and strings using `DataInputStream`/`DataOutputStream` (§18.4.3).

- To store and restore objects using `ObjectOutputStream` and `ObjectInputStream`, and to understand how objects are serialized and what kind of objects can be serialized (§18.6).

- To use the `Serializable` interface to enable objects to be serializable (§18.6.1).

- To know how to serialize arrays (§18.6.2).

- (Optional) To use `RandomAccessFile` for both read and write (§18.7).

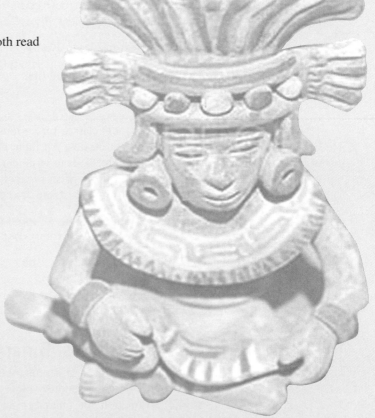

18.1 Introduction

Data stored in a *text file* is represented in human-readable form. Data stored in a *binary file* is represented in binary form. You cannot read binary files. They are designed to be read by programs. For example, Java source programs are stored in text files and can be read by a text editor, but Java classes are stored in binary files and are read by the JVM. The advantage of binary files is that they are more efficient to process than text files.

Although it is not technically precise and correct, you can envision a text file as consisting of a sequence of characters and a binary file as consisting of a sequence of bits. For example, the decimal integer **199** is stored as the sequence of three characters, **'1'**, **'9'**, **'9'**, in a text file, and the same integer is stored as a **byte**-type value C7 in a binary file, because decimal **199** equals hex C7 ($199 = 12 \times 16^1 + 7$).

Java offers many classes for performing file input and output. These classes can be categorized as *text I/O classes* and *binary I/O classes.* You learned how to read/write strings and numeric values from/to a text file using **Scanner** and **PrintWriter** in §8.8, "Text I/O." This section introduces the classes for performing binary I/O.

18.2 How is I/O Handled in Java?

Recall that a **File** object encapsulates the properties of a file or a path, but does not contain the methods for reading/writing data from/to a file. In order to perform I/O, you need to create objects using appropriate Java I/O classes. The objects contain the methods for reading/writing data from/to a file. For example, to write text to a file named **temp.txt**, you may create an object using the **PrintWriter** class, as follows:

```
PrintWriter output = new PrintWriter("temp.txt");
```

You can now invoke **PrintWriter** from the object to write a string into the file. For example, the following statement writes **"Java 101"** to the file:

```
output.print("Java 101");
```

The next statement closes the file.

```
output.close();
```

There are many I/O classes for various purposes. In general, these can be classified as input classes and output classes. An input class contains the methods to read data, and an output class contains the methods to write data. **PrintWriter** is an example of an output class, and **Scanner** is an example of an input class. The following code shows an example of creating an input object for the file **temp.txt** and reading data from the file:

```
Scanner input = new Scanner(new File("temp.txt"));
System.out.println(input.nextLine());
```

If **temp.txt** contains **"Java 101"**, **input.nextLine()** returns string **"Java 101"**.

Figure 18.1 illustrates Java I/O programming. An input object reads a stream of data from a file, and an output object writes a stream of data to a file. An input object is also called an *input stream*, and an output object is also called an *output stream*.

18.3 Text I/O vs. Binary I/O

Computers do not differentiate binary files and text files. All files are stored in binary format, and thus all files are essentially binary files. Text I/O is built upon binary I/O to provide a level of abstraction for character encoding and decoding, as shown in Figure 18.2(a). Encoding and decoding are automatically performed for text I/O. The JVM converts a

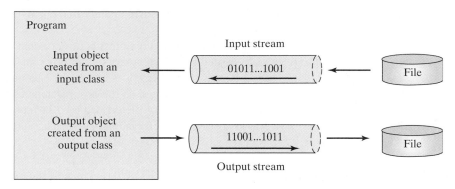

FIGURE 18.1 The program receives data through an input object and sends data through an output object.

Unicode to a file-specific encoding when writing a character and converts a file-specific encoding to a Unicode when reading a character. For example, suppose you write string **"199"** using text I/O to a file. Each character is written to the file. Since the Unicode for character '1' is **0x0031**, the Unicode **0x0031** is converted to a code that depends on the encoding scheme for the file. (Note that the prefix **0x** denotes a hex number.) In the United States, the default encoding for text files on Windows is ASCII. The ASCII code for character '1' is **49** (**0x31** in hex) and for character '9' is **57** (**0x39** in hex). So to write the characters "199", three bytes, **0x31**, **0x39**, and **0x39**, are sent to the output, as shown in Figure 18.2(a).

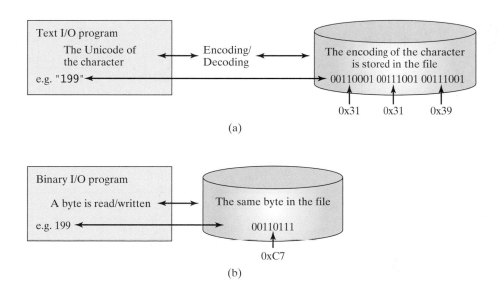

FIGURE 18.2 Text I/O requires encoding and decoding, whereas binary I/O does not.

 Note

JDK 1.5 supports *supplementary Unicode*. For simplicity, however, this book considers only the original Unicode from **0** to **FFFF**.   supplementary Unicode

Binary I/O does not require conversions. If you write a numeric value to a file using binary I/O, the exact value in the memory is copied into the file. For example, a byte-type value **199** is represented as **0xC7** ($199 = 12 \times 16^1 + 7$) in the memory and appears exactly as **0xC7** in the file, as shown in Figure 18.2(b). When you read a byte using binary I/O, one byte value is read from the input.

In general, you should use text input to read a file created by a text editor or a text output program, and use binary input to read a file created by a Java binary output program.

Binary I/O is more efficient than text I/O, because binary I/O does not require encoding and decoding. Binary files are independent of the encoding scheme on the host machine and thus are portable. Java programs on any machine can read a binary file created by a Java program. This is why Java class files are binary files. Java class files can run on a JVM on any machine.

Note

.txt and .dat

For consistency, this book uses the extension `.txt` to name text files and `.dat` to name binary files.

18.4 Binary I/O Classes

The design of the Java I/O classes is a good example of applying inheritance, where common operations are generalized in superclasses, and subclasses provide specialized operations. Figure 18.3 lists some of the classes for performing binary I/O. `InputStream` is the root for binary input classes, and `OutputStream` is the root for binary output classes. Figures 18.4 and 18.5 list all the methods in `InputStream` and `OutputStream`.

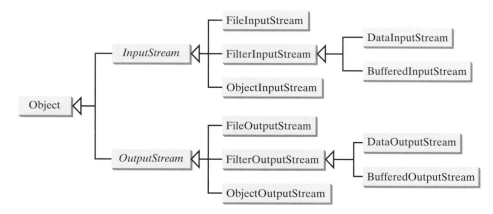

FIGURE 18.3 `InputStream`, `OutputStream`, and their subclasses are for binary I/O.

java.io.InputStream	
+read(): int	Reads the next byte of data from the input stream. The value byte is returned as an int value in the range 0 to 255. If no byte is available because the end of the stream has been reached, the value –1 is returned.
+read(b: byte[]): int	Reads up to b.length bytes into array b from the input stream and returns the actual number of bytes read. Returns –1 at the end of the stream.
+read(b: byte[], off: int, len: int): int	Reads bytes from the input stream and stores them in b[off], b[off+1], ..., b[off+len–1]. The actual number of bytes read is returned. Returns –1 at the end of the stream.
+available(): int	Returns the number of bytes that can be read from the input stream.
+close(): void	Closes this input stream and releases any system resources associated with it.
+skip(n: long): long	Skips over and discards n bytes of data from this input stream. The actual number of bytes skipped is returned.
+markSupported(): boolean	Tests whether this input stream supports the mark and reset methods.
+mark(readlimit: int): void	Marks the current position in this input stream.
+reset(): void	Repositions this stream to the position at the time the mark method was last called on this stream.

FIGURE 18.4 The abstract `InputStream` class defines the methods for the input stream of bytes.

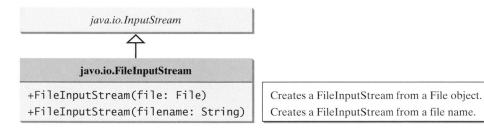

java.io.OutputStream	
+write(*int b*): *void*	Writes the specified byte to this output stream. The parameter b is an int value. (byte)b is written to the output stream.
+write(b: byte[]): void	Writes all the bytes in array b to the output stream.
+write(b: byte[], off: int, len: int): void	Writes b[off], b[off+1], ..., b[off+len–1] into the output stream.
+close(): void	Closes this output stream and releases any system resources associated with it.
+flush(): void	Flushes this output stream and forces any buffered output bytes to be written out.

FIGURE 18.5 The abstract `OutputStream` class defines the methods for the output stream of bytes.

 Note

All the methods in the binary I/O classes are declared to throw `java.io.IOException` or a subclass of `java.io.IOException`.

throws **IOException**

18.4.1   `FileInputStream`/`FileOutputStream`

`FileInputStream`/`FileOutputStream` is for reading/writing bytes from/to files. All the methods in these classes are inherited from `InputStream` and `OutputStream`. `FileInputStream`/`FileOutputStream` does not introduce new methods. To construct a `FileInputStream`, use the following constructors, as shown in Figure 18.6:

java.io.InputStream	

javo.io.FileInputStream	
+FileInputStream(file: File)	Creates a FileInputStream from a File object.
+FileInputStream(filename: String)	Creates a FileInputStream from a file name.

FIGURE 18.6 `FileInputStream` inputs stream of bytes from a file.

A `java.io.FileNotFoundException` will occur if you attempt to create a `FileInputStream` with a nonexistent file.

FileNotFound-Exception

To construct a `FileOutputStream`, use the following constructors, as shown in Figure 18.7.

java.io.OutputStream	

java.io.FileOutputStream	
+FileOutputStream(file: File)	Creates a FileOutputStream from a File object.
+FileOutputStream(filename: String)	Creates a FileOutputStream from a file name.
+FileOutputStream(file: File, append: boolean)	If append is true, data is appended to the existing file.
+FileOutputStream(filename: String, append: boolean)	If append is true, data is appended to the existing file.

FIGURE 18.7 `FileOutputStream` outputs stream of bytes to a file.

If the file does not exist, a new file will be created. If the file already exists, the first two constructors will delete the current content of the file. To retain the current content and append new data into the file, use the last two constructors by passing **true** to the **append** parameter.

IOException Almost all the methods in the I/O classes throw `java.io.IOException`. Therefore you have to declare `java.io.IOException` to throw in the method or place the code in a `try-catch` block, as shown below:

Declaring exception in the method

```
public static void main(String[] args)
    throws IOException {
  // Perform I/O operations
}
```

Using `try-catch` block

```
public static void main(String[] args) {
  try {
    // Perform I/O operations
  }
  catch (IOException ex) {
    ex.printStackTrace();
  }
}
```

Listing 18.1 uses binary I/O to write ten byte values from 1 to 10 to a file named **temp.dat** and reads them back from the file.

LISTING 18.1 TestFileStream.java

import

output stream

output

input stream

input

```java
 1 import java.io.*;
 2
 3 public class TestFileStream {
 4   public static void main(String[] args) throws IOException  {
 5     // Create an output stream to the file
 6     FileOutputStream output = new FileOutputStream("temp.dat");
 7
 8     // Output values to the file
 9     for (int i = 1; i <= 10; i++)
10       output.write(i);
11
12     // Close the output stream
13     output.close();
14
15     // Create an input stream for the file
16     FileInputStream input = new FileInputStream("temp.dat");
17
18     // Read values from the file
19     int value;
20     while ((value = input.read()) != -1)
21       System.out.print(value + " ");
22
23     // Close the output stream
24     input.close();
25   }
26 }
```

A `FileOutputStream` is created for file temp.dat in line 6. The `for` loop writes ten byte values into the file (lines 9–10). Invoking `write(i)` is the same as invoking `write((byte)i)`. Line 13 closes the output stream. Line 16 creates a `FileInputStream` for file temp.dat. Values are read from the file and displayed on the console in lines 19–21. The expression `((value = input.read()) != -1)` (line 20) reads a byte from `input.read()`, assigns it to `value`, and checks whether it is -1. The input value of -1 signifies the *end of a file*.

end of a file

The file `temp.dat` created in this example is a binary file. It can be read from a Java program but not from a text editor, as shown in Figure 18.8.

Tip

close stream

When a stream is no longer needed, always close it using the `close()` method. Not closing streams may cause data corruption in the output file, or other programming errors.

Binary data ───→

FIGURE 18.8   A binary file cannot be displayed in text mode.

 Note
Text I/O is built upon binary I/O. `PrinterWriter` and `Scanner` are implemented using binary I/O classes. An instance of `FileInputStream` can be used as an argument to construct a `Scanner`, and an instance of `FileOutputStream` can be used as an argument to construct a `PrintWriter`. You can create a `PrintWriter` to append text into a file using

```
new PrintWriter(new FileOutputStream("temp.txt", true));
```

If temp.txt does not exist, it is created. If temp.txt already exists, new data is appended to the file.   appending to text file

18.4.2   `FilterInputStream/FilterOutputStream`

Filter streams are streams that filter bytes for some purpose. The basic byte input stream provides a read method that can only be used for reading bytes. If you want to read integers, doubles, or strings, you need a filter class to wrap the byte input stream. Using a filter class enables you to read integers, doubles, and strings instead of bytes and characters. `FilterInputStream` and `FilterOutputStream` are the base classes for filtering data. When you need to process primitive numeric types, use `DataInputStream` and `DataOutputStream` to filter bytes.

18.4.3   `DataInputStream/DataOutputStream`

`DataInputStream` reads bytes from the stream and converts them into appropriate primitive type values or strings. `DataOutputStream` converts primitive type values or strings into bytes and outputs the bytes to the stream.

`DataInputStream` extends `FilterInputStream` and implements the `DataInput` interface, as shown in Figure 18.9. `DataOutputStream` extends `FilterOutputStream` and implements the `DataOutput` interface, as shown in Figure 18.10.

FIGURE 18.9   `DataInputStream` filters input stream of bytes into primitive data type values and strings.

FIGURE 18.10 `DataOutputStream` enables you to write primitive data type values and strings into an output stream.

`DataInputStream` implements the methods defined in the `DataInput` interface to read primitive data type values and strings. `DataOutputStream` implements the methods defined in the `DataOutput` interface to write primitive data type values and strings. Primitive values are copied from memory to the output without any conversions. Characters in a string may be written in several ways, as discussed in the next section.

Characters and Strings in Binary I/O

A Unicode consists of two bytes. The `writeChar(char c)` method writes the Unicode of character `c` to the output. The `writeChars(String s)` method writes the Unicode for each character in the string `s` to the output. The `writeBytes(String s)` method writes the lower byte of the Unicode for each character in the string `s` to the output. The high byte of the Unicode is discarded. The `writeBytes` method is suitable for strings that consist of ASCII characters, since an ASCII code is stored only in the lower byte of a Unicode. If a string consists of non-ASCII characters, you have to use the `writeChars` method to write the string.

The `writeUTF(String s)` method writes two bytes of length information to the output stream, followed by the modified UTF-8 representation of every character in the string s. UTF-8 is a coding scheme that allows systems to operate with both ASCII and Unicode. Most operating systems use ASCII. Java uses Unicode. The ASCII character set is a subset of the Unicode character set. Since most applications need only the ASCII character set, it is a waste to represent an 8-bit ASCII character as a 16-bit Unicode character. The modified UTF-8 scheme stores a character using one, two, or three bytes. ASCII values less than `0x7F` are coded in one byte. Unicode values less than `0x7FF` are coded in two bytes. Other Unicode values are coded in three bytes.

UTF-8 scheme

The initial bits of a UTF-8 character indicate whether a character is stored in one byte, two bytes, or three bytes. If the first bit is 0, it is a one-byte character. If the first bits are `110`, it is the first byte of a two-byte sequence. If the first bits are `1110`, it is the first byte of a three-byte sequence. The information that indicates the number of characters in a string is stored in the first two bytes preceding the UTF-8 characters. For example, `writeUTF("ABCDEF")` actually writes eight bytes to the file because the first two bytes store the number of characters in the string.

The `writeUTF(String s)` method converts a string into a series of bytes in the UTF-8 format and writes them into a binary stream. The `readUTF()` method reads a string that has been written using the `writeUTF` method.

The UTF-8 format has the advantage of saving a byte for each ASCII character, because a Unicode character takes up two bytes and an ASCII character in UTF-8 takes up only one byte. If most of characters in a long string are regular ASCII characters, using UTF-8 is more efficient.

Using **DataInputStream/DataOutputStream**

Data streams are used as wrappers on existing input, and output streams to filter data in the original stream. They are created using the following constructors (see Figure 18.9 and Figure 18.10):

```
public DataInputStream(InputStream instream)
public DataOutputStream(OutputStream outstream)
```

The statements given below create data streams. The first statement creates an input stream for file `in.dat`; the second statement creates an output stream for file `out.dat`:

```
DataInputStream infile =
  new DataInputStream (new FileInputStream("in.dat"));
DataOutputStream outfile =
  new DataOutputStream (new FileOutputStream("out.dat"));
```

Listing 18.2 writes student names and scores to a file named `temp.dat` and reads the data back from the file.

LISTING 18.2 TestDataStream.java

```
1 import java.io.*;
2
3 public class TestDataStream {
4   public static void main(String[] args) throws IOException {
5     // Create an output stream for file temp.dat
6     DataOutputStream output =                                        output stream
7       new DataOutputStream(new FileOutputStream("temp.dat"));
8
9     // Write student test scores to the file
10    output.writeUTF("John");                                         output
11    output.writeDouble(85.5);
12    output.writeUTF("Jim");
13    output.writeDouble(185.5);
14    output.writeUTF("George");
15    output.writeDouble(105.25);
16
17    // Close output stream
18    output.close();                                                  close stream
19
20    // Create an input stream for file temp.dat
21    DataInputStream input =                                          input stream
22      new DataInputStream(new FileInputStream("temp.dat"));
23
24    // Read student test scores from the file
25    System.out.println(input.readUTF() + " " + input.readDouble());  input
26    System.out.println(input.readUTF() + " " + input.readDouble());
27    System.out.println(input.readUTF() + " " + input.readDouble());
28  }
29 }
```

A `DataOutputStream` is created for file `temp.dat` in lines 6–7. Student names and scores are written to the file in lines 10–15. Line 18 closes the output stream. A `DataInputStream` is created for the same file in lines 21–22. Student names and scores are read back from the file and displayed on the console in lines 25–27.

`DataInputStream` and `DataOutputStream` read and write Java primitive type values and strings in a machine-independent fashion, thereby enabling you to write a data file on one machine and read it on another machine that has a different operating system or file structure. An application uses a data output stream to write data that can later be read by a program using a data input stream.

Caution

You have to read data in the same order and format in which they are stored. For example, since names are written in UTF-8 using `writeUTF`, you must read names using `readUTF`.

Tip

If you keep reading data at the end of a `DataInputStream`, an `EOFException` will occur. How, then, do you check the end of a file? Use `input.available()` to check it. `input.available() == 0` indicates the end of a file.

18.4.4 BufferedInputStream/BufferedOutputStream

`BufferedInputStream`/`BufferedOutputStream` can be used to speed up input and output by reducing the number of reads and writes. `BufferedInputStream`/`BufferedOutputStream` does not contain new methods. All the methods in `BufferedInputStream`/`BufferedOutputStream` are inherited from the `InputStream`/`OutputStream` classes. `BufferedInputStream`/`BufferedOutputStream` adds a buffer in the stream for storing bytes for efficient processing.

You may wrap a `BufferedInputStream`/`BufferedOutputStream` on any `InputStream`/`OutputStream` using the following constructors, as shown in Figure 18.11 and Figure 18.12:

FIGURE 18.11 `BufferedInputStream` buffers input stream.

FIGURE 18.12 `BufferedOutputStream` buffers output stream.

If no buffer size is specified, the default size is 512 bytes. A buffered input stream reads as many data as possible into its buffer in a single read call. By contrast, a buffered output stream calls the write method only when its buffer fills up or when the `flush()` method is called.

You can improve the performance of the `TestDataStream` program in the preceding example by adding buffers in the stream in lines 6–7 and 21–22, as follows:

```
DataOutputStream output = new DataOutputStream(
  new BufferedOutputStream(new FileOutputStream("temp.dat")));

DataInputStream input = new DataInputStream(
  new BufferedInputStream(new FileInputStream("temp.dat")));
```

18.5 Case Study: Copying File

This case study develops a program that copies files. The user needs to provide a source file and a target file as command-line arguments using the following command:

java Copy source target

The program copies a source file to a target file and displays the number of bytes in the file. If the source does not exist, tell the user that the file has not been found. If the target file already exists, tell the user that the file exists. A sample run of the program is shown in Figure 18.13.

FIGURE 18.13   The program copies a file.

To copy the contents from a source to a target file, it is appropriate to use a binary input stream to read bytes from the source file and a binary output stream to send bytes to the target file, regardless of the contents of the file. The source file and the target file are specified from the command line. Create an `InputFileStream` for the source file and an `OutputFileStream` for the target file. Use the `read()` method to read a byte from the input stream, and then use the `write(b)` method to write the byte to the output stream. Use `BufferedInputStream` and `BufferedOutputStream` to improve the performance. Listing 18.3 gives the solution to the problem.

LISTING 18.3   Copy.java

```
 1 import java.io.*;
 2
 3 public class Copy {
 4   /** Main method
 5     @param args[0] for source file
 6     @param args[1] for target file
 7   */
 8   public static void main(String[] args) throws IOException {
 9     // Check command line parameter usage
10     if (args.length != 2) {
```

check usage

```
11          System.out.println(
12            "Usage: java CopyFile sourceFile targetfile");
13          System.exit(0);
14        }
15
16        // Check if source file exists
17        File sourceFile = new File(args[0]);
18        if (!sourceFile.exists()) {
19          System.out.println("Source file " + args[0] + " not exist");
20          System.exit(0);
21        }
22
23        // Check if target file exists
24        File targetFile = new File(args[1]);
25        if (targetFile.exists()) {
26          System.out.println("Target file " + args[1] + " already exists");
27          System.exit(0);
28        }
29
30        // Create an input stream
31        BufferedInputStream input =
32          new BufferedInputStream(new FileInputStream(sourceFile));
33
34        // Create an output stream
35        BufferedOutputStream output =
36          new BufferedOutputStream(new FileOutputStream(targetFile));
37
38        // Display the file size
39        System.out.println("The file " + args[0] + " has " +
40          input.available()  + " bytes");
41
42        // Continuously read a byte from input and write it to output
43        int r;
44        while ((r = input.read() ) != -1)
45          output.write((byte)r);
46
47        // Close streams
48        input.close();
49        output.close();
50
51        System.out.println("Copy done!");
52      }
53    }
```

source file (line 17)
target file (line 24)
input stream (line 31)
output stream (line 35)
read (line 44)
write (line 45)
close stream (line 48)

- The program first checks whether the user has passed two required arguments from the command line in lines 10–14.

- The program uses the `File` class to check whether the source file and target file exist. If the source file does not exist (lines 18–21) or if the target file already exists, exit the program.

- An input stream is created using `BufferedInputStream` wrapped on `FileInputStream` in lines 31–32, and an output stream is created using `BufferedOutputStream` wrapped on `FileOutputStream` in lines 35–36.

- The `available()` method (line 40) defined in the `InputStream` class returns the number of bytes remaining in the input stream.

- The expression `((r = input.read()) != -1)` (line 44) reads a byte from `input.read()`, assigns it to `r`, and checks whether it is `-1`. The input value of `-1` signifies the end of a file. The program continuously reads bytes from the input stream and sends them to the output stream until all of the bytes have been read.

18.6 Object I/O

`DataInputStream`/`DataOutputStream` enables you to perform I/O for primitive type values and strings. `ObjectInputStream`/`ObjectOutputStream` enables you to perform I/O for objects in addition to primitive type values and strings. Since `ObjectInputStream`/`ObjectOutputStream` contains all the functions of `DataInputStream`/`DataOutputStream`, you can replace `DataInputStream`/`DataOutputStream` completely with `ObjectInputStream`/`ObjectOutputStream`.

`ObjectInputStream` extends `InputStream` and implements `ObjectInput` and `ObjectStreamConstants`, as shown in Figure 18.14. `ObjectInput` is a subinterface of `DataInput`. `DataInput` is shown in Figure 18.9. `ObjectStreamConstants` contains the constants to support `ObjectInputStream`/`ObjectOutputStream`.

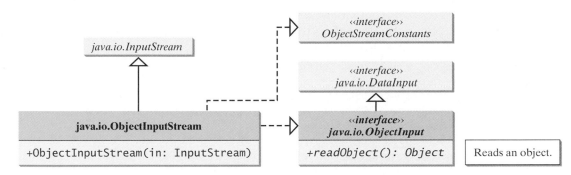

FIGURE 18.14 `ObjectInputStream` can read objects, primitive type values, and strings.

`ObjectOutputStream` extends `OutputStream` and implements `ObjectOutput` and `ObjectStreamConstants`, as shown in Figure 18.15. `ObjectOutput` is a subinterface of `DataOutput`. `DataOutput` is shown in Figure 18.10.

FIGURE 18.15 `ObjectOutputStream` can write objects, primitive type values, and strings.

You may wrap an `ObjectInputStream`/`ObjectOutputStream` on any `InputStream`/`OutputStream` using the following constructors:

```java
// Create an ObjectInputStream
public ObjectInputStream(InputStream in)

// Create an ObjectOutputStream
public ObjectOutputStream(OutputStream out)
```

Listing 18.4 writes student names, scores, and current date to a file named `object.dat`.

LISTING 18.4 TestObjectOutputStream.java

```java
1 import java.io.*;
2
3 public class TestObjectOutputStream {
```

```
 4   public static void main(String[] args) throws IOException {
 5     // Create an output stream for file object.dat
 6     ObjectOutputStream output =
 7       new ObjectOutputStream(new FileOutputStream("object.dat"));
 8
 9     // Write a string, double value, and object to the file
10     output.writeUTF("John");
11     output.writeDouble(85.5);
12     output.writeObject(new java.util.Date());
13
14     // Close output stream
15     output.close();
16   }
17 }
```

output stream

output

An `ObjectOutputStream` is created to write data into file `object.dat` in lines 6–7. A string, a double value, and an object are written to the file in lines 10–12. To improve performance, you may add a buffer in the stream using the following statement to replace lines 6–7:

```
ObjectOutputStream output = new ObjectOutputStream(
  new BufferedOutputStream(new FileOutputStream("object.dat")));
```

Multiple objects or primitives can be written to the stream. The objects must be read back from the corresponding `ObjectInputStream` with the same types and in the same order as they were written. Java's safe casting should be used to get the desired type. Listing 18.5 reads data back from `object.dat`.

LISTING 18.5 TestObjectInputStream.java

```
 1 import java.io.*;
 2
 3 public class TestObjectInputStream {
 4   public static void main(String[] args)
 5       throws ClassNotFoundException, IOException {
 6     // Create an input stream for file object.dat
 7     ObjectInputStream input =
 8       new ObjectInputStream(new FileInputStream("object.dat"));
 9
10     // Write a string, double value, and object to the file
11     String name = input.readUTF();
12     double score = input.readDouble();
13     java.util.Date date = (java.util.Date)(input.readObject());
14     System.out.println(name + " " + score + " " + date);
15
16     // Close output stream
17     input.close();
18   }
19 }
```

input stream

input

The `readObject()` method may throw `java.lang.ClassNotFoundException`. The reason is that when the JVM restores an object, it first loads the class for the object if the class has not been loaded. Since `ClassNotFoundException` is a checked exception, the `main` method declares to throw it in line 5. An `ObjectInputStream` is created to read input from `object.dat` in lines 7–8. You have to read the data from the file in the same order and format as they were written to the file. A string, a double value, and an object are read in lines 11–13. Since `readObject()` returns an `Object`, it is cast into `Date` and assigned to a `Date` variable in line 13.

ClassNotFoundException

18.6.1 The `Serializable` Interface

Not every object can be written to an output stream. Objects that can be written to an object stream are said to be *serializable*. A serializable object is an instance of the `java.io.Serializable` interface, so the class of a serializable object must implement `Serializable`.

serializable

The `Serializable` interface is a marker interface. Since it has no methods, you don't need to add additional code in your class that implements `Serializable`. Implementing this interface enables the Java serialization mechanism to automate the process of storing objects and arrays.

To appreciate this automation feature and understand how an object is stored, consider what you need to do in order to store an object without using this feature. Suppose you want to store a `JButton` object. To do this you need to store all the current values of the properties (e.g., color, font, text, alignment) in the object. Since `JButton` is a subclass of `AbstractButton`, the property values of `AbstractButton` have to be stored as well as the properties of all the superclasses of `AbstractButton`. If a property is of an object type (e.g., `background` of the `Color` type), storing it requires storing all the property values inside this object. As you can see, this is a very tedious process. Fortunately, you don't have to go through it manually. Java provides a built-in mechanism to automate the process of writing objects. This process is referred to as *object serialization*, which is implemented in `ObjectOutputStream`. In contrast, the process of reading objects is referred to as *object deserialization*, which is implemented in `ObjectInputStream`.

serialization
deserialization

Many classes in the Java API implement `Serializable`. The utility classes, such as `java.util.Date`, and all the Swing GUI component classes implement `Serializable`. Attempting to store an object that does not support the `Serializable` interface would cause a `NotSerializableException`.

NotSerializable-
  Exception

When a serializable object is stored, the class of the object is encoded; this includes the class name and the signature of the class, the values of the object's instance variables, and the closure of any other objects referenced from the initial object. The values of the object's static variables are not stored.

Note

If an object is an instance of `Serializable` but contains nonserializable instance data fields, can it be serialized? The answer is no. To enable the object to be serialized, mark these data fields with the `transient` keyword to tell the JVM to ignore them when writing the object to an object stream. Consider the following class:

non-serializable fields

transient

```java
public class Foo implements java.io.Serializable {
  private int v1;
  private static double v2;
  private transient A v3 = new A();
}

class A { } // A is not serializable
```

When an object of the `Foo` class is serialized, only variable `v1` is serialized. Variable `v2` is not serialized because it is a static variable, and variable `v3` is not serialized because it is marked `transient`. If `v3` were not marked `transient`, a `java.io.NotSerializable Exception` would occur.

Note

If an object is written to an object stream more than once, will it be stored in multiple copies? The answer is no. When an object is written for the first time, a serial number is created for it. The JVM writes the complete content of the object along with the serial number into the object stream. After the first time, only the serial number is stored if the same object is written again.

duplicate objects

When the objects are read back, their references are the same, since only one object is actually created in the memory.

18.6.2 Serializing Arrays

An array is serializable if all its elements are serializable. An entire array can be saved using `writeObject` into a file and later can be restored using `readObject`. Listing 18.6 stores an array of five `int` values, an array of three strings, and an array of two `JButton` objects, and reads them back to display on the console.

LISTING 18.6 TestObjectStreamForArray.java

```
 1 import java.io.*;
 2 import javax.swing.*;
 3
 4 public class TestObjectStreamForArray {
 5   public static void main(String[] args)
 6       throws ClassNotFoundException, IOException {
 7     int[] numbers = {1, 2, 3, 4, 5};
 8     String[] strings = {"John", "Jim", "Jake"};
 9     JButton[] buttons = {new JButton("OK"), new JButton("Cancel")};
10
11     // Create an output stream for file array.dat
12     ObjectOutputStream output =
13       new ObjectOutputStream (new FileOutputStream("array.dat", true));
14
15     // Write arrays to the object output stream
16     output.writeObject(numbers);
17     output.writeObject(strings);
18     output.writeObject(buttons);
19
20     // Close the stream
21     output.close();
22
23     // Create an input stream for file array.dat
24     ObjectInputStream input =
25       new ObjectInputStream(new FileInputStream("array.dat"));
26
27     int[] newNumbers = (int[])(input.readObject());
28     String[] newStrings = (String[])(input.readObject());
29     JButton[] newButtons = (JButton[])(input.readObject());
30
31     // Display arrays
32     for (int i = 0; i < newNumbers.length; i++)
33       System.out.print(newNumbers[i] + " ");
34     System.out.println();
35
36     for (int i = 0; i < newStrings.length; i++)
37       System.out.print(newStrings[i] + " ");
38     System.out.println();
39
40     for (int i = 0; i < newButtons.length; i++)
41       System.out.print(newButtons[i].getText() + " ");
42   }
43 }
```

output stream *(lines 12–13)*

store array *(lines 16–18)*

input stream *(lines 24–25)*

restore array *(lines 27–29)*

Lines 16–18 write three arrays into file `array.dat`. Lines 27–29 read three arrays back in the same order they were written. Since `readObject()` returns `Object`, casting is used to cast the objects into `int[]`, `String[]`, and `JButton[]`.

18.7 (Optional) Random Access Files

All of the streams you have used so far are known as *read-only* or *write-only* streams. The external files of these streams are *sequential* files that cannot be updated without creating a new file. It is often necessary to modify files or to insert new records into files. Java provides the `RandomAccessFile` class to allow a file to be read from and written to at random locations.

read-only
write-only
sequential

The `RandomAccessFile` class implements the `DataInput` and `DataOutput` interfaces, as shown in Figure 18.16. The `DataInput` interface shown in Figure 18.9 defines the methods (e.g., `readInt`, `readDouble`, `readChar`, `readBoolean`, `readUTF`) for reading primitive type values and strings, and the `DataOutput` interface shown in Figure 18.10 defines the methods (e.g., `writeInt`, `writeDouble`, `writeChar`, `writeBoolean`, `writeUTF`) for writing primitive type values and strings.

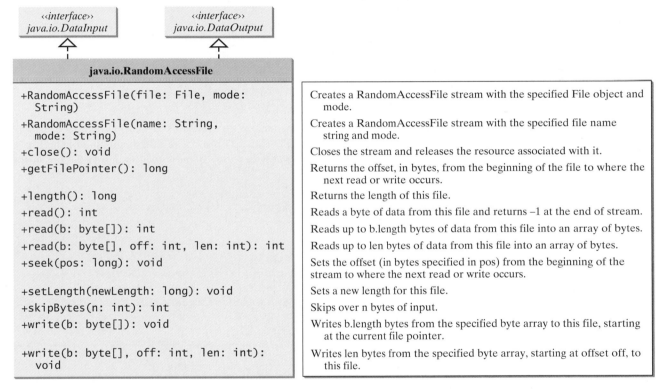

FIGURE 18.16 `RandomAccessFile` implements the `DataInput` and `DataOutput` interfaces with additional methods to support random access.

When creating a `RandomAccessFile`, you can specify one of two modes (`"r"` or `"rw"`). Mode `"r"` means that the stream is read-only, and mode `"rw"` indicates that the stream allows both read and write. For example, the following statement creates a new stream, `raf`, that allows the program to read from and write to the file `test.dat`:

```
RandomAccessFile raf = new RandomAccessFile("test.dat", "rw");
```

If `test.dat` already exists, `raf` is created to access it; if `test.dat` does not exist, a new file named `test.dat` is created, and `raf` is created to access the new file. The method `raf.length()` returns the number of bytes in `test.dat` at any given time. If you append new data into the file, `raf.length()` increases.

 Tip

Open the file with the `"r"` mode if the file is not intended to be modified. This prevents unintentional modification of the file.

file pointer

A random access file consists of a sequence of bytes. There is a special marker called *file pointer* that is positioned at one of these bytes. A read or write operation takes place at the location of the file pointer. When a file is opened, the file pointer is set at the beginning of the file. When you read or write data to the file, the file pointer moves forward to the next data item. For example, if you read an **int** value using **readInt()**, the JVM reads 4 bytes from the file pointer and now the file pointer is 4 bytes ahead of the previous location, as shown in Figure 18.17.

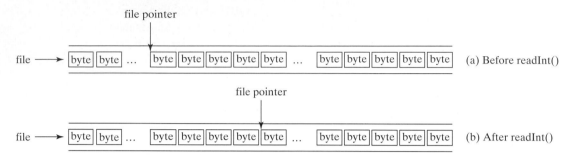

FIGURE 18.17   After reading an **int** value, the file pointer is moved 4 bytes ahead.

For a **RandomAccessFile raf**, you can use **raf.seek(position)** method to move the file pointer to a specified position. **raf.seek(0)** moves it to the beginning of the file, and **raf.seek(raf.length())** moves it to the end of the file. Listing 18.7 demonstrates **RandomAccessFile**.

LISTING 18.7   TestRandomAccessFile.java

RandomAccessFile

empty file

write

move pointer
read

```java
 1  import java.io.*;
 2
 3  public class TestRandomAccessFile {
 4    public static void main(String[] args) throws IOException {
 5      // Create a random access file
 6      RandomAccessFile inout = new RandomAccessFile("inout.dat", "rw");
 7
 8      // Clear the file to destroy the old contents if exists
 9      inout.setLength(0);
10
11      // Write new integers to the file
12      for (int i = 0; i < 200; i++)
13        inout.writeInt(i);
14
15      // Display the current length of the file
16      System.out.println("Current file length is " + inout.length());
17
18      // Retrieve the first number
19      inout.seek(0); // Move the file pointer to the beginning
20      System.out.println("The first number is " + inout.readInt());
21
22      // Retrieve the second number
23      inout.seek(1 * 4); // Move the file pointer to the second number
24      System.out.println("The second number is " + inout.readInt());
25
26      // Retrieve the tenth number
27      inout.seek(9 * 4); // Move the file pointer to the tenth number
28      System.out.println("The tenth number is " + inout.readInt());
29
30      // Modify the eleventh number
31      inout.writeInt(555);
```

```
32
33      // Append a new number
34      inout.seek(inout.length()); // Move the file pointer to the end
35      inout.writeInt(999);
36
37      // Display the new length
38      System.out.println("The new length is " + inout.length());
39
40      // Retrieve the new eleventh number
41      inout.seek(10 * 4); // Move the file pointer to the eleventh number
42      System.out.println("The eleventh number is " + inout.readInt());
43
44      inout.close();
45   }
46 }
```

close file

- A **RandomAccessFile** is created for the file named **inout.dat** with mode "**rw**" to allow both read and write operations in line 6.

- **inout.setLength(0)** sets the length to **0** in line 9. This, in effect, destroys the old contents of the file.

- The **for** loop writes two hundred **int** values from **0** to **199** into the file in lines 12–13. Since each **int** value takes 4 bytes, the total length of the file returned from **inout.length()** is now 800 (line 16), as shown in Figure 18.18.

- Invoking **inout.seek(0)** in line 19 sets the file pointer to the beginning of the file. **inout.readInt()** reads the first value in line 20 and moves the file pointer to the next number. The second number is read in line 24.

- **inout.seek(9 * 4)** (line 27) moves the file pointer to the tenth number. **inout.readInt()** reads the tenth number and moves the file pointer to the eleventh number in line 28. **inout.write(555)** writes a new eleventh number at the current position (line 31). The previous eleventh number is destroyed.

- **inout.seek(inout.length())** moves the file pointer to the end of the file (line 34). **inout.writeInt(999)** writes 999 to the file. Now the length of the file is increased by 4, so **inout.length()** returns 804 (line 38).

- **inout.seek(10 * 4)** moves the file pointer to the eleventh number in line 41. The new eleventh number, 555, is displayed in line 42.

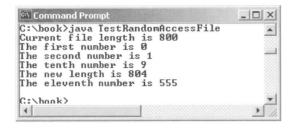

FIGURE 18.18   **TestRandomAccessFile** manipulates a **RandomAccessFile**.

18.8 (Optional) Case Study: Address Book

Now let us use **RandomAccessFile** to create a useful project for storing and viewing an address book. The user interface of the program is shown in Figure 18.19. The *Add* button stores a new address at the end of the file. The *First*, *Next*, *Previous*, and *Last* buttons retrieve the first, next, previous, and last addresses from the file, respectively.

FIGURE 18.19 AddressBook stores and retrieves addresses from a file.

Random access files are often used to process files of records. For convenience, fixed-length records are used in random access files so that a record can be located easily, as shown in Figure 18.20. A record consists of a fixed number of fields. A field can be a string or a primitive data type. A string in a *fixed-length record* has a maximum size. If a string is smaller than the maximum size, the rest of the string is padded with blanks.

fixed-length record

file ——▶ | Record 1 | Record 2 | ... | Record n | | Address 1 | Address 2 | ... | Address n |

Field 1 Field 2 ... Field k   e.g., ——▶   name street city state zip

FIGURE 18.20 Random access files are often used to process files of fixed-length records.

Let **address.dat** be the file to store addresses. A RandomAccessFile for both read and write can be created using

```
RandomAccessFile raf = new RandomAccessFile("address.dat", "rw");
```

Let each address consist of a name (32 characters), street (32 characters), city (20 characters), state (2 characters), and zip (5 characters). If the actual size of a field (e.g., name) is less than the fixed maximum size, fill it with blank characters. If the actual size of a field is greater than the fixed maximum size, truncate the string. Thus the total size of an address is $32 + 32 + 20 + 2 + 5 = 91$ characters. Since each character occupies two bytes, one address takes $2*91 = 182$ bytes. After an address record is read, the file pointer is 182 bytes ahead of the previous file pointer.

For convenience, Listing 18.8 contains two methods for reading and writing a fixed-length string.

LISTING 18.8 FixedLengthStringIO.java

```
1  import java.io.*;
2
3  public class FixedLengthStringIO {
4    /** Read fixed number of characters from a DataInput stream */
5    public static String readFixedLengthString(int size,
6        DataInput in) throws IOException {
7      // Declare an array of characters
8      char[] chars = new char[size];
9
10     // Read fixed number of characters to the array
11     for (int i = 0; i < size; i++)
12       chars[i] = in.readChar();
13
```

read characters

```
14    return new String(chars);
15  }
16
17  /** Write fixed number of characters to a DataOutput stream */
18  public static void writeFixedLengthString(String s, int size,
19      DataOutput out) throws IOException {
20    char[] chars = new char[size];
21
22    // Fill in string with characters
23    s.getChars(0, Math.min(s.length(), size) , chars, 0);         fill string
24
25    // Fill in blank characters in the rest of the array
26    for (int i = Math.min(s.length(), size) ; i < chars.length; i++)
27      chars[i] = ' ';                                             fill blank
28
29    // Create and write a new string padded with blank characters
30    out.writeChars(new String(chars));                            write string
31  }
32 }
```

The `writeFixedLengthString(String s, int size, DataOutput out)` method writes a string in a fixed size to a `DataOutput` stream. If the string is longer than the specified size, it is truncated (line 23); if it is shorter than the specified size, blanks are padded into it (lines 26–27). In any case, a new fixed-length string is written to a specified output stream. Since `RandomAccessFile` implements `DataOutput`, this method can be used to write a string to a `RandomAccessFile`. For example, invoking `writeFixedLengthString("John", 2, raf)` actually writes `"Jo"` to the `RandomAccessFile raf`, since the size is `2`. Invoking `writeFixedLengthString("John", 6, raf)` actually writes `"John "` to the `Random AccessFile raf`, since the size is `6`.

The `readFixedLengthString(int size, InputOutput in)` method reads a fixed number of characters from an `InputStream` and returns as a string. Since `RandomAccessFile` implements `InputOutput`, this method can be used to read a string from a `writeFixedLengthString(String s, int size, DataOutput out)`.

The rest of the work can be summarized in the following steps:

1. Create the user interface.

2. Add a record to the file.

3. Read a record from the file.

4. Write the code to implement the button actions.

The program is shown in Listing 18.9.

LISTING 18.9 AddressBook.java

```
1 import java.io.*;
2 import java.awt.*;
3 import java.awt.event.*;
4 import javax.swing.*;
5 import javax.swing.border.*;
6
7 public class AddressBook extends JFrame {
8   // Specify the size of five string fields in the record
9   final static int NAME_SIZE = 32;                  constant
10  final static int STREET_SIZE = 32;
11  final static int CITY_SIZE = 20;
12  final static int STATE_SIZE = 2;
13  final static int ZIP_SIZE = 5;
```

```
14    final static int RECORD_SIZE =
15      (NAME_SIZE + STREET_SIZE + CITY_SIZE + STATE_SIZE + ZIP_SIZE);
16
17    // Access address.dat using RandomAccessFile
18    private RandomAccessFile raf;
19
20    // Text fields
21    private JTextField jtfName = new JTextField(NAME_SIZE);
22    private JTextField jtfStreet = new JTextField(STREET_SIZE);
23    private JTextField jtfCity = new JTextField(CITY_SIZE);
24    private JTextField jtfState = new JTextField(STATE_SIZE);
25    private JTextField jtfZip = new JTextField(ZIP_SIZE);
26
27    // Buttons
28    private JButton jbtAdd = new JButton("Add");
29    private JButton jbtFirst = new JButton("First");
30    private JButton jbtNext = new JButton("Next");
31    private JButton jbtPrevious = new JButton("Previous");
32    private JButton jbtLast = new JButton("Last");
33
34    public AddressBook() {
35      // Open or create a random access file
36      try {
37        raf = new RandomAccessFile("address.dat", "rw");
38      }
39      catch(IOException ex) {
40        System.out.print("Error: " + ex);
41        System.exit(0);
42      }
43
44      // Panel p1 for holding labels Name, Street, and City
45      JPanel p1 = new JPanel();
46      p1.setLayout(new GridLayout(3, 1));
47      p1.add(new JLabel("Name"));
48      p1.add(new JLabel("Street"));
49      p1.add(new JLabel("City"));
50
51      // Panel jpState for holding state
52      JPanel jpState = new JPanel();
53      jpState.setLayout(new BorderLayout());
54      jpState.add(new JLabel("State"), BorderLayout.WEST);
55      jpState.add(jtfState, BorderLayout.CENTER);
56
57      // Panel jpZip for holding zip
58      JPanel jpZip = new JPanel();
59      jpZip.setLayout(new BorderLayout());
60      jpZip.add(new JLabel("Zip"), BorderLayout.WEST);
61      jpZip.add(jtfZip, BorderLayout.CENTER);
62
63      // Panel p2 for holding jpState and jpZip
64      JPanel p2 = new JPanel();
65      p2.setLayout(new BorderLayout());
66      p2.add(jpState, BorderLayout.WEST);
67      p2.add(jpZip, BorderLayout.CENTER);
68
69      // Panel p3 for holding jtfCity and p2
70      JPanel p3 = new JPanel();
71      p3.setLayout(new BorderLayout());
72      p3.add(jtfCity, BorderLayout.CENTER);
73      p3.add(p2, BorderLayout.EAST);
74
```

raf

GUI component

open file

create UI

```
75      // Panel p4 for holding jtfName, jtfStreet, and p3
76      JPanel p4 = new JPanel();
77      p4.setLayout(new GridLayout(3, 1));
78      p4.add(jtfName);
79      p4.add(jtfStreet);
80      p4.add(p3);
81
82      // Place p1 and p4 into jpAddress
83      JPanel jpAddress = new JPanel(new BorderLayout());
84      jpAddress.add(p1, BorderLayout.WEST);
85      jpAddress.add(p4, BorderLayout.CENTER);
86
87      // Set the panel with line border
88      jpAddress.setBorder(new BevelBorder(BevelBorder.RAISED));
89
90      // Add buttons to a panel
91      JPanel jpButton = new JPanel();
92      jpButton.add(jbtAdd);
93      jpButton.add(jbtFirst);
94      jpButton.add(jbtNext);
95      jpButton.add(jbtPrevious);
96      jpButton.add(jbtLast);
97
98      // Add jpAddress and jpButton to the frame
99      add(jpAddress, BorderLayout.CENTER);
100     add(jpButton, BorderLayout.SOUTH);
101
102     jbtAdd.addActionListener(new ActionListener() {         register listener
103       public void actionPerformed(ActionEvent e) {
104         writeAddress();                                     add address
105       }
106     });
107     jbtFirst.addActionListener(new ActionListener() {       register listener
108       public void actionPerformed(ActionEvent e) {
109         try {
110           if (raf.length() > 0) readAddress(0);             first record
111         }
112         catch (IOException ex) {
113           ex.printStackTrace();
114         }
115       }
116     });
117     jbtNext.addActionListener(new ActionListener() {        register listener
118       public void actionPerformed(ActionEvent e) {
119         try {
120           long currentPosition = raf.getFilePointer();
121           if (currentPosition < raf.length())
122             readAddress(currentPosition);                   next address
123         }
124         catch (IOException ex) {
125           ex.printStackTrace();
126         }
127       }
128     });
129     jbtPrevious.addActionListener(new ActionListener() {
130       public void actionPerformed(ActionEvent e) {
131         try {
132           long currentPosition = raf.getFilePointer();
133           if (currentPosition - 2 * RECORD_SIZE > 0)
134             // Why 2 * 2 * RECORD_SIZE? See the follow-up remarks
135             readAddress(currentPosition - 2 * 2 * RECORD_SIZE);
```

```
136              else
137                readAddress(0);
138            }
139            catch (IOException ex) {
140              ex.printStackTrace();
141            }
142          }
143        });
```

```
144        jbtLast.addActionListener(new ActionListener() {
145          public void actionPerformed(ActionEvent e) {
146            try {
147              long lastPosition = raf.length();
148              if (lastPosition > 0)
149                // Why 2 * RECORD_SIZE? See the follow-up remarks
```

```
150                readAddress(lastPosition - 2 * RECORD_SIZE);
151            }
152            catch (IOException ex) {
153              ex.printStackTrace();
154            }
155          }
156        });
157
158        // Display the first record if exists
159        try {
```

```
160          if (raf.length() > 0) readAddress(0);
161        }
162        catch (IOException ex) {
163          ex.printStackTrace();
164        }
165      }
166
167      /** Write a record at the end of the file */
168      public void writeAddress() {
169        try {
170          raf.seek(raf.length());
171          FixedLengthStringIO.writeFixedLengthString(
172            jtfName.getText(), NAME_SIZE, raf);
173          FixedLengthStringIO.writeFixedLengthString(
174            jtfStreet.getText(), STREET_SIZE, raf);
175          FixedLengthStringIO.writeFixedLengthString(
176            jtfCity.getText(), CITY_SIZE, raf);
177          FixedLengthStringIO.writeFixedLengthString(
178            jtfState.getText(), STATE_SIZE, raf);
179          FixedLengthStringIO.writeFixedLengthString(
180            jtfZip.getText(), ZIP_SIZE, raf);
181        }
182        catch (IOException ex) {
183          ex.printStackTrace();
184        }
185      }
186
187      /** Read a record at the specified position */
188      public void readAddress(long position) throws IOException {
189        raf.seek(position);
190        string name = FixedLengthStringIO.readFixedLengthString(
191          NAME_SIZE, raf);
192        String street = FixedLengthStringIO.readFixedLengthString(
193          STREET_SIZE, raf);
```

```
194      String city = FixedLengthStringIO.readFixedLengthString(
195        CITY_SIZE, raf);
196      String state = FixedLengthStringIO.readFixedLengthString(
197        STATE_SIZE, raf);
198      String zip = FixedLengthStringIO.readFixedLengthString(
199        ZIP_SIZE, raf);
200
201      jtfName.setText(name);
202      jtfStreet.setText(street);
203      jtfCity.setText(city);
204      jtfState.setText(state);
205      jtfZip.setText(zip);
206    }
207
208    public static void main(String[] args) {
209      AddressBook frame = new AddressBook();
210      frame.pack();
211      frame.setTitle("AddressBook");
212      frame.setDefaultCloseOperation(JFrame.EXIT_ON_CLOSE);
213      frame.setVisible(true);
214    }
215  }
```

- A random access file, `address.dat`, is created to store address information if the file does not yet exist (line 37). If it already exists, the file is opened. A random file object, `raf`, is used for both write and read operations. The size of each field in the record is fixed and therefore defined as a constant in lines 9–15.

- The user interface is created in lines 44–100. The listeners are registered in lines 102–156. When the program starts, it displays the first record, if it exists, in lines 159–164.

- The `writeAddress()` method sets the file pointer to the end of the file (line 170) and writes a new record to the file (lines 171–180).

- The `readAddress()` method sets the file pointer at the specified position (line 189) and reads a record from the file (lines 190–199). The record is displayed in lines 201–205.

- To add a record, you need to collect the address information from the user interface and write the address into the file (line 104).

- The code to process button events is implemented in lines 102–156. For the *First* button, read the record from position `0` (line 110). For the *Next* button, read the record from the current file pointer (line 122). When a record is read, the file pointer is moved `2 * RECORD_SIZE` number of bytes ahead of the previous file pointer. For the *Previous* button, you need to display the record prior to the one being displayed now. So you have to move the file pointer two records before the current file pointer (line 135). For the *Last* button, read the record from the position at `raf.length() - 2 * RECORD_SIZE`.

KEY TERMS

binary I/O 606	sequential access file 621
deserialization 619	serialization 619
file pointer 622	stream 606
random access file 621	text I/O 606

CHAPTER SUMMARY

- I/O can be classified into text I/O and binary I/O. Text I/O interprets data in sequences of characters. Binary I/O interprets data as raw binary values. How text is stored in a file is dependent on the encoding scheme for the file. Java automatically performs encoding and decoding for text I/O.

- The `InputStream` and `OutputStream` classes are the roots of all binary I/O classes. `FileInputStream`/`FileOutputStream` associates a file for binary input/output. `BufferedInputStream`/`BufferedOutputStream` can be used to wrap on any binary I/O stream to improve performance. `DataInputStream`/`DataOutputStream` can be used to read/write primitive values and strings.

- `ObjectInputStream`/`ObjectOutputStream` can be used to read/write objects in addition to primitive values and strings. To enable object serialization, the object's defining class must implement the `java.io.Serializable` marker interface.

- The `RandomAccessFile` class enables you to read and write data to a file. You can open a file with the `"r"` mode to indicate that it is read-only, or with the `"rw"` mode to indicate that it is updateable. Since the `RandomAccessFile` class implements `DataInput` and `DataOutput` interfaces, many methods in `RandomAccessFile` are the same as those in `DataInputStream` and `DataOutputStream`.

REVIEW QUESTIONS

Sections 18.1–18.2

18.1   What is a text file, and what is a binary file? Can you view a text file or a binary file using a text editor?

18.2   How do you read or write data in Java? What is a stream?

Section 18.3 Text I/O vs. Binary I/O

18.3   What are the differences between text I/O and binary I/O?

18.4   How is a Java character represented in the memory, and how is a character represented in a text file?

18.5   If you write string `"ABC"` to an ASCII text file, what values are stored in the file?

18.6   If you write string `"100"` to an ASCII text file, what values are stored in the file? If you write a numeric byte-type value `100` using binary I/O, what values are stored in the file?

18.7   What is the encoding scheme for representing a character in a Java program? By default, what is the encoding scheme for a text file on Windows?

Section 18.4 Binary I/O Classes

18.8   Why do you have to declare to throw `IOException` in the method or use a `try-catch` block to handle `IOException` for Java IO programs?

18.9   Why should you always close streams?

18.10   `InputStream` reads bytes. Why does the `read()` method return an `int` instead of a byte? Find the abstract methods in `InputSteam` and `OutputStream`.

18.11   Does `FileInputStream`/`FileOutputStream` introduce any new methods? How do you create a `FileInputStream`/`FileOutputStream`?

18.12 What will happen if you attempt to create an input stream on a nonexistent file? What will happen if you attempt to create an output stream on an existing file? Can you append data to an existing file?

18.13 How do you append data to an existing text file using `java.io.PrintWriter`?

18.14 Suppose `input` is a `DataInputStream`, `input.available()` returns 100. After invoking `read()`, what is `input.available()`? After invoking `readInt()`, what is `input.available()`? After invoking `readChar()`, what is `input.available()`? After invoking `readDouble()`, what is `input.available()`?

18.15 What is written to a file using `writeByte(91)` on a `FileOutputStream`?

18.16 How do you check the end of a file in a binary input stream (`FileInputStream`, `DataInputStream`)?

18.17 What is wrong in the following code?

```java
import java.io.*;

public class Test {
  public static void main(String[] args) {
    try {
      FileInputStream fis = new FileInputStream("test.dat");
    }
    catch (IOException ex) {
      ex.printStackTrace();
    }
    catch (FileNotFoundException ex) {
      ex.printStackTrace();
    }
  }
}
```

18.18 Suppose you run the program on Windows using the default ASCII encoding. After the program is finished, how many bytes are in the file `t.txt`? Show the contents of each byte.

```java
public class Test {
  public static void main(String[] args) throws
      java.io.IOException {
    java.io.PrintWriter output = new
    java.io.PrintWriter("t.txt");
    output.printf("%s", "1234");
    output.printf("%s", "5678");
    output.close();
  }
}
```

18.19 After the program is finished, how many bytes are in the file `t.dat`? Show the contents of each byte.

```java
import java.io.*;

public class Test {
  public static void main(String[] args) throws IOException {
    DataOutputStream output = new DataOutputStream(
      new FileOutputStream("t.dat"));
    output.writeInt(1234);
    output.writeInt(5678);
    output.close();
  }
}
```

18.20 For each of the following statements on a `DataOutputStream` out, how many bytes are sent to the output?

```
output.writeChar('A');
output.writeChars("BC");
output.writeUTF("DEF");
```

18.21 What are the advantages of using buffered streams? Are the following statements correct?

```
BufferedInputStream input1 =
  new BufferedInputStream(new FileInputStream("t.dat"));

DataInputStream input2 = new DataInputStream(
  new BufferedInputStream(new FileInputStream("t.dat")));

ObjectInputStream input3 = new ObjectInputStream(
  new BufferedInputStream(new FileInputStream("t.dat")));
```

Section 18.6 Object I/O

18.22 What types of objects can be stored using the `ObjectOutputStream`? What is the method for writing an object? What is the method for reading an object? What is the return type of the method that reads an object from `ObjectInputStream`?

18.23 If you serialize two objects of the same type, will they take same space?

18.24 Is it true that any instance of `java.io.Serializable` can be successfully serialized? Are the static variables in an object serialized? How do you mark an instance variable not to be serialized?

18.25 Can you write an array to an `ObjectOutputStream`?

18.26 Is it true that `DataInputStream`/`DataOutputStream` can always be replaced by `ObjectInputStream`/`ObjectOutputStream`?

18.27 What will happen when you attempt to run the following code?

```
import java.io.*;

public class Test {
  public static void main(String[] args) throws IOException {
    ObjectOutputStream output =
      new ObjectOutputStream(new
        FileOutputStream("object.dat"));

    output.writeObject(new A());
  }
}

class A implements Serializable {
  B b = new B();
}

class B {
}
```

Section 18.7 (Optional) Random Access Files

18.28 Can `RandomAccessFile` streams read and write a data file created by `DataOutputStream`? Can `RandomAccessFile` streams read and write objects?

18.29 Create a `RandomAccessFile` stream for the file `address.dat` to allow the updating of student information in the file. Create a `DataOutputStream` for the file `address.dat`. Explain the differences between these two statements.

18.30 What happens if the file `test.dat` does not exist when you attempt to compile and run the following code?

```
import java.io.*;

public class Test {
  public static void main(String[] args) {
    try {
      RandomAccessFile raf =
        new RandomAccessFile("test.dat", "r");
      int i = raf.readInt();
    }
    catch (IOException ex) {
      System.out.println("IO exception");
    }
  }
}
```

PROGRAMMING EXERCISES

Section 18.3 Text I/O vs. Binary I/O

18.1* (*Creating a text file*) Write a program to create a file named `Exercise18_1.txt` if it does not exist. Append new data to it if the file already exists. Write one hundred integers created randomly into the file using text I/O. Integers are separated by a space.

Section 18.4 Binary I/O Classes

18.2* (*Creating a binary data file*) Write a program to create a file named `Exercise18_2.dat` if it does not exist. Append new data to it if the file already exists. Write one hundred integers created randomly into the file using binary I/O.

18.3* (*Summing all the integers in a binary data file*) Suppose a binary data file named `Exercise18_3.dat` has been created using `writeInt(int)` in `DataOutputStream`. The file contains an unspecified number of integers. Write a program to find the total of integers.

18.4* (*Converting a text file into UTF*) Write a program that reads lines of characters from a text and writes each line as a UTF-8 string into a binary file. Display the sizes of the text file and the binary file. Use the following command to run the program:

```
java Exercise18_4 Welcome.java Welcome.utf
```

Section 18.6 Object I/O

18.5* (*Storing objects and arrays into a file*) Write a program that stores an array of five `int` values 1, 2, 3, 4 and 5, a `Date` object for current time, and a double value `5.5` into the file named `Exercise18_5.dat`.

18.6* (*Storing Loan objects*) The `Loan` class, introduced in §7.15, "Case Study: The `Loan` Class," does not implement `Serializable`. Rewrite the `Loan` class to implement `Serializable`. Write a program that creates five `Loan` objects and stores them in a file named `Exercise18_6.dat`.

18.7* (*Restoring objects from a file*) Suppose a file named `Exercise18_7.dat` has been created using the `ObjectOutputStream`. Write a program that reads the `Loan` objects from the file and computes the total loan amount. Suppose you don't know how many `Loan` objects are in the file. Use `EOFException` to end the loop.

Section 18.7 (Optional) Random Access Files

18.8*   (*Updating count*) Suppose you want to track how many times a program has been executed. You may store an `int` to count the file. Increase the count by 1 each time this program is executed. Let the program be `Exercise18_8`, and store the count in `Exercise18_8.dat`.

18.9** (*Updating address*) Modify `AddressBook` in Listing 18.9, AddressBook.java, to add an *Update* button, as shown in Figure 18.21, to enable the user to modify an address that is being displayed.

FIGURE 18.21   You can update the address record that is currently displayed.

RECURSION

Objectives

- To know what a recursive method is and the benefits of using recursive methods (§19.1).

- To determine the base cases in a recursive method (§§19.2–19.5).

- To understand how recursive method calls are handled in a call stack (§§19.2–19.3).

- To solve problems using recursion (§§19.2–19.7).

- To use an overloaded helper method to derive a recursive method (§19.5).

- To solve the Towers of Hanoi problem using recursion (§19.6).

- To draw fractals using recursion (§19.7).

- To understand the relationship and difference between recursion and iteration (§19.8).

636 Chapter 19 Recursion

recursive method

19.1 Introduction

A *recursive method* is a method that invokes itself directly or indirectly. Recursion is a useful programming technique. In some cases, using recursion enables you to develop a natural, straightforward, simple solution to a problem that would otherwise be difficult to solve. This chapter introduces the concepts and techniques of recursive programming and uses examples demonstrating how to "think recursively."

19.2 Example: Factorials

Many mathematical functions are defined using recursion. The factorial of a number n can be recursively defined as follows:

```
0! = 1;
n! = n x (n - 1)!; n > 0
```

How do you find n! for a given n? It is easy to find 1! because you know that 0! and 1! is 1 x 0!. Assuming that you know (n-1)!, n! can be obtained immediately using n x (n - 1)!. Thus, the problem of computing n! is reduced to computing (n - 1)!. When computing (n - 1)!, you can apply the same idea recursively until n is reduced to 0.

base case or stopping condition

Let factorial(n) be the method for computing n!. If you call the method with n = 0, it immediately returns the result. The method knows how to solve the simplest case, which is referred to as the *base case* or the *stopping condition*. If you call the method with n > 0, it reduces the problem into a subproblem for computing the factorial of n - 1. The subproblem is essentially the same as the original problem, but is simpler or smaller than the original. Because the subproblem has the same property as the original, you can call the method with a different argument, which is referred to as a *recursive call*.

recursive call

The recursive algorithm for computing factorial(n) can be simply described as follows:

```
if (n == 0)
  return 1;
else
  return n * factorial(n - 1);
```

A recursive call can result in many more recursive calls because the method is dividing a subproblem into new subproblems. For a recursive method to terminate, the problem must eventually be reduced to a stopping case. When it reaches a stopping case, the method returns a result to its caller. The caller then performs a computation and returns the result to its own caller. This process continues until the result is passed back to the original caller. The original problem can now be solved by multiplying n with the result of factorial(n - 1).

Listing 19.1 gives a complete program that prompts the user to enter a non-negative integer and displays the factorial for the number.

LISTING 19.1 ComputeFactorial.java

```
1 import javax.swing.JOptionPane;
2
3 public class ComputeFactorial {
4   /** Main method */
5   public static void main(String[] args) {
6     // Prompt the user to enter an integer
7     String intString = JOptionPane.showInputDialog(
8       "Please enter a non-negative integer:");
9
```

```
10      // Convert string into integer
11      int n = Integer.parseInt(intString);
12
13      // Display factorial
14      JOptionPane.showMessageDialog(null,
15        "Factorial of " + n + " is " + factorial(n));
16    }
17
18    /** Return the factorial for a specified number */
19    public static long factorial(int n) {
20      if (n == 0) // Base case                                    base case
21        return 1;
22      else
23        return n * factorial(n - 1); // Recursive call            recursion
24    }
25 }
```

The `factorial` method (lines 19–24) is essentially a direct translation of the recursive mathematical definition for the factorial into Java code. The call to `factorial` is recursive because it calls itself. The parameter passed to `factorial` is decremented until it reaches the base case of 0.

Figure 19.1 illustrates the execution of the recursive calls, starting with **n = 4**. The use of stack space for recursive calls is shown in Figure 19.2.

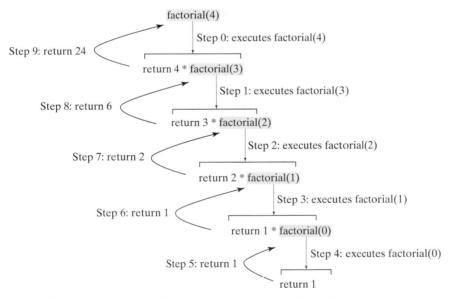

FIGURE 19.1   Invoking `factorial(4)` spawns recursive calls to `factorial`.

Caution

Infinite recursion can occur if recursion does not reduce the problem in a manner that allows it to   infinite recursion
eventually converge into the base case. For example, if you mistakenly write the `factorial`
method as follows:

```
public static long factorial(int n) {
  return n * factorial(n - 1);
}
```

The method runs infinitely and causes a `StackOverflowError`.

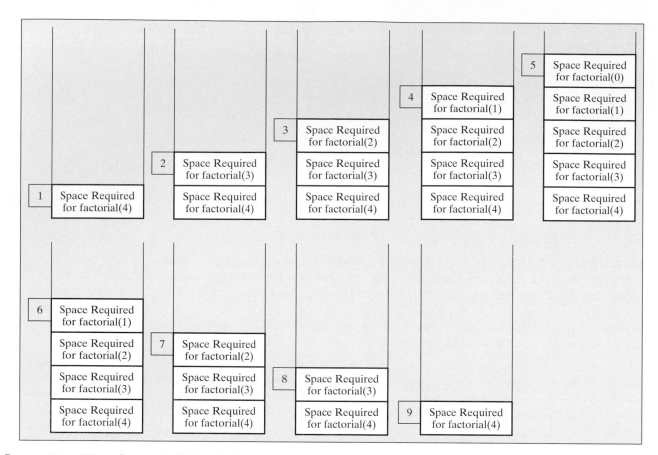

FIGURE 19.2 When `factorial(4)` is being executed, the `factorial` method is called recursively, causing memory space to dynamically change.

Pedagogical Note

It is simpler and more efficient to implement the `factorial` method using a loop. However, the recursive `factorial` method is a good example to demonstrate the concept of recursion.

19.3 Example: Fibonacci Numbers

The `factorial` method in the preceding section could easily be rewritten without using recursion. In some cases, however, using recursion enables you to give a natural, straightforward, simple solution to a program that would otherwise be difficult to solve. Consider the well-known Fibonacci series problem, as follows:

The series:	0	1	1	2	3	5	8	13	21	34	55	89	...
indices:	0	1	2	3	4	5	6	7	8	9	10	11	

The Fibonacci series begins with 0 and 1, and each subsequent number is the sum of the preceding two numbers in the series. The series can be recursively defined as follows:

```
fib(0) = 0;
fib(1) = 1;
fib(index) = fib(index - 2) + fib(index - 1); index >= 2
```

The Fibonacci series was named for Leonardo Fibonacci, a medieval mathematician, who originated it to model the growth of the rabbit population. It can be applied in numeric optimization and in various other areas.

How do you find `fib(index)` for a given `index`? It is easy to find `fib(2)` because you know `fib(0)` and `fib(1)`. Assuming that you know `fib(index - 2)` and `fib(index - 1)`, `fib(index)` can be obtained immediately. Thus, the problem of computing `fib(index)` is reduced to computing `fib(index - 2)` and `fib(index - 1)`. When computing `fib(index - 2)` and `fib(index - 1)`, you apply the idea recursively until `index` is reduced to `0` or `1`.

The base case is `index = 0` or `index = 1`. If you call the method with `index = 0` or `index = 1`, it immediately returns the result. If you call the method with `index >= 2`, it divides the problem into two subproblems for computing `fib(index - 1)` and `fib(index - 2)` using recursive calls. The recursive algorithm for computing `fib(index)` can be simply described as follows:

```
if (index == 0)
  return 0;
else if (index == 1)
  return 1;
else
  return fib(index - 1) + fib(index - 2);
```

Listing 19.2 gives a complete program that prompts the user to enter an index and computes the Fibonacci number for the index.

LISTING 19.2 ComputeFibonacci.java

```
1 import javax.swing.JOptionPane;
2
3 public class ComputeFibonacci {
4   /** Main method */
5   public static void main(String args[]) {
6     // Read the index
7     String intString = JOptionPane.showInputDialog(
8       "Enter an index for the Fibonacci number:");
9
10    // Convert string into integer
11    int index = Integer.parseInt(intString);
12
13    // Find and display the Fibonacci number
14    JOptionPane.showMessageDialog(null,
15      "Fibonacci number at index " + index + " is " + fib(index));
16  }
17
18  /** The method for finding the Fibonacci number */
19  public static long fib(long index) {
20    if (index == 0) // Base case                           base case
21      return 0;
22    else if (index == 1) // Base case
23      return 1;
24    else // Reduction and recursive calls
25      return fib(index - 1) + fib(index - 2);              recursion
26  }
27 }
```

The program does not show the considerable amount of work done behind the scenes by the computer. Figure 19.3, however, shows successive recursive calls for evaluating `fib(4)`. The original method, `fib(4)`, makes two recursive calls, `fib(3)` and `fib(2)`, and then returns `fib(3)` + `fib(2)`. But in what order are these methods called? In Java, operands are evaluated from left to right. The labels in Figure 19.3 show the order in which methods are called.

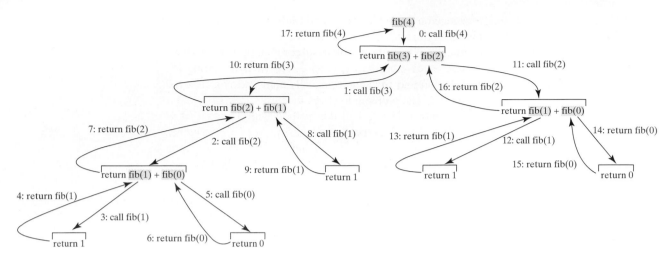

FIGURE 19.3 Invoking `fib(4)` spawns recursive calls to `fib`.

As shown in Figure 19.3, there are many duplicated recursive calls. For instance, `fib(2)` is called twice, `fib(1)` is called three times, and `fib(0)` is called twice. In general, computing `fib(index)` requires twice as many recursive calls as are needed for computing `fib(index - 1)`. As you try larger index values, the number of calls substantially increases.

Besides the large number of recursive calls, the computer requires more time and space to run recursive methods.

 Pedagogical Note
The recursive implementation of the `fib` method is very simple and straightforward, but not efficient. See Exercise 19.2 for an efficient solution using loops. The recursive `fib` method is a good example to demonstrate how to write recursive methods, though it is not practical.

19.4 Problem Solving Using Recursion

The preceding sections presented two classic recursion examples. All recursive methods have
recursion characteristics   the following characteristics:

if-else

- The method is implemented using an `if-else` or a `switch` statement that leads to different cases.

base cases

- One or more *base cases* (the simplest case) are used to stop recursion.

reduction

- Every recursive call reduces the original problem, bringing it increasingly closer to a base case until it becomes that case.

In general, to solve a problem using recursion, you break it into subproblems. If a subproblem resembles the original problem, you can apply the same approach to solve the subproblem recursively. This subproblem is almost the same as the original problem in nature but with a smaller size.

Let us consider the simple problem of printing a message for n times. You can break the problem into two subproblems: one is to print the message one time and the other is to print the message n - 1 times. The second problem is the same as the original problem with a smaller size. The base case for the problem is n == 0. You can solve this problem using recursion as follows:

```java
public static void nPrintln(String message, int times) {
  if (times >= 1) {
    System.out.println(message);
    nPrintln(message, times - 1);
  } // The base case is n == 0
}
```
recursive call

Note that the `fib` method in the preceding example returns a value to its caller, but the `nPrintln` method is `void` and does not return a value to its caller.

Many of the problems presented in the early chapters can be solved using recursion if you *think recursively*. Consider the palindrome problem in Listing 7.1. Recall that a string is a palindrome if it reads the same from the left and from the right. For example, mom and dad are palindromes, but uncle and aunt are not. The problem to check whether a string is a palindrome can be divided into two subproblems:

think recursively

- Check whether the first character and the last character of the string are equal.
- Ignore the two end characters and check whether the rest of the substring is a palindrome.

The second subproblem is the same as the original problem but with a smaller size. There are two base cases: (1) the two end characters are not same; (2) the string size is 0 or 1. In case 1, the string is not a palindrome; and in case 2, the string is a palindrome. The recursive method for this problem can be implemented in Listing 19.3.

Listing 19.3 Recursive Palindrome Method

```
1 public static boolean isPalindrome(String s) {
2   if (s.length() <= 1) // Base case
3     return true;
4   else if (s.charAt(0) != s.charAt(s.length() - 1)) // Base case
5     return false;
6   else
7     return isPalindrome(s.substring(1, s.length() - 1));
8 }
```

recursive call

The `substring` method in line 7 creates a new string that is the same as the original string except without the first and last characters in the original string. Checking whether a string is a palindrome is equivalent to checking whether the substring is a palindrome if the two end characters in the original string are the same.

19.5 Recursive Helper Methods

The preceding recursive `isPalindrome` method is not efficient, because it creates a new string for every recursive call. To avoid creating new strings, you can use the low and high indices to indicate the range of the substring. These two indices must be passed to the recursive method. Since the original method is `isPalindrome(String s)`, you have to create a new method `isPalindrome(String s, int low, int high)` to accept additional information on the string, as shown in Listing 19.4.

Listing 19.4 Palindrome Using a Helper Method

```
1 public static boolean isPalindrome(String s) {
2   return isPalindrome(s, 0, s.length() - 1);
3 }
4
5 public static boolean isPalindrome(String s, int low, int high) {
6   if (high <= low) // Base case
7     return true;
8   else if (s.charAt(low) != s.charAt(high)) // Base case
9     return false;
10  else
11    return isPalindrome(s, low + 1, high - 1);
12 }
```

recursive call

Two overloaded `isPalindrome` methods are declared. The first method, `isPalindrome(String s)`, checks whether a string is a palindrome, and the second method, `isPalindrome`

(String s, int low, int high), checks whether a substring s(low..high) is a palindrome. The first method passes the string s with low = 0 and high = s.length() - 1 to the second method. The second method can be invoked recursively to check a palindrome in an ever-shrinking substring. It is a common design technique in recursive programming to declare a second method that receives additional parameters. Such a method is known as a *recursive helper method*.

recursive helper method

Helper methods are very useful to design recursive solutions for problems involving strings and arrays. The following sections present two more examples.

19.5.1 Selection Sort

Selection sort was introduced in §6.8.1, "Selection Sort." Recall that selection sort finds the largest number in the list and places it last. It then finds the largest number remaining and places it next to last, and so on until the list contains only a single number. The problem can be divided into two subproblems:

■ Find the largest number in the list and swap it with the last number.

■ Ignore the last number and sort the remaining smaller list recursively.

The base case is that the list contains only one number. Listing 19.5 gives the recursive sort method.

LISTING 19.5 Recursive Sort Method

base case

recursive call

```
1  public static void sort(double[] list) {
2    sort(list, list.length - 1);
3  }
4
5  public static void sort(double[] list, int high) {
6    if (high > 1) {
7      // Find the largest number and its index
8      int indexOfMax = 0;
9      double max = list[0];
10     for (int i = 1; i <= high; i++) {
11       if (list[i] > max) {
12         max = list[i];
13         indexOfMax = i;
14       }
15     }
16
17     // Swap the largest with the last number in the list
18     list[indexOfMax] = list[high];
19     list[high] = max;
20
21     // Sort the remaining list
22     sort(list, high - 1);
23   }
24 }
```

Two overloaded sort methods are declared. The first method, sort(double[] list), sorts an array in list[0..list.length - 1], and the second method, sort(double[] list, int high), sorts an array in list[0..high]. The second method can be invoked recursively to sort an ever-shrinking subarray.

19.5.2 Binary Search

Binary search was introduced in §6.7.2, "The Binary Search Approach." For binary search to work, the elements in the array must already be ordered. The binary search first compares the key with the element in the middle of the array. Consider the following three cases:

- Case 1: If the key is less than the middle element, recursively search the key in the first half of the array.

- Case 2: If the key is equal to the middle element, the search ends with a match.

- Case 3: If the key is greater than the middle element, recursively search the key in the second half of the array.

Case 1 and Case 3 reduce the search in a smaller list. Case 2 is a base case when there is a match. Another base case is that the search is exhausted without a match. Listing 19.6 gives a clear, simple solution for the binary search problem using recursion.

LISTING 19.6 Recursive Binary Search Method

```
 1 public static int recursiveBinarySearch(int[] list, int key) {
 2   int low = 0;
 3   int high = list.length - 1;
 4   return recursiveBinarySearch(list, key, low, high);
 5 }
 6
 7 public static int recursiveBinarySearch(int[] list, int key,
 8       int low, int high) {                                          base case
 9   if (low > high)  // The list has been exhausted without a match
10     return -low - 1; // Return -insertion point - 1
11
12   int mid = (low + high) / 2;
13   if (key < list[mid])                                              recursive call
14     return recursiveBinarySearch(list, key, low, mid - 1);          base case
15   else if (key == list[mid])
16     return mid;
17   else
18     return recursiveBinarySearch(list, key, mid + 1, high);         recursive call
19 }
```

The first method finds a key in the whole list. The second method finds a key in the list with index from `low` to `high`.

The first `binarySearch` method passes the initial array with `low = 0` and `high = list.length - 1` to the second `binarySearch` method. The second method is invoked recursively to find the key in an ever-shrinking subarray.

19.6 Tower of Hanoi

The Tower of Hanoi problem is another classic recursion example. The problem can be solved easily using recursion, but is difficult to solve without using recursion.

The problem involves moving a specified number of disks of distinct sizes from one tower to another while observing the following rules:

- There are *n* disks labeled 1, 2, 3, ..., *n*, and three towers labeled A, B, and C.

- No disk can be on top of a smaller disk at any time.

- All the disks are initially placed on tower A.

- Only one disk can be moved at a time, and it must be the top disk on the tower.

The objective of the problem is to move all the disks from A to B with the assistance of C. For example, if you have three disks, as shown in Figure 19.4, the following steps will move all of the disks from A to B:

1. Move disk 1 from A to B.

2. Move disk 2 from A to C.

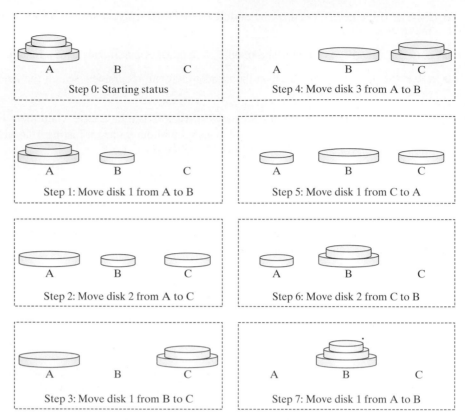

FIGURE 19.4 The goal of the Towers of Hanoi problem is to move disks from tower A to tower B without breaking the rules.

3. Move disk 1 from B to C.

4. Move disk 3 from A to B.

5. Move disk 1 from C to A.

6. Move disk 2 from C to B.

7. Move disk 1 from A to B.

 Note

The Towers of Hanoi is a classic computer science problem. There are many Websites devoted to this problem. The Website www.cut-the-knot.com/recurrence/hanoi.html is worth seeing.

In the case of three disks, you can find the solution manually. However, the problem is quite complex for a larger number of disks—even for four. Fortunately, the problem has an inherently recursive nature, which leads to a straightforward recursive solution.

The base case for the problem is $n = 1$. If $n == 1$, you could simply move the disk from A to B. When $n > 1$, you could split the original problem into three subproblems and solve them sequentially.

1. Move the first $n - 1$ disks from A to C with the assistance of tower B.

2. Move disk n from A to B.

3. Move $n - 1$ disks from C to B with the assistance of tower A.

The following method moves *n* disks from the `fromTower` to the `toTower` with the assistance of the `auxTower`:

```
void moveDisks(int n, char fromTower, char toTower, char auxTower)
```

The algorithm for the method can be described as follows:

```
if (n == 1) // Stopping condition
  Move disk 1 from the fromTower to the toTower;
else {
  moveDisks(n - 1, fromTower, auxTower, toTower);
  Move disk n from the fromTower to the toTower;
  moveDisks(n - 1, auxTower, toTower, fromTower);
}
```

Listing 19.7 gives a program that prompts the user to enter the number of disks and invokes the recursive method `moveDisks` to display the solution for moving the disks. A sample run of the following program appears in Figure 19.5.

FIGURE 19.5   The program prompts the user to enter the number of disks and then displays the steps that must be followed to solve the Towers of Hanoi problem.

LISTING 19.7 TowersOfHanoi.java

```
 1 import javax.swing.JOptionPane;
 2
 3 public class TowersOfHanoi {
 4   /** Main method */
 5   public static void main(String[] args) {
 6     // Read number of disks, n
 7     String intString = JOptionPane.showInputDialog(
 8       "Enter number of disks:");
 9
10     // Convert string into integer
11     int n = Integer.parseInt(intString);
12
13     // Find the solution recursively
14     System.out.println("The moves are:");
15     moveDisks(n, 'A', 'B', 'C');
16   }
17
18   /** The method for finding the solution to move n disks
19       from fromTower to toTower with auxTower */
```

```
20    public static void moveDisks(int n, char fromTower,
21        char toTower, char auxTower) {
22      if (n == 1) // Stopping condition
23        System.out.println("Move disk " + n + " from " +
24          fromTower + " to " + toTower);
25      else {
26        moveDisks(n - 1, fromTower, auxTower, toTower);
27        System.out.println("Move disk " + n + " from " +
28          fromTower + " to " + toTower);
29        moveDisks(n - 1, auxTower, toTower, fromTower);
30      }
31    }
32 }
```

recursion

recursion

This problem is inherently recursive. Using recursion makes it possible to find a natural, simple solution. It would be difficult to solve the problem without using recursion.

Consider tracing the program for n = 3. The successive recursive calls are shown in Figure 19.6. As you can see, writing the program is easier than tracing the recursive calls. The system uses stacks to trace the calls behind the scenes. To some extent, recursion provides a level of abstraction that hides iterations and other details from the user.

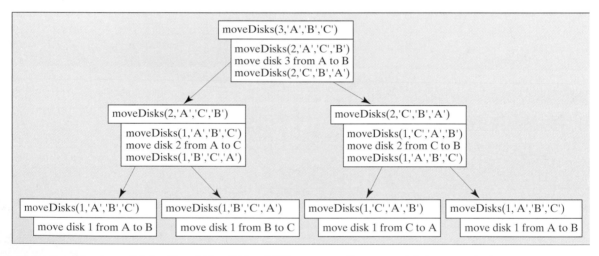

FIGURE 19.6 Invoking moveDisks(3, 'A', 'B', 'C') spawns calls to moveDisks recursively.

19.7 Fractals

A fractal is a geometrical figure, but unlike triangles, circles, and rectangles, fractals can be divided into parts that are each a reduced-size copy of the whole. There are many interesting examples of fractals. This section introduces a simple fractal, called the *Sierpinski triangle*, named after a famous Polish mathematician.

A Sierpinski triangle is created as follows:

1. It begins with an equilateral triangle, which is considered to be a Sierpinski fractal of order (or level) 0, as shown in Figure 19.7(a).

2. Connect the midpoints of the sides of the triangle of order 0 to create a Sierpinski triangle of order 1, as shown in Figure 19.7(b).

3. Leave the center triangle intact. Connect the midpoints of the sides of the three other triangles to create a Sierpinski of order 2, as shown in Figure 19.7(c).

4. You can repeat the same process recursively to create a Sierpinski triangle of order 3, 4, . . . , and so on, as shown in Figure 19.7(d).

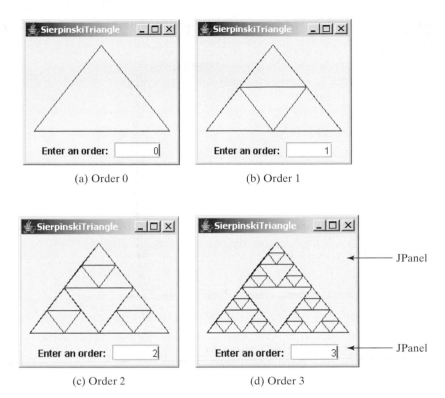

(a) Order 0   (b) Order 1

(c) Order 2   (d) Order 3

FIGURE 19.7   A Sierpinski triangle is a pattern of triangles.

The problem is inherently recursive. How do you develop a recursive solution for this problem? Consider the base case when the order is 0. It is easy to draw a Sierpinski triangle of order 0. How do you draw a Sierpinski triangle of order 1? The problem can be reduced by drawing three Sierpinski triangles of order 0. How do you draw a Sierpinski triangle of order 2? The problem can be reduced to drawing three Sierpinski triangles of order 1. So the problem of drawing a Sierpinski triangle of order n can be reduced to drawing three Sierpinski triangles of order $n - 1$.

Listing 19.8 gives a Java applet that displays a Sierpinski triangle of any order, as shown in Figure 19.7. You can enter an order in a text field to display a Sierpinski triangle of the specified order.

LISTING 19.8 SierpinskiTriangle.java

```
1 import javax.swing.*;
2 import java.awt.*;
3 import java.awt.event.*;
4
5 public class SierpinskiTriangle extends JApplet {
6   private JTextField jtfOrder = new JTextField(5); // To hold order
7   private SierpinskiTrianglePanel trianglePanel =
8     new SierpinskiTrianglePanel(); // To display the pattern
9
10   public SierpinskiTriangle() {
11     // Panel to hold label, text field, and a button
12     JPanel panel = new JPanel();
13     panel.add(new JLabel("Enter an order: "));
14     panel.add(jtfOrder);
15     jtfOrder.setHorizontalAlignment(SwingConstants.RIGHT);
16
17     // Add a Sierpinski Triangle panel to the applet
18     getContentPane().add(trianglePanel);
```

```
19        getContentPane().add(panel, BorderLayout.SOUTH);
20
21        // Register a listener
22        jtfOrder.addActionListener(new ActionListener() {
23          public void actionPerformed(ActionEvent e) {
24            trianglePanel.setOrder(Integer.parseInt(jtfOrder.getText()));
25          }
26        });
27      }
28
29      static class SierpinskiTrianglePanel extends JPanel {
30        private int order = 0;
31
32        /** Set a new order */
33        public void setOrder(int order) {
34          this.order = order;
35          repaint();
36        }
37
38        public void paintComponent(Graphics g) {
39          super.paintComponent(g);
40
41          // Select three points in proportion to the panel size
42          Point p1 = new Point(getWidth() / 2, 10);
43          Point p2 = new Point(10, getHeight() - 10);
44          Point p3 = new Point(getWidth() - 10, getHeight() - 10);
45
46          displayTriangles(g, order, p1, p2, p3);
47        }
48
49        private static void displayTriangles(Graphics g, int order,
50            Point p1, Point p2, Point p3) {
51          if (order >= 0) {
52            // Draw a triangle to connect three points
53            g.drawLine(p1.x, p1.y, p2.x, p2.y);
54            g.drawLine(p1.x, p1.y, p3.x, p3.y);
55            g.drawLine(p2.x, p2.y, p3.x, p3.y);
56
57            // Get three midpints in the triangle
58            Point midBetweenP1P2 = midpoint(p1, p2);
59            Point midBetweenP2P3 = midpoint(p2, p3);
60            Point midBetweenP3P1 = midpoint(p3, p1);
61
62            // Recursively display three triangles
63            displayTriangles(g, order - 1,
64              p1, midBetweenP1P2, midBetweenP3P1);
65            displayTriangles(g, order - 1,
66              midBetweenP1P2, p2, midBetweenP2P3);
67            displayTriangles(g, order - 1,
68              midBetweenP3P1, midBetweenP2P3, p3);
69          }
70        }
71
72        private static Point midpoint(Point p1, Point p2) {
73          return new Point((p1.x + p2.x) / 2, (p1.y + p2.y) / 2);
74        }
75      }
76    }
```

Margin notes:

listener (line 22)

set a new order (line 24)

three initial points (line 42)

draw a triangle (line 53)

top subtriangle (line 62)

left subtriangle (line 64)

right subtriangle (line 66)

main method omitted (line 75)

The initial triangle has three points set in proportion to the panel size (lines 42–44). The `displayTriangles(g, order, p1, p2, p3)` method performs the following tasks if `order >= 0`:

1. Display a triangle to connect three points **p1**, **p2**, and **p3** in lines 53–55.

2. Obtain a midpoint between **p1** and **p2** (line 58), a midpoint between **p2** and **p3** (line 59), and a midpoint between **p3** and **p1** (line 60).

3. Recursively invoke `displayTriangles` with a reduced order to display three smaller triangles (lines 63–68).

A Sierpinski triangle is displayed in a `SierpinskiTrianglePanel`. The `order` property in the inner class `SierpinskiTrianglePanel` specifies the order for the Sierpinski triangle. The `Point` class, introduced in §14.4, "Mouse Events," represents a point on a component. The `midpoint(Point p1, Point p2)` method returns the midpoint between **p1** and **p2** (lines 72–74).

19.8 Recursion versus Iteration

Recursion is an alternative form of program control. It is essentially repetition without a loop control. When you use loops, you specify a loop body. The repetition of the loop body is controlled by the loop-control structure. In recursion, the method itself is called repeatedly. A selection statement must be used to control whether to call the method recursively or not.

Recursion bears substantial overhead. Each time the program calls a method, the system must assign space for all of the method's local variables and parameters. This can consume considerable memory and requires extra time to manage the additional space.

Any problem that can be solved recursively can be solved nonrecursively with iterations. Recursion has many negative aspects: it uses up too much time and too much memory. Why, then, should you use it? In some cases, using recursion enables you to specify a clear, simple solution that would otherwise be difficult to obtain.

The decision whether to use recursion or iteration should be based on the nature of the problem you are trying to solve and your understanding of the problem. The rule of thumb is to use whichever of the two approaches can best develop an intuitive solution that naturally mirrors the problem. If an iterative solution is obvious, use it. It will generally be more efficient than the recursive option.

Note

Your recursive program could run out of memory, causing a `StackOverflowError`.

`StackOverflowError`

Tip

If you are concerned about your program's performance, avoid using recursion, because it takes more time and consumes more memory than iteration.

performance concern

KEY TERMS

base case 636	recursive method 636
infinite recursion 637	stopping condition 636
recursive helper method 641	

CHAPTER SUMMARY

- A recursive method is a method that invokes itself directly or indirectly. For a recursive method to terminate, there must be one or more base cases.

- Recursion is an alternative form of program control. It is essentially repetition without a loop control. It can be used to specify simple, clear solutions for inherently recursive problems that would otherwise be difficult to solve.

- Sometimes the original method needs to be modified to receive additional parameters in order to be invoked recursively. A recursive helper method can be declared for this purpose.

- Recursion bears substantial overhead. Each time the program calls a method, the system must assign space for all of the method's local variables and parameters. This can consume considerable memory and requires extra time to manage the additional space.

REVIEW QUESTIONS

Sections 19.1–19.3

19.1 What is a recursive method? Describe the characteristics of recursive methods. What is an infinite recursion?

19.2 Write a recursive mathematical definition for computing 2^n for a positive integer n.

19.3 Write a recursive mathematical definition for computing x^n for a positive integer n and a real number x.

19.4 Write a recursive mathematical definition for computing $1 + 2 + 3 + \cdots + n$ for a positive integer n.

19.5 How many times is the `factorial` method in Listing 19.1 invoked for `factorial(6)`?

19.6 How many times is the `fib` method in Listing 19.2 invoked for `fib(6)`?

19.7 Show the output of the following program:

```java
public class Test {
  public static void main(String[] args) {
    System.out.println(
      "Sum is " + xMethod(5));
  }

  public static int xMethod(int n) {
    if (n == 1)
      return 1;
    else
      return n + xMethod(n - 1);
  }
}
```

```java
public class Test {
  public static void main(String[] args) {
    xMethod(1234567);
  }

  public static void xMethod(int n) {
    if (n > 0) {
      System.out.print(n % 10);
      xMethod(n / 10);
    }
  }
}
```

19.8   Show the output of the following two programs:

```java
public class Test {
  public static void main(String[] args) {
    xMethod(5);
  }

  public static void xMethod(int n) {
    if (n > 0) {
      System.out.print(n + " ");
      xMethod(n - 1);
    }
  }
}
```

```java
public class Test {
  public static void main(String[] args) {
    xMethod(5);
  }

  public static void xMethod(int n) {
    if (n > 0) {
      xMethod(n - 1);
      System.out.print(n + " ");
    }
  }
}
```

19.9   What is wrong in the following method?

```java
public class Test {
  public static void main(String[] args) {
    xMethod(1234567);
  }

  public static void xMethod(double n) {
    if (n != 0) {
      System.out.print(n);
      xMethod(n / 10);
    }
  }
}
```

```java
public class Test {
  public static void main(String[] args) {
    Test test = new Test();
    System.out.println(test.toString());
  }

  public Test() {
    Test test = new Test();
  }
}
```

Sections 19.4–19.6

19.10   Show the call stack for `isPalindrome("abcba")` using the methods declared in Listing 19.3 and Listing 19.4, respectively.

19.11   Show the call stack for `selectionSort(new double[]{2, 3, 5, 1})` using the method declared in Listing 19.5.

19.12   What is a recursive helper method?

Section 19.6 Towers of Hanoi

19.13   How many times is the `moveDisks` method in Listing 19.7 invoked for `moveDisks(5, 'A', 'B', 'C')`?

Section 19.8 Recursion versus Iteration

19.14   Which of the following statements are true?

- Any recursive method can be converted into a non-recursive method.
- Recursive methods take more time and memory to execute than non-recursive methods.
- Recursive methods are *always* simpler than non-recursive methods.
- There is always a condition statement in a recursive method to check whether a base case is reached.

19.15   What is the cause for the stack overflow exception?

PROGRAMMING EXERCISES

Sections 19.2–19.3

19.1 (*Computing factorials*) Rewrite the `factorial` method in Listing 19.1 using iterations.

19.2* (*Fibonacci numbers*) Rewrite the `fib` method in Listing 19.2 using iterations.

Hint

To compute `fib(n)` without recursion, you need to obtain `fib(n - 2)` and `fib(n - 1)` first. Let `f0` and `f1` denote the two previous Fibonacci numbers. The current Fibonacci number would then be `f0 + f1`. The algorithm can be described as follows:

```
f0 = 0; // For fib(0)
f1 = 1; // For fib(1)

for (int i = 1; i <= n; i++) {
  currentFib = f0 + f1;
  f0 = f1;
  f1 = currentFib;
}

// After the loop, currentFib is fib(n)
```

19.3* (*Computing greatest common divisor using recursion*) The `gcd(m, n)` can also be defined recursively as follows:

- If `m % n` is 0, `gcd (m, n)` is n.
- Otherwise, `gcd(m, n)` is `gcd(n, m % n)`.

Write a recursive method to find the GCD. Write a test program that computes `gcd(24, 16)` and `gcd(255, 25)`.

19.4 (*Summing series*) Write a recursive method to compute the following series:

$$m(i) = 1 + \frac{1}{2} + \frac{1}{3} + \cdots + \frac{1}{i}$$

19.5 (*Summing series*) Write a recursive method to compute the following series:

$$m(i) = \frac{1}{3} + \frac{2}{5} + \frac{3}{7} + \frac{4}{9} + \frac{5}{11} + \frac{6}{13} + \cdots + \frac{i}{2i + 1}$$

19.6** (*Summing the series*) Write a recursive method to compute the following series:

$$m(i) = \frac{1}{2} + \frac{2}{3} + \cdots + \frac{i}{i + 1}$$

19.7* (*Fibonacci series*) Modify Listing 19.2, ComputeFibonacci.java, so that the program finds the number of times the `fib` method is called.

Hint

Use a static variable and increment it every time the method is called.

Section 19.4 Problem Solving Using Recursion

19.8** (*Printing the digits in an integer reversely*) Write a recursive method that displays an `int` value reversely on the console using the following header:

public static void reverseDisplay(**int** value)

For example, `reverseDisplay(12345)` displays `54321`.

19.9** (*Printing the characters in a string reversely*) Write a recursive method that displays a string reversely on the console using the following header:

```
public static void reverseDisplay(String value)
```

For example, `reverseDisplay("abcd")` displays `dcba`.

19.10* (*Occurrences of a specified character in a string*) Write a recursive method that finds the number of occurrences of a specified letter in a string using the following method header:

```
public static int count(String str, char a)
```

For example, `count("Welcome", 'e')` returns 2.

19.11** (*Summing the digits in an integer using recursion*) Write a recursive method that computes the sum of the digits in an integer. Use the following method header:

```
public static int sumDigits(long n)
```

For example, `sumDigits(234)` returns 2 + 3 + 4 = 9.

Section 19.5 Recursion Helper Methods

19.12** (*Printing the characters in a string reversely*) Rewrite Exercise 19.9 using a helper method to pass the substring high index to the method. The helper method header is:

```
public static void reverseDisplay(String value, int high)
```

19.13** (*Finding the largest number in an array*) Write a recursive method that returns the largest integer in an array.

19.14* (*Finding the number of uppercase letters in a string*) Write a recursive method to return the number of uppercase letters in a string.

19.15* (*Occurrences of a specified character in a string*) Rewrite Exercise 19.10 using a helper method to pass the substring high index to the method. The helper method header is:

```
public static int count(String str, char a, int high)
```

19.16* (*Finding the number of uppercase letters in an array*) Write a recursive method to return the number of uppercase letters in an array of characters. You need to declare the following two methods. The second one is a recursive helper method.

```
public static int count(char[] chars)
public static int count(char[] chars, int high)
```

19.17* (*Occurrences of a specified character in an array*) Write a recursive method that finds the number of occurrences of a specified character in an array. You need to declare the following two methods. The second one is a recursive helper method.

```
public static int count(char[] chars, char ch)
public static int count(char[] chars, char ch, int high)
```

Sections 19.6 Tower of Hanoi

19.18* (*Towers of Hanoi*) Modify Listing 19.7, TowersOfHanoi.java, so that the program finds the number of moves needed to move *n* disks from tower A to tower B. (Hint: Use a static variable and increment it every time the method is called.)

19.19* (*Sierpinski triangle*) Revise Listing 19.8 to develop an applet that lets the user use the Increase and Decrease buttons to increase or decrease the current order by 1, as shown in Figure 19.8(a). The initial order is 0. If the current order is 0, the Decrease button is ignored.

(a)   (b)

FIGURE 19.8   (a) Exercise 19.19 uses the Increase and Decrease buttons to increase or decrease the current order by 1. (b) Exercise 19.10 draws ovals using a recursive method.

19.20* (*Displaying circles*) Write a Java applet that displays ovals, as shown in Figure 19.8(b). The ovals are centered in the panel. The gap between two adjacent ovals is 10 pixels, and the gap between the panel and the largest oval is also 10.

Comprehensive

19.21*** (*String permutation*) Write a recursive method to print all the permutations of a string. For example, for a string **abc**, the printout is

    abc
    acb
    bac
    bca
    cab
    cba

 Hint

Declare the following two methods. The second is a helper method.

```
public static void displayPermutation(String s)
public static void displayPermutation(String s1, String s2)
```

The first method simply invokes **displayPermutation("", s)**. The second method uses a loop to move a character from **s2** to **s1** and recursively invoke it with a new **s1** and **s2**. The base case is that **s2** is empty and prints **s1** to the console.

19.22*** (*Creating a maze*) Write an applet that will find a path in a maze, as shown in Figure 19.9(a). The applet should also run as an application. The maze is represented by an 8 × 8 board. The path must meet the following conditions:

■ The path is between the upper-left corner cell and the lower-right corner cell in the maze.

- The applet enables the user to insert or remove a mark on a cell. A path consists of adjacent unmarked cells. Two cells are said to be adjacent if they are horizontal or vertical neighbors, but not if they are diagonal neighbors.
- The path does not contain cells that form a square. The path in Figure 19.9(b), for example, does not meet this condition. (The condition makes a path easy to identify on the board.)

(a) Correct path   (b) Illegal path

FIGURE 19.9 The program finds a path from the upper-left corner to the bottom-right corner.

19.23*** (*Koch snowflake fractal*) The text presented the Sierpinski triangle fractal. In this exercise, you will write an applet to display another fractal, called the *Koch snowflake*, named after a famous Swedish mathematician. A Koch snowflake is created as follows:

1. It begins with an equilateral triangle, which is considered to be the Koch fractal of order (or level) 0, as shown in Figure 19.10(a).
2. Divide each line in the shape into three equal line segments and draw an outward equilateral triangle with the middle line segment as the base to create a Koch fractal of order 1, as shown in Figure 19.10(b).
3. Repeat step 2 to create a Koch fractal of order 2, 3, . . . , and so on, as shown in Figure 19.10(c).

(a)   (b)   (c)   (d)

FIGURE 19.10 A Koch snowflake is a fractal starting with a triangle.

APPENDIXES

Java Keywords

The following fifty keywords are reserved for use by the Java language:

abstract	double	int	super
assert	else	interface	switch
boolean	enum	long	synchronized
break	extends	native	this
byte	for	new	throw
case	final	package	throws
catch	finally	private	transient
char	float	protected	try
class	goto	public	void
const	if	return	volatile
continue	implements	short	while
default	import	static	
do	instanceof	strictfp*	

The keywords **goto** and **const** are C++ keywords reserved, but not currently used, in Java. This enables Java compilers to identify them and to produce better error messages if they appear in Java programs.

The literal values `true`, `false`, and `null` are not keywords, just like literal value `100`. However, you cannot use them as identifiers, just as you cannot use 100 as an identifier.

assert is a keyword added in JDK 1.4 and **enum** is a keyword added in JDK 1.5.

---

*The `strictfp` keyword is a modifier for method or class to use strict floating-point calculations. Floating-point arithmetic can be executed in one of two modes: *strict* or *nonstrict*. The strict mode guarantees that the evaluation result is the same on all Java Virtual Machine implementations. The nonstrict mode allows intermediate results from calculations to be stored in an extended format different from the standard IEEE floating-point number format. The extended format is machine-dependent and enables code to be executed faster. However, when you execute the code using the nonstrict mode on different JVMs, you may not always get precisely the same results. By default, the nonstrict mode is used for floating-point calculations. To use the strict mode in a method or a class, add the `strictfp` keyword in the method or the class declaration. Strict floating-point may give you slightly better precision than nonstrict floating-point, but the distinction will only affect some applications. Strictness is not inherited; that is, the presence of `strictfp` on a class or interface declaration does not cause extended classes or interfaces to be strict.

Appendix B

The ASCII Character Set

Tables B.1 and B.2 show ASCII characters and their respective decimal and hexadecimal codes. The decimal or hexadecimal code of a character is a combination of its row index and column index. For example, in Table B.1, the letter A is at row 6 and column 5, so its decimal equivalent is 65; in Table B.2, letter A is at row 4 and column 1, so its hexadecimal equivalent is 41.

TABLE B.1 ASCII Character Set in the Decimal Index

	0	1	2	3	4	5	6	7	8	9
0	nul	soh	stx	etx	eot	enq	ack	bel	bs	ht
1	nl	vt	ff	cr	so	si	dle	dc1	dc2	dc3
2	dc4	nak	syn	etb	can	em	sub	esc	fs	gs
3	rs	us	sp	!	"	#	$	%	&	'
4	(	)	*	+	,	–	.	/	0	1
5	2	3	4	5	6	7	8	9	:	;
6	<	=	>	?	@	A	B	C	D	E
7	F	G	H	I	J	K	L	M	N	O
8	P	Q	R	S	T	U	V	W	X	Y
9	Z	[	\	]	^	_	`	a	b	c
10	d	e	f	g	h	i	j	k	l	m
11	n	o	p	q	r	s	t	u	v	w
12	x	y	z	{			}	~	del		

TABLE B.2 ASCII Character Set in the Hexadecimal Index

	0	1	2	3	4	5	6	7	8	9	A	B	C	D	E	F
0	nul	soh	stx	etx	eot	enq	ack	bel	bs	ht	nl	vt	ff	cr	so	si
1	dle	dc1	dc2	dc3	dc4	nak	syn	etb	can	em	sub	esc	fs	gs	rs	us
2	sp	!	"	#	$	%	&	'	(	)	*	+	,	–	.	/
3	0	1	2	3	4	5	6	7	8	9	:	;	<	=	>	?
4	@	A	B	C	D	E	F	G	H	I	J	K	L	M	N	O
5	P	Q	R	S	T	U	V	W	X	Y	Z	[	\	]	^	_
6	`	a	b	c	d	e	f	g	h	i	j	k	l	m	n	o
7	p	q	r	s	t	u	v	w	x	y	z	{			}	~	del

APPENDIX C

Operator Precedence Chart

The operators are shown in decreasing order of precedence from top to bottom. Operators in the same group have the same precedence, and their associativity is shown in the table.

Operator	Name	Associativity
()	Parentheses	Left to right
()	Function call	Left to right
[]	Array subscript	Left to right
.	Object member access	Left to right
++	Postincrement	Right to left
--	Postdecrement	Right to left
++	Preincrement	Right to left
--	Predecrement	Right to left
+	Unary plus	Right to left
-	Unary minus	Right to left
!	Unary logical negation	Right to left
(type)	Unary casting	Right to left
new	Creating object	Right to left
*	Multiplication	Left to right
/	Division	Left to right
%	Remainder	Left to right
+	Addition	Left to right
-	Subtraction	Left to right
<<	Left shift	Left to right
>>	Right shift with sign extension	Left to right
>>>	Right shift with zero extension	Left to right
<	Less than	Left to right
<=	Less than or equal to	Left to right
>	Greater than	Left to right
>=	Greater than or equal to	Left to right
instanceof	Checking object type	Left to right
==	Equal comparison	Left to right
!=	Not equal	Left to right

Operator	Name	Associativity
&	(Unconditional AND)	Left to right
^	(Exclusive OR)	Left to right
|	(Unconditional OR)	Left to right
&&	Conditional AND	Left to right
||	Conditional OR	Left to right
?:	Ternary condition	Right to left
=	Assignment	Right to left
+=	Addition assignment	Right to left
−=	Subtraction assignment	Right to left
*=	Multiplication assignment	Right to left
/=	Division assignment	Right to left
%=	Remainder assignment	Right to left

APPENDIX D

Java Modifiers

Modifiers are used on classes and class members (constructors, methods, data, and class-level blocks), but the final modifier can also be used on local variables in a method. A modifier that can be applied to a class is called a *class modifier*. A modifier that can be applied to a method is called a *method modifier*. A modifier that can be applied to a data field is called a *data modifier*. A modifier that can be applied to a class-level block is called a *block modifier*. The following table gives a summary of the Java modifiers.

Modifier	class	constructor	method	data	block	Explanation
(default)*	√	√	√	√	√	A class, constructor, method, or data field is visible in this package.
public	√	√	√	√		A class, constructor, method, or data field is visible to all the programs in any package.
private		√	√	√		A constructor, method or data field is only visible in this class.
protected		√	√	√		A constructor, method or data field is visible in this package and in subclasses of this class in any package.
static			√	√	√	Define a class method, or a class data field or a static initialization block.
final	√		√	√		A final class cannot be extended. A final method cannot be modified in a subclass. A final data field is a constant.
abstract	√		√			An abstract class must be extended. An abstract method must be implemented in a concrete subclass.

*Default access has no modifier associated with it. For example: **class Test {}**

Modifier	class	constructor	method	data	block	Explanation
native			√			A native method indicates that the method is implemented using a language other than Java.
synchronized			√		√	Only one thread at a time can execute this method.
strictfp	√	√				Use strict floating-point calculations to guarantee that the evaluation result is the same on all JVMs.
transient				√		Mark a nonserializable instance data field.

Special Floating-Point Values

Dividing an integer by zero is invalid and throws `ArithmeticException`, but dividing a floating-point value by zero does not cause an exception. Floating-point arithmetic can overflow to infinity if the result of the operation is too large for a `double` or a `float`, or underflow to zero if the result is too small for a double or a `float`. Java provides the special floating-point values `POSITIVE_INFINITY`, `NEGATIVE_INFINITY`, and `NaN` (Not a Number) to denote these results. These values are defined as special constants in the `Float` class and the `Double` class.

If a positive floating-point number is divided by zero, the result is `POSITIVE_INFINITY`. If a negative floating-point number is divided by zero, the result is `NEGATIVE_INFINITY`. If a floating-point zero is divided by zero, the result is `NaN`, which means that the result is undefined mathematically. The string representation of these three values are Infinity, -Infinity, and NaN. For example,

```
System.out.print(1.0 / 0); // Print Infinity
System.out.print(-1.0 / 0); // Print -Infinity
System.out.print(0.0 / 0); // Print NaN
```

These special values can also be used as operands in computations. For example, a number divided by `POSITIVE_INFINITY` yields a positive zero. Table E.1 summarizes various combinations of the `/`, `*`, `%`, `+`, and `-` operators.

TABLE E.1   Special Floating-Point Values

x	y	x/y	$x*y$	$x\%y$	$x + y$	$x - y$
Finite	± 0.0	± ∞	± 0.0	NaN	Finite	Finite
Finite	± ∞	± 0.0	± 0.0	x	± ∞	∞
± 0.0	± 0.0	NaN	± 0.0	NaN	± 0.0	± 0.0
± ∞	Finite	± ∞	± 0.0	NaN	± ∞	± ∞
± ∞	± ∞	NaN	± 0.0	NaN	± ∞	∞
± 0.0	± ∞	± 0.0	NaN	± 0.0	± ∞	± 0.0
NaN	Any	NaN	NaN	NaN	NaN	NaN
Any	NaN	NaN	NaN	NaN	NaN	NaN

Note

If one of the operands is NaN, the result is NaN.

Bit Operations

To write programs at the machine-level, often you need to deal with binary numbers directly and perform operations at the bit-level. Java provides the bitwise operators and shift operators defined in Table F.1.

The bit operators apply only to integer types (`byte`, `short`, `int`, and `long`). A character involved in a bit operation is converted to an integer. All bitwise operators can form bitwise assignment operators, such as =, |=, <<=, >>=, and >>>=.

TABLE F.1

Operator	Name	Example (using bytes in the example)	Description
&	Bitwise AND	10101110 & 10010010 yields 10000010	The AND of two corresponding bits yields a 1 if both bits are 1.
|	Bitwise inclusive OR	10101110 | 10010010 yields 10111110	The OR of two corresponding bits yields a 1 if either bit is 1.
^	Bitwise exclusive OR	10101110 ^ 10010010 yields 00111100	The XOR of two corresponding bits yields a 1 only if two bits are different.
~	One's complement	~10101110 yields 01010001	The operator toggles each bit from 0 to 1 and from 1 to 0
<<	Left shift	10101110 << 2 yields 10111000	Shift bits in the first operand left by the number of bits specified in the second operand, filling with 0s on the right.
>>	Right shift with sign extension	10101110 >> 2 yields 11101011 00101110 >> 2 yields 00001011	Shift bit in the first operand right by the number of bits specified in the second operand, filling with the highest (sign) bit on the left.
>>>	Right shift with zero extension	10101110 >>> 2 yields 00101011 00101110 >>> 2 yields 00001011	Shift bit in the first operand right by the number of bits specified in the second operand, filling with 0s on the left.

INDEX